1969

ok may be kept

FOURTEEN DAYS

time.

A STUDY OF
HISTORY

A STUDY OF HISTORY

BY

ARNOLD J. TOYNBEE

HON. D.LITT. OXON. AND BIRMINGHAM
HON. LL.D. PRINCETON, F.B.A.

*Director of Studies in the Royal Institute
of International Affairs
Research Professor of International History
in the University of London
(both on the Sir Daniel Stevenson Foundation)*

'Except the Lord build the house,
their labour is but lost that build it.
'Except the Lord keep the city,
the watchman waketh but in vain.'
Ps. cxxvii. 1–2

VOLUME VI

*Issued under the auspices of the Royal Institute
of International Affairs*

OXFORD UNIVERSITY PRESS
LONDON   NEW YORK   TORONTO

Oxford University Press, Amen House, London E.C. 4

EDINBURGH GLASGOW NEW YORK TORONTO MELBOURNE
WELLINGTON BOMBAY CALCUTTA MADRAS CAPE TOWN

Geoffrey Cumberlege, Publisher to the University

FIRST EDITION   1939
SECOND IMPRESSION   1940
THIRD IMPRESSION   1946
FOURTH IMPRESSION   1948

PRINTED IN GREAT BRITAIN
BY JARROLD AND SONS, LTD., THE EMPIRE PRESS
NORWICH

CONTENTS

V. THE DISINTEGRATIONS OF CIVILIZATIONS (*cont.*)

THE DISINTEGRATIONS OF CIVILIZATIONS (*cont.*)

C. THE PROCESS OF DISINTEGRATION (*cont.*)

(I) THE CRITERION OF DISINTEGRATION (*cont.*)

(d) SCHISM IN THE SOUL (*cont.*)

7. *The Sense of Unity*

IN our preliminary reconnaissance of the relations between the several alternative ways of behaviour, feeling and life in which human souls react to the ordeal of social disintegration, we have observed[1] that the sense of promiscuity, which we have just been studying in various manifestations of it, is a psychological response to a blurring and blending of the sharp individual outlines that are assumed by a civilization while it is still in growth and is therefore still differentiating itself from other representatives of its kind;[2] and in this connexion we have observed that the same experience may alternatively evoke another response—an awakening to a sense of unity—which is not only distinct from the sense of promiscuity but is its exact antithesis. The painful perturbing dissolution of familiar forms, which suggests to weaker spirits that the ultimate reality is nothing but a chaos, may reveal to a steadier and more penetrating spiritual vision the truth that the flickering film of a phenomenal world in which the forms of outward things take shape only to disappear again is an illusion which cannot for ever obscure the everlasting unity that lies behind.[3]

This spiritual truth, like other truths of the kind, is apt to be apprehended first by analogy from some outward visible sign; and the portent in the external world which gives the first intimation of a unity that is spiritual and ultimate is the unification of a human society into a universal state through a prosaically brutal process of internecine warfare between parochial states which has

[1] In V. C (i) (*d*) 1, vol. v, p. 381, above.
[2] For the differentiation that accompanies, and bears witness to, the growth of a civilization see III. C, vol. iii, pp. 377–90, above.
[3] In the Hellenic World *post Alexandrum* this revelation of unity was apprehended and given expression by Zeno, the founder of the Stoic school of philosophy (Bidez, J.: *La Cité du Monde et la Cité du Soleil chez les Stoïciens* (Paris 1932, Les Belles Lettres), p. 50). In applying his apprehension of this truth to the problem of Man's place in the Universe, Zeno parted company with the Cynics. 'Apprenant à l'homme à se considérer non comme une simple partie (μέρος), mais comme un membre (μέλος) d'un vaste organisme social, . . . Zénon donne à l'esprit purement négatif et frondeur du cynicisme un espoir positif' (ibid., pp. 29–30; cf. p. 10). For the Hellenic conception of the *Cosmopolis*, which was in large measure the Stoics' work, see V. C (i) (*d*) 7, Annex, pp. 332–8, below.

ended at last in the exclusive and unchallenged dominion of one
sole surviving belligerent.

The dawn of a sense of unity on this pedestrian political plane of
life is commemorated in the titles in which some of the universal states
that have come into existence up to date have proclaimed their rulers'
own conception of their nature and function.[1] For example, the
prince of the Eleventh Egyptiac Dynasty who was the founder of
the Egyptiac universal state styled himself 'the Uniter of the Two
Lands',[2] and his Sumeric counterpart Ur-Engur gave his similar
political handiwork the title of 'the Kingdom of Sumer and Akkad'.
Ur-Engur's successor, Dungi, abandoned this mere enumeration
of his empire's two principal component parts for the abstract and
comprehensive title of 'the Kingdom of the Four Quarters';[3] and
precisely the same formula was invented independently by the Incas
—in another hemisphere and at a Time-remove of more than three
thousand years—to designate the universal state into which they
had united the political surface of the Andean World.[4] Again,

[1] Pretensions to oecumenical power can be expressed in the action of a rite or ceremony as well as in the words of a style and title; and the Indic Society established a
practical test for pretensions of the kind in 'the antique rite of the horse-sacrifice (aśva
medha), which, according to immemorial tradition, could only be performed by a para-
mount sovereign and involved as a preliminary a formal and successful challenge to all
rival claimants to supreme power, delivered after this fashion:

' "A horse of a particular colour was consecrated by the performance of certain
ceremonies, and was then turned loose to wander for a year. The King, or his representative, followed the horse with an army, and, when the animal entered a foreign country,
the ruler of that country was bound either to fight or to submit. If the liberator of the
horse succeeded in obtaining or enforcing the submission of all the countries over which
it passed, he returned in triumph with all the vanquished rājas in his train; but if he
failed he was disgraced, and his pretensions ridiculed. After his successful return a
great festival was held, at which the horse was sacrificed" ' (Smith, V. A.: *The Early
History of India*, 3rd ed. (Oxford 1914, Clarendon Press), p. 200, quoting Dowson, J.:
Classical Dictionary of Hindu Mythology and Religion, Geography, History, and Literature
(London 1879, Trübner), s.v. Aśvamedha).

The first recorded performance of this imperial rite seems to be its celebration by
Pushyamitra, the usurper who overthrew the Maurya Dynasty—and attempted in vain
to enter into the imperial heritage of Chandragupta and Açoka—circa 185 B.C. (see
Smith, op. cit., pp. 200–2). Thereafter, upon the reintegration of the Indic universal
state by the Gupta Dynasty after a long interlude of Helleno-Nomad intrusion, the
traditional horse-sacrifice was celebrated in succession by Samudragupta, *circa* A.D. 351
(Smith, op. cit., p. 288), and by his grandson Kumāragupta (*imperabat*, A.D. 413–55)
(Smith, op. cit., p. 299). The last recorded performance of the horse-sacrifice is its
celebration by a scion of the Gupta Dynasty after the death of the Thānēsarī emperor
Harsha in A.D. 647 (Smith, op. cit., p. 313).

[2] Meyer, E.: *Geschichte des Altertums*, vol. i, part 2, 3rd ed. (Stuttgart and Berlin
1913, Cotta), p. 257. According to Breasted, J. H.: *The Development of Religion and
Thought in Ancient Egypt* (London 1912, Hodder & Stoughton), pp. 314–15, 'it was universalism expressed in terms of imperial power [by the emperors of "the New Empire" in and
after the reign of Thothmes III] which first caught the imagination of the thinking men
of the Empire, and disclosed to them the universal sweep of the Sun-God's dominion as
a physical fact', whereas 'commercial connexions, maintained from an immemorially remote past, had not sufficed to bring the great world within the purview of Egyptian thinking'. As evidence of the awakening of Egyptiac minds, in the time of 'the New Empire',
to a sense of world-unity, Breasted (op. cit., pp. 315–17) quotes a hymn to the Sun-God
which was composed in the reign of Amenhotep III (*imperabat*, *circa* 1405–1370 B.C.).

[3] Meyer, op. cit., vol. cit., p. 557. See also the present Study, V. C (i) (*d*) 6 (δ),
Annex, vol. v, p. 651, above.

[4] See V. C (i) (*d*) 6 (δ), Annex, p. 652, above, and Cunow, H.: *Geschichte und
Kultur des Inkareiches* (Amsterdam 1937, Elsevier), pp. 75–6; Markham, Sir C.: *The

the sovereign of the Achaemenian Empire, which served as a universal state for the Syriac World, asserted the oecumenical range of his rule by styling himself 'King of the Lands' or 'King of Kings'[1]—a title which was laconically translated into Greek in the one word Βασιλεύς without even an introductory definite article.[2] The same claim to exercise an oecumenical authority over a united world is embodied, with complete explicitness, in the phrase T'ien Hia—'All that is under Heaven'—which was the official title of the Sinic universal state of the Han; and the transmission, not only of this verbal formula, but also of the outlook which it conveys, from the Sinic Society to the main body of the affiliated Far Eastern Society is attested—among a mass of other evidence—by the terms of a letter from the Manchu Emperor Ch'ien Lung (*imperabat* A.D. 1735–96) to King George III of Great Britain which has been quoted already in this Study.[3] The Roman Empire which served the Hellenic World as a universal state came to be equated in the Latin language with the *Orbis Terrarum*[4] and in Greek with the Οἰκουμένη in the sense of the whole of the inhabited world; and the consciousness, in Hellenic souls, of the unity of Mankind, for which the Roman Empire provided an outward visible symbol, may be illustrated by quoting from the works of two writers of the second century of the Christian Era—one a philosopher and the other a historian—who were both of them living under the aegis of an oecumenical Roman Peace.

In a passage in which his main concern is to point out the limitations of Caesar's power, Epictetus begins by remarking:

'You see that Caesar appears to provide us with a great peace, because there are no longer any wars or battles or any serious crimes of brigandage or piracy, so that one can travel at any season and can sail from the Levant to the Ponent.'[5]

Incas of Peru (London 1910, Smith Elder), p. 173. In the Mexic World, where the establishment of an indigenous universal state by Aztec empire-builders was forestalled by a Spanish conquest, the sense of unity which thus never achieved its expression on the political plane seems to have expressed itself, by anticipation, on the religious plane in a conception of the world as a unity articulated into four quarters for ritual purposes (see Spinden, H. J.: *Ancient Civilisations of Mexico and Central America* (New York 1922, American Museum of Natural History), p. 207).

[1] Meyer, E.: *Geschichte des Altertums*, vol. iii (Stuttgart 1901, Cotta), pp. 24–6.

[2] This verbal recognition of the uniqueness of the status and office of the Achaemenian Great King was a striking act of homage on the lips of Hellenes who were defying his efforts to extend his oecumenical authority over their own city-states.

[3] In I. C (iii) (*b*), vol. i, p. 161, above.

[4] See Vogt, J.: *Orbis Romanus* (Tübingen 1929, Mohr). This scholar points out (pp. 23–7) that, while the Romans did have an inkling, in the first century of the Christian Era, that *noster orbis* was not the only one on the face of the Earth (as is indicated in such expressions as Lucan's 'orbis qua Romanus erat' (*Pharsalia*, Book VIII, ll. 211 seqq.)), nevertheless 'the equation of the Roman Empire with the entire *Oecumenē* continued to be the predominant point of view'.

[5] Epictetus: *Dissertations*, Book III, chap. 13, § 9. The sequel, in which Epictetus goes on to draw the contrast between the *Pax Augusta* and the *Pax Philosophica*, is

And this unification of the whole of Mankind under a Roman peace, which Epictetus mentions in order to belittle the achievement, is belauded by Appian in the enthusiastic introduction to his *Studies in Roman History*:

'A few more subject nations have been added by the emperors to those already under the Roman dominion, and others which have revolted have been reduced to obedience; but, since the Romans already possess the choicest portions of the land and water surface of the Globe, they are wise enough to aim at retaining what they hold rather than at extending their empire to infinity over the poverty-stricken and un-remunerative territories of uncivilized nations. I myself have seen representatives of such nations attending at Rome on diplomatic missions and offering to become her subjects, and the Emperor refusing to accept the allegiance of peoples who would be of no value to his Government. There are other nations innumerable whose kings the Romans themselves appoint, since they feel no necessity to incorporate them into their empire. There are also certain subject nations to whom they make grants from their treasury, because they are too proud to repudiate them in spite of their being a financial burden. They have garrisoned the frontiers of their Empire with a ring of powerful armies, and keep guard over this vast extent of land and sea as easily as though it were a modest farm.'[1]

In this picture of a Hadrian or an Antoninus Pius dealing with the barbarians of his own entourage with that judicious mixture of benevolence and disdain which Ch'ien Lùng employed in dealing with the ambassadors of the South Sea Barbarian King George III, we see Rome holding at bay a generation of men who are impor-tuning her to place her empire at their disposal as an instrument for giving satisfaction to a sense of unity which is demanding fulfilment in an outward political form. The Roman Emperor of Appian's day does not have to 'go out into the highways and hedges and compel them to come in, that' his 'house may be filled:'[2] so far from his being called upon to be a conqueror, his task is to act as the warden of a kingdom that 'suffereth violence, and the violent take it by force'[3]—in so far as the Emperor, in his wisdom, allows them to have their way.

In truth, neither the Roman Empire nor any other universal state could have either established itself in the first instance or maintained itself thereafter if it had not been led on to fortune upon a tide of desire for political unity which had mounted to its flood as a 'Time of Troubles' approached its climax.[4] In Hellenic

---

quoted in the present chapter, p. 16, footnote 2, and at greater length in V. C (i) (*d*) 10, p. 142, below.

[1] Appian: *Romaïca*, Prooemium, 7.　　　[2] Luke xiv. 23.　　　[3] Matt. xi. 12.

[4] This yearning to give political expression to an awakened consciousness of the unity of Mankind is not confined to the Dominant Minority and the Internal Proletariat who

history this longing—or, rather, the sense of relief at its belated
satisfaction—breathes through the Latin poetry of the Augustan

find their satisfaction for it in becoming respectively the citizens and the subjects of a
universal state: as Appian testifies, it also arises out of an analogous experience, and
finds satisfaction in an analogous way, among the External Proletariat in the no-man's-
land beyond the stationary artificial *limes* of a universal state which has not arrived at a
'natural frontier' (see V. C (i) (c) 3, vol. v, pp. 208–10, above).

In this case, as in the other, the consciousness of unity is awakened by a violent process
of external unification on the political plane of life. We have seen that, in the course of
the 'Time of Troubles' of a disintegrating civilization, the parochial states into which
the society has articulated itself in its growth-stage destroy one another through an
internecine warfare which ends in the establishment of one universal state by a sole
surviving victor. In a similar way the incessant border-warfare, along the *limes* of an
established universal state, between the garrisons on the one side and the outer barbarians on the other, results in the break-up of the primitive barbarian tribes and in their
replacement by war-bands. These war-bands conform—on a miniature scale and with a
barbarous crudity—to the pattern of the adjoining universal state to whose challenge
they are a response (see V. C (ii) (a), pp. 230–3, below: one striking example of this, which
has been noticed in V. C (i) (c) 3, vol. v, pp. 270–1, above, is the establishment of the
steppe empire of the Hiongnu in answer to that of the Sinic universal state of the Prior
Han); and one of the ways in which this conformity shows itself is the role which is
played by such war-bands, as well as by universal states, in evoking a consciousness of
unity out of an experience of *pammixia*. A war-band, like a universal state, is apt to
express this consciousness in its style and title. For example, we may see an analogue
of the Achaemenian 'Kingdom of the Lands' in the 'Pamphyli', who were one of the
bands that descended upon the derelict domain of the Minoan World in the last wave
of the post-Minoan Völkerwanderung, and an analogue of the Sinic 'All that is under
Heaven' in the 'Alemanni' who broke through the Roman *limes* and ensconced themselves in a salient between the upper courses of the Rhine and the Danube during the
bout of anarchy through which the Roman Empire passed in the third century of the
Christian Era (see V. C (i) (c) 3, Annex I, vol. v, p. 593, above). Such names tell their
own story; and the social change to which they testify is a replacement of the primitive
bonds of kinship by a pan-barbarian comradeship—based on the personal loyalty of a
comitatus to a war-lord—which is incompatible with the primitive sense of tribal particularism as well as with the complementary sense of solidarity within each tribe. (For
this change see Chadwick, H. M.: *The Origins of the English Nation* (Cambridge 1907,
University Press), pp. 162–4 and 175; eundem: *The Heroic Age* (Cambridge 1912,
University Press), pp. 391 and 443; and the present Study, V. C (ii) (a), in the present
volume, pp. 228–36, and especially pp. 231–2, below.) A classic case is that of the
war-bands (*druzhinas*) of the Scandinavian barbarian 'successor-states' of the Khazar
steppe empire in the Khazars' former sphere of influence in the Russian forests. Both
the princes and their war-bands were entirely without 'stability' (in the monastic sense
of an enduring attachment to a single community in a single place). The principalities
ranked in a definite order of precedence; a prince had to follow a *cursus honorum* which
kept him perpetually on the move from one principality to another of higher rank; and
the war-bands trekked at their masters' heels. In the twelfth century, 'as before, the
druzhina was a mixed company. In the tenth and eleventh centuries the Varangians, as
we know, had been the predominant element in them. In the twelfth century alien
elements also "join up". Besides native Slavs and Russified descendants of the
Varangians we also find recruits of alien race from East and West, members of neighbouring communities, Turks, Berendeyans, Polovci, Khazars, even Jews, Ugrians,
Liakhi, Lithuanians, and the Chuds' (Kliutschewskij, W. [Kluchevski, V.]: *Geschichte
Russlands*, vol. i (Berlin 1925, Obelisk Verlag), pp. 197–8).

This passage from an old-fashioned tribalism to a new-fangled social sense which is
individualistic in one aspect but universalistic in another is reflected in the Teutonic
barbarians' 'heroic' poetry, in which 'nationalism in the narrower sense—i.e., in the
interests of the poet's own nation or tribe—seems to be altogether wanting' (Chadwick,
The Heroic Age, p. 34; cf. p. 335; Meyer, E.: *Geschichte des Altertums*, vol. ii, part (1),
2nd ed. (Stuttgart and Berlin 1928, Cotta), p. 295). The same Universalism is likewise characteristic of the 'heroic' poetry of the Russians (Chadwick, H. M. and N. K.:
The Growth of Literature, vol. ii (Cambridge 1936, University Press), pp. 92 and 94) and
the Achaeans; and it also displays itself—in this case in combination with Anthropo-
morphism—in the religion of the Teutons, the Achaeans, and the Aryas, who, all alike,
worshipped a pantheon conceived in the image of a barbarian war-band with a war-lord
at its head (see the present Study, I. C (i) (b), vol. i, pp. 95–100; II. D (vii), vol. ii, p. 316;
II. D (vii), Annex V, vol. ii, pp. 434–7; and V. C (i) (c) 3, vol. v, pp. 230–3, above).
'The same gods were, to a large extent at least, recognized everywhere. Whether by

Age; and we children of the Western Society in the present generation are aware from our own experience how poignant this longing may be in an age when the unity of Mankind is being striven for unavailingly. In our day the universal state for which we yearn—the oecumenical commonwealth that will establish its peace from end to end of a Westernized and, by the same token, tormented world—has not yet made its epiphany even on the horizon; yet, in anticipation of its coming, its style and title— 'The Great Society'—has been coined by a twentieth-century English sociologist[1] as a Western equivalent for the Hellenic Οἰκουμένη and for the Sinic 'All that is under Heaven'.

It is this great longing for Peace on Earth after the tribulation of a 'Time of Troubles' that has moved the subjects of the founders or preservers of the universal states to venerate them as Saviours of Society[2] or actually to worship them as gods incarnate.[3] And even the historian's colder judgement will single out, as the greatest of all men of action, those oecumenical rulers—a Cyrus, an Alexander, an Augustus—who have been touched with pity for the sufferings of their fellow men and, having caught the vision of the unity of Mankind, have devoted their personal genius and their political power to the noble enterprise of translating this dearly bought ideal into a humane reality.

Alexander's vision of Homonoia or Concord[4] never faded out of the Hellenic World so long as a vestige of Hellenism remained in existence; and the compelling spiritual power of his humanitarian gospel is impressive in view of the recalcitrance of his Macedonian companions towards his efforts to induce them to fraternize with their defeated Iranian antagonists, and the equally stubborn recalcitrance of the rest of the Greeks towards his ordinance that the ruling faction in every city-state should reopen the gates to their exiled opponents of the contrary party. All but a few of the

borrowing or by identification of cults they had ceased to be merely tribal deities. . . . Tribal ideas gave way to Universalism both in the cult of higher powers and in the conception of immortality' (Chadwick: The Heroic Age, pp. 424 and 443). A parochial tribalism was likewise transcended in the abortive movements of resistance to an irresistible tide of European colonization that were set in motion among the North American Indians at different times between A.D. 1762 and A.D. 1886 by a series of barbarian prophets (see V. C (i) (c) 3, vol. v, pp. 328–32, above); and the subordination of an unusually obstinate tribal particularism to a new sense of Panarab brotherhood was the essence of the immense political achievement of the barbarian Prophet Muhammad in the Arabian hinterland of the Roman Empire.

[1] Wallas, Graham: The Great Society (London 1914, Macmillan).
[2] See V. C (ii) (a), pp. 181–213, below.
[3] See V. C (i) (d) 6 (δ), Annex, vol. v, pp. 648–57, above.
[4] The credit for having been the first to catch this vision in the Hellenic World is disputed between Alexander of Macedon and Zeno of Citium by their respective modern Western champions: W. W. Tarn (Alexander the Great and the Unity of Mankind (London 1933, Milford)) and J. Bidèz (La Cité du Monde et la Cité du Soleil chez les Stoïciens (Paris 1932, Les Belles Lettres)). See now also Tarn: 'Alexander, Cynics and Stoics' in American Journal of Philology, vol. lx, 1, Whole Number 237 (Baltimore, January 1939, Johns Hopkins University Press).

Macedonian officers whom their royal leader had cajoled or dragooned into embarking with him on the pacific adventure of taking in marriage an Iranian bride might brutally repudiate their unwanted Oriental wives as soon as Alexander had been laid in his premature grave.[1] Yet, some three hundred years after Alexander's death, we find Caesar Augustus putting Alexander's head on his Roman signet-ring as an acknowledgement of the source from which he was seeking inspiration for his arduous work of bringing a tardy peace and unity to a Hellenic World which Alexander's successors had thrown back into disunion and discord;[2] and some two hundred years after Augustus's time, again, this Alexandrine tradition of humanitarianism still had power to move so coarse-grained and brutal a soul as Caracalla's[3] to complete the process—which Julius Caesar had lavishly begun and Augustus cautiously continued—of conferring the Roman citizenship upon the subject majority in the population of the Roman Empire.[4] Nor did Alexander's example merely influence the action of these later oecumenical rulers who sat in Alexander's seat and caught from that eminence Alexander's bird's-eye view of all his fellow men; the leaven also worked its way down through the variegated strata of a Hellenic Society which had now annexed the children of four submerged alien worlds to the Hellenic internal proletariat. It was Alexander's spirit that moved one Roman centurion at Capernaum to make his humble appeal to Jesus to heal his servant by simply speaking the word without coming under his roof,[5] and that emboldened another Roman centurion at Caesarea to invite Peter to his house.[6] It was Alexander's spirit, likewise, that inspired the Greeks who had come up to Jerusalem in order to worship at the feast to ask the disciples of Jesus whether their Master would grant them an audience;[7] and we may believe that the same Alexandrine vision of the unity of Mankind was the human inspiration in the mind of Jesus himself[8] when he broke out into

[1] Seleucus set an honourable but not a widely followed example in remaining faithful to Apame.

[2] Tarn, op. cit., p. 18, citing Suetonius: *Augustus*, chap. 50. For the treachery of Alexander's successors towards Alexander's ideals see V. C (ii) (*b*), pp. 289–90, below.

[3] For Caracalla's role in Hellenic social history as a blatant example of the vulgarization of the Dominant Minority see V. C (i) (*d*) 6 (α), vol. v, p. 455, above.

[4] According to our literary authorities, Caracalla's *Constitutio Antoniniana* conferred the citizenship upon *all* inhabitants of the Empire who were still juridically *peregrini*. Mommsen disputed this and suggested that even Caracalla's extension of the franchise was perhaps limited to those inhabitants of the Empire who were already in possession of some local civic franchise. Since Mommsen's day a fragment of the text of the *Constitutio Antoniniana* itself has come to light in *Papyrus Giessen 40*, but the surviving text is so ambiguous, and the lacunae are susceptible of being filled by so many alternative and equally plausible conjectural restorations, that the discovery has not conclusively disposed of Mommsen's query. (See Jones, A. H. M.: 'Another Interpretation of the *Constitutio Antoniniana*' in *The Journal of Roman Studies*, vol. xxvi, part 2 (1936).)

[5] Matt. viii. 5–13 = Luke vii. 1–10. [6] Acts x. [7] John xii. 20–2.
[8] If Jesus's breaking of the bounds of Jewry in his intercourse with his fellow men

a paean of exultation upon learning of the Greeks' request,[1] and again when, in his encounters with the dissident woman of Samaria[2] and with the Hellenized woman of Phoenicia,[3] he broke away from an inhuman Jewish tradition of non-intercourse with unbelievers.[4]

If we are convinced that Alexander's gospel of the unity of Mankind did indeed possess this power of creating concord between souls so far removed in time and creed and class from the Macedonian warrior-visionary, then we shall find ourselves impelled to search for the source from which this extraordinary power was derived; and, if we address our inquiry in the first instance to a humanist of the modern Western school,[5] he will probably reply that the Brotherhood of Man is one of those fundamental truths which, once seen, are recognized, in the same flash, as being self-evident; and he will be likely to add that the duty and desire to serve Humanity require no sanctions outside themselves in any human heart that has become sensitively aware of its kinship with all its fellows. *Homo sum, humani nihil a me alienum puto.*[6] The validity of the principle of Altruism is taken for granted by modern Western humanists of every sect. The Communist, for instance, believes, as devoutly as the Positivist,[7] that Man's ultimate duty is owed to his fellow men in a Universe in which Humanity is monarch of all it surveys, because Man has no God above him;[8] and yet we have seen reasons for believing that the dynamic elements in Communism—the springs of the action that has made Communism a force in contemporary human affairs—are derived, albeit unconsciously, from a trinity of theistic religions, if we are right in tracing back some of these elements to Christianity and others to Christianity's two forerunners, Judaism and Zoroastrianism.[9] If we now return to our inquiry into the basis of the Human-

---

was indeed partly inspired by the spirit of Alexander, this is not to say that Jesus himself was ever conscious of acting under Alexander's influence, but simply that Alexander's spirit was 'in the air' of Palestine in Jesus's day.

[1] John xii. 23–4. The historical significance of this passage is the same whether it be accepted as a statement of historical fact or interpreted as a piece of retrospective fiction.

[2] John iv. 1–42.   [3] Mark vii. 24–30.

[4]   Iudaicum ediscunt et servant ac metuunt ius,
                tradidit arcano quodcumque volumine Moyses,
                non monstrare vias eadem nisi sacra colenti,
                quaesitum ad fontem solos deducere verpos.
                                    Juvenal: *Satires*, No. xiv, ll. 101–4.

[5] For the modern Western idolization of Humanity at large with a capital 'H'—as distinct from the idolization of some racial or tribal fraction of Mankind—see IV. C (iii) (c) 2 (α), vol. iv, pp. 300–3, above.

[6] Terence: *Heautontimorumenos*, Act I, Scene i, l. 25. Compare the lines of Menander that are quoted on p. 11, footnote 1, below.

[7] For the Positivist doctrine on this point see Caird, E.: *The Social Philosophy and Religion of Comte* (Glasgow 1885, Maclehose), p. 53.

[8] For this forlorn and forbidding aspect of Humanism see IV. C (iii) (c) 2 (α), vol. iv, pp. 302–3, above.

[9] See V. C (i) (c) 2, vol. v, pp. 178–9, above. Compare Toynbee, A. J., and Boulter, V. M.: *Survey of International Affairs, 1934* (London 1935, Milford), pp. 355–7.

ism of Alexander, shall we find the theistic vein that is latent in
Marx's Humanism anticipated in Alexander's vision?

There was, we must allow, in Alexander's life one arresting
experience on the ordinary human plane which might have been
sufficient, in and by itself, to open Alexander's eyes to the intellectual falsity and the moral indefensibility of the current Hellenic
dichotomy of Mankind into 'Hellenes' and 'Barbarians'; and that
was his sensational discovery of the unexpected virtues of his
defeated Iranian adversaries. In the hostile caricature which had
been the convention in Hellas during the interval of 146 years by
which Alexander's passage of the Hellespont was separated from
Xerxes' unluckier crossing of the same straits in the opposite
direction, the Persian grandees had been held up to odium as
monsters of luxury, tyranny, cruelty, and cowardice; and now,
when Xerxes' abortive aggression had been avenged at last up to
the hilt by Alexander's victorious *riposte*, the Macedonian champion of Hellas learnt, through the intimate and illuminating inter-.
course of warfare, that these arch-barbarians were in reality men
capable of showing a bravery in battle and a dignity in defeat
which even a Spartan might envy.[1] The deepness of the impression which this unlooked-for discovery made upon Alexander's
mind is notorious; but, if we go on to ask whether, in Alexander's
opinion, this experience of his own, or others like it, would suffice
in themselves to awaken in human souls a consciousness of the
unity of Mankind and a will to act upon this great discovery, our
evidence (scanty though it is) will inform us explicitly that the
answer is in this case in the negative. It is recorded that at Opis,
in Babylonia, Alexander once offered up a prayer that his Macedonians and his Persians might be united in Homonoia;[2] and
Plutarch reports[3] as one of Alexander's sayings:

'God is the common father of all men, but he makes the best ones
peculiarly his own.'

If this 'logion' is authentic it tells us that Alexander's anthropology differed from that of Marx in the fundamental point of
resting on an avowed theological foundation instead of professedly
hanging in the air. It tells us that Alexander discovered the truth
that the brotherhood of Man presupposes the fatherhood of God
—a truth which involves the converse proposition that, if the
divine father of the human family is ever left out of the reckoning,
there is no possibility of forging any alternative bond of purely
human texture which will avail by itself to hold Mankind together.

[1] See V. C (i) (c) 1, vol. v, pp. 51-2, above.
[2] For the significance of this prayer see Tarn, op. cit., p. 19.
[3] Plutarch: *Life of Alexander*, chap. 27 (cited in Tarn, op. cit., pp. 25 and 41).

The only society that is capable of embracing the whole of Mankind is a superhuman *Civitas Dei*; and the conception of a society that embraces all Mankind and yet nothing but Mankind is an academic chimaera.

If Alexander was indeed the Prometheus who enriched the Hellenic World with a knowledge of this heavenly truth,[1] the care with which the precious revelation was handed down to later generations is impressively attested in the teachings of a Stoic philosopher who was born not much less than four hundred years after Alexander's death.

'Slave, wilt thou not bear with thine own brother, who has Zeus to his forefather and has been begotten like a son from the same sperms, and in the same emission from Heaven, as thyself? If the station in which thou hast been posted here below happens to be one that is somewhat superior to thy brother's, wilt thou have the face to take advantage of that in order to make thyself a tyrant? Wilt thou not remember what thou art thyself and who are these thy subjects—remember, that is to say, that they are thy kinsmen and thy brothers, both in the order of Nature and in their being of Zeus's lineage?'—'Yes, but I have rights of property over them, while they have none over me.'—'Do you perceive the objects upon which your eyes are set? They are set upon the Earth and upon the Pit and upon the wretched laws of a society of corpses, instead of being set upon the laws of the Gods. . . .'[2]

'What kind of love was it that Diogenes felt for his fellow men? It was the kind that befitted a sage who was the servant of Zeus—a love that was devoted to the creature's welfare yet was at the same time submissive to the Creator's will. In virtue of this, Diogenes alone among men had every land on Earth for his native country, without there being one single spot where he did not find himself at home. When he was taken captive, he felt no homesickness for Athens or for his Athenian friends and acquaintances. He became intimate with the pirates themselves, and did his best to reform them. And when he had been sold into slavery he led just the same life in Corinth afterwards as he had led in Athens before. Nor would he have behaved any differently if he had been packed off to Ultima Perrhaebia.'[3]

Epictetus's Diogenes has won his freedom of 'the Great Society' of the Hellenic Οἰκουμένη by taking the road from Man through God to Man which Paul lays down for his Colossians. In the philosopher's colder and more sophisticated way, Diogenes too, as Epictetus portrays him, has

'put off the old man with his deeds and . . . put on the new man which is renewed in knowledge after the image of him that created him—where there is neither Greek nor Jew, circumcision nor uncircumcision,

---

[1] For the modern Western controversy over this question see p. 6, footnote 4, above.
[2] Epictetus: *Dissertationes*, Book I, chap. 13, §§ 3–5.
[3] Ibid., Book III, chap. 24, §§ 64–6.

Barbarian, Scythian, bond nor free; but Christ is all, and in all,'[1] [because Christ is God Incarnate, and] 'God that made the World and all things therein . . . hath made of one blood all nations of men for to dwell on all the face of the Earth, . . . that they should seek the Lord, if haply they might feel after him and find him—though he be not far from every one of us; for in him we live and move and have our being, as certain also of your own poets have said: "For we are also his offspring".'[2]

Thus we see a prophet of the internal proletariat of the Hellenic Society proclaiming in unison with a statesman and a philosopher of the dominant minority the truth that the unity of Mankind is a goal which men can attain by way of the common fatherhood of God and (Paul would add) through the new revelation of the common brotherhood of Christ, but not through any exclusively human endeavours in which God's leading part is left out of the reckoning. If it is true on the one hand that 'where two or three are gathered together in my name, there am I in the midst of them',[3] it is equally true—as is signified in the legend of the Tower of Babel[4]—that, 'except the Lord build the house, their labour is but lost that build it; except the Lord keep the city, the watchman watcheth but in vain'.[5] The common experience of the Hellenic 'Time of Troubles' taught this truth to Alexander the Greek and to Paul the Jew, to Epictetus the Hierapolitan bondsman[6] and to Diogenes the freeman of the city of the Οἰκουμένη; but the Hellenic Society has not been singular either in passing through great tribulation or in learning this lesson by suffering this affliction. In the Egyptiac World, more than a thousand years before Alexander made his pilgrimage to the oasis-oracle of Amon, the unity of Mankind was numbered among the mighty works of the divinity, manifested in the Sun-Disk, who was worshipped by Ikhnaton.

'The lands of Syria and Nubia and the land of Egypt—thou puttest every man in his place and thou suppliest their needs. . . . Thou art lord

---

[1] Col. iii. 9–11. In these words of Saint Paul there is perhaps an echo of some lines of Menander (fragment 533 in Koch's edition):

$$\text{ὃς ἂν εὖ γεγονὼς ᾖ τῇ φύσει πρὸς τἀγαθά,}$$
$$\text{κἂν Αἰθίοψ ᾖ, μῆτερ, ἐστὶν εὐγενής.}$$
$$\text{Σκύθης τίς; ὄλεθρος· ὁ δ᾽ Ἀνάχαρσις οὐ Σκύθης;}$$

[2] Acts xvii. 24–8. The quotation τοῦ γὰρ καὶ γένος ἐσμέν is from the exordium of Aratus's *Phaenomena*, l. 5, which had been echoed in the Stoic philosopher-poet Cleanthes' *Hymn to Zeus*, l. 4: ἐκ σοῦ γὰρ γένος εἶσ᾽ . . . or ἐκ σοῦ γὰρ γενόμεσθ᾽ . . . .

[3] Matt. xviii. 20. This Christian 'logion' is presumably derived from a Jewish 'logion' —preserved in more than one passage of the Talmudic literature—which runs: 'Where two or three are gathered together to study the Torah, the Shekinah is in the midst of them.'

[4] Gen. xi. 1–9.   [5] Ps. cxxvii. 1–2.

[6] Epictetus appears to have been born at Hierapolis (the Carian or the Syrian?) and only to have settled at Nicopolis after having been expelled from Italy (see H. Schenkl's edition of the *Dissertationes* (Leipzig 1894, Teubner), p. iv).

of them all, who wearieth himself on their behalf; the lord of every land,
who ariseth for them. . . . All far-off peoples—thou makest that whereon
they live.'[1]

And in the Western World of the present generation a truth which
has been strenuously combated by a school of Western humanists
for the past five hundred years has at last been boldly and abruptly
reaffirmed by a philosopher who is a Frenchman in culture and
a Jew by origin.

In a book entitled *Les Deux Sources de la Morale et de la Religion*[2]
the veteran metaphysician Monsieur Henri Bergson has expounded
his ethics and his politics at an age of life at which the philosopher's
intellect has received the tempering of the man's experience; and
Bergson's central theme in this work of his old age is the thesis that
there is no terrestrial road along which Man can make the transit
from a primitive Ishmaelitish tribalism to an oecumenical concord
of all Mankind. Between the tribe and Mankind there is a great
gulf fixed, and on the terrestrial plane this chasm is utterly impassable, since the social bond which holds the tribe together is a
solidarity for parochial self-defence against a world of human
enemies beyond the tribal pale; and a complete removal of this
external human pressure would threaten the tribe with dissolution
by depriving it of the hostile environment on which it depends for
its cohesion. The denizens of the deep sea, whose frames have
been built for bearing the enormous pressure of the mass of water
that weighs upon them at these formidable depths, are said to
burst asunder, long before they reach the surface, if the deep-sea
fisherman catches them in his toils and strives to drag them up to
the air and light; and in much the same way a tribe of men—
though it may be capable of expanding from the dimensions of a
kaffir kraal to a British Empire embracing one-fifth of the living
generation of Mankind and extending over a quarter of the land-
surface of the Globe—is perhaps doomed *a priori* to fall to pieces,
long before it comes within sight of attaining an oecumenical
universality, at the point, wherever this may lie, where the cen-
tripetal outer forces that have been holding it together lose their
preponderance over the centrifugal forces from within that are for
ever pushing it to dissolve apart. If ever this critical point is
reached, the human statesman who has dreamed the dream of
elevating his tribe into an oecumenical society must find himself

---

[1] Ikhnaton's hymn to the Aton, as translated in Erman, A.: *The Literature of the
Ancient Egyptians*, English translation (London 1927, Methuen), p. 290. In V. C (i)
(*d*) 6 (δ), Annex, vol. v, p. 695, with footnote 2, above, it is suggested that Ikhnaton's
proclamation of the unity of Mankind—in virtue of their common enjoyment of the
ubiquitous beneficence of the Aton—was a disinterested expression of a genuine intuition
and was not the political manœuvre of a prince whose real concern was to unify a multi-
national empire.   [2] Paris 1932, Alcan.

awakened to a harsh reality in which he is offered the cruel choice between falling back into tribalism and stumbling on into anarchy. On this showing, the attempt to make the transit to an oecumenical society from a parochial tribe is doomed *a priori* to failure so long as it is made on the terrestrial level; and the last word of Bergson's philosophy is a declaration that this transit—which Man must somehow make if he is not to perish from off the face of the Earth —can only be made across a bridge that vaults over an impassable terrestrial gulf by rising to the height of Heaven. The whole of Mankind can never dwell together in a brotherly unity[1] until men have learnt to exchange their intrinsically conflicting as well as parochial tribal loyalties for one common allegiance to a heavenly king.[2]

This is the final intuition of a modern Western philosopher who stands, in his ripe old age, at the apex of a pyramid of thought that is the cumulative product of the philosophical labours of five industrious centuries of Western mental 'output'; yet the truth which it has cost our philosophers all this time and toil to win by their own lights has been picked up casually by our anthropologists 'out of the mouth of babes and sucklings'.[3] The all but annihilated rear-guard of a Primitive Man whom a sophisticated *Homo Occidentalis* alternately pities and abhors for his ignorance of his social solidarity with the main body of Mankind outside the tribal zariba, has never ceased to take for granted the solidarity between the tribe on its narrowly circumscribed terrestrial allotment and the tribal gods in a circumambient Universe;[4] and, however parochial the 'savage's' horizon may be on the plane of sheerly human life on the surface of this planet, his soul still lives and moves in a spiritual environment with a superhuman dimension which the modern Western humanist has deliberately excluded from his reckoning. The humanist purposely concentrates all his attention and effort upon a purely human cross-section of life which he abstracts from the totality of his spiritual environment by a mental operation that is performed for the practical purpose of bringing human affairs under human control. Yet Reality cannot in truth be eluded by begging the question that is involved in the postulate that 'Man is the measure of all things';[5] and therefore the unity of Mankind can never be established in fact except within a framework of the unity of the superhuman Whole of which

[1] Ps. cxxxiii. 1.
[2] This Bergsonian thesis is examined further in Part VII, below.
[3] Ps. viii. 2.
[4] This element in the *Weltanschauung* of Primitive Man has been touched upon by anticipation in IV. C (iii) (c) 2 (β), vol. iv, p. 351, above.
[5] This saying, which is attributed to Protagoras, is alluded to by Plato in his *Theaetetus*, 183 B.

Humanity is a part. An oecumenical society must preserve or recapture those spiritual dimensions which the tribal societies possess as their birthright if the house with the broader terrestrial site is to stand as stalwartly as its terrestrially diminutive neighbour. However large its area on Earth, Man's universe cannot give Man's spirit room to breathe unless it also extends from Earth to Heaven; and our modern Western school of humanists have perhaps been peculiar, as well as perverse, in planning to reach Heaven[1] by raising a titanic Tower of Babel on terrestrial foundations in three dimensions—as though it were sheer physical distance, and not any difference in mode of spiritual being, that divided and distinguished Heaven from Earth. When we compare this grossly mundane plan of operations which has governed the outlook and behaviour of the Western Society in its Modern Age with the reactions of other civilizations to a comparable social experience, we shall become aware of a contrast. In the Sinic World, for example, the craving for unity that was evoked by a 'Time of Troubles' was never confined to the terrestrial plane.

'To the Chinese of this period the word One (unity, singleness, &c.) had an intensely emotional connotation, reflected equally in political theory and in Taoist metaphysics. And indeed the longing—or, more accurately, the psychological need—for a fixed standard of belief was profounder, more urgent and more insistent than the longing for governmental unity. In the long run Man cannot exist without an orthodoxy, without a fixed pattern of fundamental belief.'[2]

If this comprehensive Sinic way of pursuing the quest for unity may be taken as the norm,[3] and our modern Western cult of an arbitrarily insulated Humanity may be written off as something exceptional or even pathological, then we should expect to see the practical unification of Mankind and the ideal unification of the Universe accomplished *pari passu* by a spiritual effort which would not cease to be one and indivisible because it manifested itself simultaneously in diverse fields. As a matter of fact, we have

---

[1] Gen. xi. 4.
[2] Waley, A.: *The Way and its Power* (London 1934, Allen & Unwin), Introduction, pp. 69–70.
[3] There is, however, at least one modern Western scholar who claims for the camp of Humanism not only Confucius but all the Sinic philosophers with the possible exception of Mo-tse.
'Confucius eut, semble-t-il, l'idée . . . de faire reposer toute la discipline des mœurs sur un sentiment affiné de l'humanisme. . . . La conception confucienne du *jen* ou de l'homme accompli, et qui mérite seul le nom d'homme, s'inspire d'un sentiment de l'humanisme qui peut déplaire, mais qu'on n'a pas le droit de celer. . . . Seul, semble-t-il, lui paraissait bienfaisant et valable un art de la vie jaillissant des contacts amicaux entre hommes policés. . . . Sauf Mö tseu (s'il faut admettre que ce prédicateur croyait à sa rhétorique), il n'est point, dans l'antiquité, de sage chinois qui ait véritablement songé à fonder, sur des sanctions divines, la règle des mœurs. . . . La sagesse chinoise est une *sagesse indépendante* et tout humaine. Elle ne doit rien à l'idée de Dieu' (Granet, M.: *La Pensée Chinoise* (Paris 1934, Renaissance du Livre), pp. 473, 486, 489, and 588).

observed already[1] that when, after the breakdown of a civilization, a number of parochial communities are fused together into a universal state, the process of political unification is apt to be accompanied, on the religious plane of ritual and theology, by an incorporation of the diverse parochial divinities into a single pantheon which reflects, and is reflected in, the concomitant change in the order of human life on Earth.[2] As the internecine warfare between conflicting parochial states results in the supremacy of a single victor and in the subjugation of all the rest, so the parochial god of the victorious human community—an Amon-Re of Thebes or a Marduk-Bel of Babylon—becomes the high god of a pantheon into which the gods of the defeated human communities are marshalled in order that henceforth they may fetch and carry or stand and wait at the pleasure of their new master.

It will be seen, however, that the condition of human affairs which finds its superhuman reflexion in a pantheon of this kind is the situation immediately after the genesis of a universal state, and not the constitution into which a polity of that type eventually settles down in the course of the age that follows its establishment; for the ultimate constitution of a universal state is not a hierarchy which preserves its constituent parts intact and merely converts their former equality as sovereign independent states into a hegemony of one of them over the rest. A political structure which, on the morrow of its establishment, may have been accurately described as 'the Kingdom of the Lands' solidifies in the course of time into a unitary empire articulated into standardized provinces; and a corresponding process of concentration concurrently transforms the Pādishāh or King of Kings—in fact, if not in name —into a solitary autocrat who delegates his plenary authority to creatures of his own instead of simply keeping his foot upon the necks of kinglets whose forefathers had been his own forefathers' peers. In fact, in a fully seasoned universal state which, in maturing, has developed true to type, there are two salient features which dominate, between them, the entire social landscape. On the one hand there is a monarch whose task and title-deeds alike consist in keeping the peace among his subjects by the exercise of his sovereign will; and on the other hand there is the law which is the instrument for translating the monarch's will into action. And in a world of men that is governed on this plan the Universe as a

---

[1] In V. C (i) (d) 6 (δ), vol. v, pp. 529–32, above.

[2] This morphological correspondence between the universal state and the pantheon that are constructed by the Dominant Minority at the close of the 'Time of Troubles' has its analogue, in the history of the External Proletariat, in the similar correspondence between the barbarian war-band and the barbarian pantheon of Olympus or Asgard (see I. C (i) (b), vol. i, pp. 96–7; II. D (vii), Annex V, vol. ii, pp. 436–7; and V. C (i) (c) 3, vol. v, pp. 230–3, above).

whole is likely to be conceived on a corresponding pattern. If the human ruler of a universal state is at once so powerful and so beneficent that the subjects whom he has delivered from the nightmare of a 'Time of Troubles' are easily persuaded to worship him in person as a god incarnate,[1] then, *a fortiori*, they will be prone to see in him a terrestrial likeness of a heavenly ruler who is likewise unique and omnipotent—a god who is no mere God of Gods like Marduk-Bel or Amon-Re, but who reigns alone as the One True God with mere angels for his ministers and with no other god in existence to share, even in a subordinate role, a divinity which would not be truly divine if it were not strictly indivisible. Again, the law in which the human emperor's will is translated into action is an irresistible and ubiquitous force which suggests, by analogy, the idea of an impersonal 'Law of Nature': a law which governs not only the regular alternations of night and day and winter and summer but also the more wayward movements of the winds and tides and the impenetrably mysterious distribution of joy and sorrow, good and evil, and reward and punishment on those deeper levels of human life where Caesar's writ ceases to run.[2]

This pair of concepts—a ubiquitous and irresistible law and a unique and omnipotent deity—will be found at the heart of almost every representation of the unity of the Universe that has ever taken shape in human minds in the social environment of a universal state;[3] but a survey of cosmologies of this kind will show us that they tend to approximate to one or other of two distinct types.

[1] For this phenomenon of Caesar-worship in universal states see V. C (i) (*d*) 6 (δ), Annex, vol. v, pp. 648–57, above.

[2] The limitations upon Caesar's power are pointed out by Epictetus in the sequel to the passage that has been quoted in this chapter on p. 3, above:

'Can Caesar also bring us peace from fever and from shipwreck, or from conflagration or earthquake or thunderbolt? Yes, and from love? Impossible. And from grief? Impossible. And from envy? A sheer impossibility in every one of these predicaments. But, unlike Caesar, the doctrine (λόγος) of the philosophers does promise to bring us peace from these troubles too' (Epictetus: *Dissertationes*, Book III, chap. 13, § 10).

This Stoic distinction between the two different kinds of peace has (as has been pointed out by Professor N. H. Baynes in *The Journal of Roman Studies*, vol. xxv, part (1), 1935, p. 85) a Christian counterpart in:

'Peace I leave with you; my peace I give unto you. Not as the World giveth give I unto you' (John xiv. 27).

For the context of the passage of Epictetus see V. C (i) (*d*) 10, p. 142, below.

[3] The Sinic representation of the unity of the Universe which crystallized under the Ts'in and Han régimes must be declared, however, to be an exception to our rule if we are to follow the guidance of Monsieur Marcel Granet in his *La Pensée Chinoise* (Paris 1934, Renaissance du Livre). The formula in which this modern Western scholar sums up (in op. cit., p. 586) his own reading of 'l'esprit des mœurs chinoises' is 'Ni Dieu, ni Loi'; and he gives his grounds for this dictum in other passages of the same book.

'Ché Houang-ti [She Hwang-ti], quand il fonda l'Empire, pensa établir le règne de la Loi. Le régime n'a pas duré. Les Chinois l'ont honni, reprochant aux Légistes leur dureté, leur cruauté. Les Légistes étaient coupables, en effet, d'avoir cru à l'unique vertu de la discipline. . . . Ils ont eu le goût des jugements impartiaux, des évaluations objectives, des arguments concrets. Ces esprits positifs et déjà épris de rigueur scientifique n'ont obtenu qu'un succès fugitif. Les Sophistes n'ont pas réussi à faire accepter

There is one type in which the Law is exalted at the expense of
God and another in which God is exalted at the expense of the
Law. And we shall also find that the emphasis on the Law is
characteristic of the philosophies of the Dominant Minority, while
the religions of the Internal Proletariat incline to subordinate the
majesty of the Law to the omnipotence of God.

This differentiation of outlook is not difficult to understand if
we can imagine ourselves, by turns, in the position of each of the
parties. The Achaemenian Emperor and the Persian grandees
who were his ministers in the government of the Syriac universal
state were acutely conscious of the potency of a Law which was
not merely the engine of the Imperial administration but was also
a force in itself—'the Law of the Medes and Persians which
altereth not'[1] and which insists inexorably 'that no decree nor
statute which the King establisheth may be changed',[2] though the
King himself may labour till the going down of the Sun[3] to revoke the
royal decision that has passed—once made—out of the playground
of personal caprice into the realm of the immutable. On the other
hand the impotent and insignificant Jewish subjects of the Great
King, who knew nothing of the *arcana imperii*,[4] were vividly aware,
and whole-heartedly grateful, when the Great King deigned to
take notice of their plight and to speak the saving word. A Cyrus
who delivered them from a Babylonish captivity[5] and an Artaxerxes who intervened at the critical moment to avert the imminent
miscarriage of the work of reconstruction that an Ezra or a Nehemiah was carrying out under the Great King's patronage[6]—these
were personalities whose power and will for good made an enduring impression upon the 'folk-memory' of the broken peoples over
whom they had cast their beneficent aegis.

Such considerations may explain why it is that the mind of the

par les Chinois l'idée qu'il existât des termes contradictoires. De même, les Légistes
n'ont pas réussi à accréditer la notion de règle constante et la conception de la Loi
souveraine (pp. 470–1). . . .
   'Puisque tout dépend de congruences, tout est affaire de convenances. La Loi, l'abstrait,
l'inconditionnel sont exclus—l'Univers est un—tant de la Société que de la Nature. . . .
On tient à conserver à toutes les notions, même à celle de Nombre, même à celle de
Destin, quelque chose de concret et d'indéterminé qui réserve une possibilité de *jeu*.
Dans l'idée de *règle*, on ne veut guère voir que l'idée de *modèle*. La notion chinoise de
l'Ordre exclut, sous tous ses aspects, l'idée de Loi' (p. 590).
   This Sinic refractoriness to the concept of Law has its complement in an impervious-
ness to the concept of God.
   'Les Chinois n'ont aucune tendance au spiritualisme. À peine trouve-t-on la trace,
dans les croyances populaires, d'un animisme inconsistant. . . . L'incrédulité, chez tous
les sages, est totale, bien plus souriante qu'agressive. . . . Les dieux . . . *n'ont aucune
transcendance*. Trop engagés dans le concret, trop singuliers, *ils manquent aussi de per-
sonnalité*. Et chez aucun sage, en effet, aucune tendance au personnalisme ne se re-
marque, pas plus qu'au spiritualisme' (p. 587).
   [1] Dan. vi. 8 and 12; compare Esther i. 19.   [2] Dan. vi. 15.
   [3] Dan. vi. 14.   [4] Tacitus: *Annals*, Book II, chap. 36.
   [5] Isa. xliv. 28 and xlv. 1–4; Ezra i.
   [6] Ezra iv; Neh. ii.

Internal Proletariat is apt to dwell upon the omnipotence of God and the mind of the Dominant Minority upon the supremacy of the Law. It must be repeated, however, that the distinction which we are here seeking to draw between two different types of cosmology is no more than a matter of emphasis, and that, in almost every cosmology which a disintegrating civilization brings to birth, both the two fundamental concepts—the concept of God and the concept of Law—are to be found not only coexisting but also interwoven with one another, whatever their respective proportions may be. If we examine some proletarian-born religion—say, Judaism or Islam—in which the personality of God is emphasized to a degree at which it seems to overshadow and overwhelm everything else in the Universe, we find nevertheless that the human worshipper is commanded to observe a rigid law with scrupulous exactitude as the form of human service which is most pleasing in the eyes of the Almighty. Conversely, if we follow out the history of Buddhism—one of the philosophies of the Dominant Minority that carried a belief in Law to the logical extreme of denying the existence of personality, either human or divine[1]—we find this austere psychological discipline of Siddhārtha Gautama undergoing its extraordinary transformation into the 'higher religion' of the Mahāyāna in order to satisfy souls that cannot be content with a godless Universe by offering them objects of worship that are personal, immortal, and omnipotent divinities in everything but name.[2]

Having placed this reservation upon the distinction that we are seeking to establish, we may now survey, in succession, those representations of the unity of the Universe in which Law has been exalted at the expense of God, and those other representations in which God overshadows the Law which He promulgates.

In the systems in which 'Law is king of all'[3] we can watch the personality of God growing fainter as the Law that governs the Universe comes out into sharper focus.

In our own Western World, for example, within the last three hundred years, the Triune God of the Athanasian Creed has faded by stages, in an ever-increasing number of Western minds,[4] as

---

[1] Sir S. Radhakrishnan, in *Gautama the Buddha* (London 1938, Milford), pp. 31–50, contends that Siddhārtha Gautama himself did not deny the existence either of God or of the Self, and that he conceived of *Nirvāna*, not as a negation of existence, but as 'a different, deeper mode of life' which 'is peace and rest in the bosom of the Eternal'.

[2] For the metamorphosis of the Primitive Buddhism into the Mahāyāna see V. C (i) (c) 2, vol. v, pp. 133–6, above.

[3] Νόμος πάντων βασιλεύς.—Herodotus, Book III, chap. 38, quoting Pindar.

[4] See, for example, Mr. H. G. Wells' account—quoted in V. C (i) (d) 1, vol. v, p. 381, footnote 3, above—of his own successful efforts, as a boy, to eliminate from his picture of the Universe the figure of God which his mother had taken care to implant in his mind.

Physical Science, in its hitherto uninterruptedly triumphal progress, has extended the frontiers of its intellectual empire over one field of existence after another—until at last, in our day, when Science is laying claim to the whole of the Spiritual as well as the Material Universe, we see God the Mathematician fading right out into God the Vacuum. This modern Western process of evicting God to make room for Law to reign in His stead was anticipated in the Babylonic World in the eighth century B.C. when the discovery of the periodicities in the motions of the stellar cosmos[1] inveigled the Chaldaean *mathematici*, in their enthusiasm for the new science of Astrology, into transferring their allegiance from Marduk-Bel to the Seven-Planets; for these hitherto less honoured 'rulers of the heavenly spheres' were remote and inexorable powers by comparison with the old familiar tutelary deity of the Land of Shinar, whose votaries had always known where to find him and how to propitiate him, seeing that he was a god in human form with one foot firmly planted in the soil of Babylon and the other in the soil of Nippur.[2]

In the Indic World, again, when the Buddhist school of philosophy worked out to their extreme conclusions the logical consequences of the psychological law of *Karma*,[3] the divinities of the Vedic Pantheon were the most signal victims of this aggressive system of 'totalitarian' spiritual determinism. These barbaric gods of a barbarian war-band were now made to pay dearly, in their unromantic middle age, for the all too human wantonness of a turbulent youth. They suffered the same fate as the Roman patricians when these discomfited aristocrats forfeited all that was politically valuable in their ancestral privileges without obtaining the right to vote in the *concilium plebis* or to offer themselves as candidates for the Tribunate. In a Buddhist Universe in which all consciousness and desire and purpose was reduced to a succession of atomic psychological states which by definition were incapable of coalescing into anything in the nature of a continuous or stable personality, the Gods were automatically reduced to the spiritual stature of human beings on a common level of nonentity. In such a Universe, what serious difference could it make whether the fly

---

[1] See V. C (i) (c) 1, vol. v, pp. 56–7, above.

[2] For the manufacture of Marduk-Bel through an identification of the god of Babylon with the lord god of Nippur see V. C (i) (d) 6 (δ), vol. v, p. 529, above.

[3] See V. C (i) (d) 4, vol. v, pp. 427–9, above. The law under which *Karma* operates is itself conceived of as *Ṛta* or as *Dharma*. 'All things and beings are under the power of Law. They follow a certain course prescribed for them. . . . *Ṛta*, the moral order, is not the creation of a god. It is itself divine and independent of the Gods. . . . *Dharma* is the immanent order. It denotes the Law of Nature, the chain of causation. . . . "Who is, venerable sir, the King of Kings?"—"*Dharma* is the King of Kings"' (Radhakrishnan, Sir S.: *Gautama the Buddha* (London 1938, Milford), pp. 36–7, quoting the *Aṅguttara-Nikāya*, sutra 3).

on the wheel was a human gnat or a divine bluebottle? And what could it matter whether the small deer scampering through the aisles of the towering temple were mannikin mice or godling rats? Yet in their practical treatment of this wretched rabble of the self-enslaved bondsmen of Desire—this motley crowd in which men and gods were tumbling over each other pell-mell under the sage's coldly contemptuous eye—the Buddhist philosophers did still take the trouble to differentiate between the two species in one way that was wholly to the disadvantage of Man's superhuman companion in insignificance. The mouse-like human being was eligible, *ex officio humanitatis*, for admission to the only career that was worth following in a world of suffering and illusion; and from this strait way of release the rat-like god was excluded *a priori, ex officio divinitatis*. Any human being might become a Buddhist monk or nun, if only he or she could stand the ascetic ordeal; and, for this renunciation of the pleasures of *l'homme moyen sensuel*, the compensation that was offered was enormous. Even the subdued philosophy of Primitive Buddhism held out to the steadfast arhat the prospect of ultimately attaining for himself (or, strictly speaking, for his own tangled spillikin-pile of psychological states) a release from the Wheel of Existence and an entry into the oblivion of *Nirvāna*; and the flamboyant religion of the Mahāyāna, which was the Buddhist philosophy's changeling child, outbid its foster mother by bringing within the reach of any one of its human children the nobler and more inspiring aim of becoming a Bodhisattva or candidate for the sublime role of Buddhahood. Thus Buddhism, in both its philosophical and its religious presentation, did offer Man, at a price, a way out of the *impasse* in which he found himself entrapped on the Buddhist map of the Universe. On the Gods, however, the Hīnayāna and the Mahā-yāna unanimously closed the doors of mercy; for 'the Gods are laymen'.[1]

In the Hellenic World the gods of Olympus fared better than they deserved if their deserts are to be measured by the punishment that was meted out by a Buddhist justice to their Vedic cousins; for, when the Hellenic school of philosophers came to conceive of the Universe as a 'Great Society' of supra-terrestrial dimensions whose members' relations with one another were

---

[1] Thomas, E. J.: *The History of Buddhist Thought* (London 1933, Kegan Paul), p. 217. This laicity of the Gods was taken so much in earnest that in a Mahayanian sutra a chapter in which the Mahayanian Buddhist doctrine is expounded in exoteric terms that can be understanded of the people is formally addressed to the Gods, as a hint that it is an *œuvre de vulgarisation* (ibid., loc. cit.). The Buddha's own view seems to have been that 'the Gods are merely angels who may be willing to help good Buddhists, but are in no wise guides to Religion, since they need instruction themselves' (Eliot, Sir Ch.: *Hinduism and Buddhism* (London 1921, Arnold, 3 vols.), vol. i, p. xxii).

regulated by Law and inspired by Homonoia or Concord,[1] they wrote into the constitution of this *Cosmopolis* the principle of equality before the Law which was the constitutional palladium of the best conducted terrestrial Hellenic city-states. In this Hellenic philosophers' Universe the Gods were at any rate no worse off than their human fellow citizens, even if they no longer enjoyed those traditional privileges which they had never earned and had often abused. And Zeus, who had started life as the disreputable war-lord of the Olympian war-band, was now morally reclaimed and handsomely pensioned off by being elected to the Honorary Presidency of the *Cosmopolis* with a status not unlike that of some latter-day Western constitutional monarch who 'reigns but does not govern'—a king who meekly countersigns the decrees of Fate[2] and obligingly lends his name to the operations of Nature.[3]

Our survey has now perhaps made it apparent that the Law which eclipses the Godhead may present itself in a variety of modes. It is a mathematical law that has enslaved the Babylonic astrologer and the modern Western man of science; a psychological law that has captivated the Buddhist ascetic; and a social law that has won the allegiance of the Hellenic philosopher. If we pass next to the Sinic World, where the concept of Law has not found favour, we shall find the Godhead being eclipsed here again by an Order[4] which in the Sinic *Weltanschauung* presents itself as

---

[1] For this Hellenic conception of the Universe as a society see further V. C (i) (*d*) 7, Annex, below.

[2] Zeus is explicitly coupled with Fate in the famous verses of the Stoic philosopher Cleanthes which have been quoted in Part III. A, vol. iii, p. 47, footnote 1, and again in V. C (i) (*d*) 4, vol. v, p. 421, above.

[3] The brutal truth was that the only way of making Zeus respectable was to emasculate him; and this *ultima ratio* was eventually applied, in desperation, by the god's philosopher-physicians, who found their patient's lascivious propensities too difficult to cope with by any less drastic means, even for such skilful practitioners as they were. Yet this Stoic solution of the problem of Zeus was a sheer counsel of despair; and Hellenic souls did not resign themselves to it until the Hellenic Civilization was far gone in its decline. During the century immediately preceding the breakdown of 431 B.C., when the noblest souls in Hellas were being inspired by a spiritual yearning which was not yet divorced from hope, the Athenian poet Aeschylus tried to convert Zeus into the One True God of a 'higher religion'.

> Zeus! Zeus, Whate'er He be,
> If this name He love to hear
> This He shall be called of me.
> Searching earth and sea and air
> Refuge nowhere can I find
> Save Him only, if my mind
> Will cast off before it die
> The burden of this vanity.
> (Aeschylus: *Agamemnon*, ll. 160-7, Gilbert Murray's translation.)

Zeus, however, showed no inclination at all to dance to Aeschylus's piping; and the sublime poet's attempt to enlist the *ci-devant* captain of the Olympian troop in the cause of providing bread, instead of a stone, for hungry Hellenic souls was an even greater failure than his disreputable fellow countryman Onomacritus's attempt to manufacture a higher religion *de toutes pièces* (see V. C (i) (*d*) 6 (δ), Annex, vol. v, pp. 697-8, above).

[4] See the quotations from Granet on p. 16, footnote 3, above.

a kind of magical congruence or sympathy between the behaviour of Man and that of his environment.

While the action of the environment upon Man is recognized, and manipulated, in the Sinic art of geomancy, the converse action of Man upon the environment is controlled and directed by means of a ritual and an etiquette which are as elaborate and as momentous as the structure of the Universe which they mirror and at the same time modify.

'L'homme et la Nature ne forment pas deux règnes séparés, mais une *société* unique. Tel est le principe des diverses techniques qui réglementent les attitudes humaines. C'est grâce à une participation active des humains et par l'effet d'une sorte de *discipline civilisatrice* que se réalise l'Ordre universel. À la place d'une *Science* ayant pour objet la connaissance du Monde, les Chinois ont conçu une *Étiquette* de la vie qu'ils supposent assez efficace pour instaurer un Ordre total.'[1]

The Sinic way of conceiving Time and Space has furnished Sinic intelligences with

'les cadres d'une sorte d'art total: appuyé sur un savoir qui nous semble tout scolastique, cet art tend à réaliser, par le simple emploi d'emblèmes efficaces, un aménagement du Monde qui s'inspire de l'aménagement de la Société. . . . Précisons en disant que les sectes ou écoles se sont toutes proposé de réaliser un *aménagement* de la vie et des activités humaines prises dans leur *totalité*—entendez: dans la totalité de leurs prolongements, non seulement sociaux, mais cosmiques. Chaque maître professe une sagesse qui dépasse l'ordre moral et même l'ordre politique.'[2]

And, on the same principle,

'le Total, *Yi*, l'Entier, c'est le pouvoir universel d'animation qui appartient au Chef, Homme Unique. Toute la conception chinoise des Nombres (comme . . . la conception du Yin et du Yang[3] et comme . . . la conception de Tao[4]) sort de représentations sociales, dont elle n'a aucunement cherché à s'abstraire. . . . L'ordre de l'Univers n'est point distingué de l'ordre de la Civilisation.'[5]

The human master of the ceremonies who makes the World go round is the monarch of the Sinic universal state;[6] and, in virtue of the superhuman scope of his function, the Emperor was offi-

[1] Granet, op. cit., p. 24.   [2] Ibid., pp. 113 and 17.
[3] See the present Study, Part I. B, vol. i, pp. 201–3, above.—A.J.T.
[4] See the present Study, III. C (i) (c), vol. iii, p. 187, and V. C (i) (d) 4, vol. v, pp. 416–17, above.—A.J.T.   [5] Granet, op. cit., pp. 298 and 389.
[6] This Sinic conception of a magical order of the Universe with the magician himself for its hub is manifestly much less far removed from the *Weltanschauung* of Primitive Man than are the Hellenic and Indic and Babylonic and Western conceptions of Cosmic Law, analogous to Human Law, which we have examined above; and accordingly we shall not be surprised to find Sinic notions foreshadowed in our records of less highly sophisticated human readings of the relation between Man and his environment. For example, the following two passages in the Homeric Epic, which catch a Western reader's attention because they are so startlingly out of gear with the order of the Universe as it presents itself to Western intelligences, would be so immediately and

cially styled the Son of Heaven; yet this Heaven who, in the Sinic Society, was the adoptive father of the magician-in-chief, was as pale as the sky on a frosty winter day in Northern China.

'Création savante de la mythologie politique, le Souverain d'En-haut n'a qu'une existence littéraire. Ce patron dynastique, chanté par les poètes de la cour royale, n'a jamais dû jouir d'un grand crédit auprès des "petites gens", ainsi que semble le prouver l'échec de la propagande théocratique de Mö tseu [Mo-tse]. Confuciens ou Taoïstes ne lui accordent aucune considération. Pour eux, les seuls êtres sacrés, ce sont les Saints ou les Sages.'[1]

Indeed, this celestial stalking-horse of the human manipulator of the Sinic Universe had so faint a personality that, in the affiliated Far Eastern Society at the turn of the seventeenth and eighteenth centuries of the Christian Era, the Jesuit missionaries in China raised a storm when—in their eagerness to translate the doctrines of Christianity into terms that would be familiar and agreeable to their prospective converts[2]—they employed the Chinese word for Heaven, *T'ien*, to render their Latin word *Deus*. In A.D. 1693 the Papal Vicar-General of the Chinese province of Fukien, Bishop Maigrot, issued an edict prescribing that *Deus* must henceforth be rendered in Chinese no longer by the single word *T'ien* (Heaven)

completely intelligible to a Far Eastern reader that he might be tempted to indulge in the fancy that the Hellenic poet was here taking a leaf out of the Sinic classics.

ἦ γάρ σευ κλέος οὐρανὸν εὐρὺν ἱκάνει
ὥς τέ τευ ἢ βασιλῆος ἀμύμονος, ὅς τε θεουδὴς
ἀνδράσιν ἐν πολλοῖσι καὶ ἰφθίμοισιν ἀνάσσων
εὐδικίας ἀνέχῃσι, φέρῃσι τε γαῖα μέλαινα
πυροὺς καὶ κριθάς, βρίθῃσί τε δένδρεα καρπῷ,
τίκτῃ τ' ἔμπεδα μῆλα, θάλασσά τε παρέχῃ ἰχθῦς
ἐξ εὐηγεσίης, ἀρετῶσι δὲ λαοὶ ὑπ' αὐτοῦ.

Odyssey, Book XIX, ll. 108-14.

ὡς δ' ὑπὸ λαίλαπι πᾶσα κελαινὴ βέβριθε χθὼν
ἤματ' ὀπωρινῷ, ὅτε λαβρότατον χέει ὕδωρ
Ζεύς, ὅτε δή ῥ' ἄνδρεσσι κοτεσσάμενος χαλεπήνῃ,
οἳ βίῃ εἰν ἀγορῇ σκολιὰς κρίνωσι θέμιστας,
ἐκ δὲ δίκην ἐλάσωσι, θεῶν ὄπιν οὐκ ἀλέγοντες·
τῶν δέ τε πάντες μὲν ποταμοὶ πλήθουσι ῥέοντες,
πολλὰς δὲ κλιτῦς τότ' ἀποτμήγουσι χαράδραι,
ἐς δ' ἅλα πορφυρέην μεγάλα στενάχουσι ῥέουσαι
ἐξ ὀρέων ἐπὶ κάρ, μινύθει δέ τε ἔργ' ἀνθρώπων·
ὡς ἵπποι Τρῳαὶ μεγάλα στενάχοντο θέουσαι.

Iliad, Book XVI, ll. 384-93.
Cf. Hesiod: *Works and Days*, ll. 213-47, and Euripides: *Medea*, ll. 410-13.

[1] Granet, op. cit., p. 587. It will be seen that the Sinic philosophers were of one mind with their Indic *confrères* in assigning a higher rank in the hierarchy of Existence to a disciplined human being than to a volatile divinity. (For the Buddhist sages' attitude towards the gods of the Vedic Pantheon see pp. 19-20, above.)

[2] For the parallel between the abortive attempt of the Jesuits to facilitate the conversion of the Far Eastern World to Christianity, by transposing the Christian religion into terms of the Sinic philosophy, and the successful restatement of Christianity in terms of the Hellenic philosophy by the Alexandrian Fathers of the Church see V. C (i) (c) 4, vol. v, pp. 365-7, and V. C (i) (d) 6 (δ), vol. v, p. 539, above.

but by the phrase *T'ien Chu* (the Lord of Heaven);[1] in 1704 Bishop
Maigrot's edict was confirmed by a decree of Pope Clement XI;[2]
and the prospects of Catholicism in China were compromised—
as it proved, beyond rehabilitation—when, in December 1706,
Bishop Maigrot was summoned into the Emperor K'ang Hsi's
presence and was dismissed into banishment for his outrageous
presumption in venturing to dispute with the Son of Heaven
himself on the meaning of the Chinese word *T'ien*, although he
was convicted by the Emperor, in a personal colloquy, of being
quite unversed in the Sinic philosophy and even ignorant of the
Chinese language.[3]

This unhappy controversy might never have arisen if, in the
Sinic World some two thousand years before the day of the Manchu Emperor K'ang Hsi and the French Bishop Maigrot, an enrichment of the Sinic conception of the magical order of the Universe
had not brought with it a proportionate impoverishment of the
Sinic conception of the Godhead. For the *T'ien* whose personality
was so faint that a Papal Vicar-General was unwilling to recognize
in him a counterpart of the Christian *Deus* (notwithstanding the
willingness of the Son of Heaven to wield his immense authority
under an alleged mandate from this nebulous power) was an
abstraction from an earlier *Shangti* ('Supreme Ancestor')[4] whose
claim to have been a personal god would appear to be less open
to doubt.[5]

If we now turn our attention again for a moment to the Hellenic
World, and re-examine the Neoplatonic *Weltanschauung*, we may
be struck by its similarity to the Sinic *Weltanschauung* which we
have just been considering; and we shall notice that, although this
Neoplatonic conception of the Universe, unlike its Sinic counterpart, was abortive, it did nevertheless have the effect, even in

[1] Jenkins, R. C.: *The Jesuits in China* (London 1894, Nutt), p. 25.
[2] Ibid., p. 33.
[3] Ibid., pp. 28, 91, and 110–112.
[4] 'Supreme Ancestor' is the rendering of the term *Shangti* that is given in Fitzgerald, C. P.: *China, a Short Cultural History* (London 1935, Cresset Press), p. 36.
The fuller title *Hao-t'en Shangti* is analysed in Maspéro, H.: *La Chine Antique* (Paris
1927, Boccard), p. 162, footnote 1, as follows:
'La traduction de cette expression doit être considérée comme très approximative,
car son sens exact n'est en réalité pas connu. La signification de presque tous les termes
est douteuse: celle de *hao* paraît bien avoir été perdue dès le temps des Han. . . . *Chang*
[*Anglicè* '*Shang*'] peut signifier en haut, au propre, ou suprême, au figuré. Même les
mots *t'ien* et *ti* sont loin d'être simples: étant donné l'antiquité de l'expression, le sens de
t'ien est douteux; on a remarqué depuis longtemps la forme humaine donnée ancienne-
ment au caractère qui sert à écrire ce mot, ce qui semble indiquer une conception
anthropomorphique du ciel; et le mot correspondant des langues thāi, *t'en*, désigne les
dieux célestes, tandis que le ciel physique, le firmament, est désigné par le mot *fa*.
Quant au mot *ti*, il paraît être au propre une désignation des dieux célestes, et ses sens
usuels (titre rituel d'un empereur défunt, et, en général, empereur) n'en sont que des
dérivations.'
[5] In this matter of degree of personality the Sinic *Shangti* perhaps stands to the Sinic
T'ien as the Indic *Varuna* stands to the Hellenic *Uranus*.

embryo, of taking the colour out of the Solar divinity with the worship of whom Neoplatonism was associated. During the time when—in and after the bout of anarchy into which the Hellenic Society fell in the third century of the Christian Era—this last creative work of Hellenic minds was assuming the systematic shape which it wears in the fourth-century tract *De Diis et Mundo*,[1] the highly individual personalities and sharply distinctive visual forms of an Apollo and a Mithras were fading into the abstraction of a Sol Invictus,[2] and Aurelian's abstract Sol was paling in his turn into Julian's wintry Helios—a shadow-king of the Universe who, in Julian's constitution of the Cosmic Commonwealth, was relegated to the honorary presidency that had been assigned to Zeus by Zeno[3] and Cleanthes.

The substitution of Julian's Helios and Aurelian's Sol Invictus for a Mithras and an Apollo in the penultimate chapter of Hellenic history has an exact parallel in Ikhnaton's attempt to substitute the new-fangled worship of an intentionally abstract Sun-Disk for the historic worship of a Protean Amon-Re;[4] and we may speculate whether, if the Egyptiac emperor-prophet's work had not died with him, it might not have resulted in a radical revision of the whole of the Egyptiac *Weltanschauung* on lines which would have exalted the conception of Law at the expense of the conception of the Godhead.[5]

Andean history affords another instance in which the abrupt and violent intervention of an external force—in this case, the Spanish conquest—may have anticipated the working out of the ultimate consequences of the deliberate substitution of a relatively faint and tenuous representation of the One True God for a relatively clear and concrete one. We have already observed[6] that the organization of an Egyptiac Pantheon, under the presidency of Amon-Re, on the initiative of the Pharaoh Thothmes III, has an analogue in the Inca Pachacutec's organization of an Andean Pantheon under the presidency of the Sun-God of Corichanca; but there is a further

---

[1] This illuminating document can now be studied in the admirable edition by Nock, A. D.: *Sallustius 'Concerning the Gods and the Universe'*, edited with Prolegomena and Translation (Cambridge 1926, University Press).

[2] For Sol Invictus see V. C (i) (c) 2, vol. v, p. 82, footnote 4, and V. C (i) (d) 6 (δ), Annex, vol. v, pp. 649-50 and 691-4, above.

[3] There is a touch of irony in the fact that the Hellenized Syriac philosopher who reduced the Olympian war-lord to a dignified state of impotence on the pretext of paying him honour was called, in Greek, by a name which engaged him to approach Zeus in the spirit of a devotee rather than in that of a disciplinarian.

[4] For Ikhnaton's fiasco see I. C (ii), vol. i, pp. 145-6, and V. C (i) (d) 6 (δ), Annex, vol. v, pp. 695-6, above.

[5] In the opinion of Breasted, J. H.: *The Development of Religion and Thought in Ancient Egypt* (London 1912, Hodder & Stoughton), p. 332, 'it is clear that' Ikhnaton 'was projecting a world religion'.

[6] In V. C (i) (d) 6 (δ), vol. v, pp. 530-2, above. See also V. C (i) (d) 6 (δ), Annex, vol. v, pp. 652-4, above.

analogy between the histories of the Andean and Egyptiac societies on the religious plane to which we have not yet paid attention. If the Andean World had its Thothmes III in the person of the Inca Pachacutec, it also had its Ikhnaton in the person of Pachacutec's immediate predecessor the Inca Viracocha;[1] for this emperor took up, and commended to his subjects, the worship of a creator-god[2] who was the namesake of his Imperial devotee.[3] The Andean religious innovator, however, was wiser in his generation than his Egyptiac counterpart.

In his zeal for his own conception of the One True God[4] Ikhn-

[1] Viracocha *imperabat circa* A.D. 1347–1400; Pachacutec *imperabat circa* A.D. 1400–48.

[2] For this Andean creator-god see Means, P. A.: *Ancient Civilizations of the Andes* (New York 1931, Scribner), pp. 422–40; Cunow, H.: *Geschichte und Kultur des Inkareiches* (Amsterdam 1937, Elsevier), pp. 175–85. This divinity was known on the Plateau by the name of Viracocha (Means, op. cit., p. 119) and on the Coast by the name of Pachacamec (Means, op. cit., pp. 184–5), and (according to Cunow, op. cit., p. 179) the two names mean respectively 'Earth Creator' and 'World Animator'; but these two general names probably replaced a host of previous local names, since they are both of them taken from the Quichua language (Means, op. cit., pp. 422–3), which was the *lingua franca* of the Incaic Empire (see V. C (i) (d) 6 (γ), vol. v, pp. 523–4, above). Means (in op. cit., pp. 424–5) brings forward reasons for believing that this Viracocha-Pachacamec was indigenous on the Plateau; that he was originally a sky-god; and that his worship can be traced at least as far back as a period in the growth-stage of Andean history, circa A.D. 600–900, which is known among the archaeologists as Tiahuanaco II. This was a period in which, as in the time of the Incaic Empire, there was an active cultural intercourse between the Plateau and the Coast.

[3] In this matter of names the Inca Viracocha's adoption of the name of the sky-god of Tiahuanaco is analogous to the gesture which the Pharaoh Amenhotep IV made when he took to calling himself Ikhnaton ('Aton is satisfied') in preference to his proper name Amenhotep ('Amon is at rest')—with, however, the significant difference that the Inca missionary of a new religion did not go out of his way to insult the religion of his fathers. An exact parallel to the Inca Viracocha's identification of himself with a god to whom he was peculiarly devoted is to be found in the assumption of the name Elagabalus by the Roman Emperor Marcus Aurelius Antoninus *alias* Varius Avitus Bassianus (see V. C (i) (c) 2, vol. v, p. 82, footnote 4, and V. C (i) (d) 6 (δ), Annex, vol. v, pp. 685–8, above).

[4] It may be noted in passing that the Aton, like Viracocha (Cunow, op. cit., pp. 179 and 183–4), was adored by his votaries as the creator and sustainer of the Universe; and the likeness between the Pharaoh's and the Inca's respective conceptions of God—at any rate in this aspect of the divine activity—may be illustrated by a comparison between the following extracts from two hymns: the hymn to the Aton which has been recovered by our modern Western archaeologists from the debris of Ikhnaton's Counter-Thebes at Tell-el-Amarna, and of which the text may be read in Erman, A.: *The Literature of the Ancient Egyptians*, English translation (London 1927, Methuen), pp. 288–91; and a hymn to Viracocha which is translated by Means, op. cit., p. 438, from sources described on p. 477, footnote 27.

The Egyptiac hymn runs:
'Beautiful is thine appearing in the horizon of Heaven, thou living Sun, the first who lived. . . .
'Thou who createst (male children?) in women, and makest seed in men! Thou who maintainest the son in the womb of his mother, and soothest him so that he weepeth not—thou nurse in the womb. Who giveth breath in order to keep alive all that he hath made.'

The Andean hymn runs:
'O conquering Viracocha!
Ever-present Viracocha!
Thou who art without equal upon the Earth!
Thou who art from the beginnings of the World until its end!
Thou gavest life and valour to men, saying:
"Let this be a man."
And to woman, saying:
"Let this be a woman."
Thou madest them and gavest them being.

aton tilted against an established religion which by his day was virtually impregnable against attack owing to the consolidation of all its forces, human and divine, into a single hierarchy and a single pantheon by the act of Ikhnaton's own predecessor and ancestor Thothmes III a hundred years before.[1] The Inca Viracocha would not have had to reckon with so formidable a resistance if he had attempted, in Ikhnaton's fashion, to take the fortress of the established religion by assault; for in the Andean World the equivalent of the work of Thothmes III was not carried out until after Viracocha had been succeeded by Pachacutec on the throne of the Incaic Empire. Nevertheless the Inca Viracocha, in his activities on behalf of the god whose name he bore, was careful not to embroil himself with the Sun-God of Corichanca who was the ancestral patron of the Incaic Dynasty. And accordingly, when the Inca Pachacutec set himself to translate his predecessor's ideas into practice, he was able to promote the respective worships of the Creator-God and the Sun-God simultaneously and side by side—in contrast to what happened in the Egyptiac World, where Ikhnaton's tactics not only drove Aton and Amon into conflict with one another, but turned their quarrel into a fight to the death.

By contrast, the Inca Pachacutec adroitly preserved the peace between the Creator-God Viracocha and the Corichancan Sun-God by insisting upon the diversity of their natures, spheres, and roles. At his Pan-Andean synod of priests he waited till he had obtained the assembly's consent to the organization of a pantheon of the historic local divinities, with the Corichancan Sun-God at their head, before he made, on his personal initiative, the more surprising, and perhaps also more contentious, suggestion that, side by side with this consolidation of all the other existing worships of the Andean World, a separate cult of Viracocha the Creator should be instituted for the benefit of the spiritual *élite*.[2] Possibly the consent of the synod to this second of the Inca's two proposals, as well as to the first of them, was the more readily accorded because Pachacutec simultaneously proposed a differentiation in the respective material provisions that were to be made for the service of the Corichancan President of the Pantheon and for that of his creator-colleague. While the Corichancan Sun-God was endowed with estates and revenues in every province and parish of 'the Land of the Four Quarters', as was meet and right for a divinity who was the heavenly patron and counterpart of the Sapa Inca himself, the etherial Viracocha needed no special

[1] Thothmes III *imperabat solus circa* 1480–1450 B.C.; Ikhnaton *imperabat circa* 1370–1352 B.C.
[2] Means, op. cit., pp. 427–8; Markham, Sir C.: *The Incas of Peru* (London 1910, Smith Elder), pp. 97–8.

endowments or memorials in a world that must everywhere and always bear witness to its Creator's power and glory by the sheer fact of its own existence. In the whole Incaic Empire no more than two temples dedicated to Viracocha are vouched for by the surviving records of Andean history.[1]

Supposing that the wayward goddess Fortune had permitted the Incaic Empire to live out the full term of life of a universal state, instead of bringing Pizarro from the farther side of the Atlantic to make havoc of Pachacutec's work within less than a hundred years, we may speculate whether the paternal, authoritarian, collectivist régime which Pachacutec had brought to perfection would have come, in course of time, to be reflected in some representation of the Universe as a commonwealth governed, *more Hellenico*, by a social law, but with a constitution of the Spartan rather than of the Athenian pattern. If we may allow our imagination to picture the development of an Andean *Weltanschauung* on such lines as these, then perhaps—on the analogy of what happened to Zeus—we may also imagine the *ci-devant* sky-god Viracocha being relegated to an Honorary Presidency of the Cosmic Phalanstery.[2]

We have now to consider those other representations of the constitution of the Universe in which its unity presents itself as the work of an omnipresent and omnipotent Godhead, while the Law which can be discerned in the Universe's structure and movement and life is regarded as being a manifestation of God's will, instead of being thought of as a sovereign unifying force which regulates the actions of gods and men alike if it leaves any place at all in the picture for anything that could be counted as divine.

We have observed already[3] that this concept of a unity of all

[1] Means, op. cit., pp. 428–9.
[2] There is, of course, the alternative possibility that Viracocha—unlike Zeus—might have risen to the occasion of the spiritual crisis under stress of which he was suddenly called upon by his worshippers to play a greater role than that for which he had been previously cast. We have already quoted, on page 21, footnote 3, the famous lines of Aeschylus in which the Hellenic poet expresses his yearning for an epiphany of Zeus in which his worshippers might be able to discern the lineaments of the One True God. This passage of Greek poetry has a remarkable Quichuan parallel in the following passages from a hymn to Viracocha which is translated by Means, op. cit., pp. 437–8, from sources described on p. 447, footnote 26:

'Viracocha, Lord of the Universe!
Whether male or female. . . .
Where art Thou?
Would that Thou wert not hidden from this son of Thine!

Creator of the World,
Creator of Man,
Great among my ancestors,
Before Thee
My eyes fail me,
Though I long to see thee.'

[3] On pp. 15–18, above.

things through God, as well as the alternative concept of a unity of all things through Law, is conceived by human minds through an analogy from the constitution which a human universal state inclines to assume as, after its foundation, it gradually crystallizes into its final shape. In this process of crystallization we have seen that the human ruler of the universal state, who at the outset is literally a King of Kings, eliminates the client princes who were once his peers and thereby transforms his own constitutional status from a suzerainty to a monarchy in the literal sense of that word. If we now examine what happens simultaneously to the gods of the diverse peoples and lands which the universal state has absorbed into its own body politic, we shall find that there is an analogous change in the reciprocal relations of these objects of human worship. In the place of a pantheon in which a high god exercises a suzerainty over a community of other gods who were once his peers, and who have not lost their divinity in losing their independence, we see emerging a single God whose uniqueness is His essence.

This religious revolution is apt to begin with a general change in the relations between divinities and worshippers. Within the framework of a universal state there is a tendency for all divinities to divest themselves of the bonds that have hitherto bound each of them up with some particular parochial human community. A divinity who has started life as the patron *de jure* and servitor *de facto* of some single tribe or town or valley or mountain now enters on a wider field of action by learning to appeal on the one hand to the Soul of the individual human being and on the other hand to the whole of Mankind; and, as each *genius loci* simultaneously steps out into this wider world which has at last been opened up for him by human empire-builders, there tends to arise, under the aegis of a political peace, a religious competition between rival worships which ends, like the foregoing physical warfare between parochial states, in the victory of some single competitor over all the rest. The course of this religious revolution, as it worked itself out in the arena of the Achaemenian Empire, has been described by Eduard Meyer in a passage which demands quotation in our present context, not only on account of the brilliance of its observation and analysis, but also because the particular chapter of religious history that is here recorded is typical of what is apt to happen on the religious plane of life within the political framework of any universal state.

'The most persistent effects of the Achaemenian Empire—effects which are still exerting a direct influence upon our own present age—are to be found in the domain of Religion. The Achaemenian régime saw the beginning of a transformation of religions that cut very deep. This development was assisted by the fact that the Achaemenian emperors treated the religions of their subjects with a large-hearted considerateness[1] and sought to erect them into props for their own policy; but a still more potent factor was the mere existence of an empire which embraced the whole World as the Achaemenian Empire did.

'In ancient times Religion had been the most vital expression of the political community. It was the Gods that enabled the State to keep alive, to maintain itself in conflict with other Powers, and to increase in power and prosperity. But all that had changed since the national states, one after another, had been deprived, at the very least, of their political independence and had mostly been annihilated, so that the inhabitants of all the civilized countries of South-Western Asia had had to accustom themselves to seeing their fate decided by foreigners. Occasionally this experience led to a repudiation of the native divinity who had shown himself so weak and powerless that his worship had patently ceased to be worth while. But, so far as can be seen, this consequence was drawn only by isolated individuals. Among people in the mass the belief in the reality of the native divinities was too deeply rooted for there to be any possibility of the people tearing themselves away from their traditional objects of worship. And there was a way out of the dilemma which was always open: either the god was angry, or else he had helped the adversary's cause to triumph because it was the cause that deserved to win. Cyrus is in Babylon the legitimate king who has been elected by Marduk, while Nabonidus is the apostate who has been rejected. In the eyes of the Prophets of Israel the victory of the Assyrians and Chaldaeans over the Prophets' countrymen is the work of the victims' own national god. He wills to chastise his people, and even to annihilate them, because they fail to understand his true nature; and he demonstrates his power all the more dazzlingly by bestowing the gift of world domination upon a nation which knows nothing of him and which fondly imagines that he is one of the powers whom it has vanquished. Others try to console themselves with the idea by which the Delphic Oracle attempted to justify its behaviour towards Croesus: above the god there stands a still mightier power to which the god has to submit—either an inexorable Fate of an impersonal kind (the Necessity of the Orphics), or else the verdict of some supreme Ruler of the Universe.[2]

'In any case the inevitable result is a revolution in the old concept of God. Already, through a theological extension of a naïve faith, the national gods had everywhere become cosmic powers as well—powers whose creative, life-giving, preservative activity embraces Heaven and Earth. Now, with the annihilation of the National State and the cessation of public life, the political side of the divinity falls away and the universal concept alone survives. Manners and customs converge; the

---

[1] For the religious policy of the Achaemenidae see also the present Study, V. C (i) (d) 6 (δ), Annex, vol. v, pp. 704–5, above.—A.J.T.

[2] In this last sentence Meyer is, of course, referring to the alternative road which we have already reconnoitred in this chapter and which leads, not towards an Almighty God, but towards a Sovereign Law.—A.J.T.

nations mingle with one another—partly in the peaceful way of commercial intercourse, partly through the coercive action of the rulers; in many cases even the native language disappears before the face of the great languages that are the vehicles of Civilization.[1] In these circumstances the national community falls back more and more upon Religion: that is, upon the worship of the gods who are indigenous in its homeland, and upon the scrupulous observance of their ritual. This very process, however, endows the local religion with a capacity to extend its range beyond the old national frontiers. The worshippers of a given divinity are now no longer the members of the national community who have been born into that divinity's service and are beholden to him for their very existence: his worshippers are now those who acknowledge him and remain faithful to him, whether they be members of the national community or not; and this turns religion into something that is at once individual and universal. The god is no longer expected to bring public prosperity to the body politic: what every one expects of him is personal prosperity and individual advantage for the worshipper himself. And accordingly the foreigner can pray to this god just as well as some one who has inherited his relation to the god from his ancestors. So the divinity becomes an independent self-subsistent power which operates from its seat of worship and offers grace and blessing to all the World. This is how these divinities are regarded by the Achaemenian Imperial Government. The Government grants privileges and endowments to all the larger shrines; and at all of them sacrifices and prayers are offered for the well-being of the Emperor. The immediate ground for this policy is a desire to make capital for the Government out of the high prestige which the shrine possesses in the eyes of the subject population; but the Government is also moved by a genuine belief that these divinities are mighty powers and that it cannot be anything but an advantage to stand well with them.

'Thus Universalism and Individualism become the characteristic features of all religions and all worships. Every worship claims to be the highest, and if possible the only legitimate, one; every divinity claims to be a great cosmic power; and they all of them address themselves no longer—or no longer exclusively—to a national community, but primarily to each individual human being—promising him all kinds of profit, both on Earth and in the Other World, and this with greater certitude than any other god can offer. This religious revolution was not accomplished at one stroke, but it begins in the Achaemenian Age.[2] This age witnesses the prelude to the great competition between religions which fills the later centuries of Antiquity.

[1] For the spread of such *lingue franche* see the present Study, V. C (i) (*d*) 6 (γ), vol. v, pp. 483-527, above.—A.J.T.

[2] The progress of the same religious revolution during the Roman Imperial Age is noticed by Spengler, O.: *Der Untergang des Abendlandes*, vol. i (Munich 1920, Beck), pp. 576-7. A corresponding religious revolution from a public communal to a private personal relation between the Soul and God took place in the Indic World at the birth of the Mahāyāna and of Hinduism (see V. C (i) (*c*) 2, vol. v, pp. 135 and 138, above), and in the Egyptiac World during the two centuries beginning with the generation of Ikhnaton (Breasted, J. H.: *The Development of Religion and Thought in Ancient Egypt* (London 1912, Hodder & Stoughton), pp. 348-9 and 355-6).—A.J.T.

'It has also now become possible to pay respect to a divinity at a distance from his local habitation and in detachment from his native soil and from his own people; for the bond which unites god and worshipper is no longer national or political but is personal and therefore indissoluble. Slaves and merchants and artisans who are permanently expatriated carry their divinity with them, found new shrines for him, and win adherents for him in foreign parts, while conversely the stranger who arrives at a seat of worship pays the divinity the tribute of his devotion and can be permanently won for this divinity's service.

'Hence all worships begin to make an active propaganda. They either bestir themselves to widen the circle of the devotees of the shrine and to heighten its prestige and influence far and wide beyond mere parochial limits, or they seek to raise the ideas and the ritual of their religion to a status of commanding importance. For instance, the Babylonian and Egyptian priests broadcast their wisdom everywhere; the priests of the Pessinuntine Mother of the Gods, and those of kindred Anatolian and Syrian worships, enlist from all quarters a circle of fanatical adherents who are prepared to castrate themselves in the service of the divinity and to range over the face of the Earth as mendicant monks. These cults do not, any of them, make outright war upon those of the other gods: they merely relegate them to a position of inferiority, or demand at any rate a recognized position for themselves side by side with them. There are, however, certain religions that do not recognize the legitimacy of alien cults at all (the attitude of Zoroastrianism), or that even go so far as to condemn them as the most grievous sin against their own god (the attitude of Judaism). Their exclusiveness makes these religions all the more active in trying to win foreign adherents who, by their acceptance of the revelation, will save themselves from perdition and at the same time will bear witness among the nations to the power of the Only True God and will thereby raise the status of the god's worshippers in the eyes of the World. The teaching of Zarathustra, which was the religion of the ruling nation, addressed itself, from the very beginning, to the whole Human Race and therefore never had an exclusive national character. The religion of Yahweh did not completely lose, but did recast, its original nationalism under the impact of the blows of Fate which descended on the Jewish people; and, after achieving this transformation, it began to enlist proselytes all the more actively for coming late into the mission-field.

'Inwardly, too, the religions begin to become assimilated to one another. All the worships of the Oriental World now pass through the same process as the parochial worships of the cantons of Egypt. The only surviving differences between them are simply differences of name and of the minutiae of liturgical practice. In substance all these worships are now indistinguishable[1]—all gods having become sun-gods and all goddesses heaven-goddesses—and this convergence has the para-

---

[1] 'En général la religion était partout la même; les dieux seuls étaient différents; et, si leurs cultes s'étendaient quelquefois, c'était en se mêlant et non en se chassant réciproquement des contrées où ils étaient reçus.'—Œuvres de Turgot (Paris 1844, Guillaumin, 2 vols.), vol. ii, p. 621 ('Géographie Politique').—A.J.T.

doxical effect of stimulating their militant competition with each other.
Spiritually, politically, and socially the plane on which the several religions live becomes more and more uniform, and this leads to the
formation of uniform religious general ideas which present themselves
in the individual worships and individual religions with merely superficial differentiations. No one can any longer find satisfaction in the old
notion that the divinity to whom he pays devotion is a local power whose
operation is confined to a particular territory. Every one thinks of his
god as the epiphany of a universal cosmic power, which both rules the
Earth and guides the destiny of Man—as a sun-god or a heaven-god if
the divinity is male, and as a goddess of fertility or a nature-goddess if
she is female. Hence in Syria and Phoenicia "the Lord of Heaven"
(*Be'elšamîn*) acquires ever greater prestige. He is "the good god who
rewards his devotees" in the language of later inscriptions, and he is
also the Thunderer on High. Sometimes the divinity is invoked without
being named. For example, the inscriptions on Palmyrene altars of the
Hellenistic Age invoke "Him whose name is praised unto Eternity, the
Gracious, the Compassionate". Side by side with this Unnamed God,
Bêl, "the Guider of Fate", pushes his way in from Babylonia. One feels
how close the individual gods have come to one another—how, in some
sense, each of them is simply an epiphany of the others. Even the Jews,
in addressing themselves to foreigners, designate their god, not as
Yahweh, but as "the Heaven-God of Jerusalem"; and by this designation they present him to their Persian masters as the peer of Ahuramazda.'[1]

One reason why these formerly parochial and variegated divinities were thus being drawn into an ever closer conformity with one
another was because they were now subject, all alike, to the
influence of a single ensample; and this loadstone was the human
monarch of a universal state which had provided the political
container for this religious ferment.

'Après la conquête de Babylone par Cyrus, le culte mazdéen s'installa
dans cette antique métropole et un grand nombre de mages s'y établi-
rent. Entre eux et les Chaldéens, un voisinage plusieurs fois séculaire
amena des rapports de confraternité, et ainsi le mazdéisme importé en
Chaldée subit l'ascendant de la religion autochtone. Toute la théologie
des mages se pénétra d'astrologie. Dans cette astrologie chaldéo-
persique, le gouvernement du ciel, pour demeurer le patron et le modèle
des puissances terrestres, dut se prêter à une transformation. A la
hiérarchie de justiciers établie là-haut par les anciens Chaldéens, se
substitua l'idée d'une royauté sidérale analogue à l'Empire des Aché-
ménides. Puis, cette notion nouvelle d'un palais étoilé se répandit partout où s'imposait la suprématie des Perses et elle s'y perpétua dans le

---

[1] Meyer, E.: *Geschichte des Altertums*, vol. iii (Stuttgart 1901, Cotta), pp. 167–71.
Cf. eundem: *Ursprung und Anfänge des Christentums*, vol. ii (Stuttgart and Berlin 1921,
Cotta), pp. 17–19, and *Geschichte des Altertums*, vol. i, part (2), 4th ed. (Stuttgart and
Berlin 1921, Cotta), pp. 153–7.

culte. "L'inscription de Nemroud-Dagh[1] parle des trônes célestes de Zeus Oromasdès, et un bas-relief nous le montre assis sur un trône, le sceptre à la main." Hostanès se le figure de même, les anges ou messagers divins faisant cercle autour de lui. Dans des textes nombreux, on retrouve un souvenir, lointain parfois, de la croyance qui fit comparer le Maître du Monde avec le Grand Roi, et ses assesseurs avec des satrapes. C'est de là que devait venir, avec l'idée d'un Royaume des Cieux, si familière à nos esprits, la conception stoïcienne d'une Cité du Monde gouvernée par les planètes et les étoiles fixes, auxquelles les hommes sont assujettis.'[2]

The closing sentence of this last quotation brings us back to the now familiar forking-point of the road which we are attempting to survey; but this time we have not to follow out the branch leading towards a Cosmic Law, which we have explored already, but the other branch which leads towards a Unique and Omnipotent God; and in this direction the first landmark that we shall notice is the influence of the Achaemenian Monarchy upon the Jewish conception of the God of Israel.[3]

'In the Jewish religion, the [heavenly] court, by which Yahweh is waited upon, is elaborated on a Babylonian pattern, even though certain old native conceptions may account for the origin of the idea.'[4]

And, in Jewish minds, this new conception of Yahweh had worked itself out to completion by about 166–164 B.C., which appears, from internal evidence, to have been the approximate date of the writing of the prophetical part of the Book of Daniel.

'I beheld till the thrones were cast down, and the Ancient of Days did sit, whose garment was white as snow, and the hair of his head like the pure wool; his throne was like the fiery flame, and his wheel as burning fire.

'A fiery stream issued and came forth from before him; thousand thousands ministered unto him, and ten thousand times ten thousand stood before him; the judgment was set and the books were opened.'[5]

---

[1] See V. C (i) (d) 6 (δ), vol. v, p. 547, footnote 2, above.—A.J.T.
[2] Bidez, J.: La Cité du Monde et la Cité du Soleil (Paris 1932, Les Belles Lettres), pp. 7–8.
[3] The Jews appear to have taken this turning deliberately, for they rejected and contemned the science of Astrology because they perceived the fundamental incompatibility of its belief in an inexorable mathematical law with a belief in God as an omnipotent personality (Meyer, E.: Ursprung und Anfänge des Christentums, vol. ii (Berlin 1921, Cotta), p. 54).
[4] Meyer, E.: Geschichte des Altertums, vol. iii (Stuttgart 1901, Cotta), p. 172. In his Ursprung und Anfänge des Christentums, vol. ii (Berlin 1921, Cotta), pp. 58–9, the same scholar points out that Yahweh is already conceived in the likeness of an Achaemenian emperor in Zech. iii, which was written circa 519 B.C., as well as in the Book of Job, which was written about a century later.
[5] Dan. vii. 9–10. This precise and vivid picture of Yahweh in the likeness of an Achaemenian Great King appears to have been borrowed by Judaism from Zoroastrianism. According to von Gall, A.: Βασιλεία τοῦ Θεοῦ (Heidelberg 1926, Winter), p. 268, 'the Ancient of Days . . . has nothing whatever in common with the god Yahweh, whom the Jews would never have visualized in this shape; the Ancient of Days is Ahuramazda,

The Achaemenian Great King is not, however, the only monarch of a universal state in whose likeness his subjects have shaped their conceptions of an Almighty God. In the Egyptiac World, for example,

'the conception of the Sun-God as a former king of Egypt, as the father of the reigning Pharaoh, and as the protector and leader of the nation, still a kind of ideal king, resulted in the most important consequences for Religion. The qualities of the earthly kingship of the Pharaoh were easily transferred to Re. . . . The whole earthly conception and environment of the Egyptian Pharaoh were soon, as it were, the "stage properties" with which Re was "made up" before the eyes of the Nile-dweller. When, later on, therefore, the conception of the human kingship was developed and enriched under the transforming social forces of the Feudal Age,[1] these vital changes were soon reflected from the character of the Pharaoh to that of the Sun-God.'[2]

who was portrayed by the Persians as he is described in Dan. vii. 9'. Cf. Meyer, E.: *Ursprung und Anfänge des Christentums*, vol. ii, pp. 195–9. The profoundness of the effect which this Iranian image exerted upon the Syrian imagination, when once it had been transmitted from the Iranian to the Syrian province of the Syriac World, is revealed by a comparison of several scattered pieces of evidence. The most celebrated testimony is the reproduction of the passage quoted above from Daniel (vii. 9–10) in Revelation (i. 13–16), where we see a Christian writer who wishes to present a visual image of his Christ in His glory drawing upon the Iranian imagery of a Jewish work which by this time was not much less than three centuries old. It is perhaps not less significant that one of the features in this literary image is reported to have been simulated 'in real life', by means of a trick, by at least two Syrian men of action who were as far separated from one another in time as the respective authors of the Book of Daniel and the Revelation of Saint John the Divine. Both these tricksters were violent-handed futurist leaders of the Hellenic internal proletariat; and, while the respective arenas in which they fought were far apart—Eunus's arena being in Sicily and Bar Kōkabā's in Palestine—their respective birthplaces were both on Syrian soil, since Eunus is known to have come from Apamea and Bar Kōkabā was presumably Palestinian-born. If both of them practised the same trick at dates divided by so wide an interval—Eunus in the seventh decade of the second century B.C., and Bar Kōkabā in the fourth decade of the second century of the Christian Era—this must mean that in Syria, at any time during the three centuries following the publication of the Book of Daniel, a proletarian agitator who preached insurrection, and who promised to lead his insurgent followers to victory on the strength of a divine commission which he claimed to hold, would be expected to give material evidence of this divine patronage by himself performing one of the prodigies that is attributed, in the Iranian imagery, to the Ancient of Days. According to Dan. vii. 10, 'a fiery stream issued and came forth from before him', while, according to Revelation i. 16, this flame came 'out of his mouth' in the shape of 'a sharp two-edged sword'. Now, according to Diodorus, Books XXXIV–XXXV, chap. 2, §§ 6–7, Eunus 'used to emit fire and flame from his mouth, with a certain display of divine possession (ἐνθουσιασμοῦ), by means of an apparatus; and this was the setting in which he used to declaim his prophecies. He used to take a nutshell or something of the sort, bore two holes in it on opposite sides, stuff it with fire and enough fuel to keep the fire alight, and then put it into his mouth and flare out sometimes sparks and sometimes flame by blowing into it. In the days before he rose in revolt, Eunus used to declare that the Syrian Goddess had granted him an epiphany and had told him that he was to become a king' (see V. C (ii) (a), Annex II, p. 383, below). Similarly, according to Saint Jerome, *Adversus Rufinum*, Book III, chap. 31 (= Migne: *Patrologia Latina*, vol. xxiii, col. 480), Bar Kōkabā 'used to put a lighted straw into his mouth and fan it into flame by blowing into it, in order to create the illusion that he was vomiting fire'. Presumably this trick was designed to lend authority to Bar Kōkabā's claim to be the Messiah (i.e. 'the Lord's Anointed').

[1] i.e. the Egyptiac 'Time of Troubles'. For this transformation of an earlier Egyptiac conception of the kingship see also the present Study, IV. C (iii) (c) 2 (β), vol. iv, pp. 408–14, above.—A.J.T.

[2] Breasted, J. H.: *The Development of Religion and Thought in Ancient Egypt* (London 1912, Hodder & Stoughton), pp. 16–17, cited already in I. C (ii), vol. i, p. 141, above.

In the Sinic World, likewise, we find the same mental imagery already taking shape during the 'Time of Troubles' which preceded the foundation of a Sinic universal state by Ts'in She Hwang-ti. At any rate, the philosopher Mo-tse, who lived from the fifth into the fourth century B.C.,

'pour réfréner les vices des tyrans . . . évoque, à la suite des poètes de la cour royale, l'idée du Ciel Justicier, du Souverain d'En-haut, patron dynastique. Aussi parle-t-il de la Volonté du Ciel (*T'ien tche*) avec les mêmes termes, à peu près, qu'il emploie pour exiger une entière soumission aux décisions du souverain.'[1]

This pair of illustrations from the histories of other civilizations may serve to show that the course of religious evolution in the Syriac World, within the political framework of the Achaemenian Empire and its Seleucid 'successor-state',[2] was not anything exceptional, but was a normal development which exemplifies a general rule. In the political and social circumstances to which the foundation of a universal state gives rise, a number of previously parochial divinities simultaneously assume the insignia of the newly established terrestrial monarch and then compete with one another for the sole and exclusive dominion which these insignia imply, until at length one of the competitors annihilates all the other claimants and thus establishes his title to be worshipped as the One True God. This outcome of the Battle of the Gods is analogous to that of the terrestrial struggle for existence between human princes during the disintegration of a civilization; for, in the course of the two successive rounds in which this political conflict works itself out, one of the competitors first either annihilates or subjugates all his peers in the internecine warfare of a 'Time of Troubles', and afterwards peacefully yet relentlessly eliminates those of them who have temporarily survived the establishment of a universal state by reconciling themselves to becoming client princes of a victorious King of Kings—with the result that the victor-suzerain turns into a monarch who, in his final plenitude of power, is the sole embodiment of royalty and vehicle of sovereignty and source of authority in his world. There is, however, one vital point on which the analogy that we have been drawing does not hold.

In the constitutional evolution of a universal state the universal monarch whom we find enthroned in solitary sovereignty at the end of the story is usually a direct successor—in an unbroken constitutional sequence—of the Pādishāh, or overlord of client

1 Granet, M.: *La Pensée Chinoise* (Paris 1934, Renaissance du Livre), p. 495.
2 For the transmission to the Seleucid Monarchy of the Achaemenian Empire's function as a political *foyer* for acts of religious creation see Part I. A, vol. i, pp. 5–6, above.

princes, under whose auspices the story opens.[1] When an Augustus who had been content to make his authority felt in Cappadocia or Palestine or Nabataea by maintaining a general superintendence over local kings or tetrarchs was succeeded in due course by a Hadrian who administered these former principalities as provinces under his own direct rule, there was no break in the continuity of the dominant power; for Hadrian, no less than Augustus, was master of the Hellenic Οἰκουμένη in virtue of being the head of the Roman State, and he was still exercising this Roman authority in the form of the Principate—a subtle institution which was the principal heirloom in Augustus's political legacy. In fact, the universal state with which the Hellenic World had originally been endowed by Roman empire-builders had not ceased to be a Roman Empire in consequence of the subsequent process by which the former client-states had been administratively *gleichgeschaltet* through being assimilated to the provinces that had been under the direct government of the Princeps and the Senate from the beginning. On the other hand, in the corresponding and contemporary religious change, continuity, so far from being the rule, is a theoretically possible exception which it might be difficult to illustrate by historical examples.

The writer of this Study cannot, indeed, call to mind a single case in which the high god of a pantheon has ever served as the medium for an epiphany of God as the unique and omnipotent master and maker of all things. Neither the Corichancan Sun-God nor the Theban Amon-Re nor the Babylonian Marduk-Bel nor the Vedic Dyauspitar nor the Olympian Zeus has ever revealed the countenance of the One True God beneath his own Protean mask.

[1] There is, however, at least one conspicuous exception to this rule in the constitutional history of the Sinic universal state. In the first place the founder, Ts'in She Hwang-ti, attempted to carry through by force, within the span of a single reign, a process of *Gleichschaltung* which, in the constitutional history of the Roman Empire, was spread over a period of not much less than two centuries. In the second place this ruthless radicalism evoked an equally violent reaction which did not indeed destroy the universal state that had just been founded by this empire-builder of the House of Ts'in, but did depose Ts'in She Hwang-ti's dynasty in favour of a *novus homo* whose ancestors had had no part or lot in the Ts'in Dynasty's empire-building work. In the third place the *parvenu* founder of the Prior Han Dynasty tried to repair Ts'in She Hwang-ti's error, and to avoid the Ts'in Dynasty's fate, by abandoning the radical policy of *Gleichschaltung* and centralization for a conservative policy of re-establishing the *ci-devant* parochial states of the Sinic World as client kingdoms under the *parvenue* dynasty's suzerainty. In the fourth place the Han Dynasty soon discovered, by trial and error, that this attempt at political devolution was after all an anachronism; and they then reverted to Ts'in She Hwang-ti's policy of centralization—but this time with greater tact and at a gentler pace. We can transpose the constitutional history of the Sinic universal state into Hellenic terms by imagining what might have happened if the Battle of Actium had been won, not by Octavian, but by Antony and Cleopatra. In that imaginary event the Hellenic universal state which had been established by Roman arms in the course of the preceding two hundred years might have been ruled for the next four centuries by a Government seated at Alexandria and administering Roman Italy as a client republic or even as a subject province. (The psychological reaction of the Alexandrians to the chagrin of having just missed their 'manifest destiny' is examined in V. C (ii) (a), pp. 217–19 below.)

And even in the Syriac universal state, where the god who was worshipped by the Imperial Dynasty was not a divinity of this synthetic kind and was also not a product of *raison d'état*,[1] the deity through whose lineaments the existence and the nature of a One True God became apparent to Mankind was not Ahuramazda the god of the Achaemenidae: it was Yahweh the god of the Achaemenian emperors' insignificant Jewish subjects. This victory of Yahweh over Ahuramazda, and over all the other divinities of the Achaemenian Empire and its 'successor-states' who had been competing with the once parochial god of Israel and Judah for the superlative honour of becoming an epiphany of God Almighty, is the triumph that is celebrated in the Eighty-second Psalm:

'God standeth in the congregation of the mighty; he judgeth among the gods. . . .
' "I have said: *Ye are gods, and all of you are children of the Most High*;
' "But ye shall die like men, and fall like one of the princes."
'Arise, O God; judge the Earth; for thou shalt inherit all nations.'[2]

The note of this paean is not pitched too high; for, while Asshur's following had dwindled, by the time when the Jewish poem was written, to as small a company[3] as Ahuramazda's worshippers muster to-day,[4] these stricken gods' rival Yahweh—whose Chosen People was first trampled under foot by the Assyrians and then raised from the dust by the Achaemenidae—has grown into the God of Christendom and Islam as well as the God of Jewry. This contrast between the ultimate destinies of the rival divinities and the momentary fortunes of their respective followers makes it evident that the religious life and experience of generations born and bred under the political aegis of a universal state is a field of historical study which offers to the observer some striking and momentous examples of the phenomenon of *Peripeteia* or 'the reversal of roles';[5] and in fact it is not an exception, but the rule, for the particular representation of the Godhead which is singled out for becoming a vehicle of the revelation of the unity of God, in this unitary political phase of the disintegration of a civilization, to be an obscure divinity of humble antecedents. At the same time

---

[1] For the origin and nature of the Zoroastrian religion see I. C (i) (*b*), vol. i, p. 81, and V. C (i) (*c*) 2, vol. v, p. 121, above; for the religious policy of the Achaemenidae see V. C (i) (*d*) 6 (δ), Annex, vol. v, pp. 704–5, above.

[2] Ps. lxxxii. 1 and 6–8.

[3] For the remnant of the Assyrian people which continued, for some centuries after the destruction of Nineveh in 612 B.C., to worship their eponymous divinity among the ruins of the city of Asshur in which he and his worshippers had begun their common career, see IV. C (iii) (*c*) 3 (α), pp. 470–1, above.

[4] For the downfall of Zoroastrianism, and for its political cause, see V. C (i) (*d*) 6 (δ), Annex, vol. v, pp. 659–61, above.

[5] For *Peripeteia* see IV. C (iii) (*c*) 1, vol. iv, pp. 245–61, above.

this original lowliness and obscurity are not the only features that are characteristic of the divinities that are cast for this overwhelming role.

When we look into the nature and êthos of Yahweh as these are portrayed for us in the scriptures that we have inherited from his pre-Christian worshippers, two other features immediately strike the eye. On the one hand Yahweh is in origin a local divinity—in the literal sense *glebae adscriptus* if we are to believe that he first came within the Israelites' ken as the *jinn* inhabiting and animating a volcano in North-Western Arabia, and in any case a divinity who struck root in the soil of a particular parish, and in the hearts of a particular parochial community, after he had been carried into the hill country of Ephraim and Judah as the divine patron of the barbarian war-bands who broke into the Palestinian domain of 'the New Empire' of Egypt in the fourteenth century B.C.[1] On the other hand Yahweh is 'a jealous god',[2] whose first commandment to his worshipper is :'Thou shalt have no other gods before me.'[3] It is not, of course, surprising to find these two traits of provincialism and exclusiveness displayed by Yahweh simultaneously; for a god who keeps strictly to his own local domain may be expected to be equally strict in warning off any neighbouring gods who show a disposition to trespass. What is, however, surprising —and even repellent, at any rate at first sight—is to see Yahweh continuing to exhibit an unabated intolerance towards the rivals with whom he courts a conflict when, after the overthrow of the parochial kingdoms of Israel and Judah and the establishment of a Syriac universal state in the shape of the Achaemenian Empire, the *ci-devant* god of two small upland principalities steps out into a wider world and aspires, like his neighbours, to win for himself the worship of all Mankind. In this oecumenical phase of Syriac history the persistence of Yahweh in maintaining the intolerant attitude and outlook that were legacies from his parochial past was an anachronism which was undoubtedly out of tune with the

---

[1] See I. C (i) (*b*), vol. i, p. 102, and V. C (i) (*c*) 3, Annex III, vol. v, p. 611, above.

[2] Exod. xx. 5 and xxxiv. 14; Deut. v. 9 and vi. 15; Joshua xxiv. 19.

[3] Exod. xx. 3; Deut. v. 7 and vi. 14. According to Woolley, Sir L.: *Abraham* (London 1936, Faber), chap. 6, pp. 234–5 and 244, the 'jealousy' which is one of the outstanding characteristics of Yahweh the God of Moses was already characteristic of the nameless God of Abraham, of Isaac, and of Jacob with whom Yahweh came to be identified by Abraham's descendants in the Mosaic Age. In Woolley's view Abraham's God was the Family God that had been worshipped in every household in Ur, and it was of the essence of this Family God that 'he could admit no alien worshippers and have no outside interests'. In persisting in the worship of this Family God when he left the city gods of Ur behind him, Abraham became, not indeed a monotheist, but at least 'monolatrous'. It will be seen that the God of Abraham (if Woolley is right) resembled the God of Moses in the point of exclusiveness, but differed from him in not being tied to any particular locality. While the worship of Yahweh was bound up with Yahweh's successive local habitations on Sinai, at Bethel, and in Jerusalem, the God of Abraham, of Isaac, and of Jacob was worshipped by his Nomadic votaries wherever they happened to pitch their moving tents.

temper that was prevalent in that age among the host of *ci-devant* local divinities of Yahweh's kind, who for the most part were conducting their tournament in a spirit of 'live-and-let-live' and 'give-and-take'.[1] This unamiable anachronism was, nevertheless, as we shall see, one of the elements in Yahweh's character that helped him to win his astonishing victory.

It may be instructive to look into these two traits of provincialism and exclusiveness more closely, taking the provincialism first and the exclusiveness second.

The choice of a provincial divinity to be the vehicle for an epiphany of a God who is omnipresent and omnipotent and unique might seem at first sight to be an inexplicable paradox; for, while the Jewish and Christian and Islamic conception of a God with these attributes[2] has indisputably been derived, as a matter of historical fact, from the figure of a Yahweh who makes his first appearance on the terrestrial scene as the Thunderer of Sinai or as the Ba'al of Shiloh, it is equally indisputable that the theological content, as opposed to the historical origin, of the idea of God which is common to these three monotheistic religions sprung from a single Syriac root is immeasurably different from the primitive representation of Yahweh, and bears a far closer resemblance to a number of other conceptions to which, as a matter of historical fact, the Islamic-Christian-Jewish conception is either indebted less deeply or even—in some of the cases in question—not indebted at all, so far as we can tell. In point of universality the Islamic-Christian-Jewish conception of God has less in common with the primitive representation of Yahweh than it has with the picture of the high god of a pantheon—an Amon-Re or a Corichancan Sun-God or a Marduk-Bel—whose authority at any rate extends in some sense over the whole of the Universe, even though the divinity by whom this supreme power is exercised be neither omnipotent nor unique. Or, if we take as our standard of comparison the degree of the spirituality that the different conceptions of God display, here the latter-day Jewish and Christian and Islamic conception of God has more in common with the abstractions of the philosophic schools: with an Andean Viracocha, an

---

[1] The abnormality of the exclusiveness that was displayed, in different degrees of militancy, by both Judaism and Zoroastrianism in the Achaemenian Age, is noticed by Eduard Meyer in the passage quoted on p. 32, above.

[2] It was because Christianity had inherited from Judaism the conception of a God who was unique that the Hellenes looked upon the Christians as being no better than atheists (see IV. C (iii) (c) 2 (β), vol. iv, p. 348, and the passage quoted from the writings of the Emperor Julian in V. C (i) (c) 2, Annex II, vol. v, p. 584, above). 'To the mind of a Roman there was something atheistic in Yahweh's claim to be the only god in existence. For the Roman, *One* God was *no god*' (Spengler, O.: *Der Untergang des Abendlandes*, vol. ii (Munich 1920, Beck), p. 567). See further V. C (ii) (a), Annex II, in the present volume, p. 536, below.

Egyptiac Aton, a Neoplatonic Helios, a Confucian T'ien, a Stoic
Zeus, and even, perhaps, with a latter-day Western 'God the
Mathematician'. For the primitive figure of Yahweh, as we see it
(through a glass darkly) in the panorama of the Pentateuch, appears
equally gross whether we compare it with these philosophic abstractions or with our own idea of the God whose countenance has
been astonishingly revealed to us through Yahweh's features. Why
is it, then, that, in a mystery play which has for its plot the revelation of God to Man, the supreme role of serving as the vehicle for
the divine epiphany has been allotted, not to an etherial Aton or
even to an imperial Amon-Re, but to a barbaric and provincial
Yahweh whose qualifications for playing this tremendous part
might seem, on our present showing, to be so conspicuously
inferior to those of so many of his unsuccessful competitors?

The answer to this hard question may perhaps be found in calling to mind one element in the latter-day Jewish and Christian and
Islamic conception of God which we have not yet mentioned. We
have dwelt so far upon certain qualities which are as prominent
in this etherial representation of God as they are conspicuous by
their apparent absence from the character of the primitive Yahweh
—the three sublime qualities of uniqueness and omnipotence and
omnipresence. Yet, for all their sublimity, these three attributes
of the Divine Nature are in themselves no more than conclusions
of the human understanding; they are not experiences of the
human heart; and, while it is no doubt possible for a human soul
which has made its first discovery of God on the intellectual plane
to enter into communion with Him thereafter on that higher level
of spiritual intercourse on which human beings are able to love,
as well as know, their human fellow creatures, the attainment of
communion with God along a path on which the heart has to wait
upon the head is evidently 'hard and rare'. Few human souls have
succeeded, like Ikhnaton or Akbar, in winning the *Visio Beatifica*
for themselves by this intellectual approach;[1] fewer still have
succeeded, like Zarathustra, in communicating to others a vision
that has been gained in this primarily intellectual way; and this
will not surprise us when we consider what element in God's
nature it is that we have so far left out of account; for it is an
element that is no mere attribute but is rather the very essence
of the Divine Nature as it presents itself to us—an essence apart
from which the Godhead could hardly be imagined as existing or
as being capable of having any attributes ascribed to it.

For Man, God's essence is that He is a living god with whom

---

[1] For the failure of Ikhnaton and Akbar to become founders of new religions see
V. C (i) (*d*) 6 (δ), Annex, vol. v, pp. 695–6 and 699–704, above.

a living human being can enter into a spiritual relation that is
recognizably akin to his spiritual relations with the living human
beings among whom Man lives his earthly life as a social creature.
This fact of being alive is the essence of God's nature for human
souls that are seeking to enter into communion with Him, and at
the same time it is the hardest element in God's nature for human
beings to grasp, since this living god has to be apprehended by
our human faculties without the aid of those physical evidences of
life—a visibility and a tangibility—that are offered by all other
living beings that come within Man's ken. And, if it is thus the
most difficult part of the knowledge of God to know Him in this
essential way, this difficulty is evidently at its maximum for a
spiritual explorer who attempts an intellectual approach to his
divine goal, since an intellectual apprehension of God's attributes
is a way of knowing God which is more remote than any other
from the direct communion of Life with Life. The seeker after
God who takes this intellectual path is like some climber who gains
his first footing on the mountain-side at the point which is not
only farthest from the summit but which is also separated from
it by the deepest chasms and the sheerest precipices. It is manifestly less difficult—however difficult it still may be—for a human
soul which is already in enjoyment of a direct communion with
God to enlarge its comprehension of the Divine Nature by graft-
ing a branch of intellectual knowledge on to the living stem of
its intuitive religious experience. In short, the natural order of
aspiration in any human endeavour to find the way to God is the
order which is followed in Francis Thompson's poem:

> O world invisible, we view thee,
> O world intangible, we touch thee,
> O world unknowable, we know thee,
> Inapprehensible, we clutch thee!

We can now perhaps see why our latter-day Islamic-Christian-
Jewish conception of God has grown, as it has, out of the primitive
figure of Yahweh and not out of the sophisticated constructions
of the philosophers; for this quality of being alive, which is the
essence of God as Jews and Christians and Muslims believe in Him
to-day, is likewise the essence of Yahweh as he makes his appearance in the Old Testament.[1] 'For who is there of all flesh that

1 In the minds of the Israelites this property of 'life' or 'existence' in the god whose
worship they had inherited from their forefathers eventually came to loom so large that,
at least in official parlance, the genuine traditional name of the god was distorted into
conformity with a false etymology which sought to derive the name itself from the outstanding property of the god who bore it. The true form of Yahweh's name appears to
have been Yahō or Yahū; for this is the form in which it figures in the compound proper
names into which it enters—and this not only in the Hebrew names in the Old Testament, but also in certain non-Israelite names, some of which are of earlier date (e.g. in
compound names current in Shinar in the time of Hammurabi, at Hamath in the time of

hath heard the voice of the living god speaking out of the midst
of the fire, as we have, and lived?'[1]—is the boast of Yahweh's
Chosen People after his epiphany to them on Sinai. And it is this
same assurance that the god whom they worship is a living god
that nerves the Israelites to invade and occupy the Palestinian provinces of 'the New Empire' of Egypt,[2] and afterwards to match
themselves against the rival Philistine claimants to Pharaoh's derelict Palestinian heritage.[3] When this living God of Israel encounters in turn an abstract Zoroastrian Ahuramazda[4] and an abstract

Sargon, and at Damascus in the time of Esarhaddon). Moreover, Yahū is the form of
his name under which the god was worshipped in the fifth century B.C. at Elephantine
by the Jewish, or Judaeo-Samaritan, garrison of that frontier-fortress of the Achaemenian
Empire. This original Yahū has been twisted into Yahwēh to give the word the appearance of being the third person singular of the imperfect tense of the verbal root HYH,
signifying 'existence'—though the correct form of this is not *yahwēh* but *yihyēh*. In
Exodus iii. 13–15 this name is represented as being revealed by its divine owner to
Israel through the mouth of Moses; and in this place the distortion is carried a stage
farther than usual; for while in verse 15 the Lord instructs Moses to declare to Israel
that 'Yahwēh the god of your fathers . . . hath sent me unto you' and 'this is my name for
ever', in the preceding verse the Lord reveals his name to Moses, not in the third person
as Yahwēh (purporting to mean 'He is'), but in a corresponding first person as Ehyēh
(purporting to mean 'I am'). This Ehyēh is so far removed from the original Yahū that
its origin would be an enigma if we did not happen to know the intermediate term.
(For this etymological evidence of the Israelites' sense of the vitality of their god see
van Hoonacker, A.: *Une Communauté Judéo-Araméenne à Éléphantine, en Égypte, aux
vie et ve siècles av. J.-C.* (London 1915, Milford), pp. 67–73. See also Pauly-Wissowa:
Real-Encyclopädie der Classischen Altertumswissenschaft, neue Bearbeitung, Halbband
xvii, cols. 698–721, s.v. Iao.)

[1] Deut. v. 26.   [2] Joshua iii. 10.   [3] 1 Sam. xvii. 26 and 36.

[4] Ahura Mazdāh means 'God the Wise'; and in the Zoroastrian conception of him
he is as abstract as the Stoic Zeus, even if there be truth in the conjecture that the
Iranian, like the Hellenic, abstraction has been drawn out of an historical divinity who,
in the Iranian case, would be Varūna, the Aryan counterpart of the Greek Ūranus (for
this conjecture see Christensen, A.: *L'Iran sous les Sassanides* (Copenhagen 1936, Levin
& Munksgaard), p. 28). Ahuramazda was conceived of by the Prophet Zarathustra as a
One True God who was served by attendant spirits of less than divine rank—though,
in the Gathas, these spirits, too, are called *ahuras*, like God Himself. The abstractness
(see Meyer, E.: *Ursprung und Anfänge des Christentums*, vol. ii (Stuttgart and Berlin
1921, Cotta), p. 59) of the beings who constitute the Zoroastrian Host of Heaven is as
evident in Zarathustra's names for these *amesha spentas* as it is in his name for the God
whom they serve. They are called (see Christensen, op. cit., pp. 29–30) Vohū Manah
('Good State of Mind'), Asha Vahishta ('The Best Truth'), Khshathra Vairya ('The
Desirable Kingdom [of God]'), Ārmaiti ('Submission'—compare Muhammad's term
'Islām'), Haurvatāt ('Integrity' or 'Health'), Ameretāt ('Immortality'), Sraosha
('Obedience'). It is astonishing that this hierarchy of undisguised abstractions should
have been substituted by a prophet of the External Proletariat for an anthropomorphi-
cally conceived barbarian pantheon—the Iranian counterpart of the Vedic Pantheon of
the Aryas—whose members were the hereditary objects of worship of Zarathustra's
world; yet, in order to clear the Universe for exclusive occupation by the creatures—or
discoveries—of his own penetrating thought, Zarathustra had the audacity to degrade
the traditional Iranian gods (the *daēvas*) to the rank of demons in the service of another
abstraction: Angra Mainyaush (Ahriman), 'the enemy spirit' or adversary of Ahuramazda. It is still more astonishing to find that this artificial, abstract, and universal
religion gradually supplanted the traditional Iranian paganism—though this at the price
of incorporating into itself a considerable amount of incongruous pagan ritual and myth.
The secret of this success—in which Zoroastrianism is perhaps unique among religions
and philosophies of this abstract kind—can hardly be ascribed to the royal patronage
which Zarathustra won for his new faith in his own lifetime, and which was retained by
Zoroastrianism until the end of the Achaemenian régime; for the Achaemenian Emperors took care not to force upon their subjects the religion which they had embraced
for themselves (see V. C (i) (d) 6 (δ), Annex, vol. v, pp. 704–5, above); and the intolerant enforcement of a Zoroastrian orthodoxy by the Sasanidae in a later age, so far
from proving beneficial to Zoroastrianism, had a disastrous effect upon its destinies

Stoic Zeus and an abstract Constantinian Sol Invictus[1] and an abstract Neoplatonic Helios, it becomes manifest that Yahweh

$$οἶος πέπνυται, τοὶ δὲ σκιαὶ ἀΐσσουσιν.[2]$$

For the primitive figure of Yahweh has grown into the Christian conception of God by annexing the intellectual attributes of these abstractions without deigning to acknowledge the debt or scrupling to obliterate their names.[3] The completeness of Yahweh's victory in this series of encounters is pointed by its contrast with what happened when another barbaric and parochial yet aggressively living god—the divine patron of the Arabian city-state of Mecca, who was known within the Ka'bah as Allāh, 'the god' *sans phrase* —came to be identified by the Prophet Muhammad with the omnipresent and omnipotent and unique God of Jewry and Christendom.[4] The Ba'al of Mecca who was thus suddenly magnified by the fiat of a man of genius did not contribute a single new attribute to the intellectual conception of the One True God whose *alter ego* Allāh was now proclaimed to be; but he has given proof of his vitality by imposing his own provincial name upon the God of the Universe on the lips of all the myriads of human beings in every part of the World who have come to know God through embracing Islam.

(see V. C (i) (*d*) 6 (δ), Annex, vol. v, pp. 659–61, above). A more powerful adventitious aid was the eventual enlistment of the Magi (V. C (i) (*d*) 6 (δ), vol. v, p. 542, above) in the service of an upstart faith which they had at first done their utmost to stamp out (compare the enlistment of the Brahmans in the service of Hinduism (V. C (i) (*c*) 2, vol. v, pp. 137–8, above) and the enlistment of the Egyptiac priesthood in the service of the worship of Osiris (I. C (ii), vol. i, p. 144, above)). But in the main we must attribute the remarkable success of Zarathustra's religion to the force of the Prophet's character and to the truth and profundity of his ideas. The eight concepts of the Devil, the Last Judgement, Salvation, the Saviour, Transfiguration (Frashōkarati), the Millennium, the Kingdom of God (Khshathra Vairya), and Immortality, which, between them, cover so large a part of the fields of Christian and Islamic theology, are all derived from Zoroastrianism through a Jewish channel (for the Zoroastrian origin of the Jewish eschatology see von Gall, A.: Βασιλεία τοῦ Θεοῦ (Heidelberg 1926, Winter), pp. ix–x and 156–7; for the Zoroastrian origin of the Jewish belief in Immortality see ibid., p. 160).

[1] For an interpretation of Constantine's vision of the Unconquerable Christ revealing his cross athwart the disk of the Unconquerable Sun see the passage quoted from N. H. Baynes in V. C (i) (*d*) 6 (δ), Annex, vol. v, p. 693, above.

[2] *Odyssey*, Book X, l. 495, quoted in Polybius, Book XXXVI, cap. 8.

[3] In the Christian diffraction of the Unity of God into a Trinity of Persons we can observe the extent of the Christian Theology's intellectual debt to the abstract religions and philosophies with which Judaism and Christianity had collided between the sixth century B.C. and the fourth century of the Christian Era. While in the Second Person of the Trinity the quality of being a living god has been brought home to human hearts, with quite a new emotional vividness and spiritual force, by a God who has renounced the unmitigated transcendence of Yahweh in order to become incarnate, the First Person of the Trinity is represented in the iconography of the Christian Church, as He is in the Book of Daniel (see p. 34, footnote 5, above), in the likeness of the Zoroastrian representation of Ahuramazda, and the Third Person of the Trinity is virtually identical in name, as well as in function, with the first of the Zoroastrian *amesha spentas*, Vohū Manah. In this theological plagiarism Christianity has done Zoroastrianism not a wrong but a service, for 'it is not until it has been taken up into Christianity that the *Weltanschauung* of the Iranian prophet begins to have its greatest effect in the field of world history' (Meyer, E.: *Ursprung und Anfänge des Christentums*, vol. ii (Stuttgart and Berlin 1921, Cotta), p. 441).

[4] See V. C (i) (*d*) 6 (δ), Annex, vol. v, p. 688, footnote 2, above.

If this persistent quality of being alive is the obverse of Yahweh's primitive provincialism,[1] we may find that the exclusiveness which is an enduring as well as an original trait in Yahweh's character has also some value which is indispensable for the historic role which the God of Israel has played in the revelation of the Divine Nature to Mankind.

This value begins to become apparent as soon as we consider the significance of the contrast between the ultimate triumph of the 'jealous god' of two puny and ephemeral Syriac principalities and the ultimate fiasco of the high gods of the pantheons of the two neighbouring societies which, between them, ground the political structure of the Syriac World to pieces, as a pair of converging icebergs might crush a frail kayak. In respect of being rooted in the soil and of flowing with the sap of visible and tangible life, both Amon-Re and Marduk-Bel could measure themselves against Yahweh on equal terms, while they had the advantage over him in being associated, in the minds of their hereditary worshippers, with the colossal worldly success of their native Thebes and Babylon—a success which was ascribed to the zeal and prowess of these great tutelary divinities on their peoples' behalf, whereas Yahweh's people had been left, in their abasement and captivity, to solve as best they could the problem of vindicating the benevolence and omnipotence of a tribal divinity who had apparently abandoned his tribesmen in their hour of need, without lifting a finger to defend them against a ruthless alien aggressor.[2] If, in spite of these telling points in their favour, Marduk-Bel and Amon-Re were outstripped, as they were, by Yahweh in the competition between divinities under the Achaemenian régime, we can hardly avoid ascribing their failure to their innocence of Yahweh's jealous vein; for the absence of this trait was as conspicuous in the characters of both the Egyptiac and the Babylonic high god as its presence was in the character of their obscure yet victorious Palestinian rival. A freedom—for good or for ill—from the spirit of exclusiveness is implicit in the hyphen which links the two parts of these synthetic divinities' respective names; for, if jealousy had been the ruling passion of either of the original constituents in either case, then neither of these composite high gods could ever even have come into existence.[3] No wonder that Marduk-Bel and Amon-Re were as tolerant of polytheism beyond the bounds of

---

[1] Compare the effect of the same quality in enabling natural languages of an originally no more than local currency to defeat artificial languages like Esperanto in the competition for becoming *lingue franche* (see V. C (i) (d) 6 (γ), vol. v, pp. 492–3, above).

[2] For the solution of this problem which Yahweh's Jewish worshippers worked out, see the passage quoted from Eduard Meyer on p. 30, above.

[3] For the manufacture of Amon-Re and Marduk-Bel as a symptom of the sense of promiscuity in the field of Religion see V. C (i) (d) 6 (δ), vol. v, pp. 529–31, above.

their own loose-knit personalities as they were tolerant of the
disunity in their Protean selves. Both of them alike were born—or,
more accurately speaking, were manufactured—to be content with
their primal status of suzerainty over a host of other beings who
were no less divine, and not even much less potent, than they were;
and, by the same token, this congenital lack of ambition doomed
them both to drop out of the competition for a monopoly of divinity when Yahweh's devouring jealousness would as surely spur him
on to run to the end this race that had been set before them all.[1]

The same relentless intolerance of any rival was also manifestly
one of the qualities that enabled the God of Israel, after he had
become the God of the Christian Church, to outrun all his competitors once again in another Battle of the Gods which was fought
out this time in the arena of the Roman Empire. These rival
candidates for the spiritual allegiance of the Hellenic internal
proletariat were of diverse natures and origins—a Syriac Mithras,
an Egyptiac Isis, a Hittite Cybele—but they were in unanimous accord with each other, and in unanimous disagreement
with their eventual conqueror, in being ready to enter into a
compromise. They would have been willing either to partition the vast population of the Hellenic universal state into as
many separate flocks as there were competing divinities, or to find
a niche for each and all of the divine competitors in each and every
human soul, or even to allow the ingenuity of their hierophants
to incorporate these hitherto rival gods into a joint-stock company
for a common exploitation of the vast new virgin territory which
lay open to the Oriental divinities in a Hellenic World whose
native gods were now too decrepit to be capable any longer of
fighting even on their own ground in defence of their traditional

---

[1] Heb. xii. 1. The enterprise of our modern Western archaeologists has disinterred at Elephantinê, in Upper Egypt, the records of one exception to the rule
of Yahweh's jealousness which proves the rule to have had the value that we have
just attributed to it. In the Aramaic papyri relating to the affairs of the Jewish, or
Judaeo-Samaritan, garrison of Elephantinê under the Achaemenian régime we find
that in this community of Yahū-worshippers the god did not enjoy a monopoly of worship but had at least four associates—'Anath-Yahū, 'Anath-Bethel, Ašm-Bethel, Haram-
Bethel—of whom the first two, at any rate, were goddesses (see Meyer, E.: *Der Papyrusfund von Elephantine*, 2nd ed. (Leipzig 1912, Hinrichs), pp. 54–63). These associates
of Yahū at Elephantinê appear to have been, not survivals from a pre-monotheistic
phase of Yahū-worship, but accretions contributed by a Samaritan element in the community at Elephantinê (for this explanation see van Hoonacker, op. cit., pp. 73–85,
especially p. 82; for the political origin and religious history of the Samaritans see
V. C (i) (c) 2, vol. v, p. 125, footnote 1, above). The most interesting feature in the
testimony of the Elephantinê papyri from our present point of view is the fact that,
fragmentary though they are, they inform us, not only that Yahū of Elephantinê was a
less jealous god than Yahweh of Jerusalem, but also that the worship of Yahū at Elephantinê failed to survive. One of the documents is a letter, written in 408–7 B.C., which
recounts the destruction of the temple of Yahū by the local priests of the Egyptiac god
Khnum with the connivance of the Persian military commandant at Elephantinê. And
the worship of the easy-going Yahū of Elephantinê, in contrast to the worship of the
jealous Yahweh of Jerusalem, seems to have perished in the ruin of the shrine in which
it had been carried on in this particular place.

rights.[1] This easy-going, compromising spirit was fatal to the rivals of the God of Tertullian when they had to face an adversary who could not be content with a less than 'totalitarian' victory because any abatement of his own exclusive claim to divinity would be, for him, a denial of his own essence.

The most impressive testimony to the value of the jealous vein in Yahweh's êthos is perhaps afforded by a piece of negative evidence that comes from an Indic World in which the God of Israel did not begin to make his existence felt until after the religion of the Indic internal proletariat had set hard in an indigenous form[2] that it still retains to-day.[3] In the Indic World, as elsewhere, the process of social disintegration was accompanied by the development of a sense of unity, and this made itself felt very forcibly on the religious plane—as was to be expected in a society in whose *habitus* the religious vein was dominant.[4] In response to an ever more insistent craving in Indic souls to apprehend the unity of God, the myriad divinities of the Indic internal proletariat gradually coalesced or dissolved into one or other of the two mighty figures of Shiva and Vishnu.[5]

'Vishnu is really all the other gods. Just as he is identical with Brahman and Çiva, so he condescends to manifest himself in beings which do not claim to be self-existent or without beginning. It involves some partial limitation of his own nature, some Docetic assumption of a temporary form. Çaiva piety reached the same end in a different way. "Victorious is the Eternal Sthānu (the 'Steadfast' or 'Stable'), whose one body is formed by the coalescence of all the gods": so ran the dedication of King Kakusthavarman (*regnabat* A.D. 500–50) on a great tank in Mysore adjoining a temple of Çiva.'[6]

---

[1] For this decrepitude of the native Hellenic divinities by the time of the foundation of the Roman Empire see I. C (i) (*a*), vol. i, p. 57; II. D (vi), vol. ii. pp. 215–16; and IV. C (iii) (*c*) 2 (*β*), vol. iv, p. 349, above.

[2] For the elements and êthos of Hinduism see V. C (i) (*c*) 2, vol. v, pp. 137–8, above.

[3] In essentials Hinduism appears to have attained its present form by the time of the Gupta Dynasty (*imperabant circa* A.D. 350–480, or, on a stricter reckoning, *circa* A.D. 390–470: see I. C (i) (*b*), vol. i, p. 85, footnote 1, above). On the other hand, Islam—which is the vehicle in which the 'jealous god' of Israel has made his epiphany on Indian soil—did not begin to impinge upon the Hindu World, even in the outlying and isolated province of Sind, until after the beginning of the eighth century of the Christian Era, and did not sweep over Hindustan until the turn of the twelfth and thirteenth centuries (see IV. C (ii) (*b*) 2, vol. iv, pp. 99–100, above).

[4] For this dominance of the religious vein in the *habitus* of both the 'apparented' Indic and the 'affiliated' Hindu Society see the quotations from Sir Charles Eliot in III. C (iii), vol. iii, pp. 384–5 and 388, above.

[5] The stage in the process of transcending a primitive polytheism which is represented, in the history of Indic religion, by the absorption of all other divinities into either Vishnu or Shiva was never completed in the Babylonic and Egyptiac worlds. There does, however, seem to have been an inchoate and abortive tendency, in the time of 'the New Empire' of Egypt, for Amon-Re to attract into his own personality some, at least, of the other divinities of the Thothmean Pantheon—to judge by certain passages from the Egyptiac religious literature of that age that have been quoted in V. C (i) (*d*) 6 (*δ*), vol. v, p. 531, above.

[6] Carpenter, J. Estlin: *Theism in Medieval India* (London 1921, Williams & Norgate), p. 290.

With a former multiplicity of local divinities thus absorbed into the personality of one or other of two alternative Lords of the Universe, Hinduism has reached the stage that was reached by the religion of the Syriac internal proletariat[1] in the Achaemeno-Seleucid Age, when the mighty figures of Ahuramazda and Yahweh confronted one another as the two survivors on a stricken field of battle between a host of divinities who had been contending for the prize of becoming the vehicle for a revelation of the unity of the Divine Nature. This penultimate stage on the road towards the apprehension of the unity of God was attained by Hinduism at least fifteen hundred, and perhaps two thousand, years ago; and yet, in all the time that has elapsed since then, Hinduism has never taken the final step that was taken by the Syriac religion when Yahweh—intolerant of even a single peer—disposed of Ahuramazda by swallowing him whole. In Hinduism the concept of an Almighty God, instead of being unified, has been polarized round the mutually complementary and by the same token antithetic figures of two equally-matched candidates who have persistently refrained from settling accounts with one another.

In face of this strange situation we are bound to ask ourselves why Hinduism has accepted, as a solution for the problem of the unity of God, a compromise which, so far from offering a genuine solution, involves an unresolved contradiction inasmuch as it is really impossible to conceive of a godhead that is omnipresent and omnipotent—as Vishnu and Shiva each claim to be—without being at the same time unique. As soon as we put this question, the answer stares us in the face. The reason why Hinduism has come to this tragic halt within sight of a goal towards which it has travelled over so long a road is because neither Shiva nor Vishnu is a 'jealous god' in Yahweh's vehement vein. So far from that, the êthos of both these Hindu divinities bears a manifest resemblance to that of the Hittite and Egyptiac and Syriac divinities—a Cybele and an Isis and a Mithras—whom the God of Israel overthrew after he had become the God of Christianity. In the same easy-going spirit Vishnu and Shiva have always preferred a compromise to a fight to the death; and it might have been expected *a priori* that, in a world where they did not find themselves confronted by any implacable rival, they would have been able to strike their compromise with an impunity that was impossible for Mithras and Cybele and Isis in an arena in which the Christians' 'jealous god' was also one of the combatants. Yet, as it has turned out, the fortunes of Shiva and Vishnu have been hardly happier than

[1] For the Syriac counterparts of the worships of Shiva and Vishnu see V. C (i) (c) 2, vol. v, p. 138, above.

those of their counterparts in the Roman Empire. They have been spared annihilation only to meet the more ironic fate of being reciprocally frustrated and stultified by one another. And this failure to apprehend the unity of God in a world in which the God of Israel has not been on the scene seems to indicate that the jealousness of Yahweh, which at first sight is so repellent, has a value that transcends its sheer survival-value in a struggle for existence between competing divinities. Its transcendent value lies in the disconcerting fact that a divinity who is credited by his worshippers with this spirit of uncompromising self-assertion proves to be the only medium through which the profound and therefore elusive truth of the unity of God has been firmly grasped hitherto by human souls.

8. Archaism

(α) Archaism in Institutions and Ideas.

Having now taken stock of the alternative ways of behaviour and feeling that present themselves to souls who are born into a socially disintegrating world, we may pass on to a consideration of the alternative ways of life that lie open to be followed in the same challenging circumstances; and here we may begin with that way which, in our preliminary reconnaissance of this stage in our Study, we have labelled 'Archaism'[1] and have defined[2] as an attempt to remount the stream of life—breasting the current and taking salmon-leaps up cataracts and waterfalls—in the hope of regaining one of those quiet upper reaches that in 'Times of Troubles' are regretted the more poignantly the farther they have been left behind.[3]

In making an empirical survey of examples of this phenomenon of Archaism, we shall perhaps obtain a clearer view if we once again divide the landscape up into those four fields—Conduct, Art, Language, and Religion—which we have already plotted out in the course of a preceding inquiry into the sense of promiscuity.[4]

---

[1] In V. C (i) (d) 1, vol. v, p. 383, above.

[2] In V. C (i) (d) 1, vol. v, pp. 383-4, above.

[3] In recalling our definition of the term Archaism, it may be timely to remind ourselves of the limitations which we are placing upon it in this Study. For our purposes Archaism means an attempt to recapture some elements from the past *of the society of which the archaist himself is a member*. We are not taking Archaism to mean any and every attempt at a reversion to something in the Past; for we are not including in our use of the term those renaissances of elements in an 'apparented' civilization which an 'affiliated' civilization sometimes achieves. On the conception of History which we are trying to work out in this Study, such renaissances are *contacts* between different civilizations in the Time-dimension, whereas Archaism is a movement which does not range outside the bounds of the single civilization to which the archaist himself belongs. From our standpoint this difference between Archaism within the Time-horizon of a single civilization and the contact in Time between two different civilizations is more important than the feature—common to Archaism and Contact in Time—of being an attempt at a reversion to the Past.   [4] See V. C (i) (d) 6, vol. v, above.

We shall find, however, that in these two different surveys our four fields are not completely coextensive in their several areas, and that this divergence arises from an inward diversity between the two states of mind which are the respective objects of study in the two cases. The sense of promiscuity is a spontaneous, un-self-conscious feeling which sometimes asserts itself, as we have seen, in defiance of tradition and of law and of public opinion and even of the taste and conscience of the person or persons whom the sense of promiscuity is overpowering and carrying away. By contrast, Archaism is a deliberate, self-conscious policy of attempting to swim against the stream of life at the bidding of a conscience and a taste and a public opinion and a law and a tradition which spur the swimmer into attempting his arduous *tour de force*; and accordingly we shall find that in the field of conduct Archaism expresses itself in formal institutions and formulated ideas rather than in un-self-conscious manners, and in the linguistic field in points of style and theme, which are matters of convention and, as such, are amenable to the control of the will, as well as in points of vocabulary, accidence, and syntax, in which the wayward spirit of the vulgar tongue is apt to outwit the 'high-brow' purist's most straitly pedantic intentions.

If we now begin our survey by entering upon the field of institutions and ideas, our best plan of operations will be to start by taking a glance at institutional Archaism in detail and then to follow the spread of the archaistic state of mind over a wider and wider area till we arrive, in the end, at an 'ideological' Archaism which is all-pervasive because it is an Archaism-on-principle.

We have already come across one example of an archaistic resuscitation of a particular rite in our survey of civilizations that have come to a standstill on the threshold of life.[1] We have seen[2] how in Plutarch's day, which was the heyday of the Hellenic universal state, the ceremony of scourging Spartiate boys at the altar of Artemis Orthia—an ordeal which, in Sparta's prime, had been taken over from a primitive fertility-ritual and had been incorporated into the Lycurgean *agôgê*—was being practised at Sparta once again, though now with a pathological exaggeration which is one of the characteristic notes of Archaism in all its manifestations. In the Indic World, too, we have noted[3] that the horse-sacrifice, which was a traditional Indic method of asserting a title to an oecumenical authority, was resuscitated first by Pushyamitra, the usurper who overthrew the Mauryas in the second century B.C., and afterwards—more than five hundred years later—by the

---

[1] In Part III. A, vol. iii, above.   [2] In Part III. A, vol. iii, p. 77, above.
[3] In V. C (i) (*d*) 7, p. 2, footnote 1, above.

Guptas. It is easy to guess that Pushyamitra and Samudragupta in turn were moved to make this archaistic demonstration of their legitimacy by an inward doubt about the validity of their respective claims to a sovereignty on the oecumenical scale; and it was assuredly an inward loss of certainty about the boasted eternity of Rome that moved the Emperor Philip to celebrate, with the utmost solemnity and magnificence, the traditional *Ludi Saeculares* when, in A.D. 248, the Roman Empire was enjoying a momentary breathing-space in the midst of a bout of anarchy that was threatening to put an end to its very existence.[1]

If we pass from recurrent rites to permanent institutions, we shall observe that, in this age in which the Roman Commonwealth appeared to be on the point of dissolution, the revival of the *Ludi Saeculares* in A.D. 248 was followed in or about A.D. 250[2] by the re-establishment of the venerable office of the censorship. And if we cast our eyes back to the 'Time of Troubles' from which the bout of anarchy in the third century of the Christian Era was divided by a span of effective Roman Peace, we shall see the Gracchi attempting to deal with the economic and social crisis which was the aftermath of the Hannibalic War by legislating for the restoration of a system of peasant-proprietorship which they believed to have been prevalent in the *Ager Romanus* at a date more than two hundred years before their own day.[3] If we turn from the Hellenic to the Western World, we shall find an analogue of the re-establishment of the Roman censorship in the third century of the Christian Era in the re-enhancement, in the twentieth century, of the prestige and popularity of the British Crown to a height at which they had never stood at any time since the death of Queen Elizabeth in A.D. 1603.[4]

---

[1] The *Ludi Saeculares* had been first revived—or had been originally invented—by Augustus in 17 B.C., and had since then been celebrated by Claudius in A.D. 47, by Domitian in A.D. 88, by Antoninus Pius in A.D. 147 (according to Bury, J. B.: *A History of the Roman Empire from its Foundation to the Death of Marcus Aurelius* (London 1913, Murray), p. 524), and by Septimius Severus in A.D. 204. The celebration by Philip in A.D. 248 was officially in honour of the completion of the first millennium of Rome's existence, counting from the legendary date of the foundation of the city. For the symbolic meaning and psychological effect of the ritual act *condere saeculum* see Wendland, P.: *Die Hellenistisch-Römische Kultur*, 2nd and 3rd ed. (Tübingen 1912, Mohr), p. 144.

[2] The date is given as the 27th October, 251, in the so-called *Historia Augusta*, 'Valeriani Duo', chap. 5, § 4; but this can hardly be right, since by that date the Emperor Decius, who was the author of this archaistic measure, was in all probability already dead, and the true date must have been prior to the Emperor's departure from Rome for the campaign against the Goths in which he was to meet his death. (See Schiller, H.: *Geschichte der Römischen Kaiserzeit*, vol. i, part (2) (Gotha 1883, Perthes), p. 807, footnote 3.)

[3] See IV. C (iii) (c) 3 (β), vol. iv, p. 508; V. C (i) (c) 2, vol. v, pp. 70–1 and 78; and V. C (i) (d) 1, vol. v, pp. 388–9, above; and V. C (ii) (a), in the present volume, pp. 219–20, below.

[4] The prestige and popularity which the British Crown was enjoying in the year 1937 would have astonished even the most sharp-sighted observer of the politics of the United Kingdom in 1837, on the eve of the accession of Queen Victoria—supposing that

If we pass from particular institutions to constitutions extending over the whole domain of political life, we shall observe that the revalorization of the medieval institution of the Crown in Great Britain has been contemporaneous with the organization in Italy of a 'corporative state', and that this is supposed to be a restoration of a political and economic régime which was in force in 'the Middle Ages' in Northern Italy and in the rest of the medieval Western city-state cosmos, and which was based, in its original form, upon the medieval trade-guilds. This modern Western Fascist 'corporative state' is a veritable πάτριος πολιτεία ('ancestral constitution') of the kind which was so prominent a portent in a disintegrating Hellenic World both during the Hellenic 'Time of Troubles' and after the establishment of a Hellenic universal state in the shape of the Roman Empire.

The slogan 'patrios politeia' implies the claim that a newly inaugurated constitution is in reality an old-established one which is now being brought back into force after an unmerited and unfortunate interval of disuse and oblivion. In the history of the decline and fall of the Hellenic Civilization we find this claim being made, within twenty years of the breakdown of 431 B.C., by the Athenian reactionaries who succeeded, through a *coup d'état*, in imposing upon the Athenian Dêmos the short-lived oligarchic constitution of the year 411. This 'Régime of the Four Hundred' was hailed by its supporters as a return to the Constitution of Cleisthenes and perhaps even to the Constitution of Solon. In a similar tone Agis and Cleomenes—the two Spartan martyr-kings who successively staked and lost their lives on a policy of political and social Archaism in the third century B.C.—proclaimed that they were restoring the Constitution of Lycurgus and that they ought therefore to be applauded as reformers instead of being execrated as revolutionaries.[1] At Rome in the second century B.C.

our imaginary observer could have returned to life after the lapse of a hundred years. It is true that in 1937 the Crown performed a practical service—for which there had been no demand a hundred years back—as a personal link between the several fully self-governing states members of the British Commonwealth of Nations (for this latter-day role of the British Crown see Part II. B, vol. i, pp. 190–1, and IV. C (iii) (*b*) 5, vol. iv, p. 187, above). Yet a contemporary English observer would not be disposed to believe that the twentieth-century revalorization of the Crown had been wholly, or even mainly, due to any such utilitarian constitutional considerations. The deeper reason why the British Crown was now once more attracting to itself the affections and the hopes of its subjects in the United Kingdom was because the English in this generation had a feeling —which was not the less strong for being unacknowledged—that England had now passed her political zenith. It was this feeling that was sapping the prestige and popularity of Parliament—the master institution of England in her maturity—and was restoring the prestige and popularity of the Crown, which had been the master institution of an age of political adolescence to which the twentieth-century Englishman was now wistfully looking back.

[1] See Part III. A, vol. iii, pp. 76–7; V. C (i) (*c*) 2, vol. v, p. 78; and V. C (i) (*d*) 1, vol. v, pp. 388–9, above; and V. C (ii) (*a*), in the present volume, pp. 219–20, below.

the Gracchi professed—and this, no doubt, with the same good faith as their Heracleid forerunners at Sparta—to be exercising the office of the Tribunate of the Plebs in the fashion that had been intended at the time when, at the turn of the fourth and third centuries, the dissident Plebeian *imperium in imperio* had been re-absorbed into the legitimate Roman body politic in virtue of a sagacious political compromise.[1]

In the same Roman Commonwealth a hundred years later the dictatorship—which by that time had come to be the only possible instrument for appeasing a *stasis* which the Gracchi had provoked —was commended to the *ci-devant* governing class by an Augustan Archaism which was as *rusé* as the Gracchan Archaism had been *naïf*. The assassination of Octavian's adoptive father Divus Julius had shown that the sheer necessity and urgency of establishing a dictatorial régime were not enough to guarantee immunity from criminal violence to a statesman who was attempting to perform this invidious public service. So far from that, the mere admission of the need for a dictatorship was a crushing indictment of the class in whose hands the government of the Roman Common- wealth had been concentrated for the past two centuries. If the Ordo Senatorius were to be forced to confess that a dictator could no longer be dispensed with, then it would be confessing in the same breath its own complete political and moral failure; and the fate of Caesar the dictator-god had shown that it was impossible to extort this confession from the Roman aristocracy without driving them, in the act, into a homicidal frenzy of exasperation. The adoptive Caesar Octavianus might lack the genius of the genuine Caesar the God, but he did possess, in the highest degree, the capacity for learning by experience; and, when the crime of 44 B.C. confronted Octavian with the problem of how to wield Caesar's powers without courting Caesar's fate, he contrived a solution which earned him the titles of Augustus and Pater Patriae and enabled him to become the true founder of the long-yearned- for Hellenic universal state.[2]

Augustus's solution of the political crux of the age was to 'save the face' of the Ordo Senatorius by tacitly inviting its members to collaborate with him in an open constitutional conspiracy. The unavowed bargain which he induced them to accept was a 'division of powers' in which Augustus received the substance while the

---

[1] For this chapter of the constitutional history of the Roman Republic see IV. C (iii) (b) 9, vol. iv, p. 205; IV. C (iii) (c) 3 (β), vol. iv, p. 508; V. C (i) (c) 2, vol. v, pp. 70–1; V. C (i) (d) 1, vol. v, pp. 388–9, above; and V. C (ii) (a), pp. 219–20, below.

[2] For Augustus's role and achievement see V. C (i) (d) 6 (δ), Annex, vol. v, pp. 648–9, above, and V. C (ii) (a), in the present volume, pp. 187 and 190, below.

Senate retained the form; and the offer—which would have been rejected as an insult by the *ci-devant* Roman governing class in its heyday—was accepted by their epigoni with alacrity and gratitude. In consequence, Augustus died in his bed at a ripe old age more than forty years after he had settled down into his dictatorship under the disarming title of Princeps Senatus; and throughout those four decades every urgent autocratic act that he had performed had been juridically warranted by the constitutionally well-established powers of the traditional republican magistracies which the Senate had officially conferred upon him. *De facto* the nature and scope and effect of these powers were magnified out of all recognition by being combined in the person of a single incumbent upon whom they had been conferred in some cases in perpetuity and in the rest with a frequency of iteration which had no historical precedent. Yet this patent fact that the ancient republican magistracies amounted cumulatively to a dictatorship was never allowed—either by Augustus of the one part or by the Senate of the other—to disturb the constitutional fiction that the Princeps Senatus was wielding no power which was alien to the ancient republican constitution of the Roman Commonwealth; and this archaistic constitutional make-believe actually provided so solid a foundation for a new political structure that the Augustan Principate endured for the best part of three hundred years.[1]

It is also significant that the meticulous respect that was shown by Augustus, throughout the period of his constitutional rule, for the theory of the sovereignty of the Senate, was equalled and even surpassed towards the close of this three-hundred-years' period after having been cast aside, with various degrees of brutality, by the first emperor's earlier successors from Tiberius onwards. In the breathing-spaces in that half-century of political convulsions, between A.D. 235 and A.D. 284, which was the prelude to a liquidation of the Augustan Principate to make way for an absolute monarchy on the Sasanian pattern, the Senate found itself once again being treated with an honour which it had seldom known since the death of Augustus himself. The struggle against the proletarian dictatorship of Maximinus Thrax was conducted by the Gordians—and, after their deaths, by Maximus and Balbinus —as the Senate's nominees and mandatories. And even after Gallienus had deprived the Ordo Senatorius of their last shreds

---

[1] It will be seen that Divus Caesar, with his reckless radicalism, is the Hellenic counterpart of a Sinic Ts'in She Hwang-ti, while Augustus, with his artful Archaism, is the counterpart of Liu Pang, the *novus homo* who became the founder of the Prior Han Dynasty. (For this contrast between Ts'in She Hwang-ti and Liu Pang see V. C (i) (*d*) 7, p. 37, footnote 1, above. For the general distinction between the two classes of saviours with the sword who respectively fail and succeed in an attempt to establish a universal state see V. C (ii) (*a*), pp. 186–91, below.)

of effective power,[1] and after Aurelian had given the Hellenic
World a foretaste of the despotism that was to be imposed upon
it, once for all, by Diocletian within less than ten years of Aurelian's
death, we find the Army engaging with the Senate in an unprecedented contest in courtesy in which each party insisted, *more
Japonico*, that the other should accept the honour of electing
Aurelian's successor, until at last the Senators admitted defeat by
consenting to nominate one of their own number. In A.D. 275 it
was strange indeed to see a proletarian soldiery submitting to the
command of a cultivated civilian who was already seventy-five
years old; but it was even stranger—when the anxieties and
fatigues of his incongruous task brought the aged Emperor Tacitus
to his grave within six months of his investiture with the purple
—to see his virile successor Probus, who was a peasant-soldier of
the same rough Illyrian stock as Aurelian and Diocletian, declining
to assume the Imperial title, though he was already the candidate of the Army and the master of the Empire *de facto*, until
he had asked for and obtained the Senate's ratification of the
Army's choice. Thus, in the constitutional history of the Roman
Commonwealth, the Senate was never treated with a greater
show of deference than at a moment when it was on the point of
losing the last shadow of a sovereignty which by that time
had been in abeyance *de facto* for the best part of four centuries.[2] So strong was the archaistic impulse in a society which
was obsessed with the problem of self-preservation under a threat
of imminent death.

If we turn from a disintegrating Hellenic to a disintegrating
Sinic World, we shall be able here to observe the emergence of
a constitutional Archaism of a more comprehensive scope, extending
from public into private life and from institutions to ideas.

The challenge of the Sinic 'Time of Troubles' produced a
spiritual ferment in Sinic minds which displayed itself both in
the Confucian humanism of the fifth century B.C.[3] and in the later

---

[1] According to Parker, H. M. D.: *A History of the Roman World from A.D. 138 to 337*
(London 1935, Methuen), pp. 178–81, Gallienus (*imperabat solus* A.D. 260–8) made
Senators ineligible for appointment to military commands and perhaps also deprived
the Senatorial governors of provinces of their authority over the troops stationed in their
districts. (This conjecture is based on Aurelius Victor, *De Caesaribus*, 33, 34, as read in
the light of the evidence of inscriptions.)

[2] The Senate's loss of control over the reins of government *de facto* is to be dated
neither from the victory of Augustus over Antony at Actium in 31 B.C. nor from the
formation of the Second Triumvirate in 43 B.C. nor from the formation of the First
Triumvirate in 60 B.C., but rather from the civil war of 90–81 B.C. The Sullan restoration
was already an archaistic *tour de force*; and it was the tragedy of the Roman constitu-
tionalists of the generation of Cicero and Cato Minor that they had been born into an
age in which the dictatorship was overdue and in which the surviving simulacrum of
Senatorial government was a delusive anachronism.

[3] For the humanistic êthos of Confucius himself see the passages quoted from Granet
in V. C (i) (*d*) 7, p. 14, footnote 3, above.

and more radical schools of the 'Politicians' and 'Sophists' and 'Legists';[1] but this burst of spiritual activity was ephemeral.

'Ce sont les efforts tentés par les gouvernements de potentats (dont certains jouaient les despotes éclairés) pour édifier l'État sur un ordre social rénové qui sont à l'origine des concurrences corporatives et des polémiques sectaires par lesquelles se signalent les vᵉ, ivᵉ et iiiᵉ siècles. Beaucoup d'idées fécondes furent alors brillamment défendues. Aucune n'a réussi à modifier profondément la mentalité des Chinois. . . . Comme les solutions proposées l'attestent, toute l'activité de pensée que ces problèmes ont provoquée a été déterminée par une crise sociale où le système féodal et la conception traditionnelle de l'Étiquette auraient pu sombrer. L'ordre féodal, cependant, est, pour le fond, demeuré vivace. L'agitation philosophique qui donne tant d'intérêt à la période des Royaumes Combattants a abouti au triomphe de la scolastique. Un conformisme archaïsant a renforcé le prestige de l'Étiquette et de tout le vieux systeme de classifications, de comportements, de convenances.'[2]

This revulsion towards the Past can be seen at its clearest in the fate which overtook the Confucian humanism.

'En même temps que s'atténuait l'inspiration humaniste, s'accroissait l'attachement à un décorum archaïsant. Plutôt qu'à observer les comportements de l'homme en cherchant à affiner le sens de la dignité humaine, les héritiers infidèles du Maître s'employèrent à subordonner l'ensemble du savoir à l'étude des traditions rituelles.'[3]

From this attitude of mind it is a short step to the Archaism-on-principle of Tong Chong-chu (*vivebat circa* 175–105 B.C.), an Imperial civil servant of the Prior Han régime who succeeded in making a *reductio ad absurdum* of the bureaucratic outlook by working out a system for subjecting every administrative act to the test of an historical precedent.

'C'est en se servant des précédents, c'est-à-dire grâce à une interprétation des faits de l'histoire, qu'on justifiera, mais aussi qu'on pourra condamner, les décisions du prince et de ses conseillers. Ceux-ci et leurs décrets se trouveront jugés par le Ciel et le peuple, dès qu'un savant, ayant produit un *fait historique*, l'aura interprété en montrant quel fut, jadis, dans une *situation déclarée analogue* à telle situation actuelle, le jugement du peuple et du Ciel.'[4]

Another example of Archaism-on-principle in a different sphere is the cult of a largely fictitious Primitive Teutonism which has

---

[1] For a conspectus of the sects and schools of thought which were brought into existence by the ordeal of the Sinic 'Time of Troubles' see Granet, M.: *La Pensée Chinoise* (Paris 1934, Renaissance du Livre), Book IV, chaps. 1–3, and Waley, A.: *The Way and its Power* (London 1934, Allen & Unwin), Introduction.

[2] Granet, op. cit., pp. 423–4 and 417–18.

[3] Ibid., p. 553. A still later stage in the metamorphosis of Confucianism, when it degenerated into sheer sorcery, has been touched upon in V. C (i) (d) 6 (δ), vol. v, pp. 549 and 555–6, above.

[4] Granet, op. cit., p. 577.

been one of the provincial products of a general archaistic movement of Romanticism in the modern Western World.

This curious superstition has arisen within the last hundred
years in certain provinces of Western Christendom in which the
current vernacular happens to be some twig of the Teutonic
branch of the Indo-European family of languages. The postulates
are that the Teutonic language has been spoken, *ab initio*, by a
blonde and blue-eyed race; that this race is autochthonous in
Northern Europe; and that the region, the race, and the language
are all of them uniquely noble.[1] After having afforded a harmless
antiquarian gratification to some nineteenth-century English historians and instilled a perhaps more tiresome racial self-conceit
into some twentieth-century American ethnologists, this cult of
an imaginary Primitive Teutonism has latterly revealed its true
nature by becoming—in the watchword 'Blood and Soil'—the
palladium of the post-war National-Socialist Movement in the
German Reich. We are here confronted with an exhibition of
Archaism which would be pathetic if it were not so sinister.[2] A
great modern Western nation which has been brought, by the
spiritual malady of this Modern Age,[3] within an ace of an irretrievable national collapse, has apparently lost faith in the panoply
of a modern Western culture which has not availed to save it from
this dreadful experience; and, in a desperate effort to find a way
out of the trap into which the recent course of history has inveigled
it, this distraught and disillusioned Germany has turned away from
a future prospect of interminable humiliation and horror, and has
doubled back upon its own historical past. This is, no doubt, a
trail which has only to be retraced in the reverse direction in order
to lose itself sooner or later in the darkness of the primeval forest
out of which our common Teutonic ancestors first emerged into
notoriety some two thousand years ago; but it remains to be
proved that the *Urwald* is an earthly paradise!

In this latter-day German archaistic resort to a fancied saving
grace of the pristine tribal lair and the primitive tribal stock there
is a touch of the Sinic style of Archaism with its *flair* for the
primitive solidarity between the human tribe and the tribe's non-
human environment; but in this modern Western variation on a

---

[1] The racial facet of this delusion has been examined already in this Study in II. C (ii)
(a) 1, vol. i, pp. 207–49, above.

[2] At the moment of revising this passage for publication in November 1938 the
German National-Socialist cult of 'Blood and Soil' had already earned this epithet. For,
although it had not so far precipitated a European War, it had already let loose, inside
the Reich, an outburst of savage Anti-Semitism.

[3] Germany's troubles in the present generation can be ascribed, without dispute, to
the contemporary *Zeitgeist* of the Western Society of which Germany herself is a
fraction, though it might be more difficult to arrive at an agreement on the minor
question of assessing the relative responsibilities of the Germans and their neighbours.

Sinic theme the subtle Sinic touch is incongruously combined with the simple animal instinct which prompts a baby kangaroo in the zoological gardens of a great metropolis to take refuge in its mother's pouch after it has been put out of countenance by the collective stare of an inquisitive crowd of human spectators.

Yet another form of Archaism-on-principle is the hankering after 'a return to Nature' or to 'the simple life';[1] and in our modern Western Society, since the days of Jean-Jacques Rousseau and Marie Antoinette, this itch has been apt to seek relief in a variety-show of cranks and affectations—in unfavourable contrast to the corresponding reaction of the Taoist sages of a disintegrating Sinic World, who turned their minds towards the soberer simplicity of the archaic village communities out of which the now decadent Sinic Society had originally sprung.[2]

'L'idéal politique des maîtres taoïstes paraît avoir été un régime de minuscules communautés paysannes. Dans une bourgade isolée, un saint (vénéré comme un dieu du sol) peut, de la façon la plus modeste, exercer ses pouvoirs indéfinis. Tchouang tseu déclare que tout va bien dans l'Empire lorsqu'on laisse libre cours aux traditions locales qu'il nomme les maximes villageoises.'[3]

This archaistic ideal is commended in the nineteenth chapter of the *Tao Te King*:[4]

Banish wisdom, discard knowledge,
And the people will be benefited a hundredfold.
Banish human kindness, discard morality,
And the people will be dutiful and compassionate.
Banish skill, discard profit,
And thieves and robbers will disappear.
If when these things are done they find life too plain and unadorned,
Then let them have accessories;
Give them Simplicity to look at, the Uncarved Block to hold,
Give them selflessness and fewness of desires.

In the eightieth chapter of the same work the same ideal picture is drawn again, but this time with a vividness which conveys, in

---

[1] This hankering, which in one aspect is an expression of archaistic-mindedness, has another aspect in which it is a gesture of *abandon* (see V. C (i) (d) 1, vol. v, p. 377, and V. C (i) (d) 2, vol. v, p. 403, above).

[2] See Hackmann, H.: *Chinesische Philosophie* (Munich 1927, Reinhardt), pp. 109–10, for the view that this hankering after a return to 'the simple life' is a symptom of social senescence.

[3] Granet, op. cit., p. 547. While the Taoists were the chief advocates of an archaistic return to the simple life during the final paroxysm of the Sinic 'Time of Troubles' in the fourth and third centuries B.C., this idea was not the monopoly of any one of the numerous Sinic schools of philosophy that were evoked by the challenge of being born into that terrible age. There was, for instance, an archaistic vein in the philosophy of Mencius (*vivebat*, 372–289 B.C.) (Hackmann, H.: *Chinesische Philosophie* (Munich 1927, Reinhardt), pp. 187–9 and 192–4).

[4] The following English translations are taken from Waley, A.: *The Way and its Power* (London 1934, Allen & Unwin).

a few strokes of the Sinic brush, the essence of an Archaism that is elaborated by Plato in page after page of *The Republic* and *The Laws*.

'Given a small country with few inhabitants, he could bring it about that though there should be among the people contrivances requiring ten times, a hundred times less labour, they would not use them.[1] He could bring it about that the people would be ready to lay down their lives and lay them down again in defence of their homes, rather than emigrate. There might still be boats and carriages, but no one would go in them; there might still be weapons of war, but no one would drill with them. He could bring it about that "the people should have no use for any form of writing save knotted ropes, should be contented with their food, pleased with their clothing, satisfied with their homes, should take pleasure in their rustic tasks. The next place might be so near at hand that one could hear the cocks crowing in it, the dogs barking; but the people would grow old and die without ever having been there." '[2]

To an English reader of the *Tao Te King* the note of this passage is already familiar in Gray's *Elegy Written in a Country Churchyard*; and in the England of the present writer's day this archaic life was still being lived—in an unbroken continuity with the Past—by some, at least, of the inhabitants of the tract of Yorkshire country-side in which he wrote these lines. If there is any grain of truth in Tong Chong-chu's belief that the lessons of History may elucidate the signs of the times,[3] it may be surmised that, to-day, there are children already born in London or in Leeds who will live to be overwhelmed by a passionate archaistic impulse to throw away their motor-cars and wireless sets and Lewis guns and bombing-planes in order to free their hands for handling 'the poor crooked scythe and spade' that are fabled once upon a time to have bestowed a homely happiness upon the modern English urban proletariat's far-off rustic ancestors when, in an unwittingly Taoist vein, 'they kept the noiseless tenor of their way along the cool sequester'd vale of life'.

(β) *Archaism in Art.*

The vogue of Archaism in Art is something so familiar to modern Western Man that he is apt to take it for granted without ever becoming conscious of it. For the most conspicuous of the

---

[1] Compare the legend of the latter-day Chinese pilot that has been recounted in III. C (i) (c), vol. iii, pp. 188-9, above.—A.J.T.
[2] The passage within double quotation marks is, in Waley's view, a quotation from an earlier Taoist work (see Waley, op. cit., p. 242, footnote 1). In more concrete and prosaic terms this Taoist Sinic idea is also expressed by the Positivist Western philosopher Comte in his suggestion that the great national states of the modern Western World should be broken up into *Kleinstaaten* on the scale of the Grand Duchy of Tuscany (see Caird, E.: *The Social Philosophy and Religion of Comte* (Glasgow 1885, MacLehose), pp. 239-40).
[3] See p. 56, above.

arts is Architecture; in almost every great city of the Western World
in A.D. 1938 at least nine-tenths of the buildings then standing were
less than a hundred years old;[1] and our modern Western architecture had already been falling under the dominion of Archaism at
the time—by then a hundred years back—when this orgy of building had begun.[2] Thus the worker who travels twice a day between
his suburban dormitory and his urban factory or office has registered automatically, on his visual memory, the print of innumerable Neo-Gothic railway-stations and churches, while, if he is a
worker in New York, his eye will have become equally well
accustomed to the millions of square feet of Neo-Colonial[3] brick-
work that cast a cloak of archaistic decency over the steel-and-
concrete skeletons of the sky-scrapers. If our breadwinner is not
in too much of a hurry to glance at the marble bas-relief that
crowns the entrance to that Colonial-brick-skinned mammoth
office-building, he may find to-day that the lines of the carving
have been cunningly reduced to the clumsy stiffness of the pre-
Romanesque Dark Ages;[4] and, if he actually has the leisure to step
into the Neo-Gothic ironwork of this municipal art gallery, he may
stumble here into a roomful of 'Pre-Raphaelite' pictures.

This triumph of Archaism over the visual arts is, indeed, one
of the dominant features in our modern Western urban landscapes;
but it is not, of course, a phenomenon that is peculiar to our

---

[1] The European traveller becomes aware of this as soon as he visits the United States
or any other overseas country that is Western in its culture. At first he is surprised to
find that cities which are not more than one hundred or two hundred years old can look
—when viewed from bus-roof or train-window—so little different from the cities of his
own European home, which can count their age in thousands of years instead of hundreds. It is only on second thoughts that it occurs to him that, in all but one or two of
the European cities that are to-day in the full swim of modern Western life, nine-tenths
of the buildings are no older than ten-tenths of those in Buffalo or Pittsburgh. This
is true not only of Manchester and Berlin, but even of London and Cologne and Paris
and Milan.

[2] In this connexion it may be well to draw attention once again to the distinction,
pointed out on p. 49, footnote 3, above, between Archaism within the limits of the
experience of a single society and that contact in the Time-dimension between two
different civilizations which displays itself in what is commonly called a renaissance.
In the modern Western World, for example, the Neo-Gothic Archaism of the architecture of the past hundred years has been a reaction against the fashion, which had been
prevalent for some three or four centuries before that, of discarding almost every
vestige of a native Western style in order to ape the alien architecture of the Hellenes.

[3] The Americans use the term 'Colonial' for the eighteenth-century style of architecture which the English call 'Georgian'.

[4] The primitivism of one school of modern Western sculpture has suggested the
following reflexions to a contemporary Western biologist:
'To my mind, the closest analogy to the evolution of a given group is the history of
the art and literature of a civilization. The clumsy primitive forms are replaced by a
great variety of types. Different schools arise and decline more or less rapidly. Finally
a period of decline sets in, characterized by Archaism like that of the last ammonites.
And it is difficult not to compare some of the fantastic animals of the declining periods
of a race with the work of Miss Sitwell, or the clumsy but impressive with that of
Epstein. The history of an animal group shows no more evidence of planning than does
that of a national literature. But both show orderly sequences which are already pretty
capable of explanation.'—Haldane, J. B. S.: *Possible Worlds* (London 1928, Chatto &
Windus), p. 43.

Western Society. If a Londoner travels to Constantinople instead of travelling to New York, and watches the pageant of the sun setting over the ridge of Stamboul, he will see, silhouetted against the sky-line, dome after dome of the mosques which—under an Ottoman régime that has provided the main body of Orthodox Christendom with its universal state[1]—have been constructed, with a profoundly archaistic servility, upon the pattern of the Big and the Little Haghía Sophía: the two Byzantine churches whose audacious defiance of the fundamental canons of the classical Hellenic order of architecture had once upon a time proclaimed in stone the emergence of an infant Orthodox Christian Civilization out of the wreckage of a Hellenic World which had already ceased to live.[2]

If we turn to the decline and fall of this Hellenic Society to which our own, as well as the Orthodox Christian, is affiliated, and watch what the cultivated Emperor Hadrian was doing with his wealth and leisure in the pale clear sunshine of a Hellenic 'Indian Summer',[3] we shall see him spending a considerable part of both in furnishing his suburban villa with expertly manufactured copies of the masterpieces of Hellenic sculpture of the archaic period (that is to say, the seventh and sixth centuries B.C.). The taste of a generation of connoisseurs who were too highly refined to appreciate the obvious and were too exquisitely sensitive not to shiver at the mildest touch of a frost in which they could recognize the herald of an approaching winter, found the masterliness of the Hellenic sculptor's art in its fifth-century maturity too self-confident—and at the same time perhaps too painfully close to the verge of the débâcle—to be valued quite at its proper worth. On the other hand the archaic style appealed to the sophisticated intellects of Hadrian's generation as something precious and *recherché*, while it captivated their unconscious selves by instilling a suggestion of the dewy freshness of dawn into the still and stale air of a monotonous evening. In combination, these two distinct motives for preferring the archaic to the classical style made an irresistible appeal to the Hellenic *virtuosi* of Hadrian's day. And similar considerations will explain why it was that, in the latter stages of the long-drawn-out dotage of the Egyptiac Society, the artistic style of 'the Old Kingdom'—the style which had distinguished the growth-stage of Egyptiac history in a remote antiquity

[1] See Part III. A, vol. iii, pp. 26–7; IV. C (ii) (*b*) 1, vol. iv, p. 70; V. C (i) (*c*) 1, vol. v, p. 54; and V. C (i) (*c*) 4, vol. v, p. 348, above.
[2] In IV. C (ii) (*a*), vol. iv, pp. 54–5, above, it has been argued that the Byzantine breach with a Hellenic past in the domain of Architecture was deliberate.
[3] For the view that an ostensible 'Golden Age' of the Hellenic World, during the reigns of the Roman Emperors Nerva to Marcus inclusive, was really no more than an 'Indian Summer', see IV. C (ii) (*b*) 1, vol. iv, pp. 58–61, above.

before the beginning of the 'Time of Troubles'—was taken as a pattern by the Saïte Pharaohs of the Twenty-Sixth Dynasty after an interval of some two thousand years.

(γ) *Archaism in Language and Literature.*[1]

When the spirit of Archaism is moved to express itself in the field of Language and Literature, the supreme *tour de force* to which it can address itself here is to bring a 'dead language'[2] to

[1] In this field, Archaism—in the sense of a deliberate return to some form of language or style of literature or range of thought and feeling that has fallen into disuse—has to be distinguished from a mere conservatism which clings, perhaps more often than not out of sheer inertia and with no deliberate policy at all, to a form of language that has ceased to be intelligible or to a style of literature that has ceased to be serviceable or to a range of thought and feeling that has ceased to come natural. The commonest examples of such linguistic and literary conservatism are to be found in one or other of the two moulds of legal formulae and religious liturgies: for instance, in the Norman-French tags in our twentieth-century English judicial and parliamentary procedure, and in the Latin Liturgy of the Catholic Church. Other examples of the preservation, in a living liturgy, of a language that is dead in every other usage are the survival of the Attic κοινή, Old Slavonic, and Classical Georgian in different versions of the Liturgy of the Orthodox Christian Church; the survival of Classical Syriac, Classical Armenian, Classical Coptic, and Ge'ez in different versions of the Liturgy of the Monophysite Christian Church; the survival of Classical Syriac in the Liturgy of the Nestorian Christian Church; and the survival of Classical Hebrew in the religious life of Jewry. The Egyptiac Society is perhaps unique in having performed twice over the *tour de force* of preserving a form of language until it has become unintelligible—and this not merely in a liturgy but in a profane literature. 'As far back as we can trace it, the Egyptian language displays signs of being carefully fostered'; the works of literature that were written in this Classical Egyptian during the Egyptiac 'Time of Troubles' and the earlier days of the Egyptiac universal state (*circa* 2424–1770 B.C.) 'were read in the schools five hundred years later; and from their language and style no one dared venture to deviate'. The spoken language, however, went its own way, until 'finally . . . .the difference . . . became so great that the classical language could scarcely be understood by ordinary people. In the great revolution at the end of the Eighteenth Dynasty which we associate with the name of Amenophis IV [Ikhnaton] these shackles also were broken. Men began to write poetry in the actual language of the day; and in it is composed the beautiful Hymn to the Sun, the manifesto of the Reformed Religion. But, whereas the other innovations of the heretical régime disappeared after its collapse, this particular one survived—doubtless because the conditions hitherto existing had become impossible.' Once more, however, a cultural conservatism was to prevail in Egyptiac intelligences over a human thirst for life. The 'New Egyptian Literature, which, as we might suppose, had set out to be really popular, did not long pursue this course. . . . For something like five centuries this later literature appears to have been cultivated, and then its language also became a dead one, which the boys at school had to learn!' (Erman, A.: *The Literature of the Ancient Egyptians*, English translation (London 1927, Methuen), pp. xxiv–xxvi; see also the present Study, IV. C (ii) (*a*), vol. iv, p. 55, footnote 3, and V. C (i) (*d*) 6 (γ), vol. v, p. 496, above).
This incorrigible conservatism which clings blindly to whatever it may happen to have in hand is evidently not the same thing as an Archaism which deliberately drops what it has been holding in order to set the hand free for grasping at some lost treasure of the Past.
[2] The term 'dead language' is ordinarily used to describe a language which has fallen into disuse merely as a spoken vernacular, while remaining in use as a vehicle for Ritual or Law or Science or even for Belles Lettres; but, strictly speaking, a language which is in this position (e.g. Latin in the position which it now occupies in the modern Western World) is only half dead. The truly dead languages are those of which some inscribed or written monument has been recovered by the ingenuity of our modern Western archaeologists after the rediscovered language has been not merely in disuse but in oblivion for hundreds or thousands of years—a sequence of death, burial, and disinterment which has been the history of Etruscan, Lycian, Ancient Egyptian both 'Old' and 'New' and 'Demotic', Sumerian, Akkadian, Elamite, Urartian, the Old Persian of the Achaemenian inscriptions, Tokharian, and so on. The criterion of 'deadness' in this stricter sense is that the disinterred texts have to be deciphered either from internal evidence or by the lucky discovery of some bilingual or multilingual

life again by putting it back into circulation as a living vernacular; and such an attempt is being made to-day, under our eyes, in several places in our Westernized World.

In this instance the impulse has come from the modern Western movement of Nationalism, which we have defined in this Study as a transference of interest from the whole to the part and as a withdrawal of loyalty from the Creator in order to bestow it upon the creature.[1] A community that has succumbed to this grave spiritual malady is apt to resent its cultural debt to the society of which it is itself a fragment, and in this frame of mind it will put itself to great trouble and inconvenience for the sake of transposing its culture into a shape that can be certified as being parochially 'national' throughout. One of the staples of such a 'national culture' is a 'national language'; and, while most of the nationalized communities of the modern 'Great Society' have found their 'national language' ready to hand, there are some which have been reduced to the laborious and ludicrous expedient of fabricating the 'mother-tongue' that they are determined to possess, in the temper of a *nouveau riche* who furnishes himself with portraits of appropriate ancestors. In our latter-day Westernized World the would-be self-sufficient nations that have found themselves destitute of natural linguistic resources have all taken the road of Archaism as the readiest way of obtaining a supply of the linguistic commodity of which they are in search. At the present moment there are at least five nations in our world that are engaged in producing a distinctive national language of their own by the process of putting back into circulation as a living vernacular some language which has long since ceased to be current in any but an academic sphere. The five nations whom the writer of this Study has in mind are the Norwegians, the Irish, the Ottoman Turks, the Greeks, and the Zionist Jews; and it will be seen from this roll-call that none of them is a chip of the original block of Western Christendom. The Norwegians and the Irish are respectively remnants of an abortive Scandinavian and an abortive Far Western Christian Civilization which came into collision with the Roman Christendom in the first chapter of our Western history and were successively defeated and devoured by this more puissant neighbour.[2] The Ottoman Turks and the Greeks are recently Western-

inscription in which one of the other languages employed is some language that has never ceased to be studied (as, for example, a key to Ancient Egyptian was found in the Rosetta Stone, on which one version of the text is engraved in the Attic κοινή). Some of these genuinely dead languages (e.g. Etruscan and Lycian) still remain undeciphered because no illuminating bilingual inscription has been found. There is probably no example of any attempt to resuscitate a language that is 'dead' in this stricter sense.

[1] See Part I. A, vol. i, p. 9; IV. C (iii) (b) 4 and 5, vol. iv, pp. 156–90; IV. C (iii) (c) 2 (α), vol. iv, p. 261; and IV. C (iii) (c) 2 (β), vol. iv, p. 303, above.
[2] See II. D (vii), vol. ii, pp. 322–60, above.

ized contingents of the Iranic Society in the one case and of the main body of the Orthodox Christian Society in the other. The Zionist Jews are a fragment of a fossil of alien origin which has been embedded in the body of Western Christendom since its pre-natal days.

The need which the Norwegians feel to-day for the production of a modern Norwegian national language is the historical consequence of a political eclipse under which the Kingdom of Norway lay from A.D. 1397, which was the date of the Union of Calmar,[1] until A.D. 1905, when Norway at length recovered her complete political independence. During the greater part of this period of more than 500 years—from 1397, that is to say, until 1814— Norway was politically united with Denmark under conditions which made her culturally as well as politically subordinate to her sister kingdom; and in these circumstances the indigenous Scandinavian literature in the Norse language—a literature which was now no more than a decadent relic of an abortive Scandinavian Civilization—gave place in Norway to a version of the modern Western literature which was written in Danish by Norwegian hands,[2] though on Norwegian lips its pronunciation was modified into harmony with the contemporary Norwegian vernacular. Thus, when the Norwegians set themselves tentatively *post* 1814, and resolutely *post* 1905, to fit themselves out with a national culture which was to be complete according to the specifications of a conventional French or English pattern, they found themselves without any literary medium, except one of foreign mintage, for conveying modern Western ideas, and without any mother-tongue except a peasant *patois* which had ceased to be a vehicle for the long since extinct Scandinavian literature without ever having been refashioned into a vehicle for a Norwegian version of the modern literature of the Western World. Confronted with this awkward gap in the linguistic department of their national outfit, the Norwegian nationalists have been trying to produce a Norwegian language that will serve peasant and townsman alike by fulfilling simultaneously both the two requirements of being national and being cultivated; and the method that they have followed has

---

[1] See II. D (v), vol. ii, p. 175, above.

[2] In Norway the indigenous Scandinavian literature in the Norse language died out in the fourteenth century; and by the sixteenth century Old Norse had ceased to be generally intelligible to the literate public in Norway—as is testified by Laurents Hanssøn and other sixteenth-century Norwegian men-of-letters who on this account were already beginning to make translations out of foreign languages not into Norse but into Danish for the benefit of Norwegian readers. On the other hand, in Iceland, where the indigenous Scandinavian literature in Norse had attained its greatest brilliance (see II. D (iii), vol. ii, pp. 94–6, and II. D (vii), vol. ii, pp. 356–9, above), there has been no comparable break in the tradition, either linguistic or literary. Any one who is literate in the living form of Icelandic Norse can still read the Classical Icelandic Norse literature without difficulty down to the present day.

been to provide a substitute for an orally Norwegianized Danish (the *Bokmaal*) by cultivating the contemporary Norwegian vernacular into a New Norse (*Ny Norsk*)[1]—in the hope that a *patois* which has shown its mettle in the past by providing the linguistic resources for the creation of a Classical Scandinavian literature may prove strong enough to-day to stand the strain of being suddenly called upon to serve as a vehicle for the ponderous mental panoply of modern Western Man.[2]

These Norwegian nationalists' Irish contemporaries and counterparts are seeking a similar solution for a linguistic problem of their own which is the same in substance while presenting greater difficulties in almost every detail. In Ireland the British Crown has played the political role of the Danish Crown in Norway,[3] and this with much the same linguistic and cultural consequences. The language of the politically dominant Power has come to be the channel through which the dominated people has obtained its

[1] A satirical caricature of the *Maalstrevers'* endeavours has been drawn by Ibsen in *Peer Gynt*:

> But ere modern times began
> 'Twas the great Orang-utan
> O'er the forest ruled supreme,
> As he chose could fight and scream. . . .
> Ah, but then the foreign yoke
> Came and marred the speech he spoke;
> On the ape descended quite
> Twice two hundred years of night. . . .
> I have striven to protect
> Our primeval dialect,
> To restore it, and to preach
> General liberty of screech:
> Screeched myself, to show the ways
> It was used in tribal lays.
>
> (G. M. Gathorne-Hardy's translation.)

[2] While the stimulus which has moved the Norwegian *Maalstrevers* to act has been the modern Western psychosis of Nationalism, the confidence that has nerved them to attempt their *tour de force* has been fortified by the fact that the Norse language has acquitted itself brilliantly once before as a medium for a literature. This archaistic inspiration of the *Maalstrever* movement is apparent in the work of its originator, Ivar Aasen (*vivebat* A.D. 1813–96). Aasen's essay in creating a New Norse literary language was eclectic. He did not try (as some of his successors have tried) to keep within the limits of this or that local living Norwegian dialect; he wrote in a composite language for which a number of different dialects were laid under contribution; and in making his selection he showed an unmistakable preference for those elements in the living Norse *Sprachgut* that were the most closely akin to the Old Norse of the Classical Scandinavian literature, without paying so much attention to the utilitarian consideration of whether the living elements of speech that happened to possess this archaistic title to nobility were also the elements that enjoyed the widest contemporary currency. In this indirect way the Old Norse language of the Classical Scandinavian literature has made its influence felt in the formation of the New Norse that has been called into existence in order to serve as an instrument for modern Western thought. On the other hand the *Maalstrevers* have found it impracticable to extend their sources of linguistic supply by drawing direct upon the vocabulary or upon the style of the extant literature in Old Norse, owing to the remoteness of the Classical Scandinavian literature from that of the modern West in subject and setting and ēthos.

[3] Since a Danish reader might take objection to this comparison, the English author of this Study will anticipate his critic by making the admission that England has much more to regret in looking back on her behaviour towards Ireland than Denmark has in looking back on hers towards Norway.

access to the literary sources of the modern Western culture; but in the Irish case the resulting difficulties have been aggravated by two unfortunate facts: in the first place the intrusive Teutonic English is far more alien from the native Celtic Irish than Danish is from the sister Norwegian twig of the same Scandinavian branch of a single Teutonic stem;[1] and in the second place the English language has latterly supplanted the Irish language in Ireland not merely as the medium of culture and government but also as the vernacular tongue of the common people—except for a small minority of the peasantry in a few remote and backward districts along the western coast.[2] Accordingly, in Ireland it is an even greater *tour de force* than it is in Norway to attempt to conjure a cultivated national language out of a peasant *patois*; and in these more desperate circumstances the Irish have resorted to an expedient of which the Norwegians have fought shy. The Irish have tried to lend a rubble foundation the strength to bear the weight of the massive superstructure which they are proposing to build upon it by grouting it with the vocabulary of an ancient and long since extinct literature[3]—in the hope that, through being reconditioned in this exotic way, it may become capable of serving as a vehicle for the modern Western culture. A foreign observer of this Irish experiment may well feel that Archaism could no farther go—at any rate in the linguistic field. Yet, if the observer happens to be an Englishman, it would ill become him to smile at the extravagance of the nationalism of his Irish neighbours. He would do better to reflect that, if—as seems only too probable—the archaistic *tour de force* of attempting to rehabilitate the Irish

---

[1] This difference, however, has counted for less than might have been expected; for in the sight of the Norwegian *Maalstrevers*—who have warped their vision by wearing the spectacles of Nationalism—the Danish language is not a sister Scandinavian language to be called in aid, but a hostile foreign language to be expelled from the national territory. The negative process of eliminating everything Danish from the literary language of Norway has been the most assiduous and the most successful of the activities of the *Maalstrever* movement; and for the sake of getting rid of a Danish word these Norwegian linguistic nationalists do not hesitate to alloy their New Norse with an outlandish vocabulary which is neither Scandinavian nor even Teutonic but French, Latin, or Greek in origin.

[2] This replacement of Irish by English as the vernacular language of the great majority of the Irish people is a recent event. As lately as a hundred years ago Irish was still prevalent among the peasantry in all parts of the island outside the Dublin Pale and the Ulster Plantations. This spread of English at the expense of Irish is to be explained partly by the sheer impassability of the gulf between the two languages (which made it impossible to blend them and therefore necessary to make a choice between them) and partly by the advantage which English acquired through becoming an oecumenical *lingua franca*. Thanks to its attainment of this status, English was employed as a matter of course in the nineteenth century as the vehicle for the spread of education in Ireland; and it was also propagated unintentionally by every Irish emigrant to the United States of America who eventually came home to settle down—or even merely to pay a passing visit to his family.

[3] This indigenous Irish literature did not survive the tribulations of the seventeenth century of the Christian Era, and its *floruit*—the age in which its surviving masterpieces were composed—was a thousand years before that.

language proves to be a disastrously heavy incubus upon the cultural life of a small and till recently backward people, then this will be one more item on the list of unhappy legacies that Ireland has inherited from her ill-starred political association with the English observer's own country.

The linguistic Archaism in which the Ottoman Turks have been indulging under the late President Mustafā Kemāl Atatürk's régime is perhaps more wanton than the Norwegian, but certainly less tragic than the Irish, excursion along the same regressive path. Modern Ottoman Turkish—as it was until the other day, when the archaizers took it in hand—was a language which, in point of vocabulary, was in much the same condition as modern English, and this for much the same reasons. The ancestors of the modern Turks, like those of their English contemporaries, were outer barbarians who had trespassed on, and squatted in, the derelict domain of a broken-down civilization; and the descendants of both sets of barbarians have made the same use of the vehicle of language as a means for acquiring a tincture of civilization. Just as the English have enriched their meagre primitive Teutonic vocabulary by loading it with a wealth of borrowed French and Latin and Greek words and phrases,[1] so the 'Osmanlis have encrusted their plain Turkish with innumerable jewels of Persian and Arabic speech.[2] The result, in both cases, has been to endow a poverty-stricken barbarian language with a richness in means of expression which might be envied by the great culture-languages themselves; and the English-speaking peoples, for their part, are still modestly content to enjoy this borrowed abundance without dreaming of repudiating it as a national disgrace. The nationalism of the English-speaking peoples is, however, a native growth and therefore a mild one; for Nationalism is a cultural virus which appears to work with a potency that is proportionate to its novelty. At any rate, this spiritual infection from the West has been taken so seriously by the Ottoman Turks that they have come to the conclusion that they would be unworthy of their Eurasian Nomad ancestors if they forbore to purify their ancestral language from the foreign accretions which it has acquired in the course of an unfortunate but ephemeral episode in its long and glorious history. When it is remembered that the Persian and Arabic element in Modern Turkish is at least as large and as important proportionately as the French and Latin and Greek element in Modern

[1] In taking on board this exotic cargo the medieval English were not guilty of the same wanton extravagance as the modern Norwegians (see p. 66, footnote 1, above). They were filling an empty hold and not jettisoning one cargo in order to make room for another.

[2] See V. C (i) (d) 6 (γ), vol. v, p. 516, above.

English, it will be seen that, in this enterprise of cleansing his
native tongue, the Ghāzi set himself a task with which none but
a hero could grapple; and the Turkish hero's method of setting
about it was the method which he had previously employed in
ridding his native country of the alien elements in its population.
In that graver crisis Mustafā Kemāl had evicted from Turkey an
old-established and apparently indispensable Greek and Armenian
middle class, on the calculation that, when once the social vacuum
had been produced, sheer necessity would compel the Turks to fill
it by taking upon their own shoulders social tasks which hitherto
they had lazily left to others. On the same principle the Ghāzi
afterwards evicted the Persian and Arabic words from the Ottoman
Turkish vocabulary; and, by this drastic measure, he demonstrated what an astonishing intellectual stimulus can be given to
mentally sluggish peoples (such as his Turks and our English are)
when they find their mouths and ears remorselessly deprived of
the simplest verbal necessities of life. In these dire straits the
Turks have latterly been ransacking Cuman glossaries, Orkhon
inscriptions, Uighur sutras, and Chinese dynastic histories in order
to find—or fake—a genuine Turkish substitute for this or that
sternly prohibited Persian or Arabic household word; and for an
English spectator these frantic lexicographical labours at Angora
and Stamboul are an awe-inspiring spectacle; for they give him an
inkling of tribulations that the future may hold in store for English-
speakers too, if ever the day should come when 'pure English' in
the literal sense is required of us by some masterful 'Saviour of
Society' as a sacrifice on the altars of our English 'blood and soil'.

If we turn from modern Turkey to modern Greece we shall
find here a linguistic Archaism which has the same political background as the Irish and Norwegian examples which we have
already examined—with the Turks in Greece taking the place of
the English in Ireland and of the Danes in Norway as the political
villains of the piece. Rather more than a hundred years ago the
Greek insurgents against the Ottoman Pādishāh succeeded, thanks
to the intervention of a Western France and England and a Westernized Russia, in carving out of a moribund Ottoman Empire
the nucleus of a sovereign independent Greek national state, and
they then at once set out to lead a new life as a fledgling Greek
nation on Western lines. For this cultural adventure, however,
they found themselves equipped linguistically with nothing better
than a peasant *patois*[1] which was incapable, as it stood, of serving

[1] At the time of the foundation of the present Greek national state (A.D. 1829-32)
the Modern Greek *patois* was by no means so near the point of extinction as the Modern
Irish *patois* was at the time of the foundation of the Irish Free State (A.D. 1921). On the
other hand it was not (as the Modern Norwegian *patois* was in A.D. 1905) the common

as a vehicle for expressing the ideas of the contemporary West, in whose intellectual life these politically emancipated Greeks were now eager to participate. In their impatience at this obstacle in their Westward path the Greeks anticipated the Irish in resorting to the expedient of reconditioning their *patois* for its strange and exacting new task by grouting it with injections of an antique form of the language—a form which in the Greek case had long since fallen out of use in every sphere except the Liturgy of the Greek-speaking patriarchates of the Orthodox Church. But, in making this same experiment of producing a new language by calling an old one back to life, the Greeks have had to wrestle with a problem which is the antithesis of the difficulty which has confronted the Irish. Whereas the Irish have been handicapped, like the Turks, by the scantiness of the nutriment that they have been able to extract for a living *patois* out of a dead culture-language, the modern Greeks have been overwhelmed by an *embarras de richesses*. For the liturgical Greek which has served their turn is not, like Old Irish (and Old Norse), the fragile blossom of a culture that died in its infancy. The liturgical Greek is the Attic κοινή; and, in audaciously drawing upon this reservoir of Ancient Greek, with its vast floating wealth of Pagan as well as Christian literature, the patriots who have been trying to force the growth of a Modern Greek culture-language have been in danger, not of seeing their irrigation-channel run dry, but of bringing down a spate which might obliterate the living *patois* instead of invigorating it. In fact, the besetting temptation in the path of this Modern Greek linguistic Archaism has been to draw upon the resources of Ancient Greek too lavishly; for, in themselves, these resources are almost inexhaustible; and the short cut to the supply of any Modern Greek linguistic need is always to open yet another Attic sluice-gate. These archaistic excesses have provoked a modernist reaction; and the artificial 'language of the purists' (ἡ καθαρεύουσα) has been answered in a caricature of the 'popular language' (ἡ δημοτική) which is no less artificial in its own contrary way, since it pounces upon every vulgarism that it spies in the gutter, while it avoids every classicism with as prim a pedantry as the champions of the opposing purism display in ejecting even the healthiest Turcicisms and Italianisms from their stilted vocabulary. This battle in a Westernized Greece between the advocates of alternative

language of the whole population of the new kingdom. Even within its original narrowly drawn frontiers—which excluded large Greek-speaking and still larger Greek-feeling populations—the Kingdom of Greece included considerable tracts in which the vernacular of the peasantry was not Greek at all. In Attica, for instance, the capital of the new kingdom, which had been placed at Athens, was surrounded by an Albanian-speaking peasantry.

artificial languages has been as bitter in its way as the feud between Constantinians and Venizelists.[1]

Our fifth instance of linguistic Archaism in the 'Great Society' of the present day is the reconversion of Hebrew into a vernacular language of everyday life on the lips and in the ears of the Zionist Jews from the Diasporà who have settled in Palestine;[2] and this is the most remarkable case of all the five; for, whereas none of the other four languages in question, not even the Irish, has ever quite ceased to be spoken or heard, more than twenty-three centuries have passed since the original Hebrew vernacular was supplanted by Aramaic in Palestine itself,[3] while even in North-West Africa, where the Hebrew language was introduced by the Israelites' neighbours the Phoenicians and not by the Israelites themselves, it does not seem to have lingered on much later than the lifetime of Saint Augustine (*decessit* A.D. 430).[4] For more than two thousand years past the language that a Jewish child has learnt at its mother's knee has been the mother-tongue of one or other of the Gentile peoples among whom Jewry has been dispersed abroad: Aramaic or Greek or Latin; Arabic or Castilian; German[5] or Russian or English.[6] For all this length of time, until within living memory, Hebrew has survived only as the language of the liturgy of the Jewish Church and of the scholarship that is concerned with the study of the Jewish Law. And then, in the course of a single generation, this 'dead language' has been brought out of the synagogue and has been converted into a vehicle for conveying the modern Western culture—at first in a newspaper

[1] Greece is perhaps the only country in Christendom—either Orthodox or Western —in which popular disturbances over the question of translating the Bible out of a classical language into the vulgar tongue have been excited, not against a veto upon the project of translation, but against a threat to carry the project into effect!

[2] Zionism has been touched upon already in this Study in II. D (vi), vol. ii, pp. 252–4, above.

[3] Hebrew was ceasing to be spoken by the Jewish community in Palestine as early as the third quarter of the fifth century B.C. on the testimony of Nehemiah (Neh. xiii. 24, already quoted in V. C (i) (*d*) 6 (γ), vol. v, p. 499, footnote 5, above). At the present day the Aramaic which supplanted Hebrew (see I. C (i) (*b*), vol. i, pp. 80–1, and V. C (i) (*d*) 6 (γ), vol. v, p. 491, above) and which was afterwards supplanted in its turn by Arabic has likewise become extinct in Palestine and all but extinct throughout Syria. The Aramaic language's last surviving Syrian citadel is the Jabal Qalamūn, an isolated range of hills which rises beyond the north-eastern fringe of the Ghūṭah of Damascus and juts out farther in the same direction into the Hamād. In this fastness an Aramaic dialect is still spoken in the villages of Maʿlūlah, Bakhʿah and Jubb ʿAdīn. 'The dialect differs very considerably from the vernacular Syriac of the Nestorian Christians in Persia and Kurdistan, so that the communities are not mutually intelligible. The dialect of these villages is said to be largely mixed with Arabic, and is never written. Classical Syriac is here and elsewhere used in the liturgies of some of the churches' (British Admiralty Naval Staff Intelligence Division: *A Handbook of Syria, including Palestine* (London 1920, H.M. Stationery Office), p. 196).

[4] See III. C (i) (*a*), vol. iii, p. 138, footnote 3, above.

[5] That is, the Jewish dialect of German known as Yiddish (Jüdisch).

[6] The Gentile language spoken by a particular Jewish community at a particular date has not, of course, always been the language of the country in which that community has been domiciled at the moment. For example, at the present moment the Jews in the ex-Ottoman countries speak Castilian and the Jews in Poland German.

press in the so-called 'Jewish Pale' in Eastern Europe, and now latterly in the schools and the homes of the Jewish community in Palestine—where the children of Yiddish-speaking immigrants from Europe and English-speaking immigrants from America and Arabic-speaking immigrants from the Yaman and Persian-speaking immigrants from Bukhārā are all growing up together to speak, as their common language, a tongue which, in Palestine, has not been heard on children's lips since the days of Nehemiah.

These five cases of linguistic Archaism in our contemporary Westernized World are all in some degree abnormal in the sense of being, all of them, cases in which a community that is not one of the original members of the Western Society has resorted to Archaism in the linguistic field as one of its ways and means of qualifying itself for naturalization by fitting itself out with all the equipment that any nation is expected to possess if it is to be admitted to the Western comity. Yet the very fact that Archaism should have come in so handy for this purpose seems to indicate that there must be a strong archaistic vein in our latter-day Western nationalism, at any rate in its linguistic facet.

This alliance between linguistic Archaism and linguistic Nationalism in the modern, or 'post-modern', Western World has a parallel in the Hellenic World in the days of the Hellenic universal state.

'In Roman Imperial times the antiquarian interest in local dialects is reflected in the revival of their use in parts of Greece where for some two centuries previously the Attic κοινή had been in general use, at least in inscriptions. So, for example, in the case of Lesbian, Laconian, and to some extent in Elean, where examples of rhotacism reappear in the first and second centuries A.D. It is impossible to determine in every case whether this was a wholly artificial revival of a dialect which had long ceased to be spoken, or was an artificial elevation to written use of a dialect which had survived throughout the interval as a *patois*. The latter is true of Laconian; but for most dialects we have no adequate evidence as to the length of their survival in spoken form.'[1]

In the Hellenic World, however, this symptom of social decline in the shape of linguistic Archaism was no mere adjunct of a parochial nationalism, but was something more pervasive than that,

[1] Buck, C. D.: *Introduction to the Study of the Greek Dialects* (Boston 1910, Ginn), p. 161. In the anthology of inscriptions in non-Attic Greek dialects that forms part of this book the author has included one archaistic inscription in Lesbian Aeolic which can be dated from internal evidence to some year between 2 B.C. and A.D. 19 [No. 24], and four archaistic inscriptions in Laconian Doric [Nos. 70–3] which all date from the second century of the Christian Era—a century in which the Hellenic craze for Archaism was at its height in every field. The reason why it can be asserted with assurance that the Laconian dialect continued to be spoken as a peasant *patois*, during the interval between its natural demise and its artificial revival as a culture-language worthy of being inscribed on stone, is that this dialect continues to be spoken down to the present day along the remote and isolated eastern seaboard of Laconia. This 'Tsakonian' *patois* is the only surviving form of spoken Greek that is not derived from the Attic κοινή.

and very much more important. For in the course of the disintegration of the Hellenic Society this movement asserted itself not only in official or semi-official records but also in the field of literature.

If you examine a book-case filled with a complete collection of the books, written in Ancient Greek before the seventh century of the Christian Era,[1] that have survived until the present day, you will soon notice two things: first that the overwhelmingly greater part of this surviving corpus of Ancient Greek literature is written in the Attic dialect, and second that, if this Attic part of the corpus is arranged chronologically, it falls apart into two distinct groups. In the first place there is an original Attic literature which was written at Athens in the fifth and fourth centuries B.C. by Athenians[2] who were writing, un-self-consciously and unaffectedly, in the language which they themselves were at the same time speaking and hearing in the course of their daily life in their native country. In the second place there is an archaistic Attic literature which was produced over a period of some six or seven centuries —from the last century B.C. to the sixth century of the Christian Era—and was the work of authors who for the most part did not live at Athens and did not speak Attic as their native tongue— indeed, a number of them were not born speakers of any dialect of Greek at all.

The geographical range over which these Neo-Attic writers are distributed is almost as wide as the Οἰκουμένη itself. If we take half a dozen of the non-Christian names, without calling upon the Christian Fathers, we can muster Josephus of Jerusalem and Aelian of Praeneste and Marcus Aurelius of Rome and Lucian of Samosata and Julian of Constantinople (or, ought we to say, 'of Paris'?) and Procopius of Caesarea. Yet, in spite of this wide diversity of origin, the Neo-Atticists display an extraordinary uniformity in one point which, for them, was the essence of their work. In their Attic vocabulary and Attic syntax and Attic style they are, one and all, frank and servile and shameless imitators. They have even bequeathed to us some of the grammars and the glossaries—indispensable tools of their literary craft—which they

---

[1] This *terminus ante quem* has to be inserted because, from the eighth to the fifteenth century of the Christian Era inclusive, a copious literature in the Ancient Greek language was produced in the Orthodox Christian World, and much of this medieval Greek literature (which corresponds to the medieval Latin literature of Western Christendom) has also survived. On the criterion laid down at the beginning of this chapter (see p. 49, footnote 3, above) this medieval Greek literature is the offspring, not of Archaism, but of 'Contact in Time'.

[2] Athenians in the geographical sense of natives of Attica, but not necessarily in the political sense of citizens of the Athenian state. For example, the advocate Lysias, whose Attic is unsurpassed in its purity, was politically a resident alien whose devotion to Athens did indeed win for him the Athenian franchise, but did not avail to enable him to retain it.

laboriously compiled for themselves by making a minute and exact study of the linguistic idiosyncrasies of their ancient Athenian en-samples. They were determined to make their pens proof against solecisms, and they achieved their ambition. Indeed, their success in the game of archaistic writing is vouched for by the very fact that the works of these Neo-Atticists have been preserved in quantities that are at first sight astonishingly voluminous—by comparison either with the actual volume of the surviving Athenian Classics or with the probable volume of the Ancient Greek literature as a whole.

The explanation is that, at the critical time, on the eve of the final dissolution of the Hellenic Society, when the question 'to be or not to be' was being decided for each and every Ancient Greek author by the prevailing literary taste of the day, the test question for copyists was 'Is it pure Attic?' rather than 'Is it great litera-ture?'; and the certified specimens of pure Attic were apt to be picked out for recopying on their formal Attic merits, without any invidious discrimination between a Plato of Athens and a Lucian of Samosata. The consequence is that we find ourselves in posses-sion of a number of works in Neo-Attic which have comparatively little intrinsic merit; and, if some miracle were to give us the chance of making over again, for ourselves, the choice that has actually been made for us by the Atticomaniac copyists of the Imperial and the Post-Imperial Age, we would gladly exchange this mediocre Neo-Attic stuff for one-tenth of that quantity of the mighty works of Greek literature which are now lost to us. Among these lost works are almost all the masterpieces of the third and second centuries B.C.; and these were allowed to drop out of circulation for ever simply because the great Greek writers of that age, like their greater predecessors in the fifth and fourth centuries, wrote un-self-consciously and unaffectedly in the current Greek of their own time and place, and therefore wrote for the most part in a vulgar Attic κοινή[1] which the Neo-Attic archaizers of the succeed-ing age—with their laboriously cultivated hyper-sensitiveness to fine shades of language and style—found almost too excruciating to read and a fortiori uninviting to copy out. Why spend labour on preserving these horrors when the only sure result would be to imperil the Attic purism of future generations?

It is this perversely archaistic outlook that has deprived us of all but a fragment of the work of Polybius of Megalopolis (vivebat circa 206–128 B.C.),[2] an author whose surviving literary remains

---

[1] For this Attic κοινή see V. C (i) (d) 6 (γ), vol. v, pp. 494–5, above.
[2] For the life of Polybius as an illustration of the movement of Withdrawal-and-Return see III. C (ii) (b), vol. iii, pp. 310–18, above.

proclaim him to have been one of the four greatest historians who ever wrote in Ancient Greek from beginning to end of the life-span of the Hellenic Society,[1] and who—perhaps just because he had so much to tell—was content to write in the pedestrian style of his generation. This loss of the work of Polybius is merely one conspicuous illustration of the severity of the losses that have been inflicted upon us by the Neo-Attic Archaism of the Imperial Age of Hellenic literary history. The Greek literature that was written neither in original nor in archaistic Attic has been reduced to shreds and tatters; and the papyri which our modern Western archaeologists have recovered from deposits made in Egypt in the Ptolemaic and the Roman Age have restored to us less of the vulgar Attic Greek literature of the Hellenic 'Time of Troubles' than might have been expected. The truth is that the Epimethean fixation upon an Attic literary past took possession of Greek minds at the very time when Greek texts began to be deposited in Egypt in consequence of the conquest of the Achaemenian Empire by Alexander. And thus even to-day, when we have had the benefit of half a century of papyrological enterprise and ingenuity, our extant specimens of non-archaistic post-Alexandrine Greek litera-ture are still substantially confined to two sets of works: on the one hand the bucolic poetry of the third and second century B.C., which was preserved as a literary curiosity for the sake of its precious Doric; and on the other hand the Greek text of the Jewish and Christian Scriptures—the Septuagint crowned by the New Testament—which was safeguarded by a religious conviction that these linguistically bizarre specimens of the Attic κοινή with an Aramaic flavouring were direct utterances of the Living God.[2]

The Atticism which triumphed in the Archaistic Age of Hellenic history was not the only literary exercise in which the archaists indulged. Our surviving body of Neo-Attic Greek literature has its pendants in the Neo-Ionic pieces of Lucian[3] and in the Neo-Homeric epic poetry which was cultivated by a long line of anti-quarian scholars[4] ranging from Apollonius Rhodius, whose lifetime

[1] Two of the four are, of course, indisputably Thucydides and Herodotus; and most Hellenists would probably allow Polybius the third place. As for the fourth place, in the humble opinion of the writer of this Study it should be assigned, not to Xenophon, but to Procopius.

[2] It was this belief in the verbal inspiration of the Bible that compelled even the most Attically educated of the Christian Fathers to assess the value of this stylistically bar-barous farrago on its intrinsic spiritual merits. If they had not been under the discipline of this religious categorical imperative, we may suspect that the vocabulary and style of the Greek Bible would have been intolerable for the Origens and Basils and Gregories and John Chrysostoms.

[3] e.g. his Περὶ τῆς Ἀστρολογηΐης and his Περὶ τῆς Συρίης Θεοῦ.

[4] 'My learned friend'—a form of reference which is in use between fellow barristers in the Law Courts in London at the present day—is the stock epithet for a poet in the language of those Latin poets of the last century B.C. who had learnt their trade from the Greek poets of the Alexandrian school! This usage of the word *doctus* tells a tale.

extended from the third into the second century B.C., through Quintus Smyrnaeus in the fourth century of the Christian Era to Nonnus Panopolitanus, who may have lived to see the fifth century pass over into the sixth.[1]

The archaistic resuscitation of the Attic dialect of Greek to serve as a vehicle for a voluminous Neo-Attic literature has an exact parallel in Indic history in the resuscitation of Sanskrit in comparable volume for a similar purpose.[2]

The original Sanskrit had been the vernacular of the Eurasian Nomad horde of the Aryas, who had broken out of the Steppe and had flooded over Northern India, as well as over South-Western Asia and Northern Egypt, in the second millennium B.C.;[3] and on Indian ground this language which had come in on the lips of barbarian invaders had been preserved in the Vedas, a corpus of religious literature which had become one of the cultural foundations of an Indic Civilization that had arisen on the site of the Aryas' Indian camping-grounds after the dust of the Aryan invasion had subsided. By the time, however, when this Indic Civilization had broken down and entered upon the path of disintegration,[4] Sanskrit had passed out of current usage and had become a classical language which continued to be studied because of the enduring prestige of the literature that was enshrined in it. As a medium of communication in everyday life, Sanskrit had by this time been replaced by a number of younger local vernaculars which were all alike derived from Sanskrit but which had come, in process of time, to be so far differentiated both from their parent and from one another that—from a practical, if not from a philological, point of view—they had become separate languages.[5] One of these

[1] This linguistic Archaism which is so prominent a feature of the Greek literature of the decline and fall was no doubt stimulated by a literary convention which had established itself in Hellas long before the breakdown of 431 B.C. This convention consisted in allocating a particular dialect to a particular genre of literature, whatever might be the native dialect of the author by whom this genre was being practised. For example, the Attic tragedians of the fifth century B.C. wrote their choruses in an artificial kind of Doric which had come to be recognized as the proper medium for lyrics; and as early as the eighth or seventh century B.C., or whatever the date may have been at which Hesiod was writing, the Homeric dialect—an archaic Ionic with a tincture of Aeolic in it—had become so completely *de rigueur* for any Greek poet who was writing in hexameters that it was employed by the Ascran author of *The Works and Days* as a matter of course, though this Homeric Greek was almost as remote from Hesiod's native Boeotian Aeolic as it was from the native Attic κοινή of Apollonius and Quintus and Nonnus.

[2] This resuscitation of Sanskrit is also discussed in this Study in V. C (i) (c) 3, Annex II, vol. v, p. 606, footnote 3, above.

[3] For the long and widely divergent ramifications of the Völkerwanderung of the Aryas see I. C (i) (b), vol. i, pp. 104-7, and p. 111, footnote 1; II. D (vii), vol. ii, pp. 388-91; and V. C (i) (c) 3, vol. v, pp. 263-4, above.

[4] In other contexts (e.g. in I. C (i) (b), vol. i, p. 87, and in IV. C (ii) (b) 1, vol. iv, pp. 66-7, above) we have seen reason to date the breakdown of the Indic Civilization before the birth of Siddhārtha Gautama the Buddha, and perhaps even before the end of the eighth century B.C.

[5] Franke, R. O.: *Pāli und Sanskrit in ihrem historischen und geographischen Verhältnis*

prākrits—the Pālī of Ceylon—was employed as the vehicle of the Hinayanian Buddhist Scriptures, and several others were employed by the Emperor Açoka (*imperabat* 273–232 B.C.) as vehicles for the edicts which he caused to be inscribed at various places in his extensive dominions.[1]

Açoka's object in varying the prākrit which he employed according to the locality in which he was employing it was to make sure that his edicts should be intelligible to the local population in each of the districts where they were inscribed. Intelligibility was for him a major consideration, to which he sacrificed the trivial convenience of establishing a single standard official language for the whole of his empire. And the ruler of a universal state who thus forbore to insist upon the use of any one current local vernacular at the expense of the rest would presumably have scouted, *a fortiori*, the suggestion that he should address his subjects in a language which—like Sanskrit in Açoka's day—had long since passed out of spontaneous use. Nevertheless, just such an artificial revival of Sanskrit was started, at a point within the frontiers of Açoka's empire,[2] at latest immediately after, and possibly even before, the Emperor Açoka's death;[3] and this archaizing linguistic movement steadily extended its range[4] until, by the sixth century of the Christian Era, the triumph of the Neo-Sanskrit language over the prākrits was complete on the Indian mainland[5]—leaving Pālī to survive as a literary curiosity in the solitary island fastness of Ceylon.

Thus our extant corpus of Sanskrit literature, like our extant corpus of Attic Greek literature, falls into two distinct portions:

auf Grund der Inschriften und Münzen (Strassburg 1902, Trübner), pp. 65–6, 90, and 139–40. The geographical lines of division between these local prākrits were not clear-cut; the respective ranges of the various dialectical peculiarities overlapped (op cit., p. 126).

[1] See V. C (i) (*d*) 6 (γ), vol. v, p. 498, above.

[2] The geographical centre of dispersion of this archaistic movement for the revival of Sanskrit is shown by the epigraphical evidence to have been the Ganges-Jumna Duab between the foot of the Himalayas and the city of Mathurā (Franke, op. cit., p. 83).

[3] Franke (in op. cit., p. 87) dates the beginning of the Neo-Sanskrit movement before the end of the third century B.C.

[4] The spread of the use of Neo-Sanskrit from its starting-point in the Ganges-Jumna Duab into other parts of India was gradual, and some of the stages can be dated. In inscriptions Neo-Sanskrit did not begin to replace Pālī in any part of the Indic World until the last century B.C. (Franke, op. cit., pp. 50–1); and, even in Northern India, it was not until the second century of the Christian Era that Neo-Sanskrit inscriptions became so numerous relatively to inscriptions in Pālī (ibid., p. 52). In the Deccan Pālī was still holding the field in the second century of the Christian Era, and only began to give way to Neo-Sanskrit in the third century; and in this region some Pālī inscriptions have been discovered which date from as late as the fourth century (ibid., p. 51). There are also extant a number of documents in a mixed language—part Pālī and part Neo-Sanskrit—and these can be arranged in a series showing the gradual transition from a Pālī with an infusion of Sanskrit in it to a Sanskrit with a trace of Pālī in it (ibid., pp. 53–4). In the first century of the Christian Era Pālī was still predominant in the grammatical terminations, but in the second century the Sanskritisms became much more sharply pronounced (ibid., p. 59).   [5] Ibid., p. 53.

an older portion which is original and a younger portion which is imitatively archaistic.[1]

Up to this point we have confined our attention to matters of language and style, without pausing to consider that this linguistic Archaism is unlikely to have been cultivated as an end in itself.[2] It is, however, manifestly improbable *a priori* that even a pedant would condemn himself to the hard labour of resuscitating a language which had passed out of circulation unless he were moved by some strong desire to make use of the 'dead language', when he had duly succeeded in reviving it, in order to convey to his fellow men some literary message—a complex of emotions or a system of ideas—which was of capital importance in the archaist's own estimation. We must therefore go on to inquire into the literary purposes for which the Neo-Sanskrit and the Neo-Attic linguistic vehicles were actually employed. Were they used for mere literary exercises in genres which were just as much *vieu jeu* as their linguistic medium? Or was there a contrast between the Archaism of the medium and the spirit of the ideas and emotions which the medium was made to convey?

If we put this question first apropos of the Neo-Sanskrit literature we shall find that the archaic vehicle has in fact been used principally for the conveyance of something which is not merely new but is also charged with a creative vitality; for the main use to which the Neo-Sanskrit language has been put has been to serve as a vehicle for the Scriptures of the Mahāyāna and Hinduism;

[1] In the Attic Greek literature the original and the archaistic portions are not only distinct, but are separated from one another chronologically, as we have seen, by an interval of not much less than a quarter of a millennium between the latest Athenian works in original Attic and the earliest non-Athenian works in Neo-Attic. In making a corresponding survey of the Sanskrit literature it is impossible to draw so sharp a line. The Sanskrit Epic, for example, which, in the form in which it has come down to us, is undoubtedly a work of the Neo-Sanskrit Age, may also (as is pointed out in V. C (i) (c) 3, Annex II, in vol. v, above) contain an original Sanskrit element which it is impossible now to disengage from its Neo-Sanskrit recensions and accretions. Thus, in the Epic, we have one outstanding work of Sanskrit literature which cannot be classified as belonging wholly either to the Neo-Sanskrit or to the original Sanskrit stratum.

[2] Before leaving the subject of purely linguistic Archaism we may take notice, in the Syriac World, of the epic poet Firdawsī's policy of restricting to a minimum the quota of the Arabic vocabulary in the New Persian language in which he was writing. (For the infusion of Arabic into New Persian see I. C (i) (b), vol. i, p. 80, above, and V. C (i) (d) 6 (γ), vol. v, p. 501, above.) This is undoubtedly a case of linguistic Archaism; but Firdawsī's archaistic impulse was not very strong; for it did not occur to him to write in Pehlevi, and he was probably unaware of the existence of the two dialects of Old Iranian—uncontaminated by any Semitic taint—that are familiar to us as the respective vehicles of the Achaemenian inscriptions and of the oldest stratum of the Avesta.

The archaistic purge by which Firdawsī relieved the New Persian language of an intrusive Arabic vocabulary has a parallel in which New Persian has been the victim instead of being the beneficiary. The Hindī form of Hindustānī 'was derived from Urdū by ejecting all words of Arabic and Persian birth, and substituting in their place words borrowed or derived from the indigenous Sanskrit' (*The Imperial Gazetteer of India*, new edition (Oxford 1907, Clarendon Press), p. 366, quoted already in V. C (i) (d) 6 (γ), vol. v, p. 518, footnote 2, above). It is one of the curiosities of history that these Hindu archaists should have been missionaries of an alien religion and culture.

and these were a pair of new-born 'higher religions'—Hinduism being a direct product of the religious experience of the internal proletariat of the Indic Society, while the Mahāyāna was a metamorphosis of the Buddhist philosophy of the Indic dominant minority.[1] Was the Neo-Attic language turned to any corresponding account? The answer is in the affirmative; for the corpus of Neo-Attic literature includes both the works of the Neoplatonic philosophers and those of the Christian Fathers. Yet, if we leave our answer at that, it will be misleadingly incomplete; for neither the Neoplatonic Philosophy nor the Christian Theology was the 'subject-matter' for the sake of which the Attic language was so laboriously reconstructed. That tremendous labour of love and learning was lavished upon a dead Attic dialect without any intention of using it to convey a living message. The purpose of the Atticists was indeed the exact contrary of that. The vision that inspired them was the prospect of re-creating a linguistic medium through which they would be able to walk—for all the world like Alice through her looking-glass—out of the living social environment of their own time and place into a dead social environment which could only be recaptured, if it could ever be recaptured at all, by the magic of a literary make-believe.

'Eloquence was now not valued because it affected the practical decisions of the Present, but because it transported men into the Past. Probably more than any other generations of men, before or since, the Greeks of the first Christian centuries found their pleasure in living by imagination in a Past five hundred years gone by. The events of those hundred and eighty years long ago, from the Battle of Marathon to the death of Demosthenes, stood out in peculiar illumination; all that followed was grey. It was as if those hundred and eighty years were the only ones that counted in human history: things had then really happened, events in which it was worth being interested. When you went from the commonplace streets of your town into the hall where a great orator was to speak and submitted yourself to that flow of words, the rhetoric acted, as some drugs do, to carry you into a wonder-world. If the cities of the Greek World had ceased for centuries to have the determination of great events in their hands, the Greeks could still, as in an opium dream, find themselves among the multitude in the Pnyx and listen to Demosthenes thundering against Philip. How much the interval of time between the fourth century B.C. and the present was considered, as far as was possible, non-existent, one may see by the rhetorical sermons of Maximus of Tyre, a contemporary of Marcus Aurelius. They are full of illustrative references and anecdotes, but no allusion, I think, to anything later than the fourth century B.C., except a few references to Epicurus in the third century, and a solitary reference to Carneades in the second. We forget, while the spell of Maximus

[1] See V. C (i) (c) 2, vol. v, pp. 133–8, above.

holds us, that such a thing as Rome, such a person as Caesar, has ever existed. A still odder indication of this habit of thought may be found in a reference to Stoics in the *Protrepticus* of Iamblichus, a Greek writer of an even later century than Maximus of Tyre—an indication all the more striking because it is incidental and not supposed, apparently, to cause any surprise. Iamblichus, round about the year A.D. 300, refers to the founders of the Stoic school as οἱ νεώτεροι.[1] His standpoint is that of Pythagoras or Plato, and thus philosophers of the third century B.C. appear as "the moderns" or "the more recent"—philosophers separated from Iamblichus by an interval of time as great as separates us from Dante or Chaucer! Centuries later than the third century B.C. do not count.'[2]

This pathetic endeavour to circumvent the remorseless flow of Time by dodging back into a dead and buried Past through a literary door made of mirror-glass began on the morrow of the breakdown of the Hellenic Society and was never abandoned so long as anything that could call itself Hellenism remained in existence. On the morrow of the breakdown we find Plato representing his fictitious dialogues as taking place, not at the time when the author himself was thinking the thoughts which the dialogues expound, or when he was putting these thoughts into words or setting the words down on paper: every dialogue is deliberately ascribed to some date that is prior to the death of Socrates; and for Plato the judicial murder of Socrates in 399 B.C., rather than the outbreak of the Atheno-Peloponnesian War in 431 B.C., was the symbolic catastrophe which proclaimed the breakdown of the Hellenic Civilization. The *dramatis personae* are carefully chosen to fit these imaginary dates, and their ages and outlooks are portrayed in conformity with this archaistic regression.[3] Since Plato (*vivebat circa* 430–347 B.C.) himself was born immediately after the outbreak of the fatal war, and was still a young man at the time of the inexpiable judicial murder, the Time-span involved in this Platonic Archaism is not more than half a lifetime. This, however, was only the first move in a game that was to be played, as the centuries passed, with an ever-growing extravagance until, in the Hellenic World of the second century of the Christian Era, we are treated to the spectacle of a new Socrates being commemorated by

[1] Page 118 of the Teubner text.
[2] Bevan, E. R.: 'Rhetoric in the Ancient World' in *Essays in Honour of Gilbert Murray* (London 1936, Allen & Unwin), pp. 208–10.
[3] 'His dialogues are not only a memorial to Socrates, but also to the happier days of his own family. Plato must have felt the events of the end of the fifth century keenly, but he is so careful to avoid anachronisms in these dialogues that no one could ever guess from them that they were written after Kritias and Charmides had met with a dishonoured end' (Burnet, J.: *Greek Philosophy: Part I, Thales to Plato* (London 1914, Macmillan), pp. 208–9. Cf. pp. 211–13). For the detachment which was a different and a deeper response of Plato's soul to the challenge of social disintegration see V. C (i) (d) 1, vol. v, pp. 394–6, above, and V. C (i) (d) 10, in the present volume, pp. 132–48, below.

a new Xenophon. Arrian's digest of Epictetus's dissertations is a conscious repetition of Xenophon's act in writing the *Memorabilia*; and the Nicomedian public servant of a Roman Imperial Government can never forget that his literary mission is to follow in the footsteps of an Athenian man-at-arms and man-of-letters who was Arrian's senior by about five hundred years, and whose life had been lived, and *Weltanschauung* been formed, in utterly different social circumstances.

Strange though this Neo-Atticism may appear, the most extraordinary feat of linguistic and literary Archaism in the Hellenic World in the Imperial Age has still to be recorded. In this age, once again, a captive Greece succeeded in captivating her Roman conqueror;[1] and this time she led him a dance; for she now prevailed upon him to fall into step with her retreat, after having once upon a time carried him along with her in the last halting stage of her broken advance; and for the Roman this reverse movement in the train of his Greek Muse meant harking back, not to the glories of an original Attic literature of the fifth and fourth centuries B.C., but to the crudities and curiosities of his own ancestors' first attempt to reclothe Greek literature in a Latin dress.

This disease of literary Archaism which the Romans caught from the Greeks in the Imperial Age did not begin to show itself in Latin literature until about a hundred years after Greek literature had succumbed to it; but, when once the infection had taken, its ravages were rapid; and before the end of the second century of the Christian Era the Latin version of Hellenism was quite as far gone as its Greek ensample in a decline that could only end in utter sterility.

The sickening of the Latin genius with this fatal malady can be observed in Tacitus's *Dialogus de Oratoribus*, which is represented as having taken place in the sixth year of the reign of the Emperor Vespasian (A.D. 74–5).[2] One of the topics of the dialogue[3] is a disputation over the relative merits of 'the ancients' and 'the moderns'; and, although the cause of 'the moderns' is championed in spirited language by an advocate who holds up to scorn the perversity of those archaists 'who read Lucilius in preference to Horace and Lucretius in preference to Virgil',[4] the argument is eventually broken off because the cause of 'the ancients' is assumed to be invincible.[5] The Latin literary Archaism of Tacitus's genera-

---

[1] Horace: *Epistolae*, Book II, Ep. i, l. 156.   [2] Tacitus: *Dialogus*, chap. 17, § 3.
[3] Chaps. 14–26.   [4] Tacitus: *Dialogus*, chap. 23, § 2.
[5] Tacitus: *Dialogus*, chap. 27, *init*. The rest of the work is devoted to considering not *whether*, but *why*, the eloquence of 'the ancients' (i.e. of Latin orators of the last generation before the establishment of the *Pax Augusta*) was superior to that of 'the moderns' (i.e. the characters in the dialogue and their younger contemporaries of Tacitus's own generation). In this inquiry Tacitus starts from a change for the worse in

tion[1] kept, however, within the bounds of moderation, since the oldest 'ancients' with whom the speakers in the *Dialogus* are seriously concerned are those of the generation of Cicero. Thereafter the deterioration was rapid, for Tacitus himself may have lived to see the principate of Hadrian, and the Latin poet whom Hadrian preferred to Virgil was not the austere Lucretius but the uncouth Ennius. The still more exotic taste of Marcus Aurelius's African tutor Fronto found the greatest merit in the most archaic Latin literature that had survived; and Fronto's Archaism was pushed to a further degree of extravagance by his disciple Aulus Gellius.[2]

The bilingual folly of this Greek and Latin literary Archaism of the second century of the Christian Era might have been pilloried as the extreme case of its kind, if it were not a matter of attested historical fact that, in this wild-goose chase, Hellenism has been outrun by Sinism.

'Les Chinois, quand ils parlent et quand ils écrivent, s'expriment uniformément en employant des formules consacrées. . . . La littérature chinoise est une littérature de centons. Quand ils veulent prouver ou expliquer, quand ils songent à raconter ou à décrire, les auteurs les plus originaux se servent d'historiettes stéréotypées et d'expressions convenues, puisées à un fonds commun. Ce fonds n'est pas très abondant et, d'ailleurs, on ne cherche guère à le renouveler. Une bonne partie des thèmes qui ont joui d'une faveur permanente se retrouvent dans les productions les plus anciennes et les plus spontanées de la poésie chinoise. . . . Le rôle des centons n'est pas moins grand dans la prose que dans la poésie, dans le style savant que dans la langue vulgaire. . . . Un lecteur attentif des Annales chinoises hésite constamment: veut-on lui présenter des faits particuliers, singularisés, ou lui apprendre ce qu'il convient de faire ou de ne pas faire? La rédaction en termes rituels

---

domestic life: modern parents do not give the same personal attention as their predecessors gave to the upbringing of their children, but leave it all to servants. He goes on to discuss the changes in the system of apprenticeship for public speaking; and here he has some severe strictures to make upon the modern schools of rhetoric. But his most trenchant point is that fine oratory is the fruit of turbulent times, and that the inevitable price of good government is an atmosphere of dullness which gives human wits no stimulus. 'Magna eloquentia, sicut flamma, materia alitur et motibus excitatur et urendo clarescit' (chap. 36, § 1). Already, half-way through the principate of Augustus, 'longa temporum quies et continuum populi otium et assidua senatus tranquillitas et maxime principis disciplina ipsam quoque eloquentiam sicut omnia alia pacaverat' (chap. 38, § 2). 'Nemo eodem tempore adsequi potest magnam famam et magnam quietem' (chap. 41, § 5). These concluding chapters of the *Dialogus* are a brilliant essay on the theme that Caesar's peace (unlike the Peace of God) is a Yin-state which is not at all conducive to creativity. In a work of a later generation on the same subject (Longinus [?]: *De Sublimitate*, chap. 44), Tacitus's political explanation of the decay of eloquence is re-examined, but is rejected in favour of the alternative thesis that the root of the evil is not the public vice of despotism but the private vices of avarice and self-indulgence.

[1] The fictitious date of the *Dialogus* is placed by Tacitus, *more Platonico*, about half a generation earlier than the author's own *floruit*.

[2] For this Latin literary and linguistic Archaism of the Antonine 'Indian Summer' in the second century of the Christian Era see Parker, H. M. D.: *A History of the Roman World from A.D. 138 to 337* (London 1935, Methuen), pp. 47–8.

s'explique-t-elle simplement par un parti pris de stylistes ou bien l'histoire n'a-t-elle à conter qu'une succession d'incidents rituels? Il n'y a pas à décider: en fait, le goût des formules toutes faites n'est que l'un des aspects d'une adhésion générale à une morale conformiste. . . . Comme les annalistes, les philosophes chinois sont des conteurs d'historiettes. Dans les ouvrages de tous genres, on trouve, utilisées à satiété, les mêmes anecdotes — si bien qu'un lecteur occidental lisant pour la première fois une œuvre chinoise éprouve presque immanquablement une impression de déjà lu.'[1]

When even the earliest of our surviving specimens of Sinic literature—the poetry collected in the *She King* which apparently dates from the Sinic Civilization's growth-stage—already displays this archaistic mental orientation towards the Past, we shall not be surprised to find literary Archaism carrying all before it in the succeeding age of disintegration, and capturing, quickly and completely, the Confucian school of philosophy.

'La passion d'enseigner en commentant signale le fléchissement du goût pour les formes pragmatiques d'enseignement auxquelles Confucius dut apparemment son prestige. Le Maître avait essayé de faire reconnaître la valeur d'une psychologie positive en habituant ses disciples à réfléchir en commun à propos d'incidents journaliers. Ses successeurs enseignèrent en *commentant* les vers du *Che King* aussi bien que les formules du *Tch'ouen ts'ieou*, les aphorismes chers aux devins tout comme les adages des maîtres des cérémonies. Dès la fin du ve siècle, on pouvait les accuser de ne s'attacher qu'à un savoir livresque et de n'accorder de valeur qu'aux semblants rituels.'[2]

If this were a verdict on the Hellenic thought of the Neo-Attic Age, there might be nothing more to be said; but in studying the actions of Sinic souls we must never forget to reckon with the dexterity of a Sinic genius which delights in the use of unpromising means for the attainment of unexpected ends.

'Si les auteurs s'appliquent à parler par proverbes, ce n'est point qu'ils pensent de façon commune; c'est que la bonne façon, et la plus fine, de faire valoir leur pensée, est de la glisser dans une formule éprouvée dont elle empruntera le crédit. Les centons possèdent une sorte de force, neutre et concrète, qui peut, de façon latente, se particulariser à l'infini, tout en conservant, dans les applications les plus singulières, un égal pouvoir d'inviter à agir. . . . Les poèmes du *Che King* qui sont écrits dans la langue la plus proverbiale sont assurément ceux (l'opinion publique en fait foi) où se sont signifiées les pensées les plus subtiles. La même règle vaut pour les œuvres de tous les temps, de tous les genres. Les poésies les plus riches en expressions consacrées sont les plus admirées. Dans aucune, les formules convenues ne se pressent autant que dans ces sortes de méditations mystiques où le

[1] Granet, M.: *La Pensée Chinoise* (Paris 1934, Renaissance du Livre), pp. 57, 58, 68, 69, and 70.   [2] Ibid., p. 553.

lyrisme chinois donne sa note la plus haute. La densité en centons ne mesure pas seulement le savoir traditionnel du poète: la densité la plus forte est la marque de la pensée la plus profonde.'[1]

This Sinic art of turning the trick of literary Archaism from a barren conceit into a potent charm, whose compelling power can strike down to the subconscious fundament of the Soul and then stir it to the depths, will be no secret to any Jewish or Christian or Islamic writer who has had the good fortune to have been equipped for his work by being educated in accordance with the tradition of his forefathers; for the language of the Bible or the Qur'ān will have been imprinted on his memory in his childhood as indelibly as the language of the Sinic Classics on the memory of the Far Eastern litteratus; and a mind thus inalienably enriched with the treasures of its native spiritual heritage will be master of that alchemy which knows how to evoke something new out of an allusion to something old or, in other words, how to transmute an act of mimesis into an act of creation.

(δ) *Archaism in Religion.*

In the field of Religion, as in the fields of Language and Art and Institutions, it is possible for a Western student of history at the present day to study the phenomenon of Archaism at first hand within the limits of his own social environment.

Within the past hundred years France, England, and Germany in turn have each been the scene of an archaistic religious movement. In France and in England this religious Archaism has been the expression of a homesickness for the ceremonial and the atmosphere of a medieval Western Christianity; and it is a remarkable spectacle to see this homesickness overcoming two modern Western institutions that have travelled so far from their medieval Christian origins as the Positivist school of philosophy and the Anglican Church: an artificial philosophy that has been manufactured in a Humanistic workshop,[2] and a parochial Protestant

---

[1] Ibid., pp. 65 and 68; cf. pp. 73-4.

[2] The Humanism which has been one of the governing principles of our Western culture in its so-called 'Modern Age' has been touched upon already in IV. C (iii) (c) 2 (α), vol. iv, pp. 300-3, and in V. C (i) (d) 7, in the present volume, p. 8, above. Comte's purpose in appropriating the trappings of a medieval Western Christianity for the use of his own 'Religion of Humanity' was not, of course, to revive the worship of the god who had previously been honoured with these rites. On the contrary, Comte was determined to replace the Christians' personal God by a collective Humanity, and to present this 'vrai Grand Être' to his own Positivist disciples as the proper recipient for the traditional divine honours. Comte's 'Religion of Humanity' has been touched upon already in IV. C (iii) (c) 2 (α), vol. iv, pp. 300-1, above, in this aspect, as an example of the idolization of an ephemeral self. And this element of anti-Christian idolatry in 'the Religion of Humanity' is, of course, much more important than the element of pseudo-Christian Archaism with which we are concerned in the present context.

This pseudo-Christian Archaism, which Comte (*vivebat* A.D. 1798–1857) gradually worked out on lines of his own (see Caird, E.: *The Social Philosophy and Religion of*

Church that is borne upon the political establishment of one of the national states of the modern Western World. Yet this regression of a French Positivism and a British Anglo-Catholicism towards the religion of medieval Western Christendom is not so startling a phenomenon as the corresponding movement of Hauerism in post-war Germany, where the spiritual strain to which the German people has been continuously subject since July 1914 has eventu-

Comte (Glasgow 1885, MacLehose), pp. 238–47, and Berdyaev, N.: *The Meaning of History* (London 1936, Bles), pp. 163–4), was perhaps originally suggested to his mind by the ideas of two thinkers of an older generation, Joseph de Maistre (*vivebat* A.D. 1754–1821) and C. H. de Rouvroy, Comte de Saint-Simon (*vivebat* A.D. 1760–1825). De Maistre was a thorough-going archaist who advocated a revival of the Hildebrandine *Respublica Christiana* under the exclusive and absolute sovereignty of the Pope as the only effective antidote to the Revolution; and his ideas were already familiar by the time when Comte was growing up (de Maistre's masterpiece, *Du Pape*, was finished in 1817 and published in 1819 (Lyon, Rusand, 2 vols.)). Saint-Simon's aim was different; for to his mind the institutions of medieval Western Christendom were outworn, and he wished to replace them by modern equivalents which would perform corresponding functions. Science was to be substituted for the Church, and Industry for Feudalism. These Saint-Simonian ideas were set forth in an unfinished work, *Nouveau Christianisme* (Paris: Bossange, Sautelet), which was published in 1825; and in 1826 Comte wrote his *Considerations on the Spiritual Power* (English translation in *Early Essays on Philosophy translated from the French of Auguste Comte* by Henry Dix Dutton (London, n.d., Routledge)), in which he propounded his own scheme for enlisting an ecclesiastical Archaism in the service of an anthropolatrous Paganism. 'The social condition of the most civilized nations imperiously demands the formation of a new spiritual order as the first and chief mode of ending the Revolutionary Period which began in the six-teenth century and thirty years ago entered on its last stage' (p. 297). 'It would be easy to form empirically a clear idea of the functions of the modern spiritual power by a careful study of those which devolved upon the Catholic clergy at the period of their greatest vigour and complete independence, that is to say, from about the middle of the eleventh to nearly the end of the thirteenth century. . . . For every social relation that fell within the province of the Catholic clergy, an analogous attribute will be found in the new political system as a function of the modern spiritual power' (p. 298). We must emancipate ourselves 'from the pernicious prejudices generally inspired by the Critical Philosophy towards the spiritual system of the Middle Age' (p. 299). On the other hand, due allowance must be made for 'the extreme difference' between the medieval and the modern state of Western Civilization (p. 299); and on this head Comte criticizes de Maistre and the other contemporary philosophers of 'the retrograde school'. 'In them we may remark the radical inconsequence which consists in directly transferring to modern societies considerations exclusively drawn from the observation of medieval societies so essentially different. Associated, moreover, as they invariably are, with projects for restoring a system whose destruction, already almost completed, is hence-forward irrevocable, they tend in the present state of men's minds rather to fortify than to uproot the general prejudice against every spiritual power' (p. 351, footnote 2). The details of Comte's own system were afterwards worked out in a *Positivist Calendar* (1849), in which 'Benefactors of Humanity', *more Alexandri Severi* (see V. C (i) (d) 6 (δ), vol. v, p. 549, above), were substituted for Saints, and thereafter (in 1852) in *The Catechism of Positivism or Summary Exposition of the Universal Religion in Thirteen Syste-matic Conversations between a Woman and a Priest of Humanity* (English translation, second edition: London 1883, Trübner, with a reprint, at the end, of the *Positivist Calendar*). In the latter work Comte's thesis that Catholicism, on new intellectual foundations, will finally preside over the spiritual life of a reorganized Modern Society (*Positive Philosophy*, vol. v, p. 344) is illustrated by the presentation of Humanity as an 'incomparable goddess' (*Catechism*, English translation, p. 58) in the lineaments of the Theotókos.

'Never will Art be able worthily to embody Humanity otherwise than in the form of Woman. . . . The Symbol of our goddess will always be a woman of thirty with her son in her arms' (*Catechism*, pp. 84 and 99).

In taking the traditional image of the Theotókos and renaming it 'Humanity', Comte was following a precedent which had been set by the Christian Church itself when, in its formative age in the early centuries of the Christian Era, it had made its own image of Mary in the traditional likeness of Isis or Ishtar or Cybele.

It is only in England, and not in his native France, that Comte's dream of establishing a Positivist Church with a corporate life and an order of public worship has come true.

ally betrayed its severity in the desperateness of the reaction in which a certain number of tormented German souls are now seeking to find relief.

Professor Hauer is adjuring his countrymen not merely to repudiate a modern phase of the Western Civilization which to-day, in retrospect, may well be looked askance at by any of its children, but actually to break away from the Western Christianity which is the common primal root and stem of every modern branch of the Western Society. The watchword of Professor Hauer is 'Back to the paganism in which our Teutonic forebears found happiness before they were captivated by an alien Judaistic super- stition and an alien Romance culture'. The Hauerites' bugbear is Charlemagne, who in their eyes has been the arch-betrayer of the German Race. They cannot forgive this all-powerful German master of an infant Western Europe for having employed his power in suppressing the paganism of the Saxon barbarians in the outer darkness beyond the north-east frontier of the Austrasian dominions; for, in incorporating Saxony into Western Christen- dom, Charlemagne, in the Hauerites' view, was capturing for Christ and for Rome the last continental stronghold of a pure and undefiled German culture.[1] And they picture the German pagan- ism which Charlemagne stamped out—and which they themselves are now proposing to revive—in a shape which bears no recog- nizable likeness to the historical worship of the deified war-lord Woden and his deified war-band.[2] The religion with which the Primitive Germans are credited by the Hauerites is a worship of the One True God through the symbol of physical light; and, in their sophisticated enthusiasm for this imaginary religious intuition of their primitive ancestors, they would almost have us believe that the valley of the Spree, and not the valley of the Nile, was the scene of Ikhnaton's enlightenment.

In 1938 it was impossible for an English observer to tell how seriously this Neo-Pagan movement in Germany had to be taken as an indication of the religious destiny of the Western World as a whole; but he could hardly be mistaken in citing this portent of Hauerism as evidence that Western souls were no longer proof

[1] Less hysterical modern students of Charlemagne's work will be inclined to censure the Austrasian militarist, not for setting out to reclaim his Saxon neighbours from their pestilent barbarism by converting them from their barren paganism, but for attempting to achieve an admirable social purpose by means of the pernicious instrument of military force. In the present Study Charlemagne's behaviour towards the Saxons has been criticized on this ground already in II. D (v), vol. ii, p. 167; II. D (vii), vol. ii, pp. 345–6; IV. C (iii) (c) 2 (β), vol. iv, pp. 322–3; IV. C (iii) (c) 3 (α), vol. iv, pp. 488–90, and IV. C (iii) (c) 3 (β), vol. iv, p. 523, above.

[2] For this by no means primitive pagan religion of the North-European external proletariat of the Hellenic World in its 'heroic age' see V. C (i) (c) 3, vol. v, pp. 230–3. above. The historical religion of the German participants in a post-Hellenic Völkerwan- derung is reflected, not in Professor Hauer's theology, but in Herr Hitler's politics.

against being captivated by a religious Archaism even when this offered itself in an extravagant fancy-dress.

The three living examples of Archaism in the religious field which have met our eyes in the contemporary Western World[1] are none of them impressive; for, while the German movement is patently rabid, the French and English movements are no less patently sentimental. If we now transfer our attention from our own world to the Hellenic, and concentrate it upon that moment in the Hellenic Society's disintegration when Augustus was bringing a Hellenic 'Time of Troubles' to an end by establishing a Hellenic universal state, we shall encounter here an experiment in religious Archaism which may command our admiration.

'The revival of the State religion by Augustus is at once the most remarkable event in the history of the Roman religion, and one almost unique in religious history. . . . The belief in the efficacy of the old cults had passed away among the educated classes; . . . the mongrel city populace had long been accustomed to scoff at the old deities; and . . . the outward practice of religion had been allowed to decay. To us, then, it may seem almost impossible that the practice, and to some extent also the belief, should be capable of resuscitation at the will of a single individual, even if that individual represented the best interests and the collective wisdom of the State. For it is impossible to deny that this resuscitation was real; that both *pax deorum* and *ius divinum* became once more terms of force and meaning. Beset as it was by at least three formidable enemies, which tended to destroy it even while they fed on it, like parasites in the animal or vegetable world feeding on their hosts— the rationalizing philosophy of syncretism,[2] the worship of the Caesars,[3] and the new Oriental cults[4]—the old religion continued to exist for at least three centuries in outward form, and to some extent in popular belief.'[5]

This long-enduring success of Augustus's enterprise of reviving the native religion of the Roman people is remarkable indeed; for

[1] If it be asked why Protestantism has been omitted from a list in which Anglo-Catholicism has been included, the answer is that Anglo-Catholicism is, while Protestantism is not, an example of Archaism in the sense in which the term is used in this Study. In our terminology Protestantism is a case, not of Archaism within the compass of the life of a single civilization, but of the 'Contact in the Time-dimension' between two different civilizations; for, in its endeavour to return to the practice and the spirit of the Primitive Church and to recover this spirit and practice by taking the Canon of Scripture as its exclusive authority, Protestantism was seeking to establish a direct contact with the extinct Syriac Civilization which was the source of the Jewish head-waters of the stream of Christianity. On this showing, the modern Western religious movement known as Protestantism falls into the same category as the medieval Italian and modern Transalpine Western intellectual and aesthetic movement known as the Renaissance, which was an attempt to establish a direct contact with Hellenism. (For the popular confusion of this Renaissance of Hellenism with the radiation of the medieval Italian culture into Transalpine Europe see IV. C (iii) (c) 2 (α), vol. iv, p. 275, footnotes 1 and 2, above.) Both Protestantism and the Western Renaissance are discussed in Part X, below.
[2] See V. C (i) (d) 6 (δ), vol. v, p. 547, above.—A.J.T.
[3] See V. C (i) (c) 2, vol. v, p. 80, and V. C (i) (d) 6 (δ), Annex, vol. v, pp. 648–50, above.—A.J.T.
[4] See II. D (vi), vol. ii, pp. 215–16, and V. C (i) (c) 2, vol. v, pp. 81–2, above.—A.J.T.
[5] Warde-Fowler, W.: *The Religious Experience of the Roman People* (London 1911,

at first sight the Roman statesman's experiment might appear to a modern Western observer to have been not less cold-blooded than the French philosopher Comte's and not less crack-brained than the German professor Hauer's. We may pay tribute to Augustus's insight in recognizing that the spiritual void in the souls of his countrymen and contemporaries must be filled with something or other by any would-be Saviour of Society who was seriously setting himself to heal the wounds of the Hellenic World with the balm of a Roman Peace; for the Romans could not confer an outward peace upon their neighbours until they had established an inward peace within themselves. We may acknowledge Augustus's perspicacity in perceiving that the sophisticated philosophies of the dominant minority were 'caviare to the vulgar',[1] and that the Caesar-worship in which he was capitalizing the popular gratitude towards himself was at best a fair-weather cult which could not be expected to outlast the temporary reprieve that Augustus's exertions had won for the Hellenic Society and for the Roman Commonwealth.[2] We may also sympathize with Augustus's desire to stem the tide of *pammixia* and proletarianization by damming back the inflow of 'the new Oriental cults'. But when we have conceded all this, we may still find it difficult to understand why Augustus should have attempted the *tour de force* of bringing the native Roman religion back to life. Why did he not put the whole of his Roman treasure in the Greek gods of Athens and Delphi and Eleusis in an age which found Rome already completely acclimatized to the Hellenic culture and at least half-conscious that it was now her mission to salvage a Hellenic Society which she had done so much to wreck in the preceding chapter of Roman and Hellenic history? These Greek divinities might lack the vitality of their aggressive Oriental rivals, but no competitor could eclipse their matchless dignity and grace. Why, then, was Augustus not content with the notable addition that he had made to the array of Roman shrines in which these Greek divinities were installed?[3] Was not his Roman religious task fulfilled when he had received into his own house on the Palatine with all due honour the Greek Apollo who, at the crisis of Augustus's career, had sent him victorious in the decisive naval engagement below the cliffs of Actium?[4]

Macmillan), pp. 428–9. The whole of Lecture xix should be read by any one who wishes to obtain a comprehensive view of Augustus's archaistic work in the field of Religion.
[1] See V. C (i) (d) 6 (δ), vol. v, pp. 559–62, above.
[2] See V. C (i) (d) 6 (δ), Annex, vol. v, pp. 649–50, above.
[3] See V. C (i) (d) 6 (δ), vol. v, pp. 528, above.
[4]
   Actius haec cernens arcum intendebat Apollo
  desuper: omnis eo terrore Aegyptus et Indi,
 omnis Arabs, omnes vertebant terga Sabaei.
      Virgil: *Aeneid*, Book VIII, ll. 704–6.

Why must he go on to experiment in the extravaganza of attempting also to revive the native Roman religion in its primitive unhellenized nakedness? The ethics of this brutally business-like Roman religion of 'Do ut des' must be laughed away as childish if they were not to be condemned as immoral; and, as for the quaint rites in which this Roman commerce between men and gods had been transacted since the dawn of history, they could hardly be taken seriously nowadays by any one but an antiquary.[1] Would not the resuscitation of this ridiculous native hocus-pocus compromise, instead of crowning, the rest of Augustus's endeavours to win back for Religion at Rome the repute and authority which it had lost? What, then, could have moved so astute a statesman as Augustus to pin his faith to this relic of a primitive past as his sovereign means for evoking that spiritual rally in Roman souls on which the statesman-saviour no doubt rightly set such store?

The vindication of Augustus's apparently unpromising essay in religious Archaism is to be found in the sequel; for, if we date the Augustan reinstatement of the primitive Roman religion from his celebration of the *Ludi Saeculares* in 17 B.C.,[2] we shall find that Augustus's work of archaistic reconstruction lasted not merely for three centuries, but for four;[3] that, even at the end of that long

---

[1] The existing fragments of the *Antiquitates Rerum Divinarum* of Marcus Terentius Varro (*vivebat* 116–28 B.C.) show that the prince of Roman antiquaries made his study of the official religion of the community into which he had been born in a spirit of thorough-going scientific detachment.

[2] This is a more significant date than 12 B.C., which was the year in which Augustus became Pontifex Maximus; for the celebration of the *Ludi Saeculares* was an act of religious policy for which Augustus was free to choose his own time, whereas the date of his assumption of the office of Pontifex Maximus was determined for him by the length of the life of the previous incumbent. If Augustus had abused his dictatorial powers in order to anticipate Lepidus's death by evicting him from an office of which the traditional tenure was for life, the would-be restorer of the prestige of the native Roman religion would simply have been defeating his own purpose.

[3] Three centuries is the duration claimed for Augustus's work by Warde-Fowler in the passage quoted above; and it is true (see Geffken, J.: *Der Ausgang des Griechisch-Römischen Heidentums* (Heidelberg 1920, Winter), pp. 20–5) that in Rome itself, as well as all over the Roman Empire, *circa* A.D. 240–60, there seems to have been a sudden cessation of pagan cults, on the negative evidence of a widespread breaking off of the serial records of acts of worship in inscriptions. At Rome the records of the proceedings of the Arval Brethren and those of the celebration of the rite of the Taurobolium both alike break off in A.D. 241. On the Nubian border of Egypt, at Ethiopian Talmis, and in the Fayyūm, there are corresponding breaks in the local records after the years A.D. 244, 248, and 250 respectively. At Olympia the last victor inscription is of the year A.D. 261, and the last cult inscription is of the year A.D. 265. In Macedonia, where the inscriptions testify to an increase of ritual and liturgical activity in the second quarter of the third century of the Christian Era, the records break off, nevertheless, in A.D. 265. It is only in Attica and in Syria that the series of inscriptions runs on through the third century without a break. At the turn of the third century and the fourth century, however, there was a deliberate and systematic revival of pagan worships all over the Empire by the pagan emperors of the Diocletianic school who were at war with Christianity (see V. C (i) (d) 6 (δ), vol. v, pp. 565–6, and V. C (i) (d) 6 (δ), Annex, vol. v, p. 650, footnote 3, above); and this revival gave another hundred years' lease of life to the Augustan paganism at Rome, as well as to the pagan worships of other parts of the Empire.

Time-span, it did not simply fall to pieces of itself but was deliberately demolished by the fanaticism of the pagan archaist-emperor's latter-day Christian successors Gratian and Theodosius;[1] and that, so far from being accepted with the indifference with which so many similar acts of religious sabotage were received in other parts of the Hellenic World of the age,[2] this attack upon the once artificially resuscitated paganism of Rome aroused a heart-felt opposition which expressed itself first in a fifteen-years-long constitutional struggle over an altar and statue of Victory (A.D. 382–94)[3] and finally in a military *pronunciamiento*—engineered by the pagan Frankish mercenary Arbogastes—in which the Christian soldier-emperor Theodosius's title to the Imperial office was audaciously disputed by the pagan professor of literature Eugenius (A.D. 392–4).[4] The tenacity to which these facts bear witness is evidence that Augustus had, after all, been as competent a builder in his reconstruction of Religion at Rome as in the rest of his handiwork; and we must infer that he knew what he was about when he insisted upon reviving the primitive native Roman religion besides completing the acclimatization of the Greek religion on Roman soil. Augustus must have divined that this native religion, crude and discredited though it might be, had a hold on Roman hearts which an imported Hellenism could never acquire on its own merits, however nicely it might suit the taste of cultivated Roman palates. He therefore deliberately grafted these foreign slips on to a native stem; and this was the secret of the strength of the stately tree whose grain almost turned the edge of a Christian axe four hundred years later.[5]

If we turn from the Hellenic World to the Japanese offshoot of the Far Eastern Society, we shall find, in a latter-day Japanese attempt to revive the native Japanese variety of Primitive Pagan-

[1] See IV. C (iii) (b) 12, vol. iv, pp. 226–7, above.

[2] It is true that the pagan revolt in the West which was headed by the rhetor Eugenius in A.D. 392–4 had been anticipated at Alexandria by a similar revolt, likewise under professorial leadership, in A.D. 391 (Geffken, op. cit., p. 157). On the other hand the cessation of the Olympian Games, after their last celebration in the year A.D. 393 (ibid., p. 159), does not seem to have made the same stir as the removal of the altar and statue of Victory from the Senate House at Rome.

[3] The altar and statue of Victory were removed from the Senate House at Rome by the orders of the Emperor Gratian in A.D. 382; and this act—which was intended to be, and was taken as being, symbolic—moved the cultivated pagan aristocracy of the capital to protest with all the vigour that was compatible with their loyalty to the Imperial Government. The last petition for restitution was rejected in A.D. 394. The statue had been brought to Rome from Tarentum and set up in the Curia Julia by Caius Julius Caesar.

[4] Fuller accounts of the last stand of Augustus's archaistically reconstructed Roman paganism will be found in Gibbon, E.: *The History of the Decline and Fall of the Roman Empire*, chap. xxxviii; and in Dill, S.: *Roman Society in the Last Century of the Western Empire* (London 1905, Macmillan), Book I: 'The Tenacity of Paganism'.

[5] The compositeness of the grain of the Roman paganism that was given this long new lease of life through the arts of Augustus is illustrated by the fact that the statue over which this Roman paganism fought its last fight was a piece of Greek workmanship.

ism which is traditionally known as Shinto,[1] another essay in religious Archaism which has points in common, not only with Augustus's achievement and with Professor Hauer's conceit, but also with the religious policy which Bismarck attempted to carry out after the foundation of the Second German Reich.

In degree of extravagance the revival of Shinto shows a greater likeness to Hauerism than to Augustus's work; for, whereas the native Roman paganism which Augustus successfully revived was in his time still 'a going concern' in the sense that it had never been officially disestablished, the movement for the resuscitation of the native Japanese paganism did not begin until more than a thousand years had passed since this primitive religion had been partly supplanted, partly absorbed, and partly informed[2] by the higher religion of the Mahāyāna. The Mahāyāna began to make its spiritual conquest of Japan in the course of the sixth century of the Christian Era[3]—more than two hundred years before the date at which Christianity was thrust upon Saxony at Charlemagne's sword-point. And the archaistic revival of Shinto was started in the seventeenth century of the Christian Era[4]—at a date which was likewise rather more than two hundred years before a 'return to Woden' began to be preached in modern Germany.

In Japan, as in Germany, the first phase of the movement was academic. The Japanese resuscitation of Shinto was put in train by a Buddhist monk named Keichū (*vivebat* A.D. 1640–1701) whose interest in the subject seems to have been primarily philological;[5] Keichū was followed by Motoori Norinaga (*vivebat* A.D. 1730–1801), who was not only a scholar but was also a theorist applying his scholarship to an imaginary reconstruction of an obliterated ancestral faith;[6] and Motoori Norinaga was followed in his turn

---

[1] Shinto means 'the Way of the Numina' (to use an impersonal Latin word which may be a better translation of the Japanese original than 'gods' or 'spirits'). See Holtom, D. C.: *The National Faith of Japan: A Study in Modern Shintō* (London 1938, Kegan Paul, Trench, Trubner), pp. 13–14. The modern revival of Shinto is known as Fukko Shinto ('Restoration Shinto') (ibid., p. 44).

[2] See V. C (ii) (c) 2, vol. v, p. 97, footnote 3, and p. 147, footnote 1; V. C (i) (d) 6 (δ), vol. v, p. 528, footnote 2, above.

[3] In this first chapter of its history in Japan the Mahāyāna, while nominally professed by all subjects of the Emperor, was not in fact comprehended and assimilated by Japanese souls outside the narrow limits of a sophisticated court circle. The propagation of the Mahāyāna among the masses, in popular forms which the common man could understand, did not begin until after the onset of a 'Time of Troubles' in the latter part of the twelfth century of the Christian Era (see V. C (i) (c) 2, vol. v, pp. 97–8, above).

[4] Its antecedents can, however, be traced back as far as the fifteenth century (Holtom, op. cit., pp. 39–41).

[5] There was a general revival of Japanese studies at and after the close of the seventeenth century (Murdoch, J.: *History of Japan*, vol. iii (London 1926, Kegan Paul), p. 468). Holtom (op. cit., pp. 45–8) presents, as Motoori's principal predecessor, not Keichū but Kamo-no-Mabuchi (*vivebat* A.D. 1697–1769).

[6] In Japan in the middle of the eighteenth century there was a general romantic revival of interest in the Japanese national past (Murdoch, J.: *History of Japan*, vol. i (London 1910, Kegan Paul), p. 11). Motoori himself was both anti-rationalist and Anti-Sinic (Murdoch, op. cit., vol. iii, pp. 476–90). In this Anti-Sinism Motoori had had

by Hirata Atsutané (*vivebat* A.D. 1776–1843), who was not only a theorist but was also a controversialist, and who launched an attack, in the name of Shinto, upon the exotic religion of the Mahāyāna and the exotic philosophy of Confucianism.[1]

It will be seen from the dates that the archaistic revival of a primitive Japanese paganism was put in hand, like Augustus's resuscitation of a primitive Roman paganism, immediately after the foundation of a universal state; for in Japanese history the universal state that put an end to an antecedent 'Time of Troubles' was the Tokugawa Shogunate which was the fruit of the successive labours of Nobunaga and Hideyoshi and Ieyasu in the later decades of the sixteenth and the earlier decades of the seventeenth century of the Christian Era.[2] Whereas, however, the reinstatement of the Roman paganism was carried out almost at one stroke by the fiat of a political dictator, the revival of Shinto began as a work of private enterprise[3] which took two hundred years to advance—or regress—from the Varronian objectivity of a Keichū to the Rosenbergian militancy of a Hirata Atsutané.

The Neo-Shinto movement had just arrived at this militant stage when the Japanese universal state was prematurely shattered by the impact of an aggressively expanding Western Civilization. The rigorously maintained artificial isolation which had enabled the Japanese to live for a quarter of a millennium as though Japan were 'All that was under Heaven' had to be abandoned in the third quarter of the nineteenth century of the Christian Era in favour of a diametrically opposite strategy of self-defence in which Japan was to hold her own in a no longer avoidable Western environment by learning to live as one of the nations of a Westernized World. And when, upon the Revolution of 1867–8, this abrupt change from a negative to a positive attitude towards the outer world was given a symbolic expression in the liquidation of the Tokugawa Shogunate and the official restoration of an Imperial Dynasty which had been reigning (though not always governing) in an unbroken succession since the dawn of Japanese history,[4] the now

forerunners. Kada Adzumaro (*vivebat* A.D. 1669–1736) had presented to the authorities in A.D. 1735 a memorial advocating Japanese as against Sinic studies; and the campaign against an alleged contamination of Japanese by Sinic culture had been continued by Mabuchi (see Murdoch, op. cit., vol. iii, pp. 473–5).

[1] The facts mentioned in this paragraph are taken from Anesaki, M.: *History of Japanese Religion* (London 1930, Kegan Paul), pp. 307–9.

[2] See IV. C (ii) (*b*) 2, vol. iv, pp. 88, 92, and 94; and V. C (i) (*d*) 6 (δ), Annex, vol. v, pp. 655–7, above, as well as V. C (ii) (*a*), in the present volume, pp. 186, 188–9, and 191, below.

[3] The Tokugawa régime had a leaning towards Buddhism and regarded the Neo-Shinto movement with suspicion as a threat to the security of the Tokugawa Shogunate. The Neo-Shintoists' idealization and deification of the Imperial House did, in fact, prepare the ground for the Restoration of A.D. 1868.

[4] During the Japanese 'Time of Troubles' and universal state the Imperial Dynasty at Kyoto had, of course, been leading an obscure and shadowy existence on sufferance

militant Neo-Shinto movement so exactly accorded with a *Zeit-geist* in which a no longer practicable xenophobia was being converted into terms of the archaistically romantic Nationalism of the modern West that it looked for a moment as though a once academic conceit was now to have its fortune made for it by being taken under the potent patronage of the new régime.

'The first step taken by the new Government in regard to Religion was an attempt to establish Shinto as the religion of the State. The . . . National Cult Department . . . an institution for ceremonial observance, having little to do with matters of really religious or political significance . . . was given the highest position among the government offices, and Shinto was proclaimed the national cult or State Religion.[1] This meant at the same time a vigorous suppression of Buddhism, because it was a foreign religion and had flourished under the protection of the Shogunate Government. All privileges granted to the Buddhist clergy were abolished, and a large part of the properties belonging to the Buddhist institutions was confiscated. A reign of persecution was started. Buddhists were driven out of the syncretic Shinto sanctuaries which they had been serving for ten centuries or more. Buddhist statues, scriptures and decorations in those temples were taken out and set on fire or thrown into the water. The "purification" of the Shinto temples was achieved, and the severance of Buddhism and Shinto ruthlessly carried out. . . .[2]

'At one time it seemed as if Buddhism would be swept away by the persecution, but the danger brought Buddhist leaders to united action. . . . In the official circles, too, some realized that an entire suppression of Buddhism was neither desirable nor possible,[3] and the Government was induced gradually to modify their religious policy. The National Cult was replaced by an Ecclesiastical Board in 1872,[4] under which a central board of preachers was to superintend religious instructions. . . . The Board was abolished in 1877, and the Buddhist bodies were granted autonomy. Shinto was treated in the same way;[5] and its church bodies

from the militarists who were governing—or misgoverning—the Japanese World in the Imperial Dynasty's name.

[1] This Department of Shinto was set up as early as the first month of the first year of Meiji (A.D. 1868), and was reorganized three times before the close of the fourth year of the Meiji Era. Official instructors in Shinto were appointed by the Imperial Government in November 1870 (Holtom, op. cit., pp. 54–5).—A.J.T.

[2] For further details of this persecution see Holtom, pp. 56–8.—A.J.T.

[3] The persecution was producing a disturbing and disruptive effect at a time of stress in which there was an urgent need for national stability and unity (Holtom, pp. 58–9).—A.J.T.

[4] While the National Cult Department had been concerned exclusively with Shinto, the new Ecclesiastical Board or Department of Religion had Buddhism as well as Shinto under its aegis (Holtom, p. 59). After having failed, between A.D. 1868 and A.D. 1872, to drive Buddhism off the field by force, the Imperial Government next tried, from 1872 to 1875, to brigade Buddhism with Shinto and to drill the pair of them into working in double harness as a dual state religion (ibid., pp. 59–61). In 1875 this second experiment in regulating the relations between Church and State was abandoned in its turn.—A.J.T.

[5] The Imperial Government gave up the last remnants of its control over the appointment and dismissal of priests of private sects—Buddhist and Shinto alike—in A.D. 1884 (Holtom, p. 62).—A.J.T.

gradually emerged out of the State Religion,[1] while the ceremonies in
the Court and the communal Shinto cult were regarded as having
nothing to do with religious teaching, but as civic institutions.[2] Thus
subsided the frenzy of Shinto revival.'[3]

The Western reader will not have failed to notice the curious
analogy between this unsuccessful offensive which was launched
against the Mahayanian Buddhist Church by a new régime in
Japan and the contemporary attack—likewise ending in failure—
which was made upon a Christian Catholic Church by a new
régime in Germany. Like Bismarck, the architects of the Japanese
Imperial Restoration were intoxicated by their success in endowing
their country with a new political structure which appeared to
answer to the needs of the times; and, like Bismarck again, they
conceived it to be their duty, and imagined it to lie within their
power, to make the new Nationalism prevail in the religious as
well as in the secular sphere. In Japan, as in Germany, the
nationalists had to be taught by a humiliating experience that the
'higher religions' which have sprung from the ruins of disintegrating civilizations with a message to deliver to all Mankind cannot
easily be dragooned to suit the momentary exigencies of parochial
politics.[4]

Our survey of Archaism in the field of Religion has not been
exhaustive; for the examples which we have cited from the histories of three civilizations—the Western, the Hellenic, and the
Far Eastern—can all be duplicated if we go farther afield. If

[1] The legal separation of the autonomous private Shinto sects from the state-regu-
lated public Shinto establishment was carried out in A.D. 1882 (Holtom, op. cit., pp.
67–8). In 1938 thirteen private Shinto sects enjoyed official recognition, and their
aggregate membership was estimated at little less than 17,400,000 (ibid., p. 69).
Of these sects, six had been already in existence in the Tokugawa Period (A.D. 1600–
1867), six had come into existence during the Meiji Period (A.D. 1868–1912), and
one, which took final shape in the Meiji Period, had existed in the Tokugawa Period in
an inchoate form (Kato, Genchi: *A Study of Shintō, the Religion of the Japanese Nation*
(Tokyo 1926, Meiji Japan Society), p. 1). 'The one conspicuous point of identity
between the Shintō of the State and that of the people lies in the deities that are honoured. The *kami* of Sect Shintō and those of State Shintō are for the most part one
and the same' (Holtom, op. cit., p. 69). The private Shinto sects differ from State Shinto
and resemble the 'higher religions' in the point of having personal founders (ibid.,
p. 68; Kato, op. cit., p. 210).—A.J.T.

[2] See V. C (i) (*d*) 6 (δ), Annex, vol. v, p. 707, footnote 2, above. On this point Kato,
in op. cit., pp. 2–3, expresses the opinion 'that even this State Shintō, which some
Japanese go so far as to speak of as no religion at all, is in reality nothing short of evidence
of a religion interwoven in the very texture of the original beliefs and national organization of the people, camouflaged though it may be as a mere code of national ethics and
State rituals, and as such apparently entitled only to secular respect. . . . Shintō—the
State Shintō as well as the Sectarian Shintō—is in very truth a religion.' This authori-
tative Japanese opinion must carry weight.—A.J.T.

[3] Anesaki, M.: *History of Japanese Religion* (London 1930, Kegan Paul), pp. 334–6.

[4] This is a truth against which the ministers of the 'lower religions' rebel. In the
words of a priest of the Atago [State Shinto] Shrine of Kyoto, quoted by Holtom, op.
cit., p. 293:
'The shrines are Religion. They are real Religion. They are perfect Religion. If the
statement will be permitted, it may be said that Christianity and Buddhism are side
movements in Religion. They are incomplete religions. They are secondary religions.'

we glance, for instance, at the Hindu World under the British Rāj,
we may espy in the Arya Samāj[1] an analogue of the Neo-Shinto
movement in its early days under the Tokugawa Shogunate. If we
glance at the Babylonic World, we may see in Nabonidus an
emperor of the Babylonic universal state who might have anticipated Augustus's archaistic *tour de force* if he had not come to
grief through being too poor a politician and too keen an archaeologist. And, if we glance at the Iranic World, we may recognize a
contemporary parallel to Professor Hauer's extravaganza of proposing to resuscitate a pre-Christian German paganism in the not
less extravagant conceit, with which some play has been made in
the Turkey of President Mustafā Kemāl Atatürk, of bringing back
to life a dead and buried pre-Islamic Turkish wolf-worship.[2] Perhaps, however, we have already carried our survey far enough to
bring out the psychological relation between the phenomenon of
religious Archaism and the experience of social disintegration.

(ε) *The Self-Defeat of Archaism.*

If we now turn back and take a synoptic view of all the four fields
in which we have been watching Archaism at work, we shall notice
that in each field one or two of the examples which we have examined
in order to discover what Archaism is are also illustrations of an
apparent tendency in Archaism for the movement to defeat itself.

In the field of Institutions we can watch the two Heracleidae at
Sparta, and in their footsteps the two Gracchi at Rome, embark
on the archaistic enterprise of re-establishing an ancestral constitution which is still nominally in force but which has admittedly
been ignored and even violated with a scandalous laxity. The
young reformers are whole-heartedly sincere and enthusiastic in
their pursuit of their archaistic aim; and yet their well-meant
activities produce results which are the exact opposite of their
single-minded intentions.[3] Instead of achieving a reform they
actually let loose a revolution which does not come to rest again
until it has swept the last remnants of the πάτριος πολιτεία away.
Again, in the field of Art, we see a Pre-Raphaelitism which is
athirst to drink at the fountain-head of the Western artistic tradition being led by its archaistic quest into an anti-realism that dries
up all the water brooks and leaves a desert in which nothing can

---

[1] An account of the Arya Samāj will be found in Farquhar, J. N.: *Modern Religious
Movements in India* (New York 1919, Macmillan), pp. 101–29.
[2] We do know something about the pre-Islamic Nestorian Christianity which gained
some hold upon the Turks in Central Asia before they began to drift into Dār-al-Islām
(see II. D (vi), vol. ii, pp. 236–8, and V. C (i) (c) 3, vol. v, p. 250, above); but it
might be difficult to identify with assurance the mortal remains of a Turkish wolf-totem
which, if authentic, must be pre-Christian as well as pre-Islamic.
[3] Plutarch brings out this point in his *Comparison of Agis and Cleomenes with the
Gracchi*, chap. 5.

live except the demon of Futurism. In the field of Language we see the efforts to call back to life an extinct form of Turkish or Hebrew or Irish succeeding in their *tour de force* of conjuring articulate and intelligible speech out of the silence of the grave—but this only at the price of defeating the archaists' own intentions by composing a new language which the simpletons who once spoke the original language as their mother-tongue might find it difficult either to speak or to understand.[1] In the field of Religion we see the would-be archaist Julian embarrassing the official representatives of a paganism which he is trying to bolster up by expecting these priests of Hellenic divinities to behave as though they were clergy of the Christian Church;[2] and we also see another would-be religious archaist, Nabonidus, positively enraging the priesthood of the Babylonic World to a degree of exasperation at which they are ready to welcome the alien invader Cyrus with open arms as a liberator from an indigenous régime which has insisted upon making itself intolerable.

These instances of Archaism defeating itself are too numerous and too consistent to be dismissed as mere tricks of Chance. It looks as though there must be something in the essence of Archaism that drives it into self-defeat in frustration of its conscious purpose; and we may be able to put our finger on this disconcerting factor when we remind ourselves that Archaism sets out to be no mere academic exercise but a practical way of life, and that what it promises to do is to grapple with the urgent human problem of combating the malady of social disintegration. If he is to justify his pretensions the archaist has to convince the philistine majority of his public that the nostrum which he is offering them is demonstrably capable of restoring an ailing social system to health. In fact, the archaist is pledged to 'make things work' again; and this formidable commitment compels him to become a man of action instead of remaining the pure archaeologist that, in his heart, he would probably prefer to be.

---

[1] There is a story—*ben trovato, se non vero*—that an eminent scholar of pure English extraction, who had spent his life in Dublin on the archaistic task of resuscitating the Irish language, at last made up his mind to harvest the reward for his long labour of love by holding converse with the survivors of an Irish-speaking peasantry on the banks of the Shannon. By the time when he reached his destination our scholar's eagerness had mounted to such a pitch that he burst into a torrent of his own Neo-Irish in the face of the first native whom he encountered on alighting from the train. After listening in silence for a minute or two with a look of blank incomprehension on his face, the native interrupted the visitor's flow of speech by remarking politely, in excellent English: 'I am sorry, but I don't know any German.' The scholar's choice vocabulary—culled from ancient Irish epics—had been no more intelligible to the bilingual westerner than so much Double-Dutch; and, finding himself thus surprisingly addressed in a language which he could not recognize as being either English or Irish, he had jumped to the conclusion that the gentleman who was addressing him must be one of those German engineers who were at that time superintending the construction of the Shannon Dam.
[2] See V. C (i) (c) 2, Annex II, vol. v, p. 584, above.

The point may be illustrated by considering the contrast between an archaeologist's and a dentist's way of dealing with a decayed tooth. When an archaeologist disinters a palaeolithic burial his business is to preserve his trove in a glass case in the exact condition in which he found it below the sod; so all that he has to do to the skeleton's teeth is to coat them with some chemical that will arrest their decay at the point which it has already reached. His problem is a simple one; for in the museum curator's keeping these teeth have no further function except to lie still and be looked at; their biting days are over once for all. The dentist's problem is not so easily solved; for what the dentist has to do with the decayed tooth of his living patient is not to provide an archaeologically-minded public with an informative 'museum piece', but to provide a live human being with a tooth that will stop aching and get back to work; so the dentist sets about 'restoring' the tooth in a way that would outrage the archaeologist's sense of professional honour. The dentist's first act is to whittle away the surviving remnant of the authentic original tooth by grinding out all the rotten parts; his second act is to fill the cavity, which he has thus deliberately enlarged, with foreign matter that will bite as hard as though it were the natural ivory. When the dentist has accomplished each of these two things he proudly assures his patient that he has given the old tooth a new lease of life; but this admirable dentistry would infuriate our archaeologist if he fancied himself as a headhunter. 'This charlatan', he would protest, 'professes to have restored that tooth when, as a matter of fact, as you can verify if you will look, he has removed the greater part of what was left of the real tooth and has then tried to cover his fraudulent tracks by inserting a mass of foreign matter which has been skilfully designed to deceive the layman's eye and make him believe that the "denture" at which he is looking is a genuine antiquity and not (as it really is) a fake. This so-called dentistry is nothing but an impudent deception of a credulous public.'

We may leave our two *dramatis personae* to continue an argument in which they will never be able to agree; but, if we have made it clear that Archaism is a kind of dentistry and not a kind of archaeology—notwithstanding the similarity of the names and the archaist's mistaken belief that they mean the same thing—then we may find that we have arrived at an explanation of the paradoxical fact that Archaism so often ends in defeating its own quite sincerely archaeological intentions. The archaist would, in fact appear to be condemned, by the very nature of his enterprise, to be for ever trying to reconcile Past and Present; and the proneness of their competing claims to prove incompatible is the weakness o

Archaism as a way of life. The archaist is on the horns of a dilemma which is likely to impale him, whichever way he may lean. If he tries to restore the Past without taking the Present into consideration, then the impetus of Life—an elemental force which he can never arrest—will shatter into fragments the brittle shell that he is bent on retrieving. On the other hand, if he consents to subordinate his whim of resuscitating the Past to the task of making the Present *viable*, then, in the name of restoration, he will be led on and on into 'scrapping' so much of what is left of the Past, and introducing so much new masonry to reinforce the remnant, that his pious work of 'reconstruction' will be difficult to distinguish from the Vandalism of naked demolition and replacement. On either alternative the archaist will find, at the end of his labours, that unwittingly or unwillingly he has been playing the futurist's game. In labouring to perpetuate an anachronism he will in fact have been opening the door to some ruthless innovation that has been lying in wait outside for this very opportunity of forcing an entry.

9. *Futurism*

(α) *The Relation between Futurism and Archaism.*

There is an antithesis between Futurism and Archaism that is brought out by the mere juxtaposition of the two words; yet the obvious difference of orientation which distinguishes these two ways of life is not so significant as are the characteristic features that they have in common. Futurism and Archaism are, both alike, attempts to break with an irksome Present by taking a flying leap out of it into another reach of the stream of Time without abandoning the plane of mundane life on Earth. And these two alternative ways of attempting to escape from the Present but not from the Time-dimension also resemble one another in the further point of being *tours de force* which prove, on trial, to have been forlorn hopes.[1] The two movements differ merely in the direction —up or down the Time-stream—in which they make their two equally desperate sorties from a position of present discomfort and distress which neither the futurist nor the archaist has any longer the heart to hold; and this difference of direction is not a difference of kind. At the same time, Futurism does differ materially from Archaism in the degree in which it goes against the grain of human nature; for, while human beings are prone to seek refuge from a disagreeable Present by retreating into a familiar Past,[2] they are

[1] These points of likeness between Futurism and Archaism have been touched upon, by anticipation, in V. C (i) (d) 1, vol. v, pp. 383–5, above.
[2] An illustration of this tendency on the political plane is the well-known human

equally prone to cling to a disagreeable Present rather than strike out into an unknown Future.

The spectacle of Time perpetually marching forward over the corpse of a Present that Time's scythe is perpetually mowing down is so appalling to human minds that they are apt to recoil into a passionate yearning for continuity, in the spirit of the mortal worshipper's prayer to an immortal God in the Hundred and Second Psalm:

'I said: "O my God, take me not away in the midst of my days: thy years are throughout all generations.

' "Of old hast thou laid the foundation of the Earth, and the Heavens are the work of thy hands.

' "They shall perish, but thou shalt endure; yea, all of them shall wax old like a garment; as a vesture shalt thou change them, and they shall be changed;

' "But thou art the same, and thy years shall have no end.

' "The children of thy servants shall continue, and their seed shall be established before thee." '[1]

In this expression of the pathos of Syriac souls in one chapter of the long-drawn-out disintegration of the Syriac Society we see Humanity seeking to win an exemption from the doom of being carried away on the inexorable flow of the Time-stream by catching at the skirts of a divine Eternity which is naïvely conceived of as a Present prolonged into infinity.[2]

This natural human horror at the ever imminent prospect of the annihilation of a Present which can never really be prolonged can no doubt be counteracted, and even overcome, either by a philosophical fortitude in facing hard facts without flinching or by a religious intuition of a 'larger hope' lightening the darkness of death.

The philosophical response to the challenge of Mutability is to

weakness of recalling 'elder statesmen' to power in times of political crisis (as, for example, they were recalled in many of the countries that were belligerents in the General War of 1914–18). This is one of the classic examples of a vein of Archaism that is instinctive and unreasoning. A rational calculation would lead to the conclusion that these 'elder statesmen' are the last people to whom a community can safely commit its destinies in an emergency, since, *ex hypothesi*, these 'dug-outs' are doubly incapacitated—in the first place by the lassitude of old age and secondly, and more seriously, by the obsoleteness of their outlook and their habits. It is virtually impossible for them to be abreast of the times, considering that the experience on which they have been formed is bound to have been thrown out of date by the very onset of the crisis which the 'elder statesmen' have to thank for their recall.

[1] Ps. cii. 24–8.

[2] The yearning that is expressed in this passage is foredoomed to frustration, not because it is utterly impossible under all conditions for the Human Soul to enter into God's mode of being by attaining union with Him, but because it is not possible to achieve this spiritual transfiguration without rising above the mundane plane of life. The prayer in the last verse is for a continuity of human social life in This World as a miraculous special dispensation from the 'law'—truly cited in the three preceding verses—which condemns all the works of God's creation, *qua* creatures, to be ephemeral. As a statement, and a magnificent statement, of this 'law', vv. 25–7, without vv. 24 and 28, have already been quoted in II. C (ii) (*b*) 1, vol. i, p. 285, above.

be heard in the concordant voices of an Epicurean poet and a Stoic
emperor whose consensus on this crucial point reveals a fundamental unity of outlook at the heart of two classic expressions of
the Hellenic philosophy which are superficially antagonistic to one
another.[1]

Lucretius strikes a note which is as true to the temper of his
Master as it is remote from the spirit that is vulgarly attributed to
the Epicurean school:

> cedit enim rerum novitate extrusa vetustas
> semper, et ex aliis aliud reparare necessest. . . .
> materies opus est ut crescant postera saecla,
> quae tamen omnia te vita perfuncta sequentur;
> nec minus ergo ante haec quam tu cecidere, cadentque.
> sic alid ex alio nunquam desistet oriri,
> vitaque mancipio nulli datur, omnibus usu.[2]

This Epicurean poetry is echoed by Marcus Aurelius in Stoic
prose:

'You are afraid of Change? But nothing can happen without Change;
it is something that is of the essence of the nature of the Universe. You
cannot even take a hot bath without the fuel undergoing one kind of
change, or digest your dinner without the food undergoing another. In
fact, without the possibility of Change there could be no satisfaction for
any of our needs; and in this light it becomes evident that, when it is
your own turn to change into something other than yourself, this is all
in the day's work—just another necessity of Nature. . . . In Nature's
hands the sum of things is like a lump of wax. At one moment she
moulds it into a toy horse; then she kneads up the horse in order to
mould the same stuff into a toy tree; then she makes it into a mannikin,
and then into something else. The duration of each of these successive
shapes is infinitesimally short, but where is the grievance? Does it do
a packing-case any more harm to be broken up than it does it good to be
knocked together?'[3]

The religious response to the challenge which Philosophy meets
in this way is to be found in the New Testament in two variants
of one simile:

'That which thou sowest is not quickened except it die,'[4]
and

'Except a corn of wheat fall into the ground and die it abideth alone,
but if it die it bringeth forth much fruit.'[5]

---

[1] For the relation between Epicureanism and Stoicism see V. C (i) (d) 1, vol. v, p. 394,
above, and V. C (i) (d) 10, passim, in the present volume, pp. 132–48, below.
[2] Lucretius: De Rerum Natura, Book III, ll. 964–5 and 967–71.
[3] Marcus Aurelius Antoninus: Meditations, Book VII, chaps. 18 and 23.
[4] 1 Cor. xv. 36.
[5] John xii. 24.

In these flashes of religious light[1] an apparently merciless sacrifice of a sensitive Present to a callous Future is seen as an illusion in which the growing-pains of a single immortal soul have been falsely construed into a war to the knife between two irreconcilable adversaries. On this view the underlying reality is not an inconsequent Mutability but a triumphant Withdrawal-and-Return—a reality which is as glorious as the illusion is repulsive.[2] Yet, whether they thrill us with their ecstasy or impress us with their fortitude, these two diverse reactions to the prospect of annihilation still testify with one accord to the unnaturalness of a Futurism which spurns the Present instead of clinging to it and which springs forward to meet the Future instead of cowering back to put off the moment of its inevitable impact.

Here is a psychological *tour de force* which is keyed to a distinctly higher pitch than its archaistic alternative; and, in view of this striking difference between Futurism and Archaism in degree

[1] It is curious to observe the diffraction of these beams of light from the New Testament in the labyrinthine preciosity of a modern Western poet. Yet it is indeed the same spiritual truth that is declared in Edmund Spenser's *Faerie Queene*, Canto vii, Stanza 58, in the judgement given by Nature in the contest between Mutability and Jove for the lordship of the Universe:

> I well consider all that ye have sayd,
> And find that all things stedfastnes doe hate
> And changed be: yet being rightly wayd
> They are not changed from their first estate;
> But by their change their being doe dilate;
> And turning to themselves at length againe,
> Doe worke their owne perfection so by fate:
> Then over them Change doth not rule and raigne;
> But they raigne over Change, and doe their states maintaine.

The hope of transfiguration which is implicit in this movement of Withdrawal-and-Return is enlarged upon in the following stanzas in the eighth canto of the same poem:

> When I bethinke me on that speech whyleare,
> Of Mutability, and well it way:
> Me seemes, that though she all unworthy were
> Of the Heav'ns Rule; yet very sooth to say,
> In all things else she beares the greatest sway.
> Which makes me loath this state of life so tickle
> And love of things so vaine to cast away;
> Whose flowring pride, so fading and so fickle,
> Short time shall soon cut down with his consuming sickle.
>
> Then gin I thinke on that which Nature sayd,
> Of that same time when no more Change shall be,
> But stedfast rest of all things firmely stayd
> Upon the pillours of Eternity,
> That is contrayr to Mutabilitie:
> For all that moveth doth in Change delight,
> But thence forth all shall rest eternally
> With Him that is the God of Sabbaoth hight:
> O that great Sabbaoth God, grant me that Sabbath's sight.

[2] The two passages here quoted from the New Testament have been quoted already—the Pauline passage at greater length—in the analysis of the movement of Withdrawal-and-Return in III. C (ii) (*b*), vol. iii, p. 258, above. In the two passages of Greek poetry that are quoted on the preceding page of the same volume the opposite belief that the appearance of annihilation is no illusion but is an ultimate as well as inexorable reality is expressed with a poetic pathos which reflects the same mood of resignation as the Stoic and Epicurean note of philosophic fortitude, notwithstanding the difference of tone between these two alternative variations on one theme.

of abnormality, it is remarkable to observe that a lighter penalty is exacted for the wider aberration. While Archaism, as we have seen,[1] is frequently required to pay the crushing penalty of defeating its own aim by collapsing into Futurism, we shall find that Futurism is sometimes rewarded for its greater transgression by being allowed to transcend itself through rising into Transfiguration. If we may liken the catastrophe of Archaism to the crash of a motor-car which skids right round on its tracks and then rushes to destruction in the opposite direction to that in which the unhappy driver was steering before the machine escaped from his control, the happier experience of Futurism may be likened to that of a passenger on board a motor-driven vehicle who believes himself to be travelling in a terrestrial omnibus and observes, with deepening dismay, the ever-increasing roughness of the *terrain* over which he is being carried forward, until suddenly—at the moment when it looks and feels as though an accident can no longer be staved off—the vehicle rises from the ground at a turn of the unseen pilot's wrist and soars over crags and chasms in its own element. While the archaist driver of our imaginary motor-car fares worse than he has had reason to fear, the futurist passenger in our imaginary aeroplane fares better than he has had any right to expect.

(β) *The Breach with the Present.*

The Breach in Manners.

The futuristic, like the archaistic, way of breaking with the Present can be studied empirically in a number of different fields of social activity; but we need not always map these out on precisely the same lines. We may vary the map to suit the subject; and in our study of Futurism it may prove convenient to deal separately with Manners and with Institutions; to bring Language and Literature and the Visual Arts together under the common head of Secular Culture; and to take Religion by itself, as we have taken it before in our studies of Archaism and of the Sense of Promiscuity.

In the field of Manners the first gesture in which Futurism is wont to advertise itself is the exchange of a traditional for an outlandish costume; and in the ubiquitously—though still no more than superficially—Westernized World of the present day[2] we have already been offered the spectacle of a host of non-Western societies, from China to Peru, abandoning a hereditary and distinctive

---

[1] In V. C (i) (d) 8 (ε), pp. 94–7, above.
[2] For the superficiality of the Westernization (so far as it has yet gone) of the surviving non-Western Societies see I. B (iii), vol. i, pp. 35–6, above.

dress and conforming to a drably exotic Western fashion as an outward and visible sign of their voluntary or involuntary enrolment in a vastly swollen Western internal proletariat.

The most famous, as well as the earliest, example of a forcible process of external Westernization is the shaving of beards and banning of kaftans in Muscovy at the turn of the seventeenth and eighteenth centuries of the Christian Era by order of Peter the Great.[1] In the third quarter of the nineteenth century this Muscovite revolution in costume was emulated in Japan. And in our own Post-War Age similar circumstances have evoked similar acts of tyranny in a number of non-Western countries in which a long-postponed course of Westernization is now being taken by forced marches under the lash of local dictators. In the forcibly Westernized Turkey of President Mustafā Kemāl Atatürk the unveiling of the women[2] has been the counterpart of the shaving of the men in the forcibly Westernized Muscovy of Peter the Great; but in the Islamic World of this age the main battle of Futurism in the field of dress has been fought over the question of masculine headgear, which in this society has been traditionally invested with a greater social and even political significance than any other article of dress.[3] The landmarks in the progress of this struggle are the Turkish law of November 1925 which has made it compulsory for all male Turkish citizens to wear hats with brims,[4] and the corre-

---

[1] The shaving of Muscovite beards was executed not merely by Peter's orders but actually by the futurist Tsar's own hand upon certain conspicuous countenances. This was, in fact, the gesture by which Peter, upon his return from his Western tour in the autumn of A.D. 1698, elected to announce his programme of forcible Westernization to some of the dignitaries of his hitherto Byzantine empire when they presented themselves in order to welcome him home; and we may be sure that this 'positive act', performed by the Tsar in person, had a greater effect upon the Muscovite imagination than the elaborate official regulations, *more Occidentali*, by which it was followed up. Some details of Peter's futuristic campaign against the traditional Muscovite costume have already been set out in III. C (ii) (*b*), vol. iii, p. 283, footnote 1, above. In taking this plunge into a forcibly imposed sartorial Futurism, Peter was blindly perpetuating the methods, while abruptly reversing the policy, of his recent predecessors on the Muscovite Imperial Throne. Before Peter's accession the Government of Muscovy had been more conservative than the people, and its exercise of a tyrannical authority in the domain of dress had therefore taken the form of a veto upon innovations. In the reign of Peter's own father Alexei (*imperabat* A.D. 1645–76) the wearing of Polish costume had been forbidden by a law of A.D. 1675 (see Brückner, A.: *Peter der Grosse* (Berlin 1879, Grote), p. 218); and in the same reign the offence of adopting the Western style of coiffure had been punished by excommunication and dismissal from office (Brückner, op. cit., p. 220). The father's tyrannical Conservatism, however, was a mild affliction by comparison with the son's tyrannical Futurism; for Peter's father had merely been lagging a short distance behind a small minority of his subjects, whereas Peter was forging far ahead of the vast majority of his.

[2] See Toynbee, A. J., and Boulter, V. M.: *Survey of International Affairs, 1928* (London 1929, Milford), pp. 202–3.

[3] See ibid., pp. 203–5, and *Survey of International Affairs, 1936* (London 1937, Milford), pp. 777–8, as well as Toynbee, A. J.: *Survey of International Affairs, 1925*, vol. i (London 1927, Milford), pp. 73–5.

[4] The passage of this law had the effect of forcing all male Turkish citizens into making a breach with one of the outward observances of Islam; for the Islamic form of prayer requires the worshipper both to keep his head covered and to touch the ground with his forehead; and it is impossible to observe both these prescriptions in any head-

sponding decrees of Rizā Shāh Pehlevī of Iran and King Amānallāh of Afghanistan which followed in 1928.[1]

The Islamic World in the twentieth century of the Christian Era is not the only arena in which a hat with a brim has been adopted as the battle-crest of a militant Futurism. In the Syriac World in the fourth decade of the second century B.C. the High Priest Joshua—who was the leader of a faction in Jewry which was eager at that time to repudiate at least the external trappings of the Jewish community's native cultural heritage—was not content to advertise his programme by the verbal gesture of hellenizing his own name from Joshua into Jason. The 'positive act' which provoked the demonic reaction of the Maccabees was the adoption by the younger priests of the Temple in Jerusalem, at Joshua's instigation, of the broad-brimmed felt sun-hat which was the distinctive headgear of the pagan dominant minority in the Achaemenian Empire's Hellenic 'successor-states'. In the sight of

dress with a brim. In the summer of the year 1929 the writer of this Study noticed the embarrassment which the new law was then inflicting upon the devout worshippers in the Mosque of Sultan Mehmed Fātih in Stamboul (see Toynbee, A. J.: *A Journey to China* (London 1931, Constable), p. 69); and it is difficult not to suspect—though perhaps no less difficult to prove—that this was one of the effects which the law was deliberately designed to produce. It is noteworthy that this futuristic imposition of the Western brimmed hat upon male Turkish citizens in 1925 followed hard upon the heels of a short-lived archaistic fashion of wearing the *qalpāq*, a brimless black lambskin cap which was a trivial part of the Ottoman Turks' heritage from the Eurasian Nomad minority of their ancestors. It will be seen that the wearing of the *qalpāq* was the equivalent, in the field of dress, of the linguistic Archaism that has been purifying the Ottoman Turkish language of the non-Turkish elements in its vocabulary (see V. C (i) (d) 8 (γ), pp. 67–8, above). The change from the archaistic Eurasian *qalpāq* to the futuristic Western Homburg hat was abrupt; for as late as April 1923, when the writer of this Study paid his first visit to Angora, he soon discovered that the hat which he had brought on his own head from London was anathema in Anatolia because in Turkish eyes it was then still a symbol of the imperialism of the Western Powers and of the self-assertiveness of the Orthodox and Gregorian Christian *ra'īyeh*. The *qalpāq*, which was so soon to be supplanted by this ex-enemy headgear, had already supplanted the *fez*; and the *fez*, too, had been an innovation in its day. It had been introduced by Sultan Mahmūd II (*imperabat* A.D. 1808–39) as an alternative to the invidiously distinctive variety of headgear that had previously been either obligatory or customary in the Ottoman Empire. It is noteworthy that Mahmūd does not appear to have made the wearing of the *fez* compulsory except for public servants.

[1] Rizā Shāh banned the sugar-loaf-shaped felt *kulāh*—which, on the evidence of Achaemenian bas-reliefs, had been the customary Persian male headgear since at least the fifth century B.C.—but he was prudent enough to make a compromise with the susceptibilities of his subjects in selecting his compulsory substitute. Instead of following the precedent of the Turkish law of November 1925, Rizā Shāh constrained his male subjects to wear, not the civilian Western hat of the day, but the so-called *Kulāh Pehlevī*, a fancy head-dress, designed by the Shah himself, more or less on the pattern of the contemporary headgear of officers in the French Army. King Amānallāh—who had to deal with a population which was still more conservative than that of Persia—made the mistake which Rizā Shāh avoided. Amānallāh did attempt to follow the Turkish example; and this was the crowning folly that cost him his throne (see V. C (i) (c) 3, vol. v, p. 333, above, and V. C (ii) (a), in the present volume, p. 234, below). On the other hand, in the relatively progressive 'successor-state' of the Ottoman Empire that has been established in 'Irāq, the first sovereign, King Faysal b. Husayn, exercised an even greater prudence than Rizā Shāh; for the 'Faysal cap' which he introduced is modelled, not on the peaked cap of the French Army, but on the soft and brimless forage-cap of the British Army, in which any devout Muslim can perform his prayer-drill without impediment.

the orthodox Palestinian Jews of the day this spectacle was as shocking as it would be to the eyes of our twentieth-century Palestinian Arab Muslims if the Grand Mufti of Jerusalem were to air himself in the Haram-ash-Sharīf with a sola topee on his head. And in the Jewish case in point the rapid progress of the futurist furore was soon to give the puritans reason; for the young priests of Yahweh did not confine their revolutionary cult of Hellenism to the wearing of the *petasus*. Their Hellenic headgear was not so shocking as the Hellenic nakedness with which they practised Hellenic sports in a Hellenic palaestra. Hellenic athletic competitions led on to Hellenic dramatic festivals; and, almost before the conservatively orthodox majority of the Palestinian Jewish community had realized what was happening, the 'raging tearing campaign' of Futurism had arrived at its sacrilegious culmination.

'They shall pollute the sanctuary of strength and shall take away the daily sacrifice, and they shall place the abomination that maketh desolate.'[1]

Jason's futuristic campaign had started as a voluntary movement; and, for all its radicalism, it had not trespassed beyond the limits of a secular field of action in which it might give offence to Jewish taste without driving Jewish consciences to desperation. But the Jewish High Priest Jason had been working under the patronage of the Seleucid Emperor Antiochus Epiphanes; and the patron held in the hollow of his hand a client who was merely the prelate of one of those diminutive temple-states which were embedded

---

[1] Dan. xi. 31. The crescendo movement of Jason's futurist 'ramp' is depicted, in colours which are as vivid as they are unflattering, in a celebrated passage in the Second Book of Maccabees:

'After the passing of Seleucus [IV] and the accession of Antiochus the God Manifest (so called), Jason the brother of Onias wormed his way into the High Priesthood. He achieved this by petitioning the King and promising him 360 talents of silver per annum, besides 80 talents from other sources of revenue. In addition he undertook to levy another 150 talents if he were also empowered by royal authority to establish a physical training centre (γυμνάσιον) and a youth club (ἐφηβεῖον) and to register the inhabitants of Jerusalem as citizens of Antioch. The King gave his assent; and the new High Priest had no sooner taken up the reins of office than he set himself to transform his countrymen into Hellenes. He brushed aside the royal charter that had been secured to the Jews by the efforts of John the father of Eupolemus, and he made havoc of their lawful institutions in order to make room for impious innovations. He took a peculiar pleasure in installing his physical training centre under the very shadow of the citadel, enrolling the pick of the youth, and putting them into slouch hats (ἀσμένως ... τοὺς κρατίστους τῶν ἐφήβων ... ὑπὸ πέτασον ἦγαγεν). Indeed, the unparalleled profanity of Jason, who behaved more like an enemy of Religion than like a High Priest, gave Hellenism such a vogue and Renegadism such an impetus that the priests lost interest in the Liturgy, looked down upon the Temple, neglected the sacrifices and cared for nothing but to enter themselves for competitions in discus-throwing and to take their part in all the impious performances in the ring. They despised what their forefathers had honoured, and regarded Hellenic notions as the best in the world. In retribution for this they were overtaken by serious misfortunes and received their punishment at the hands of the very nation whose ways they had admired and wanted to ape in every particular. The laws of Heaven cannot be defied with impunity, as the sequel will show' (2 Macc. iv. 7–17).

here and there in the vast body politic of the Seleucid Empire.[1]
When it suited Antiochus's convenience he sold Jason's office over
Jason's head to a rival aspirant[2] who was not only a higher bidder
for the Jewish High Priesthood but was also a more violent futurist;
and, when the evicted Jason descended upon Jerusalem from his
asylum in Transjordan and expelled his supplanter by a *coup de
main*, Antiochus promptly took advantage of the opening given
him by this act of Jewish rebellion in order to intervene personally
with a high hand. He marched on Jerusalem; crushed the revolt;
installed a Macedonian garrison; confiscated the treasure of the
Temple for the benefit of his own insatiable exchequer; and put
(as he supposed) the finishing touch to the work of Hellenization,
in which Jason had played his part as pioneer, by courteously
identifying 'the Heaven-God of Jerusalem'[3] with the Olympian
Zeus and graciously providing the necessary statue of the god—
portrayed in the Emperor's own image—to fill the void in a hitherto bleakly vacant Holy of Holies.[4] 'The Abomination of Desolation,
spoken of by Daniel the Prophet, standing where it ought not,'[5]
was the swift and fearful nemesis of Joshua-Jason's futuristic
escapade.[6]

The ultimate outcome of this Jewish essay in Futurism in the
second century B.C. was not a triumph like Peter the Great's but
a fiasco like Amānallāh's; for the Seleucid Power's frontal attack
upon the Jewish religion evoked a Jewish reaction of a violence[7]
with which Epiphanes and his successors found themselves unable
to cope.[8] Yet the fact that this particular essay in Futurism

---

[1] For these temple-states, which were the debris of shattered civilizations, see IV. C
(iii) (c) 2 (β), vol. iv, p. 312, footnote 1, and p. 422, footnote 3; IV. C (iii) (c) 3 (α),
vol. iv, p. 471; and IV. C (iii) (c) 3 (β), vol. iv, pp. 515-18, above.

[2] We have no record of the Jewish name which was hellenized into Menelaus by
Joshua-Jason's supplanter (Bevan, Edwyn: *Jerusalem under the High Priests* (London
1904, Arnold), p. 80).

[3] For this description of Yahweh, under which the tribal god of Jewry had been commended by the Jews themselves to the notice of the Pagan World, see the passage quoted
from Eduard Meyer in V. C (i) (d) 7, p. 33, above.

[4] For the measures taken by Antiochus Epiphanes at Jerusalem see Bevan, op. cit.,
pp. 81-2.

[5] Mark xiii. 14; cf. Matt. xxiv. 15.

[6] The swiftness of the nemesis is impressive if it is true that Antiochus's devastating
act of introducing the Hellenic idol into the Jewish Holy of Holies followed within eight
years of Jason's apparently innocuous act of putting his young priests into Hellenic hats.

[7] See V. C (i) (c) 2, vol. v, pp. 68 and 72-3, above.

[8] Eduard Meyer, in *Ursprung und Anfänge des Christentums*, vol. ii (Stuttgart and
Berlin 1921, Cotta), p. 143, makes a suggestive comparison between Antiochus Epiphanes
and the Hapsburg Emperor Joseph II. The Seleucid Empire was already labouring
under the shock of its collision with Rome by the time when Antiochus Epiphanes (no
doubt unwittingly) challenged Jewry to a fight to the death with the Emperor's Hellenism. Within ten years of the conquest of Coele Syria by Antiochus the Great in 198 B.C.
the Seleucid conqueror of the Ptolemy had been routed by Scipio Asiagenus at Magnesia
and had been compelled, as part of a peace settlement which was dictated to him by the
Roman Government, to consent to a drastic limitation of Seleucid armaments. And
Antiochus Epiphanes himself had been publicly humiliated by a Roman Commissioner
before the walls of Pelusium (see V. C (i) (d) 6 (γ), Annex I, vol. v, p. 628, footnote 2,

happens to have been abortive does not make it any the less instructive; and one of the points which it illustrates is the impossibility of indulging in Futurism within fore-appointed limits. The essence of Futurism is a breach with the present; and, when once there has been a lesion at any point in the fabric of social life, the rent will extend itself and the threads will continue to unravel—even if the original rift was minute and even if the point at which it was made lay on the outermost fringe of the web. The êthos of Futurism is intrinsically 'totalitarian'; and the evidence which points to this conclusion is by no means confined to the single instance which has led us up to it. Just as the Jew who takes to wearing the *petasus* soon learns to frequent the palaestra and the amphitheatre, so the Muscovite who has been dragooned into wearing a Western wig goes on to dance the fashionable Western dances and play the fashionable Western card-games, while in a later generation the Turk in a Homburg hat and the Persian in a Pehlevī cap cannot be kept off the football field or out of the cinema hall. In these cases, as in that, the abandonment of a traditional style of dress leads on to a general revolution in manners; and this is not the end of the futurist rake's progress. For, while in the Islamic World to-day the post-war fever of Futurism is still in the innocuous preliminary external stage of the Jewish movement under Jason's brief régime, Japan, who anticipated Turkey by three-quarters of a century in discarding her traditional male costume, is already being haunted by the spectre of 'dangerous thought', while in Russia —where the change of costume occurred about a century and three-quarters earlier than in Japan—the process has culminated in our day[1] in a campaign against the ancestral religion of the land

above) only a few months before he stormed the walls of Jerusalem and desecrated the Temple. The main lines of Epiphanes' ill-starred policy can all be traced back to the effects of Roman pressure. His abortive campaign of forcible Hellenization was an ill-judged effort to reinvigorate his empire by consolidating it. His abortive invasion of Egypt was a hazardous attempt to take advantage of the Romans' preoccupation with Perseus in order to secure a belated territorial compensation for the loss of the former possessions of the Seleucid Monarchy north-west of Taurus. The financial straits which tempted Antiochus to resort to the fatal expedient of robbing his Jewish subjects of their temple-treasures were the price of his own costly military adventure in Egypt following upon the payment of the heavy war-indemnity which had been exacted by the Romans from his predecessor Antiochus the Great. Before the Seleucid Government was pushed or led into these fatal courses in consequence of its encounter with Rome, its yoke had weighed lightly, by comparison with the rival Ptolemaic Government's yoke, upon its Oriental subjects' necks (see V. C (i) (c) 2, vol. v, p. 65, above).

[1] The pace of Futurism in Russia has, of course, been much slower than the pace at which it moved in Palestine in the second century B.C.; for while, as we have seen, the installation of 'the Abomination of Desolation' in the Holy of Holies may have followed within eight years of the adoption of the *petasus* by Joshua-Jason's young men, there is an interval of no less than 228 years between the date of Peter the Great's effective accession to power in A.D. 1689 and the date of the Bolshevik Revolution of A.D. 1917. This difference of pace is evidently due to one signal difference in the course of events. The hand which placed the statue of Zeus Olympius in the Temple of Yahweh at Jerusalem was the hand of an alien intruder; and the fact that Antiochus was not a Jew but a Greek accounts both for the swiftness with which the Palestinian drama reached its culmina-

which is being conducted with a far more powerful 'drive' than Antiochus was able to put into his casual assault upon the traditional worship of Yahweh.

On this showing, we may expect to see Futurism invade the sanctuary of Religion sooner or later in any society in which this contagious way of life has once asserted itself in the trivial and frivolous spheres of dress and recreation; but in its victorious advance from the outworks to the citadel of the Soul a futuristic movement has to traverse the intermediate zones of Politics and Secular Culture; and we must therefore take a survey of its effects in these two fields before pursuing our inquiry into the supreme effort to break with the Present which Futurism makes when it turns its batteries upon the ancestral religion of a society whose less intimate ancestral institutions have already been razed to the ground in the earlier stages of the offensive.

The Breach in Institutions.

In the political sphere Futurism may express itself either geographically in the deliberate obliteration of existing landmarks and boundaries or socially in the forcible dissolution of existing corporations, parties, and sects or 'liquidation' of existing classes or abolition of existing organs or offices of state; and it may be convenient to survey separately some of the outstanding examples of its operation in these two different fields, though in practice a futuristic political revolution is apt to extend over both fields if it has succeeded in making headway in either one of them.

The classical example of a systematic obliteration of landmarks and boundaries for the express purpose of producing a breach of political continuity is the redrawing of the political map of Attica by a successful revolutionary, Cleisthenes the Alcmaeonid, *circa* 507 B.C. Cleisthenes' aim was to transform a loosely-knit polity, in which the claims of kinship had hitherto usually prevailed over those of the community whenever the two allegiances had come into conflict, into a unitary state in which the obligation of citizenship would in future override all lesser loyalties. He perceived that these lesser loyalties, which he wished to weaken or break, were strong in virtue of their possessing 'a local habitation and a name';[1] and accordingly he replaced—or at any rate overlaid—the

tion and for the fierceness of the reaction which eventually rendered the whole movement abortive. If Joshua-Jason's Seleucid patron and master had had the wisdom to refrain from intervening in person, and had left the Jewish futurist movement to work itself out at its own natural pace under exclusively Jewish auspices, it is conceivable that the first century of the Christian Era might have witnessed an eradication of the worship of Yahweh by Jewish hands instead of witnessing, as it did, the outburst of Jewish Zealotism which culminated in the great Romano-Jewish War of A.D. 66–70 (see V. C (i) (c) 2, vol. v, p. 68, above).

[1] Shakespeare: *A Midsummer Night's Dream*, Act v, Scene 1, l. 17.

traditional Attic *phylae* and *phratriae* and *genê* with a brand-new set of artificially invented and arbitrarily delimited *phylae* and *trittyes* and *dêmi* which would foster the allegiance of their members to the all-embracing city-state of Athens of which these new geographical circumscriptions, unlike the old kin-groups, were mere articulations without any prior or independent life of their own.[1]

This precedent from Hellenic history has been followed in our Western World by the makers of the French Revolution—whether consciously, as part of their cult of Hellenism, or because they lighted independently upon the same means for compassing an identical end. Aiming at the political unification of France as Cleisthenes had aimed at that of Attica, these French political futurists did in fact adopt the Cleisthenic device of abolishing the old provincial boundaries and levelling the old internal customs barriers in order to turn France into a unitary fiscal area subdivided for administrative convenience into departments whose monotonous uniformity and strict subordination were intended to efface the memory of the historic provinces with their persistent traditions of diversity and autonomy. To-day the departments of France bid fair to prove, as the demes of Attica proved, the most durable monuments of the revolution whose fiat first traced their boundaries on the map; and already this feat of geographical Futurism in France has had repercussions in other parts of

[1] Cleisthenes' revolutionary reconstruction of the political map of Attica was justified by its fruits; for it did produce precisely that overriding sense of loyalty to the state which it had been intended to produce; and, with this artificial reinforcement, the Athenian civic consciousness developed a strength and tenacity which could bear comparison even with the Spartiates' public spirit. The brilliance of Cleisthenes' success as a revolutionary may perhaps be accounted for in part by the fact that this Athenian political futurist was also the scion of a noble house with a strong family tradition. At any rate, whether for this or for some other reason, Cleisthenes was one of those rare revolutionaries that have had the insight to understand the potency of Conservatism and the wisdom to harness this mighty social force for their own purposes. When Cleisthenes set himself to replace the four historic *phylae* of Attica with ten brand-new *phylae* of his own invention, he took pains to invest his new creations with an air of antiquity and a halo of sanctity. He solved the delicate problem of providing his new ten tribes with names by drawing up a panel of a hundred names of mythical Attic heroes and then persuading the Oracle at Delphi (where the Alcmaeonidae had influence) to designate ten as being the most appropriate (Aristotle: *Institutions of Athens*, chap. 21). The Cleisthenic 'tribes' thus started life with a religious sanction which soon gave them as powerful a hold upon the allegiance of the citizens enrolled in them as if they had been in existence since time immemorial; and this new allegiance to the ten Cleisthenic tribes, in contrast to the old allegiance to the four Ionic tribes, had the effect of fortifying, instead of competing with, the members' simultaneous allegiance to the Athenian city-state. (It is true that in Attica the Ionic tribes, too, in their day, may have started as artificial articulations of the body politic which were copied, in this case, from Miletus or some other city-state of Ionia in which these tribes were an indigenous institution representing the several 'swarms' of migrants in the post-Minoan *Völkerwanderung* whose political union in their new place of settlement had brought a new body politic to birth (see II. D (iii), vol. ii, pp. 97-8, above). But, if the introduction of the Ionic tribes into Attica really had been an anticipation of Cleisthenes' invention of his ten tribes, the earlier political revolution had miscarried; for by Cleisthenes' time the Ionic tribes in Attica had become incorporated into the indigenous kin-group organization of *phratriae* and *genê*.)

Europe. It is true that the departments on the French model which were instituted under the Napoleonic régime in those tracts of Italy, Germany, and the Low Countries that were incorporated into the Napoleonic Empire and its client states did not survive the downfall of Napoleon and the consequent reduction of France to her old limits by the re-establishment of the frontiers of A.D. 1792. Yet, although these departments in the French Revolutionary style *in partibus peregrinorum* were themselves ephemeral, their negative effect upon the political map of Europe has been lasting and profound; for in the short period of their currency they did effectively obliterate the pre-existing political landmarks, and thereby they cleared the ground for the erection of a united Italy and a united Germany whose makers have been persistently inspired by the pattern of a united France until, in our own day, they have turned imitation into caricature by carrying it to 'totalitarian' lengths.[1] In Germany under the National-Socialist régime Herr Hitler has been following out at any rate one of 'the Ideas of 1789' in his move to replace the *Länder* of the Reich, with their unwelcome historic associations of dynastic particularism, by *Gaue* in which the essential unity of the Reich will be proclaimed in the very artificiality of these new-fangled geographical articulations.[2]

While Herr Hitler has been experimenting—with a caution that seems alien from the Nazi êthos—in this enterprise of remapping 'the Third Reich' on futuristic lines, his 'opposite number' Monsieur Stalin has given characteristic expression to the Bolshevik êthos in the geographical field by carrying to completion a far more radical rearticulation of the internal divisions of the Soviet Union.

The thoroughness of the breach of continuity which has been made by Stalin in this sphere becomes apparent when the new administrative map of the Union of Soviet Socialist Republics[3] is superimposed upon the old administrative map of the Russian Empire; for it would be hard to find a sector where the two sets of lines coincide. The autonomous Uzbeg khanates and Cossack republics have been swept away as unceremoniously as the subdivisions of those territories that used to be under the direct administration of St. Petersburg; and these old administrative

[1] See V. C (i) (*d*) 6 (γ), Annex I, vol. v, pp. 636–42, above.

[2] In theory the *Gaue* into which the National-Socialist Party has been remapping 'the Third Reich' for certain purposes are archaistic restorations of the tribal communities into which the German-speaking population of the Continent of Europe was divided in the Dark Ages, before the establishment of the Holy Roman Empire. The practical purpose, however, which these new *Gaue* are intended to serve is the futuristic aim of obliterating the vestiges of the dynastic states into which Germany broke up as the Holy Roman Empire weathered away.

[3] See the English text of the Constitution (Fundamental Law) of the Union of Soviet Socialist Republics adopted [on the 5th December, 1936] at the Extraordinary Eighth Congress of Soviets of the U.S.S.R. (Moscow 1937, Co-operative Publishing Society of Foreign Workers in the U.S.S.R.), chap. 2, arts. 13 and 22–7.

units have been replaced by a complicated hierarchy of new ones
—ranging from the constituent states of the Union down to a
number of autonomous republics and districts within their respective borders—which bears no relation whatsoever to the old administrative 'lay-out'. Stalin's motive in carrying out his geographical revolution has been the same as Hitler's and Cleisthenes'.
His aim, like theirs, has been to make sure that the common
allegiance of his fellow citizens to the commonwealth as a who!e
shall be stronger than their parochia! allegiance to any lesser
geographical unit. In pursuing this identical aim, however, Stalin
has acted with a subtlety in which he is perhaps a pioneer. Whereas his predecessors and contemporaries have all alike sought to
attain their purpose of weakening the existing parochial loyalties
by effacing the landmarks to which these loyalties have attached,
Stalin has pursued the exactly contrary policy of satisfying, and
even anticipating, the cravings of parochialism on the shrewd
calculation that an appetite is more likely to be stifled by satiety
than it is to be extinguished by starvation.

Stalin has perceived in advance that one of the most formidable
impediments to the triumph of the Marxian 'ideology' among the
peoples of the Soviet Union is likely to be the attraction of the
alternative 'ideology' of Nationalism—a competing Western political idea which has already captured some of the most highly
cultivated peoples of the Union, such as the Ukrainians, Georgians,
and Armenians, and which is likely to continue to spread until its
leaven—or virus—will have infected even the most remote and
backward tribes in the mountain-fastnesses of the Caucasus and
Altai and in the tundras beyond the Arctic Circle. Recognizing
that this unwelcome triumph of Nationalism is at least as probable
as the triumph of the Communism which it is his mission to promote, Stalin has set himself to prevent the plague of Nationalism
from taking a virulent form by applying the homoeopathic treatment of inoculation. He has thrown open to the peoples of the
Union so wide a scope for the satisfaction of nationalist proclivities
as to reduce to a minimum the danger that nationalist grievances
may be used as a 'red herring' to draw the peoples' feet away from
the path of Communism which Stalin wishes them to tread.

In this field, at any rate, Stalin knows what he is about; for he
is himself a Georgian by birth and he has thus had a direct experience of the stimulating effect of the old Imperial Russian policy
of repression upon national movements among non-Russian subjects of the Tsar. It is therefore perhaps not improbable—in the
light of the sequels to the French Revolution of A.D. 1789 and to
the Attic Revolution of 507 B.C.—that the futuristic recasting of the

administrative map of the Soviet Union under Stalin's auspices may prove to be the most durable monument of the Russian Revolution of A.D. 1917. And in that event Stalin—who in other connexions may chiefly be remembered as a politician who slily shepherded his silly sheep back out of the Marxian wilderness in the direction of the bourgeois fold—will also have a second title to fame as a statesman whose brilliant political homoeopathy saved some sixteen per cent. of the land-surface of the planet from being ravaged by the Western political plague of Nationalism with the extreme virulence that is symptomatic of an 'ideological' germ when it is attacking bodies social that have not been preconditioned for resisting it.

Unhappily the homoeopathic treatment which the All-Union Communist Party, under Stalin's inspiration, have applied to the problem of Nationalism within the frontiers of the Soviet Union has not been their policy in dealing with corporations and parties and sects and classes. In this field their Futurism has taken the form of a 'totalitarian' intolerance, and here their pernicious example—which has itself been inspired by the outlawry of the Noblesse in the French Revolution—has been all too faithfully followed by the National-Socialist Party in Germany.

As for the breach in Institutions which takes the form of an abolition of existing organs or offices of state, we may cite, as a classical example, the abolition of the Roman Consulate by the Roman Emperor Justinian.[1]

The Breach in Secular Culture and in Religion.

In the field of Secular Culture the classic expression of Futurism is the symbolic act of the Burning of the Books. In the Sinic World the Emperor Ts'in She Hwang-ti, who was the revolution-ry first founder of the Sinic universal state,[2] is said to have systematically confiscated and burnt the literary remains of the philosophers who had flourished during the Sinic 'Time of Troubles', for fear that a transmission of this 'dangerous thought' might thwart his own design of inaugurating a brand-new order of society.[3] And in the Syriac World the Caliph 'Umar, who was the veritable reconstructor of the Syriac universal state after it had been in abeyance during a millennium of Hellenic intrusion upon the Syriac World,[4] is reported to have written, in reply to an

[1] See V. C (ii) (a), p. 224, below.   [2] See V. C (ii) (a), p. 187, below.
[3] According to Hackmann, H.: Chinesische Philosophie (Munich 1927, Reinhardt), 171, the 'dangerous thought' that Ts'in She Hwang-ti was particularly anxious to suppress was the Mencian version of Confucianism.
[4] For the Arab Caliphate as a 'reintegration' or 'resumption' of the Achaemenian Empire see I. C (i) (b), vol. i, pp. 73–7, above.

inquiry from a general who had just received the surrender of the city of Alexandria and had asked for instructions as to how he was to dispose of the famous library,

'If these writings of the Greeks agree with the Book of God, they are useless and need not be preserved; if they disagree, they are pernicious and ought to be destroyed.'[1]

According to the legend, the contents of a library which had been accumulating for more than 900 years were thereupon condemned to be consumed as fuel for the heating of the public baths.

Whatever may be the proportions of fiction and fact in these tales that attach to the names of 'Umar and Ts'in She Hwang-ti, the burning of the books at Münster under the militant Anabaptist régime of A.D. 1534–5,[2] and in the whole of Germany after the advent of Herr Hitler to power on the 30th January, 1933, is authentic history; and the motive which inspired our modern Western National Socialists was undoubtedly that which the legend ascribes to the Sinic futurist dictator.

Herr Hitler's Turkish contemporary President Mustafā Kemāl Atatürk succeeded in producing an even sharper breach with the Turkish cultural heritage by means of a less drastic but possibly more effective device. The Turkish dictator's aim was nothing less than to wrench his fellow countrymen's minds out of their inherited Iranic cultural setting and to force them, instead, into a Western cultural mould; but, as an alternative to burning the books in which the treasures of Iranic culture are enshrined, he contented himself with insisting upon a change of Alphabet. A law which was duly passed by the Great National Assembly at Angora on the 1st November, 1928, gave legal currency in Turkey to a version of the Latin Alphabet which had been worked out for the conveyance of the Turkish language at the dictator's order; and the same law went on to prescribe that all newspapers, magazines, pamphlets, advertisements, and public signs must be printed in the new Alphabet on and after the coming 1st December; that all business of public services, banks, and companies must be conducted in it, and all books printed in it, on and after the 1st January 1929; that all administrative and legal forms, documents, and records must be conceived in it on and after the 1st June 1929; and that, as from the last-mentioned date, the public was to correspond in the new Alphabet with government departments

---

1 The anecdote is recounted by Gibbon in his inimitable manner (*The History of Decline and Fall of the Roman Empire*, chap. li).
2 For this outbreak at Münster in these years see V. C (i) (*c*) 2, vol. v, pp. 167 and above. For the particular incident of the Burning of the Books see Carew Hunt, R. 'John of Leyden' in *The Edinburgh Review*, No. 507, vol. 249, January 1929, p. 86.

banks, and companies.[1] The passage and enforcement of this law
made it unnecessary for the Turkish Ghāzī to imitate the Arab
Caliph's melodramatic gesture. The classics of Arabic, Persian,
and Ottoman Turkish literature had now been effectively placed
beyond the reach of a rising generation of Turkish boys and girls
who might otherwise perhaps have been beguiled by the taste of
these forbidden fruits into rebelling against the destiny of Westernization to which they had been devoted by the will of their dictator.
There was no longer any necessity to burn the ancient books when
the Alphabet that was the key to them had been put out of currency. They could now be safely left to rot on their shelves in the
assurance that they would soon be as completely undecipherable
as a Sinic scroll or a Babylonic tablet to the whole of the Turkish-
reading public save for a negligible handful of specialist scholars.[2]

In the banning of a script or the burning of a book the breach
with a cultural tradition is symbolized in a physical act; but the
essence of cultural Futurism is a mental revolution, and this may
be effectively carried through without being advertised in any
outward visible sign. The destruction of the library at Alexandria,
for example (if we may believe that the legend contains some
kernel of fact), was only one particular expression of the impulse
to break with Hellenism which was inherent in Primitive Islam;[3]
and this impulse itself was inherited by the Primitive Muslims
from Christian and Jewish predecessors; for the revolt of Islam
was merely the victorious climax of a persistent attempt—perpetually sustained and renewed in despite of repeated discourage-
ments and failures—to liberate a submerged Syriac Civilization
from the incubus of a Hellenism which had originally imposed
itself on the Syriac World by naked force of arms.[4] In its first
phase this Syriac reaction against Hellenism had taken the form
of an archaistic recoil into the native Syriac tradition by way of
a pathologically meticulous observance and elaboration of the
Mosaic or the Zoroastrian law.[5] In its later phases the same

---

[1] See Toynbee, A. J., and Boulter, V. M.: *Survey of International Affairs, 1928*,
III A (viii), especially pp. 228–30.
[2] The change of Alphabet in Turkey in A.D. 1928 has been touched upon already in
IV. C (ii) (*a*), vol. iv, pp. 52–4, above, where it has been pointed out that the change
has been due to a deliberate act of policy and not to a loss of technique.
[3] At a later stage, of course, the Syriac Civilization in a more sophisticated Islamic
guise drew more copiously upon the mental riches of the Hellenic culture than it had
ever been willing to draw in times when it had still been politically and even militarily
subject to a Hellenic ascendancy. This cultural contact between the Syriac and Hellenic
societies in the Age of the 'Abbasid Caliphate is examined further in Part IX, below.
[4] For this role of Islam in the conflict between the Syriac and Hellenic cultures see
I. C (i) (*b*), vol. i, pp. 90–1; II. D (vi), vol. ii, p. 235; II. D (vii), vol. ii, pp. 285–8; and
V. C (i) (*d*) 6 (δ), Annex, vol. v, pp. 675–8, above.
[5] This phenomenon of 'Zealotism', which is one of the regular psychological con-
comitants of the contact of civilizations in the Space-dimension, is examined further in
Part IX, below.

reaction found a futurist expression in a campaign to reconvert
from Hellenism the *ci-devant* Syriac masses who in the meantime
had been converted to this alien culture in a more or less superficial way through being forcibly enrolled in the Hellenic internal
proletariat. This subterranean mental strife, which gradually prepared the ground for 'Umar's lightning victory in a more flamboyant form of warfare, is described in the following passage from
the pen of a modern Western master of the subject:

'The supremacy of the intellect and the disciplined acquisition of
knowledge by the understanding, which finds its perfected expression
in the [Hellenic] philosophical systems—though it is also striven after
by Judaism, in Sirach, in his pursuit of the *Chokmah* or Divine Wisdom,
as well as in the interpretation of the Law—is ousted by the forces of
emotion: the longing for redemption and for the gift of a peace that
passeth all understanding; the longing for a direct union with the supernatural world of God. This longing finds its satisfaction in the expec-
tant approach to the Godhead and in the mystical, intuitive form of
knowledge (*Gnosis*) to which this opens the way. In spite, or rather just
by reason, of its intellectual derangement, this *Gnosis* has the power to
create an inner sense of certainty, to overcome doubt, and to lull the
understanding to sleep; and so the mediator between God and Man—
the "Son"—calls the simple souls to him and reveals this knowledge to
them, while they, for their part, make it their own with alacrity and
carry it with ease. The grain of truth that lies in *credo quia absurdum*[1]
has found here an ideal expression. The phrase towers high above all
the repeated attempts—from Paul's spurts of rabbinical logic onwards—
to unite and harmonize faith with the rational form of knowledge. It
enunciates the contradiction between them quite clearly without any
mitigation of its harshness. . . .'[2]

'What we are witnessing here is the passing of the sceptre from the
educated to the uneducated—from the upper strata, whose creative
force and capacity for achievement are exhausted,[3] to the masses below
them. The process moves steadily forward towards completion during
the early centuries of the Christian Era, and it manifests itself first in
the great religious movement that sets in at the birth, and even before
the birth, of the Empire. This is the framework within which Christianity spreads[4] until finally it conquers all its competitors (though not

---

[1] For the authentic words of Tertullian see V. C (i) (d) 6 (δ), vol. v, p. 564, above.—
A.J.T.

[2] In the passage here omitted Eduard Meyer depreciates the attempts of Clement of
Alexandria and Origen and their successors to restate the creed of Christianity in terms
of Hellenic philosophy. For a different appreciation of the work of these Christian
Fathers see the present Study, V. C (i) (c) 4, vol. v, pp. 366–7, and V. C (i) (d) 6 (δ),
vol. v, p. 539, above.—A.J.T.

[3] The degeneration of creative into dominant minorities has been examined in this
Study in IV. C (iii) (a), vol. iv, pp. 123–4 and 131–2; V. C (i) (a), vol. v, p. 20; and V.
C (i) (b), vol. v, pp. 23–35, above.—A.J.T.

[4] The futurist note can in fact be heard in those passages from the New Testament
and from the works of Saints Ambrose and Augustine that have been quoted in this
Study respectively in IV. C (iii) (c) 1, vol. iv, pp. 246–9, and in V. C (i) (d) 6 (δ),
vol. v, p. 564, footnote 4, above. In those other contexts they have been quoted for the

without being influenced and modified by them profoundly). But the movement has a far wider sweep than that. It embraces every department of cultural, spiritual, and social life and attains a complete supremacy with the establishment of the absolute military monarchy and the régime of the soldier-emperors from the third century onwards.'[1]

On the intellectual plane the triumph of Futurism is consummated when the heirs of the intellectual tradition of a once creative but now merely dominant minority proclaim their own mental bankruptcy by positively repudiating the cultural heritage which they have failed to defend against the futurist attack and voluntarily embracing the anti-intellectual faith which has been the deadliest weapon of their futurist assailants.[2] The Hellenic Enlightenment had extinguished its own lamp long before Justinian set the seal upon an accomplished fact by closing the now benighted Athenian schools.[3]

The illustrations of Futurism in this intellectual sphere that have come to our attention at an earlier point[4] have been drawn from the histories of the Hellenic and Sinic and Indic civilizations in the course of their disintegration; but there are other illustrations nearer home that stare us in the face; for a futurist assault upon the intellectual heritage of our Western Society is a recent yet already conspicuous feature of our own current history. This contemporary Western vein of anti-intellectual Futurism is in fact a common element in movements which might seem at first sight to be remote from one another. The same animus can be detected in the harmlessly theoretical speculations of the gentle French philosopher Bergson and in the militantly practical policy of the Fascist and Communist worshippers of the idol of 'the Totalitarian State'.[5]

Thought and literature are not, of course, the only provinces of secular culture in which the heritage of the Present from the Past is exposed to a futurist attack. There are other worlds for Futurism to conquer in the visual and aural arts; and in another context[6]

testimony which they bear to an objective truth—the operation of the principle of περιπέτεια or 'the reversal of roles'—which is one of the fundamental facts of life. But in enunciating an objective truth these passages also incidentally express a subjective state of mind, and that is the spirit of the futurist who feels it to be his mission to cast out and tread under foot the salt that has lost his savour (Matt. v. 13).—A.J.T.

[1] Meyer, E.: *Ursprung und Anfänge des Christentums*, vol. i (Berlin and Stuttgart 1921, Cotta), pp. 289–90. Compare the quotation from C. G. Jung in V. C (i) (d) 6 (δ), vol. v, pp. 567–8, above.

[2] This metamorphosis of philosophies into religions has been examined in V. C (i) (d) 6 (δ), vol. v, pp. 545–68, above.

[3] For the closing of the University of Athens by Justinian in A.D. 529 see IV. C (iii) (c) 2 (α), vol. iv, pp. 272–3, above, and V. C (ii) (a), in the present volume, pp. 223–4, below.   [4] See V. C (i) (d) 6 (δ), vol. v, pp. 545–68, above.

[5] For the idolatrous worship of states see IV. (iii) (c) 2 (α) and (β), vol. iv, pp. 261–423, above. For modern Western Man's emotional revolt against his intellectual heritage see Watkin, E. I.: *Men and Tendencies* (London 1937, Sheed & Ward).

[6] In IV. C (ii) (a), vol. iv, pp. 51–2, above.

we have already had occasion to take notice of the impulse which, in our own Western World in our own day, is leading us to abandon our traditional Western styles of music and dancing and painting and sculpture in favour of outlandish innovations. It is, in fact, our modern Western innovators in those fields who have coined the word 'Futurism' in order to apply it to their own handiwork in assertion of a claim to originality. In their case this boast is proved false by the testimony of a bizarre borrowed plumage which flagrantly betrays its incongruous Tropical African and pseudo-Byzantine origins. The title 'futurist' might have been assumed with better right by the genuine Byzantine school of architecture and the other visual arts which, in an offensive that started in the third and triumphed in the sixth century of the Christian Era, made itself mistress of the entire domain of a moribund Roman Empire by attacking and supplanting the Hellenic school with one hand and the Egyptiac with the other.[1]

There is one notorious form of Futurism in the field of the visual arts which stands on common ground between the two spheres of Secular Culture and Religion, and that is Iconoclasm. The Iconoclast resembles the modern Western champion of cubist painting or syncopated music in his repudiation of a traditional form of Art, but he is peculiar in confining his hostile attentions to Art in association with Religion, and in being moved to this hostility by motives that are not aesthetic but are theological. The essence of Iconoclasm is an objection to a visual representation of the Godhead or of any creature, lower than God, whose image might become an object of idolatrous worship; but there have been differences in the degree of rigour with which this common underlying principle has been translated into practice by different Iconoclastic schools. The most celebrated school is the 'totalitarian' one that is represented by Judaism and, in imitation of Judaism, by Islam.

'Thou shalt not make unto thee any graven image, or any likeness of anything that is in heaven above or that is in the earth beneath or that is in the water under the earth. Thou shalt not bow down thyself to them nor serve them; for I the Lord thy god am a jealous god.'[2]

This ban upon all visual art without exception is the logical form of Iconoclasm for a religion which claims to be coextensive with life itself and which therefore refuses to recognize any distinction between one sphere of life which is religious and another which is secular. On the other hand the Iconoclastic movements which have arisen within the bosom of the Christian Church have accommodated themselves to a distinction which Christianity, in con-

---

[1] See IV. C (ii) (a), vol. iv, pp. 51 and 54-5, above.   [2] Exod. xx. 4-5.

trast to both Judaism and Islam, has always accepted from the
earliest date to which we can trace back the Christian *Weltanschauung*. Though the eighth-century outbreak of Iconoclasm in
Orthodox Christendom and the sixteenth-century outbreak in
Western Christendom may have been respectively inspired, at any
rate in part, by the examples of Islam in the one case and of Judaism in the other, they did not either of them follow the Judaico-
Islamic school in going the length of banning the visual arts *in
toto*. They did not carry their offensive into the secular field; and
even in the strictly religious field, to which both the Western
and the Orthodox Christian Iconoclasts confined their attack, the
latter eventually acquiesced in a compromise with their Iconodule
adversaries which might seem to have given the 'image-worship-
pers' the best of the bargain. In return for the concession that
all three-dimensional representations of persons who were objects
of Christian adoration should thenceforth be banned by a tacit
common consent the Orthodox Christian Iconoclasts conceded,
for their part, that two-dimensional representations should be
countenanced even in the religious sphere;[1] and this arbitrary and
irrational ecclesiastical distinction between sculpture and painting[2]
was justified of its political fruits, since it did bring a permanent
truce to the controversy over images in the Orthodox Church.

In Iconoclasm the spirit of Futurism in the religious field has
expressed itself symbolically in a physical act of destruction which
is comparable to the burning of books and the banning of scripts
in the secular sphere; but here too the same spirit also can be, and
has been, at work without any visible advertisement of its activity;
and the Iconoclastic movements which we have just been passing
in review are manifestations of a Futurism in the religious field
which extends beyond Iconoclasm over a vastly wider range of religious life. In our surveys of the internal and external proletariats[3]
that are generated by the schism in the body social of a broken-
down and disintegrating civilization we have observed that both
branches of the Proletariat have been apt to express in religious,
as well as in political and economic, forms their revolt against the
ascendancy of a dominant minority and their repudiation—which

[1] Officially the images were restored in Orthodox Christendom in A.D. 843 without
any limitations or reservations; but the perpetuation of the Iconoclasts' ban in respect of
three-dimensional representations was not the less effective for being unavowed (see
Bury, J. B.: *A History of the East Roman Empire, A.D. 802–867* (London 1912, Macmillan), pp. 152–3).
[2] Presumably the distinction was based on the qualification of the term 'image' by the
epithet 'graven' in the Second Commandment. Yet the commandment goes on (in the
passage quoted above) to forbid the use of visual art in general, *sans phrase*, and it has
never occurred either to the Jews or to the Muslims to draw the distinction which is
the basis of the present practice of the Orthodox Christian Church.
[3] See V. C (i) (c) 2 and 3, *passim*, in vol. v, above.

is partly the cause of the revolt, and partly its consequence—of that dominant minority's cultural heritage. We have traced the origins of the 'higher religions' (in so far as their appearance on the scene of mundane history may be explicable in sociological terms) to the reactions of internal proletariats; and we have likewise found that external proletariats have tended to assert their social individuality on the religious plane either by appropriating to themselves some peculiar version, or perversion, of a 'higher religion' or alternatively by creating a barbarian pantheon of their own in the likeness of a war-lord's war-band. The spirit in which these proletarian-born religions are embraced by their human foster-parents—as distinct from the sometimes utterly different spirit which these religions reveal in themselves—is manifestly an expression of Futurism in the sense which we have given to the word in this Study; and, on this showing, Futurism in the religious field extends over an enormous range—which need not be re-explored here,[1] since we have attempted to survey it already in bringing the Proletariat on to our stage.

(γ) *The Self-Transcendence of Futurism.*

Futurism is a way of life which leads those who seek to follow it into a barren quest of a goal that is intrinsically unattainable. Yet though the quest is barren and may be tragic it need not be without value or importance; for it may guide the baffled seeker's feet into a way of peace[2] along which he will perhaps allow himself to be drawn now that he has stumbled upon it apparently by chance, though he might not have been willing deliberately to choose it in the first instance.

Futurism in its primitive nakedness is, as we have seen,[3] a counsel of despair which, even as such, is a *pis aller*; for the first recourse of a soul which has despaired of the Present without having lost its appetite for life on the mundane level is to attempt to take a flying leap up the Time-stream into the Past; and it is only when this archaistic line of escape has been tried in vain, or has shown itself, without need of trial, to be manifestly impracticable, that the Soul will nerve itself to take the less natural line of Futurism[4] as a last resort, and will attempt, in a recoil from some

---

[1] It will suffice to recall our previous references to the forcible suppression of the Hellenic paganism by the Christian Roman Emperors Gratian and Theodosius the Great (see IV. C (iii) (*b*) 12, vol. iv, pp. 226–7, and V. C (i) (*d*) 8 (δ), in the present volume, p. 89, above).
   [2] Luke i. 79.   [3] In V. C (i) (*d*) 9 (α), pp. 97–101, above.
   [4] Futurism is not only less natural than Archaism psychologically: it is also sociologically more difficult than Archaism to embark upon (though not more difficult to carry through to success, considering that Archaism and Futurism are both intrinsically incapable of succeeding). The reason why Futurism is more difficult than Archaism to launch is to be found in the fact (which we have noticed in V. C (i) (*d*) i, vol. v, p. 398,

grievously shattered hope, to leap out of a blank and dreary Present, not up-stream into a Past which is at any rate familiar, even if it be now beyond recapture, but down-stream into a Future that is conceived of as a state in which the shattered hope can be repaired and resumed and realized.

The nature of this pure—and by the same token purely mundane—Futurism can best be illustrated by citing some of the classic historical examples of it.

In the Hellenic World, for instance, in the second century B.C. thousands of Syrians and other highly cultivated Orientals were deprived of their freedom, uprooted from their homes, separated from their families, and shipped overseas to Sicily and Italy to serve as a 'labour-force' for plantations and cattle-ranches in areas that had been devastated in the Hannibalic War.[1] For these expatriated slaves, whose need for a way of escape out of the Present was extreme, an archaistic recoil into the Past was out of the question. They could not dream of finding their way back to Syria; and, even if the physical feat of repatriation had been practicable, they could hardly feel homesick for an alien Seleucid régime or for the Seleucids' equally alien Achaemenian or Neo-Babylonian or Assyrian predecessors. The pre-Assyrian cosmos of Syriac city-states in which their ancestors had once been truly at home was now buried deep in oblivion. These Syriac slaves who had been conscripted into the ranks of a Hellenic proletariat in a new world overseas could therefore not look back; they could only look forward; and so, when their oppression became intolerable and they were goaded into physical revolt, the objective which they set before their eyes, in order to give themselves heart in their almost desperate enterprise, was to bring to pass an entirely new thing. They made it their aim to establish a kind of inverted Roman Commonwealth in which the existing order of Hellenic Society was to be turned upside down by an exchange of roles between the present slaves and their present masters. The project was audacious, but in the circumstances it was not fantastic. In a universe in which it had been possible for the insurgent slaves themselves to suffer the extreme change of fortune which they had already experienced, what reason was there to suppose that the top-dog of to-day was immune from the possibility of meeting the same fate to-morrow, or that the bottom-dog of to-day, for his

above) that, while Archaism makes its first appearance in the ranks of the Dominant Minority, Futurism first arises in the Proletariat. This makes the launching of an archaistic enterprise relatively easy and that of a futuristic enterprise relatively difficult, because, in any disintegrating society, the Dominant Minority is *ex hypothesi* in the saddle and the Proletariat *ex hypothesi* under the harrow.

[1] See II. D (vi), vol. ii, pp. 213–16; III. C (i) (*b*), vol. iii, pp. 168–71; and V. C (i) (*c*) 2, vol. v, pp. 66 and 69–70, above.

part, was debarred from the possibility of living to see his own
fortune's wheel come round again full circle?

In an earlier chapter of Syriac history the Jews had reacted in
a similar way to the destruction of the sovereign independent
Kingdom of Judah.[1] After they had been swallowed up in the
Neo-Babylonian and Achaemenian Empires and been scattered
abroad among the Gentiles they could not hope with any conviction for an archaistic return to the Pre-Exilic dispensation in which
Judah had lived a life of parochial isolation. A hope that was to
be convincing must not be conceived in terms of a social environment which had disappeared beyond recall; and, since they could
not live without some lively hope of extricating themselves from
a present in which they were unwilling to acquiesce, the Post-
Exilic Jews were driven into looking forward to the future establishment of a Davidic kingdom in a shape which had no precedent
in Judah's political past. The Jews now dreamt of the epiphany
of a scion of David's House who would restore David's kingdom
in the only fashion that was now conceivable in a world which had
been first shattered and then refashioned by the sweeping strokes
of a Sargon and a Nebuchadnezzar and a Cyrus. If the New
David was effectively to reunite all Jewry under his rule—and
what but this was his mission?—in an age in which the living
generation of Jews was scattered over the face of the Earth, then
he must gird himself to acquire a dominion to which his forebears
had never aspired in the highest flights of their ambition. He must
wrest the sceptre of the world-empire from the hands of its present
holder and must make Jerusalem become to-morrow what Susa was
to-day and what Babylon had been yesterday. In order to reunite the
Jews he must now reign as King of Kings over Jews and Gentiles
alike. And why, after all, should the coming champion of Jewry not
attain this pinnacle of power and glory? In a world in which a Cyrus
or Seleucus could rise and a Cambyses or Antiochus the Great could
fall with the speed of the lightning when it flickers between the
Earth and the Firmament,[2] why should not a Zerubbabel have as
good a chance of world dominion as a Darius, or a Judas Maccabaeus as an Antiochus Epiphanes, or a Bar Kōkabā as a Hadrian?[3]

A similar dream once captivated the imaginations of 'the Old
Believers' in the Russian province of Orthodox Christendom. In
the eyes of these Raskolniks the Tsar Peter's version of Orthodoxy
was no Orthodoxy at all; and yet at the same time it was impossible

---

[1] The Jewish reaction has been discussed in IV. C (iii) (b) 12, vol. iv, pp. 224–5;
V. C (i) (c) 2, vol. v, pp. 68–9; and V. C (i) (d) 6 (δ), Annex, vol. v, pp. 657–9, above.
[2] Luke x. 18.
[3] For the belief in the omnipotence of Chance which is apt to prevail in times of
social disintegration—and this with equal potency, whether the belief be unconscious
or unavowed or explicit—see V. C (i) (d) 4, vol. v, pp. 412–19, above.

to imagine the old ecclesiastical order triumphantly reasserting itself in the teeth of a secular government that was now omnipotent as well as Satanic. The Raskolniki were therefore driven to hope for something which had no precedent, and that was for the epiphany of a Tsar-Messiah who would be able as well as willing to undo the Tsar-Antichrist's sacrilegious work and restore the Orthodox Faith in its pristine purity because he would combine absolute mundane power with perfect piety. The Raskolniki hugged this wild hope, because their only alternative was the bleak prospect of waiting grimly for the Last Judgement.[1]

The significant common feature of these historic exhibitions of naked Futurism is that the hopes in which the futurists have sought refuge and relief have all been set upon a purely matter-of-fact fulfilment in the ordinary and familiar mundane way; and this feature is conspicuous in the Futurism of the Jews—about which we happen to be unusually well informed because it has left behind it a documentary record of its history.

After the destruction of the Kingdom of Judah by Nebuchadnezzar in 586 B.C. the Jews again and again put their treasure in the hope of establishing a new Jewish state on the same purely mundane plane whenever the play of oecumenical politics gave them even the slightest encouragement for embarking on a fresh attempt to translate their dream into reality.[2] The brief bout of anarchy through which the Achaemenian Empire passed between the death of Cambyses and the triumph of Darius the Great saw Zerubbabel's attempt (*circa* 522 B.C.) to make Jerusalem the capital of a new Davidic Kingdom.[3] In a later chapter of history the longer interregnum in the rule of the Hellenic dominant minority over its subject territories on Syriac ground west of Euphrates—an interregnum which was merely the incidental and temporary by-product of a family quarrel between the Seleucid and the Roman representatives of the domineering alien power[4]—was mistaken by

---

[1] See Wallace, D. Mackenzie: *Russia* (London 1877, Cassell, 2 vols.), vol. ii, chap. xx, pp. 12–13; Brückner, A.: *Peter der Grosse* (Berlin 1879, Grote), pp. 535–8; Mettig, C.: *Die Europäisierung Russlands im 18. Jahrhundert* (Gotha 1913, Perthes), pp. 161–72.

[2] This dream was dreamed, in the years immediately after the Exile, by the author of the Book of the Prophet Ezekiel (Meyer, E.: *Geschichte des Altertums*, vol. iii (Stuttgart 1901, Cotta), pp. 180–1); and the first attempt to translate it into reality was made by the first party of Jewish exiles in Babylonia who availed themselves of Cyrus's permission to them to return to Judaea. 'There was as yet no thought of founding a church; the intention was to restore the political community, or at any rate a fraction of it, a "remnant", which was to provide a nucleus for the Messianic Empire that was shortly to be expected' (ibid., p. 192).

[3] For Zerubbabel's enterprise and its failure see ibid., vol. iii (Stuttgart 1901, Cotta), pp. 194–6; eundem: *Der Papyrusfund von Elephantine*, 2nd ed. (Leipzig 1912, Hinrichs), p. 68; Gall, A. von: Βασιλεία τοῦ Θεοῦ (Heidelberg 1926, Winter), pp. 188–97.

[4] For the family likeness, displayed in a similarity of constitutional structure, between the Roman Commonwealth and the Seleucid Monarchy see IV. C (iii) (c) 2 (β), vol. iv, pp. 311–13, above.

the Jews for a triumph of the arms of the Maccabees;[1] and a majority of the Palestinian Jewish community[2] were so heedlessly carried away by this mirage of mundane success that they were willing—as 'Deutero-Isaiah' had been willing four hundred years earlier[3]—to throw overboard the now long-consecrated tradition that the founder of a new Jewish state must be a son of David, and to cry 'Hosanna' to a son of Hasmon instead, just because at the moment the Maccabee might appear to have accomplished what should have been a Davidic Messiah's appointed mundane task.[4] Nor were the Jews cured of their crudely futuristic hope of a new mundane Jewish commonwealth when in due course the Hellenic political ascendancy, from which Palestine had temporarily been released when the Romans had hamstrung the Seleucid Monarchy,[5] was reimposed in the more formidable shape of a dominion exercised *in partibus Syriacis* by Rome herself.

It was, of course, inevitable that Rome should eventually fill a vacuum which Rome herself had created. However unwillingly, she was bound to step into her Seleucid victims' shoes; and, considering that the Jews had been no match for their old Seleucid masters until the Romans had deliberately tilted the scales in the Jewish insurgents' favour, it was evident that a Jewish community whose political fortunes Rome had made by one touch of her little finger would find their new Roman masters irresistible when once Pompey had decided to remove the Hasmonaean pawn from the Palestinian square of Rome's oecumenical chess-board. If the

[1] Tacitus's biting censure of this Jewish error of political judgement has been quoted already in V. C (i) (*d*) 1, vol. v, p. 390, footnote 3, above. In a different context the unhappy outcome of the Maccabees' divagation into politics has been discussed in V. C (i) (*d*) 6 (δ), Annex, vol. v, pp. 657–9, above.

[2] It was to the credit of the Pharisees that they did not let themselves drift with the tide of popular feeling, but parted company with the Maccabees just when, and just because, the Maccabees put their treasure in the establishment of an earthly kingdom.

[3] 'Deutero-Isaiah'—the sixth-century writer of a politico-religious work which has been appended to the genuine text of the real Isaiah and now figures there as chaps. xl–lv—hails Cyrus, the founder of the Achaemenian Empire, as the Lord's Anointed (Isa. xlv. 1), in the wild hope that the Persian conqueror may be moved to bestow his world-empire upon the Jews!

[4] For the new era which Simon Maccabaeus inaugurated in 142 B.C. to commemorate the establishment of his new Jewish state, see V. C (i) (*d*) 9 (β), Annex, in the present volume, p. 344, footnote 3, below. So far from being able to claim descent from David, the Hasmonaeans were not even members of the Tribe of Judah. As priests they traced their origin back, not to Judah, but to Levi. Davidic Messianism came into its own again after the 'mediatization' of the Hasmonaean principality by Pompey in 63 B.C. (Lagrange, M.-J.: *Le Messianisme chez les Juifs* (Paris 1909, Gabalda), p. 10).

[5] In the year 162 B.C. the Seleucids' stud of war-elephants at Apamea was literally hamstrung, in execution of instructions from the Senate at Rome, by the orders of Roman commissioners who were visiting the military head-quarters of the Seleucid Empire on a tour of precautionary inspection (see V. C (i) (*c*) 3, vol. v, p. 215, footnote 3, above). This barbarity cost the chairman of the commissioners, Gnaeus Octavius, his life, since it was one of the outrages that moved Leptines to assassinate him (for the hamstringing of the elephants see Appian: *Studies in Roman History*, 'Rome and Syria', chap. 46; for the assassination of Octavius see the present Study, V. C (ii) (*a*), in the present volume, p. 219, footnote 1, below).

Jews had been unable to shake off by their own unaided efforts the yoke of a Seleucid Monarchy which had been only one, and that by no means the strongest one, of five contemporary Great Powers in the Hellenic arena, how could the Jews hope to measure themselves against a Rome who in the meantime had swept away not only the Seleucid Monarchy but every other rival Power in the Hellenic World and had thereby transformed her own sole surviving empire into a state that was universal and omnipotent? The answer to these questions was as clear as day to the Idumaean dictator Herod. He never forgot that he was ruler of Palestine solely by the grace of Rome and of Augustus; and so long as he reigned over the Palestinian Jews he contrived to save them from the nemesis of their own folly.[1] Yet, instead of being grateful to Herod for teaching them so salutary a political lesson, his Jewish subjects would not forgive him for being right;[2] and as soon as his masterly—and masterful—hand was removed they took the bit between their teeth and bolted down their futuristic path till they crashed into the inevitable catastrophe.[3] Nor, even then, did a single physical demonstration of Rome's omnipotence suffice. The experience of A.D. 66–70 was not enough to cure the Jews of Futurism. The Diasporà had to repeat the appalling experiment in A.D. 115–17, and the Palestinian Jewry to make yet another trial of it in A.D. 132–5,[4] before the hope of a new mundane Jewish commonwealth was finally extinguished.[5] Bar Kōkabā in A.D. 132–5 was pursuing the same end by the same means as Zerubbabel about the year 522 B.C.[6] It had taken the Jews more than six and a half centuries to learn by an agonizing process of trial and error that Futurism simply would not work.[7]

If this were the whole Jewish story it would not be an interesting

---

[1] So long as Herod the Great was on the throne the Messianic movement in Jewry was tentative and undecided (Lagrange, op. cit., p. 12).

[2] Messianism began to raise its head after Herod had turned against Religion in 25 B.C. The first Messianic conspiracy—in which the wife of Herod's brother Pheroras played a leading part—was hatched *circa* 7–6 B.C. (ibid., pp. 13 and 16).

[3] The first serious Messianic crisis was precipitated by Herod the Great's death in 4 B.C. Messianic insurrections became frequent after the death of Herod Agrippa I in A.D. 44 (ibid., pp. 17 and 21–2).

[4] For these Jewish insurrections against the Roman Imperial Government see the authorities cited in V. C (i) (c) 2, vol. v, p. 68, footnote 3, above.

[5] The word 'finally' holds good, notwithstanding the recent rise of Zionism; for Zionism is a mimesis of the contemporary Nationalism of the Western World and is not a revival of the Jewish Futurism which was extinguished at last in the blood of the followers of Bar Kōkabā.

[6] Bar Kōkabā's coinage seems to show that he set up a regular Jewish state (see ibid., pp. 317–18).

[7] The impracticability of Futurism is reflected in the spirit of the Apocalyptic genre of literature in which it found expression. 'C'est un recul très caractérisé du sentiment religieux tel qu'on le trouve dans les grands prophètes et les psalmistes — recul mal dissimulé par un élan disproportionné vers l'inaccessible et l'insondable. . . . L'apocalypse, tournée toute entière vers l'avenir, se préoccupe surtout des révolutions attendues. . . . Les maîtres, moins attentifs aux circonstances de l'intervention divine, sont dominés par les idées absolues qui doivent être la règle de la vie.'—Ibid., pp. 135 and 147.

one, for it would be nothing but a monotonously repetitive record
of the inevitable and well-deserved misfortunes of a stiff-necked
people that was its own worst enemy. But this obstinate pursuit
of Futurism is, of course, only half the story—and the less important half at that. The whole story is that, while some Jewish souls
went on clinging to a mundane hope in the teeth of a succession
of disillusionments, other Jewish souls—and even some of the
same souls in a different mood or through a different spiritual
faculty—were gradually taught by the repeated failure of this
earthly quest to put their treasure elsewhere. In the process of
discovering the bankruptcy of Futurism the Jews made the further
tremendous discovery of the existence of the Kingdom of God;
and century by century these two progressive revelations—one
negative but the other positive—were being unfolded simultaneously. The expected founder of the new mundane Jewish commonwealth was conceived of, appropriately enough, as a king of
human flesh and blood who would not miraculously live for ever
but would prosaically found a hereditary dynasty.[1] Yet the title
under which this future Jewish empire-builder was predicted—
and under which every successive pretender to the role was
acclaimed, from Zerubbabel through Simon Maccabaeus down to
Simon bar Kōkabā[2]—was not *melek*, which in the Hebrew vocabulary was the simple word for 'king' with no special connotations:
the word that became current and consecrated in this special
futurist sense was *meshiḥa*,[3] meaning 'the Anointed', and this was
an abbreviation for 'the Anointed of the Lord'. Thus, even if
only in the background, the god of the Jews was associated with
the hope of the Jews from the beginning; and as the mundane
hope inexorably faded away the divine figure loomed ever larger
until, in the end, it dominated the whole horizon.

To call a god in aid is not, of course, in itself an unusual procedure. It is probably as old a practice as Religion itself for a
person or people that is embarking on some formidable enterprise
to invoke the protection of their traditional tutelary divinity; and
it would have been strange if the Syrian slaves had not called upon
the name of the Dea Syra, Atargatis,[4] when they rose in revolt
against their Greek masters and Roman rulers in Sicily, or if the

---

[1] On this point see Gall, A. von: Βασιλεία τοῦ Θεοῦ (Heidelberg 1926, Winter),
pp. 256–7.
[2] For the recognition of Simon (or Symeon) bar Kōkabā as the Messiah by Rabbi
Aqiba see ibid., p. 395, and Lagrange, op. cit., p. 316.
[3] According to von Gall, op. cit., p. 173, footnote 1, the title which in Greek is translated Χριστός and transliterated Μεσσίας is the Aramaic equivalent *meshiḥa* of an original
Hebrew *meshiah*.
[4] See V. C (i) (c) 2, vol. v, p. 130, footnote 5, and V. C (i) (d) 7, in the present volume,
p. 34, footnote 5, above, and V. C (ii) (a), Annex II, in the present volume, p. 383,
below.

Jews had not called upon the name of Yahweh when they ventured to measure their strength against the might of a Darius or an Antiochus or a Nero or a Trajan or a Hadrian. The new departure lay not in the claim—expressed in the title 'Messiah'—that the people's human champion had the sanction of a god behind him;[1] what was new, and also momentous, was the conception of the patron divinity's nature and function and power; for, while Yahweh did not cease to be thought of as the parochial god of Jewry in a certain sense, it was in another and wider aspect than this that he was pictured as the divine protector of 'the Lord's Anointed'.

This widening of the conception of the protecting divinity was indeed imperatively demanded by the mundane situation of the day; for the Jewish futurists *post* 586 B.C. were, after all, engaged upon no ordinary political enterprise. They had set their hands to a task which was, humanly speaking, an impossible one; for, when they had failed to preserve their independence, how could they rationally hope to reconquer it—and, what is more, to supplant their own conquerors in the lordship of the World—by the strength of their own right arm? To succeed in this tremendous undertaking they must have behind them a god who was not only competent to see fair play but was also capable of redressing a balance that, on any human reckoning, was hopelessly inclined against this god's terrestrial protégés. If the protégés were engaged on a forlorn hope, then the protector must be nothing less than omnipotent—and it would follow from this that he must also be actively and whole-heartedly righteous; for only an all-powerful godhead who cared for righteousness above everything else would be both able and willing to exert himself with effect on behalf of a people whose cause was just but whose worldly position was insignificant.

'For he that is mighty hath done to me great things, and holy is his name. . . .

'He hath showed strength with his arm; he hath scattered the proud in the imagination of their hearts.

'He hath put down the mighty from their seats and exalted them of low degree.'[2]

This, and nothing less than this, must be the power and the performance of the divinity who stood behind the devoted human leader of a futurist forlorn hope; and it was not only the Jewish

---

[1] For a survey of other instances in which a mundane power that has come to feel itself unequal to its task has called a god in aid and has placed itself under this divine patron's aegis, see V. C (i) (*d*) 6 (δ), Annex, vol. v, pp. 649–57, above.
[2] Luke i. 49 and 51–2.

futurists that were forcibly led by their experience in the realm of politics to this conclusion in the realm of theology. The Yahweh who revealed himself behind the Jewish Messiah had his counterparts in the Ahuramazda who was the god behind the Zoroastrian Saošyant (Saviour)[1] and in the Helios who was the god of Aristonicus's Heliopolitae.[2] In the same hard school of Futurism three separate contingents of proletarians made—each independently, under as many different names and aspects[3]—the same sublime discovery of the One True God.[4]

When once this discovery has been made, a drama which, up to this point, has been played on a terrestrial stage by human actors with mundane aims acquires a new protagonist and at the same time is transposed into a higher spiritual dimension. The human champion who has been the hero hitherto—in virtue of being cast for the part of leading his brethren out of a mundane Wilderness into a mundane Promised Land—now sinks to a subordinate role, while the divinity who has originally been called in aid merely in order to give supernatural power to the human elbow of 'the Lord's Anointed' now comes to dominate the scene. God comes to be recognized as the sole but sufficient saviour of a people that has learnt by bitter experience that its human champion is after all impotent, under any auspices, to save it in its dire extremity. The human champion himself cannot be made equal to what has now proved to be a superhuman task by the expedient of consecrating him with a divine unction. A human Messiah is not enough. God himself must condescend to play the part, which He alone can effectively play, of serving His people as their saviour and their king.[5]

---

[1] See V. C (i) (d) 11, p. 163, footnote 1, below.

[2] For the Heliopolitae see IV. C (iii) (c) 3 (β), vol. iv, p. 507; V. C (i) (c) 2, vol. v, pp. 69–70 and 179–82; V. C (i) (d) 1, vol. v, p. 384; and V. C (i) (d) 6 (δ), Annex, vol. v, p. 692, footnote 2, above, and V. C (i) (d) 11, Annex I, in the present volume, p. 351, below.

[3] For the contrast between the two different aspects of the One True God which were apprehended respectively in the Jewish conception of Yahweh and in the Zoroastrian conception of Ahuramazda see V. C (i) (d) 7, pp. 43–4, above.

[4] This discovery has already been dealt with—as an aspect of the sense of unity—in V. C (i) (d) 7, pp. 37–49, above. In other contexts (e.g. in V. C (i) (c) 2, vol. v, p. 82, footnote 4, and in V. C (i) (d) 6 (δ), Annex, vol. v, pp. 649–57, above) it is pointed out that the rulers of universal states are apt (under pressure of the same political necessity that drives the leaders of proletarian futurist émeutes) to fall back upon the sanction of a tutelary deity to make good the failure of their own personal prestige.

[5] The emergence of the conception of Yahweh as king in the course of the development of the religion of Post-Exilic Jewry is traced in detail by Freiherr A. von Gall in Βασιλεία τοῦ Θεοῦ (Heidelberg 1926, Winter). 'The hope of a Messiah—i.e. the hope for the reappearance of a king of David's line—can, of course, be only of purely Jewish Post-Exilic origin. The impulse from which this hope started was given by the short-lived kingdom of Zerubbabel. But as far as the majority of the Jews were concerned it seems—so far as we can judge from the surviving literature—that the national form of Messianic hope was still rejected even then. For pious Jews in the mass, Yahweh was and remained the king of the expected new kingdom. This yearning for the kingship of Yahweh himself was stronger than the yearning for the kingship of Yahweh's Anointed'

By this time any modern Western psycho-analyst who is reading these lines and knows his duty will be raising his eyebrows. 'What you have proclaimed as a sublime spiritual discovery turns out,' he will interject, 'now that you have explained what you mean, to be nothing but a surrender to that infantile desire to escape from reality which is one of the besetting temptations of the human psyche. You have described how some unhappy people who have foolishly set their hearts on an unattainable aim attempt to shift the intolerable burden of being saddled with an impossible task from their own shoulders to those of a series of intended substitutes. Their first conscript is a purely human champion; then, when he cannot avail, they exchange him for a human champion whose humanity is reinforced by an imaginary divine backing; and finally, when even "the Lord's Anointed" breaks down, the fools in desperation signal S.O.S. to a wholly fictitious divine being whose alleged omnipotence is expected to make up for the proven impotence of his human inventors. For the psychological practitioner this rake's progress in escapism is as familiar a story as it is a melancholy one.'

In taking account of this criticism we shall readily agree with the psycho-analyst's strictures upon the childishness of calling on a supernatural power to perform a mundane task which we have first wilfully chosen for ourselves and have then discovered to be beyond our own strength. We shall also find, on consideration, that many of the futurists whom we have had under observation have in fact fallen into this spiritual error and have duly paid the material penalty which our psychological practitioner would no doubt have predicted. In the Jewish case in point there were certain schools of Jewish futurists who did persuade themselves that Yahweh would take upon himself his worshippers' self-appointed mundane tasks and would miraculously make up for

(ibid., p. 250). In von Gall's belief the title of king—which was already applied to Yahweh before the destruction of the mundane kingdom of Judah in 586 B.C.—was originally a mere cult title which he bore (in accordance with a Canaanite practice that was pre-Israelite and non-Israelite) in his capacity of city-god of the *ci-devant* Jebusite city of Zion (ibid., pp. 41–2). According to von Gall it was this originally perhaps no more than formal title that suggested the later idea of conceiving of Yahweh as king in a more significant sense. Von Gall follows the growth of the idea in 'Deutero-Isaiah' [i.e. Isa. xl–lv] (pp. 178–88) and in the Books of the Law (pp. 199–208). He seeks to demonstrate that in the Achaemenian Age this hitherto purely native Jewish notion of Yahweh's kingship came to be informed and enriched by the Zoroastrian notion of a Last Judgement that was to be conducted by Ahuramazda (pp. 219–45). And he shows how the conception of Yahweh the god-king of Zion eventually enlarged itself in Jewish minds from the idea of a parochial tutelary divinity of a Palestinian highland fastness into that of a universal and omnipotent godhead who was king of the whole World and of all Mankind, and who would one day exercise, from his seat in Zion, the royal prerogative of oecumenical dominion that was already his by right. This direct reign of Yahweh from Zion was to be inaugurated by a general judgement in which Gentiles as well as Jews would be summoned to present themselves in Zion before the universal god-king-judge's judgement-seat (ibid., pp. 235–6).

their natural disappointments; and these Jewish futurists did, as we have seen, all come to a bad end. There was the melodramatic suicide of the Zealots who faced hopeless military odds[1] in the fanatical faith that the Lord of Hosts would be a host in himself on the side of his self-constituted human instruments; and there has been the prosaic self-stultification of the Quietists who have argued from the same erroneous premisses[2] to the exactly opposite —but in the end not less hopeless—practice of abstaining from taking any action of their own in a mundane cause which they have decided to register as God's affair.[3] At the same time, however, we shall remember that the fanaticism of the Zealots and the Quietism of the *Agudath Israel* are not the only responses to the challenge from the Hellenic dominant minority that were made by the Jewish contingent of the Hellenic internal proletariat. There was the response of the school of the Rabbi Johanan ben Zakkai[4] and there was the response of the Christian Church;[5] and, while these two other responses both resemble Quietism in the negative feature of being non-violent, they differ from Quietism and Zealotism alike in the far more important positive point that they have ceased to set their heart upon the old mundane purpose of Futurism and have put their treasure, instead, in a purpose which is not Man's but God's and which therefore can only be pursued in a spiritual field of supra-mundane dimensions.

This point is of capital importance because it disposes, in these cases, of the criticism which our psycho-analyst can direct against both the Zealots and the Quietists with such deadly effect. To call in God cannot be denounced as an infantile attempt to escape from the hard necessity of facing the defeat of a human endeavour if, in the act of invocation, the human actor simultaneously withdraws his *libido* from his previous mundane aim. And conversely, if the act of invocation does produce so great and so good a spiritual effect as this in the human soul that performs it, that would appear *prima facie* to give ground for a belief that the power which has been invoked is not a mere figment of the human imagination. At any rate, the onus of proof may now reasonably be laid upon

---

[1] See V. C (i) (c) 2, vol. v, p. 68, above.

[2] The Quietists hold in common with the Zealots the erroneous idea that God will have made it His own business to fulfil a purpose which His worshippers have chosen for themselves and which is therefore intrinsically mundane. On the other hand they charge the Zealots with impiety (and in this they are surely right) for supposing that, for the accomplishment of a purpose which *ex hypothesi* God has indeed made His own to the best of His worshippers' belief, God can have any need of help from human volunteers. If we accept, for the sake of the argument, the premiss from which both the Quietists and the Zealots start, we must find in the Quietists' favour.

[3] For this attitude, which is illustrated by the present aloofness of the *Agudath Israel* from Zionism, see V. C (i) (c) 2, vol. v, p. 76, and V. C (i) (c) 2, Annex III, vol. v, p. 588, above.   [4] See V. C (i) (c) 2, vol. v, pp. 75–6, above.

[5] See V. C (i) (c) 2, vol. v, pp. 72–4, above.

the sceptic; and, pending his reply, we may allow ourselves to hold that our description of this spiritual reorientation as a discovery of the One True God was after all correct. A human make-believe about the future of This World has given place to a divine revelation of the existence of an Other World. Through the disappoint-ment of a mundane hope we have been admitted to an apocalypse or discovery of a reality which has been there all the time behind the scenes of the narrow man-made stage that has hitherto set the limits of our field of vision and of action.[1] The veil of the Temple has been rent in twain.

It remains for us to take note of some of the principal stages in the accomplishment of this immense feat of spiritual reorientation.

The social circumstances in which Man gains his first inkling that God's purpose is other than, and better than, Man's own, are vividly depicted in the following analysis of the religious experi-ence of the peoples of the Syriac and Babylonic worlds under the Achaemenian régime:

'The complete state of blessedness, on which human hopes are set, is [evidently] not granted by the Divinity to his worshippers in this present time; if it were, the faithful would be bound to triumph over all their adversaries and to see the supremacy of their god acknowledged by all other nations. This means that the full power of the Divinity is not destined to manifest itself until some future date; at the present moment the Divinity is still engaged in a struggle. The process of shap-ing the World is not yet at an end; the ideal state of things has not yet been attained; the adversaries have not yet been annihilated. It is quite natural that such eschatological hopes should assume the most lively shape among nations, and in religions, which are being subjected to some particularly severe pressure—such hopes were developed by the Prophets of Judah from as early a date as Isaiah's. But they were not alone in this; for Zarathustra's teaching likewise conceives of life as a struggle between two great powers—a struggle which is to close with the victory of Ahuramazda.[2] The struggle is pictured on the lines of the Gods' great struggles at the creation of the World—a creation that has not reached its complete conclusion—and so Eschatology becomes a repetition and transformation of the creation-myths.[3] This is the

[1] The quest that originally led us into this Study was the hope of seeing through the 'shimmer of relativity in the foreground of historical thought' (Part I. A, vol. i, p. 16, above). We have already observed that the ordeal of social disintegration may awaken a sense of unity (V. C (i) (d) 7, in the present volume, pp. 1–49, above). And we have noted how the two successive blows of the Crucifixion and the Ascension evoked the Acts of the Apostles (II. D (iv), vol. ii, pp. 111–12, above).

[2] According to the same scholar (Meyer, E.: *Ursprung und Anfänge des Christentums,* vol. ii (Stuttgart and Berlin 1921, Cotta), p. 113), Zoroastrian influences played their part in the translation of the Jewish conception of the Last Judgement from political into ethical terms.—A.J.T.

[3] Compare von Gall, op. cit., p. 236: 'The Kingdom of God, which manifests itself at the end of all things, also existed at the beginning of all things' (citing Deut. xxxiii. 5, and Ps. lxxiv. 12). Compare, further, Spengler, O.: *Der Untergang des Abendlandes,* vol. i (Munich 1920, Beck), p. 614, apropos of the *Weltanschauung* of the Western

point in which the Babylonic Mythology has exercised its greatest influence. It has become the basis of a general conception which has found its way into religions of the most diverse kinds.'[1]

The essence of this conception is that a mundane scene which was once looked upon as a stage for human actors (either with or without superhuman backers) is now regarded as a field for the progressive realization of the Kingdom of God. At first, however, this new idea of the transfiguration of one world by the spiritual irruption of another world of a higher spiritual dimension largely clothes itself, as is to be expected, in imagery that is derived from the old futurist idea of a mundane kingdom which is distinguished from the present state of mundane affairs simply by its position in the Time-stream and by its standard of mundane well-being, and not by any intrinsic difference of spiritual quality. Against this mental background 'Deutero-Isaiah' draws the lineaments of a Kingdom of God[2] which transcends, while including, the idea of a mundane kingdom,[3] but transcends it merely in the point that both Man and Nature are depicted as experiencing a supernatural and miraculous beatification, and not in the deeper sense of exceeding the familiar mundane dimensions of spiritual experience. 'Deutero-Isaiah's' Kingdom of God is really nothing but a new Earthly Paradise—a Garden of Eden adapted to the requirements of a human society which is still mundane though it is no longer primitive—and a distinct advance in spiritual insight is achieved when this new Earthly Paradise comes to be thought of as only a transitory state[4] which may last, perhaps, for a Millennium but which is destined, at the end of its allotted term, to pass away with the passing of This World itself.

This World must pass in order to give place to an Other World beyond it; and it is in that Other World that the true Kingdom of God is now seen to lie; for the king who is to reign during the

---

Civilization: 'To-day, in the sunset of the Scientific Age, at the stage when Scepticism is winning the day, the clouds part, and the morning landscape stands out once more with unmistakable clarity.'—A.J.T.

1 Meyer, E.: *Geschichte des Altertums*, vol. iii (Stuttgart 1901, Cotta), pp. 173–4.

2 See von Gall, op. cit., pp. 181–3.

3 The mundane kingdom which is included in 'Deutero-Isaiah's' Kingdom of God is imagined (see the present chapter, p. 122, footnote 3, above) as an Achaemenian Empire in which Cyrus has taken Zion instead of Susa for his capital and the Jews instead of the Persians for his ruling race, because the God of Israel has revealed to him that it is He (and, by implication, not Ahuramazda) who has enabled Cyrus to conquer the World (Isa. xlv. 1–6). In this day-dream 'Deutero-Isaiah' is exposing himself, with a vengeance, to the censure of our imaginary psycho-analyst. He is conscripting Yahweh to inspire Cyrus to turn the feats of Persian arms to the benefit of the Jews in order that the latter may be compensated for their inability to preserve the independence of their own petty principality of Judah by being invested with the lordship of a universal state! Jewry's thirst to gain a new mundane kingdom was so deep that the Jewish prophet was prepared to recognize the Gentile as 'the Lord's Anointed' (Isa. xlv. 1) if that would secure the fulfilment of these Jewish hopes.

4 See von Gall, op. cit., index, s.v. *Zwischenreich*.

Millennium on a glorified Earth is not yet God himself but is merely a Messiah who is God's terrestrial deputy. 'The Lord's Anointed' is, indeed, now portrayed as a supernatural figure, and is no longer thought of as an historical human potentate—a Cyrus or a Zerubbabel or a Simon Maccabaeus or a Simon bar Kōkabā —who is singular only in having God's authority behind him. This supernatural Messiah is all of a piece with a world that has been reconverted into an Earthly Paradise for the last Millennium of its existence. But it is manifest that the construction of a miraculous Millennium in This World, pending the replacement of This World by another, is an untenable attempt at a compromise between two ideas which are not only quite distinct but are also in the last resort mutually incompatible. The first of these ideas is the hope of a mundane kingdom which in no way differs from the present in its spiritual quality and is merely projected into the future in order to give scope for make-believe. The second idea is that of a Kingdom of God which is not in Time at all—either present, future, or past—and which differs from all temporal mundane states in the radical way of being in a different spiritual dimension, but which, just by virtue of this difference of dimension, is able to penetrate our mundane life and, in penetrating, to transfigure it.[1] For making the arduous spiritual ascent to the vision of Transfiguration from the mirage of Futurism the eschatological scheme of a Millennium may be a convenient mental ladder; but when once the height has been scaled the ladder can be allowed to fall away; and therewith the mundane Futurism which has evoked a vision of the Other World in response to the challenge of its own unescapable bankruptcy will at last have been completely transcended.

'The Pharisaic pietist had already learnt under the Hasmonaeans to turn away from This World to Heaven, to the future; and now, under Herod, all the current of national feeling which had been set running during the last generations in such strength beat against a blind wall, and itself found no outlet save through the channels opened by the Pharisee. It was among the people bent down beneath that iron necessity that the transcendental beliefs, the Messianic hopes, nurtured in the Pharisaic schools, spread and propagated themselves with a new vitality. The few books of Pharisaic piety which have come down to us—*Enoch*, the *Psalms of Solomon*, the *Assumption of Moses* and others—show us indeed what ideas occupied the minds of writers, but they could not

[1] Physical similes for spiritual truths are bound to be imperfect and are not unlikely to be misleading; but, in terms of our modern Western Physical Science, the spiritual action of the Other World on This World might perhaps be likened to the play of Radiation upon Matter or to the sweep of a comet's tail through a cluster of planets. This simile of Radiation has been employed already in V. C (i) (*d*) 1, vol. v, pp. 396–7, above. For some alternative similes see V. C (i) (*d*) 11, in the present volume, pp. 157–61, below.

have shown us what we learn from our Gospels: how ideas of this order
had permeated the people through and through; how the figure of the
Coming King, "the Anointed One", the "Son of David", how definite
conceptions of the Resurrection, of the Other World, were part of the
ordinary mental furniture of that common people which hung upon the
words of the Lord. . . . But . . . the Christ whom the Christian worshipped was not the embodiment of any single one of those forms which
had risen upon prophetic thought; in Him all the hopes and ideals of
the past met and blended; the heavenly Son of Man and the earthly
Son of David, the Suffering Servant of the Hebrew Prophet and the
Slain God of the Greek Mystic, the Wisdom of the Hebrew sage and
the Logos of the Greek philosopher, all met in Him; but He was more
than all.'[1]

10. *Detachment*

Our inquiries into the nature and working of Futurism and
Archaism have now led us to the conclusion that neither of these
two ways of life is permanently *viable* and that the failure of both
of them is accounted for by the same fatal error. They are both
doomed to fail because both are attempts to perform the impossible
acrobatic feat of escaping from the Present without rising above
the spiritual plane of mundane life on Earth.[2] The difference
between them is a superficial difference of direction; and a flying
leap out of the Present which aims at alighting in another reach
of the Time-stream is bound to land disastrously on the rocks just
the same whether the leaping fish's unattainable goal happens to
lie up stream or down it. Archaism, as we have seen, defeats itself
by veering round disconcertingly in mid air and recoiling like a
boomerang along a futurist course which runs exactly counter to
its aim, while Futurism transcends itself—in the act of coming
disastrously to grief—by rending the veil of mundane appearances
and bringing into view, beyond them, an Other World of a higher
spiritual dimension. The way of life in this Other World is thus
revealed to human souls on Earth through a recognition of the
bankruptcy of one of the two alternative ways of seeking a change
of life without leaving the mundane level; the mystery of Transfiguration is apprehended in a reaction against the fallacy of
Futurism. But the bankruptcy of Archaism—which the archaist,
in his pursuit of his own fruitless quest, is equally bound to recognize sooner or later—may also bear fruit in a spiritual discovery.
The recognition of the truth that Archaism is not enough is a
challenge to which the baffled archaist must respond by taking

---

[1] Bevan, E.: *Jerusalem under the High Priests* (London 1904, Arnold), pp. 158 and 162.
[2] See V. C (i) (*d*) 1, vol. v, pp. 383–5; V. C (i) (*d*) 9 (α), in the present volume,
pp. 97–8; and V. C (i) (*d*) 9 (γ), pp. 118–19, above.

some new spiritual departure, unless he is prepared to resign himself to an irretrievable spiritual defeat; and his line of least resistance is to convert a flying leap that is heading for disaster into a
flight that will evade the problem of landing by taking permanent
leave of the ground. An experience of the impracticability of
Archaism inspires a philosophy of Detachment; and we shall do
well to examine this simpler way of rising above the mundane
level[1]—a way which is the archaist's last resort when he finds
himself at bay—before we venture to peer into the mystery of
Transfiguration.

The experience of life which leads to the conclusion that the
only way of life which solves the problem of life is to detach oneself from life has been sketched with an elegant irony in the
following imaginary dialogue from the pen of a Hellenic man-of-
letters who lived in the Age of the Antonines without mistaking an
'Indian Summer'[2] for a return of spring.

Charon: 'I will tell you, Hermes, what Mankind and human life
remind me of. You must, before now, have watched the bubbles rising
in the water under the play of a fountain—the froth, I mean, that makes
the foam. Well, some of those bubbles are tiny, and these burst at once
and vanish, while there are others that last longer and attract their
neighbours till they swell to a portentous bulk—only to burst without
fail sooner or later in their turn, as every bubble must. Such is human
life. The creatures are all inflated—some to a greater and others to a
lesser degree—and there are some whose inflation lasts as long as the
twinkling of an eye, while others cease to be at the moment of coming
into being; but all of them have to burst sooner or later.'

Hermes: 'Your simile is as apt as Homer's simile of the leaves.'[3]

Charon: 'Yet, ephemeral though these human beings are, you see,
Hermes, how they exert themselves and compete with one another in
their struggles for office and honours and possessions—though one day
they will have to leave all that behind and come to our place with nothing
but one copper in their pockets. Now what do you think? Here we are
on an exceeding high mountain. Shan't I shout to them at the top of
my voice and warn them to abstain from useless exertions and to live
their lives with Death constantly in mind? I will say to them: "You
silly fellows, why are you so keen on all that? You had better stop putting yourselves through it. You are not going to live for ever. None of
these earthly prizes is everlasting; and nobody, at death, can carry away
any of them with him. One day, as sure as fate, the owner will be gone
—as naked as he came—and his house and estate and money will pass
for ever after to a constant succession of alien possessors."' Supposing I

---

[1] This philosophy of Withdrawal-without-Return has been touched upon already, by
anticipation, in III. C (ii) (*b*), vol. iii, pp. 254–5, above.

[2] For this diagnosis of the so-called 'Golden Age' of Hellenic history under the
régime of the Antonines see IV. C (ii) (*b*) 1, vol. iv, pp. 58–61, above.

[3] Quoted in this Study in III. C (ii) (*b*), vol. iii, p. 257, above.—A.J.T.

were to shout this at them, or something like it, and could make myself
heard, don't you think they might stand to benefit enormously and might
also become vastly more sensible than they now appear to be?'

Hermes: 'I am afraid, Charon, you are suffering under an amiable
delusion. I don't think you realize the condition to which they have
been reduced by their ignorance and self-deception. Even with a gimlet
you couldn't now open their ears—they have plugged them and plugged
them with wax (as Odysseus treated his companions for fear that they
might hear the Sirens singing). They wouldn't be able to hear you,
even if you screamed till you burst. In the world of men Ignorance
produces the same effect as Lethe in your Hades. All the same, there
are a few of them who have refused to put the wax into their ears; and
these few do see life steadily, know it for what it is, and incline towards
the truth.'

Charon: 'Then shan't we shout to *them*, anyway?'

Hermes: 'Well, even that would be superfluous. You would only be
telling them what they knew already. You can see how pointedly they
have drawn away from the rest and how disdainfully they are laughing
at what is going on. Obviously they are finding no satisfaction at all in
all that, and are planning to make a "get-away" from Life and to seek
asylum with you. You know they are not exactly loved by their fellow
creatures for showing up their follies.'

Charon: 'Well played, sirs! But how terribly few there are of them,
Hermes.'

Hermes: 'Quite as many as are wanted.'[1]

Having thus brought on to our stage the exponents of the
philosophy of Detachment, we may stay to watch them performing
their spiritual exercises. We shall find, as we look on, that the
practice of Detachment rises through successive degrees from an
initiatory act of still reluctant resignation to a climax at which the
adept deliberately aims at self-annihilation.

The attitude of mere resignation is illustrated by the consensus
between an Epicurean poet and a modern Western Hellenist who
has been professor and poet in one.

> Quae mala nos subigit vitai tanta cupido?
> certa quidem finis vitae mortalibus adstat
> nec devitari letum pote quin obeamus . . .
> nec prorsum vitam ducendo demimus hilum
> tempore de mortis nec delibare valemus,
> quo minus esse diu possimus forte perempti,
> proinde licet quot vis vivendo condere saecla;
> mors aeterna tamen nilo minus illa manebit,
> nec minus ille diu iam non erit, ex hodierno
> lumine qui finem vitai fecit, et ille,
> mensibus atque annis qui multis occidit ante.[2]

[1] Lucian: *Charon*, 21.
[2] Lucretius: *De Rerum Natura*, Book III, ll. 1077-9 and 1087-94.

A lighter English echo of these massive Lucretian lines can be
heard in the following verses of Housman's:

> From far, from eve and morning
> And yon twelve-winded sky,
> The stuff of life to knit me
> Blew hither: here am I.
>
> Now—for a breath I tarry
> Nor yet disperse apart—
> Take my hand quick and tell me,
> What have you in your heart.
>
> Speak now, and I will answer;
> How shall I help you, say;
> Ere to the wind's twelve quarters
> I take my endless way.[1]

The effort of making this act of resignation to Death may be
eased by the reflection that Death automatically draws his own
sting, since he cannot extinguish life without also extinguishing
consciousness, pain, and desire.

> Nil igitur mors est ad nos neque pertinet hilum,
> quandoquidem natura animi mortalis habetur;
> et, velut anteacto nil tempore sensimus aegri,
> ad confligendum venientibus undique Poenis
> omnia cum belli trepido concussa tumultu
> horrida contremuere sub altis aetheris oris,
> in dubioque fuere utrorum ad regna cadendum
> omnibus humanis esset terraque marique,
> sic, ubi non erimus—cum corporis atque animai
> discidium fuerit quibus e sumus uniter apti—
> scilicet haud nobis quicquam (qui non erimus tum)
> accidere omnino poterit sensumque movere,
> non si terra mari miscebitur et mare caelo.[2]

Here again there are English echoes playing round the Latin
theme.

> Men loved unkindness then, but lightless in the quarry
> I slept and saw not; tears fell down, I did not mourn;
> Sweat ran and blood sprang out and I was never sorry:
> Then it was well with me, in days ere I was born.[3]

And since this peace-before-birth is a mirror of the peace-
after-death from which it is barely separated in time by the brief

---

[1] Housman, A. E.: *A Shropshire Lad*, xxxii.
[2] Lucretius: *De Rerum Natura*, Book III, ll. 830–42.
[3] Housman, A. E.: *A Shropshire Lad*, xlviii.

convulsion of life, the living Englishman may keep up his courage
by thinking of the dead Roman.

> The gale, it plies the saplings double,
> It blows so hard, 'twill soon be gone:
> To-day the Roman and his trouble
> Are ashes under Uricon.[1]

It is the same consolation that is offered by a Stoic philosopher
in less harsh language:

'He sounds the retreat, throws open the door, and calls to you
"Come". Come whither? Why, to nowhere very dreadful, but only to
where you came from. Come to something that is familiar and akin.
Come to the elements: fire to fire, earth to earth, breath to breath,
moisture to moisture.'[2]

Death automatically brings oblivion; and anyway the enjoyment
of life has limits which are inexorable because they are inherent
in the nature of life itself. Life is a movement which has its own
proper curve and span. Its secret lies in a succession; and therefore time unduly drawn out can bring nothing but satiety and
boredom.

'When you have come to the end of the time that has been allowed
you for watching the procession and taking part in the festivities, will
you make a fuss', asks our Stoic philosopher, 'on getting the signal to
leave, about making your bow and saying "thank you" for the treat and
then taking your departure?'—'Yes I will, because I still want to go on
having a good time.'—'You are not the only one. But, after all, festivities can't last for ever. So you really must come away and take your
leave with at least a show of gratitude and good grace. You must make
way for others. Others have to put in an appearance as you have done
in your time, and when they present themselves they must be found
room and lodging and board. But, if the first-comers won't get out of
their light, there will be nothing left for them. Don't be greedy; don't
be insatiable; don't take up the whole world.'[3]

Time is up, and, what is more, you are not likely to enjoy
yourself if you overstay your welcome.

> Praeterea versamur ibidem atque insumus usque
> nec nova vivendo procuditur ulla voluptas.
> sed, dum abest quod avemus, id exsuperare videtur
> cetera; post aliut, cum contigit illud, avemus
> et sitis aequa tenet vitai semper hiantis. . . .
> omnia perfunctus vitai praemia marces. . . .
> nunc aliena tua tamen aetate omnia mitte,
> aequo animoque agedum humanis concede: necessest.[4]

---

[1] Housman, A. E.: *A Shropshire Lad*, xxxi.
[2] Epictetus: *Dissertationes*, Book III, chap. 13, § 14.
[3] Ibid., Book IV, chap. 1, §§ 105–6.
[4] Lucretius: *De Rerum Natura*, Book III, ll. 1080–4, 956, 961–2.

Nor does the nemesis of satiety lie in wait only for individual human beings; it overtakes whole generations.

> Nil erit ulterius quod nostris moribus addat
> posteritas: eadem facient cupientque minores.[1]

In fact,

'One generation passeth away and another generation cometh, but the Earth abideth for ever. . . . The thing that hath been, it is that which shall be, and that which is done is that which shall be done, and there is no new thing under the Sun.'[2]

These words of a Syriac sceptic whose mind had perhaps been chilled by a breath of the cold wind of Hellenic philosophy are echoed—in accents that are chillier still—in the meditations of a Roman Stoic sage:

'The rational soul ranges over the whole Cosmos and the surrounding void and explores the scheme of things. It reaches into the abyss of boundless Time and not only comprehends, but studies the significance of, the periodic new birth (τὴν περιοδικὴν παλιγγενεσίαν[3]) of the Universe. These studies bring the rational soul to a realization of the truth that there will be nothing new to be seen by those who come after us and that, by the same token, those who have gone before us have not seen anything, either, that is beyond our ken. In this sense it would be true to say that any man of forty who is endowed with moderate intelligence has seen—in the light of the uniformity of Nature—the entire Past and Future.'[4]

The purchase given by tedium for levering the Soul away from its attachment to life is so familiar a commonplace of the philosophers that an anthology of variations on the theme culled from Seneca's works alone would be almost enough to fill a volume.[5]

Nor need any one wait till he has reached the point of satiety in order to make the, after all, obvious discovery that mundane life, as it is lived by the *homme moyen sensuel*, is at best insipid.

> Lie down, lie down, young yeoman;
> The Sun moves always west;
> The road one treads to labour
> Will lead one home to rest.
> And that will be the best.[6]

---

[1] Juvenal: *Satires*, No. 1, ll. 147–8.   [2] Eccles. i. 4 and 9.

[3] For the history of this word παλιγγενεσία see V. C (i) (*b*), vol. v, p. 27, footnote 2, above.—A.J.T.

[4] Marcus Aurelius Antoninus: *Meditations*, Book XI, chap. 1 (compare Book VII, chap. 49, and the present Study, IV. C (i), vol. iv, p. 28, footnote 2, above). 'The entire past and future' (πάντα τὰ γεγονότα καὶ τὰ ἐσόμενα) sounds like a reminiscence of a Hesiodic formula (τά τ' ἐσσόμενα πρό τ' ἐόντα (*Theogony*, l. 32; cf. l. 38)). If there is really a reminiscence of Hesiod here, it illustrates the change of mood that had come over Hellenic minds between Hesiod's and Marcus's day; for Hesiod imagined that he needed the inspiration of the Muses to gain a knowledge which in Marcus's view is known to the average man of forty as a matter of course.

[5] See, for example, Seneca: *Epistulae Morales*, Ep. xxiv, § 26; Ep. lxxvii, §§ 6 and 17–20; Ep. lxxviii, § 26.   [6] Housman, A. E.: *A Shropshire Lad*, vii, *ad fin.*

That is depressing; but (since sordidness is worse than insipidity) it is not so repulsive as this:

> Tu vero dubitabis et indignabere obire?
> mortua cui vita est prope iam vivo atque videnti,
> qui somno partem maiorem conteris aevi
> et vigilans stertis nec somnia cernere cessas
> sollicitamque geris cassa formidine mentem.[1]

This drabness of the plain man's life is painful enough. Yet it is not so excruciating as that morbid restlessness of the idle rich which Lucretius depicts with deadly acumen in a passage that has been quoted near the beginning of this Study as an epitome of the state of mind of the Dominant Minority.[2]

Any one who has ever been in this state of mind, or who has even had an inkling of it at second hand through being haunted by Lucretius's lines, will be inclined to agree with Seneca that life is a synonym for punishment;[3] and he may even be persuaded to agree with Lucretius that life is a Hell on Earth:

> Atque ea nimirum quaecumque Acherunte profundo
> prodita sunt esse, in vita sunt omnia nobis. . . .
> hic Acherusia fit stultorum denique vita.[4]

Lucretius's intuition is Macbeth's experience:

> Better be with the dead,
> Whom we, to gain our peace, have sent to peace,
> Than on the torture of the mind to lie
> In restless ecstasy. Duncan is in his grave;
> After life's fitful fever he sleeps well.[5]

But Macbeth lives on to sound still deeper depths of horror.

> To-morrow and to-morrow and to-morrow
> Creeps in this petty pace from day to day
> To the last syllable of recorded time;
> And all our yesterdays have lighted fools
> The way to dusty Death. Out, out, brief candle!
> Life's but a walking shadow, a poor player
> That struts and frets his hour upon the stage

---

[1] Lucretius: *De Rerum Natura*, Book III, ll. 1045–9.
[2] Ibid., ll. 1053–70, quoted in I. C (i) (*a*), vol. i, p. 55, above. This is another Lucretian theme on which Seneca has composed variations: e.g. in *De Tranquillitate*, chap. 2, §§ 6–15 (where Lucretius, Book III, l. 1068, is quoted), and in *Ep. Mor.* iii, § 5.
[3] 'Si velis credere altius veritatem intuentibus, omnis vita supplicium est.'—Seneca: *Ad Polybium*, chap. 9, § 6.
[4] Lucretius: *De Rerum Natura*, Book III, ll. 978–9 and 1023. The intervening lines are occupied with an ingenious analysis of the genuine terrestrial equivalents of the legendary tortures of Tantalus, Tityus, and Sisyphus and the legendary horrors of Tartarus, Cerberus, and the Furies. (For a hypothesis regarding the origin of these Hellenic legends see V. C (ii) (*a*), Annex II, pp. 522–3, below.)
[5] Shakespeare: *The Tragedy of Macbeth*, Act III, Scene 2, ll. 19–23.

> And then is heard no more: it is a tale
> Told by an idiot, full of sound and fury,
> Signifying nothing.[1]

If life is as grim as that, death must be, by comparison, agreeable.

> Numquid ibi horribile apparet, num triste videtur
> quicquam, non omni somno securius exstat?[2]

Seneca justifies his equation of life with punishment[3] by comparing the experience of living with that of being adrift on a stormy sea 'from which the only haven is the harbour of death'.[4]

> Suave, mari magno turbantibus aequora ventis,
> e terra magnum alterius spectare laborem;
> non quia vexari quemquamst iucunda voluptas,
> sed quibus ipse malis careas quia cernere suave est.[5]

But, if that is sweet, it must be sweeter still to be totally insensible: to know nothing of others' feelings, besides feeling nothing oneself.

> Ay, look: high heaven and earth ail from the prime foundation;
>   All thoughts to rive the heart are here, and all are vain:
> Horror and scorn and hate and fear and indignation—
>   O why did I awake? When shall I sleep again?[6]

'When you will', replies the philosopher; for the time to take action is at hand, and there are effective ways of detaching oneself from life that can be followed if only one is in earnest to the point of willing not merely the desirable end but also the arduous means.

'Ethical prowess (ἀρετή) can and will produce felicity (εὐδαιμονίαν) and invulnerability (ἀπάθειαν) and well-being (εὔροιαν) . . . and there is one way only by which well-being can be reached: the way of Detachment (ἀπόστασις) from all morally neutral values (τῶν ἀπροαιρέτων). You must not allow yourself to have a sense of property in anything; you must surrender everything to God and to Chance . . . and must concentrate upon one thing only—the thing that is truly your own, and in which no outside power can interfere.'[7]

Spiritual exercises in the practice of Detachment fill many of these 'Leaves from a Stoic Philosopher's Note-Book' out of which

---

[1] Ibid., Act v, Scene v, ll. 19–28.
[2] Lucretius: *De Rerum Natura*, Book III, ll. 976–7.
[3] See the sentence quoted on p. 138, footnote 3, above.
[4] Seneca: *Ad Polybium*, chap. 9, § 7: 'In hoc tam procelloso et ad omnes tempestates exposito mari navigantibus nullus portus nisi mortis est.'
[5] Lucretius: *De Rerum Natura*, Book II, ll. 1–4.
[6] Housman, A. E.: *A Shropshire Lad*, xlviii; the same theme is handled with a lighter touch in li.
[7] Epictetus: *Dissertationes*, Book I, chap. 4, § 3, and Book IV, chap. 4, § 39.

the foregoing sentences have been culled.[1] But if we follow the path of Detachment far enough we shall find ourselves sooner or later turning from a Hellenic to an Indic guide; for, far though the disciples of Zeno may go, it is the disciples of Gautama that have had the courage to pursue Detachment all the way to its logical goal of self-annihilation.[2]

Detachment is, indeed, a matter of degree. One may play at it in the game of a sophisticated 'return to Nature' that was played by a Marie Antoinette in her Parisian dairy and by a Theocritus in his Coan harvest-field.[3] One may carry this game to the length of a pose,[4] as it was carried by a Diogenes in his tub and by a Thoreau in his wigwam.[5] One may genuinely stake one's life— as an anchorite in the desert or as a yogi in the jungle—upon the efficacy of this would-be solution of the problem which life presents. But a traveller along the path of Detachment who is to reach the goal and win the reward must do more than stake his life on the quest; he must detach himself from life to the point of being in love with nothing but its negation.[6]

To do this, of course, means flying in the face of human nature, and even a willing spirit may be tempted to humour the weakness of the flesh by accepting the assistance of a god to waft it on its way towards so formidable a destination.

> With the great gale we journey
>   That breathes from gardens thinned,
> Borne in the drift of blossoms
>   Whose petals throng the wind;
>
> Buoyed on the heaven-heard whisper
>   Of dancing leaflets whirled
> From all the woods that autumn
>   Bereaves in all the World.

---

[1] e.g. see also Book I, chap. 29, περὶ εὐσταθείας, and Book II, chap. 2, περὶ ἀταραξίας.

[2] The Epicurean Hellenic ideal of imperturbability (ἀταραξία) seems to have been conceived and pursued independently in a disintegrating Sinic Society by Hsün-tse, the founder of a school of Confucian philosophy which was the antithesis of the school of Mencius (see Hackmann, H.: Chinesische Philosophie (Munich 1927, Reinhardt), p. 201). But the Sinic, like the Hellenic, sages seem to have flinched from going to Indic extremes.

[3] See V. C (i) (d) 1, vol. v, p. 377; V. C (i) (d) 2, vol. v, p. 403; and V. C (i) (d) 8 (α), in the present volume, pp. 58-9, above. The game that is described in Theocritus's Seventh Idyll and in Lucretius's De Rerum Natura, Book II, ll. 20-33 (on which Seneca has embroidered in Ep. Mor. xc, §§ 40-3), is also portrayed in the picture by Giorgione that goes by the name of La Fête Champêtre.

[4] A Detachment that is no more than a game or a pose may be suspected of being Abandon masquerading in a pretentious disguise (see V. C (i) (d) 2, vol. v, p. 403, above).

[5] See Thoreau, H. D.: Walden, or Life in the Woods (Boston 1854, Houghton Mifflin).

[6] It is the aim of the Hinayanian Buddhist sage to make his way, through exercises in spiritual concentration, into other and higher worlds of which the keynote is a toning down of feelings to a 'veiled indifference (Nivṛta-Avyakṛta)' (Stcherbatsky, Th.: The Conception of Buddhist Nirvana (Leningrad 1927, Academy of Sciences of U.S.S.R.), p. 11).

And midst the fluttering legion
Of all that ever died
I follow, and before us
Goes the delightful guide,

With lips that brim with laughter
But never once respond,
And feet that fly on feathers,
And serpent-circled wand.[1]

If one is really going to walk over the edge of a precipice, is it
not best to let oneself be led over it in this agreeable way by
Hermes Psychopompus? Perhaps it is better to make certain of
the guide's identity before putting ourselves in his hands. And,
when we look into it, we shall find that the bearer of this imposing
Hellenic title is a will-o'-the-wisp who also answers to the Nordic
name of the Pied Piper of Hamelin. The Piper hypnotizes children into falling in at his heels; but the trance in which they follow
him does not end for them in an escape from life; it ends instead
in their sitting in darkness and the shadow of death in the bowels
of a mountain into which the deceitful magician entices them.
And, even without having the Teutonic fairy-tale to warn him, the
Indic candidate for arhatship knows by intuition that the Hellenic
expedient of a conducted tour to *Nirvāna* is a snare and a delusion.
If one takes an anaesthetic, one cannot commit hara-kiri; and in
order to achieve the greater *tour de force* of spiritual self-annihilation one must be alertly aware, from first to last, of what one is
about. The key that unlocks the gate of *Nirvāna* is not an aesthetically agreeable hypnosis but an arduous and painful mental strife
of the kind that is prescribed in the following passage from a
work of the Hinayanian Buddhist philosophy.

'In one who abides surveying the enjoyment in things that make for
grasping, craving (*tanhā*) increases. Grasping is caused by craving,
coming into existence by grasping, birth by coming into existence, and
old age and death by birth. . . . Just as if a great mass of fire were burning of ten, twenty, thirty or forty loads of faggots, and a man from time
to time were to throw on it dry grasses, dry cow-dung, and dry faggots;
even so a great mass of fire with that feeding and that fuel would burn
for a long time. . . .

'In one who abides surveying the misery in things that make for
grasping, craving ceases. With the ceasing of craving, grasping ceases;
with the ceasing of grasping, coming into existence ceases; with the
ceasing of coming into existence, birth ceases; and, with the ceasing of
birth, old age and death cease. Grief, lamentation, pain, dejection, and
despair cease. Even so is the cessation of all this mass of pain.'[2]

[1] Housman, A. E.: *A Shropshire Lad*, xlii.
[2] *Upādāna-sutta*, ii. 84, quoted in Thomas, E. J.: *The History of Buddhist Thought*
(London 1933, Kegan Paul), p. 62.

The reward that awaits the whole-hearted seeker after Detachment at his journey's end is described by our Hellenic philosopher in a characteristically political simile.

'You see that Caesar appears to provide us with a great peace, because there are no longer any wars or battles or any serious crimes of brigandage or piracy, so that one can travel at any season and can sail from the Levant to the Ponent.[1] But tell me now: can Caesar also bring us peace from fever and from shipwreck, or from conflagration or earthquake or thunderbolt? Yes, and from love? Impossible. And from grief? Impossible. And from envy? A sheer impossibility in every one of these predicaments. But, unlike Caesar, the doctrine (λόγος) of the philosophers does promise to bring us peace from these troubles too.[2] And what does that doctrine tell us? "My children", it says, "if you listen to me, then, wherever you are and whatever you are doing, you will not be overtaken by sorrow or by anger or by a consciousness either of constraint or of frustration. You will go through with it in a state of invulnerability (ἀπαθεῖς διάξετε), in which you will be free from all these ills." This is a peace that is proclaimed not by Caesar (how *could* Caesar proclaim it for us?) but by God through the voice of Philosophy (διὰ τοῦ λόγου). And the philosopher who possesses that peace is master of the situation even when he is single-handed. For he can look the World in the face as he thinks to himself: "Now no evil can befall me. For me there exists no such thing as a brigand or an earthquake. For me there is nothing anywhere but peace, nothing but imperturbability (πάντα εἰρήνης μεστά, πάντα ἀταραξίας)."'[3]

This Hellenic simile veils a metaphysical belief which is embraced in its elemental nakedness by a hardier Indic school of thought.

'The world-process is . . . a process of co-operation between . . . subtle, evanescent elements; and such is the nature of *dharmas* that they proceed from causes and steer towards extinction. Influenced by the element *avidyā*, the process is in full swing. Influenced by the element *prajñā*, it has a tendency towards appeasement and final extinction. In the first case streams of combining elements are produced which correspond to ordinary men; in the second the stream represents a saint.[4] The complete stoppage of the process of phenomenal life corresponds to a Buddha. . . . The final result of the world-process is its suppression:

---

[1] This sentence has been quoted already, apropos of the actual *Pax Augusta*, in V. C (i) (*d*) 7, p. 3, above.—A.J.T.
   [2] These sentences have been quoted already in V. C (i) (*d*) 7, p. 16, footnote 2, above.—A.J.T.
   [3] Epictetus: *Dissertationes*: Book III, chap. 13, §§ 11–13.
   [4]   With his body still alive
                     The saint enjoys some feeling,
                     But in Nirvāna consciousness is gone
                     Just as a light when totally extinct.

   Verses quoted by Candrakirti, and, after him, by Stcherbatsky, Th.: *The Conception of Buddhist Nirvana* (Leningrad 1927, Academy of Sciences of U.S.S.R.), p. 184.

Absolute Calm.[1] All co-operation is extinct and replaced by immut-
ability (*Asamskṛta = Nirvāna*). . . . The Absolute (*Nirvāna*) is inanimate,
even if it is something. It is sometimes, especially in popular literature,
characterized as bliss; but this bliss consists in the cessation of unrest
(*duhkha*). Bliss is a feeling, and in the Absolute there neither is a feeling
nor conception nor volition nor even consciousness. The theory is that
consciousness cannot appear alone without its satellites, the phenomena
of feeling, volition, &c.; and the last moment in the life of a Bodhisattva,
before merging into the Absolute, is also the last moment of consciousness in his continuity of many lives.'[2]

This absolute Detachment has perhaps never been attained, or
at least never as a permanent state, outside the school of the Indic
philosopher Siddhārtha Gautama.[3] As an intellectual achievement

[1]
                      The body has collapsed,
                      Ideas gone, all feelings vanished,
                      All energies quiescent
                      And consciousness itself extinct.
                                        Ibid.

[2] Stcherbatsky, Th.: *The Central Conception of Buddhism and the Meaning of the Word
'Dharma'* (London 1923, Royal Asiatic Society), pp. 74 and 53. The same author, in
The Conception of Buddhist Nirvana (Leningrad 1927, Academy of Sciences of U.S.S.R.),
p. 40, describes the Hinayanian conception of *Nirvāna* as representing 'some indefinite
essence of . . . forces which were active in phenomenal life but are now extinct and
converted into eternal death'. See also, however, Radhakrishnan, Sir S.: *Gautama the
Buddha* (London 1938, Milford), pp. 41–6, cited in this Study already in V. C (i) (*c*) 2,
vol. v, p. 134, footnote 1, and in V. C (i) (*d*) 7, in the present volume, p. 18, footnote 1,
above, for the view that *Nirvāna*, in Siddhārtha Gautama's own conception of it, is not
a negation of existence but is 'a different, deeper mode of life' which 'is peace and rest
in the bosom of the Eternal'.
[3] The *Nirvāna* that is the normal and permanent goal of the Hinayanian Buddhist
arhat was, however, perhaps apprehended as a rare and fleeting experience by Plotinus,
whose Neoplatonism was the last of the schools of Hellenic philosophy.
  'The ecstatic trance, in which the distinction between the mind and its ideas, the self
and self-knowledge, passes away, is not, so Plotinus would have us believe, a mere
swooning and eclipse of the Soul while the World goes booming on, but a flight of the
Alone to the Alone. Sense and spiritual contemplation and mystic union are psychological states corresponding to cosmic climes, and growth in self-knowledge may be
described also as a journey of the Soul through the Universe to its far-off home. Only
this should be noted, that the actual attainment of the noetic state, when once the
Soul has been released from the bondage of rebirth, brings a cessation of what we
regard as personal existence. The heaven of the Nous has no place for memory of the
Soul's past lives, and Being there is not an immortality that denotes conscious continuity;
it is rather a blissful forgetfulness. And the last stage of identification with the One is a
complete loss of identity' (More, P. E.: *Hellenistic Philosophies = The Greek Tradition
from the Death of Socrates to the Council of Chalcedon: 399 B.C.–A.D. 451*, vol. ii (Princeton
1923, University Press), pp. 197–8).
  On this showing, Plotinus's *Visio Beatifica* might be described as an entry into *Nirvāna*
that is momentary instead of being permanent, but which is genuine for so long as it
lasts. On the other hand the common essence of the Neoplatonic and the Hinayanian
Buddhist experience is apparently not to be found in the experience of either the
Christian or the Islamic school of mysticism.
  '*Fanā*', an important technical term of Sūfism, meaning "annihilation, dissolution".
The Sūfi who attains perfection must be in a kind of state of annihilation. . . . The
origin of the Muslim conception of *fanā*' has . . . to be sought in Christianity, from which
it seems to be borrowed. This conception simply means the annihilation of the individual human will before the will of God—an idea which forms the centre of all Christian
mysticism. The conception thus belongs to the domain of ethics and not in the slightest
degree to that of metaphysics, like the *nirvāna* of the Hindu. . . . The author of the
Kashf al-Mahjub expressly states that *fanā*' does not mean loss of essence and destruction of personality, as some ignorant Sūfis think' (*Encyclopaedia of Islam*, vol. ii (London
1927, Luzac), p. 52).

it is imposing; as a moral achievement it is overwhelming; but it has a disconcerting moral corollary; for perfect Detachment casts out Pity, and therefore also Love, as inexorably as it purges away all the evil passions.

The intellectual reasonableness of this appalling moral conclusion is most easily demonstrable in the case of the Gods, for whom the human philosophy of Detachment can hardly find room except in the contemptible role of spoilt children of the Universe.[1]

The habitat of these unedifying privileged beings is the nearest thing to an unearned *Nirvāna*[2] (a virtual contradiction in terms!) that Epicurus admits into his Cosmos.

> Apparet divom numen sedesque quietae
> quas neque concutiunt venti nec nubila nimbis
> aspergunt neque nix acri concreta pruina
> cana cadens violat semperque innubilus aether
> integit, et large diffuso lumine rident.
> omnia suppeditat porro Natura neque ulla
> res animi pacem delibat tempore in ullo.[3]

This Lotus-Eaters' 'no-man's-land'[4] was necessarily incommensurable with, and therefore also necessarily insulated from, the habitat of Mankind.

> Illud item non est ut possis credere, sedes
> esse deum sanctas in mundi partibus ullis.
> tenvis enim natura deum longeque remota
> sensibus ab nostris animi vix mente videtur;
> quae quoniam manuum tactum suffugit et ictum,
> tactile nil nobis quod sit contingere debet.
> tangere enim non quit quod tangi non licet ipsum.
> quare etiam sedes quoque nostris sedibus esse
> dissimiles debent—tenues, de corpore eorum.[5]

It follows that neither the world which Mankind inhabits nor Mankind itself is of the Gods' creation. And, apart from the sheer physical impossibility of the hypothesis, what conceivable motive could the Gods have had for creating anything, even if they had had the power?

---

[1] The tendency of Philosophy to depreciate God in magnifying Law has been examined in V. C (i) (*d*) 7, pp. 18–28, above.

[2] In Stcherbatsky, Th.: *The Conception of Buddhist Nirvana* (Leningrad 1927, Academy of Sciences of U.S.S.R.), p. 15, it is pointed out that the saints in the Hinayanian *Nirvāna* are, like the gods in the Epicurean μετακόσμια (see footnote 4, below), quiescent, inactive, and possessed of bodies of a special atomic structure.

[3] Lucretius: *De Rerum Natura*, Book III, ll. 18–24.

[4] The term is strictly applicable; for Epicurus parked his gods in his μετακόσμια, which, in the language of our modern Western astronomy, might perhaps be translated as 'inter-nebular spaces'.

[5] Lucretius: *De Rerum Natura*, Book V, ll. 146–54.

Quid enim immortalibus atque beatis
gratia nostra queat largirier emolumenti
ut nostra quicquam causa gerere aggrediantur?
quidve novi potuit, tanto post, ante quietos
inlicere ut cuperent vitam mutare priorem?[1]

Nor, whatever the myths may say, have the Gods ever intervened in human affairs, any more than they have been responsible
for bringing the human race into existence.

Omnis enim per se divom natura necessest
immortali aevo summa cum pace fruatur
semota ab nostris rebus seiunctaque longe.
nam privata dolore omni, privata periclis,
ipsa suis pollens opibus, nil indiga nostri,
nec bene promeritis capitur neque tangitur ira.[2]

And Lucretius's point has been anticipated, in still more shocking
lines of Latin verse, by his predecessor Ennius:

Ego deum genus esse semper dixi et dicam caelitum,
sed eos non curare opinor quid agat humanum genus;
nam, si curent, bene bonis sit, male malis, quod nunc abest.

It would indeed be uncomplimentary to hold the Gods responsible for works which 'ail from the prime foundation'.

Quod si iam rerum ignorem primordia quae sint,
hoc tamen ex ipsis caeli rationibus ausim
confirmare aliisque ex rebus reddere multis,
nequaquam nobis divinitus esse paratam
naturam rerum: tanta stat praedita culpa.[3]

But there is another and a deeper reason why it would be impious to credit the Gods with having anything to do with the
World, and this is that a perfect Detachment is the very hall-mark
of Divinity.

'Being blissful and incorruptible means having no bothers oneself and
causing none to others, and this in turn means being detached from all
feelings of anger or of gratitude. All that kind of thing is a sure sign of
infirmity.'[4]

In a famous work of Indic literature a god is duly made to glory
in the Detachment which, in the passage just quoted, is attributed
by a Hellenic philosopher to the Godhead *a priori*.

[1] Ibid., Book V, ll. 165–9.
[2] Ibid., Book II, ll. 646–51.
[3] Ibid., Book V, ll. 195–9.
[4] Epicurus, quoted in Diogenes Laertius: *The Lives of the Philosophers*, Book X,
chap. 139: τὸ μακάριον καὶ ἄφθαρτον οὔτ' αὐτὸ πράγματ' ἔχει οὔτ' ἄλλῳ παρέχει, ὥστ'
οὔτ' ὀργαῖς οὔτε χάρισι συνέχεται· ἐν ἀσθενεῖ γὰρ πᾶν τὸ τοιοῦτον. This passage is also to be
found in a Latin translation in Cicero: *De Natura Deorum*, Book I, chap. 17 (section 45).
The same equation of action with infirmity is made in a passage of Plotinus which has
been quoted in this Study in III. C (ii) (*b*), vol. iii, p. 254, footnote 4, above.

'I am indifferent to all born things; there is none whom I hate, none whom I love.'[1]

These words are placed in the mouth of a god, but it is a human ideal that they express; for the tribe of philosophers is not less prone than the tribes of Thracians and Ethiopians[2] to portray the Gods in their human makers' image; and the same poem elsewhere extols the same inhumanly complete Detachment as the hall-mark, not of divinity, but of perfection in the soul of a human being.

'He whose mind is undismayed in pain, who is freed from longings for pleasure, from whom passion, fear and wrath have fled, is called a man of abiding prudence, a saintly man. He who is without affection for aught, and whatever fair or foul fortune may betide neither rejoices in it nor loathes it, has wisdom abidingly set.'

'The man whose every motion is void of love and purpose, whose works are burned away by the fire of knowledge, the enlightened call "learned".'

'The learned grieve not for them whose lives are fled nor for them whose lives are not fled.'[3]

To the Indic sage's mind this heartlessness is the adamantine core of philosophy; and the same conclusion was reached independently by the Hellenic philosophers as a result of following likewise to the bitter end a parallel line of escape from life. The Hellenic sage who had struggled out into the sunshine of enlightenment might perhaps feel a greater sense of social obligation to return to the Cave where the vast majority of his former fellow prisoners were still languishing;[4] but this difference, such as it was, between the Hellenic and the Indic philosopher's code was superficial; for, even if he did return, the Hellenic philosopher was merely to go through the motions of showing mercy upon his suffering fellow creatures. He was not only free, but was in duty bound, to leave his heart behind him. This personal obligation, which the Hellenic philosopher remorselessly laid upon himself, to preserve at all costs his hard-won invulnerability has been described by a modern Western scholar[5] in terms so startling that we might be inclined to suspect him of rhetorical exaggeration if there were not chapter and verse to warrant every statement to which he commits himself.

'The Wise Man was not to *concern* himself with his brethren . . . he was only to serve them.[6] Benevolence he was to have, as much of it as

---

[1] Bhagavadgītā, ix. 29 (English translation by Barnett, L. D. (London 1920, Dent), pp. 129–30).
[2] See the quotation from Xenophanes at the beginning of Part I. A, vol. i, p. 1, above.
[3] Bhagavadgītā, ii. 56–7; iv. 19; ii. 11 (Barnett's translation (cited in footnote 1, above), pp. 94, 104, 88).
[4] For Plato's simile of the Cave see III. C (ii) (b), vol. iii, pp. 249–52, above.
[5] Bevan, E. R.: *Stoics and Sceptics* (Oxford 1913, Clarendon Press), pp. 66–7.
[6] 'The sage will not feel pity, because he cannot feel it without himself being in a pitiful state of mind; but everything else that is done by those who do indulge in that

you can conceive; but there was one thing he must not have, and that was love. Here, too, if that inner tranquillity and freedom of his was to be kept safe through everything—here too, as when he was intending to acquire objects for himself, he must engage in action without desire.[1] He must do everything which it is possible for him to do, shrink from no extreme of physical pain, in order to help, to comfort, to guide his fellow men, but whether he succeeds or not must be a matter of pure indifference to him. If he has done his best to help you and failed, he will be perfectly satisfied with having done his best. The fact that you are no better off for his exertions will not matter to him at all. Pity, in the sense of a painful emotion caused by the sight of other men's suffering, is actually a vice.[2] The most that can be allowed when the Wise Man goes to console a mourner, is that he should feign sympathy as a means of attaining his object; but he must take care not to feel it. He may sigh, Epictetus says, provided the sigh does not come from his heart.[3] In the service of his fellow men he must be prepared to sacrifice his health, to sacrifice his possessions, to sacrifice his life; but there is one thing he must never sacrifice: his own eternal calm.'[4]

emotion will also be done by him—and this readily and high-mindedly. He will succour a sorrowful neighbour without joining in his grief. He will give a helping hand to the castaway, hospitality to the exile, alms to the destitute. . . . He will allow a mother's tears to purchase the freedom of her son, will release the prisoner from his chains and the gladiator from his barracks, and will even give burial to the criminal's corpse. But he will do all this without any mental agitation or any change of countenance' (Seneca: *De Clementia*, Book II, chap. 6, §§ 1–2).—A.J.T.

[1] 'If you are kissing a child of yours—or a brother, or a friend—never put your imagination unreservedly into the act and never give your emotion free rein, but curb it and check it (like the mentors who stand behind the conqueror in his triumphal car to prompt him to remember that he is only a human being). It is up to you to be your own prompter and to remind yourself that the being whom you love is mortal, so that what you are loving is not your own property. It has been given to you only temporarily, and the gift is not irrevocable or absolute. It is like a fig or a bunch of grapes that one has at the appointed season; and if one goes on craving for it in wintertime one is a fool. It is equally foolish to crave for one's son or one's friend out of season; that is just another form of asking for figs in winter. . . . Indeed, there is no harm in accompanying the act of kissing the child by whispering over him: "To-morrow you will die"' (Epictetus: *Dissertationes*, Book III, chap. 24, §§ 85–8). The whole chapter—which is entitled 'The impropriety of being emotionally affected by what is not under one's control'—is more or less apposite.—A.J.T.

[2] 'Pity is a mental illness induced by the spectacle of other people's miseries, or alternatively it may be defined as an infection of low spirits caught from other people's troubles when the patient believes that those troubles are undeserved. The sage does not succumb to suchlike mental diseases. The sage's mind is serene and is immune from being upset by the incidence of any external force. The noblest ornament of human nature is greatness of soul; but such greatness is not compatible with grief; for grief bruises the mind and prostrates it and shrivels it up; and the sage does not allow that to happen to him—even in calamities that are his own. . . . Pity is next-door neighbour to pitifulness (*misericordia vicina est miseriae*). . . . Pity is a vice of minds too prone to be appalled at the sight of misery. If you expect the sage to feel pity, you might almost as well expect him to weep and wail at somebody else's funeral' (Seneca: *De Clementia*, Book II, chap. 5, §§ 4–5, and chap. 6, § 4).—A.J.T.

[3] 'I do not say that it is inadmissible to groan; the point is that the groan must not come from the heart' (Epictetus: *Dissertationes*, Book I, chap. 18, § 19). It would perhaps be unfair to Epictetus to overlook the fact that this precept is given apropos of a physical pain afflicting oneself. At the same time Dr. Bevan is no doubt fairly entitled to assume that the precept has a wider application than this in Epictetus's philosophy. —A.J.T.

[4] 'The sage will always keep the same calm and unmoved countenance—which he could not do if he permitted himself to feel sorrow' (Seneca: *De Clementia*, Book II, chap. 5, § 5).—A.J.T.

Nor, among the dominant minority in a disintegrating Hellenic Society, was this repulsive ideal a mere uncoveted monopoly of a handful of pedants and prigs. The most sensitive and lovable and popular of all the Latin poets has deliberately drawn his hero in the unfeeling philosopher's image; and his heartlessness is the sign in which Aeneas conquers at the crisis of his career, when he successfully steels himself—like an oak standing up to a storm—against Anna's supreme appeal on Dido's behalf.

Mens immota manet; lacrimae volvuntur inanes.[1]

A modern Western Hellenist has used his art to preach this sophisticated philosophy in the name of the plain man. In the grave—'in the nation that is not'—sings a Shropshire Lad,

> Lovers lying two by two
> Ask not whom they sleep beside,
> And the bridegroom all night through
> Never turns him to the bride.[2]

Yet, in pressing its way to a conclusion which is logically inevitable and at the same time morally intolerable, the philosophy of Detachment ultimately defeats itself; and it is in vain that its exponents wring a grudging recognition of their fortitude, and even of their nobility, out of the petrified hearts of their audience. In the very act of unwilling admiration we are vehemently moved to revolt. It was the sorrows of Dido and not the virtues of Aeneas that appealed to Saint Augustine in his unregenerate youth; and he lived to write as a saint in middle age: 'It is not true that "No god ever enters into relations with Man"—even if Plato did say so, as Apuleius says he did.'[3] The philosophy of Detachment does not, after all, provide a solution for the problem which it sets out to solve; for in consulting only the head and ignoring the heart it is arbitrarily putting asunder what God has joined together.[4] This philosophy falls short of the truth by refusing to take account of the Soul's duality in unity; and therefore the philosophy of Detachment has to be eclipsed by the mystery of Transfiguration. The Hīnayāna makes way for the Mahāyāna,[5] Stoicism for Christianity, the arhat for the Bodhisattva,[6] the sage for the saint.

---

[1] Virgil: *Aeneid*, Book IV, l. 449.
[2] Housman, A. E.: *A Shropshire Lad*, xii.
[3] Augustine, *De Civitate Dei*, Book IX, chap. 16, quoting Apuleius: *De Deo Socratis*, chap. 4, § 21 (edited by Lütjohann, Chr.: Greifswald 1878, Kunike): 'Nam, ut idem Plato ait, "nullus deus miscetur hominibus [θεὸς δὲ ἀνθρώπῳ οὐ μίγνυται.—*Symposium*, 203 A]", sed hoc praecipuum eorum sublimitatis specimen est, quod nulla adtrectatione nostra contaminantur.'   [4] Matt. xix. 6.
[5] For the eruption of the Mahāyāna out of the Hīnayāna see V. C (i) (c) 2, vol. v, pp. 133-6, and V. C (i) (d) 6 (δ), vol. v, p. 552, above.
[6] For the antithesis between Bodhisattva and arhat see further V. C (i) (d) 11, p. 164, footnote 3, below.

II. *Transfiguration*

We have found that the experience of being constrained to live in the adverse social environment of a disintegrating civilization confronts the Soul with a spiritual problem which is, no doubt, demanding a solution all the time but which can be more or less successfully ignored or evaded so long as the Soul is able to float lazily on the flowing tide of a civilization that is still in growth. When this latent problem of life is forced upon the Soul's attention by the hard fact that a way of life which has hitherto been taken for granted is now failing to work, the Soul is driven into searching for a substitute, and we have already passed in review three different attempts to find one; but, so far, our survey has brought us each time to the dead end of a blind-alley. The way of Archaism ends in self-defeat, the way of Futurism in self-transcendence, the way of Detachment in self-stultification. There is, however, one way left for us still to explore, and that is the way to which we have provisionally given the name of Transfiguration.[1]

As we gird up our loins to take this fourth and last turning a clamour of disapproving and derisive voices assails our ears. Shall we allow ourselves to be intimidated by this chorus of protest? Shall we abandon at this point a course of exploration which has hitherto proved as disappointing as it has been laborious? It is tempting to yield to the promptings of weariness and disillusionment. Yet, before we do give in, it may be well to consider whether we really wish to resign ourselves to remaining imprisoned in a city of destruction—like rats in a trap—so long as there is still one possible egress left untried. And it may also be well to ask ourselves whether the hostile chorus is really a bad augury. For whose, after all, are these voices that are eager to deter us? When we look the hostile chorus in the face we see before us nothing more formidable than the sullen countenances of the baffled philosophers and futurists (the archaists have been so deeply discouraged by their own fiasco that they have not had the heart to join in the outcry). Are these familiar companions of our previous journeys now likely to give us good advice? Will they not be prone to be unduly discouraged by their own unfortunate experience, and unduly sceptical about an alternative road which might conceivably arrive at the goal which the roads of Futurism and Detachment have failed to reach? And is their unquestionable eminence in their respective spheres of action and of thought a cogent reason for accepting their authority? May not this be the moment to remind ourselves of the principle of περιπέτεια—'the reversal of

---

[1] See V. C (i) (*d*) 1, vol. v, pp. 390 and 396–7, above.

roles'—upon which we have stumbled at an earlier stage of our inquiry?[1] This principle of irony and paradox is mighty in its operation. A study of history reveals in every act and scene of the play the truth that

'God hath chosen the foolish things of the World to confound the wise; and God hath chosen the weak things of the World to confound the things which are mighty.'[2]

This truth which we can thus verify empirically is also known to us intuitively. And in the light and the strength of it we may brave the disapproval of futurists and philosophers alike by stepping boldly out in the footprints of a guide who is neither Simon bar Kōkabā nor Hermes Psychopompus.

'The Jews require a sign and the Greeks seek after wisdom; but we', writes Paul to the Corinthians, 'preach Christ Crucified—unto the Jews a stumblingblock and unto the Greeks foolishness.'[3]

Why is Christ Crucified a stumbling-block to futurists who have never succeeded in eliciting the sign which they require? And why is He foolishness to philosophers who for their part have never succeeded in discovering the wisdom after which they seek? If we press these two questions, we may not only put ourselves in a position to take a more exact measure of those two spiritual blind-alleys: we may also (and this is of much greater moment) be able to make some progress in exploring the mysterious way of life along which the Apostle is beckoning us.

Christ Crucified is foolishness to the philosopher (be he of a Greek or of an Indian school) because the philosopher's ultimate aim is Detachment; and therefore the philosopher cannot comprehend how any reasonable being who has once attained that forbidding goal can be so perverse as deliberately to relinquish what he has so hardly won. What is the sense of withdrawing simply in order to return?[4] This passes the understanding of a philosopher who knows by his own experience how heavy a toll of fortitude and perseverance the feat of withdrawal must have taken from any human being who has successfully achieved it. And *a fortiori* the philosopher is completely nonplussed at the notion of a God who has not even had to take the trouble to withdraw from an unsatisfactory World, because He is completely independent of it by virtue of His very divinity, but who nevertheless deliberately enters into the World, and subjects Himself there to the utmost agony

---

[1] In IV. C (iii) (c) 1, vol. iv, pp. 245–61, above. See also V. C (i) (d) 6 (δ), vol. v, pp. 561–5, above.
[2] 1 Cor. i. 27, quoted already in IV. C (iii) (c) 1, vol. iv, p. 249, above.
[3] 1 Cor. i. 22–3.
[4] For the contrast between the pagan philosopher's withdrawal and the Christian mystic's withdrawal-and-return see III. C (ii) (b), vol. iii, pp. 249–63, above.

that God or Man can undergo, for the sake of a race of beings of an immeasurably inferior order. 'God so loved the World that He gave His only begotten Son?'[1] That is the last word in folly from the standpoint of a seeker after Detachment. 'He saved others; himself he cannot save!'[2]

The fact is that

'Mankind has two different ideals before it; and I do not see how the ideal of Detachment is compatible with the ideal of Love. If we choose one, we must forgo the other; each ideal appears faulty when judged by the measure of the other. With the one goes to a large extent the intellect of Ancient Greece and of India, with the other the Christian Church and the hearts of men, the *anima naturaliter Christiana*; for neither in Greece nor India nor China have the philosophers been the whole of the people—nor their philosophy the whole of the philosophers.

'There have been things tending to obscure this divergence between the two ideals. The language used by the Stoics or Buddhists about benevolence may often be taken to be inspired by the Christian ideal of Love. On the other hand the Christian ideal has involved Detachment from many things, from "the care of this world and the deceitfulness of riches"[3] and the lusts of other things, and much of the language used about this sort of Detachment in Christian books may seem to point to the ideal of Ancient Greece and India.[4] The Stoic sage strenuously labouring to do good and indifferent whether good is done, sighing with his stricken friend, but not from the heart, is a figure serving well to bring home to us the difference. And we may see, I think, that the Stoics and sages of India could say no less without giving up their whole scheme.

'If the supreme end is Tranquillity, of what use would it be to set the Wise Man's heart free from disturbance by cutting off the fear and desire which made him dependent upon outside things, if one immediately opened a hundred channels by which the World's pain and unrest

[1] John iii. 16. This view of what God's feeling and attitude and purpose and action may be seems to have been a Syriac discovery (see V. C (ii) (*a*), p. 276, footnote 5, below). [2] Mark xv. 31. [3] Matt. xiii. 22.
[4] For example, the following words of Saint John of the Cross might readily be taken in a Stoic or Hinayanian Buddhist sense at a first reading:

'There is no Detachment if desire remains.... Detachment ... consists in suppressing desire and avoiding pleasure; it is this that sets the Soul free, even though possession may be still retained. It is not the things of This World that occupy or injure the Soul, for they do not enter within, but rather the wish for, and desire of, them, which abide within it. The affection and attachment which the Soul feels for the creature renders the Soul its equal and its like, and the greater the affection the greater will be the likeness. Love begets a likeness between the lover and the object of his love' (Saint John of the Cross: 'The Ascent of Mount Carmel' in *The Mystical Doctrine of Saint John of the Cross* (London 1934, Sheed & Ward), p. 10).

This Christian practice of Detachment differs, nevertheless, from the pagan practice in a fundamental point which is indicated by the inclusion of the words 'for the creature'. And these three words give the key, not only to this passage, but to the whole spirit and aim of the Christian mysticism. The unspoken—because unquestioned—premiss of the argument is that the motions of affection and attachment are only to be inhibited in so far as they are directed towards the creature and not towards the Creator. The aim of the Christian practice of Detachment is not to mortify love but to vivify it when it is a love of God. And the truth that 'love begets a likeness between the lover and the object of his love' is as true of the love of God as it is of the love of the things of This World.
—A.J.T.

could flow into his heart through the fibres, created by Love and Pity, connecting his heart with the fevered hearts of men all round? A hundred fibres!—one aperture would suffice to let in enough of the bitter surge to fill his heart full. Leave one small hole in a ship's side, and you let in the sea. The Stoics, I think, saw with perfect truth that if you were going to allow any least entrance of Love and Pity into the breast, you admitted something whose measure you could not control, and might just as well give up the idea of inner Tranquillity at once. Where Love is, action cannot be without desire; the action of Love has eminently regard to fruit, in the sense of some result beyond itself—the one thing that seems to matter is whether the loved person really is helped by your action. Of course you run the risk of frustrated desire and disappointment. The Stoic sage was never frustrated and never disappointed. Gethsemane, looked at from this point of view, was a signal breakdown. The Christian's Ideal Figure could never be accepted by the Stoic as an example of his typical Wise Man.'[1]

No, and neither could the Stoic's Ideal Figure ever be accepted conversely by the Christian as a prototype of his Christ or even as an analogue of his Christian saint. The shortcomings of the pagan philosophy from the Christian standpoint have been starkly exposed by a saint—who has the advantage of being a philosopher as well—in an argument which proceeds from the Christian postulates that 'God is Love'[2] and that 'perfect Love casteth out fear'.[3]

'In the Hellenic philosophy there are two schools of thought with regard to those mental emotions which are called in Greek πάθη and in Latin either "perturbations" (in the usage of Cicero and others) or "affections" (alias "affects") or else "passions" (a more exact translation of the Greek, which is employed, for example, by Apuleius). These perturbations or affections or passions are declared by one school to attack the sage too [as well as the plain man], only in the sage they are moderate and subject to reason, so that the mind maintains its supremacy and imposes on these passions a system of laws which restrain them within proper bounds. This school is the Platonico-Aristotelian. . . . But there is another school, represented by the Stoics, which does not admit that the sage is attacked by any passions of this kind at all. . . . When all is said, [however,] the difference of view, in regard to passions and mental perturbations, between the Stoics and other philosophers is infinitesimal; for both schools agree in seeking to make the mind and reason of the sage immune from the passions' dominion. . . . The Christian doctrine[, on the other hand,] subordinates the mind itself to God, to be ruled—and aided—by Him, and subordinates the passions to the mind, to be governed—and curbed—by it until they are converted into instruments of justice. Consequently in our Christian discipline the question that is asked is not *whether* the religious mind feels anger, but *why* it feels it; not *whether* it feels sadness, but *what* makes it sad;

---

[1] Bevan, E. R.: *Stoics and Sceptics* (Oxford 1913, Clarendon Press), pp. 69–70.
[2] 1 John iv. 8 and 16.   [3] 1 John iv. 18.

and not *whether* it feels fear, but *what* it is afraid of. To be angry with
the sinner in order that he may receive correction; to be sorry for the
sufferer in order that he may win liberation; to be fearful for the soul in
peril lest it may go to perdition: I can hardly imagine these emotions being
deliberately condemned by any one in his senses. Yet even the emotion
of pity is usually censured by Stoics. . . . Far better, far more humane,
and far more consonant with religious feeling is what Cicero says in his
praise of Caesar: "None of your virtues is more admirable or more
lovable than your sense of pity." After all, what is pity but sympathy
in our own heart for somebody else's misery—a sympathy which
peremptorily commands us to give our help if we can? And this emotion
works in the service of reason when pity is bestowed without prejudice
to justice—as, for example, when we give to the needy or forgive the
penitent. Yet, while such a master of language as Cicero did not hesitate to call this sense of pity a virtue, the Stoics are not ashamed to
include it in the catalogue of the vices. . . . [Well,] if emotions and affections which come from a love of the good and from a holy charity
are to be called vices, we might as well allow the real vices to be called
virtues. . . .

'If we are entirely without these emotions while we are subject to the
infirmity of this [earthly] life, that really means that there is something
wrong with our way of living. The Apostle abhorred and castigated
certain persons whom he has described as being, among other things,
without natural affection;[1] and one of the psalms, likewise, censures
those of whom it says: *I looked for some to take pity, but there was none.*[2]
To be entirely without pain while we are in this place of misery is
assuredly "a state which can only be purchased at a prohibitive price in
inhumanity of mind and in insensibility of body"—as has been felt, and
been put into words, even by one of the secular men-of-letters. On this
showing, the state which in Greek is called ἀπάθεια[3] (and which in Latin
would be called "impassibility" if that were a possible Latin word)[4] may
be a thoroughly good state, and even an extremely desirable one,[5] but
is quite incompatible with this life if we understand this state (which is
a mental, not a physical, experience) to mean living without those
affections which assail us, and upset our minds, in an irrational way.
This is the verdict, not of nonentities, but of the most profoundly
religious and extremely just and holy souls. *If we say that we have no
sin, we deceive ourselves, and the truth is not in us.*[6] "Invulnerability"
(ἀπάθεια) in this sense will not be achieved until Man is without sin. As

---

[1] Rom. i. 31.   [2] Ps. lxix. 20.
[3] This Greek word ἀπάθεια is rendered in this Study (for reasons given in V. C (i) (d) 1,
vol. v, p. 394, footnote 1, above) by the English word 'invulnerability' and not by the
English word 'apathy'.—A.J.T.
[4] This word which Saint Augustine has coined on the pattern of a Greek original,
only to reject it as an inadmissible monstrosity, has, of course, since been adopted as a
technical term in the theological vocabulary of the Western Christian Church.—A.J.T.
[5] In examining and criticizing the Peripatetic and Stoic ideal of 'Imperturbability'
Saint Augustine quotes (*De Civitate Dei*, Book IX, chap. 4, *ad fin.*), as an illustration of
the admirable element in it, the Virgilian line (*Aeneid*, Book IV, l. 449) which has been
quoted in this Study in V. C (i) (d) 10, p. 148, above.—A.J.T.
[6] I John i. 8.

things actually are, a life without outward misdemeanour is as good a life as we can aspire to; but any one who imagines that he is living without sin is not achieving freedom from sin but is merely rejecting the chance of forgiveness. On the other hand, if "invulnerability" is to be taken in the other sense of a state in which the mind is completely proof against any feeling, surely every one would consider an insensibility of this degree to be something worse than all the vices. So, while it can be said without absurdity that the perfect state of beatitude will know no sadness and will feel no prick of anxiety, nobody who is not altogether blinded to the truth will say that in that state there will be no love and no joy. If, however, "invulnerability" merely means a state in which there is no fear to terrify us and no anguish to torment us, such "invulnerability" is to be shunned in this life if we desire to live it, as it should be lived, in God's way, but it is to be frankly hoped for in that blessedly happy life which is promised to us as our everlasting future condition. . . .

'The eternal life of blessed happiness will have a love and a joy which will be not only right states of feeling but also assured states, while it will be wholly free from anxiety and anguish. . . . As for the commonwealth—or society—of the irreligious who are living not in the way of God but in the way of Man . . . it is convulsed by these depraved feelings, which upset it like mental diseases. And, if this commonwealth has any citizens who make some show of controlling such emotions and more or less keeping them within bounds, they become elated with such an irreligious pride that any success that they may have in reducing their mental distress is counterbalanced by a proportionate degree of mental inflation, while if there are a few of them who—moved by a vanity which is as inhuman as it is rare—have set their hearts on making themselves entirely proof against being affected by any emotion whatever in any way, such creatures merely lose their last shred of humanity without ever attaining to a true tranquillity. For a thing does not become right just through being hard, or wholesome just through being stupid.'[1]

Having followed Saint Augustine in this counter-attack upon the philosophers in whose sight Christ Crucified is foolishness,[2]

---

[1] Saint Augustine: De Civitate Dei, Book IX, chaps. 4 and 5, and Book XIV, chap. 9.

[2] The first draft of the present chapter drew from Professor Gilbert Murray, who kindly read it at that stage, a defence of the philosophers which the writer of this Study is glad to be able now to incorporate into the final draft, in the hope that it may serve here as a corrective to any bias in his own presentation of the issue between the way of Detachment and the way of Transfiguration.

'You take late Stoicism in one of its most over-intellectualized doctrines as standing for Greek philosophy altogether: mere intellect as against Christian love. But compare Zeno, fragment 263, where the thing that binds his πολιτεία together is Ἔρως, and that Ἔρως a god. Compare also fragment 88, where the motive spirit is not merely an anima rationalis, but also creates beauty. This is different from pure intellectualism. Again, according to Aristotle, Metaphysics, 1072 B, the Final Cause produces motion by being loved. It is the love of God, Ἔρως, that produces all the motion of the World. Of course they tended to shrink from the use of the word Ἔρως, just as the Christians did; but Epicurus's Φιλία is pretty strong. Fragment 52: ἡ Φιλία περιχορεύει τὴν Οἰκουμένην κηρύττουσα δὴ πᾶσιν ἡμῖν ἐγείρεσθαι ἐπὶ τὸν μακαρισμόν—it dances round the World calling us to awaken to our blessedness. Also fragment 28: we must run risks for the sake of Φιλία. Compare fragments 23 and 78, where the two things that matter are Σοφία and Φιλία.'

The writer of this Study heartily agrees that there is a strong vein of Christianity In

we may go on to deal with the futurists for whose feet He is a stumbling-block.

The Crucifixion is a stumbling-block in the way of Futurism because the death on the Cross bears out—by a logic of events that leaves nothing more to be said—the declaration of Jesus that His Kingdom is not of This World;[1] and, for the Jewish Zealot, this declaration is a contradiction in terms which is not just fatuously illogical but is shockingly impious. The sign which the futurist requires is the announcement of a kingdom which will be bereft of all meaning if it is not to be a mundane success. With what intent has Yahweh promised to send his Chosen People a king who will reign over them as 'the Lord's Anointed'? And by what token will this Messiah be recognized? The Messiah's token and task is to be, as we have seen,[2] the seizure of the sceptre of world-dominion out of the hands of some Darius or Antiochus or Caesar, and the raising of the Jews to the rank of ruling race in place of the Persians or the Macedonians or the Romans, as the case may be.

'Thus saith the Lord to his Anointed, to Cyrus [or Zerubbabel or Simon Maccabaeus or Simon bar Kōkabā or whatever may be the name of the hero of the hour], whose right hand I have holden, to subdue nations before him (and I will loose the loins of kings, to open before him the two-leaved gates; and the gates shall not be shut):

' "I will go before thee and make the crooked places straight; I will break in pieces the gates of brass and cut in sunder the bars of iron; and I will give thee the treasures of darkness[3] and hidden riches of secret places." '[4]

How was this authentically futurist conception of a Messiah to be reconciled with the words of a prisoner who answered Pilate

'Thou sayest that I am a king',[5]

and then went on to give so fantastic an account of the royal mission on which he claimed that God had sent him?

'To this end was I born, and for this cause came I into the World, that I should bear witness unto the truth.'[6]

The disconcerting words might perhaps be contested or ignored,

many of the exponents of Hellenism—and, conversely, a strong vein of Hellenism in many of the exponents of Christianity. In quoting Hellenic expressions of the philosophy of Detachment and Christian expressions of the religion of Love he has not meant to imply either that the Christians have never fallen below the ideal of Love or that the Hellenes have never risen above the ideal of Detachment. He has not been attempting to make a critique of either Christianity or Hellenism. His sole concern has been to bring out the respective meanings of Detachment and Transfiguration by quoting testimonies that his readers will accept as *loci classici*.

[1] John xviii. 36.   [2] In V. C (i) (*d*) 9 (γ), pp. 120–3, above.
[3] It was not the Jews but the Macedonians who eventually appropriated the contents of the Achaemenian treasuries.—A.J.T.
[4] Isa. xlv. 1–3 (i.e. 'Deutero-Isaiah'), cited in V. C (i) (*d*) 9 (γ), p. 122, above.
[5] John xviii. 37.   [6] John xviii. 37.

but the malefactor's death could neither be undone nor be explained away; and we have observed, in the classic case of Peter's ordeal, how grievous this stumbling-block was.[1]

The Kingdom of God, of which Christ Crucified is King, is in fact spiritually incommensurable with any kingdom that could ever be founded or ruled by a Messiah envisaged as an Achaemenian world-conqueror who has been turned into a Jew and been projected into the future. As far as this *Civitas Dei* enters into the Time-dimension at all, it is not a mere dream of the future but is a spiritual reality which is at all times present in This World[2] besides existing—and, indeed, just because it exists—as well in an Eternity and an Infinity that are in a supra-mundane spiritual dimension.[3] If there are any moments in Time which can in some sense be regarded, in a Christian *Weltanschauung*, as historical dates of particular irruptions of God's Kingdom into This World, they are moments that are hallowed by descents of the Holy Ghost —upon Jesus at his baptism or upon the Apostles on the Day of Pentecost.[4] When

'they asked of him saying: "Lord, wilt thou at this time restore again the Kingdom to Israel?" . . . he said unto them: "It is not for you to

---

[1] See V. C (i) (d) 1, vol. v, pp. 392–3, above.
[2] The interpretation of Luke xvii. 21 has been discussed in V. C (i) (d) 1, vol. v, p. 396, footnote 1, above.
[3] See V. C (i) (d) 9 (γ), p. 131, footnote 1, above.
[4] This is perhaps the point where the gulf between the conception of Transfiguration and the conception of Futurism is at its narrowest. For, while on the one side the transfiguration of This World through its irradiation by the Kingdom of God is conceived of as being in some sense apprehensible as an historical process in Time, it is also true on the other side, as we have had occasion to notice already, that in the *Weltanschauung* of Futurism the difference between the present régime against which the futurist is in revolt and the future kingdom on which his hopes are set is not regarded as being simply —or even, 'in the last analysis', essentially—determined by the difference between the present and the future tense of the verb 'to be'.

When he is driven into a corner by the bankruptcy of his mundane policy the futurist eventually admits, as we have seen (in V. C (i) (d) 9 (γ), pp. 128–31, above), that the stormy advent of the kingdom of his hopes will be in the nature of an apocalypse rather than of an act of creation. The triumphant destruction of the present dispensation, when this is at last duly achieved, will not be like the clearing of a hitherto encumbered site for the erection of a brand-new building. It will be like the rending of a veil in order to bring into view a hitherto invisible kingdom that has been in existence in the background all the time and has merely been awaiting the hour appointed for its revelation. Even at the earlier stage at which the futurist's hope of a substantial mundane success has not yet evaporated he will be willing to admit that the catastrophe to which he is looking forward is in the nature of a revolution; and, as we have observed in another context (in IV. C (iii) (b) 1, vol. iv, pp. 135–6, above), Revolution shares with Revelation the particular feature that concerns us here. The outbreak of a revolution in the bosom of a body social is not an event that can be explained in terms of that body alone without reference to anything existing outside it. The superficial phenomenon of the violent substitution of new elements for old elements in the structure of the body in which the revolution is taking place is always found to be the effect of a less obvious yet more significant piece of action in a larger field; and this action consists in the play, upon the revolutionary body, of some external force which must, *ex hypothesi*, have been in operation, and therefore in existence, before the outbreak of the revolution of which this foreign body has been the cause.

On this showing, it would seem as though the abstract conception of Futurism cannot be minted into the coin of concrete thought without being stiffened by the addition of a transfigurational alloy which is decidedly foreign to it.

know the times or the seasons which the Father hath put in his own power. But ye shall receive power after that the Holy Ghost is come upon you." [1]

The presence of the Kingdom of God in This World is manifested in the operation of the Spirit; and this operation, which since the beginning of Time has never been withheld—though it may now and then have been suddenly intensified—transfigures the World and, in transfiguring, redeems it, according to a tenet that is at the same time a touchstone of Christianity.

'In the conception of the Church—that is, the organized body of believers—as a thing in itself, to be worked for and fostered, lies the true point of difference between Catholicism and Gnosticism, between Aphraates and *The Acts of Thomas*. To the convert of Judas-Thomas there was literally nothing left on this Earth to live for. . . . The old civilization was doomed, but this religious Nihilism puts nothing in its place. To the orthodox Christian, on the other hand, the Church stood like Aaron between the dead and the living, as a middle term between the things of the Next World and of This. It was the Body of Christ and therefore eternal; something worth living for and working for. Yet it was in the World as much as the Empire itself.'[2]

But how can the Kingdom of God be authentically in This World and yet also be essentially not of it?[3] This is a question which we are bound to ask but cannot be sure of being able to answer, since it brings to light an apparent contradiction in our conception of the relation between the subject and the object of the act of Transfiguration, and this problem may be intractable to attempts to solve it in terms of logic; but, if we are willing to acknowledge that the nature of Transfiguration is a mystery that passes our understanding—as we have seen that it has passed the understanding of philosophers whose intellects have certainly not been inferior to ours!—we may perhaps be rewarded for a sober recognition of the limits of our intellectual power by finding ourselves able to peer into the mystery through the imagery that conveys the intuition of the poets.

Perhaps the simplest image of the relation of the Kingdom of God to This World is a geometrical simile. We may liken their relation to that between a cube and one of the squares that are presented by the solid figure's faces. If the cube were not there the square would not be there either; yet this does not mean that the relation of square to cube is that of part to whole; for part and whole must be things of the same kind, whereas square and cube are figures of different dimensions.

[1] Acts i. 6–8.
[2] Burkitt, F. C.: *Early Eastern Christianity* (London 1904, Murray), pp. 210–11.
[3] This question is implicit in John xvii. 16 and in 1 John ii. 15–17.

This simile incidentally brings out one of the differences between the Christian conception of the Kingdom of God and the Hellenic conception of the *Cosmopolis*;[1] for the 'City of Zeus' is described by Marcus Aurelius as 'a supreme commonwealth' of which the 'City of Cecrops' and the other commonwealths of that order 'are no more than houses'.[2] In this description the relation between a mundane commonwealth and the *Cosmopolis* is clearly defined as a relation of part to whole; and this means that the *Cosmopolis*, unlike the *Civitas Dei*, is conceived of as being a society of the same spiritual dimensions as the oecumenical empire of Rome or the parochial city-state of Athens. If, in the imagery of our simile, we once more represent our mundane society by a square, then the *Cosmopolis* will assume the likeness, not of a cube, but of the surface of a chess-board, which differs geometrically from the single chequer in nothing but the superficial feature of extending over an area that is sixty-four times larger.

An alternative image of the relation between the *Civitas Dei* and This World may be drawn from a recent enrichment of our archaeological knowledge which has been a surprising and exciting consequence of our acquisition of the art of flying.

The new technique of aerial photography has lately been revealing to us traces of the handiwork of our human predecessors which for ages past have been totally invisible to successive generations of human beings who have been living and working—ploughing and building—on the very sites on which these traces are imprinted. So long as we have had our feet on the ground, in immediate contact with these enduring marks which our predecessors' labours have left on the face of the Earth, we have been totally blind to something that has been lying there under our noses. It is only in the air that our eyes have been opened; for it is not until we have parted company with the surface of the Earth, and have climbed in our aeroplane to an altitude at which we seem to have lost all contact with the ground for practical purposes, that we begin to enjoy this novel enhancement of our powers of visual observation. The fact is that the hitherto unobserved physical traces of past human activities consist of undulations or discolorations which are so slight in themselves that they are only visible in a field of vision of a vastly wider sweep than can be commanded by an eye that is approximately on their level. To be perceived they must be caught in a bird's-eye view;[3] and, now that we are

---

[1] See V. C (i) (d) 7, Annex, pp. 332–8, below.
[2] Marcus Aurelius Antoninus: *Meditations*, Book III, chap. 11, and Book IV, chap. 3, quoted in V. C (i) (d) 7, Annex, p. 335, below.
[3] Even on a bird's-eye view the traces that are a matter of colour and not of contour are often invisible on the bare ground and only come to light in the springing corn; for

able to emulate the vision of a hawk or kite by training upon the ground from an aeroplane a camera fitted with a telescopic lens, we can demonstrate to the astonished yokel, whom we have taken up with us on our survey-flight, that his native village lies within the circumvallation of a Roman camp of which he and his forebears have never suspected the existence—although they have in fact been sleeping every night within that historic rampart, and have been crossing it daily as they have plodded to and fro between their cottages and their fields, from generation to generation.

The relation of the English village to the Roman camp offers us an image of the relation between This World and the *Civitas Dei* that may give us some further insight into that mystery. At any rate, if we work the simile out, we shall find that it presents a number of illuminating aspects.

In the first place we see two settlements—camp and village—coexisting on the same site. In the second place we see that it is possible for them to coexist—in defiance of the geometrical axiom that two different objects cannot simultaneously occupy the same space—because the respective modes of their simultaneous existence are not identical in quality. The fields and cottages of the village provide the inhabitants with physical food and shelter; the ramparts of the camp have provided them with institutions and ideas in virtue of which they are now living together as social animals. In the third place we see that, although the village is palpable whereas the camp is not even visible except on a bird's-eye view, the inhabitants of the site are dependent on the camp, as well as on the village, for commodities which are necessities of life. Indeed, the camp's contribution is, if anything, more important than the village's if it is true, as it seems to be, that, in the course of the evolution of Life, Sub-Man had to become a social animal as a preliminary step towards becoming human.[1] Without the social heritage which they have derived from the invisible empire of which the camp has been an outpost, the inhabitants of the palpable village would find themselves unable to keep up that social co-operation which is the necessary moral condition for the upkeep of their material well-being.

There is yet another point, which is perhaps the most significant of the truths that our simile brings to light; and this is that the existence of the empire, and its effect on the villagers' lives, are

the cause of the discoloration is a slight change in the chemical composition of the soil through a replacement of the natural strata by man-made deposits consisting in part of the debris of human artifacts; and, even in an aeroplane photograph, this local difference in the soil may not be apparent except when it is reproduced—and, in the process, exaggerated—in the colour and height and thickness of a crop that has been sown on the site.

[1] See I. C (iii) (*c*), vol. i, p. 173, footnote 3, above.

facts which are entirely independent of the beneficiaries' awareness of them. The moment at which the yokel first descried the outline of the camp—as he leant over the side of the aeroplane with the archaeologist at his elbow to tell him where to look and what to look for—was not, of course, the moment at which he first began to draw benefit from the legacy of the oecumenical empire of which the camp was once a local *point d'appui*. As a matter of fact, he began to draw his profit in times before he was born or conceived; for the social heritage which he derives from the empire has been handed down to him by a long line of ancestors. And the fact of the empire's existence has been having its effect just the same, even though the villagers may not have been aware till this moment that their village lay within the empire's bounds—and perhaps not even aware that there was any such thing as this empire within their horizon.

Even if they do now begin to perceive—as a consequence of a belated Pisgah-sight from the cock-pit of a newly invented flying-machine—some glimmer of what the empire has been doing all the time for them, as well as for their forefathers, their belated discovery of the empire is even now not likely to extend very far beyond the immediate neighbourhood of their own local habitat. Will the local clue that has just been given them enable them to infer that the empire that has swum into their ken has a vastly wider ambit than the field of vision which has been opened up to them by a single flight in an aeroplane circling just above their home parish? Have they the imagination to picture in their mind's eye the long roads running from camp to camp, and through forum and municipium, till they lead to Rome and out of Rome again to the banks of the Danube and the Euphrates and to the fringes of the Syrian and the Libyan desert? Can they conceive of a Roman Peace which spreads its mantle over Dura and Durostorum and Timgad as well as over Verulam and Chester? And can they comprehend that the effect which the Roman Empire is having upon their own lives is also being exerted upon the lives of their contemporaries in distant countries under different climes? It hardly seems probable that a majority of the latter-day beneficiaries of the Roman Empire will have gained even an inkling of the full extent of the Roman domain, or of the full range of the Imperial Government's operation, from their discovery of the presence of a Roman camp within the bounds of their English parish; and we can conceive of a state of affairs in which all knowledge of the Roman Empire has been irretrievably lost; for even those physical traces that are, as it happens, still visible from the air might easily have vanished completely in the course of the centuries that went by before aeroplanes were invented. If that had been the order of events, and if our air-survey had therefore after all brought no Roman camp into view on the site of our English village, would this defeat for Archaeology have wiped off the slate of History either the fact or the effect of the Roman Empire's existence? The answer is, of course, in the negative; and the truth which we can grasp in its mundane application to the Roman Empire can be seen by analogy to be true of the Kingdom of God—and of that Kingdom's King.

'That was the true light which lighteth every man that cometh into the World. He was in the World, and the World was made by Him, and the World knew Him not.'[1]

To know Him—and, through Him, the Kingdom over which He reigns—it is not enough for our yokel in his aeroplane to see the World with the eye of a hawk. The man must be given an eye which not only magnifies but also penetrates into other dimensions. What he needs is the eye of a poet,

> To see a world in a grain of sand
> And a heaven in a wild flower,
> Hold Infinity in the palm of your hand,
> And Eternity in an hour.[2]

And the poet who has this vision of the transfiguration of This World by the Kingdom of God must also be something of a prophet, for he must have an intuition of the Godhead which poetry alone cannot give him. The act of Transfiguration is a mystery because it is an act of God and an effect of God's presence—and this is a truth which has been less obscure to the Jewish futurist than to the Greek philosopher.

'The world which was set forth in the philosophy of Poseidonius had many features in common with the world of "Enoch", but "Enoch's" world was not an end in itself. "Enoch" tells us of the World to show us that everything in it is prepared for the inevitable Judgement of the Most High. . . . There is no Great Day in the world of Poseidonius . . . [and] this is the world that Israel refused to accept. The rarefied air of the Stoic heaven was one in which the Jew did not easily breathe. . . . He demanded an ultimate reward for his labour, even at the price of punishment for his faults: otherwise the World seemed to him meaningless. And so, when the Jew does contemplate the World as a whole, as is done in "Enoch", it is all placed under the eye of God, who made it and whose Judgement upon it will give it its meaning. . . . In the last resort the difference between Poseidonius and "Enoch", between late Hellenic Civilization and the Jews that refused to be dominated by it, is symbolized in the sentence from the Fourth Book of Ezra, which says

---

[1] John i. 9-10. [2] Blake, William: *Auguries of Innocence.*

directly and in so many words: "The Most High hath not made one world, but two".[1] This is the essential thing, the central doctrine that animates all the Apocalypses. . . . And those who cling to the belief that human history is not altogether meaningless and that it marches, however slowly and haltingly, to a definite goal, ought to regard the ideas enshrined in books like "Enoch" with sympathy.'[2]

In this revelation of a reality which the veil of Futurism masks until it is rent, the relation between the Kingdom of God and This World can be seen—now no longer in an image but direct (albeit still darkly, through a glass)[3]—as a manifestation of God's all-pervading presence and activity.

> O world invisible, we view thee,
> O world intangible, we touch thee,
> O world unknowable, we know thee,
> Inapprehensible, we clutch thee!
>
> Does the fish soar to find the ocean,
> The eagle plunge to find the air—
> That we ask of the stars in motion
> If they have rumour of thee there?
>
> Not where the wheeling systems darken
> And our benumbed conceiving soars!—
> The drift of pinions, would we hearken,
> Beats at our own clay-shuttered doors.
>
> The angels keep their ancient places—
> Turn but a stone and start a wing!
> 'Tis ye, 'tis your estrangèd faces,
> That miss the many-splendoured thing.[4]

But how in fact can God's will be done on Earth as it is in Heaven? In the technical language of Theology the omnipresence of God involves His immanence in This World and in every living soul in it, as well as His transcendent existence on supra-mundane planes of being. In the Christian conception of the Godhead His transcendent aspect is displayed in Gōd the Father and His immanent aspect in God the Holy Ghost; but the distinctive and also crucial feature of the Christian Faith is the doctrine that the Godhead is not a Duality but a Trinity in Unity, and that in His aspect as God the Son the other two aspects are unified in a Person who, in virtue of this mystery, is as accessible to the human heart as He is incomprehensible to the human understanding. In the person of Christ Jesus—Very God yet also Very Man—the divine society and the mundane society have a common member who in

---

[1] 4 Ezra vii. 50.
[2] Burkitt, F. C.: *Jewish and Christian Apocalypses* (London 1914, Milford), pp. 31–3.
[3] 1 Cor. xiii. 12.   [4] Thompson, Francis: *In No Strange Land.*

the order of This World is born into the ranks of the Proletariat and dies the death of a malefactor, while in the order of the Other World He is the King of God's Kingdom—and a King who is God Himself and not God's less-than-divine deputy.[1]

[1] This Christian conception of Christ the King has points both of likeness to and of difference from both of the two Jewish conceptions of Yahweh the King (see V. C (i) (d) 9 (γ), p. 126, footnote 5, above) on the one hand, and of the Messiah on the other. Christ is, like Yahweh, a king who is also God; but at the same time Christ's divinity differs from Yahweh's in being not exclusively transcendent; and on this account Christ's kingship can be felt as a concrete and personal exercise of royal authority, whereas the awful remoteness and aloofness of the God of Israel from his worshippers makes it difficult for them to conceive of Yahweh's kingship as a real function which is something more than a formal title of honour. In this point of realism—and it is a point of capital importance—the figure of Christ the King bears less resemblance to that of Yahweh the King than to that of the Messiah; and it is no accident that the very name of Christ is derived historically from the title (in its Greek dress) of the king whose coming was awaited by the Jewish futurists. The Christian idea of Christ's kingship agrees with the Jewish expectation of the Messiah's kingship in conceiving of the kingship as a reality; but at the same time it differs from this Jewish expectation in believing the king to be God instead of expecting him to be a man sent by God as His human deputy. This point of difference—and it is of not less capital importance than the point of likeness—between the Christian view of Christ and the Jewish view of the Messiah comes out in the significant fact that the connotation of the word 'Christ' has been exactly reversed in the process of being taken over into the Christian out of the Jewish vocabulary. In its literal and original meaning of 'the Lord's Anointed' the title 'Christ' signifies that its bearer is himself some one other than, and lower than, God who has invested him with his office. On the other hand, in the Christian usage the name 'Christ' signifies that its bearer is God besides being the man who bears the name of Jesus. For a Christian, calling Jesus 'Christ' proclaims Him to be God as well as man, while for a Jew the addition of the title 'Christ' to the name Jesus would rule out the possibility of Jesus being a god (e.g. one of the false gods worshipped by the Gentiles), and would certify that he was a purely human emissary of Yahweh.

On this criterion the Zoroastrian figure of the Saošyant or Son of Man, who is to be the king of the *Zwischenreich* for the period of the Millennium (see V. C (i) (d) 9 (γ), pp. 126 and 130-1, above), is to be classed with the Jewish figure of the Messiah who is to be the king of the future Jewish universal state, and not with the Christian figure of Christ who is the king of the Kingdom of God. It is true that the Saošyant is credited with certain apparently superhuman qualities and powers, but it is none the less clear that he is conceived of as being, like the Jewish Messiah, both less than divine and other than the One True God. The essential humanity of the Saošyant is guaranteed by his lineage—he is to be of the seed of Zarathustra, as the Messiah is to be of the seed of David—and his relation to Ahuramazda, like the relation of Yahweh's Anointed to Yahweh, is that of an agent and emissary, not that of an aspect or avatar. (See Gall, A. von: Βασιλεία τοῦ Θεοῦ (Heidelberg 1926, Winter), index, s.vv. *Saošyant* and *Menschensohn*.)

In the Jewish conception of the Messiah the point of capital importance about his birth is his legitimate descent in the male line from David, and this of course rules out all idea of the Messiah being born of a virgin (see V. C (ii) (a), p. 268, footnote 5, below). According to von Gall, op. cit., p. viii, however, Jesus rejected the role of the Jewish Messiah in identifying himself with the Zoroastrian Son of Man, and, according to the Zoroastrian Mythology (ibid., pp. 126 and 418-19; cf. Meyer, E.: *Ursprung und Anfänge des Christentums*, vol. ii (Stuttgart and Berlin 1921, Cotta), p. 68), both the Son of Man and the Primal Man, of whom the Son of Man is an avatar, are virgin-born. Apart from his virgin birth, the Zoroastrian Son of Man has other features and prerogatives—'pre-existence, a touch of something godlike, Last Judgement, Ascension into Heaven' (von Gall, op. cit., p. 414)—which the Jewish Messiah lacks. The difference between the indigenous Jewish conception of the Messiah and the new figure introduced by the importation, into Jewish minds, of the Zoroastrian conception of the Son of Man is pointed out by Lagrange, M.-J.: *Le Messianisme chez les Juifs* (Paris 1909, Gabalda), p. 96:

'Le Messie . . . élevé à ces hauteurs, est désormais au niveau des conceptions eschatologiques les plus étendues et les plus spiritualisées. Il pourra figurer beaucoup plus aisément que le Messie, fils de David, roi d'Israël et conquérant. Mais il faut constater aussi que ce n'est plus le même personnage. Ce n'est pas une solution du problème posé par des conceptions nouvelles et par la tradition sur l'homme-Messie; c'est l'option exclusive d'un des deux éléments qu'il eût fallu concilier.'

But how can two natures—one divine and the other human—be both present at once in a single person? We must be able to give some answer to this question if we are to be sure that we are not just reciting a meaningless form of words when we say that the link between the Kingdom of God and the Society of This World consists in the possession of a common member who is truly native to each of these two diverse spiritual climes. Answers, cast in the form of creeds, have been worked out by Christian Fathers in terms of the technical vocabulary of the Hellenic philosophers; but this metaphysical line of approach to the problem is perhaps not the only one open to us. We may find an alternative starting-point in the postulate that the divine nature, in so far as it is accessible to us, must have something in common with our own; and, if we look for one particular spiritual faculty which we are conscious of possessing in our own souls and which we also can attribute with absolute confidence to God—because God would be spiritually inferior even to Man (*quod est absurdum*) if this faculty were not in Him but were nevertheless in us—then the faculty which we shall think of first as being common to Man and God will be one which the philosophers wish to mortify,[1] and that is the faculty of Love.

This stone which both Zeno and Gautama have so obstinately rejected is become the head of the corner[2] of the temple of the New Testament.[3] In the instruction given to Nicodemus, Love is

[1] See V. C (i) (*d*) 10, pp. 145–8, and the present chapter, pp. 150–4, above.

[2] Matt. xxi. 42 (quoting Ps. cxviii. 22). In this Study this text has been quoted already in IV. C (iii) (*c*) 1, vol. iv, p. 248, above.

[3] Love has also become the axle-tree of the vehicle of the Mahāyāna; and its conquest of Buddhism is more surprising than its outburst in Christianity; for the Christian religion of Love is in conscious and deliberate revolt against the Stoic philosophy of Detachment, whereas the Mahayanian religion of Love purports to be fulfilling the Hinayanian law and not destroying it—though, in Hinayanian eyes, the Mahayanian Bodhisattva is a Hinayanian arhat *manqué* (see V. C (i) (*d*) 10, p. 148, above). The Bodhisattva is in fact an arhat who, at the moment when his age-long efforts to attain Detachment have brought him at last to the brink of *Nirvāna*, refrains from immediately entering into his rest through taking the final step that would precipitate him into the bliss of self-annihilation, and decides, instead, to postpone the consummation of his own spiritual career—and this, may be, for countless ages more—in order to devote himself to the self-imposed task of helping other beings, by communicating to them some of the light of his own enlightenment, to reach, and perhaps to pass, the verge on which the Buddha-to-be now himself stands voluntarily poised (see Thomas, E. J.: *The History of Buddhist Thought* (London 1933, Kegan Paul), pp. 169–72). A follower of Christ will agree with the follower of the Mahāyāna that the Bodhisattva who, for love of his fellows, forbears to drink of the liberating elixir of Lethe when the cup is at his lips, is overcoming the Self in a far profounder sense than the arhat who exercises his duly earned right to consummate his own self-annihilation without being deterred by any pity for a groaning and travailing creation. The labour of Love to which the Bodhisattva dedicates himself is not unworthy to be compared with the self-sacrifice of Christ; and there is a Mahayanian counterpart of the Christian Kingdom of God in the Paradise into which a being who finds himself in the toils of This World may be born at his next birth if in his present life he has called, in a spirit of true faith, upon the name of the Bodhisattva whose name is Amitābha ('Measureless Light') or Amitāyus ('Measureless Life'). It is true that this analogy is imperfect. In the first place Amida is not God; in the second place his Paradise is not an eternal abode, but only a *Zwischenreich* beyond which the nonentity of *Nirvāna* still *patet immane et vasto respectat hiatu*

revealed as being both the motive that moves God to redeem Man
at the price of incarnation and crucifixion,[1] and the means that
enables Man to win access to God.[2] The working of Love in
God's heart—in moving God to suffer death on the Cross—is
brought out in the Synoptic Gospels in their account of the circumstances in which Jesus announces to His disciples that His
destiny is the Passion instead of being a Jewish Messiah's conventional worldly success. He forbears to reveal to them this, for
them, appalling truth until His divinity has been guessed by Peter
and has been manifested in the Transfiguration; but, as soon as
He has made His epiphany as God, He at once breaks silence
about His Passion.[3] The meaning of these revelations in this
sequence surely is that a Love which loves to the death is the
essence of God's nature. As for the working of Love in human
hearts as a means of access for Man to God, it is extolled as the
sovereign—and sole indispensable—means to this supreme end of
Man in the thirteenth chapter of the First Epistle of Paul the
Apostle to the Corinthians. And, if we try to take a comprehensive
view of the constitution of the *Civitas Dei*, and inquire what
miraculous spiritual force it is that makes it possible for its diverse
members, human and divine, to dwell together in unity,[4] we find
that Love is the life-blood of this supra-mundane body social and
the *arcanum imperii*[5] of its divine king. The secret is divulged in
the fourth chapter of the First Epistle General of John. The love
of God for Man—as manifested to Man in Christ Crucified—
calls out in Man an answering love for God; and this love of Man
for God (which is also a manifestation of the spirit of a Godhead who is immanent in the Soul of Man, as He is in all things)[6]

(Eliot, Sir Charles: *Japanese Buddhism* (London 1935, Arnold), p. 106); and in the
third place the bliss of Amida's 'Pure Land' is depicted as that of a sort of etherial
Lotus-Eaters' Garden of Eden (ibid.), like the bliss enjoyed by the Hellenic gods in
the Epicurean *intermundia* (see V. C (i) (d) 10, p. 144, above). There is, however, one
feature of capital importance that is common to the *Civitas Dei* as conceived of by Saint
Augustine and to the Paradise of Amida as conceived of by, for example, Ryōyo Shogei
(*vivebat* A.D. 1314–1420), a Japanese Mahayanian Father who was the Seventh Patriarch
of the Jōdo Sect (see V. C (i) (c) 2, vol. v, pp. 96–103, above), and who taught that
'Amida is omnipresent and his Paradise is simply absolute reality—if we can change our
point of view and see things as they really are, we can be in the Pure Land here and
now' (Eliot, op. cit., p. 385). (For the vein of personal devotion (*bhakti*) in the Mahāyāna see V. C (i) (c) 2, vol. v, pp. 134–6, and V. C (i) (c) 4, vol. v, pp. 361–2, above;
for the Japanese adaptation of the Mahayanian cult of Amitābha see cap. cit., vol. cit.,
pp. 96–103, above.)

[1] John iii. 13–17.   [2] John iii. 3–8.

[3] For this association between Jesus's prediction of His Passion and the immediately
antecedent revelations of His divinity see V. C (i) (c) 2, vol. v, p. 74, and V. C (i) (d) 1,
vol. v, pp. 392–3 above, and V. C (ii) (a), Annex II, in the present volume, p. 383, below.

[4] Ps. cxxxiii. 1.   [5] Tacitus: *Annals*, Book II, chap. 36.

[6] This love of Man for God, which is both a response to, and a manifestation of, God's
love for Man, is expounded as follows by Saint Thomas Aquinas: *Summa Theologiae*,
2 a, 2 ae. Q. 24. Art. 2: 'Charity (*Caritas*) is a kind of friendship (*amicitia*) of Man
towards God, which is founded upon the communication [by God to Man] of eternal
bliss. This communication, however, is of the order, not of the gifts of Nature, but of

flows on Earth along the channel of Man's love for his human brother.

'Beloved, if God so loved us, we ought also to love one another. No man hath seen God at any time. If we love one another, God dwelleth in us and His love is perfected in us.'[1]

In virtue of this Love which is equally human and divine and which is therefore able to circulate through all the members of the *Civitas Dei*, the Kingdom of God has a peace of its own which is not the philosophic peace of Detachment.[2] It is in these negative terms that the Peace of God is enigmatically proclaimed by Christ the King:

'Peace I leave with you; my peace I give unto you. Not as the World giveth give I unto you.'[3]

The riddle is wrestled with—and read, perhaps, as far as it can be read by human minds on Earth—in the following passage of Saint Augustine's *magnum opus*:

'The peace of the Heavenly Commonwealth (*caelestis civitatis*) is a perfectly organized and perfectly harmonious common participation in the enjoyment of God and of one another in God (*societas fruendi Deo et invicem in Deo*).[4] . . . The commonwealth of the irreligious, in which

the gifts of Grace, because, as is written in Romans vi. 23, "the gift of God is eternal life". It follows that Charity itself likewise exceeds the capacity of Nature; but something that exceeds the capacity of Nature cannot either be natural or be acquired through natural faculties, because a natural effect cannot transcend its own cause. It follows that Charity cannot either be implanted in us by Nature or be acquired by natural powers. It can only be acquired by an inpouring of the Holy Spirit, who is the love of the Father and the Son, and whose indwelling in us is identical with the creation of Charity in us (*cuius participatio in nobis est ipsa Caritas creata*).'

This divine transfiguration of the human Soul has also been described by Plato (*Theaetetus*, 176 A–B) in words that he puts into the mouth of Socrates:

'Evil cannot cease to be, for there must ever be something that is the antithesis of the good; and it cannot be situate in Heaven; so it must necessarily haunt This World and prey upon Mortality. So one must seek to fly, as quickly as may be, hence thither. This flight consists in becoming as like to God as it is possible for Man to be (φυγὴ δὲ ὁμοίωσις θεῷ κατὰ τὸ δυνατόν). And becoming like to God means becoming rationally righteous and holy (ὁμοίωσις δὲ δίκαιον καὶ ὅσιον μετὰ φρονήσεως γενέσθαι).' In these three sentences Plato successively rejects the mundane Utopias of Archaism and Futurism; takes the path of Detachment; and pushes on to the goal of Transfiguration without halting at the station of *Nirvāna*. If he had added, with Saint Thomas, that Transfiguration (ὁμοίωσις) cannot be achieved by Man's natural powers, but only by a gift of God's grace, this passage would have been completely Christian. And in another passage (*Letters*, No. 7, 341 C–D), where he writes of 'light caught from a leaping flame', he has come very near to describing the miracle of Pentecost. Transfiguration is, as we have seen (in III. C (ii) (*a*), vol. iii, pp. 245–6, above), the ideal relation for which Mimesis is an unsatisfactory substitute. If we now ask ourselves what it is in Transfiguration that Mimesis lacks, we shall answer, with Saint Thomas, that it is the gift of God's grace.

[1] 1 John iv. 11–12. For the modern Western philosopher Bergson's intuition of the truth that a common love for the One True God is the only feeling that can effectively take the place, and fulfil the function, of that common hatred of some human enemy which is the emotional bond between the members of a primitive society, see V. C (i), (*d*) 7, pp. 12–13, above, and Part VII, below.

[2] For the contrast which Epictetus draws between the *Pax Augusta* and the *Pax Zenonica* see V. C (i) (*d*) 7, pp. 3 and 16, footnote 2, and V. C (i) (*d*) 10, p. 142, above.   [3] John xiv. 27.

[4] This definition is also given, in the same words, in the passage quoted in V. C (i) (*d*) 11, Annex II, p. 367, below.—A.J.T.

God does not bear rule or receive obedience—an obedience that consists in offering sacrifice to Him alone, so that the mind rules the body, and the reason the vices, with uprightness and loyalty—such a commonwealth will be without the reality of justice. For, although the mind may appear to be ruling the body, and the reason the vices, quite creditably, neither of them will be at all properly fulfilling its task if it is not itself serving God in the way in which God Himself has ordained that He should be served. For how can a soul be mistress of the body and of the vices if it is ignorant of the True God and is not amenable to His rule? . . . The very virtues that it believes itself to possess—the virtues through which it rules the body and the vices—are vices rather than virtues if this soul addresses them to the winning or the holding of anything except God. For, while some people consider that the virtues are genuine and sincere precisely when they are addressed to themselves and are not cultivated for any ulterior object, the truth is that in such conditions they become puffed up and conceited, and are accordingly to be accounted not virtues but vices. What gives life to a physical organism is something which does not proceed from it but which is above it; and, analogously, what gives happiness in life to a human being is something which does not proceed from human nature but which is above human nature.'[1]

The last sentence of this passage perhaps points to the solution of that spiritual problem which is inexorably presented to the Soul by the poignant experience of mundane life in a disintegrating society. We have found that it is impossible to escape from an intolerable Present either by taking flying leaps up or down the stream of Time or again by seeking to achieve a complete Detachment from life at the cost of annihilating the Self. We have now gained a glimpse of an alternative way of life which does promise

'to give light to them that sit in darkness and in the shadow of death, to guide our feet into the way of peace';[2]

and this happy issue out of our afflictions is to be found in enrolling ourselves as citizens of a *Civitas Dei* of which Christ Crucified is king. This way of taking our departure from the City of Destruction is not an act of truancy; it is 'a withdrawal according to plan'; and the plan—as Christ's Passion proclaims—is not to save ourselves by escaping from a dangerous and painful mundane entanglement, but to seize the initiative in order, at our own peril, to save the City of Destruction from its doom by converting it to the Peace of God. For the human citizen of the City of God who is still in the flesh, this movement of spiritual withdrawal-and-return may entail—if the soldier is singled out for special

[1] Saint Augustine: *De Civitate Dei*, Book XIX, chaps. 13, 24, and 25.
[2] Luke i. 79.

honour—an act, not of truancy, but of martyrdom; but the martyr's goal is not Gautama's goal of self-annihilation: it is Christ's goal of self-fulfilment through self-surrender. 'To this end was I born, and for this cause came I into the World.'[1]

The member of a disintegrating mundane society who has taken this road has a surer hope, and therefore a deeper happiness, than the merely 'once-born' member of a mundane society that is still in growth; for he has learnt the saving truths that 'the Most High hath not made one world, but two',[2] and that the human wayfarer who still finds himself a sojourner in This World is not on that account beyond the pale of the Other World but is travelling all the time within the domain of the Kingdom of God and is at liberty to live as a citizen of this omnipresent commonwealth here and now, if he is willing with all his heart to pay allegiance to Christ the King and to take upon himself those obligations of citizenship which Christ has consecrated by voluntarily fulfilling them in person. This entry into the Kingdom of God is a second birth;[3] and, for the 'once-born' denizen of This World, the discovery that it is possible to obtain this freedom[4] is like finding treasure hid in a field, or finding one pearl of great price.[5] Such a trove is to be bought even at the cost of selling all that the finder has. And the reckoning of spiritual values that is made in these two parables of the Kingdom of God has been anticipated by the testimony of the first and greatest and most Christian of all the Hellenic philosophers:

'In the struggle that will decide whether good or evil is to prevail in us the issue is immeasurably greater than at first sight it might seem to be; and therefore we must not allow ourselves to be carried away by anything in the World—not by honours, not by riches, not by power, and not by poetry either. For none of these things is worth the price of neglecting Righteousness and the rest of what constitutes Virtue. . . . We must do everything that lies in our power to attain to Virtue and Wisdom in This Life. The prize is so splendid and the hope is so great.'[6]

---

[1] John xviii. 37. [2] 4 Ezra vii. 50, quoted already on p. 162, above.
[3] John iii. 3–8. [4] Acts xxii. 28. [5] Matt. xiii. 44–6.
[6] Plato: *Respublica*, 608 B, and *Phaedo*, 114 C. These two passages are brought into this relation with each other by More, P. E., in *Christ the Word = The Greek Tradition from the Death of Socrates to the Council of Chalcedon: 399 B.C.–A.D. 451*, vol. iv (Princeton 1927, University Press), p. 175, footnote 8. The original Greek runs: Μέγας . . . ὁ ἀγών, . . ., μέγας, οὐχ ὅσος δοκεῖ, τὸ χρηστὸν ἢ κακὸν γενέσθαι, ὥστε οὔτε τιμῇ ἐπαρθέντα οὔτε χρήμασιν οὔτε ἀρχῇ οὐδεμιᾷ οὐδέ γε ποιητικῇ ἄξιον ἀμελῆσαι δικαιοσύνης τε καὶ τῆς ἄλλης ἀρετῆς (608 B) . . . ἀλλὰ . . . χρὴ . . . πᾶν ποιεῖν ὥστε ἀρετῆς καὶ φρονήσεως ἐν τῷ βίῳ μετασχεῖν· καλὸν γὰρ τὸ ἆθλον καὶ ἡ ἐλπὶς μεγάλη (114 C). With these passages of Plato, More, in loc. cit., brings into comparison Sophocles: *Electra*, ll. 1491–2: λόγων γὰρ οὐ νῦν ἐστιν ἀγών, ἀλλὰ σῆς ψυχῆς πέρι, and also Saint Athanasius: *Ep. ad Episc. Aegypti et Libyae*, chap. 21 (Migne, J.-P.: *Patrologia Graeca*, vol. xxv, col. 588): ὡς τοῦ περὶ παντὸς ὄντος ἡμῖν ἀγῶνος. The same reckoning of spiritual values is to be found in Mark viii. 36–7 (= Matt. xvi. 26, and Luke ix. 25), and in Lucretius: *De Rerum Natura*, Book III, ll. 1071–5 (already quoted in I. C (i) (a), vol. i, p. 55, footnote 3, above).

(e) PALINGENESIA

We have now completed our survey[1] of four experimental ways of life which are so many exploratory attempts to find some practicable alternative to a familiar habit of living and moving at ease in a growing civilization. When this comfortable road has been remorselessly closed by the catastrophe of a social breakdown, these four ways present themselves as the alternative possible by-passes. One piece of knowledge that we have gained from our survey of them is some notion of the essential differences between their respective natures.

We have found that the paths of Archaism and Futurism are two alternative substitutes for the growth of a civilization which are both of them incompatible with growth of any kind, since they both deliberately aim at a breach of continuity, and the principle of continuity is of the essence of the movement of growth in whatever terms we may try to describe or define it. Archaism is an attempt to take a flying leap out of the mundane Present backwards into an already vanished mundane Past, while Futurism is an attempt to take a similar leap forwards into a still invisible mundane Future. In both of these *tours de force* the would-be breach of continuity is precisely what makes the spiritual acrobatic feat attractive to those souls that attempt it; and the common vice of Futurism and Archaism is thus not only manifest but also manifestly fatal. Futurism and Archaism are sheer negations of growth, and that is the whole of their tragedy. On the other hand, Detachment and Transfiguration, which are another pair of alternative substitutes for the swan-path of a growing civilization, both differ alike from Archaism and from Futurism in what is the capital point; for, unlike Archaism and Futurism, Detachment and Transfiguration are both of them reactions to the breakdown of a civilization which are still, in themselves, ways of growth—if we are to judge by the criterion of growth that we have tried to work out in an earlier part of this Study.[2]

The essential feature in which the movements of Detachment and Transfiguration diverge from those of Archaism and Futurism is, as we have seen, that they are not attempts to escape from the Present without abandoning the level of mundane life, but are endeavours to act upon a belief that there can be no salvation from that sickness of the Soul which the breakdown of a civilization brings to light through any less radical remedy than a change of spiritual clime or dimension;[3] and this is another way of saying

[1] In V. C (i) (d) 8–11, above.
[2] See Part III. C (i) (c) and (d), vol. iii, pp. 174–217, above.
[3] See V. C (i) (d) 1, vol. v, p. 394, above.

that both Detachment and Transfiguration are examples of that 'transference of the field of action' from the Macrocosm to the Microcosm which manifests itself qualitatively in the spiritual phenomenon of 'etherialization'.[1] If we are right in believing that these are symptoms of growth, and right again in believing that every example of human growth will always be found to have a social as well as an individual aspect,[2] and if we are also bound to assume *ex hypothesi* that the society to whose growth the movements of Detachment and Transfiguration thus bear witness cannot be any society of the species 'civilizations'—considering that a disintegrating society of that species is the City of Destruction from which either movement is an endeavour to escape—then we can only conclude that the movements of Detachment and Transfiguration bear witness to the growth of a society, or societies, of some other kind or kinds.

Is the singular or the dual the right number to use in referring to the social medium in which our two movements of Detachment and Transfiguration take place? The best way to approach this question may be to ask ourselves another: What is the difference between the two movements of Detachment and Transfiguration in terms of social growth? If they are both of them manifestations of social growth and yet are different from one another, does their difference reflect a distinction between two species of society which differ specifically from one another as well as from the species called 'civilizations'? Or does the difference between Detachment and Transfiguration reflect a difference of social growth which is not one of kind but merely one of degree? Are the two movements both of them manifestations of the growth of a single species of society—and perhaps even of a single unique representative of this species—at two different points on a course that runs through a succession of stages from genesis towards prime? When we put our question in this way, we shall see that we already have grounds for giving it the second of the two possible answers; for we have already apprehended[3]—though this not yet in terms of growth but so far only in terms of direction—the relation which our two movements bear to one another. While Detachment is a simple movement of sheer withdrawal, Transfiguration is a compound movement whose first beat is likewise a withdrawal but whose second beat is a return. The difference between an act of

---

[1] See Part III. C (i) (c) and (d), vol. iii, pp. 174–217, above.

[2] This belief follows from the fact that Man is 'by nature a social animal', in the sense that Man's pre-human ancestors did not, and could not, become human until they had first attained to sociality. (For Aristotle's thesis and Eduard Meyer's argument in favour of it see I. C (iii) (c), vol. i, p. 173, footnote 3, above.)

[3] In V. C (i) (d) 1, vol. v, pp. 394–7; V. C (i) (d) 10, in the present volume, pp. 132–3; and V. C (i) (d) 11, p. 151, footnote 4, above.

withdrawal and an act of withdrawal-and-return[1] is not a difference between one road and another but merely a difference in the number of stages traversed. And these two different degrees of progress may both be attained on a single road along which both the travellers are moving in the same direction.

The actual identity of the road in the case of the two progresses here in question can be tested and confirmed by taking account of the goal. We have seen what is the goal of that movement of withdrawal-and-return which we have called Transfiguration. The aim of Transfiguration is to give light to them that sit in darkness[2] and to make the darkness comprehend this light that is shining in it;[3] and this aim is pursued by seeking the Kingdom of God in order to bring its life, which is 'the light of men',[4] into action—or rather into visibility, since God is in action always and everywhere—in the field of life in This World. The goal of Transfiguration is thus the Kingdom of God. And there is a manifest difference, which is not just one of place but rather one of dimension and of kind, between this *Civitas Dei* and the pair of mundane Utopias—a 'City of Cecrops' and a 'City of the Sun'—that are the respective goals of Archaism and of Futurism. But what is the relation between the *Civitas Dei* and the *Nirvāna* that is the goal of Detachment? Are these two supra-mundane goals of human endeavour two mutually exclusive alternatives? Or is only one of the two truly a goal, while the other is merely a halting-place on the way? We have seen already that the second of these two theoretical possibilities is the fact. The Hinayanian Buddhist arhat, for whom *Nirvāna* is the be-all and end-all, is, in terms of Bergson's simile,[5] like the driver of a locomotive who has mistaken a station for the terminus; and the arhat's misapprehension is shared by the Bodhisattva who, out of compassion towards other living beings, stays poised on the brink of *Nirvāna* for aeons of aeons. The Bodhisattva is like an engine-driver who, having come within view of the station and having seen that the signal just this side of it permits him to pass, pulls up at the signal-box and quixotically sets the signal against himself. But there is also another driver whose train is neither the Hīnayāna nor the Mahāyāna, and that is the Christian mystic who recognizes the station for what it is and manfully opens the throttle again, after the momentary pause which the time-table prescribes, without being deterred by the blackness of the tunnel that engulfs the track

---

[1] The nature of this compound *motif* of Withdrawal-and-Return has been examined in III. C (ii) (*b*), vol. iii, pp. 248–63, above.
[2] Luke i. 79.　　　[3] John i. 5.　　　[4] John i. 4.
[5] See the passage of Bergson that has been quoted in III. C (ii)(*a*), vol. iii, pp. 234–5, above.

when this station has been left behind. This driver knows that he has not yet reached the terminus; and his will to reach it is so strong that it carries him through that 'dark night' in which the road that leads to the goal of the movement of Transfiguration makes its crucial reversal of direction from 'withdrawal' towards 'return'.[1]

It would thus appear that, in bearing witness to the growth of some kind of society that is neither a civilization nor a Utopia, the two movements of Detachment and Transfiguration are two pieces of evidence for a single passage of life. Both of them are reactions to the disintegration of a civilization; and, in the imagery of the Sinic *Weltanschauung*, the disintegration of a civilization discharges itself, as we have seen, in a full cycle of the alternating rhythm of Yin-and-Yang.[2] In the first beat of the rhythm a Yang-movement which has been destructive passes over into a Yin-state which is a peace of exhaustion; but the rhythm is not arrested at the dead point (as the philosophy of Detachment seeks to quench Life in *Nirvāna*); it passes over again from the Yin-state into a Yang-movement which, this time, is not destructive but is creative (like the Christian Faith that carries the Soul on beyond Detachment into Transfiguration). This double beat of the rhythm of Yin-and-Yang is that rendering of the *motif* of Withdrawal-and-Return on which we stumbled not far from the beginning of the present Part of our Study, and for which we there provisionally coined the name of Schism-and-Palingenesia.[3] Our intervening study of 'schism'—first in the Body Social and then in the Soul—has been long and laborious; but it has led us to the threshold of 'palingenesia' at last.

In this Study the word 'palingenesia', like the word 'proletariat',[4] has been commandeered to serve our purpose; and in the act of laying hands upon it we have noted[5] that its literal meaning—'recurrence of birth'—has in it an element of ambiguity. The 'recurrence' might refer exclusively to the event of birth or alternatively its reference might extend to the nature of the thing born; and, while in the latter use the word 'palingenesia' would mean a repetitive rebirth of something that has been born before, in the former use it would mean an unprecedented new birth of something that is now being born for the first time. We have observed

---

[1] See the passages quoted from Bergson in loc. cit. and in III. C (ii) (*b*), vol. iii, pp. 255–6, above.

[2] For Yin-and-Yang see Part II. B, vol. i, pp. 201–4; for the analysis of the disintegration of a civilization in terms of Yin-and-Yang see V. C (i) (*b*), vol. v, p. 26, above.

[3] In V. C (i) (*b*), vol. v, p. 27, above.

[4] For the sense in which the word 'proletariat' is used in this Study see I. B (iv), vol. i, p. 41, footnote 3, above.

[5] In V. C (i) (*b*), vol. v, p. 27, footnote 2, above.

in the same place that a recurrent birth of some identical thing was probably the idea in the minds of the Stoic philosophers by whom (as far as can be ascertained) the word 'palingenesia' was originally coined; but we have kept a free hand for ourselves to use the word in our own context in either of two meanings that are both of them equally legitimate. We have now to decide for ourselves which of the alternative meanings we are to adopt.

Are we to use 'palingenesia' in the sense of a rebirth of the actual civilization that is in course of disintegration? This would be a literal application of one of the two possible meanings of the word; but this cannot be our meaning; for it is a meaning which expresses the aim, not of Transfiguration, but of Archaism.[1]

Then is our 'palingenesia' to mean, not, perhaps, the literal rebirth of an existing civilization that is in disintegration, but the replacement of this now irretrievably damaged specimen by another representative of the same species? This cannot be our meaning either; for that is the aim, not of Transfiguration, but of Futurism; and, if the process is repeated *ad infinitum* and is translated from the mundane on to the cosmic scale, the result is the cyclic rhythm[2] which, in the history of Hellenic thought, was proclaimed to be the fundamental 'law' of the Universe by Stoic and Epicurean philosophers who apparently were not put out by the incongruity between their rotativist conception of the nature of Reality and their ethical aim of Detachment.

The Indic philosophers who have pursued the same aim have had the courage to bend their theories into conformity with it, and have set themselves to break the Wheel of Existence as the only sure way of escape from being broken on it. Is the *Nirvāna* that is attained by a complete extinction of desire the 'palingenesia' that we have in mind? No, that is impossible; for *Nirvāna* and 'palingenesia' are terms that are mutually exclusive. The very definition of *Nirvāna* is that this is the state that supervenes when birth has ceased to recur; and, however far-fetched the imagery to which we may have recourse in attempting the impossible feat of depicting 'a perfect and absolute blank', we can be certain beforehand that this particular image will have no place in our picture.

---

[1] In this archaistic meaning παλιγγενεσία is synonymous with ἀποκατάστασις—the noun of which the verb is used in. Mark ix. 12: 'Elias verily cometh first and restoreth (ἀποκαθιστᾷ) all things.' In the Jewish *Weltanschauung* of Jesus's age this archaistic 'restoration' was not an end in itself, but was merely a prelude to the fulfilment of the futuristic hope of a Messianic kingdom; and the Archaism had accordingly acquired a certain Messianic tinge. Elias' restoration of Israel to its state in the age before the beginning of the Syriac 'Time of Troubles' was to be not just a restoration but a supernaturally glorified revision of the vanished past (see V. C (i) (d) 9 (γ), pp. 130-1, above).

[2] For the cyclic theory of the rhythm of the Universe see IV. C (i), vol. iv, pp. 23-38, above.

Nirvāna may be a new state—whether of existence or of non-existence or of both or of neither—but the process by which this state of absolute negativity is reached cannot be conceived of as a 'birth' by any stretch of the imagination.

There is one other alternative meaning which the word 'palin-genesia' can bear. If it means neither the rebirth of a disintegrating mundane society nor the new birth of another representative of the same mundane species nor yet the attainment of a supra-mundane state which is reached by escaping from all birth of every kind, it can only mean an attainment of another supra-mundane state to which the image of birth can be illuminatingly applied because this other state is a positive state of life—though this in a higher spiritual dimension than the life of This World. That is the 'palingenesia' of which Jesus speaks to Nicodemus,[1] and which He proclaims in another place in the same Gospel as the sovereign aim of His own birth in the flesh.

'I am come that they might have life, and that they might have it more abundantly.'[2]

That is a 'palingenesia' in which the work of creation is resumed, but not as a 'vain repetition'.

> Neuen Lebenslauf
> Beginne
> Mit hellem Sinne,
> Und neue Lieder
> Tönen darauf.[3]

The theogony which the Muses had once recited to one of the shepherds of Ascra at the moment when a growing Hellenic Civilization had been bursting into flower[4] finds its antiphony in another theogony which was sung to shepherds of Bethlehem by

---

[1] John iii. 3–8.   [2] John x. 10.

[3] Goethe: *Faust*, ll. 1622–6, quoted already in II. C (ii) (*b*) 1, vol. i, p. 289, above. Dey, J.: Παλιγγενεσία (Münster i. W. 1937, Aschendorff), pp. 161–2 and 167–8, points out that, in Saint Paul's theology, the spiritual rebirth of the Soul is conceived of as the beginning of a process, not as the end of one. This Pauline 'palingenesia' does not bring with it a simultaneous and instantaneous spiritual perfection. It rather introduces into the Soul a spiritual leaven, and Time and Effort are of the essence of the subsequent process of leavening the lump.

[4] In retrospect it is manifest that Hesiod's poetry is a product of the eve of the brief flowering-time of the Hellenic culture; but such an account of Hesiod's place in history would have astonished and exasperated the poet himself. Hesiod believed that he was living in the last stage of a long course of social decline; and his cry of anguish (*Works and Days*, ll. 174–201) at the harrowing thought that he has been born into the Iron Age is the most poignant passage of any in his surviving poems. Was Hesiod tragically mistaking the ferment of growth for the disintegration of decay? Or was he anticipating, in a flash of intuition, one of the two possible answers to a question which was to be propounded by Plato long afterwards, on the morrow of the Hellenic Society's breakdown? Plato once asked himself, as we have seen (in IV. C (i), Annex, vol. iv, pp. 585–8, above), whether the true catastrophe of a civilization might prove to be its rise and not its fall. Was Hesiod answering this question before it had been framed?

angels[1] at a moment when a disintegrating Hellenic Society was suffering the last of the agonies of its 'Time of Troubles' and was falling into the coma of a universal state. The birth of which the angels then sang was not a rebirth of Hellas and not a new birth of other societies of the Hellenistic species. It was the birth in the flesh of the King of the Kingdom of God.

(II) AN ANALYSIS OF DISINTEGRATION

(a) THE RELATION BETWEEN DISINTEGRATING CIVILIZATIONS AND INDIVIDUALS

The Creative Genius as a Saviour.

The problem of the relation between civilizations and individuals has already engaged our attention in the course of our attempt, in an earlier part of this Study,[2] to analyse the process of growth; and, now that we have come to the point at which we must attempt to make a corresponding analysis of the process of disintegration, the same problem presents itself again. This time, however, we need not start from first principles, as we found it advisable to start when the problem confronted us first; for the elements of this problem are the same in both sets of circumstances. If the institution which we call a society consists in the common ground between the respective fields of action of a number of individual souls,[3] then we may take it that this is its constant and uniform consistency so long as it is in existence at all. In respect of this fundamental point it makes no difference whether the society happens to be in growth or in disintegration. In either of these two possible phases of social life it is equally true that the source of action is never the society itself, but is always some individual soul;[4] that the action which is an act of creation is always performed by a soul which is in some sense a superhuman genius;[5] that the genius expresses himself, like every living soul, through action upon his fellows;[6] that in any society the creative personalities are always in a minority;[7] and that the action of the genius upon souls of common clay operates more rarely by the perfect method of direct illumination than through the second-best expedient of a kind of social drill which enlists the faculty of mimesis in the souls of the uncreative rank-and-file and thereby

[1] For this assonance between Hesiod: *Theogony*, ll. 1–34, and Luke ii. 8–20, see further V. C (i) (d) 11, Annex I, pp. 363–4, below.
[2] In III. C (ii) (a), vol. iii, pp. 217–48, above.
[3] For this definition of what a society really is, see ibid., p. 230, above.
[4] Ibid., pp. 230–1, above.   [5] Ibid., pp. 232–4, above.
[6] Ibid., pp. 234–7, above.   [7] Ibid., pp. 237–44, above.

enables them to perform 'mechanically' an evolution which they could not have performed on their own initiative.[1] All this is ground that is fundamental to the problem of the relation between a civilization and the individual souls that are its 'members', whatever the phase through which the civilization may be passing; and, since we have covered this ground already, we need not go over it again, but may proceed at once to look into the more superficial features in which the fundamentally constant and uniform relation between the society and the individual does differ according to whether the society happens to be moving in one or the other of its two alternative directions.

What differences, then, can we detect? Do we find, for instance, that, when a society stops growing and begins to disintegrate, the individuals who take the lead are no longer creative personalities? If the change from growth to disintegration did involve such a change as this in the nature of the society's leadership, then that would be a difference which could hardly be treated as superficial; but as a matter of fact we have discovered already that the difference in the leadership of a society when it is growing and when it is disintegrating is not the difference between creativity and the absence of it. For, while it is true that one of the symptoms of social breakdown and causes of social schism is the degeneration of a minority that has been able to take the lead in virtue of being creative into a minority that attempts to retain the lead by sheer physical domination,[2] we have also seen that the Secession of the Proletariat—which is the answer that the Dominant Minority evokes from the members of the society whom it shuts out from its now closed and privileged circle—is achieved under the leadership of creative personalities for whose activity there is now no scope except in the organization of opposition to the incubus of uncreative powers that be.[3] Thus the change from social growth to social disintegration is not accompanied—either as cause or as effect—by an extinction of the creative spark in the souls of individuals or by a change from creative to uncreative leadership. Creative personalities continue to arise and also continue to take the lead in virtue of their creative power. All that happens is that they now find themselves compelled to do their old work from a new *locus standi* in a society which, in breaking down, has been rent by a schism.

[1] III. C (ii) (*a*), vol. iii, pp. 244–8, above.
[2] For this degeneration of a creative into a dominant minority see I. C (i) (*a*), vol. i, pp. 53–5; V. C (i) (*a*), vol. v, pp. 17–20; and V. C (i) (*c*) 1, vol. v, pp. 35–58, above. For the inherent weakness in the device of mimesis which is at least partly responsible for this disaster see III. C (ii) (*a*), vol. iii, pp. 245–8; III. C (ii) (*b*), vol. iii, p. 374; and IV. C (iii) (*a*), vol. iv, pp. 122–33, above.
[3] See V. C (i) (*b*), vol. v, pp. 29–35, above.

Then does the difference lie in the occasion that brings a potential creativity into action? In a growing civilization, as we have seen,[1] a creative personality comes into action by taking the lead in making a successful response to some challenge which confronts him in common with the uncreative rank-and-file of the society of which they are all 'members'. In a disintegrating civilization Challenge-and-Response is still the mould of action in which the mystery of creation takes place,[2] but the creative leader's task now begins at a different stage and has a different objective. In a growing civilization the creator is called upon to play the part of a conqueror who replies to a challenge with a victorious response; in a disintegrating civilization the same creator is called upon to play the part of a saviour who comes to the rescue of a society that has failed to respond because the challenge has worsted a minority that has ceased to be creative and that has sunk into being merely dominant. Perhaps we have here put our finger upon the true nature of the change in the relation between the rank-and-file of a society and its creative leader when the society passes out of growth into disintegration. It is a difference in the character of the spiritual warfare that the society is waging. In terms of this military simile, a growing society is taking the offensive and therefore looks for the leadership of a conqueror who will show it how to capture fresh ground for its advance, whereas a disintegrating society is trying to stand on the defensive and therefore requires its leader to play the more thankless—but by the same token perhaps also more heroic—part of a saviour who will show it how to hold its ground in a rearguard action.

It follows that, in a disintegrating society, the would-be saviour will appear in diverse guises that will vary with his choice of his defensive strategy and tactics. There will be would-be saviours *of* a disintegrating society who will refuse to despair of the Present and will lead forlorn hopes in an endeavour to turn the tide and to convert the rout into a fresh advance, without being willing to 'retreat according to plan' for the sake of even temporarily breaking off contact with an enemy who has at any rate momentarily gained the upper hand. There will also be saviours *from* a disintegrating society who will seek salvation along one or other of four alternative possible ways of escape which we have reconnoitred already.[3] The saviours who belong to these other four schools will all agree in ruling out the idea of trying to hold the present front line, and *a fortiori* the idea of trying to push it forward. They will all begin

---

[1] In II. C (ii) (*b*), vol. i, pp. 271–338, and Part II. D, vol. ii, *passim*, above.

[2] Challenge-and-Response cannot fail to be found anywhere where there is Life, since our formula is simply a description of Life itself in terms of Will.

[3] In V. C (i) (*d*) 8–11, pp. 49–168, above.

operations by executing a strategic retreat from the disintegrating social structure of the mundane Present; but it is only in this first negative step that they will take the same line. The saviour-archaist and the saviour-futurist will try to evade the problem of facing defeat by attempting to elude the enemy altogether. The archaist will seek to elude him by making a forced march to a position so far to the archaist's own rear, and so deeply ensconced in the jungle-clad fastnesses of the Past, that the enemy will never be able to follow him up. The futurist will seek to achieve the same result by the bolder method of putting his troops on board aeroplanes and landing them far in the rear, not of his own lines, but of the enemy's. There remain the two alternative strategies of Detachment and Transfiguration, and the saviour from a disintegrating society who follows one or the other of these will appear in quite a different guise. Along the path of Detachment he will present himself as a philosopher taking cover behind the mask of a king, and along the path of Transfiguration as a god incarnate in a man.[1] Let us try to apprehend the present object of our study as he passes through this series of Protean metamorphoses.

The Saviour with the Sword.

The would-be saviour *of* a disintegrating society is necessarily a saviour with a sword; but a sword may be either drawn or sheathed, and the swordsman may be discovered in either of two corresponding postures. Either he may be laying about him with naked weapon in hand, like the Gods in combat with the Giants as they are depicted on the Delphic or on the Pergamene frieze, or else he may be sitting in state, with his blade out of sight in its scabbard, as a victor who has 'put all enemies under his feet'.[2] The second of these postures is the end towards which the first is a means; and, though a David or a Hêraklês, who never rests from his labours until he dies in harness, may be a more romantic figure than a Solomon in all his glory or a Zeus in all his majesty, the labours of Hêraklês and the wars of David would be aimless exertions if the serenity of Zeus and the prosperity of Solomon were not their objectives. The sword is only wielded in the hope of being able to use it to such good purpose that it may eventually have no more work to do; but this hope is an illusion; for it is only in fairyland that swords cut Gordian knots which cannot be untied by fingers. 'All they that take the sword shall perish with the sword'[3]

---

[1] According to Pauly-Wissowa: *Real-Encyclopädie der Klassischen Altertumswissenschaft*, 2nd edition, Halbband v, col. 1215, this conception of the Saviour as a god incarnate is an Oriental idea which is foreign to the connotation of the Greek word σωτήρ in its original Hellenic usage. On this question see V. C (ii) (a), Annex II, *passim*, below.
[2] 1 Cor. xv. 25 (a reminiscence of Ps. cx. 1).   [3] Matt. xxvi. 52.

is the inexorable law of real life; and the swordsman's belief in a conclusive victory is an illusion. While David may never be allowed to build the Temple, Solomon's building is built only to be burnt by Nebuchadnezzar; and, while Hêraklês may never win his way in this life to the heights of Olympus, Zeus plants his throne upon the formidable mountain's summit only to court the doom of being hurled in his turn into the abyss into which his own hands have already cast the Titans.[1]

Why is it that a disintegrating society cannot, after all, be saved by the sword even when the swordsman is genuinely eager to return the weapon to its scabbard at the earliest possible moment and to keep it there—unused and unseen—for the longest possible period of time? Is not this twofold action of drawing and sheathing again a sign of grace which ought to have its reward? The warrior who is willing to renounce, at the first opportunity, the use of an instrument which he is only able now to lay aside because he has just used it so successfully must be a victor who is also a statesman, and a statesman who is something of a sage. He must have a large measure of saving common sense (σωφροσύνη) and at least a grain of the more etherial virtue of self-control (ἐγκράτεια).[2] The renunciation of War as an instrument of policy is a resolution which promises to be as fruitful as it is noble and wise; and, whenever it is taken with sincerity, it always arouses high hopes.

> Iam Fides et Pax et Honos Pudorque
> priscus et neglecta redire Virtus
> audet, apparetque beata pleno
> Copia cornu.[3]

In these lines, written to be sung at a public celebration of the beginning of a new era of Hellenic history which was to reproduce a happier past,[4] Horace seems to be consciously chanting the palinode to Hesiod's poignant lament over the reluctant retreat of the two saving goddesses Aedôs and Nemesis from Earth to Olympus under pressure of the onset of the Age of Iron.[5] Why

---

[1] In the theodicy of Aeschylus Zeus succeeds in avoiding the doom that has overtaken his predecessors Uranus and Cronos (see *Agamemnon*, ll. 160–83, and Professor Gilbert Murray's reconstruction of the denouement of the Promethean Trilogy which has been touched upon in this Study in Part III. B, vol. iii, pp. 116–17, above). Aeschylus did not foresee the humiliation that was to be inflicted upon Zeus by the philosophers of a later age of Hellenic history, whose policy towards Zeus was to bind him on his Olympian throne in gilded chains in order that he might serve their turn as a *roi fainéant* for their *Cosmopolis* (see V. C (i) (d) 7, pp. 20–1, above, and V. C (i) (d) 7, Annex, pp. 337–8, below).

[2] For this virtue—which is one of those that find scope in societies that are in disintegration—see V. C (i) (d) 1, vol. v, p. 377, and V. C (i) (d) 2, vol. v, pp. 399–403, above.

[3] Horace: *Carmen Saeculare*, ll. 57–60.

[4] For the *Ludi Saeculares* as an expression of Archaism see V. C (i) (d) 8 (α), p. 51, with footnote 1, above.

[5] Hesiod: *Works and Days*, ll. 197–201. (For Hesiod's philosophy of history see V. C (i) (e), p. 174, footnote 4, above.)

are these seemingly legitimate expectations doomed to be disappointed—as they were in the signal failure of the *Pax Augusta*
to achieve the perpetuity that was of the essence of the poet's
hopes? Is there, then, 'no place of repentance'?[1] Can the Trium-
vir who has once perpetrated, and profited by, the proscriptions
never truly transfigure himself into a Pater Patriae? The answer
to this agonizing question has been given in an Horatian ode by an
English poet upon the return of a Western Caesar from a victorious
campaign in which the victor seemed at last to have triumphantly
completed his military task. A poem which purports to be a paean
in honour of a particular victory sounds the knell of all Militarism
in its last two stanzas:

> But thou, the War's and Fortune's son,
> March indefatigably on;
> And, for the last effect,
> Still keep the sword erect.
>
> Besides the force it has to fright
> The spirits of the shady night,
> The same arts that did gain
> A power, must it maintain.[2]

This classically phrased verdict upon the career of the earliest
would-be saviour with the sword in the modern history of our
Western Civilization has a sting in its tail which pricks with a still
sharper point in the nineteenth-century *mot* that 'the one thing
which you cannot do with bayonets is to sit on them'. An instrument that has once been used to destroy life cannot then be used
to preserve life at the user's convenience. The function of weapons
is to kill; and a ruler who has not scrupled 'to wade through
slaughter to a throne' will find—if he tries to maintain his power
thereafter without further recourse to the grim arts which have
gained it—that sooner or later he will be confronted with a choice
between letting the power slip through his fingers or else renewing
his lease of it by means of another bout of bloodshed. The man
of violence cannot both genuinely repent of his violence and permanently profit by it. The law of *Karma* is not evaded so easily
as that. The Saviour with the Sword may perhaps build a house
upon the sand but never the house upon a rock.[3] And he will not
be able to build for Eternity vicariously by the expedient of a
division of labour between a blood-guilty David and an innocent
Solomon; for the stones with which Solomon builds will have been
of David's hewing; and the veto pronounced against the father—

---

[1] Μετανοίας γὰρ τόπον οὐχ ηὗρε.—Heb. xii. 17, apropos of Esau.
[2] Marvell, Andrew: *An Horatian Ode upon Cromwell's Return from Ireland.*
[3] Matt. vii. 24–9.

'Thou shalt not build an house for my name, because thou hast been a man of war and hast shed blood'[1]—spells doom for a house built by the son on the father's behalf.

This ultimate failure of all attempts to win salvation with the sword is not only proclaimed in poetry and myth and legend; it is also demonstrated in history; for 'the iniquity of the fathers' who have had recourse to the sword is visited 'upon the children unto the third and fourth generation'.[2] In our own day the descendants of the Protestant English military colonists whom Cromwell planted in Ireland to hold a conquered Catholic country down have been evicted from their ancestors' ill-gotten estates by the very weapons of violence and injustice to which they owed their cursed heritage; and, at the moment when these words were being written in August 1937, the wealth of a British community of business men in a treaty-port and settlement at Shanghai which had been founded on the iniquity of 'the Opium War' of A.D. 1840–2 was being destroyed by Japanese and Chinese hands which had been schooled in Militarism by the example of past British success in temporarily transmuting military violence into commercial profit. Nor are these two judgements of History exceptional. The classic saviours with the sword have been the captains and the princes who have striven to found or have succeeded in founding or have succeeded in preserving or have striven to preserve the universal states into which the disintegrating civilizations pass when they have lived through their 'Times of Troubles' to the bitter end; and, although the passage from 'Time of Troubles' to universal state is apt to bring with it so great an immediate relief for the tormented children of a disintegrating society that they sometimes show their gratitude to the successful founder of a universal state by worshipping him as a god,[3] we shall find, when

[1] 1 Chron. xxviii. 3.   [2] Exod. xx. 5 and xxxiv. 7; Num. xiv. 18.
[3] For the deification of political potentates in general, and of the sovereigns of universal states in particular, see V. C (i) (d) 6 (δ), Annex, vol. v, pp. 648–57, above. It has been suggested in that context that it would hardly be possible for a ruler to secure formal worship as a god without having already won the gratitude and affection of his subjects in the capacity of a human saviour; and indeed the deification of a ruler might almost be described as the translation of this spontaneous popular feeling into official language. But, if it be true that no ruler who has not been recognized as a saviour can be a successful candidate for deification, it is by no means true that, conversely, the official conferment of divine honours is a necessary consequence of the existence of the feeling which it presupposes. For example, the feeling for a living Augustus which is expressed by Virgil in the passages in which he hails the founder of the Hellenic universal state as a god (see V. C (i) (d) (δ), Annex, p. 648, with footnote 4, above) is matched in depth and sincerity by the feeling which is expressed for the same Roman Emperor in a work written more than a quarter of a century after his death by Philo of Alexandria. In his *Legatio ad Gaium*, §§ 143–7, the Jewish philosopher salutes Augustus with a paean of praise.
'What of the hero who towered above the ordinary level of human nature in all the virtues, and who—to signify his combination of supreme dictatorial power with supreme distinction of character—was the first to be called Augustus (a title which he did not inherit from his forefathers like an heirloom, but which he did transmit to his

we come to study these universal states more closely,[1] that they are at best ephemeral, and that if, by a *tour de force*, they obstinately outlive their normal span they have to pay for this unnatural longevity by degenerating into social enormities[2] which are as pernicious in their way as either the 'Times of Troubles' that precede the establishment of universal states or the interregna that follow their break-up at the normal age.

The association between the histories of universal states and the careers of would-be saviours with the sword does not merely testify in a general way to the inefficacy of force as an instrument of salvation: it enables us to survey the evidence empirically by giving us a convenient clue for sorting out the would-be saviours of this kind and marshalling them in an order in which it becomes possible to pass them in review.

The first to march past will be the tragic battalion of would-be saviours with the sword who have slashed—with blades as futile as the Danaids' sieves—at the welling wars of a 'Time of Troubles'.

In the Hellenic 'Time of Troubles' (*circa* 431–31 B.C.) we can perceive, in the first generation, the gallant figure of a Lacedae-

---

successors fraught with a dignity with which he himself had first invested it)? At the moment when Augustus took charge of the government of the World, he found the World's affairs in a state of perturbation and confusion. Islands were competing for primacy with continents, and continents with islands, under the leadership and championship of the most eminent men in Roman public life. More than that, the prime divisions of the Habitable World were struggling for political supremacy—Asia against Europe and Europe against Asia—and the nations of the two contending continents had risen up, even from the ends of the Earth, and had set themselves to wage devastating wars against one another in all habitable lands and on all navigable seas. Everywhere there were battles and sea-fights, until almost the entire human race was on the verge of complete annihilation through mutual slaughter—but for one man, one leader, Augustus, who deserves to be called the Averter of Catastrophe (ἀλεξίκακον). This is that Caesar who calmed the storms that had broken in every quarter, and who cured the plagues that had descended from South and East—upon Hellenes and Barbarians alike—and had run like wildfire right away to West and North, disseminating horrors over the intervening lands and seas. This is he who did not merely loosen, but actually struck right off, the fetters in which the World had lain fast bound and crushed. This is he who put an end both to open wars and to clandestine wars in the shape of brigandage. This is he who cleared the sea of pirates and filled it with merchantmen. This is he who salvaged all the city-states and set them at liberty; who brought order out of disorder (ὁ τὴν ἀταξίαν εἰς τάξιν ἀγαγών); who tamed and reconciled all the unsociable, savage nations; who multiplied Hellas in a host of replicas of herself (ὁ τὴν μὲν Ἑλλάδα Ἑλλάσι πολλαῖς παραυξήσας); who hellenized the most vital sections of the world of Barbarism; the Guardian of Peace; the distributor, to each and all, of what was their due; the benefactor who bestowed, without stint, on the public every gift that he had to give, and who never in his life hoarded up for himself any treasure that was fine or good.'

This prose of Philo's is as magnificent a tribute, in its way, as Virgil's verse. Yet this Jewish enthusiast for Augustus and his work would have rejected as a shocking blasphemy any suggestion that he should express his gratitude towards a human saviour by paying him those divine honours that, in Philo's belief, were payable exclusively to the One True God. Philo can have been under no temptation to worship his human hero Augustus in place of the God of Israel—though it is possible that Philo's mind may have moved in the inverse direction and that his conception of the providence of God may have been influenced by his acquaintance with the providence of Augustus (for this interesting conjecture see Charlesworth, M. P.: *The Virtues of a Roman Emperor* (London 1937, Milford), p. 18).   [1] In Part VI, below.

[2] For the social enormities that are the alternatives to revolutions see IV. C (iii) (b) 1, vol. iv, pp. 135–7, above.

monian Brasidas giving his life to liberate the Greek city-states in
Chalcidicê from an Athenian yoke—only to have his work undone
within less than half a century by other Lacedaemonian hands
which were to open the way for a Philip of Macedon to place a
heavier yoke upon the neck of every state in Hellas save Sparta
herself.[1] At Brasidas' heels stalks the sinister figure of his countryman and contemporary, Lysander, who successfully liberated the
Greek city-states along the Asiatic shores of the Aegean and gave
the Athenian 'thalassocracy' its *coup de grâce*—only to bring upon
the former subjects of Athens the chastisement of Lacedaemonian
scorpions in place of Attic whips and to set his own country's feet
upon a path that was to lead her, in thirty-three years, from
Aegospotami to Leuctra. Thereafter each successive generation
adds some figure to our parade. We see a Theban Epaminondas
liberating the Arcadians and Messenians and punishing Sparta as
Lysander had punished Athens—only to stimulate the Phocians to
inflict the same punishment on Thebes herself. We see a Macedonian Philip ridding Hellas of the Phocian scourge and being
hailed as 'friend, benefactor, and saviour'[2] by the Thebans and
Thessalians who had been the principal sufferers from it—only to
extinguish the freedom of these two Hellenic peoples that once had
been so naïve as to 'think the whole world of him'.[3] And we see
an Alexander seeking to reconcile the Hellenes to a Macedonian
hegemony by leading them on the quest of making a common
prize of the entire Achaemenian Empire—only to lose for Macedon
the hegemony which his father had won for her, and to feed the
flames of Hellenic civil war by pouring into the rival war-chests
of his own successors a treasure which the Achaemenidae had been
accumulating for two centuries.[4]

A parallel and contemporary procession of unsuccessful saviours
with the sword can be observed in that other half of the Hellenic
World which lay to the west of the Adriatic.[5] We have only to
recite the catalogue of their names—Dionysius the First and
Dionysius the Second, Agathocles and Hiero and Hieronymus— in
order to perceive that the failure of each of these dictators in turn
is proclaimed in the bare fact of his needing a successor to grapple
with the same task all over again. In another context[6] we have seen
that the problem of saving Hellenism in the west by establishing

[1] For the relations between Sparta, the Chalcidians, and Macedon between 432 and
338 B.C. see III. C (ii) (b), Annex IV, vol. iii, pp. 480–6, above.
[2] Demosthenes: *De Corona*, chap. 43.   [3] Ibid.
[4] See IV. C (iii) (c) 3 (α), vol. iv, p. 485; V. C (i) (c) 2, vol. v, pp. 62–4; and
V. C (i) (d) 11, in the present volume, p. 155, footnote 3, above; and V. C (ii) (b),
pp. 289–90 and 318–19, below.
[5] See III. C (ii) (b), vol. iii, p. 357, footnote 1, and IV. C (iii) (c) 2 (β), Annex I, vol.
v, p. 590, above.
[6] In III. C (ii) (b), vol. iii, p. 312, above.

an *union sacrée* which would be strong enough to resist the dual pressure of Syriac rivals from Africa and barbarian interlopers from Italy remained unsolved until the fertile seed-bed of Hellenic culture in Sicily was devastated by being turned into the arena of a struggle for oecumenical dominion between Carthage and Rome.

The 'Times of Troubles' of other civilizations present similar spectacles. In the Sumeric 'Time of Troubles' (*circa* 2677–2298 B.C.) we find Sargon of Agade (*dominabatur circa* 2652–2597 B.C.) being besought by the Assyrian pioneers beyond Taurus to deliver them out of the hand of the local barbarians;[1] and we see Naramsin (*dominabatur circa* 2572–2517 B.C.) representing himself on a notorious stele as the deliverer of the plains of Shinar from the depredations of the highlanders of Gutium.[2] But Naramsin's, if not Sargon's, title to rank as a saviour is impugned by the ensuing bout of Gutaean domination over the heart of the Sumeric World (*circa* 2429–2306);[3] for this barbarian counterstroke was the nemesis of Akkadian militarism. In the Orthodox Christian World the same battalion of would-be saviours is represented by figures who are more sympathetic without being more effective. In the main body of Orthodox Christendom we see Alexius Comnenus (*imperabat* A.D. 1081–1118)[4] snatching a prostrate East Roman Empire out of the jaws of Normans and Saljūqs with all the intrepidity of a David rescuing his lamb from the lion and the bear.[5] And a century later we see a Theodore Lascaris refusing to despair of the republic after the unprecedented and overwhelming catastrophe of A.D. 1204, and turning at bay, behind the walls of Nicaea, against the Frankish conquerors of the holy city of Constantine. But all this Byzantine heroism was in vain. For in the tragic history of the East Roman Empire the French Goliath who came prowling on the Fourth Crusade did not, after all, share the fate of the Norman bear and the Saljūq lion; and the eventual recapture of Constantinople by Michael Palaeologus, which seemed at the moment to have crowned Theodore Lascaris' work with a posthumous success, proved in the sequel only to have sealed the East Roman Empire's doom by showing the 'Osmanlis the way from the Asiatic to the European side of the Black Sea Straits.[6] In the history of the Russian offshoot of the Orthodox Christian

1 See I. C (i) (b), vol. i, p. 110, and V. C (i) (c) 3, vol. v, p. 262, above.
2 For the self-exposure of militarism in this work of Sumeric art see V. C (i) (c) 3, vol. v, p. 262, above, and V. C (ii) (b), in the present volume, p. 296, below. For the nemesis of Naramsin's militarism see also I. C (i) (b), vol. i, p. 109, and V. C (i) (c) 3, vol. v, p. 203, above.　　3 See V. C (i) (c) 3, vol. v, p. 262, above.
4 See IV. C (iii) (c) 2 (β), Annex II, vol. iv, pp. 619–20, above, and V. C (ii) (b), in the present volume, p. 298, below.　　5 1 Sam. xvii. 34–6.
6 For the Nicene Greek reoccupation of Constantinople as a prelude to the establishment of a universal state in Orthodox Christendom by the 'Osmanlis see Part III. A, vol. iii, p. 27, above, and V. C (ii) (b), in the present volume, p. 298, footnote 7, below.

Society we may discern counterparts of an Alexius Comnenus and
a Theodore Lascaris in Alexander Nevski (*regnabat* A.D. 1252–63)
and Dmitri Donskoi (*regnabat* A.D. 1362–89), who wielded their
swords for the salvation of the Russian World, during its separate
'Time of Troubles' (*circa* A.D. 1078–1478), from the simultaneous
assaults of Lithuanian pagans and Teutonic Crusaders on the
north-west[1] and of Mongol Nomads on the south-east.[2] These
Russian heroes of Orthodox Christendom were happier in their
generation than their Greek peers, since the fort which they held
so valiantly against such heavy odds was not, in the next chapter
of the story, to fall into alien hands. Yet Alexander and Demetrius
were no more successful than Alexius or Theodore in fulfilling
their personal task of bringing a 'Time of Troubles' to an end.

These saviours with the sword whose lot has fallen in 'Times
of Troubles' are patently cast in the mould of Hêraklês without
a touch of Zeus; but the next battalion that comes marching at
their heels consists of half-castes between the Herculean and the
Jovian type who are not dispensed from performing Hercules'
labours but are also not condemned to perform them without any
hope of obtaining Jove's reward. These Jovian Herculeses or
Herculean Joves are the forerunners of the successful founders of
universal states. They play the part of a Moses to a Joshua or an
Elias to a mundane Messiah or a John the Baptist to a Christ[3]
(if the would-be saviours of a mundane society may properly be
brought into comparison with the harbingers of a kingdom which
is not of This World). Some of these forerunners die without
passing over Jordan or obtaining more than a Pisgah-sight of the
Promised Land, while there are others who succeed in forcing the
passage and in momentarily planting the standard of their kingdom
on the farther bank; but these audacious spirits who seek to wrest
a premature success out of the hands of a reluctant Destiny are
visited, for their temerity, with a punishment that is escaped by
their peers who recognize, and bow to, their fate; for the universal
states which they prematurely set up collapse, like houses of cards,
as swiftly as they have been erected; and the jerry-builders'
abortive labours only find a place in history as a foil to display the
solidity of the work of successors who retrieve the disaster by re-
building the fallen edifice in granite instead of pasteboard.

The Moses who dies in the Wilderness is represented in Hellenic
history by a Marius, who showed the way for a Julius to follow
in the next generation, though Marius's own hesitant and clumsy

---

[1] See II. D (v), vol. ii, p. 172, and Part III. A, Annex II, vol. iii, p. 424, above.
[2] See II. D (v), vol. ii, p. 154, and V. C (i) (*c*) 3, vol. v, pp. 311–12, above.
[3] For the analogy between Elias and John the Baptist see Matt. xvii. 10–13, and
Mark ix. 11–13.

moves towards the establishment of an egalitarian dictatorship not only failed to introduce a reign of order but grievously aggravated an existing state of anarchy. In the Japanese offshoot of the Far Eastern Society we may perceive—in a different social setting— a more constructive counterpart of Marius in a Nobunaga who girt up his loins to break in the wild horses of an unbridled feudalism.[1] And Nobunaga, in his turn, has a more sympathetic Andean counterpart in an Inca Viracocha who spent in heroically stemming the torrent of Chanca invasion an energy which might otherwise have earned the reward of anticipating the achievements of a Pachacutec.[2] In the main body of Orthodox Christendom the career of the Inca Viracocha is matched by that of the 'Osmanlī Bāyezīd Yilderim, who came within an ace of anticipating Mehmed the Conqueror's double achievement of capturing Constantinople and settling scores with Qāramān, when 'the Thunderbolt' was blasted in mid-action by the sudden and irresistible impact of a still mightier military force.[3] In the main body of the Far Eastern World the Manchu restoration of a Mongol-built universal state was more to the credit of the forerunner Nurhachi (*regnabat* A.D. 1618–25), who never set foot inside the Great Wall, than it was to the credit of his *fainéant* successor Shun Chih (*imperabat* A.D. 1644–61), in whose reign the seat of the Manchu power was triumphantly transferred from Mukden to Peking. In the Sumeric World the task of throwing off a Gutaean yoke was taken in hand by Utuchegal of Erech (Uruk) before it was carried through by Ur-Engur of Ur.

Next to this vanguard who see, but never set foot on, the Promised Land comes a second company of forerunners who momentarily subdue the monster of anarchy—but this not so decisively that he cannot raise his head or show his teeth again.

In the Hellenic World a Pompey and a Caesar divided between them the task of reforming a Roman anarchy into a Roman Peace —only to share the guilt of undoing their common work by turning their arms against each other.

> Heu quantum inter se bellum, si lumina vitae
> attigerint, quantas acies stragemque ciebunt. . . .
> ne, pueri, ne tanta animis adsuescite bella
> neu patriae validas in viscera vertite vires.[4]

[1] Nobunaga assumed dictatorial power *de facto* in A.D. 1568, and he was effectively master of more than half the provinces of Japan when he met a premature death by violence in A.D. 1582 (Sansom, G. B.: *Japan, A Short Cultural History* (London 1932, Cresset Press), pp. 397 and 401).

[2] For the Inca Viracocha's career see II. D (iv), vol. ii, pp. 102–3, above. In the Inca's career, as in Marius's, the outstanding feat was the stemming of a tide of barbarian invasion.

[3] For the 'Osmanlī Bāyezīd Yilderim's career see II. D (iv), vol. ii, p. 102, above.

[4] Virgil: *Aeneid*, Book VI, ll. 828–9 and 832–3.

But remonstrance fell on deaf ears; the rival war-lords condemned a world which it was their joint mission to save to be scarified by another bout of Roman civil war; and the victor triumphed only to be 'rejected', like Esau, 'when he would have inherited the blessing', and to find 'no place of repentance, though he sought it carefully with tears'.[1] Caesar did not expiate the deaths of Pompey and Cato by his famous clemency[2] in the hour of his apparent omnipotence. The slayer who had stayed his sword from further slaughter had nevertheless to die by the daggers of defeated adversaries whose lives he had spared; and in dying this tragic death Caesar bequeathed yet another bout of civil war as his unwilled legacy to a piteous world which he had sincerely desired to save. The sword had to take a further toll of life and happiness before the task which Caesar and Pompey had so lightly thrown to the winds was well and truly executed at last by Caesar's adopted son.

Augustus did succeed, after the overthrow of the last of his adversaries, in demobilizing the swollen armies that were left on his hands on the morrow of the Battle of Actium;[3] and in the Sinic World Ts'in She Hwang-ti performed the same hazardous feat of statesmanship after he had destroyed the last rival of Ts'in by the conquest and annexation of Ts'i.[4] But this touch of grace in the heart of the violent-handed Sinic Caesar did not reprieve his handiwork. The Sinic universal state which the Ts'in Emperor had put together fell to pieces at his death;[5] and the work had to be done all over again by Han Liu Pang.

In Syriac history Ts'in She Hwang-ti and Divus Julius have their counterpart in Cyrus, the would-be bringer of a *Pax Achaemenia* to a world that had been lacerated by a *furor Assyriacus*. It was in vain that Cyrus (as the story goes) paid heed to the sign sent from Heaven by Apollo and repented of the evil that he thought to do[6] unto Croesus.[7] Instead of burning his vanquished adversary alive, Cyrus took Croesus for his trusted counsellor—only (according to the Herodotean tale)[8] to lose his life, years afterwards, through acting on bad advice which Croesus had given

---

[1] Heb. xii. 17, quoted on p. 180, footnote 1, above.

[2] See V. C (i) (c) 2, vol. v, p. 78, above.

[3] For the penitence of Augustus see V. C (i) (c) 2, vol. v, p. 78; V. C (i) (d) 5, vol. v, p. 435; V. C (i) (d) 6 (δ), Annex, vol. v, p. 648, above; and V. C (i) (d) 7, Annex, in the present volume, p. 332, footnote 1, below. This penitence evoked a gratitude which in turn expressed itself in a deification of the repentant militarist (see the third of the four passages here cited).

[4] See Cordier, H.: *Histoire Générale de la Chine*, vol. i (Paris 1920, Geuthner), pp. 200 and 202.

[5] See V. C (i) (d) 4, vol. v, p. 418, above.   [6] Jer. xviii. 8.

[7] The story is told by Herodotus in Book I, chaps. 86–7, and has been cited in this Study already—in its application to Croesus—in IV. C (iii) (c) 1, vol. iv, p. 252 above.   [8] Herodotus, Book I, chaps. 206–14.

him in good faith. The last word on Cyrus's career was spoken by the queen of the Nomads when she promised to satisfy the Persian war-lord's insatiable appetite for blood; and Tomyris duly carried out her threat on the stricken field by filling a wine-skin with the blood of the slain and dabbling in it the lips of Cyrus's corpse. Nor was it only Cyrus himself who perished by the stroke of the weapon which he had drawn; for the death of the Achaemenid empire-builder was capped by the collapse of his imposing edifice. Cambyses played the same havoc with Cyrus's *Pax Achaemenia* as a Gaius and a Nero played with Octavian's *Pax Augusta*; and Darius had to salvage Cyrus's ruined work, as Vespasian salvaged Augustus's and Liu Pang Ts'in She Hwang-ti's.

In the same Syriac World more than a thousand years later, when the Arab war-lord 'Umar brought a long interlude of Hellenic intrusion to a tardy end by emulating the Persian war-lord Cyrus's lightning-swift feats of conquest, the captor of Jerusalem showed the same clemency as the captor of Sardis—only to demonstrate once again that, for the would-be saviour with the sword, there is 'no place of repentance'. Once again a sword-built edifice collapsed as soon as the builder's sword-arm had been put out of action. After 'Umar's death his work—like Cyrus's—was first shamefully wrecked and then brilliantly salvaged—though, in the history of the Caliphate, Cambyses' and Darius's roles were both of them played, turn and turn about, by the versatile genius of a single Arab statesman. Mu'āwīyah coldly condemned a world that had just been exhausted by the last round of an inconclusive struggle between Rome and Persia to be further harried by an Arab civil war in order that the astute Umayyad might filch the political heritage of the Prophet Muhammad out of the incompetent hands of the Prophet's own cousin and son-in-law.[1]

In the Japanese offshoot of the Far Eastern World we see Hideyoshi bringing the work of his master Nobunaga to the verge of completion[2]—only to divert his energies, with a Julian levity, to the wanton enterprise of carrying the flame of war into Korea[3] before stamping out the last embers of it in Japan, with the result that Hideyoshi's work had to be re-performed after his death[4] by Ieyasu at the cost of a Battle of Sekigehara[5] and a siege of Ōsaka.[6] In genius Hideyoshi was as conspicuously superior to Ieyasu as Julius was to Octavian; and the moral of both the Japanese and the Hellenic story is that of Aesop's fable of the Hare and the Tortoise.

---

[1] For the irony of this outcome of Muhammad's political career see V. C (i) (*d*) 6 (δ), Annex, vol. v, pp. 675–7, above.
[2] Sansom, G. B.: *Japan, A Short Cultural History* (London 1932, Cresset Press), p. 403.
[3] In A.D. 1592.   [4] In A.D. 1598.   [5] In A.D. 1600.   [6] In A.D. 1614–15.

A mediocre ability which never deviates from the pursuit of a single aim may go farther in politics than a wayward genius which is master of everything except its own caprice. Yet this moral is perhaps not borne out by the history of the establishment of the Mughal Rāj which served as a universal state for the Hindu World. In this Mughal version of the play Bābur was the Cyrus whose work was undone by a Humāyūn who was as unfortunate as 'Alī and as disastrous as Cambyses; and Akbar was the Darius who retrieved the disaster and reconstructed the edifice; yet, if Bābur and Akbar were to be measured against one another in respect of either genius or caprice, it would be Akbar and not Bābur who would carry off the palm.[1] If we turn our attention from the Mughal Rāj, which was the first to provide the Hindu World with a universal state, to the British Rāj, which took up the same task after the Mughal Rāj had prematurely broken down, we shall notice, here too, a distinction between the respective achievements of two successive generations of British empire-builders: the generation of the Wellesleys (circa A.D. 1800–30), who revealed the promise of a *Pax Britannica* when they broke the power of Tipu Sahib in Mysore and of the Marāthās in the Deccan; and the generation of the Lawrences (circa A.D. 1830–60), who turned promise into performance by breaking the still more formidable power of the Sikhs in the Panjab and then riding the storm of a Mutiny in which the newly launched ship of British state in India came as near to foundering as the Achaemenian Empire came in the general revolt against the tyranny of Cambyses.

There is, however, a third company in our battalion of fore-runners, and this is composed of Herculeses who hand on to successors the fruits of their own labours without ever tasting these fruits for themselves, but also without any break or setback. In the Babylonic World, Nabopolassar (*imperabat* 626–605 B.C.) spent his life in compassing the death of the Assyrian tiger in order that Nebuchadnezzar (*imperabat* 605–562 B.C.) might sit, unchallenged, on the throne of a Neo-Babylonian Empire which could not stand secure until Nineveh lay in ruins. In the Indic World, when the Indic universal state which had been founded by the Mauryas was re-established by the Guptas, Samudragupta (*imperabat circa* A.D. 330–75) played Nabopolassar to Chandragupta II's Nebuchadnezzar (Chandragupta II Gupta *imperabat circa* A.D. 375–413).[2] These forerunners whose heritage is transmitted in peace are not far from being true founders of universal states; and, if we now pass to these, we shall find the roll-call easy to recite.

---

[1] For Akbar's genius see V. C (i) (d) 6 (δ), Annex, vol. v, pp. 699–704, above.
[2] See V. C (i) (d) 9 (β), Annex, pp. 341–2, below.

The true founder of the Hellenic universal state was Augustus (rather than Divus Julius); of the Sumeric, Ur-Engur;[1] of the Egyptiac, Mentuhotep IV[2] (the prince of the Eleventh Dynasty who reigned *circa* 2070/60–2015 B.C. and established the so-called 'Middle Empire'). In Egyptiac history Mentuhotep IV has a double in the person of Amosis[3] (the first sovereign of the Eighteenth Dynasty and the founder of the so-called 'New Empire') owing to the extraordinary restoration of the Egyptiac universal state after an interlude of barbarian rule.[4] If we pass from the Egyptiac to the Andean World, we shall find that the Inca Pachacutec's claim to be the true founder of the Andean universal state —a claim which is implicit in the title 'World Changed for the Better'[5]—is borne out by the facts of Andean history.[6] And, to continue our catalogue, Nebuchadnezzar (rather than Nabopolassar) was the true founder of the Babylonic universal state,[7] and Chandragupta Maurya the founder of the Indic universal state,[8] while Chandragupta II Gupta[9]—an Indic empire-builder who lived and reigned nearly 700 years after Chandragupta Maurya's day—is entitled to rank as the second founder of the Indic universal state, since it was he who made the decisive contribution[10] to its reconstruction after an interlude of Hellenic intrusion. To resume: Han Liu Pang (rather than Ts'in She Hwang-ti) was the true founder of the Sinic universal state; Darius I (rather than Cyrus) the true founder of the Syriac universal state; and Mu'āwīyah (rather than 'Umar) the true second founder of the Syriac universal state, inasmuch as Mu'āwīyah was the true founder of the Arab Caliphate which took up and carried through the Achaemenian Empire's uncompleted task[11] after an interlude of Hellenic intrusion upon Syriac ground which had lasted for the better part of a millennium.[12] In the main body of Orthodox Christendom the *Pax Ottomanica*, which performed the functions of a universal

---

[1] See I. C (i) (*b*), vol. i, p. 106; V. C (i) (*d*) 6 (γ), vol. v, p. 497; and V. C (i) (*d*) 6 (δ), Annex, vol. v, pp. 650–1, above; and V. C (ii) (*b*), in the present volume, pp. 296–7, below.

[2] See I. C (ii), vol. i, p. 137, and p. 140, footnote 2; II. D (v), vol. ii, p. 112; IV. C (ii) (*b*) 2, vol. iv, p. 85; V. C (i) (*c*) 3, vol. v, p. 267; and V. C (i) (*d*) 6 (δ), vol. v, p. 530, above.   [3] See I. C (ii), vol. i, p. 138, above.

[4] For this peculiar feature of Egyptiac history see ibid., pp. 138–9, above.

[5] For the meaning of the title 'Pachacutec' see further V. C (ii) (*a*), Annex I, p. 374, footnote 2, below.

[6] See I. C (i) (*b*), vol. i, p. 121, and II. D (iv), vol. ii, p. 103, above.

[7] See II. D (v), vol. ii, p. 138, above.   [8] See I. C (i) (*b*), vol. i, p. 86, above.

[9] For the Gupta Dynasty's role in Indic history see ibid., p. 85, above.

[10] This decisive contribution was the annexation of the Saka 'satrapy' in Western India; and that event, which took place at some date in the last decade of the fourth century of the Christian Era (see ibid., p. 86, above, and V. C (i) (*c*) 3, Annex II, vol. v, p. 604, above), must have been the work of Chandragupta II Gupta (*imperabat* A.D. 375–413).

[11] See I. C (i) (*b*), vol. i, pp. 76–7, above.

[12] Alexander the Great broke into Syria in the year 333 B.C.; the Emperor Heraclius evacuated Syria in A.D. 638.

state, was established by Mehmed 'the Conqueror' of Constantinople.[1] In the Russian offshoot of Orthodox Christendom the
founder of the universal state was the Tsar Ivan III (*imperabat*
A.D. 1462–1505), since the decisive event in the expansion of the
Principality of Moscow into an oecumenical empire was the annexation of the Republic of Novgorod in A.D. 1478.[2] In the main body
of the Far Eastern World the *Pax Mongolica* was established by
Chingis Khan. In the Japanese offshoot of the Far Eastern Society
the true founder of the universal state was Ieyasu (rather than
Hideyoshi). In the Hindu World the true founder of the Mughal
Rāj was Akbar[3] (rather than Bābur), while the true founders of the
British Rāj were the Lawrences (rather than the British empire-
builders of the preceding generation).

To the eyes of an historian of a later age, who can see the careers
of these founders of universal states in the light of a distant sequel,
their Jovian figures do not stand out as being strikingly different
from the Herculean figures of their predecessors. But to the eyes
of a contemporary observer, who cannot see things in perspective,
there seems to be all the difference here between failure and success. The founders of the universal states appear at the moment
to have triumphantly achieved a success which their predecessors
have striven for manfully but in vain; and the genuineness of this
success appears to be guaranteed not merely by the effectiveness
of the founders' own lives and deeds (however eloquently these
facts may speak), but most decisively of all by the prosperity of the
founders' successors. Solomon's glory is the most telling evidence
for David's prowess. Let us therefore now continue our survey of
saviours with the sword by passing in review these Solomons who
are born into the purple. The swords of the *porphyrogeniti* are
speciously muffled in the folds of an imperial robe; and, if ever we
see them show their true colours by displaying the hidden blade,
we shall always find that this act of self-betrayal has been prompted
by wantonness and not enjoined by necessity. If salvation with the
sword is to be 'justified of her children',[4] it must be now, in this
Solomonian generation, or never in the whole history of the disintegrations of civilizations. So let us inspect our Solomons closely.

---

[1] In the estimation of later generations of 'Osmanlis it was Mehmed the Conqueror
who raised the Ottoman Power to the rank of an oecumenical empire; but the credit
for this achievement properly belongs neither to Mehmed the Conqueror (*imperabat*
A.D. 1451–81) nor to his forerunner Bāyezīd the Thunderbolt (*imperabat* A.D. 1389–1402),
but to their predecessor Murād I (*imperabat* A.D. 1360–89), since the decisive event in
the establishment of the *Pax Ottomanica* was the conquest of Macedonia in A.D. 1371–2,
and not the capture of Constantinople in A.D. 1453.
[2] See IV. C (ii) (*b*) 2, vol. iv, p. 88; V. C (i) (*c*) 3, vol. v, p. 312, above; and
V. C (ii) (*b*), in the present volume, p. 309, below.
[3] See V. C (i) (*c*) 3, vol. v, p. 304, above. The decisive event which raised the Mughal
Rāj to the rank of an oecumenical empire was the annexation of Gujerat in A.D. 1572.
[4] Matt. xi. 19; Luke vii. 35.

The reigns of these Solomons constitute those relatively happy periods of partial peace and prosperity which look like 'Golden Ages' if we confine our view to the life-spans of the universal states in which they occur, but which can be seen to be really 'Indian Summers' as soon as we extend our field of vision to include the whole life-span of the civilization in whose history the coming and going of a universal state is only one of a number of incidents in a long tale of disintegration.[1] An empirical survey of these 'Indian Summers' will bring out two salient features of this historical phenomenon. We shall find that they display a striking uniformity of character combined with an equally striking inequality of duration.

We have seen that the Hellenic 'Indian Summer' began at the accession of the Emperor Nerva in A.D. 96 and ended at the death of the Emperor Marcus in A.D. 180; and these eighty-four years amount to not much less than a quarter of the total duration of a *Pax Romana* which, in the terms of the conventional chronology which dates by public events, may be reckoned to have begun in 31 B.C., on the morrow of the Battle of Actium, and to have ended in A.D. 378, on the day of the Battle of Adrianople. The 'Indian Summer' which the main body of the Far Eastern World enjoyed under the *Pax Manchuana* lasted rather longer than this, if its beginning is to be equated with the definitive subjugation of the South by the Emperor K'ang Hsi in A.D. 1682, and its end with the death of the Emperor Ch'ien Lung in A.D. 1796. In the history of the Egyptiac Society the 'Indian Summer' of 'the New Empire' lasted longer still—from the accession of Thothmes I *circa* 1545 B.C. to the death of Amenhotep III in 1376 B.C. But all these spans are surpassed in the duration of the 'Indian Summer' of 'the Middle Empire', which was the original Egyptiac universal state; for this first Egyptiac 'Indian Summer' was almost coeval with the Twelfth Dynasty, which reigned, from first to last, *circa* 2000–1788 B.C.;[2] and, even if we date the onset of winter from the death of Amenemhat III in 1801 B.C.,[3] the spell of sunshine covers half the total duration of a *Pax Thebana* that lasted in all for about four centuries, if its beginning is to be equated with the accession of Mentuhotep IV *circa* 2070/2060 B.C.[4] and its end with the irruption of the Hyksos *circa* 1660 B.C.[5]

These 'Indian Summers' that have lasted through successive

---

[1] For the nature of these 'Indian Summers' see IV. C (ii) (*b*) 1, vol. iv, pp. 58–61, above.

[2] See I. C (ii), vol. i, p. 137, and IV. C (ii) (*b*) 2, vol. iv, p. 85, above.

[3] Meyer, E.: *Geschichte des Altertums*, vol. i, part (2), 3rd ed. (Stuttgart and Berlin 1913, Cotta), p. 301.

[4] Ibid., p. 257, the present Study and chapter, p. 190, above.

[5] Meyer, op. cit., vol. cit., pp. 302 and 305.

reigns, and in at least one case for almost the whole period of a dynasty, differ notably in length from other 'Indian Summers' which are also manifestly authentic examples of the same social phenomenon, but which have not outlasted the reign of some single sovereign with whose name they are identified.

In the history of the Sumeric universal state, for instance, the 'Indian Summer' was confined to the reign of the Emperor Dungi (*imperabat circa* 2280–2223 B.C.), whose death was followed by a rapid onset of winter. In the history of the Andean universal state the 'Indian Summer' of Tupac Yupanqui's reign (*imperabat circa* A.D. 1448–82) began to fade out in the reign of his immediate successor Huayna Capac;[1] and the first touch of frost made itself felt in the feud between Huayna Capac's rival heirs, before the Incaic Empire—and, with it, the Andean Civilization itself—was wiped out by the sudden swoop of a storm-cloud from the unsuspected farther shore of a distant Atlantic. In Indic history a Mauryan 'Indian Summer' in the reign of the Emperor Açoka (*imperabat* 273–232 B.C.) was followed in 185 B.C. by the blight of Pushyamitra's usurpation of power,[2] while a Guptan 'Indian Summer' in the reign of Kumaragupta I (*imperabat* A.D. 413–55) was followed, in the very year of the serene emperor's death, by the blight of an irruption of Eurasian Nomads which was the first wave of a devastating deluge.[3] The Sinic 'Indian Summer' scarcely extended beyond the limits of the reign of the Emperor Han Wuti (*imperabat* 140–87 B.C.), whose 'forward policy' against the Eurasian Nomads was possibly the 'beginning of evils' in the history of a Prior Han Dynasty which both attained and passed its zenith in Wuti's lifetime.[4] In the history of the *Pax Mongolica* in the main body of the Far Eastern Society the 'Indian Summer' in the reign of the Great Khan Qubilay (*imperabat* A.D. 1259–94) was followed in A.D. 1368 by the eviction of the Mongols from Intramural China.[5] In the history of the Arab Caliphate the celebrated 'Indian Summer' in the reign of Hārūn-ar-Rashīd (*imperabat* A.D. 786–809) shines out so brilliantly thanks to the depth of the darkness in which this pool of light is framed. The splendours of an 'Abbasid Caliph who was profiting by the cumulative results of the labours of a long line of Umayyad predecessors are set off on the one hand by an antecedent bout of anarchy in which Hārūn's 'Abbasid forebears had wrested the Caliphate out of the Umayyads' grasp, and on the

[1] For this view see Means, P. A.: *Ancient Civilizations of the Andes* (New York 1931, Scribner), p. 274.
[2] See I. C (i) (*b*), vol. i, p. 86, above.   [3] See ibid., p. 85, above.
[4] See V. C (i) (*c*) 2, vol. v, p. 142, footnote 4, and V. C (i) (*c*) 3, vol. v, p. 271, above, and V. C (ii) (*b*), in the present volume, p. 295, below.
[5] See II. D (v), vol. ii, p. 121; IV. C (ii) (*b*) 2, vol. iv, p .87; and IV. C (iii) (*c*) 3 (α), vol. iv, p. 491, above.

other hand by a subsequent débâcle, in which Hārūn's 'Abbasid successors fell into a humiliating bondage to their own Turkish body-guard.

In the main body of Orthodox Christendom the *Pax Ottomanica* produced its 'Indian Summer' in the reign of Suleymān the Magnificent (*imperabat* A.D. 1520–66)—an 'Osmanli prince who emulated 'in real life' the legendary glory of his Davidic namesake. Suleymān's Western contemporaries were affected like the Queen of Sheba by the vastness of this latter-day Solomon's dominions and the abundance of his wealth and the grandeur of his buildings; 'there was no more spirit in' them.[1] Yet the curse which the biblical Solomon lived to bring down on himself was also incurred by Suleymān. 'The Lord said unto Solomon: "Forasmuch as this is done of thee, and thou hast not kept my covenant and my statutes which I have commanded thee, I will surely rend the kingdom from thee and will give it to thy servant." '[2] In another context[3] we have observed that Suleymān the Magnificent was the Ottoman Pādishāh who sapped the foundations of the Ottoman social system by making the first breach in the fundamental rule that the Pādishāh's Slave-Household must be recruited from persons who were infidel-born, and that Muslim freemen should be ineligible for enlistment *ex officio religionis*.[4] In tolerating the enrolment of Janissaries' sons among the '*Ajem-oghlans*, Suleymān opened the flood-gates for a disastrous dilution of the Janissary Corps; and this self-inflicted catastrophe duly rent the kingdom from the 'Osmanli Pādishāh and gave it to his 'human cattle' the *ra'īyeh*.

If we now turn our eyes from the main body of Orthodox Christendom to its offshoot in Russia, we may hesitate at first sight to recognize a counterpart of Suleymān the Magnificent in his contemporary Ivan the Terrible (*imperabat* A.D. 1533–84). Are a reign of terror and an 'Indian Summer' compatible? The two atmospheres will strike us as being so sharply antipathetic to one another that we may question the possibility of their co-existing in a single place and time. Yet the record of Ivan the Terrible's achievements may compel us to admit that his reign was an 'Indian Summer' of a sort;[5] for this was the reign which saw the prince of

[1] 1 Kings x. 5.   [2] 1 Kings xi. 11.
[3] In Part III. A, vol. iii, pp. 44–5, above.
[4] See ibid., pp. 34–5, above.
[5] There are other reigns in the histories of other universal states which we may be content to annotate with a question-mark. In the history of the Tokugawa Shogunate, which fulfilled the functions of a universal state in the disintegration of the Far Eastern Civilization in Japan, can we, for example, discern two shafts of autumn sunlight flickering round the reigns of the Shoguns Iemitsu (*fungebatur* A.D. 1622–51) and Yoshimune (*fungebatur* A.D. 1716–44)? The reader may perhaps find his own answers to this pair of questions if he consults Sansom, G. B.: *Japan, A Short Cultural History* (London 1932, Cresset Press), p. 447, and Murdoch, J.: *A History of Japan*, vol. iii (London 1926, Kegan Paul), p. 314.

Muscovy assume the style and title of an East Roman Emperor and justify this audacity by the conquest of Qāzān and Astrakhan and the opening-up of the White Sea and Siberia. This was assuredly an 'Indian Summer', albeit with thunder in the air; and this reading of Ivan the Terrible's reign is confirmed by the sequel. Before the Emperor's death a shadow was thrown athwart the sinister sunlight of his reign by the outcome of a war for the acquisition of a sea-board on the Baltic which dragged on even longer than the war subsequently waged for the same purpose by Peter the Great,[1] but which ended in a miserable failure that was at the opposite pole from Peter's brilliant success. And when Ivan had gone to his account the strokes of misfortune fell thick and fast upon the body politic which he left behind him. The year 1598 saw the extinction of the House of Rurik, and the years 1604–13 saw a temporary collapse of the Russian Orthodox Christian universal state[2] from which it did not fully recover till the reign of Peter the Great.

If we now glance back at our catalogue of 'Indian Summers' that have endured for longer than a single reign, we shall observe that these too, for all their staying-power, have succumbed to the onset of winter in the end. In the Hellenic World Marcus was followed by Commodus, and Alexander Severus by 'the Thirty Tyrants'. In the main body of the Far Eastern Society Ch'ien Lung was followed by Hung Hsiu-ch'uan.[3] In the Egyptiac World in the days of 'the New Empire' Amenhotep III was followed by an Amenhotep IV who has made himself notorious under his self-chosen title of Ikhnaton, while in the days of 'the Middle Empire' the long series of majestically alternating Amenemhats and Senwosrets gave way at last to a dynasty in which no fewer than thirteen

---

[1] Ivan the Terrible's War of Livonia lasted for twenty-five years (from A.D. 1558 to 1583); Peter's Northern War lasted for twenty-two years (from A.D. 1700 to 1721: see III. C (ii) (b), vol. iii, p. 283, footnote 3, above).

[2] This period of collapse at the close of the first chapter in the history of the Russian Orthodox Christian universal state has been remembered by Posterity as the 'Time of Troubles' *par excellence* (see I. C (i) (a), vol. i, p. 53, footnote 2; II. D (v), vol. ii, pp. 157 and 176; IV. C (ii) (b) 2, vol. iv, pp. 90 and 91; V. C (i) (c) 3, vol. v, p. 311, footnote 2, above; and V. C (ii) (b), in the present volume, p. 311, below); and it is from this original Russian use of the phrase that we have borrowed it, in this Study, to denote one particular stage in the disintegration of any broken-down civilization. This stage is the chapter that opens with the breakdown itself and closes with the partial recovery that accompanies the eventual establishment of a universal state; and in the history of the Russian Orthodox Christendom the 'Time of Troubles' in this technical sense would run from the decline of the power of the Principality of Kiev in the last quarter of the eleventh century of the Christian Era (see Kliutschewskij, W. [Kluchevski, V.]: *Geschichte Russlands*, vol. i (Berlin 1925, Obelisk Verlag), p. 166) to the union between the Principality of Moscow and the Republic of Novgorod in A.D. 1478. The later period of collapse in the early years of the sixteenth century which goes by the name of the 'Time of Troubles' in the Russian tradition would, in our terminology, be a 'recurrence' of an earlier 'Time of Troubles' which had been temporarily—but only temporarily—surmounted by the establishment of a *Pax Muscoviana*.

[3] For this leader of the Far Eastern internal proletariat in the revolutionary movement of resurgence that bears the name 'T'aip'ing', see V. C (i) (c) 2, vol. v, p. 107, footnote 1, above.

ephemeral emperors successively seized and lost the Imperial Throne within the brief span of a quarter of a century.[1]

Our survey of 'Indian Summers' has thus, it would appear, been leading us to the conclusion that the careers of the Solomons decisively refute, instead of decisively vindicating, the claim of the sword to be convertible into an instrument of salvation; for, whether an 'Indian Summer' lasts out the life of a dynasty or comes and goes within the briefer span of a single reign, we have seen that it is in any case essentially something transitory. The glory of Solomon is a glory that fades; and, if Solomon is a failure, then David—and David's forerunners—have wielded their swords in vain. The truth seems to be that a sword which has once drunk blood cannot be permanently restrained from drinking blood again, any more than a tiger who has once tasted human flesh can be prevented from becoming a man-eater from that time onwards. The man-eating tiger is, no doubt, a tiger doomed to death; if he escapes the bullet he will die of the mange. Yet, even if the tiger could foresee his doom, he would probably be unable to subdue the devouring appetite which his first taste of man-meat has awakened in his maw; and so it is with a society that has once sought salvation through the sword. Its leaders may repent of their butcher's work; they may show mercy on their enemies, like Caesar, and demobilize their armies, like Augustus; and, as they ruefully hide the sword away, they may resolve in complete good faith that they will never draw it again except for the assuredly beneficent, and therefore legitimate, purpose of preserving the peace against criminals still at large within the borders of their tardily established universal state or against barbarians still recalcitrant in the outer darkness. They may clinch this resolution with an oath and reinforce it with an exorcism; and for a season they may appear to have successfully achieved the pious *tour de force* of bitting and bridling Murder and harnessing him to the chariot of Life; yet, though their fair-seeming *Pax Oecumenica* may stand steady on its grim foundation of buried sword-blades for thirty or a hundred or two hundred years, Time sooner or later will bring their work to naught.

Time is, indeed, working against these unhappy empire-builders from the outset; for sword-blades are foundations that never settle. Exposed or buried, these blood-stained weapons still retain their sinister charge of *karma*; and this means that they cannot really turn into inanimate foundation-stones, but must ever be stirring—

---

[1] These thirteen emperors, who reigned from first to last *circa* 1788/5–1760 B.C., appear to have all belonged to a single dynasty, though the Imperial Crown seems to have made its rapid transit from head to head by violence more often than not (see Meyer, E.: *Geschichte des Altertums*, vol. (i), part (2), 3rd ed. (Stuttgart and Berlin 1913, Cotta), p. 302).

like the dragon's-tooth seed that they are—to spring to the surface again in a fresh crop of slaying and dying gladiators. Under its serene mask of effortless supremacy the Oecumenical Peace of a universal state is fighting, all the time, a desperate losing battle against an unexorcised demon of Violence in its own bosom; and we can see this moral struggle being waged in the guise of a conflict of policies.

Can the Jovian ruler of a universal state succeed in curbing that insatiable lust for further conquests which was fatal to Cyrus?[1] And, if he cannot resist the temptation *debellare superbos*, can he at any rate bring himself to act on the Virgilian counsel *parcere subiectis*?[2] When we apply this pair of tests to Jovius's performance, we shall find that he seldom succeeds in living up for long to his own good resolutions.

If we choose to deal first with the fortunes of the conflict between the alternative policies of expansion and of non-aggression in the relations of a universal state with the peoples beyond its pale, we may begin by considering the Sinic case in point, for there could have been no more impressive declaration of a determination to sheathe the sword than Ts'in She Hwang-ti's immense work of consolidating the unco-ordinated fortifications of the former Contending States of the Sinic World, where these had marched with the Eurasian Steppe, into the single continuous rampart of his Great Wall.[3] Yet Ts'in She Hwang-ti's good resolution to refrain from stirring up the Eurasian hornets' nest was broken, as we have seen, less than a hundred years after the Ts'in emperor's death, by the 'forward policy' of his Han successor Wuti.[4] In the history of the Hellenic universal state the founder himself set a practical example of moderation to his successors by abandoning his attempt to carry the Roman frontier to the Elbe,[5] before he bequeathed to them his famous counsel to be content with preserving the Empire within its existing limits, without attempting to extend it.[6] Augustus's attitude is illustrated by Strabo's account of a current controversy over the question whether the Augustan rule might allow of a British exception.[7] And, although this particular breach of the rule was eventually committed with an apparent impunity, Trajan afterwards demonstrated the soundness of Augustus's judgement when he ventured to break the rule on the grand scale by attempting to realize Crassus's and Julius's and

---

[1] See p. 188, above. [2] Virgil: *Aeneid*, Book VI, l. 853.
[3] See II. D (v), vol. ii, p. 119, and V. C (i) (c) 3, vol. v, p. 270, above.
[4] See V. C (i) (c) 3, vol. v, p. 271, above.
[5] See V. C (i) (c) 3, Annex I, vol. v, p. 593, above.
[6] Dio Cassius: *History of Rome*, Book LVI, chap. 33.
[7] This passage of Strabo has been quoted in II. D (vii), vol. ii, p. 282, footnote 4, above.

Antonius's dream of conquering the Parthian Empire. The price of a momentary advance from the hither bank of Euphrates to the foot of Zagros and the head of the Persian Gulf was an intolerable strain upon the Roman Empire's resources in money and men. Insurrections broke out not only in the newly conquered territories between the conqueror's feet but also among the Jewish Diasporà in the ancient dominions of the Empire in his rear;[1] the clear sky of a nascent Hellenic 'Indian Summer' was momentarily overcast; and it took all the prudence and ability of Trajan's successor Hadrian to liquidate the formidable legacy which Trajan's sword had bequeathed to him. Hadrian promptly evacuated all his predecessor's Transeuphratean conquests; yet he was able to restore only the territorial, and not the political, *status quo ante bellum*. Trajan's act of aggression made a deeper mark on Transeuphratean Syriac minds than Hadrian's reversal of it; and we may date from this epoch the beginning of a change of temper in the Transeuphratean tract of the Syriac World which was fostered by Roman relapses into a recourse to the sword[2] until the reaction in Iran declared itself at length in sensational fashion in the revolutionary replacement of an Arsacid King Log by a Sasanid King Stork,[3] and the consequent resumption of that militant counter-attack against the Hellenic intruder which had succeeded in evicting Hellenism from its footholds in Iran and 'Irāq in the second century B.C., but had latterly been in suspense since the conclusion by Augustus, in 20 B.C., of a Romano-Parthian 'peace with honour'. Under the auspices of the second pādishāh of the Sasanian line the Trajanic breach of the Augustan rule in A.D. 113–17 found its nemesis in A.D. 260 in a repetition of the disaster which had been inflicted upon Roman arms in 53 B.C. by the Parthians.[4]

In Egyptiac history we see the Theban sword that had been drawn in a *Befreiungskrieg* by Amosis (*imperabat* 1580–1558 B.C.) and wielded in a *revanche* by Thothmes I (*imperabat* 1545–1514 B.C.)

---

[1] For the insurrection of the Jewish Diasporà in Cyrene and Egypt and Cyprus in A.D. 115–17 see V. C (i) (c) 2, vol. v, p. 68, footnote 3; and V. C (i) (d) 9 (γ), in the present volume, p. 123, above.

[2] Trajan's error of A.D. 113–17 was repeated by Marcus in A.D. 162–6, by Septimius Severus in A.D. 195–9, and by Caracalla in A.D. 216–18. These three Roman wars of aggression were accompanied by annexations which carried the Roman frontier eastward from the Middle Euphrates to the Khābūr and thereby recaptured for Hellenism a belt of Syriac territory which had been liberated from the Seleucidae by the Arsacidae at the turn of the second and the last century B.C. But this recovery of ground in Mesopotamia was offset in 'Irāq by the indiscriminate barbarity of Marcus's and Severus's soldiery, who sacked the citadel of Hellenism at Seleucia as mercilessly as the head-quarters of the Arsacid power at Ctesiphon. And it was a still worse blow for Hellenism when the twice perpetrated sack of Seleucia-Ctesiphon in the second century of the Christian Era was avenged by Sapor's twice perpetrated sack of Antioch in A.D. 253 and 258–9.   [3] See V. C (i) (c) 3, vol. v, p. 216, above.

[4] In A.D. 260, as in 53 B.C., a Roman army laid down its arms; but the captivity of Valerian was more humiliating than the death of Crassus.

being deliberately sheathed by the Empress Hatshepsut (*imperabat* 1501–1479 B.C.)—only to be wilfully drawn and wielded again by Thothmes III (*imperabat* 1479–1447 B.C.) as soon as Death had removed Hatshepsut's restraining hand.[1] The *karma* of the Militarism which governed the policy of 'the New Empire' for the next hundred years (*circa* 1479–1376 B.C.) could not be extinguished by Ikhnaton's passionate repudiation of a policy which he had inherited from four predecessors—any more than the nemesis of Nebuchadnezzar's militarism could be averted by Nabonidus's childish device of ignoring the unwelcome realities of his imperial heritage and seeking to forget the cares of state in the delights of archaeology. Nor, in the history of the Indic universal state, could Açoka's renunciation of War as an instrument of his imperial policy[2] save the noble emperor's successors from losing the Maurya power by the same lethal arts that Açoka's grandfather Chandragupta had employed in gaining it.

In the history of the Ottoman Power Mehmed the Conqueror (*imperabat* A.D. 1451–81) deliberately limited his ambitions to the enterprise of making his *Pax Ottomanica* conterminous with the historic domain of Orthodox Christendom (not including its off-shoot in Russia);[3] and he resisted all temptations to encroach upon the adjoining domains of Western Christendom and the Iranic World. But—partly, no doubt, because his hand was forced by the aggressiveness of Ismā'īl Shāh Safawī—Mehmed's successor Selīm the Grim (*imperabat* A.D. 1512–20) broke Mehmed's self-denying ordinance in Asia,[4] while Selīm's successor Suleymān (*imperabat* A.D. 1520–66) committed the further error—which was ultimately still more disastrous and which could not be excused on Selīm's plea of *force majeure*—of breaking the same self-denying ordinance in Europe as well. In consequence the Ottoman Power was rapidly worn down by the grinding friction of a perpetual warfare on two fronts against adversaries whom the 'Osmanli could

---

[1] In thus standing out as an exception to a rule that prevailed afterwards as well as before, Hatshepsut's reign in the series of the Eighteenth Egyptiac Dynasty has a Syriac analogue in the reign of the Umayyad Caliph 'Umar II (*imperabat* A.D. 717–20). When 'Umar succeeded to the throne at Damascus he recalled the Arab army that was besieging Constantinople (see II. D (v), Annex, vol. ii, p. 400; and III. C (ii) (*b*), vol. iii, pp. 275–6, above); and he also tried, though this in vain, to withdraw his troops from the half-conquered territory of Transoxania (see II. D (v), vol. ii, p. 141; and II. D (vii), Annex VIII, vol. ii, pp. 446–52, above). It is noteworthy that 'Umar II was the only member of his dynasty who took his profession of Islam seriously (see V. C (i) (*d*) 6 (δ), Annex, vol. v, p. 675, above).

[2] The resolution which Açoka took and kept, after he had been convinced of the wickedness of War by his personal experience of the horrors of his own successful war of aggression against Kalinga, has been touched upon in V. C (i) (*d*) 6 (δ), Annex, p. 682, above.

[3] For this feature of the policy of Mehmed Fātih see I. C (i) (*b*), Annex I, vol. i, pp. 369–71, above.

[4] See I. C (i) (*b*), Annex I, vol. i, pp. 384–8, above.

repeatedly defeat in the field but could never put out of action. And this Selimian and Suleymanian perversity came to be so deeply ingrained in the statecraft of the Sublime Porte that even the collapse that followed Suleymān's death did not produce any lasting revulsion in favour of a Mehmedian moderation. The squandered strength of the Ottoman Empire had no sooner been recruited by the statesmanship of the Köprülüs than it was expended by Qāra Mustafā on a new war of aggression against the Franks which was intended to carry the Ottoman frontier up to the eastern bank of the Rhine. Though he never came within sight of this objective, Qāra Mustafā did emulate Suleymān the Magnificent's feat of laying siege to Vienna. But in A.D. 1682-3, as in A.D. 1529, the boss of the Danubian carapace of Western Christendom[1] proved to be too hard a nut for Ottoman arms to crack; and on this second occasion the 'Osmanlis did not fail before Vienna with impunity. The second Ottoman siege of Vienna evoked a Western counter-attack which continued, with no serious check, from A.D. 1683 to A.D. 1922, and which did not expend itself until the 'Osmanlis had not only been bereft of their empire but had even been compelled to renounce their ancestral Iranic culture as well, as the price of retaining possession of their homelands in Anatolia.[2]

In thus wantonly stirring up a hornets' nest in Western Christendom, Qāra Mustafā, like Suleymān before him, was committing the classic error of Xerxes when the successor of Darius[3] launched his war of aggression against Continental European Greece and thereby provoked a Hellenic counter-attack which immediately tore away from the Achaemenian Empire the Greek fringe of its dominions in Asia, and which ultimately led to the destruction of the Empire itself when the work begun by the sea-power of Athens under the auspices of Themistocles was taken up and completed by the land-power of Macedon under the auspices of Alexander. In the history of the Hindu World the Mughal Rāj produced its Xerxes in the person of the Emperor Awrangzīb (imperabat A.D. 1659-1707), whose unsuccessful efforts to assert his authority over Mahārāshtra by force of arms provoked a Marāthā counter-attack which ultimately destroyed the authority of Awrangzīb's succes-

---

[1] For the Danubian Hapsburg Monarchy's function as a carapace see I. C (iii) (b), vol. i, p. 156, footnote 1; II. D (v), vol. ii, pp. 177-90; and V. C (i) (c) 3, vol. v, pp. 325-7, above.

[2] See II. D (v), vol. ii, pp. 186-8, and Part III. A, vol. iii, pp. 46-7, above.

[3] Darius had, of course, extended the bounds of the Empire in his day—as, for that matter, had Trajan's predecessor Augustus and Suleymān's predecessor Mehmed the Conqueror. But the wars of Darius, like those of Augustus and Mehmed, differed from the wars of the Emperor's successors in the vital matter of the objective. Darius was seeking, not to expand his dominions ad infinitum, but on the contrary to bring their expansion to a definitive close by finding and establishing a 'scientific frontier' (see Meyer, E.: Geschichte des Altertums, vol. iii (Stuttgart 1901, Cotta), p. 96).

sors in the metropolitan provinces of their empire on the plains of Hindustan.[1]

It will be seen that, on the first of our two tests of ability to sheathe the sword, the rulers of universal states do not make a very good showing; and, if we now pass from the test of non-aggression against peoples beyond the pale to our second test of toleration towards the populations that are already living under the vaunted *Pax Oecumenica*, we shall find that Jovius fares hardly better in this second ordeal—though the receptivity which we have seen[2] to be characteristic of empire-builders might seem likely, on the face of it, to make toleration come easy to them.

The Roman Imperial Government, for example, made up its mind to tolerate Judaism and abode by this resolution in the face of severe and repeated Jewish provocations; but its forbearance was not equal to the more difficult moral feat of extending this tolerance to a Jewish heresy that had set itself to convert the Hellenic World. In the very first collision between the Roman authorities and the Christian Church the Imperial Government took the extreme step of making the profession of Christianity a capital offence; and this declaration of war to the death was the only one of Nero's acts of savagery that was not rescinded by the tyrant's successors on the Imperial Throne.[3] The motive of this proscription of Christianity as a *religio non licita* by the rulers of the

---

[1] It may be noted that the British Rāj in India—which has been established on the ruins of the Mughal Rāj and has taken over its function of providing a *Pax Oecumenica* for he Hindu World—has passed through a phase of boundless ambition which was reminiscent of the temper of an Awrangzīb and a Xerxes and a Qāra Mustafā and a Suleymān the Magnificent and a Thothmes III and a Trajan. The vastness and rapidity of the achievements of the British empire-builders of the generation of the Wellesleys so far turned their successors' heads that they seem for a moment to have dreamed of carrying their frontier north-westward from the banks of the Jumna to the banks of the Oxus (see V. C (i) (c) 3, vol. v, pp. 305–6, above). The extent of these British ambitions in Asia in the 'eighteen-thirties' may be gauged by the range and audacity of the reconnaissances that were made by Burnes (see loc. cit., p. 305, footnote 2) on the eve of the Anglo-Afghan War of A.D. 1838–42; but the annihilation of the British army that occupied Kābul and the execution of Stoddard aі d Conolly when they pushed on, in Burnes' footsteps, to Bukhara caused the British empire-builders to abandon once for all any idea of dealing with the Afghans and the Uzbegs as they had dealt with the Mughals and the Marāthās. The invasion and annexation of Sind in A.D. 1843 raised a controversy among the British themselves in which the policy of aggressive expansion in Asia was attacked on grounds of morality as well as on those of expediency; and, although the annexation of Sind in 1843 was followed in 1849 by the annexation of the Panjab, the British Rāj has never sought to trespass beyond the North-West frontier which it inherited in that year from the *ci-devant* Sikh principalities. The subsequent alternating trials of a 'close border' and a 'forward' policy have been a mere matter of military tactics; and this tactical controversy does not reflect any variation of political aim. The steadiness of the British-Indian Government's determination never to repeat the error of A.D. 1838 is revealed in its refusal to make any territorial profit out of its victories over Afghanistan in the wars of A.D. 1879 and A.D. 1919. (For the latter-day policy of the British Rāj on this frontier see V. C (i) (c) 3, vol. v, pp. 306–8, above.)

[2] In V. C (i) (d) 6 (α), vol. v, pp. 439–45, above.

[3] This point is made by Tertullian in *Ad Nat.*, Book I, chap. 7 (Migne, J.-P.: *Patrologia Latina*, vol. i, col. 567): 'Permansit, erasis omnibus, hoc solum institutum Neronianum.'

Hellenic universal state is as significant as the sequel. The element in Christianity that was intolerable to the Imperial Government was the Christians' refusal to accept the Government's claim that it was entitled to compel its subjects to act against their consciences.[1] The Christians were disputing the sword's prerogative; and, in defence of its *laesa majestas*, the weapon which Augustus had contrived to sheathe came shooting out of its scabbard again, like a snake out of its hole, to join battle, this time, with a spiritual power which could never be defeated by the strokes of a temporal weapon. So far from checking the propagation of Christianity, the martyrdoms proved to be the most effective agencies of conversion;[2] and the eventual victory of the Christian martyr's spirit over the Roman ruler's blade bore out Tertullian's triumphantly defiant boast that Christian blood was seed.[3]

The Achaemenian Government, like the Roman, set itself in principle to rule with the consent of the governed and was likewise only partially successful in living up to this policy in practice.

[1] This question of principle, which underlay the practice of imposing the death-penalty in case of a refusal to perform, on demand, the outward formalities of the ritual of Caesar-worship, is brought out clearly by Meyer, E.: *Ursprung und Anfänge des Christentums*, vol. iii (Stuttgart and Berlin 1923, Cotta), pp. 510–19. The same scholar points out in op. cit., vol. cit., pp. 552–65, that during the Hellenic 'Indian Summer' the Roman Imperial authorities deliberately forbore to carry the execution of their policy to its logical conclusion. Between Nero and Decius, Domitian was the only emperor who personally took the initiative in ordering a persecution (p. 553); and, while Trajan did not repeal the Neronian decree that had made the profession of Christianity a capital offence, he mitigated its practical working by ruling that the initiative in procuring convictions was not to be taken by the public authorities and that anonymous denunciations were to be ignored as an abuse which *et pessimi exempli nec nostri saeculi est* (*Correspondence between Trajan and Pliny the Younger*, No. 97 [98]). Thereafter Hadrian ruled (without formally revoking Trajan's ruling) that denunciations of Christians must take the form of an action at law; that the prosecutor must prove, not merely that the defendant was a Christian, but that he had committed a specific offence against the law; and that, if he failed to win his case, he himself should be liable to punishment (Seeck, O.: *Geschichte des Untergangs der Antiken Welt*, vol. iii, 2nd ed. (Stuttgart 1921, Metzler), p. 295). Under these rulings the profession of Christianity, while still officially proscribed, was largely, though never more than precariously, tolerated (Meyer, op. cit., vol. cit., pp. 562–4). This humanely inconsequent compromise did not outlast the *saeculum* for which it was devised. Even before the 'Indian Summer' faded out, the Government of the Emperor Marcus was swept into a campaign of persecution by the fury of a populace which had turned savage under the double scourge of war and plague (Seeck, op. cit., vol. cit., pp. 297–9); and, when the storm broke, it was not long before the Government of the Emperor Decius abandoned the Trajanic compromise and imposed a test on every subject of the Empire (see V. C (i) (c) 2, vol. v, p. 76, above). 'In accordance with the "law" which governs the religious development of the Imperial Age from first to last, the fanaticism that moved the populace to its deeds [of violence] gradually mounted from below upwards. Just as the new religion itself gradually forced its way up into the dominant social strata, so likewise the hatred of Christianity which was entertained by its opponents spread *pari passu*. The two currents that here met and broke in waves against one another were currents of an identical nature' (Seeck, op. cit., vol. cit., p. 301).

[2] 'You cannot fail to see that our having our heads cut off or being crucified or being thrown to the beasts or into bondage or to the flames or being subjected to all the other forms of torture does not make us abandon our profession of faith. On the contrary, the more of these martyrdoms that there are, the more we increase in numbers through the excess of conversions over martyrdoms.'—Justin: *Dialogus*, chap. 110 (Migne, J.-P.: *Patrologia Graeca*, vol. vi, col. 729).

[3] 'Plures efficimur quoties metimur a vobis; semen est sanguis Christianorum.'— Tertullian: *Apologeticus*, chap. 50 (Migne, J.-P.: *Patrologia Latina*, vol. i, col. 535).

It did succeed in winning the allegiance of the Phoenicians and the Jews, but it failed in the long run to conciliate either the Babylonians or the Egyptians. The magnanimity with which the Tyrians were forgiven by Cambyses for their refusal to serve against their Carthaginian kinsfolk,[1] and the Jews forgiven by Darius for Zerubbabel's abortive essay in high treason,[2] sufficed to confirm a loyalty which these two Syriac peoples were inclined in any case to feel towards a Great King whose sword had saved them from Babylonian oppressors in the one case and in the other from Greek competitors. But the conciliation of the Babylonian priesthood by Cyrus and of the Egyptian priesthood by Darius was an ephemeral *tour de force*; no tact or cajolery could permanently reconcile the heirs of the Babylonic and Egyptiac civilizations to an alien domination; and Egypt and Babylon never ceased to rise in revolt till Babylon was crushed by Xerxes and Egypt by Ochus.[3]

The 'Osmanlis had no better success in conciliating their *ra'īyeh* —notwithstanding the wideness of the scope of the cultural, and even civil, autonomy that they conceded to them in the *millet* system.[4] The liberality of the system *de jure* was marred by the high-handedness with which it was applied *de facto*; the Ottoman Government was never able completely to win the *ra'īyeh*'s hearts;[5] and the perilously practical fashion in which they displayed their disloyalty, as soon as a series of Ottoman reverses afforded an

---

[1] See Herodotus, Book III, chaps. 17 and 19.

[2] See V. C (i) (*d*) 9 (γ), in the present volume, p. 121, above

[3] See V. C (i) (*c*) 2, vol. v, pp. 94 and 123, and V. C (i) (*c*) 4, vol. v, pp. 347-8, above, and V. C (ii) (*a*), Annex II, in the present volume, p. 442, below.

[4] Mehmed the Conqueror himself (see IV. C (iii) (*c*) 2 (β), Annex II, vol. iv, p. 622, above) went so far to meet the susceptibilities of his non-Muslim subjects that one of his first acts after his capture of Constantinople was to invite the clergy of the Orthodox Church to elect a new Oecumenical Patriarch; and, when they presented George Scholarius as their candidate, the Ottoman master of the Orthodox Christian World took care to ratify the election in accordance with the procedure that had been customary under the East Roman Imperial régime (see Phrantzis, G.: *Chronicon*, Book III, chap. 11, ed. by Bekker, I. (Bonn 1838, Weber), pp. 304-7).

[5] The friendly relations between Muslims and Dhimmīs which prevailed in the earlier days of the Ottoman régime are described in Gibb, H. A. R., and Bowen, H.: *Islamic Society and the West*, vol. i (London 1939, Milford), chap. 14 (see the passage quoted in the present Study, IV. C (ii) (*b*) 1, vol. iv, p. 69, footnote 1, above). For the subsequent change from friendliness to antagonism see op. cit., vol. i, chap. 13. The growth of this antagonism can be measured and dated by the history of the relations between the two communities in the trade-guilds. Originally the Muslim and Dhimmī practitioners of the same trade belonged to the same guild, which would include all the masters of that craft without distinction of religion. From about the middle of the seventeenth century of the Christian Era onwards, however, the guilds began to split into fractions corresponding to the religious divisions between the craftsmen (Gibb and Bowen, op. cit., vol. i, chap. 6). The date of this untoward social change is significant. It coincides with the period of anarchy between the death of Suleymān the Magnificent and the advent of the statesmen of the House of Köprülü (see the present chapter, pp. 207-8 and 208-9, and V. C (ii) (*b*), p. 299, below). Compare the corresponding coincidence in date between the Decian persecution of the Christian Church and the period of anarchy through which the Roman Empire passed between the death of Marcus and the accession of Diocletian.

opening for treachery on the *ra'īyeh*'s part, gave the successors of Selīm the Grim some reason to regret that this ruthless man of action had been deterred (if the tale were true),[1] by the joint exertions of his Grand Vezīr Pīrī Pasha and his Sheykh-al-Islām Jemālī, from carrying out a plan to exterminate the Orthodox Christian majority of his subjects—as he did in fact exterminate an Imāmī Shī'ī minority.[2]

In exerting himself, with success, to defeat Sultan Selīm's atrocious project, Sheykh Jemālī was moved not merely by his own personal feelings of humanity but by the standing orders of the Islamic Canon Law which it was the Sheykh's professional duty to uphold. The *Sheri'ah* required the Commander of the Faithful, or his deputy, to give quarter to non-Muslims who were 'People of the Book'[3] if these forbore to resist the sword of Islam by force of arms, and so long as they gave and kept an undertaking to obey

---

[1] See Hammer, J. von: *Histoire de l'Empire Ottoman* (Paris 1835–43, Bellizard, Barthès, Dufour et Lowell, 18 vols.+Atlas), vol. iv, pp. 364–5. (This story has been referred to already in V. C (i) (d) 6 (δ), Annex, vol. v, p. 706, footnote 1, above.)
'C'est surtout pour les chrétiens et les Grecs de Constantinople que Djemali fut un véritable ange sauveur, lorsqu'après le massacre des schiis, Sélim eut conçu l'idée non moins pieuse d'organiser une tuerie générale des chrétiens, ou du moins de leur retirer leurs églises. A cette occasion, il proposa à Djemali cette question captieuse: lequel est le plus méritoire, de subjuguer le monde entier, ou de convertir les peuples à l'islamisme? —Le moufti, qui ne devina pas les intentions de Sélim, répondit que la conversion des infidèles était incontestablement l'œuvre la plus méritoire et la plus agréable à Dieu. Aussitôt Sélim ordonna au grand-vizir de changer toutes les églises en mosquées, d'interdire le culte des chrétiens, et de mettre à mort tous ceux qui refuseraient d'embrasser l'islamisme. Le grand-vizir, effrayé de cet ordre sanguinaire, se consulta avec Djemali, qui, sans le savoir, avait, par son fetwa, sanctionné l'arrêt de mort des chrétiens; le résultat de leur conférence fut le conseil donné secrètement au patriarche grec de demander à comparaître devant le Sultan. Sélim refusa d'abord d'aquiescer à la prière du patriarche; mais il finit par se rendre aux représentations du grand-vizir et du mufti. Le patriarche, accompagné de tout son clergé, fut donc admis à paraître devant le sultan à Andrinople; il appuya ses réclamations sur l'engagement solennellement pris par Mohammed II, lors de la conquête de Constantinople, de ne point convertir les églises en mosquées et de laisser aux chrétiens le libre exercice de leur culte; il invoqua avec éloquence le Koran, qui défend la conversion par la force et ordonne la tolérance envers les nations non musulmanes, moyennant le paiement de la capitation. L'acte constatant la promesse signée par Mohammed II avait été détruit dans un incendie; mais trois vieux janissaires qui, soixante ans auparavant, avaient assisté au siège de Constantinople, attestèrent que le Sultan avait en effet engagé sa parole sur ces trois points aux députés qui lui avaient apporté les clefs de la ville dans un bassin d'or. Sélim respecta les dispositions du Koran et la parole de son aïeul pour ce qui regardait la liberté du culte; mais il ajoutait que la loi ne disait pas que d'aussi beaux édifices que les églises chrétiennes dussent être profanés plus longtemps par l'idolâtrie. En conséquence, il ordonna de changer toutes les églises de Constantinople en mosquées, de réparer celles qui étaient près de tomber en ruines et d'en élever d'autres en bois, afin de ne point porter atteinte au droit des nationaux et des étrangers professant le christianisme. Si Sélim, grâce à l'humanité du grand-vizir Piri-Pacha et du moufti Djemali, n'a pas souillé la fin de son règne par un massacre général des infidèles, comme il en avait souillé le commencement par le massacre des hérétiques, il leur enleva toujours leurs plus beaux temples.'
[2] For Selīm's massacre of the Shī'ah in Anatolia in A.D. 1514 see I. C (i) (b), Annex I, vol. i, pp. 362 and 384, above.
[3] On a strict interpretation of this term the only peoples who could claim the status were the Jews and the Christians; but in Islamic practice the same privileges were accorded by analogy to the adherents of other 'higher religions'—in the first place to the Zoroastrians and eventually to the Hindus as well. See IV. C (iii) (b) 12, vol. iv, pp. 225–6; and V. C (i) (d) 6 (δ), Annex, vol. v, p. 674, footnote 2, above.

the Muslim authorities and to pay a super-tax. This was, in truth, the principle which had been followed by the Primitive Arab Muslim empire-builders, and their faithfulness to it is one of the considerations that account for the amazing rapidity with which they accomplished their work. As soon as the preliminary raids gave place to permanent conquests on the grand scale, the Caliph 'Umar intervened to protect the conquered populations against the rapine, and even against the rights, of the Arab Muslim soldiery;[1] it was 'Uthmān's unwillingness to abandon 'Umar's policy that cost the third of the Caliphs his life;[2] and in this matter the Umayyads[3] showed themselves worthy successors of the 'Rightly Guided' Four. Mu'āwiyah set an example of tolerance[4] which was followed not only by the later Umayyads[5] but also by the earlier 'Abbasids.[6] Yet the latter days of the 'Abbasid régime did not pass[7] without being disgraced by outbreaks of mob violence against Christian subjects of the Caliphate who had by this time dwindled in numbers from a majority to a minority of the population as a result of the mass-conversions to Islam that heralded the break-up of the universal state and the approach of a social interregnum.[8]

In the history of the Mughal Rāj in India Awrangzīb departed from a policy of toleration towards Hinduism which Akbar had bequeathed to his successors as the most important of their *arcana imperii*;[9] and this departure was swiftly requited by the downfall of the empire which Akbar had built up.[10]

Our survey has revealed the suicidal importunity of a sword that has been sheathed after having once tasted blood. The polluted weapon will not rust in its scabbard, but must ever be itching to

[1] 'Umar's policy was emulated, in the history of the expansion of our own Western Society, in the efforts of the Spanish Crown to protect its 'Indian' subjects against the rapacity and brutality of the Spanish *conquistadores* (see Kirkpatrick, F. A., in *The Cambridge Modern History*, vol. x, pp. 260–9 and 277).

[2] For the nature of 'Umar's policy and the causes of 'Uthmān's assassination see Wellhausen, J.: *Das Arabische Reich und sein Sturz* (Berlin 1902, Reimer), pp. 21 and 27–31. For the liberality of the Arab Caliphate towards its non-Muslim subjects in general, as well as in particular cases, see op. cit., pp. 15–16, 18–20, 188–90, 206.

[3] See V. C (i) (d) 6 (δ), Annex, vol. v, pp. 675–7 and 704–5, above.

[4] Wellhausen, op. cit., p. 84.

[5] See, for example, the eulogy of the Caliph Yazīd I (*imperabat* A.D. 680–3) from the pen of a Christian chronicler which has been quoted in V. C (i) (c) 3, vol. v, p. 226, above.

[6] See V. C (i) (d) 6 (δ), Annex, vol. v, pp. 677–8 and 706, above.

[7] The turning-point seems to have come in the caliphate of Mutawakkil (*imperabat* A.D. 847–61).

[8] For these outbreaks, which were reminiscent of those against the Christian 'Diasporà' in the Roman Empire in the reign of the Emperor Marcus (p. 202, footnote 1, above), see Tritton, A. S.: *The Caliphs and their Non-Muslim Subjects* (London 1930, Milford), especially chaps. 4 and 9.

[9] Tacitus: *Annals*, Book II, chap. 36.

[10] On the other hand it must be admitted that an earlier universal state which had stood on the same ground had anticipated Akbar's toleration without escaping Awrangzīb's punishment. The Guptas had adhered to Hinduism without persecuting Buddhism (see V. C (i) (d) 6 (δ), Annex, vol. v, pp. 706, above), yet their empire had been as ephemeral as the Mughal Rāj was.

leap out again—as though the disembodied spirit of the would-be saviour who first had recourse to this sinister instrument could now find no rest until his sin of seeking salvation along a path of crime had been atoned for by the agency of the very weapon which he once so perversely used. An instrument that is powerless to save may yet be potent to punish; the penitently sheathed sword will still thirst implacably to carry out this congenial duty; and it will have its way in the end when it has Time for its ally. In the fullness of Time the din of battle which has ebbed away towards the fringes of Civilization till it has passed almost out of ear-shot[1] will come welling back again in the van of barbarian war-bands that have gained the upper hand over the garrisons of the *limes* by learning from them, in the effective school of a perpetual border warfare, the winning tricks of the professional soldier's trade;[2] or, more terrifying still, the dreadful sound will come welling up again in the resurgence of an Internal Proletariat that has turned militant once more—to the consternation of a Dominant Minority which has been flattering itself that this *profanum vulgus* has long since been cowed or cajoled into a settled habit of submissiveness. The spectres of war and revolution that have latterly passed into legend[3] now once again stalk abroad, as of old, in the light of day; and a *bourgeoisie* which has never before seen bloodshed now hastily throws up ring-walls round its open towns out of any materials that come to hand: mutilated statues and desecrated altars and scattered drums of fallen columns and inscribed blocks of marble reft from derelict public monuments.[4] These pacific inscriptions are now anachronisms; for the 'Indian Summer' is over; the 'Time of Troubles' has returned; and this shocking calamity has descended upon a generation which has been brought up in the illusory conviction that the bad times of yore have gone for good![5]

[1] In the heyday of the *Pax Romana* an observer who travelled from Rome to Cologne would have met with no troops on his road, between his last sight of the garrison of the capital and his first sight of the garrison of the frontier along the Rhine, save for a single *cohors urbana* which was stationed at Lyons; and this detachment was only 1,200 men strong (see Mommsen, Th.: *The History of Rome: The Provinces from Caesar to Diocletian* (London 1886, Bentley, 2 vols.), vol. i, p. 88, footnote 3).

[2] See V. C (i) (*c*) 3, *passim*, in vol. v, above, and Part VIII, *passim*, below.

[3] See the passages of Aelius Aristeides' *In Romam* quoted in V. C (i) (*c*) 4, vol. v, pp. 343–4, above.

[4] Of all the improvised fortifications of this type that the writer of this Study has seen, the example that speaks most eloquently to the eye is the wall of the antique citadel that looks down to-day, with an air of open-mouthed amazement, upon the new-fangled capital city of the Turkish Republic at Angora. The historian's mind will also be conscious of a still more dramatic contrast between these fortifications round the citadel of Angora and the famous inscription on the wall of the Temple of Augustus; for this contrast embodies in visual form the whole tragedy of the relapse from an 'Indian Summer' into a recurrent 'Time of Troubles'.

[5] Ibn Khaldūn (*Muqaddamāt*, McG. de Slane's translation (Paris 1863–8, Imprimerie Impériale, 3 vols.), vol. ii, pp. 46–8) points out that, while both the sword and the pen are indispensable instruments of all governments at all times, the sword is at a premium and the pen at a discount at the beginning of an empire's career, when it is being founded,

We have now followed the high tragedy of the saviours with the sword into an act in the drama which makes it plain, in retrospect, that our *dramatis personae* have been foredoomed to failure. But lost causes are the mothers of heroism; and we should be denying ourselves the sight of some of the finest examples of the type of hero that we are now passing in review if we coldly turned our backs upon the stage of history at this poignant moment. Upon the recurrence of the 'Time of Troubles', Zeus yields the stage to Hêraklês once more; and, if we sit the play out, we shall bear witness, when the curtain falls, that we have never seen Hêraklês show himself to such advantage as in this forlorn hope.

In Hellenic history this sympathetic part was played by a series of Illyrian soldiers—Claudius, Aurelian, Probus, Carus—who were successively invested with the purple because they had the courage to wear it in an age when it had become a veritable shirt of Nessus, and who duly justified their sensational rise to fortune by indefatigably striking off one after another of Anarchy's hydra-heads until they had cleared the field for the entry of their Jovian compatriot Diocletian. In the recurrence of the Egyptiac 'Time of Troubles' after the decease of the Twelfth Dynasty we may espy the handiwork of some forgotten Egyptiac Aurelian in a slight and transient but unmistakable rally of the Egyptiac Society *circa* 1760 B.C.;[1] and in the duplicate recurrence of the same tribulations in the days of 'the New Empire' after the death of Amenhotep III we can discern four indubitable counterparts of our four Illyrian heroes in the soldierly figures of the fighting pharaohs Seti I and Ramses II and Merneptah and Ramses III.[2] These Egyptiac saviours, like their Illyrian counterparts in Hellenic history, were *novi homines*, and so was the tradesman Minin who rose up to deliver the Russian branch of Orthodox Christendom from the troubles of A.D. 1604–13. Minin, however, had a companion-in-arms, Prince Pojarski, who had been recruited from the ranks of the Russian dominant minority; and the role of saviour in a recurrent 'Time of Troubles' has sometimes even been assumed by a vigorous scion of an imperial dynasty whose previous decadence has been the immediate cause of the catastrophe. Such were the careers of the Achaemenid Great King Artaxerxes Ochus (*imperabat* 358–338 B.C.) and of the 'Osmanli Pādishāh Murād IV (*imperabat* A.D. 1623–40); and the demonic vein that reveals itself

and again at the end, when it is breaking up, while, in between, there is a middle period of security, prosperity, and ease during which, conversely, the sword is at a discount and the pen at a premium.

[1] See Meyer, E.: *Geschichte des Altertums*, vol. i, part (2), 3rd ed. (Stuttgart and Berlin 1913, Cotta), p. 302.

[2] See I. C (i) (*b*), vol. i, pp. 92–3 and 100–2; IV. C (ii) (*b*) 2, vol. iv, p. 85; IV. C (iii) (*c*) 2 (*β*), vol. iv, p. 422; and V. C (i) (*c*) 3, vol. v, p. 269, above.

in the êthos of both of these grim militarists is perhaps an indication that their common effort to turn back the course of dynastic history was too extreme a *tour de force* for flesh and blood to undertake with impunity. We may close our catalogue of 'Illyrians' with the name of one saviour of this class who was not either a *porphyrogenitus* or a *novus homo*. In the middle of the nineteenth century of the Christian Era, when the T'aip'ing insurrection was on the point of sweeping a degenerate successor of Ch'ien Lung off the Imperial Throne at Peking, the Ts'ing Dynasty obtained a fifty years' reprieve thanks in large measure to the prowess of a general who came in consequence to be known among his own compatriots as 'Chinese Gordon', but who really—to confess the shocking truth—was a 'South Sea Barbarian' whose sword-arm had been hired by the Emperor in his dire extremity though the Son of Heaven knew very well that this mercenary saviour's barbarous blood had not in it even a tincture of the celestial ichor of the Children of Han.

We need not now linger much longer over a history that continues to repeat itself; but we may observe that, if the 'Illyrians' faithfully fulfil their task, their prowess may make it possible for Hercules Redivivus to withdraw in favour of Jupiter Redux. The labours of Aurelian opened the way for Diocletian to make his entry on to the stage as a second Divus Julius, and for Constantine, in his turn, to play Augustus to Diocletian's Caesar. And these second founders of the Hellenic universal state have their counterparts in the histories of other civilizations. In the Sumeric World, for example, Ur-Engur's Empire of Sumer and Akkad was refounded by an Amorite prince of Babylon, Hammurabi, after it had been wrecked by a successful revolt on the part of its Elamite subjects,[1] and had lain in ruins thereafter for not less than two and a half centuries.[2] In the main body of Orthodox Christendom the demonic exertions of the 'Osmanli Pādishāh Murād IV were followed up by the constructive labours of the Albanian vezīrs of the House of Köprülü (*fungebantur* A.D. 1656–76; 1687–8; 1689–91; 1697–1702; 1710),[3] who gave the *Pax Ottomanica* a new lease of

---

[1] For this catastrophe and its sequel see V. C (ii) (*b*), pp. 297–8, below.

[2] There was an interval of 233 years between the capture of the Emperor Ibisin of Ur in 2180 B.C. and the accession of the Emperor Hammurabi of Babylon in 1947 B.C.; and it took Hammurabi many years of hard labour to accomplish his task of restoring unity and peace to the Sumeric World by welding together again, after so long an interval, the fragments into which the original Empire of Sumer and Akkad had been broken up.

[3] The succession of Grand Vezīrs of the House of Köprülü was as follows: Mehmed 1656–61; Mehmed's son Ahmed 1661–76; Mehmed's son-in-law Siāwush 1687–8; Mehmed's son Mustafā 1689–91; Mehmed's nephew Hüseyn 1697–1702; Mustafā's son Nu'mān 1710. The family ability for administration and diplomacy showed itself in varying measure in all but the last of these six members of the House. On the debit side we have, however, to place Qāra Mustafā, who was Grand Vezīr, with irretrievably

life that lasted until the outbreak of the great Russo-Turkish War of A.D. 1768–74. In the Russian offshoot of Orthodox Christendom the second founder of the universal state was the Tsar Peter the Great (*imperabat de jure inde ab* A.D. 1682, *sed de facto tantum inde ab* A.D. 1689), who roused the Russian body social out of a torpor in which it had lain since the convulsions of A.D. 1604–13 by giving it a potent injection of an alien culture.[1]

The re-establishment of a universal state after its overthrow in a recurrent 'Time of Troubles' has in some cases been accomplished to such good effect that it has resulted in a return of at least a pale similitude of the long-since departed 'Indian Summer'. In the Russian offshoot of Orthodox Christendom, for example, the 'Indian Summer' which had visited Muscovy in the reign of Ivan IV (*imperabat* A.D. 1533–84), thanks to the foundation of a universal state by Ivan III (*imperabat* A.D. 1462–1505), returned at the accession of Catherine II (*accessit* A.D. 1762), and lasted, this time, till the death of Alexander I (*obiit* A.D. 1825), thanks to the re-establishment of the Russian universal state on a new basis by Peter the Great (*imperabat* A.D. 1682–1725). And in the Hellenic World Diocletian and Constantine did their work so well when they reconstructed, on new foundations, the dilapidated political edifice of Julius and Augustus, that they made it possible for the Emperor Justinian to radiate all the glory of a Solomon—in his codification of the Roman Law and his building of the dome of the Church of the Holy Wisdom and his recovery of the Empire's lost dominions in Africa and Italy[2]—though Justinian did not begin to reign (*imperabat* A.D. 527–65) until 149 years had passed since the defeat and death of Valens at the Battle of Adrianople,[3] 243 since the accession of Diocletian, 292 since the death of Alexander

disastrous results, from 1676 to 1683. Qāra Mustafā was not a Köprülü, but he came from Merzifūn, in the neighbourhood of the Köprülüs' home-town of Vezīr Köprü in North-Eastern Anatolia, and on this account he was given his education by the generosity of Mehmed Köprülü—a bad day's work for the Ottoman Empire!

[1] It is interesting to observe that the Romanov Emperor who was the second founder of the Muscovite oecumenical empire in the Russian offshoot of Orthodox Christendom resorted (no doubt, quite independently) to an expedient which had already been adopted by the Köprülü vezīrs who were the second founders of the Ottoman oecumenical empire in the main body of Orthodox Christendom. The identical cure for an identical disease which was applied with successful results in both cases was to invigorate an anaemic body social by a process of blood transfusion (in a metaphorical sense). The Köprülüs had drawn their supply of fresh life-blood from the Orthodox Christian *ra'īyeh* of the Pādishāh (see II. D (vi), vol. ii, pp. 222–8, above); Peter drew his from the free peoples of Western Christendom (see III. C (ii) (b), vol. iii, pp. 278–83, above).

[2] In the opinion of the writer of this Study this glory of Justinian's was purchased—like that of so many other princes of the same Solomonian type—at a cost which was socially disastrous, as witness the immediate and abysmal and never-retrieved collapse of the Hellenic body social, as well as the Roman body politic, after the vainglorious emperor's death. (On this point see IV. C (iii) (c) 2 (β), vol. iv, pp. 326–8, above, and the present chapter in the present volume, pp. 223–5, below.)

[3] Justinian has a happier Indic counterpart in the Emperor Harsha (*imperabat* A.D. 606–47), who entered upon his auspicious reign some 130 years after the Huns had dealt with the Guptas as the Visigoths dealt with Valens.

Severus, and 347 since the death of Marcus in A.D. 180: a date that had marked the end of the original 'Indian Summer' which had lightened for a time the darkness of a disintegrating Hellenic Society in the Age of the Antonines before the recurrence of the Hellenic 'Time of Troubles' in the third century of the Christian Era.

At this eleventh hour in the long decline of the Hellenic Civilization, Justinian's Solomonian glory was a luxury out of season which had to be paid for at a fancy price; and, forty-five years after Justinian's death, a bill of a staggering magnitude was duly presented to the magnificent emperor's devoted successor Heraclius when he was summoned from Carthage to defend Constantinople against a Persian invader whose advance-guard had by then already pushed its way unhindered right across the Asiatic torso of Justinian's Mediterranean empire—from the banks of the Khabūr to the shores of the Bosphorus. Heraclius, with his ominous name, is a typical representative of the saviour with the sword in his final appearance on the stage, when the tragic actor once for all lays aside a Jovian mask that has now become utterly incongruous, and once more plays Hêraklês in the only scene that it is any longer possible for even a Hêraklês to play. This scene is the death of a 'Die-Hard'; a 'Die-Hard' is a soldier who offers up his life for a cause when he is convinced that all but Honour is already lost; and, as a classic example of the type, the Roman Emperor Heraclius is worthy to rank with the British Colonel Inglis whose call to his men first put the phrase into currency.[1]

Heraclius spent twenty-four years out of a reign of thirty-one on the desperate enterprise of trying by force of arms to prevent the Syriac provinces of the Hellenic universal state from shaking off at last an incubus of Hellenic domination which had been weighing upon them ever since the overthrow of the Achaemenian Empire by the arms of Alexander the Great. The sword of Heraclius could not avail to stem a tide of Syriac resurgence which had been flowing for at least eight centuries in the Transeuphratean, and for at least four centuries in the Ciseuphratean,

---

[1] In the verbal armoury of English party politics in the twentieth century of the Christian Era the term 'Die-Hard' has come to be used as a shaft of ridicule to be shot at a politician who makes a parade of his intention of 'dying in the last ditch' in defence of some political cause that is patently lost, and this particularly if his opponents have reason to expect that the *poseur* will prudently resign himself to the inevitable when it actually comes to the point. This latter-day connotation of play-acting does not, however, attach to the sobriquet in its origin. The authentic 'Die-Hards' are an infantry regiment of the British Army; and the Fifty-Seventh won their nickname as a title of honour at the Battle of Albuera in A.D. 1811. In an engagement in which the regiment was being mown down by the enemy's fire, their commander, Colonel Sir William Inglis, as he fell desperately wounded, cried 'Die hard, Fifty-Seventh! Die hard'; and the regiment gained the name of 'Die-Hards' for themselves by taking their fallen Colonel at his word.

territories of the Syriac World by the time when Heraclius was called in to Hellenism's rescue. The Syriac counter-attack was by then already victorious on the deeper planes of life—in religion, in language, in architecture, in art—and, even on the superficial planes of politics and war, the liberation, by Syriac arms, of the homeland of the Syriac culture had already been momentarily anticipated during the recurrence of the Hellenic 'Time of Troubles' in the third century of the Christian Era, when Zenobia of Palmyra had brought the whole of Syria under her rule and had even pushed her outposts across the Taurus and the Nile.[1] It is evident that Heraclius in the seventh century was courting disaster by venturing to repeat Aurelian's barely successful counterstroke.[2] Heraclius did succeed, at the end of eighteen years of strenuous and audacious campaigning, in pushing the Persian invader back from Chalcedon to Tabrīz and imposing on the Sasanian Empire a peace-settlement which restored the territorial *status quo ante bellum*. Yet the Persian champion of Syriac liberty had no sooner laid down his arms than an Arab champion stepped into his place in the arena and pitted his fresh vigour against a war-worn Roman Army; and this immediate return, from an unexpected quarter, of a tide which Heraclius had thought himself to have stemmed for good, was a challenge to which the weary emperor's spirit was not equal. In his fight to save Syria from the Arabs Heraclius abandoned after six years a struggle which he had kept up for eighteen years against the Persians, and withdrew from Antioch to Constantinople to die there broken-hearted.[3]

Heraclius is not the only famous 'Die-Hard' whose figure looms up for a moment in the last scene of the tragedy of the disintegration of the Hellenic Society. The historic fame of the African emperor has been outshone by the legendary glory of a British prince who is reputed to have spent his life, and met his death, in a vain effort to roll back a tide of barbarian invasion from the coasts of Ultima Thule; and the legend of Arthur possibly reflects —through the double refraction of Welsh epic and French romance[4] —the authentic history of an Artorius[5] who did indeed surpass his fellow Roman Heraclius in stoutness of heart if he faced his fearful

---

[1] For the historical relation between Zenobia's 'successor-state' of the Roman Empire in Syria and Mu'āwīyah's see I. C (i) (*b*), vol. i, p. 74, footnote 4, and II. D (i), vol. ii, p. 11, above.

[2] See III. C (ii) (*b*), vol. iii, p. 269, footnote 4; and IV. C (iii) (*c*) 2 (*β*), vol. iv, p. 330, above.

[3] See II. D (vii), vol. ii, pp. 287–8, above.

[4] For the attractiveness of the Welsh imagination of 'the Heroic Age' to a 'medieval' Western taste see II. D (vii), vol. ii, pp. 339–40, above.

[5] For a faint indication of a possibility that the historical Artorius may have been a less attractive character than the legendary Arthur, see V. C (i) (*c*) 3, Annex III, vol. v, p. 609, footnote 2, above.

odds, and died his 'Die-Hard's' death, in defending, not the all but impregnable citadel of the Hellenic World,[1] but an outlying and exposed province which had been abandoned by the Central Government and had lost touch with the torso of the Empire before ever Artorius drew his sword.

If we turn our eyes from the Hellenic scene to the spectacle of other dissolving societies and crumbling empires, the mouths of other 'Die-Hards' will answer our roll-call with their 'Morituri te salutamus'. In the dotage of the 'Abbasid Caliphate of Baghdad—in an age when the glory of Hārūn had long since been eclipsed by the humiliations that Hārūn's successors had suffered at the hands of barbarian praetorians and heretical Buwayhid mayors of the palace,[2] and when only two generations were still to run before the advent of the annihilating catastrophe of A.D. 1258—we see the Caliph Nāsir (*imperabat* A.D. 1180–1225), whose reign happened to fall in the trough between the Saljūq and the Mongol wave of a Eurasian Nomad Völkerwanderung, showing the hardihood to profit from this momentary relief by successfully re-establishing the rule of the Commander of the Faithful in regions, beyond the bounds of the metropolitan province of 'Irāq, where the authority of Nāsir's predecessors had been merely nominal for some three centuries past.[3] In the death-agonies of the Ottoman Empire we catch a glimpse of an intrepid 'Die-Hard' in the figure of 'Osmān Pasha successfully delaying for nearly five months the descent of a Russian avalanche from the Balkans upon Constantinople by his stand at Plevna from the 20th July to the 10th December, 1877.

[1] The strength of Constantinople lay in a masterly collaboration between Art and Nature that saved the city from capture in the crisis of A.D. 626 (see II. D (v), Annex, vol. ii, p. 400, above). At a moment when Heraclius himself—at the head of an expeditionary force into which he had drafted the best of what remained of the Roman Army—was engaged in the far interior of Asia on a thrust at the Sasanian Empire's heart (see III. C (ii) (*b*), vol. iii, p. 269, footnote 4, and IV. C (iii) (*c*) 2 (*β*), vol. iv, p. 330, above), the Emperor's base of operations at Constantinople had to withstand a concerted attack from the Persians on the Asiatic and the Avars on the European side. The city was saved by the Roman Navy's command of the waters of the Straits, which made it impossible for the two hostile forces to join hands.

[2] For the domination of the Buwayhids at Baghdad see I. C (i) (*b*), Annex I, vol. i, p. 356, above.

[3] See the article on Nāsir in the *Encyclopaedia of Islam*. This caliph had the temerity to implicate himself in the military struggles between the 'successor-states' of the Caliphate in Iran and the Oxus-Jaxartes Basin, and he succeeded in temporarily making himself master of Khuzistan by successively playing off the Khwārizmshāh against the Saljūq and the Mongol against the Khwārizmshāh. This hazardous play with an unstable Balance of Power was less statesmanlike than the simultaneous efforts that Nāsir made to rehabilitate the Caliphate by peaceful means. On the one hand he tried to heal the ancient religious schism in Islam by conciliating the Shī'ah of both the Imāmī and the Ismā'īlī persuasion. On the other hand he tried to rally the princes of Dār-al-Islām round his own person by reorganizing the religious order of the *Futuwwa* into something like an order of knighthood with himself as its head. Nāsir's rally was perhaps in Ibn Khaldūn's mind when he wrote (*Muqaddamāt*, McG. de Slane's translation (Paris 1863–8, Imprimerie Impériale, 3 vols.), vol. ii, p. 121) that 'sometimes, when an empire is in the last stage of its existence, it suddenly gives such an imposing exhibition of strength as to create the impression that its decay has been arrested. But this is merely the last flare of a light that is on the point of going out.'

But 'Osmān and Nāsir and Arthur and Heraclius alike must yield
the palm of valour to those Inca 'Die-Hards' who—after the deaths
of Huascar and Atahualpa and the fall of Cuzco and Ollantay-
Tampu and the overthrow, in the twinkling of an eye, of an Andean
universal state which it had taken three centuries to build up[1]—
still refused to despair of a republic which had just been annihilated before their eyes by irresistible invaders from an unknown
world that lay beyond the Andean horizon.[2] In the fastnesses of
the Vilcapampa Mountains the Inca Manco dared—without gunpowder, and even without steel—to defy a Spanish victor who was
already armed with European lethal inventions that have since been
turned by their inventors to such terrible account. Manco died
unconquered; and, when one of his sons, Sayri Tupac, capitulated,
the other, Titu Cusi Yupanqui, still carried on the unequal
struggle. These men of the Bronze Age held out against the men
of the Explosive Age for thirty years before Vilcapampa fell at
length and the last of the Incas, Tupac Amaru, was taken prisoner
and put to death by a Spanish Viceroy of Peru in A.D. 1571.[3]

The Saviour with the Time-Machine.

The salvation *of* a disintegrating society is so unpromising a task,
and the sword so clumsy an instrument for its execution, that it
is not surprising to find other schools of saviours arising as the
process of disintegration takes its course in spite of all the swordsmanship of Jovius and Herculius. These other schools all agree
with one another, in opposition to the saviours with the sword, in
professing to pursue a negative aim. The mundane Present which
the swordsman is still struggling to salvage is for them a City
of Destruction which it is neither possible nor desirable to save.
Salvation *from*, and not *of*, Society is therefore their common
watchword; but this is the highest common factor in their several
purposes; for each of these four schools, as we have seen,[4] follows
out the aim of salvation from Society along a different path of
escape, and they differ further in their choice of instruments and
in their drawing of the bounds of the city whose dust they are proposing to shake from off their feet. Let us begin by reviewing those
archaist and futurist saviours from Society who draw the line at
the mundane Present without abandoning the whole plane of life
on Earth, and whose instrument is a 'time-machine' which is to

---

[1] See I. C (i) (*b*), vol. i, p. 122, above.

[2] The shattering effect of this unheralded catastrophe upon the *moral* of the Incas'
subjects (see V. C (i) (*c*) 2, vol. v, pp. 90–3, above) is the foil against which we should
appraise the fortitude of the 'Die-Hard' remnant of the Incas themselves.

[3] See Markham, Sir Clements: *The Incas of Peru* (London 1910, Smith Elder),
pp. 256 and 274–96.

[4] In the present chapter, pp. 177–8, above.

transport them, by some stroke of magic, clean out of a Present which has gone awry into a still unblemished Past or a not yet blemished Future.

The notion of a 'time-machine' has been conceived by Lewis Carroll in a passage of his *Sylvie and Bruno* and applied by Mr. H. G. Wells in a fascinating book which has *The Time-Machine* for its title. Mr. Wells makes use of Lewis Carroll's conceit in order to carry his readers, on the wings of his imagination, vast distances up and down the Time-stream—with pauses here and there to view an exotic landscape through the pilot-showman's seductive lens. This conducted tour in the 'time-machine' is a parable of the recent achievements of a modern Western *Homo Mechanicus* in extending the range of his knowledge of, and power over, the Material Universe. But a conceit out of which Mr. Wells has fashioned a hymn of whole-hearted praise to Mr. Straker[1] has been turned to account by its subtle inventor for the deeper purpose of moving our *Homo Mechanicus* not to self-praise but to self-criticism, and perhaps to self-abasement, by a touch of satire which pulls the handy man up short by reminding him of the limitations of what can be done by clockwork.

Lewis Carroll's thrust goes home because his point is a simple one. He allows his ingenious clockwork-maker to outwit Nature and cheat Destiny in one move of the game—only to find that he might just as well have spared himself the pains, since in the next move Destiny and Nature compass the self-same results that they would have produced anyway if the little man had never tried to monkey with them. In Lewis Carroll's fable the observer who holds the magic watch confidingly sets back the hands when he sees the bicyclist come to grief, as he spins round the corner, over the cardboard box that has tumbled out of the draper's cart. At the magician-mechanic's sleight of hand Time duly recoils, and this time the philanthropist promptly snatches up the treacherous box before the bicyclist arrives on the scene. *Hi presto*—the trick has worked! For the bicyclist, spinning recklessly round the corner as before, is this time not caught out by colliding with an unexpected obstacle, but shoots on smoothly down the street. Yet, alas! the appearance of one moment is given the lie by the reality of the next; for, when the moment arrives at which, in the first version of the playlet, the bicyclist was lying cut and bleeding after taking his toss, lo and behold! the same moment reveals him in the same plight in the second version—just as though Philanthropy and Magic had not, after all, conspired together to whisk away the stumbling-block from in front of the luckless rider's giddy wheel.

[1] For Mr. Straker see Shaw, G. B.: *Man and Superman, passim.*

In this Lucianic parable Lewis Carroll was gently hinting to his complacent Western contemporaries that it was a vain imagination to fancy that mundane realities could be exorcized by mechanical arts. And this apologue of the generation of the velocipede may be capped by another drawn from the everyday experience of the generation of the automobile. A driver whose car is running badly may throw out the clutch, with a sigh of relief, when his road happens to bring him, in the course of its ups and downs, to the head of a gentle downward incline. 'So free-wheeling is the remedy for engine-trouble', our motorist lazily ruminates. 'How extraordinary that so simple a solution should never have been hit upon before.' But as he sits back and congratulates himself, the incline suddenly plunges into a steep descent, and on the instant he remembers that his brakes, as well as his engine, are out of order. No chance of avoiding a crash now except by going back into bottom gear! But by this time the car is racing so swiftly downhill that the result of putting in the clutch now is to strip the cogs off the gear-wheels and to check the car's impetus with a jerk that sends it skidding across the road through a dry-stone wall which masks a precipice.

The moral of our post-Carrollian parable is that the new-fangled 'time-machine' is as incapable as the old-fashioned sword is of permanently eliminating Violence when once Violence has entered in. The driver who free-wheels down the slope does succeed, for a moment or two, in silencing the noise and stilling the jolts and jars of a labouring engine; but the disaster that overtakes him the moment after proves his remedy to have been worse than the disease. The car that now lies overturned at the bottom of the ravine, with its gears stripped and its driver's corpse pinned under the steering-wheel, is in a worse case than the car which, only just now, was travelling right-side-up along the road—however disagreeably its engine might have been knocking and its ignition have been missing fire.

It was, no doubt, theoretically possible that the gentle incline which has lured the unfortunate driver to his horrid fate might have continued all the rest of the way to his journey's end; and if luck had so far favoured him he might have free-wheeled on in fine style till gravity brought him to a standstill at the door of the Roadside Hotel. To translate our imagery into terms of a piece of history that has several times engaged our attention before, we can imagine a devout Jew, who has taken to heart the lesson of Bar Kōkabā's failure, seeking salvation in the manipulation of the 'time-machine' without being taught by another disaster that he has not yet discovered a sure way of extricating himself from the endless chain of Violence. Our Jewish Quietist—and his descendants for the next sixty generations—may succeed in living, without disaster, in an archaistic and a futuristic Utopia simultaneously. They may successfully render themselves insensible to the painfulness of the mundane Present by a minute observance of a God-given law and by a patient expectation of a Kingdom of God which is to be established on Earth in God's own good time by God's omnipotence alone, without the lifting of one human finger. Yet, even if an unconscious but unconscionable desire 'that we also may be like all the nations'[1] had not inveigled the sixty-first generation of our Jewish Quietists into a hazardous attempt to put itself into gear with the militant nationalism of a twentieth-century Western World,[2] one single example of a recourse to the 'time-machine'— and this an experiment which, up to date, has escaped a crash but has not yet evaded a question-mark—would hardly avail to invalidate a conclusion that is forced upon us by the rest of the historical evidence. This conclusion is that—as a rule which is not disproved by its exceptions—the would-be saviour with the 'time-machine' is apt, sooner or later, to become so embarrassingly entangled in the intricacies of his own clockwork that he is constrained in the end to throw the ingenious piece of mechanism aside and to pick up in despair his predecessor's rusty sword which Straker has so far contemptuously left to lie in the gutter where Bayard dropped it.

If we wish to test this rule by an empirical survey it may be convenient to review in the first place the saviour-archaists who have set the 'time-machine' to jump backwards, and in the second place the saviour-futurists who have jerked the lever of fantasy in the opposite direction to make the machine jump forwards. In the sequel to both of these manœuvres we shall see a primitive demon of Violence who has been deftly shown out of the door come slyly creeping in again through the window.

In considering the archaistic variation on this theme we may begin with an illustration which we have examined in this Study already in another context.[3] The notion of a 'Nordic Race' which is hypothetically superior to the rest of Mankind in virtue of its physical descent was first conceived and launched by de Gobineau as a neat verbal retort to the grim physical violence which, in the French Revolution, the Jacobins had used upon the Noblesse. De Gobineau effectively exploded the pedantic antiquarianism of those revolutionary leaders of a French proletariat who had sought to

---

[1] 1 Sam. viii. 20.
[2] For this interpretation of Zionism see II. D (vi), vol. ii, pp. 252–4, above.
[3] In II. C (ii) (a) 1, vol. i, pp. 216–21, and in V. C (i) (d) 8 (α), in the present volume, pp. 56–8, above.

lend an air of respectability to their act of vengeance against a French dominant minority by representing themselves as descendants of the wronged and cultivated Gauls, while their adversaries were held up to odium, and condemned to extermination, as descendants of the barbarous and outrageous Franks. But this amiably academic French political *jeu d'esprit* began to breed a violence of its own when it passed out of de Gobineau's hands into those of a Nietzsche and a Houston Stewart Chamberlain whose caricatures of de Gobineau's theme helped to inspire the masters of the Second German Reich to act the part of 'the Blond Beast' in the real life of the international arena. And now, in the third generation, the platonically archaistic *Essai sur l'Inégalité des Races Humaines* has borne an ultra-Jacobin harvest in the Anti-Semitic enormities of a Third German Reich which has taken the French archaist's fantasy in deadly earnest and has based its policy, at home and abroad, upon a doctrine of 'Blood and Soil'.

This sinister metamorphosis of Archaism into Anti-Semitism in the latest chapter of the history of the Western Civilization has a Hellenic parallel. The eventual establishment of the Hellenic universal state in the form of a Roman Empire left a sting of resentment in the hearts of the citizens of Alexandria, who could not forget that, if the Battle of Actium had gone the other way, their own city might have become the metropolis of the Hellenic world-state.[1] A Greek *bourgeoisie* who, two hundred years back, had remained unmoved by the stirring call of a Spartan hero and had felt no temptation to follow Cleomenes into the streets in order to wrest their liberty by force of arms from the hands of a Macedonian autocrat[2] were now roused at last when the prize of civic pre-eminence was wrested away by an upstart Oscan city from an Alexandria whose citizens could point to the Tomb of Alexander himself and the Museum and Library of Ptolemy Soter[3] as their own city's unchallengeable title-deeds to metropolitan rank.[4] In

---

[1] For this unfulfilled historical possibility see V. C (i) (d) 7, p. 37, footnote 1, above.

[2] Plutarch: *Lives of Agis and Cleomenes*, chap. 58 (see further V. C (ii) (a), Annex II, pp. 381 and 391, below).

[3] That Ptolemy I was the founder of the Museum and Library is probable but not quite certain in the present state of our knowledge.

[4] There is some evidence to show that, as a result of her annexation to the Roman Empire after the Battle of Actium, Alexandria lost, not only her perhaps rather nebulous primacy among the cities of the Hellenic World, but also some of the solid substance of her municipal self-government (see Jones, A. H. M.: *The Cities of the Eastern Roman Provinces* (Oxford 1937, Clarendon Press), pp. 311–12). It must be added that, according to the same authority (pp. 304 and 471), the Romans were only carrying farther a process of *Gleichschaltung* which the Ptolemies had already begun. A civic council of Alexandria seems to have existed under the earlier Ptolemies, but to have been abolished by the later Ptolemies before the Roman conquest. No doubt the 'totalitarian' structure of the Ptolemaic state and the 'servile' character of native Egyptian social life under the Ptolemaic régime (see IV. C (ii) (b) 2, vol. iv, p. 85, footnote 5, above) made an unpropitious environment for Hellenic political institutions.

an age when the political liberation of Alexandria was no longer
even a forlorn hope, but had become a sheer impossibility, successive generations of Alexandrian city-fathers now intrepidly, though
inconsequently, offered up their lives on the altar of civic pride by
assuming, in face of the Roman Imperial authorities, an attitude
of defiance which left a reluctant Caesar no choice but to pronounce the death-sentence. The 'Acts of the Pagan Martyrs' in
the reigns of Claudius and Trajan and Hadrian and Commodus
were still being treasured by the Greek community in Egypt in the
third century of the Christian Era, as is witnessed by the narratives,
dating from that later age, that have been recovered in part by the
ingenuity of our modern Western papyrologists.[1] But the piquant
name which has been given to these anonymous works of Greek
literature by our Western scholars is misleading in at any rate one
point that is of capital importance. These martyrs to the civic
pride of Alexandria may resemble the martyrs to the religious faith
of the Christian Church in the courage, and even truculence, with
which they refused to bow the knee to an Imperial Government
which held them physically at its mercy. But the Christian martyr's
glory of being the victim of a violence with which he had never
polluted his own hands was not shared with Stephen and Polycarp
by Lampon and Isidore and Antoninus and Appian. These Alexandrian recalcitrants against Roman authority had Jewish blood on
their hands before their own blood was shed by a Roman sword
which might fairly claim in this case to be vindicating a *laesa
majestas*. The Greeks of Alexandria, who were impotent to assail
the Roman Imperial Government itself with any missiles except
innocuous words, were wont to satisfy their craving to vent their
spite in some more effective way than this by massacring their
Jewish neighbours.[2] From the Jewish community in Alexandria
it was occasionally possible for the Greek community to take a toll
of lives before the Roman garrison could intervene; and these
Alexandrian Jews were odious to the Alexandrian Greeks because

---

[1] For the fragments of this genre of Egyptian Greek literature of the Imperial Age
that have turned up on scraps of third-century papyrus see Meyer, E.: *Ursprung und
Anfänge des Christentums*, vol. iii (Stuttgart and Berlin 1923, Cotta), pp. 539–48; and
Bell, H. I.: *Juden und Griechen im Römischen Alexandreia* (Leipzig 1927, Hinrichs),
pp. 14–44.

[2] These periodic massacres of Jews by Greeks in an Alexandria whose Greek citizens
were smarting under a Roman yoke that had been weighing upon their city's neck since
the Battle of Actium will remind a Western reader, in the present generation, of the
persecution of the Jews in a post-war Germany by National-Socialist Gentiles who
were smarting under the *Versailler Diktat* and who sought relief for their feelings by
hitting the Jews, who happened to be at their mercy, as proxies for the Gentile victors
in the General War of 1914–18. It was, of course, these non-German Gentiles, and not
the German Jews, who had beaten Germany in the field and then dictated the terms
of peace. But, so long as Germany was disarmed, the true authors of the *Versailler
Diktat* were beyond her reach; and in these circumstances the Nazis seized upon the
German Jews as vicarious targets for a German stroke of revenge.

the Romans deliberately favoured them as a make-weight against
the flagrant disloyalty of the Greek citizens of the second city of the
Empire. Fragmentary though our evidence is, it would hardly be
rash to assume that some guilt, direct or indirect, for the shedding
of Jewish blood could be brought home to every one of those
Alexandrian Greek 'martyrs' who were condemned to death by the
Roman Government in the course of the first two centuries of the
Christian Era.[1]

We have now found two cases—one in Western and the other in
Hellenic history—in which an attempt to evade hard present facts
by harking back to an irretrievably lost state of past national or
civic glory has only resulted in a savage outbreak of Anti-Semitism.
And the same spectacle—which would be comic if it were not
tragic—of a saviour-archaist finding himself constrained to throw
away his new-fangled 'time-machine' and snatch up his predecessor's old-fashioned sword instead is afforded by the histories of
would-be constitutional reformers who have sought salvation in an
attempt at a return to some ancestral constitution or 'patrios
politeia'.[2]

In the second phase of the Hellenic 'Time of Troubles' we have
seen[3] this ironic fate overtaking a pair of Heracleidae at Sparta and
a pair of Gracchi at Rome. In each of these two parallel political
tragedies the originator of the reform movement—a Lacedaemonian Agis and a Roman Tiberius—had a horror of violence and
lawlessness which was so genuine and so extreme that the would-be
reformer actually allowed himself to be murdered by political
opponents who did not scruple to resort to these 'methods of

---

[1] At an earlier stage in the establishment of the Roman domination over the non-
Roman sections of a Hellenic dominant minority the Greek ruling class in the Seleucid
Monarchy had produced a 'pagan martyr' who had the hardihood to strike at a representative of Rome herself, instead of seeking defenceless scapegoats among Rome's
Oriental protégés. In the year 162 B.C., at Laodicea, Gnaeus Octavius, the chairman
of a Roman commission of inspection, was assassinated by a Greek nationalist named
Leptines (see V. C (i) (d) 9 (γ), p. 122, footnote 5, above). The assassin aggravated the
enormity of his offence by boasting of it in retrospect; and thereafter—with a view to
saving his city and his sovereign from the consequences of his act—he voluntarily
repaired to Rome, unfettered and unguarded; delivered himself into the hands of the
Roman Government; and made a jaunty appearance at the bar of the Senate. From
first to last he prophesied that the Romans would not touch a hair of his head; and the
denouement proved him right. For the Senate characteristically preferred the diplomatic advantage of retaining a grievance of the first order against the Seleucid Government to the emotional satisfaction of avenging their murdered representative; and
accordingly they took care not to accede to the Antiochene Government's proposal that
the Senate should inflict on Leptines whatever punishment they might think good.
Roman diplomacy kept the diplomatic incident open at the price of letting the criminal
go scot free (see Polybius, Book XXXI, chap. 33, and Book XXXII, chap. 3; Meyer,
op. cit., vol. ii, pp. 237–9).
[2] This particular expression of Archaism has been examined already in V. C (i) (d)
8 (α), pp. 52–6, above.
[3] In Part III. A, vol. iii, pp. 76–7; IV. C (iii) (b) 9, vol. iv, p. 205; IV. C (iii) (c) 3
(β), vol. iv, p. 508; V. C (i) (c) 2, vol. v, pp. 70–1 and 78; V. C (i) (d) 1, vol. v, pp. 388–
9; V. C (i) (d) 8 (α), in the present volume, pp. 52–3; and V. C (i) (d) 8 (ε), p. 94,
above.

barbarism', in the conviction that this was a lesser evil than it would be for him to give the lie, by getting in the first blow, to the very principles that he was upholding at his own peril. Yet even these two martyrs to a belief in Non-Violence had in one sense brought their deaths upon their own heads by having stooped, on their side, to a violence which was not redeemed by the fact that it was not physical. Before they lost their lives by the hands of some of their countrymen, both Agis and Tiberius had already broken some of the fundamental laws of their country's constitution; and this in itself was enough to stultify the endeavours of statesmen whose political programme was the thesis of the sacrosanctity of a constitutional heritage. The martyr hands that were innocent of having literally shed blood cannot be acquitted of the charge of having wielded the figurative sword of illegality; and the martyrs each inspired a successor who drew from the tragedy of his predecessor's fate the disastrous moral that his fatal error had been a lack of 'realism'.

In girding themselves for the task of making a second attempt to carry out their predecessors' enterprise a Cleomenes at Sparta and a Gaius at Rome did not forbear to draw and use the physical sword which had been abjured by an Agis and a Tiberius.[1] This second pair of 'tough-minded' reformers atoned for their recourse to violence by meeting, after a delusive momentary success, with the same failure and the same death as their 'tender-minded' predecessors. And their fate, in its turn, led a third pair of political adventurers to act on the theory that 'realism', if it was to do its work, must be carried to the point of a 'totalitarian' ruthlessness. By putting this theory into practice, Sulla—at the cost of proscribing half Rome and devastating all Samnium—did succeed, half a century after Tiberius Gracchus's death, in imposing something which passed for a 'patrios politeia' and in making this travesty of his country's ancestral constitution last long enough to allow the cold-blooded dictator himself to die comfortably in his bed. Sulla's Spartan counterpart Nabis did not in the end escape the assassin's knife; yet Nabis, too, lived long enough not only to complete the social revolution into which Agis' reform had been turned on Cleomenes' sword's point, but also to bring Messene and Argos, as well as Lacedaemon, under his tyrannically subversive rule, and to baffle a Roman commander who had just succeeded in beating the Macedonians.

If we turn again from Hellenic to Western history we may ob-

---

[1] Cleomenes appears to have resorted to violence without hesitation or compunction. Gaius Gracchus was torn in two ways and never whole-heartedly abandoned the gentle for the violent path (on this point see V. C (ii) (a), Annex II, pp. 378 and 392, below).

serve in the present context that our Civil War in England was precipitated by endeavours that had been made, in all good faith, to vindicate for the Parliament at Westminster a historic prerogative which, in its champions' belief, had been unlawfully set aside by a Royal Power that had recently been fortifying itself with a new administrative technique of Italian provenance.[1] And we may further observe that the soldier whose sword brought victory to the Parliament's cause played far greater havoc with the Constitution, in his autocratic role of Lord Protector of the Commonwealth, than King Charles had ever sought to play while he was sitting precariously on the throne of his ancestors. In the same Western World in our own day a Cromwellian violence has been used in Italy by a dictator who claims that by this means he has managed to give his countrymen back their 'patrios politeia' in the shape of his 'corporative state'.[2]

In the tragedy of Ottoman history we can see the two Hellenic series, Agis–Cleomenes–Nabis and Tiberius–Gaius–Sulla, reproduced in the series Selīm III–Mahmūd II–Mustafā Kemāl. Sultan Selīm (*imperabat* A.D. 1789–1807) was the first Ottoman statesman to take in hand the task of saving the heritage of his ancestors when the jeopardy into which it had fallen had been startlingly revealed by the disastrous outcome of the Russo-Turkish War of 1768–74.[3] Like Agis and Tiberius Gracchus, Sultan Selīm set himself to restore a 'patrios politeia' which had been the palladium of the State; like them, he found himself driven to pursue reform along the paradoxical path of innovation; and like them, again, he died a violent death at the hands of political opponents whom he had the courage to defy but not the ruthlessness to crush. In the next act of the Ottoman play Mahmūd II (*imperabat* A.D. 1808–39) played Cleomenes' and Gaius's part with all the ruthlessness of Sulla and all the patience of Bismarck. For an opportunity to avenge his predecessor, Mahmūd waited, not ten years, like Gaius, but eighteen;[4] during all that time he kept his own counsel, in contrast to Gaius's almost ostentatious display of his intention to seek revenge; and in consequence Mahmūd succeeded in extirpating the Janissaries and dying in his bed as comfortably as Sulla himself. Why was it, then, that this Ottoman play required a third act, and Sultan Mahmūd a successor? The reason was that Sultan Selīm's would-be archaizing reform had turned in Sultan Mahmūd's hands into a Westernizing revolution which even Mahmūd forbore to carry right through. Mahmūd required a successor

---

[1] See III. C (ii) (*b*), vol. iii, pp. 350–63, above.
[2] See V. C (i) (*d*) 8 (α), p. 52, above.   [3] See Part III. A, vol. iii, p. 48, above.
[4] Ibid., pp. 49–50, above.

because, 'under the strenuous conditions of the Modern World', the 'Osmanlis could not hold their own if they halted half-way between their broken-down indigenous institutions and an imperfectly assimilated Westernism. A 'totalitarian' Westernizer was needed to finish Mahmūd's work if the 'Osmanlis were to be saved; and in our own day this third Ottoman saviour has appeared in the person of President Mustafā Kemāl Atatürk. The Ghāzi has been able to carry his people with him along a road of Westernization *à outrance*, on which their forefathers would never have followed the Sultans, thanks to the Greek invasion of Anatolia in A.D. 1919–22; for this home-thrust opened the eyes of the Ottoman Turks to the truth that they were fighting now for their very existence and no longer just for their empire.[1]

This survey of would-be saviours with the 'time-machine' in the ranks of the Dominant Minority may close with two cases in which the revulsion from the 'time-machine' to the sword took place within a single lifetime.

The Roman Emperor Julian set himself to reinstate and reinvigorate by peaceful means the religion and culture of Hellenism when these had been pushed to the wall by a Christianity that had been enjoying an Imperial patronage since the conversion of Constantine. The moment when Julian was enabled to put this policy in hand—upon his receipt of the news of the death of the Emperor Constantius while Julian himself was on the march from Gaul to Constantinople—was separated by an interval of no more than fifteen months (December, A.D. 361–March, A.D. 363) from the moment when the new master of the Hellenic World marched on eastwards into the domain of the Sasanidae on a campaign in which he was to lose his life. These fifteen months were all the time that Julian had for putting his policy into effect; yet, short though this span was, it was long enough to see the Apostate's original policy change in two respects. Instead of being able to restore the pre-Constantinian régime and pre-Christian dispensation in their authentic shapes, Julian found himself constrained to wage his cultural and religious war on Christianity by organizing a pagan Antichurch on a Christian pattern[2] which was as alien as Christianity itself was from the genuine Hellenic êthos; and at the same time Julian failed to live up to his ideal of an enlightened tolerance. He was quickly disappointed of his romantically unrealistic expectation that, as soon as the Christian Church was deprived of its recent advantage of enjoying official support, a Hellenism that had really been moribund long before the conversion of Constantine would

---

[1] See II. D (v), vol. ii, pp. 187–8, above.
[2] See V. C (i) (c) 2, Annex II, vol. v, p. 584, above.

recapture its lost ground by the use of no other weapons than its own intrinsic merit and charm. In his treatment of his Christian subjects Julian had already crossed the line dividing a contemptuous toleration from a hostile discrimination before his activities in the field of domestic affairs were suspended by his departure for the Persian War; and, if it had been his fate to return victorious, it is difficult to believe that he would not have blackened his reputation sooner or later by crossing, in turn, the further line between discrimination and persecution.[1]

Julian's failure in the fourth century of the Christian Era to put the clock back to a pre-Constantinian hour of Hellenic history was not more signal than Justinian's failure to accomplish the lesser *tour de force* of putting the clock back to Constantine's time in the sixth century. Justinian set himself to restore the Constantinian régime in all its aspects. Once again, as of old, the Empire was to be Latin-speaking, Orthodox, and integral; yet, in every sphere, the autocrat's endeavours to achieve his archaistic aim resulted in a sensational self-defeat.

Justinian's wars for the recovery of the provinces that had fallen into barbarian hands merely devastated the Imperial territories that were reconquered while it impoverished those that had hitherto remained intact; and the conquests bought at this price proved ephemeral. In extirpating the Ostrogoths the would-be *Restitutor Orbis Romani* was actually clearing the ground for an immediate occupation of Italy by the more barbarous Lombards, and in extirpating the Vandals he was redeeming a patrimony in Ifrīqīyah for the Berbers and the Arabs.[2] Justinian was no more fortunate in his ecclesiastical policy. The ecclesiastical war which he waged against the Monophysitism of his subjects in the Oriental provinces was as unsuccessful as his military warfare against the barbarians, since it utterly failed of its intended effect of making the Catholic Church oecumenical once more in fact as well as in name. Justinian did not succeed in brow-beating Syria and Egypt back into Orthodoxy.[3] What he did achieve was to alienate their affections so deeply and so lastingly that, in the next two generations, they welcomed the Persian armies of Chosroes and the Arab armies of 'Umar as deliverers from a Melchite yoke. As for the closing of the schools at Athens and the building of the Church of Saint Sophia at Constantinople, the first of these two of Justinian's

[1] Julian's failure to establish in the Roman Empire a Neoplatonic Church in lieu of the Christian Church has been touched upon in V. C (i) (c) 2, vol. v, p. 147; V. C (i) (d) 6 (δ), vol. v, pp. 565-7; V. C (i) (c) 2, Annex II, vol. v, p. 584; and V. C (i) (d) 6 (δ), Annex, vol. v, pp. 680-3, above.
[2] See III. C (i) (b), vol. iii, p. 162, above.
[3] This failure of Justinian's Anti-Monophysite campaign has been touched upon already in V. C (i) (d) 6 (δ), Annex, vol. v, p. 679, above.

acts gave the *coup de grâce* to Hellenic learning and the second to Hellenic architecture; and, while it is true that the intellectual tradition of Plato and the architectural tradition of Ictinus were both of them already *in articulo mortis* by the time when Justinian thus sped them on their way to death,[1] these parting shots at Hellenism were nevertheless strange gestures from an enthusiast for a Roman Empire whose historic *raison d'être* had been to serve as a Hellenic universal state. It might seem equally strange that the Consulate, which had been the classic magistracy of the Roman Commonwealth, should have been abolished by an emperor who had undertaken the task of codifying the Roman Law;[2] yet this particularly conspicuous act of constitutional Vandalism was all of a piece with Justinian's legal enormity of abrogating the authority of the original texts on which his *Code* and *Digest* and *Institutes* were based, as soon as these compilations were published.

Hasty, ill arranged, and incomplete though they might be,[3] Justinian's new law books were at least a mighty monument of the Latin language; yet, when the emperor who had just re-established the authority of the Constantinopolitan Imperial Government over the Latin-speaking lands of Africa and Italy had to supplement the law which he had codified, he found it advisable, as a matter of practical convenience, to publish his *novellae* in Greek! There could have been no more ironical illustration of the self-frustration of Justinian's policy; for the publication of his own new legislation in Greek was an admission of the fact that in his day the Latin speech of the City of Constantine was being supplanted by a Levantine vernacular;[4] this linguistic revolution at Constantinople bore witness, in its turn, to the devastation and depopulation of the Imperial City's Latin-speaking European hinterland; and for this social catastrophe in the Latin-speaking provinces in the Balkan Peninsula Justinian himself bore a heavier responsibility than any

[1] For the senile decay of the Athenian intellect see IV. C (iii) (c) 2 (α), vol. iv, pp. 269–74; V. C (i) (d) 6 (δ), vol. v, pp. 563–7; and V. C (i) (d) 8 (γ), in the present volume, pp. 78–80, above; for the abandonment of the Hellenic style of architecture see IV. C (ii) (a), vol. iv, pp. 54–5, above.

[2] For the abolition of the Consulate by Justinian see V. C (i) (d) 9 (β), p. 111, above.

[3] For the contrast in spirit, aim, and efficacy between Justinian's codification of the Roman Law and the contemporary codification of monastic law in Saint Benedict's Rule see III. C (ii) (b), vol. iii, pp. 265–6, above. Justinian fell between two stools. While on the one hand his compilations were an inferior substitute for the originals out of which they were excerpted, on the other hand they still reflected the social conditions of a more highly cultivated age faithfully enough to be inappropriate to the social conditions of the ruder age into which they were launched (on this latter point see Taylor, H. O.: *The Mediaeval Mind* (London 1911, Macmillan, 2 vols.), vol. ii, pp. 242 and 248).

[4] The Greek in which Justinian's *novellae* were cast was an official variety of the Attic κοινή which had been minted in the chancelleries of the Hellenic 'successor-states' of the Achaemenian Empire and had remained current, under the Roman régime, in the Greek and Oriental provinces of the Hellenic universal state; but the colloquial Greek which was replacing a colloquial Latin in the streets and fora of Constantinople in Justinian's day was no doubt already in transition from the κοινή to Romaic.

other man[1]—an invidious distinction for a Roman Emperor whose own native province was Dardania, and who delighted in being able in consequence to boast that Latin was his mother-tongue.[2] Yet, while during Justinian's reign Greek thus gained on Latin in those Balkan territories of the Empire, including the capital itself, in which the Dardanian emperor was eager to keep Latin alive, Justinian was equally unsuccessful in his linguistic policy in the Oriental provinces. South-east of Taurus Justinian's intentions in regard to the Greek language were the opposite of what they were north-west of the Bosphorus; for in Syria and Egypt he was indirectly working to keep alive the established Greek ecclesiastical language of a Catholic Church whose cause he was championing against Monophysite dissenters. Yet, just because the Greek language was traditionally associated with the Orthodox Faith in this part of the Empire, the successful resistance of the Monophysites to Justinian's pressure on Orthodoxy's behalf was reflected in the linguistic field in the adoption of the Syriac and Coptic vernaculars as vehicles for a Monophysite liturgy and literature, in place of a Greek which was now doubly odious in Oriental Christian ears as an alien tongue which was the sign oral of the Melchites. This unfortunate identification, in the Oriental provinces, of the Greek language with a losing ecclesiastical cause was the direct result of Justinian's policy; and it sealed the doom of Greek in a region in which the κοινή had been the unchallenged vehicle of culture and administration for not much less than nine hundred years.

These interlocking failures of Justinian's policy in diverse fields amount, all told, to a total bankruptcy; and the story of this fiasco can be recapitulated in one sentence. Justinian produced results which were the opposite of his intentions because his pursuit of Archaism invariably led him into a use of force.

The saviour-archaists whom we have passed in review up to this point have all been representatives of the Dominant Minority; but there is a second company of saviours of the same class who arise in the External Proletariat when its liberty, or even its very existence, is threatened by the aggressiveness of some expanding civilization. When an external proletariat is fighting for its life against a civilization which, almost *ex hypothesi*, is its superior in material force, the members of the hard-pressed primitive society inevitably look back with regret to the easier and less anxious life which their forefathers used to lead before this external pressure began to disturb their peace. This regret for a happiness that is past may turn into a dream of harking back to it; and a people that

---

[1] See IV. C (iii) (c) 2 (β), vol. iv, pp. 327-8 and 397-8, abov
[2] See ibid., p. 326, footnote 2, above.

is dreaming this dream will lend a ready ear to a prophet who promises to translate it into reality. A collision with external forces which has brought disaster and distress in its train is thus apt to excite a movement for jumping clear of the Present and landing safe—by a backward twist of the magic lever of the 'time-machine'—in some previous stage of existence in which the harrassed society's life was once free from ills that have since been brought upon it by its undesired contact with a hostile and corroding alien presence.

This archaistic reaction to the painful experience of collision with an alien social force for which the victim is no match is not, of course, peculiar to societies of the primitive species. A primitive society that has been drawn into the External Proletariat of some expanding civilization is in no different case from a civilization that has collided with a more powerful society of its own species. In this identical situation the weaker party—be it a civilization or a primitive society—is apt to make an identical response; and the particular response that we here have in view is examined in greater detail, under the title of 'Zealotism',[1] in a later part of this Study that is concerned with the contact between civilizations in the Space-dimension.[2] In the present place we need not explore further the psychological phenomena in which 'Zealotism' displays itself, but may confine ourselves to a review of the saviours of the 'Zealot' type who arise in the External Proletariat.

There is no reason in theory why these barbarian saviour-archaists should have recourse to violence in working out their way of salvation;[3] but an empirical survey will show that in practice the barbarian saviour with the 'time-machine' refrains from taking to the sword still more rarely than his counterpart who tries to take the same archaistic way of escape out of the miseries of a disintegrating civilization. Indeed, the only non-violent barbarian saviours with the 'time-machine' whom we shall find ourselves able to muster are those prophets who arose among the Red Indians when these primitive inhabitants of North America were being overwhelmed by an immense wave of inflowing European population which was aggressively sweeping westward from coast to coast of the continent.[4] And even the followers of these Red Indian preachers of salvation through non-resistance were driven in the end, by sheer despair, to hasten the consummation of their doom by taking up arms.[5] The rest of the barbarian saviours of this class

[1] This term has been coined out of the name 'Zealots', which was applied to a party in Jewry that made itself notorious in the conflict between Jewry and Rome in the first and second centuries of the Christian Era. [2] Part IX, below.
[3] On this point see V. C (i) (c) 3, vol. v, p. 331, footnote 1, above.
[4] For these Red Indian prophets see V. C (i) (c) 3, vol. v, pp. 328–31, above.
[5] Ibid., pp. 331–2, above.

present themselves with the 'time-machine' in one hand and the sword in the other. Their posture is that of the Horatii holding the Transtiberine bridgehead against Lars Porsenna; but their fate is more cruel than that of the legendary Roman heroes, for the barbarian swordsmen's heroism seldom avails to purchase for their tribesmen the time to break the bridge before the invader can pass; and in facing enormous odds in a vain attempt to place their home beyond the reach of the aggressor's arm they more often meet the death of those two Horatii who fell than they escape with their lives like the two slain Roman heroes' brother Publius. The Redskin Sitting Bull wiping out Custer's troop of United States cavalry and surviving the feat to die in his bed in Canada is a far rarer figure in the annals of barbarian Archaism on the war-path than the Sūdānī standard-bearer at the Battle of Omdurman indomitably offering his breast to the machine-gun bullets as he still holds the Mahdi's standard defiantly aloft with his feet astride the corpses of his fallen comrades.[1]

This barbarian martyr may stand as the type of a tragic company whose roll-call is too long for us to recite. *Honoris causa* we may single out the names of Caesar's Arvernian victim Vercingetorix and Justinian's Ostrogoth victim Totila and Charlemagne's Saxon victim Widukind.[2] We may recall the scene of the Negus Theodore blowing out his own brains as he charged, like a lion at bay, out of the ring-wall of a fortress which he had obstinately deemed impregnable until his Magdala was on the point of capture by a British expeditionary force. We may mourn 'Abd-al-Qādir's heroic failure to save Algeria, and 'Abd-al-Karīm's to save the Moroccan Rīf, and Shamyl's to save the Highlands of the Caucasus, from a modern Western imperialism that has armed itself with the lethal weapons of 'the Machine Age'; and we may pay equal respect to a Viriathus who failed to save his Lusitania from a Roman imperialism[3] which was in effect as irresistible as our own, even though it was not equipped with our present technical facilities for the wholesale destruction of life and property. We may appreciate the intractability, while abhorring the savagery, of a Stenka Razin and a Pugachev[4] who successively led the revolt of the Cossack marchmen of the Russian Orthodox Christendom against the relentless determination of a Muscovite imperialism to round up these semi-barbarians[5] into the corral of a Russian universal state,

---

[1] For the Mahdī Muhammad Ahmad's leadership of a revolt of the Kordofānī Arabs against the penetration of the Nilotic Sudan by an Egypto-Ottoman imperialism equipped with Western weapons see ibid., pp. 209, footnote 3, 294–6, 321, footnote 3, and 324, above.　　　　　　　　　　　　　　　　　　　　　　[2] See ibid., p. 319.

[3] For the trapping of the barbarians in the Iberian Peninsula see ibid., pp. 205–6, above.　　　　　　　　　　　　[4] See V. C (i) (c) 2, vol. v, p. 104, above.

[5] The Cossacks, who were marchmen from the standpoint of the Russian Orthodox

and break them in to leading the servile life of an internal proletariat.[1] And we may lay a wreath on the graves of the obscure
heroes who captained the Nairi highlanders in their stand against
the Assyrians,[2] the Transcaspian Türkmens in their stand against
the Russians,[3] the Araucanians in their stand against the Spaniards,[4]
and the Maoris[5] and the Pathans[6] in their stand against the British.

After this review of would-be saviours with the 'time-machine'
who have taken the direction of Archaism, we must complete our
present survey by reviewing their futurist counterparts; but we
may not find it easy here to draw any hard-and-fast line of demarcation. To begin with, we have seen[7] that it is in the very nature of
Archaism to defeat itself by breaking down into Futurism; and we
have just been giving ourselves an empirical demonstration of the
working of this historical 'law' in our survey of archaist-saviours
in the ranks of the Dominant Minority. In one instance after
another we have found that, in the act of resorting to the violence
into which their Archaism leads them against their will, these
enthusiasts for a vanished Past have veered round, involuntarily
but unavoidably, out of an archaistic into a futuristic course. The
same transmutation of Archaism into Futurism can be observed
in the ranks of the External Proletariat; and here the change is not
only promoted by a tendency that is innate in Archaism, and is not
only precipitated by a resort to force, but is also foreshadowed, and
perhaps even fore-ordained, in the history of the genesis of the
body social in which the transmutation takes place.

In other contexts[8] we have observed that, within the brief Time-
span of some 6,000 years during which the species of societies that
we have agreed to call 'civilizations' has been in existence up to
date, the radiation of the civilizations that have already come and
gone has travelled so far and so fast that it has long since made its
mark upon every primitive society that it has not destroyed. And
it is safe to assume that this brand of an alien culture will have
burnt deep into the flesh of a *ci-devant* primitive society that has
come to such close quarters with an expanding civilization as to

Christendom (see II. D (v), vol. ii, pp. 155-7, and V. C (i) (*c*) 3, vol. v, pp. 313-15,
above), were in origin members of the external proletariat of the Golden Horde (see
V. C (i) (*c*) 3, vol. v, p. 283, above).
    [1] For the eventual success of the Russian Imperial Government in turning the
Cossacks into 'running dogs' of a Muscovite imperialism see V. C (i) (*c*) 3, vol. v,
pp. 313-15, above.
    [2] See II. D (v), vol. ii, p. 135, and IV. C (iii) (*c*) 3 (α), vol. iv, p. 475, above.
    [3] See V. C (i) (*c*) 3, vol. v, p. 323, footnote 3, above.
    [4] See V. C (i) (*c*) 3, vol. v, p. 322, above.
    [5] See ibid.
    [6] See ibid., pp. 305-8, and 332-3, and the present chapter and volume, p. 201, foot-
note 1, above.
    [7] In V. C (i) (*d*) 8 (ε), pp. 94-7, above.
    [8] In Part II. A, vol. i, pp. 185-7, and in V. C (i) (*c*) 3, vol. v, pp. 196-7, above.

have been conscripted into its imperious neighbour's external proletariat. It is therefore also safe to predict that even the most fanatically archaistic-minded leader of an external proletariat will find himself unable to carry his Archaism to 'totalitarian' lengths. When he has done his utmost, his tribe will still retain some tincture of the very civilization from which its would-be saviour has been striving to keep its life clear; and this alien cultural tincture will infuse a vein of Futurism into the Archaism of the saviour-archaist himself.

This ineradicable element of Futurism in the life and leadership of an external proletariat that is reacting in the 'Zealot' way to the pressure of an aggressive civilization is most evident in the field of military technique. For the Red Indian saviour-archaists were perhaps unique among their kind in carrying their objection to the use of the White Man's tools to the point of forbidding their followers to use in self-defence the fire-arms with which their White assailants were engaged in annihilating them.[1] In other cases the leaders who have arisen to preach salvation-through-Archaism to the rank-and-file of hard-pressed societies of either species have usually allowed—and frequently enjoined—at least this one exception in the practical application of their saving principle; and, in granting to their followers this single licence of fighting an aggressive alien enemy with his own weapons, they have unintentionally opened in their curtain-wall a breach which can never be closed again but which will be worn ever wider by an inflow of alien influences that will start as a trickle to end in a flood. The impossibility of borrowing this or that element of an alien culture at choice, without eventually making an unconditional surrender to the intrusive alien force, is a fundamental law of the contact of cultures which is examined in this Study in other places.[2] In the present context we are only concerned with this 'law' in so far as it throws light upon the cause of the change of orientation from Archaism to Futurism which is so frequently to be observed in the reaction of an external proletariat towards the dominant minority against which it is up in arms. When once the barbarian has adopted the weapons of the enemy civilization there are two clear alternatives before him: either he will succumb to the enemy through failing to master the borrowed art, or else he will survive through learning in time to beat his master at his own game. If

[1] For this remarkable veto see V. C (i) (c) 3, vol. v, p. 331, above.
[2] See V. C (i) (d) 9 (β), pp. 106–7, above, and Part IX and X, *passim*, below. For the particular operation of this law in the intercourse between an external proletariat and a dominant minority across the stationary frontier of a universal state see V. C (i) (d) 6 (α), vol. v, pp. 459–80, and V. C (i) (d) 7, in the present volume, p. 4, footnote 4, above; and Part VIII, *passim*, below.

we translate this pair of alternatives, as we must, from their literal application in the limited field of military technique into terms that cover the whole of life, we shall conclude that an external proletariat has a choice between being exterminated by the dominant minority with which it is at grips or else overcoming its adversary and stepping into his shoes. And this is, in effect, a choice between an Archaism which spells defeat and a Futurism which may be the key to victory. A barbarian saviour-archaist who is resolved at all costs to avoid the romantic doom of a Vercingetorix must embrace the futuristic ambition of a Visigothic war-lord whose 'dream was to see "Gothia" substituted for "Romania" and Atawulf seated on the throne of Caesar Augustus'.[1]

In the ranks of the External Proletariat, Atawulf—in this mood of his unregenerate youth[2]—may stand as the type of the saviour-futurist. And this Visigothic raider of a Hellenic universal state is an exceptionally articulate representative of a host of barbarian war-lords who have been impelled by a usually quite unreflective appetite for loot and fame to lead their war-bands into the derelict domain of a disintegrating society where the unsophisticated barbarian interlopers may still find an eldorado when the delicately nurtured heirs of the kingdom have already perished miserably there of want and exposure. When Atawulf thus supplants Honorius, the first thing that is apt to strike an observer is the contrast between the triumphant avenger of Vercingetorix and the discomfited successor of Caesar. What can there be in common between the war-lord who is making his fortune by the sword and the emperor who has lost the courage to use the weapon even in defence of his heritage? Yet we have seen[3] that the Goth's victorious swordsmanship has been learnt in a Roman school; and if we now look into the next chapter of the story we shall perceive that Caesar's barbarian conqueror is a barbarous caricature of Caesar himself, instead of being, as might appear at first sight, a 'noble savage' whose act of rapine is all but justified in equity by the immensity of the splendid robber's moral superiority over his degenerate victim.

In the history of the expansion of the Hellenic Civilization at any rate, the radiation of the expanding society's political institutions and ideas among the barbarians round about is almost as much in

---

[1] Orosius, P.: *Adversum Paganos*, Book VII, chap. 43, quoted already in V. C (i) (*c*) 3, vol. v, p. 227, above.
[2] The tendency, illustrated by Atawulf's second thoughts, for a victorious barbarian saviour-futurist to experience a revulsion from Violence towards Gentleness, and from Satanism towards Conservatism, has been examined ibid., pp. 223–7, above. This tendency is also illustrated, as we have there seen, by the careers of a Theodoric, a Yazīd, and even an Alaric.
[3] In V. C (i) (*d*) 6 (α), vol. v, pp. 459–69, above.

evidence as the radiation of its military technique. In another context[1] we have seen how the republicanism which was one of the prominent political tendencies of Hellenism in its growth-stage spread from its cradle in Hellas into the barbarian hinterland of the Hellenic World until, by the time when Tacitus was writing his *Germania*, this new-fangled Hellenic institution, in its north-westward line of advance through Italy and Gaul, had supplanted its old-fashioned predecessor, the patriarchal hereditary monarchy, among all the peoples—including even the recent immigrants of Teutonic speech—on the left bank of the Rhine, while it had already begun to undermine the traditional form of kingship among the Transrhenane Frisians and Cherusci. By Tacitus's day, however, at the turn of the first and second centuries of the Christian Era, this typical institution of the growth-stage of the Hellenic Society, which was then still winning converts on the verge of Ultima Thule, had, of course, long since lost its hold upon the heart of the Hellenic World; for by this time more than five hundred years had passed since the growth of the Hellenic Civilization had been cut short by the breakdown of the year 431 B.C.; and a republicanism which was bound up with a phase of Hellenic history which had thus ended in disaster had soon been unceremoniously elbowed away from its native ground by a Macedonian counter-attack of patriarchal monarchy[2] and by the rise, under this and other constitutional masks, of would-be saviours with the sword. In an age in which the Hellenic institutional wave of republicanism was still making its way, unspent, in the North European barbarian no-man's-land beyond the Rhine, the following wave of dictatorship had already arrived at the frontiers of a Hellenic universal state which owed both its creation and its preservation to a monopoly of dictatorial power in the hands of Caesar Augustus. In the next chapter of Hellenic history this second wave, in its turn, travelled on into the Transrhenane no-man's-land in the wake of its precursor, and its progress was marked by a repetition, *in partibus barbarorum*, of the institutional revolution which had already taken place in a disintegrating Hellenic World.

During the interval between the generation of Tacitus, who was writing in the early days of the Hellenic 'Indian Summer', and the generation of Ammianus Marcellinus, who lived to record the Empire's irretrievable military disaster at Adrianople in A.D. 378, both the budding republicanism of the barbarian communities in the neighbourhood of the Roman *limes* and the sheltered

---

[1] In V. C (i) (c) 3, vol. v, p. 213, footnote 1, above.
[2] For this anachronistic recrudescence of patriarchal monarchy in the heart of the Hellenic World between 379 B.C. and 168 B.C. see III. C (ii) (b), Annex IV, vol. iii, pp. 485–7, above.

patriarchalism of the remoter barbarians beyond the range of the frontier war-zone[1] were blighted by the malignant growth of a new form of government[2] which a Hellenic political philosopher would have diagnosed as 'tyranny' and would have assigned, in his classification of constitutions, to the same category as the contemporary Caesarism of the Roman Empire.

'The binding force formerly possessed by kinship was now largely transferred to the relationship between "lord" and "man", between whom no bond of blood-relationship was necessary. . . . The form of government truly characteristic of "the Heroic Age" . . . is an irresponsible type of kingship resting not upon tribal or national law—which is of little account—but upon military prestige. . . . The princes of "the Heroic Age" appear to have freed themselves to a large extent from any public control on the part of the tribe or community. . . . The force formerly exercised by the kindred is now transferred to the *comitatus*, a body of chosen adherents pledged to personal loyalty to their chief. . . . The result of the change is that the man who possesses a *comitatus* becomes largely free from the control of his kindred, while the chief similarly becomes free from control within his community.'[3]

Is this profound revolution in the institutional life of a primitive society that has been conscripted into an external proletariat a phenomenon that is peculiar to the history of the North European external proletariat of the Hellenic Society? Or is it a revolution that is apt to overtake any external proletariat as a consequence of its relations with a disintegrating civilization across the stationary frontier of a universal state? The second of these two alternative possibilities would appear to be the nearer to the truth; for the passages that have just been quoted from the work of a modern Western scholar all refer to both of two external proletariats of which the author is here making a comparative study. And, if the historical evidence reveals the war-lord, with his war-band, thus asserting himself, in an unmistakably identical fashion, among the Teutonic-speaking barbarians beyond the pale of the Roman Empire and among the Greek-speaking barbarians in the continental hinterland of the Minoan 'thalassocracy', we may venture to infer that an Atawulf who repeats the exploits of a Pelops and an Atreus[4] is a typical example of a type of barbarian saviour-futurist that is apt to make its appearance in the external proletariat of any

[1] For the survival of the patriarchal monarchy in Tacitus's day among the Suebi, the Goths, and the Swedes see V. C (i) (c) 3, vol. v, p. 213, footnote 1, above.
[2] See V. C (i) (d) 7, p. 4, footnote 4, above.
[3] Chadwick, H. M.: *The Heroic Age* (Cambridge 1912, University Press), pp. 365, 390–1, and 443.
[4] Pelops, like Atawulf, acquired his kingdom by marrying a royal heiress; and Atreus, in his turn, succeeded to the heritage of the Perseidae thanks to a marriage connexion —though in this case the lady was the barbarian interloper's sister and the degenerate emperor's mother, in contrast to the affair of Galla Placidia, who was Honorius's sister and Atawulf's bride.

disintegrating civilization. We need not call the roll of Atawulf's peers; for, in bringing the External Proletariat on to our stage in an earlier chapter, we have already made so many of them march past us at the head of their warriors[1] that the figure of the barbarian saviour-futurist is by this time familiar to us. In this place it is perhaps more pertinent to observe that, however distinctive in themselves, and distinct from one another, our Atawulf-type and Vercingetorix-type may be, it is by no means easy to be sure in every case whether a barbarian saviour with the 'time-machine' belongs to the Gallic archaist's or to the Gothic futurist's company.

In the External Proletariat, at any rate, a distinction which is plain in principle is in practice difficult to draw because the replacement of a saviour-archaist by a saviour-futurist as the leader on the barbarians' side in the tug-o'-war along the frontiers of a universal state takes place by way, not of an abrupt mutation, but of a gradual evolution;[2] and in the course of this long-drawn-out chapter in the history of the struggle between the External Proletariat and the Dominant Minority there will be some barbarian leaders who will remain archaists with impunity and others who will become futurists without escaping disaster.

As examples of the type of the triumphant barbarian archaist we may cite the obscure leaders of the Scythians who foiled Darius's attempt to extend the Achaemenian Empire on to the Black Sea Steppe; the Cheruscan leader Arminius who foiled Augustus's attempt to extend the Roman Empire into the North European Forest;[3] the Sa'ūdī leaders of the Wahhābīs[4] who threw off *circa* A.D. 1830 the Egypto-Ottoman yoke which Mehmed 'Alī had fastened upon their necks only about twelve years before at the cost of a nine years' war (*gerebatur* A.D. 1810–18);[5] and the Gutaeans who not only held out when they were assaulted in their native mountain fastnesses by Naramsin (*dominabatur circa* 2572–2517 B.C.), but survived to take their revenge upon a disintegrating Sumeric Civilization—whose earlier convulsions had launched the

---

[1] See V. C (i) (*c*) 3, *passim*, in vol. v, pp. 194–337, above.
[2] See V. C (i) (*c*) 3, vol. v, pp. 208–10, above, and Part VIII, *passim*, below.
[3] See V. C (i) (*c*) 3, vol. v, p. 205, and V. C (i) (*c*) 3, Annex I, vol. v, p. 593, above.
[4] See V. C (i) (*c*) 3, vol. v, pp. 294–6 and 333–4, above.
[5] Even at the cost of this amount of time and blood and treasure Mehmed 'Alī would probably have gained no more ground in Arabia than Darius gained in Scythia as the result of a single campaign, if the 'Osmanli empire-builder had not had, and taken, the opportunity to enhance the fighting power of his troops by borrowing from the Western World a discipline and a technique which were alien from the Ottoman spirit of that age, though the West itself had perhaps learned these arts in an Ottoman school (see Part III. A, vol. iii, p. 38, footnote 2, and IV. C (iii) (*c*) 2 (γ), vol. iv, p. 450, above). This adventitious aid enabled Mehmed 'Alī in Arabia to emulate Justinian's achievement in Italy. But his *tour de force* of asserting the dominion of a Cairene Government over the Najd was just as ephemeral as Justinian's analogous *tour de force* of asserting the dominion of a Constantinopolitan Government over the Basin of the Po (which Justinian's exertions merely converted from a Gothia into a Lombardy).

Akkadian militarist upon his career of aggression—when, less than a hundred years after Naramsin's death, the Gutaean war-bands descended upon the Sumeric Society's homeland on the plains of Shinar and kept their yoke upon their victims' necks for four successive generations (*circa* 2429–2306 B.C.).[1]

As examples of unsuccessful barbarian futurists we may cite from the history of the Hellenic World the Suevian war-lord Ariovistus,[2] and the obscurer war-lords[3] of the Cimbri and the Teutones,[4] who dreamed the dream of Atawulf five hundred years too soon and paid the penalty for their precocity by encountering, not Honorius, but Marius and Caesar. These successive roles which were played by an Ariovistus and an Atawulf on the North European front of the Roman Empire have their analogues on its West African front in the careers of a Jugurtha who came within an ace of succeeding[5] at the stage at which Ariovistus failed, and a Gildo who only just failed[6] at the stage at which Atawulf was successful. In an intermediate age, and at the eastern extremity of the North European front, we see a Decebalus who had the makings of a Theodoric being blasted by the thunderbolt of a Juppiter Trajanus. From the history of the main body of the Orthodox Christian Society we may cite the Serb war-lord Stjepan Dušan (*dominabatur* A.D. 1331–55), who achieved the success of a Theodoric (though his achievement was as ephemeral as his Ostrogothic counterpart's) at a stage of the Orthodox Christian 'Time of Troubles' which corresponds to the times of Jugurtha and Ariovistus in the history of the Hellenic World.[7] If we turn to the history of the 'Great Society' of the Westernized World of our own age we may cite, from the vast company of its *dramatis personae*, King Amānallāh of Afghanistan, who has come to grief through recklessly forcing the pace in attempting to put into effect a policy of salvation-through-Futurism[8] which his moderate and circumspect Wahhābī contemporary King 'Abd-al-'Azīz of Sa'ūdī Arabia has been carrying out with signal success.[9]

---

[1] See I. C (i) (*b*), vol. i, p. 109; V. C (i) (*c*) 3, vol. v, pp. 203 and 262, and the present chapter and volume, p. 184, above, and V. C (ii) (*b*), pp. 296–7, below.

[2] See V. C (i) (*c*) 3, vol. v, pp. 219 and 223, above.

[3] Ariovistus has been raised out of a like obscurity, not by any prowess of his own, but by the accident that his Roman conqueror Caesar was as great a master of the pen as he was of the sword, whereas Marius merely performed, without recording, his feat of exterminating the Cimbri and Teutones.

[4] See V. C (i) (*c*) 3,.vol. v, p. 218, above.

[5] See IV. C (iii) (*c*) 3 (β), vol. iv, p. 507, and V. C (i) (*c*) 3, vol. v, p. 218, above.

[6] For the wave of barbarian aggression which began to beat upon the West African front of the Roman Empire in the last quarter of the fourth century of the Christian Era, see V. C (i) (*c*) 3, vol. v, p. 221, above.

[7] For the Serb domination over Macedonia in the latter part of the Orthodox Christian 'Time of Troubles' see V. C (i) (*c*) 3, vol. v, pp. 293–4, above.

[8] See V. C (i) (*c*) 3, vol. v, pp. 332–3, and V. C (i) (*d*) 9 (β), in the present volume, p. 103, above.

[9] See V. C (i) (*c*) 3, vol. v, pp. 333–4, above.

We can also cite at least one unsuccessful barbarian leader who is bafflingly amphibious. Is the Sicel leader Ducetius (*ducebat circa* 466–440 B.C.) to be classified as an archaist or as a futurist? At first glance we may see nothing but an archaist in the man who led the last of the native barbarians in their last stand against the Greek colonists of Sicily. Is not this a hero of the same class as the Red Indian Chief Sitting Bull or the Sūdānī standard-bearer at the Battle of Omdurman? But a closer examination of Ducetius brings to light one futuristic feature after another.

In the first place Ducetius's original enterprise, with its ambitious aim of uniting all the surviving Sicel communities into a single commonwealth, was manifestly inspired by the example of two miniature empires which had recently been exercised by Greek city-states over Sicel perioeci—the empires which had been won respectively for Agrigentum by her despot Theron (*dominabatur circa* 488–472 B.C.) and for Syracuse by the Deinomenidae *dominabantur circa* 485–466 B.C.).[1] In the second place Ducetius not only emulated the ambitions of contemporary Greek empire-builders in Sicily but also imitated the methods of contemporary Hellenic statesmanship; for the device by which he sought to give his new Sicel commonwealth cohesion was to 'synoecize' it into a city-state *à la grecque* with its civic centre at Palice.[2] In the third place, after he had courted and incurred disaster by falling foul of Agrigentum and Syracuse simultaneously,[3] Ducetius threw himself on the mercy of his victorious Syracusan adversaries and acquiesced in their decision to send the defeated Sicel patriot into an honourable exile at Corinth—the mother-city of Syracuse in the heart of Hellas. In the fourth and last place Ducetius, so far from becoming estranged from the alien civilization which had now proved itself more than a match for his barbarian arms, became instead so complete a convert to Hellenism that he eventually returned from Corinth to Sicily, not as a refugee who had broken out of prison and was shaking the dust of his captivity from off his feet, but as the Sicel leader of a new swarm of Greek

[1] For these Agrigentine and Syracusan 'empires' see V. C (i) (*c*) 3, vol. v, pp. 211–12, above; for the Deinomenidae see III. C (ii) (*b*), vol. iii, p. 357, footnote 1, above. Ducetius's attempt to set up a Sicel empire in Sicily which was to take the place of both these Greek empires was made immediately after the Deinomenids' fall from power.

[2] Herein Ducetius anticipated by a whole generation the Macedonian King Perdiccas II's creative achievement of inducing the Chalcidian Greek communities ἐπὶ Θράκης to 'synoecize' themselves at Olynthus *circa* 432 B.C. (see III. C (ii) (*b*), Annex IV, vol. iii, p. 480, above).

[3] Compare the similar—and similarly disastrous—error of statesmanship which was committed by the Rîfî barbarian saviour-archaist 'Abd-al-Karîm in A.D. 1925, when, not content with being at war with the Spaniards, he invaded the French Zone of Morocco and thereby drove the French into a military co-operation with the Spaniards which sealed the Rîfî patriot's doom (see Toynbee, A. J.: *Survey of International Affairs*, 1925, vol. i (London 1927, Milford), Part II, sections (vi)–(viii)).

colonists. When death overtook him thereafter on the soil of his native island, it found him engaged once again, in this last phase of his career, on his original enterprise of attempting to unite all the surviving Sicel communities into a single commonwealth organized, *more Hellenico*, as a city-state. But Ducetius had not been blind to the lesson of his previous failure, and this time he started to build his Sicel state round a Greek nucleus. This was the significant difference between Ducetius's first experiment in 'synoecism' at Palice and his second experiment at Calacte. And if Fate had granted him the time to carry this second essay in empire-building to completion his Sicel hands would have reared a political structure with a Greek apex and a Sicel base which would have conformed exactly to the Hellenic pattern of the antecedent Siceliot Greek empires which had centred, not on Calacte, but on Syracuse and Agrigentum.

The case of Ducetius illustrates the difficulty of sorting out into an archaist and a futurist group, with a hard-and-fast line of demarcation between them, the would-be saviours with the 'time-machine' who have arisen in the External Proletariat. But when we turn to the Internal Proletariat we shall perhaps not reckon *a priori* on being confronted by any corresponding problem. One of the hall-marks of membership of the Internal Proletariat is an apparently congenital inability to make the archaistic response to the challenge of social catastrophe. It can therefore be taken for granted that every would-be saviour with the 'time-machine' who arises in the Internal Proletariat will be a saviour-futurist; and this certainty might be expected to simplify the rest of our present survey. There is, however, one complication, and that lies in the fact that the futurist leaders of the Internal Proletariat are not all of them drawn from the Internal Proletariat's own ranks.[1]

At an earlier point in this Study we have noticed the proclivity of the Dominant Minority to succumb to a process of 'proletarianization' which takes the form of 'vulgarization' when the Internal and not the External Proletariat is the proletarian object of the Dominant Minority's mimesis.[2] And in the present chapter we have seen that this transfer of social allegiance to the Internal Proletariat from the Dominant Minority, which in a Commodus is the last extravagance of a wanton luxury, may be the first necessity of a baffled idealism in a Gaius Gracchus. It is, indeed, one of the tragic ironies of the Dominant Minority's fate that the idealists who arise in its ranks should tread the same path of social

[1] See V. C (i) (c) 2, vol. v, p. 71, above.
[2] For this phenomenon of 'vulgarization' see V. C (i) (d) 6 (α), vol. v, pp. 445-59, above.

migration as the wastrels. And it is even more tragically ironical
that Gracchus should involuntarily work far greater havoc through
a nobility to which Commodus could never rise than Commodus
can work through a vulgarity into which Gracchus would never
fall. Yet this is the melancholy truth. For, while Commodus
rapidly reduces himself to impotence by a course of social truancy
which is also one of spiritual demoralization, Gracchus's spirit is
fortified by a decree of social outlawry which is passed upon him,
not by any viciousness in himself, but by the impenitence of adversaries in his own household who cannot forgive him for calling in
question the right of his own class to the enjoyment of its ill-gotten
privileges. And so, in the sequel, Commodus is uneventfully
swallowed up by a slough in which he has delighted to wallow,
whereas Gracchus breathes a demonic energy and an explosive
driving-force into the souls of the proletarians into whose company
he has been thrust by the hostile hands of his own kin and kind.

This revolutionary alliance between an outcast saviour-archaist
and an outcast Internal Proletariat is perhaps in some sense fore-
ordained from the very beginning of the archaist's career, though
it is no part of his original intentions or expectations. The essential
feature and supreme attraction of the 'patrios politeia' which the
archaist originally sets out to re-establish is its freedom from social
cankers that are penalties of social breakdown and symptoms of
social disintegration. His aim is to restore the moral health of
Society, and his prescription for dealing with the Proletariat is not
to set it in the seat of the Dominant Minority but to abolish both
classes at one stroke by closing the breach between them. But the
social physician who undertakes to heal the body social by getting
rid of the Proletariat in this way is committing himself to a policy
of righting the wrongs of the proletarians; for the schism in Society
can only be repaired by restoring to its proletarian members the
'stake' in Society of which they have been wrongfully deprived.[1]
And this plank in the archaist-reformer's platform is an insuperable stumbling-block for his fellow members of the Dominant
Minority, because the Proletariat's loss has been the Dominant
Minority's gain. In their eyes the archaist's programme of reform
is sheer treason against the reformer's own class, while in his eyes
their opposition simply shows them up as hypocrites whose pro-
fessions of public spirit disgracefully break down as soon as their
pockets are touched. Misunderstanding breeds alienation; and,
when the tension rises to breaking-point and the Dominant

[1] For the original meaning of the Latin word *proletarii*—i.e. persons whose only
'stake' in Society is the fruit of their own physical procreation—see I. B (iv), vol. i, p. 41,
footnote 3, above.

Minority casts the contumacious reformer out, the thwarted and disillusioned idealist now almost joyfully parts company with his own kin and kind and throws himself—crying 'I will be your leader'—into the arms of a Proletariat which by this time is waiting with arms outstretched to receive him. The Proletariat is content to take the archaist-outcast at the Dominant Minority's valuation. In their eyes he is a champion of the proletarian cause who has sacrificed for their sake everything in the world except their gratitude and trust; and they give practical expression to these by adopting the outlaw as their leader. This dramatic situation is one which we have encountered in this Study before. 'The stone which the builders rejected, the same is become the head of the corner.'[1] Paul turns away from the Jews who refuse him a hearing, and delivers his rejected message of salvation to the Gentiles' open ears. And, while in Jewish eyes the Pharisee-Apostle of Christ is an odious renegade, in Paul's eyes the Jewry of his generation is an Esau sacrilegiously repudiating his birthright.

When we pass in review the legion of saviour-futurists who have led the Internal Proletariat in their desperate revolts against an intolerable oppression, we see turncoats—or outcasts—from the ranks of the Dominant Minority fighting shoulder to shoulder with comrades who are proletarian-born, and in the confusion of the conflict the social antecedents of each dust-begrimed and blood-bespattered figure are not always easy to ascertain.

In the wave of insurgency that swept across the Hellenic World in the seventh decade of the second century B.C.,[2] a movement which was launched in Sicily by the Syrian slave Eunus and the Cilician slave Cleon was taken up in Asia Minor by a pretender to the throne of the Attalids who was denounced by his opponents as a bastard.[3] With which of his contemporaries is Aristonicus to be classed? With Eunus or with Tiberius Gracchus? Eunus assumed the royal name Antiochus when he proclaimed himself king of a community of freedmen; and another insurrection of the slaves in Sicily was captained by a Salvius who called himself King Tryphon. This Salvius-Tryphon was adopting as his throne-name a *sobriquet* that had been borne as a nickname by an adventurer who in the preceding generation had momentarily usurped the diadem of the Seleucidae. And this Diodotus-Tryphon's role at Antioch had been as equivocal as Aristonicus's role at Pergamum. In the third and last act of the Sicilian tragedy, which was

---

[1] Matt. xxi, 42, quoting Ps. cxviii, 22. Compare Mark xii. 10; Luke xx. 17; Acts iv. 11; Eph. ii. 20; 1 Pet. ii. 7. The passage has been quoted in this Study already in IV. C (iii) (c) 1, vol. iv, p. 248, and in V. C (i) (d) 11, in the present volume, p. 164, above.

[2] See V. C (i) (c) 2, vol. v, pp. 68–71, above.

[3] Strabo: *Geographica*, Book XIV, chap. 38 (p. 646); Justin: *Historiae Philippicae*, Book XXXVI, chap. 4, § 6.

played about half a century after the last of the local slave-revolts had been crushed,[1] the enterprise of establishing an Anti-Rome on Sicilian ground was taken up by an insurgent who, so far from being of servile blood, was a true-born son of Pompey the Great. Sextus Pompeius[2] was driven into the arms of a beaten but un-reconciled proletariat when the Second Triumvirate included his name in their proscription-list. And thereafter, with Sicily for his head-quarters and with Oriental freedmen in command of his fleet, he avenged the defeats of Eunus and Salvius on the children of the Rupilii and Luculli and emulated the atrocities of the Cilician pirates who had been swept off the seas by this Roman outlaw's father.

Before he gained possession of his maritime stronghold in Sicily, Sextus had found asylum in a Pyrenaean fastness in the country of the Lacetani; and from this Spanish base of operations he had repeated the exploits of Sertorius,[3] a refugee-partisan of Marius who, in an earlier round of a hundred-years-long Roman civil war, had held out in Spain for a decade against the elsewhere victorious lieutenants and successors of Sulla. It was an extraordinary feat of arms for the master of a couple of backward provinces to keep at bay, for that length of time, the forces of a Roman Government which not only held Rome itself but also commanded the resources of all the rest of the Roman Empire. What was the secret of Sertorius's astonishing success? When we look into the history of this Roman outlaw, we find that after he had actually been driven out of Spain into Morocco by a Sullan expeditionary force he was able to recover his foothold in the Peninsula thanks to being invited by the recently conquered Lusitanians to come over and help them against the imperialism of the Roman outlaw's own compatriots.[4] In other words, Sertorius (*in Hispania militabat circa* 82–72 B.C.) was able to set Rome at defiance because he had been invested with the mantle of Viriathus (*militabat circa* 150–140 B.C.). A barbarian people who had been forcibly transferred from the external to the internal proletariat of an aggressively expanding civilization in consequence of the failure of a native leader to stem the tide of Roman conquest, now called in one of their conquerors to deliver them from a yoke in which they had not yet learnt to acquiesce; and in this last act of the Spanish tragedy the Roman turncoat avenged the defeat of the Lusitanian patriot.

[1] The second of the slave-revolts in Sicily had lasted from about 104 to 100 B.C.; Sextus Pompeius's occupation of the island lasted from about 43 to 36 B.C.
[2] See V. C (i) (c) 2, vol. v, p. 71, above.   [3] See ibid.
[4] Like Hamilcar Barca a hundred and fifty years or so before him and the Arab Muslim conquerors some eight hundred years later, Sertorius made his descent on Spain from Africa at the head of a force which included a contingent of Berber troops.

In Italy in the same impious age we see the Roman senator Catiline (*insurgebat* 63–62 B.C.)[1] treading in the footprints of the runaway gladiator Spartacus (*insurgebat* 73–71 B.C.).[2] In the modern Western World we can espy, among the renegades from a dominant minority who put themselves at the head of the insurgent German peasants in A.D. 1524–5,[3] a counterpart of Aristonicus in the ex-Duke of Württemberg Ulrich, and counterparts of Sertorius and Sextus Pompeius in the knights Florian Geyer and Götz von Berlichingen. And in the Westernized Russian World of our own day we ourselves have lived to see the dreams of Spartacus and Catiline translated into reality by the hand of a master-revolutionary who was not a workman and not a peasant and not (as Pugachev had been)[4] a Cossack and not (as Minin had been)[5] a butcher. The extraordinary genius who succeeded in establishing a 'Dictatorship of the Proletariat' on the ruins of the empire of Ivan the Terrible and Peter the Great was not himself of proletarian origin. Lenin[6] was baptized as Vladímir Ulianov, and the father who gave him this respectable name was a gentlemanly official in the Imperial civil service.

This survey of revolutionary leaders of the Internal Proletariat who have been recruited from the ranks of the Dominant Minority will perhaps have sufficed to show that the political prophet without honour who withdraws as an outlaw to return as a saviour on a different social plane is a figure of far-reaching historical importance. We shall not learn much about the true character and worth of these social migrants by taking note of the provisional verdict that has been passed on them by their contemporaries, for it is a matter of common form for them to be execrated as turncoats by their own kin and kind and to be lauded as martyrs by their new-found comrades. We must form our own opinion on the evidence before us; and this empirical method seems likely to lead us on the whole to a favourable judgement; for, if we repeat our roll-call, we shall find that the ne'er-do-wells of the type of Catiline and the desperadoes of the type of Sextus Pompeius and Sertorius are outnumbered by the disinterested and self-sacrificing idealists—among whom we must reckon not only an Agis and a Cleomenes and a Tiberius and a Gaius Gracchus, who will be accorded the title by a general consensus, but also, at least provisionally, an Aristonicus and a Lenin, whose claim—if we do give them the benefit of the doubt—will evoke a volley of indignant protests. The final judgement on satanist-saviours such as these

---

1 See V. C (i) (c) 2, vol. v, p. 71, above.   2 See ibid., p. 70, above.
3 For the Peasants' Revolt see ibid., p. 167, above.
4 See the present chapter, p. 227, above.   5 See ibid., p. 207, above.
6 See V. C (i) (c) 2, vol. v, pp. 179–80 and 181–8, above.

must be left to Time and History; but in regard to the outlaw-saviours in general there are certain matters of fact which we may venture to state here and now. In the first place these outlaws are apt to include in their number some of the noblest souls that are ever born into the Dominant Minority of a disintegrating civilization. In the second place their nobility is the cause of their being cast out by their own kin and kind. In the third place this is the cause of their adoption as leaders by their new proletarian comrades. In the fourth place the 'clouds of glory' which these social migrants trail, as they make their painful transit across a monstrous social gulf, do not thereafter 'fade into the light of common day'. The outlook and ideals and standards and examples with which the saviour-outcasts' advent irradiates the Internal Proletariat's murky native 'ideology' are the only elements of the futurist *Weltanschauung* that survive the inevitable failure of the futurists' forlorn hope. After 'the City of the Sun' has shown itself to have been a 'City of Destruction', the alien light in which it was momentarily and bewilderingly apparelled can still be seen shining above the smoking ruins and the blood-soaked sod; and then at last this glory can be recognized for what it is. It is the celestial light that streams from the mansions of the City of God.[1]

Now that we have followed the saviour-outlaw to his journey's end, and have recognized the source of the light which this torch-bearer carries with him, we need not go on to call the roll of the native proletarian leaders with whom he throws in his lot, since we have reviewed these once already in bringing the Internal Proletariat on to our stage.[2] Our survey of would-be saviours with the 'time-machine' may therefore close at this point with a summary of our findings; and these can be stated in a single sentence: the 'time-machine' has proved to be the fraud which it was accused of being by its quizzical inventor.[3] This pretentious piece of clockwork is not, after all, an effective substitute for the sword. The sword's results cannot be attained without shedding blood and taking life; and such murderous work can only be done by dint of the sword's cutting edge. That is why the would-be saviour with the 'time-machine' invariably rejects his new-fangled instrument and gets to work again with his well-proved weapon as soon as things become serious—just as, in our British warfare in the eighteenth century, the Scottish clansmen used to throw their muskets away and draw their claymores

---

[1] The track which this light imprints, in its transit, on the sensitive medium of legend is examined, in one particularly momentous test case, in V. C (ii) (a), Annex II, pp. 376–539, below.

[2] In V. C (i) (c) 2, *passim*, in vol. v, pp. 58–194, above.

[3] For Lewis Carroll's elegant exposure of the catch in the mechanism of the 'time-machine' see the present chapter, p. 214, above.

whenever they were coming to close quarters with the 'redcoats'.

Our present inquiry, as far as we have yet carried it, has shown us that, while there may be no salvation in the sword, there is none in clockwork either. But happily these are not the only means of salvation to which human souls have had recourse in response to the challenge of a disintegrating civilization. We must carry the inquiry farther.

The Philosopher masked by a King.

A means of salvation that does not invoke the aid of either 'time-machine' or sword was propounded in the first generation of the Hellenic 'Time of Troubles' by the earliest and greatest of Hellenic adepts in the art of Detachment.

'There is no hope of a cessation of evils[1] for the states [of Hellas]— and, in my opinion, none for Mankind—except through a personal union between political power and philosophy and a forcible disqualification of those common natures that now follow one of these two pursuits to the exclusion of the other. The union may be achieved in either of two ways. Either the philosophers must become kings in our states, or else the people who are now called kings and potentates must take— genuinely and thoroughly—to philosophy.'[2]

In suggesting this cure for social troubles which were not peculiar to the Hellenic World of Plato's day but which are apt (as the Hellenic sage divined) to beset the mundane life of Man in all times and places and circumstances, Plato is at pains to disarm, by forestalling, 'the plain man's' criticism of the philosopher's prescription. He introduces his proposal as a paradox which is likely to bring down upon the sage's head a deluge of ridicule and disrepute. If he doesn't look out he will be mobbed, and he will be lucky if he isn't massacred! Yet, if Plato's paradox is a hard saying for laymen—be these kings or commoners—it is an even harder saying for philosophers. Is not the very aim of Philosophy a Detachment from Life?[3] And are not the pursuits of Detachment and of Salvation incompatible to the point of being mutually exclusive? How can one set oneself to salvage a City of Destruction from which one is rightly struggling to be free? How, then, is the sage to reconcile the spiritual exercise to which

---

[1] Plato's phrase κακῶν παῦλα ταῖς πόλεσι sounds like a reminiscence of Thucydides' phrase ἀρχὴ μεγάλων κακῶν τῇ Ἑλλάδι which has been quoted in this Study in IV. C (ii) (b) 1, vol. iv, p. 62, above. The outbreak of the Atheno-Peloponnesian War, to which the Thucydidean phrase refers, was the social débâcle from which Plato was fain to rally the Hellenes of his own generation.

[2] Plato: Respublica: 473 D, repeated in 499 B and 501 E. The passage has been quoted already in this Study in Part III. A, vol. iii, p. 93, above.

[3] See V. C (i) (d) 10, pp. 132-48, above.

he has dedicated his life with a residual scruple of conscience which he can neither justify without ceasing to be a philosopher nor overcome without ceasing to be a man?

In the sight of the philosopher the incarnation of self-sacrifice —Christ Crucified—is a personification of folly.[1] Yet few philosophers have had the courage to avow this conviction, and fewer still to act upon it, without at the same time giving Conscience something of her due. For the adept in the art of Detachment has to start as a man who is encumbered with the common human feelings and who is born, *ex hypothesi*, into a 'Time of Troubles'. The sorrows and sufferings of the age, which have impelled this human being to follow the philosophic way of life, are manifestly pressing no less cruelly upon his contemporaries. He cannot ignore in his neighbour a distress of which his own heart gives the measure, or pretend that a way of salvation which is commended by his own experience would not be equally valuable to his neighbour if only it were pointed out to him. Is our philosopher, then, to handicap himself by lending his neighbour a helping hand? In this moral dilemma it is vain for him to take refuge in the Indic doctrine that Pity and Love are vices,[2] or in the Plotinian doctrine that 'action is a weakened form of contemplation'.[3] Nor can he be content to stand convicted of intellectual and moral inconsistencies of which the Stoic Fathers—a Zeno and a Cleanthes and a Chrysippus—are roundly accused by Plutarch. This eclectic *malleus Stoicorum* is able to quote texts in which the third of the three doctors condemns the life of academic leisure in one sentence and recommends it in another within the limits of a single treatise.[4] And, in so far as these philosophers of the Stoic school did declare in favour of self-sacrifice in the cause of social service, Plutarch charges them with having failed to practise in their lives the conduct which they were preaching in their publications and their lectures.[5] We need not attempt to ascertain whether Plutarch's damaging accusations against Zeno and Zeno's disciples are altogether well founded. But we may remind ourselves of Plato's reluctant decision that the adepts who had mastered the art of Detachment could not be permitted to enjoy for ever afterwards the sunlight into which they had so hardly fought their way. With a heavy heart he condemned his perfected philosophers to redescend into the Cave for the sake of helping their

---

[1] 1 Cor. i. 23, already quoted in V. C (i) (d) 11, p. 150, above.
[2] See V. C (i) (d) 10, pp. 144-8, above.
[3] Plotinus: *Ennead* III, viii, 4, quoted in this Study in III. C (ii) (b), vol. iii, p. 254, above.
[4] See the two passages quoted from Chrysippus's *De Vitis*, Book IV, in chapters 2 and 20, respectively, of Plutarch's *De Stoicorum Repugnantiis*.
[5] Ibid., chap. 2.

unfortunate fellow men who were still sitting 'in darkness and in
the shadow of death, fast bound in misery and iron';[1] and it is
impressive to see this grievous Platonic commandment being
dutifully obeyed by Epicurus.

The Hellenic philosopher whose ideal was a state of unruffled
Imperturbability (ἀταραξία) was also, apparently, the one and only
private individual before Jesus of Nazareth to acquire the Greek
title of Saviour (σωτήρ). That honour was normally a monopoly of
princes and a reward for services of a public nature.[2] Epicurus's
unprecedented distinction was an unsought consequence of the
cool-headed philosopher's good-humoured obedience to an irresistible call of the heart.[3] And the fervour of the gratitude and
admiration with which Epicurus's work of salvation is extolled in
the poetry of Lucretius makes it clear that, in this case at least,
the title was no empty formality but was the expression of a deep
and lively feeling which must have been communicated to the
Latin poet through a chain of tradition descending without a break
from Epicurus's own contemporaries who had known him, and
adored him, in the flesh. The Lucretian hymn of praise to a
saviour who has braved the direst terrors and dared the farthest
flights in order to liberate his fellow men from the prison-house of
Superstition has been quoted in this Study already in a different
context.[4] In another passage the same poet compares his Master's
writings to the flowery pastures of the honey-bees, and declares
these 'golden sayings' to be worthy of immortal life because they
dissipate the terrors of the mind and push back the walls of the
World.[5] In a third passage Lucretius hails his saviour-philosopher
as a god in words which Virgil afterwards adapted to the apotheosis of a saviour-statesman.

> Deus ille fuit, deus, inclyte Memmi,
> qui princeps vitae rationem invenit eam quae
> nunc appellatur sapientia, quique per artem
> fluctibus e tantis vitam tantisque tenebris
> in tam tranquillo et tam clara luce locavit.[6]

---

1 Plato: *Respublica*, 520, and Ps. cvii, 10, quoted in III. C (ii) (b), vol. iii, pp. 251–2,
above. A catalogue of Hellenic philosophers who 'did take their share of the burden
of public life, instead of being good for nothing but intellectual work, and making that
an excuse for living out their lives in peace and quiet', is given by Aelian: *Variae Historiae*, Book III, chap. 17.

2 See Pauly-Wissowa: *Real-Encyclopädie der Klassischen Altertumswissenschaft*, 2nd
ed., second series, Halbband v, col. 1214. Ibid., col. 1218, it is pointed out that σωτήρ
is not yet used as a standing epithet of Christ in the Pauline Epistles.

3 For this see the evidence cited by Professor Gilbert Murray in V. C (i) (d) 11,
p. 154, footnote 2, above.

4 Lucretius: *De Rerum Natura*: Book I, ll. 62–79, quoted in II. C (ii) (b) 1, vol. i,
p. 299, above.

5 Lucretius: *De Rerum Natura*, Book III, ll. 1–17.

6 Ibid., Book V, ll. 8–12, imitated by Virgil in *Eclogue* I, ll. 6–10 (see V. C (i) (d)
6 (δ), Annex, vol. v, p. 648, footnote 4, above).

This paean may sound extravagant in Christian ears; and yet,

> If we would speak true,
> Much to the Man is due

> Who from his private gardens, where
> He lived reservèd and austere
> (As if his highest plot
> To plant the bergamot),[1]

could bring himself, for the sake of his fellow men, to play the uncongenial part of a saviour-king at the cost of sacrificing an Imperturbability which, for this sage who had sought and found it, was the pearl of great price.

The paradoxical history of Epicurus brings out the grievousness of the burden which the philosophers have to take upon their shoulders if, in setting themselves to carry out Plato's prescription, they follow the alternative of themselves becoming kings; and it is therefore not surprising to find that Plato's other alternative—of turning kings into philosophers—has proved highly attractive to every philosopher with a social conscience, beginning with Plato himself. After considering the possibility that 'sometime—either in the boundless Past or in the Present (in some non-Hellenic clime, far beyond our horizon) or else in the Future—first-rate philosophers somehow have been or are being or will be constrained to undertake the government of a state',[2] Plato goes on to examine the alternative possibility that 'there might be sons of kings or potentates who were born philosophers'. And he submits that when they had been born with this natural endowment it would not be absolutely inevitable that they should be carried off, and that—however difficult it might be for them to be saved alive —it would at the same time hardly be possible to maintain that no single one among them all would ever be saved in all time.[3] In this passage Plato exerts his great powers of persuasiveness to demonstrate the theoretical possibility that a saviour of souls from the wreck of a disintegrating society might be thrown up by the fortuitous operation of Time and Nature and Chance.[4] But a theory which satisfies the intellect of a thinker in his arm-chair may not avail in practice to relieve him of the necessity of shouldering a social burden which will fall remorselessly on the philosopher's own shoulders if he cannot find any one else to play the part of Atlas.

---

[1] With these lines of Marvell's on Cromwell compare Aristocreon's couplet on Chrysippus, quoted by Plutarch in op. cit., chap. 2.

[2] Plato: *Respublica*, 499 C.   [3] Ibid., 502 A–B.

[4] This theoretically possible but practically improbable Platonic means of salvation may be compared with the Epicurean means of creation through one 'infinitesimal swerve' (*exiguum clinamen*) of a single atom (see Lucretius: *De Rerum Natura*, Book II, l. 292).

The answer to the question whether it is practical politics for our philosopher to count upon the spontaneous generation of philosophically minded princes will depend, of course, upon the actual frequency of the occurrence of this natural phenomenon; and a survey of the histories of the disintegrations of civilizations up to date will show that the miracle is quite as rare as Plato admits it to be in his disarming apologia for this tentative solution of his problem. In another context[1] we have come across two princes—born into two different worlds at dates more than a thousand years apart—who each made it his mission to use his princely power for promoting the moral unity of Mankind without having been prompted, so far as we know, by any philosopher-mentor. 'Behold how good and how pleasant it is for brethren to dwell together in unity'[2] was at any rate never suggested to Alexander the Great by a tutor who held that all non-Hellenes, and especially those in Asia, were slaves by nature, and whose political ideal, even for a Hellenic commonwealth, was a dominant minority living parasitically upon the fruits of the labours of a servile proletariat.[3] And, if it is certain that Alexander did not learn his lesson from Aristotle, it is at least not proven that he learnt it from any other source than his own experience of things human and divine.[4] Nor is there any evidence to impugn Ikhnaton's title to originality—though we know so much less about Ikhnaton's upbringing and antecedents than we know about Alexander's that in this Egyptiac case the *argumentum ex silentio* is far from being conclusive. The most that we can say is that, in the present state of our knowledge, both Ikhnaton and Alexander would appear to fall within Plato's category of kings' sons who were born philosophers, who lived to reign, and who attempted, on the throne, to translate into political practice a philosophy that was apparently all their own.[5] At the same time we shall find that these two

---

[1] In V. C (i) (d) 7, pp. 6–12, above.　　　　　[2] Ps. cxxxiii. 1.

[3] The extremeness of the contrast between Alexander's vision of Homonoia and Aristotle's conception of Hellenism as a cultural superiority carrying with it a title to political and economic privileges is brought out in Tarn, W. W.: *Alexander the Great and the Unity of Mankind* (London 1933, Milford), p. 4. For Aristotle's gospel of social salvation through caste see the present Study, Part III. A, vol. iii, pp. 93–7, above.

[4] The evidence on this question is brilliantly examined by Tarn in op. cit.

[5] We are bound to speak in these guarded terms in presenting Alexander's and Ikhnaton's claims to originality; for, while it is hardly conceivable that Alexander can have acquired direct from Ikhnaton himself the philosophical idea which was common to these two princes—considering that, in all probability, Alexander did not even know that such a person as Ikhnaton had ever existed—it is not inconceivable that the Macedonian and the Theban philosopher-king may have each derived the idea, quite independently of one another, from a common source. On the one hand we know that the conception of a brotherhood of all Mankind through the common beneficence of God, as this is expressed in Ikhnaton's Hymn to the Aton, was anticipated in Egyptiac literature in an earlier hymn—written at least a generation before Ikhnaton's day—which was addressed not to the Aton but to the tutelary god of Thebes who had been raised by Ikhnaton's predecessor Thothmes III to the divine presidency of a Pan-Egyptiac

names exhaust our list; and this result of an empirical test will lead us to the conclusion that, if the philosopher is really in earnest in his quest for a philosophically minded prince who will satisfy the demands of the philosopher's social conscience and will thereby absolve the philosopher himself from going into politics, then the philosopher cannot afford simply to sit back and let Nature, uncontrolled, take her utterly wayward course. He must personally take a hand to the extent at any rate of developing and improving upon Nature where she shows herself susceptible of philosophic cultivation. If the philosopher wishes to insure against the risk of being called upon to play Atlas himself, he must be willing at least to play Atlas' mentor.

This solution of the philosopher's moral problem has been propounded by the Stoic Father Chrysippus.

'The sage', he says, 'will readily put up with the institution of kingship, because he will turn it to account. And if he cannot be

Pantheon under the title of Amon-Re (for this anticipation of Ikhnaton's intuition see V. C (i) (d) 6 (δ), Annex, vol. v, p. 695, footnote 2, above). On the other hand we know that a deep impression was made upon Alexander's mind by what passed between him and the priests of Amon when he visited the god's oracle-shrine in the Oasis of Siwah in 331 B.C. According to Plutarch (*Life of Alexander*, chap. 27), Alexander wrote to his mother Olympias that he had received certain private answers from the oracle which he would communicate to her, and her only, on his return. This message, if authentic, might of course be no more than a hint of the declaration, which the oracle is reported to have made to Alexander, that his true father was not Philip the son of Amyntas but was the god himself. And while this declaration was taken seriously by Alexander—who could hardly help being thrilled at hearing himself hailed as the son of a divinity whom the Hellenes identified with Zeus—it might have meant no more on the lips of the Egyptiac priests themselves than an official recognition of Alexander as a legitimate heir to the throne of a Pharaoh who had continued to bear the title of an adopted son of Re long after he had ceased in fact to be regarded as being himself a living god (see IV. C (iii) (c) 2 (β), vol. iv, pp. 412–13, and V. C (i) (d) 6 (δ), Annex, vol. v, p. 653, above). It is possible, however, that even if these were the words and the meaning of the oracle of Amon when it was consulted by Alexander there may still have been something more than that in the Egyptiac divinity's communication to the Hellenic war-lord; and some such larger message may be the source of Alexander's saying that 'God is the common father of all men, but he makes the best ones peculiarly his own' (Plutarch: *Life of Alexander*, chap. 27, quoted in V. C (i) (d) 7, p. 9, above). Did the oracle go on to tell Alexander that, in so far as his divine parentage was not a mere official formality but was a living spiritual truth, this parentage was no single human being's peculiar prerogative, and that, in making the best of his children peculiarly his own, God was charging them with the mission of bringing their fellow men to perceive and live up to the truth that all men were brothers in virtue of God's common fatherhood? In other contexts (in I. C (ii), vol. i, pp. 140–4, and IV. C (iii) (c) 2 (β), vol. iv, p. 413, above) we have seen that the principal *motif* in the drama of Egyptiac religious history was the gradual admittance of the common man to a share in certain religious hopes and consolations which had originally been the monopoly of a divine king and his privileged courtiers. This gradually achieved realization of the spiritual brotherhood of all men may have been furthered by the elevation of Amon, the originally parochial god of Thebes, to the status of a high god who was the common lord and benefactor of all Mankind up to the farthest limits of the sweep of Pharaoh's sceptre (for the elevation of Amon to this position by the Emperor Thothmes III see V. C (i) (d) 6 (δ), vol. v, pp. 530–1, and V. C (i) (d) 6 (δ), Annex, vol. v, pp. 653–4 and 695, above). Was the brotherhood of Mankind through the common fatherhood—or at any rate the common providence—of God one of the special tenets of the worship of Amon-Re from Thothmes III's time onwards? And was this mystery successively and independently learnt from the lips of Amon's priests by Ikhnaton in the fourteenth and by Alexander in the fourth century B.C.?

King himself he will be at the King's elbow both in peace and in war (συμβιώσεται βασιλεῖ καὶ στρατεύσεται μετὰ βασιλέως).'[1]

And more than a century before these words were written by Chrysippus the policy which they formulate had been put into action by Plato.

No less than three times in his life Plato voluntarily, though reluctantly, emerged from his Attic retreat and crossed the sea to Syracuse in the hope of converting a Sicilian despot to an Athenian philosopher's conception of a prince's duty. In his encounter, on his first visit, with the hard-bitten Dionysius I, Plato's expectations may not have been great; but his hopes rose higher when the founder of the second dynasty of Syracusan despots was succeeded by a son who had been saved by his father's criminal success in wading through slaughter to a throne from the horrid necessity of gaining his own throne by so unpropitious a method. Plato's failure to make a philosopher-king out of Dionysius II was the great practical disappointment of Plato's life. Yet the unexpected barrenness of his second and third visits to Syracuse was partially redressed by the unexpected fruitfulness of the first; for the shaft which, on that first campaign, the Attic archer had shot into the Sicilian air had smitten the heart of a statesman who became the brother-in-law of each of the Dionysii in turn besides being the uncle of the younger of them. 'When', Plato wrote long afterwards in retrospect, 'I conversed with Dio, who was then still quite a young man, and instructed him in my notions of the principles of ethics as a practical ideal for him to act upon, I suppose I had no idea that, all unwittingly, I was really in some sense paving the way for a future overthrow of despotism.'[2] In the fullness of time Dio put down from his seat a nephew and brother-in-law who had refused to play that part of philosopher-king for which Plato had perhaps rather arbitrarily cast him; and, when Dio, installed in Dionysius's place, brought down upon himself the tragic verdict of being *capax imperii nisi imperasset*,[3] the enterprise which had proved too much for this self-consciously enlightened Syracusan prince was executed by the un-self-consciously public-spirited Corinthian freeman Timoleon.[4]

Plato's relation to Dio is the classic example of the influence of the philosopher behind the throne in a situation in which the monarch and his mentor are in immediate personal contact. In later acts of the Hellenic 'Time of Troubles' this situation is

---

1 Chrysippus: *De Vitis*, Book I, quoted by Plutarch: *De Stoicorum Repugnantiis*, chap. 20.

2 Plato's Letters, No. 7, 327 A.

3 Tacitus: *Histories*, Book I, chap. 49.

4 See IV. C (iii) (*c*) 2 (β), Annex I, vol. iv, pp. 589–91, above.

reproduced in the relation of the Borysthenite[1] Stoic philosopher
Sphaerus to the Spartan King Cleomenes III,[2] and in the relation
of the Cumaean Stoic philosopher Blossius to the Roman states-
man Tiberius Gracchus and to the Pergamene revolutionary
Aristonicus.[3] In the history of the Hindu World the acts of the
Emperor Akbar—the founder of a Mughal Rāj which served as a
Hindu universal state—reflect the results of the Emperor's personal
converse with a number of diverse spiritual advisers: Muslim,
Zoroastrian, Christian, and Jain.[4] In the history of the Western
World in its so-called 'modern' chapter we can likewise discern in
the acts of a Frederick and a Catherine and a Joseph the results
of the personal intercourse between these 'enlightened' Hohenzol-
lern and Muscovite and Hapsburg monarchs and the contemporary
French philosophers from Voltaire downwards.[5]

Such direct personal relations are no doubt the most effective;
but it is not impossible for a philosopher-mentor to find ways and
means of exerting his influence on less onerous terms. For example, when the founder of the Stoic school was besought by the
restorer of the Macedonian monarchy to come over into Macedonia and help him,[6] Zeno did not choose to leave his Attic
cloister in order to hang about a Pellan court, but sent his disciples
Persaeus and Philonides as his proxies.[7] Nor is it only on princes

---

[1] Sphaerus was a Borysthenite according to Plutarch (*Lives of Agis and Cleomenes*, chap. 23), but a Bosporan [i.e. a native of the Cimmerian, not the Thracian, Bosporus?] according to Diogenes Laertius (*Lives of the Philosophers*, Book VII, chap. 177).

[2] Since, according to Plutarch, op. cit., loc. cit., Sphaerus's sojourn at Sparta, in the course of which the future king imbibed the philosopher's teaching, had already begun when Cleomenes was still a child, it may be conjectured that Sphaerus's influence was a factor in the political career not only of Cleomenes but also of the Agiad saviour-king's Eurypontid predecessor and ensample Agis IV (see Bidez, J.: *La Cité du Monde et la Cité du Soleil chez les Stoïciens* (Paris 1932, Les Belles Lettres), p. 38).

[3] See V. C (i) (c) 2, vol. v, pp. 179–80, above.

[4] For Akbar's mentors, and for this eclectically minded monarch's attempt to found a new 'fancy religion' of his own by combining some of the elements of their respective doctrines, see V. C (i) (d) 6 (δ), Annex, vol. v, pp. 699–704, above.

[5] The eighteenth-century French philosophers were admittedly inspired by seven-teenth-century English forerunners; the writings of these English philosophers had been an academic response to the political challenge of a conflict between Crown and Parlia-ment; and the English revolutions of the seventeenth century had been precipitated by a previous impact of Italian institutions and techniques and ideas upon Transalpine Europe (for the political reaction that was evoked, in England, by the enhancement of the royal power through an infusion of Italian efficiency, see III. C (ii) (b), vol. iii, pp. 357–63, above).

[6] For Antigonus's bent towards philosophy see V. C (i) (c) 2, vol. v, p. 132, above, and Tarn, W. W.: *Antigonus Gonatas* (Oxford 1913, Clarendon Press), chap. 8: 'Antigonus and his Circle.'

[7] Though Persaeus was Zeno's favourite disciple (and incidentally his fellow country-man), he does not appear to have proved himself an altogether satisfactory substitute for the Master himself; and he had an unfortunate end after his Macedonian pupil-patron had eventually disposed of him by making him exchange a mentor's job for a viceroy's. Antigonus placed Persaeus in command of the Macedonian garrison of Corinth; and here, in 243 B.C., the philosopher-in-harness allowed himself to be taken by surprise by the soldier-statesman-in-embryo Aratus of Sicyon. Thus Zeno's experiment in playing mentor to a prince at second hand did not turn out very well; and the philosopher who did have an effect upon King Antigonus Gonatas' life and work was neither Zeno's disciple nor Zeno himself but Bion the Borysthenite—a free lance who atoned for his

who are his own contemporaries that a philosopher-mentor is able to produce an effect at second hand. For, when the Stoic emperor-philosopher Marcus Aurelius (*vivebat* A.D. 121–80) mentions, in the roll-call of his spiritual creditors,[1] the names of two Stoic philosophers—Sextus of Chaeronea and Quintus Junius Rusticus—who had personally instructed him in his youth, he is citing only the last of many links in a golden chain of Stoic mentors of Roman statesmen which can be traced back without a break, through a quarter of a millennium and more, from the age of Marcus and Rusticus to the age of Scipio Aemilianus (*vivebat circa* 185–129 B.C.) and Panaetius.

This Rhodian Stoic Father of the second century B.C., who had sat, with Blossius, at the feet of Antipater of Tarsus, was the mentor of Marcus in a deeper sense than either Rusticus or Sextus. For, though the two Stoic tutors of the future emperor may have been the most celebrated representatives of their school in their day, they would never have had an opportunity to do their work had it not been for their distant Rhodian predecessor who had planted the first shoots of Stoicism in Roman soil. And the chain of philosopher-mentors that runs back from Rusticus to Panaetius has its parallel in the chain of statesmen-pupils that can be traced from Marcus through Domitian's victims Herennius Senecio and Arulenus Rusticus and Vespasian's victim Helvidius Priscus and Nero's victims Seneca and Thrasea Paetus and Claudius's victim Caecina Paetus and Caecina's wife Arria, who showed her husband how to die, till we come to Cato Minor—the Roman Stoic proto-martyr[2]—and finally to Panaetius's own pupil Gaius Laelius Sapiens, a contemporary of Scipio Aemilianus and Tiberius Gracchus who managed to live into the early years of the Roman century of revolution (133–31 B.C.) without allowing himself to be robbed of his sweetness and serenity.

The chain of Stoic mentors that runs back to Panaetius from the Emperor Marcus's tutors Rusticus and Sextus has a Neoplatonic parallel. Maximus of Ephesus (*vivebat circa* A.D. 300–71), who was the personal instructor of the Emperor Julian (*vivebat* A.D. 331–63), was himself a disciple of Aedesius, who had been in his day the favourite disciple of Iamblichus; and the nonsense which

disreputability by taking the trouble to answer in person the philosophically inclined prince's call. According to a modern Western scholar (Tarn, op. cit., p. 235),

'It is probable that Bion's relations with Antigonus were very much closer than written tradition gives us any idea of. Among the fragmentary notices that remain relative to the two men or to their sayings, the parallels in language are too frequent and curious to be accidental.'

In support of this view, Tarn (op. cit., p. 236, footnote 47) quotes six examples.
1 This roll-call occupies the first book of Marcus's *Meditations*.
2 For Cato Minor and the influence of his example on later generations of Roman aristocrats see V. C (i) (d) 1, vol. v, p. 390, and V. C (i) (d) 3, vol. v, p. 405, above.

Iamblichus had imported into the philosophy of Porphyry and Plotinus had been principally inspired by a work from the pen of a Babylonian medicine-man (a namesake of the Emperor Julian's) who had practised his trade on Hellenic ground in the reign of Marcus Aurelius.[1] This Julian the medicine-man stands to Julian the Emperor as the philosopher Panaetius stands to the Emperor Marcus.

There are also cases of a philosopher exerting an influence upon a prince or statesman across a gulf of time without any chain of intermediaries. For example, Gaius Gracchus was manifestly influenced by the ideas of his elder brother Tiberius's mentor Blossius[2]—though it is certain that Blossius died seven years before the year of Gaius's first tribunate,[3] and uncertain whether Gaius had been in personal touch with Blossius even in the years before the date of the philosopher's flight from Italy after the murder of Tiberius.[4] Timoleon, again, can hardly have been unaffected by the ideas of his precursor Dio's mentor Plato[5] when he accepted the mission of sailing to Syracuse in Dio's wake—though by the year in which Timoleon set sail Plato had been some three years dead,[6] and there is no record of any personal intercourse between the Attic philosopher and the Corinthian statesman during Plato's lifetime. The Indic philosopher Siddhārtha Gautama exerted his influence upon the Mauryan Emperor Açoka after a Time-interval of more than two centuries, if the Buddha died in 487 B.C. and Açoka came to the throne in 273 B.C. But perhaps the most extraordinary example of this exertion of influence at long range is Confucius's effect upon the minds and lives of the two Manchu emperors K'ang Hsi and Ch'ien Lung.

The first of these two Confucian princes did not begin to reign until more than two thousand years had passed since his mentor's death; the Far Eastern Society into which K'ang Hsi was born was sundered from the Sinic Society, in whose bosom Confucius himself had lived and taught, by a social interregnum which deepened the gulf dug by Time; and K'ang Hsi himself was not

---

[1] For the abortive Neoplatonic Church which Iamblichus tried to found and Julian to establish see V. C (i) (d) 6 (δ), vol. v, pp. 565–7, and V. C (i) (d) 6 (δ), Annex, vol. v, pp. 680–3, above. For the Emperor Julian's debt to the Babylonian medicine-man of the same name see V. C (i) (d) 6 (δ), Annex, vol. v, p. 680, footnote 3, above.

[2] For Blossius's relation to Tiberius Gracchus and to Aristonicus see V. C (i) (c) 2, vol. v, pp. 179–80, above.

[3] Gaius Gracchus was Tribune of the Plebs for the first time in 123 B.C.; Blossius had committed suicide after the defeat of Aristonicus in 130 B.C.

[4] Blossius appears to have fled from Italy to Pergamum in 132 B.C., and it was only in this year that Gaius Gracchus returned to Italy from Spain.

[5] For Plato's general idea of the right relation between philosophy and politics see the passage quoted from *The Republic* on p. 242, above. For Dio's spiritual debt to Plato, as this was estimated by Plato himself, see Plato's Seventh Letter, *passim*.

[6] Timoleon sailed in 344 B.C.; Plato had died in 347 B.C.

even a native-born son of the Far Eastern Civilization, but was a cultural convert from a horde of recently installed barbarian conquerors. The influence of Confucius upon K'ang Hsi was a brilliant posthumous consolation prize for the disappointment, in Confucius's own lifetime, of the hopes of a Sinic sage whose offers of service had been rejected by the Sinic princes of the day;[1] and this posthumous reversal of fortune was as ironic as it was extreme, for, in offering h.mself in the role of mentor, the Sinic sage had not just been making a half-hearted compromise with an importunate conscience in the manner of his Hellenic and Indic counterparts. In Confucius's eyes the role which Confucius never succeeded in playing effectively until long after his death was no grudgingly paid debt to the ineradicable human nature of the social animal under the sage's cloak: it was for him the only role in which a philosopher could properly follow his spiritual calling.[2]

Our survey of philosopher-mentors has revealed some notable instances of successful education. The state of the Indic World under the rule of Gautama's pupil Açoka and that of the Hellenïc World under the rule of Panaetius's pupil Marcus bear out Plato's contention[3] 'that social life is happiest and most harmonious where those who have to rule are the last people who would choose to be rulers'. And there are other enlightened monarchs who, though they may not have quite lived up to that standard, have at any rate testified to the truth. Antigonus Gonatas, for example, 'when he saw his son behaving all too violently and insolently towards his subjects, said to him "Don't you know, my boy, that our monarchy is only a glorified slavery?" '[4] 'Frederick William called himself "the field marshal and finance minister of the King of Prussia", Frederick the Great "the first servant of the State".'[5] Yet, in spite of a few successes such as these, our general conclusion will be that the device of serving Humanity through the soul of a king—as a ventriloquist talks to his audience through the mouth of his puppet—is not a satisfactory solution of the philosopher's personal problem of paying his moral debt to Society without abandoning his own precious Detachment.

We observe that a Dionysius II, who had been born and brought

---

[1] Confucius's career of contemporary failure and posthumous success has been cited as an example of Withdrawal-and-Return in III. C (ii) (b), vol. iii, pp. 328–30, above.

[2] In Confucius's view the ultimate purpose of self-cultivation, which was the Superior Person's first duty, was the purification of his neighbour and of the entire community. Confucius thought of himself, not as a happily detached sage, but as an unfortunately unemployed man of action (see Maspéro, H.: *La Chine Antique* (Paris 1927, Boccard), pp. 466–7 and 543).

[3] In *Respublica* 520 D, quoted in this Study already in III. C (ii) (b), vol. iii, p. 252, above.   [4] Aelian: *Variae Historiae*, Book II, chap. 20.

[5] Bruford, W. H.: *Germany in the Eighteenth Century* (Cambridge 1935, University Press), p. 28.

up in the purple, turned out to be as unpromising a subject for Plato's educative efforts as a Dionysius I who had had to seize his power by force; and neither of the two Dionysii is so discouraging a case for the experimental philosopher as their kinsman Dio; for Dio had the double advantage of possessing an aptitude for philosophy without being either a reigning despot or a despot's heir apparent; yet his mere proximity to a throne had spoilt Dio to a degree which made it almost a foregone conclusion that he would come to grief in the high-minded enterprise on which he eventually embarked. Dio aspired to transfigure his native city-state of Syracuse into Plato's ideal commonwealth by appearing in the role, not of saviour-despot, but of saviour-liberator; but the sequel to his *coup* of ejecting his despot-nephew Dionysius was tragically ironic. The would-be liberator lived to commit a tyrant's crimes before dying a tyrant's death which left the coast clear for his evicted kinsman to come back again. And the sequels to the labours of other philosopher-kings and philosopher-statesmen have been equally disappointing. Though Timoleon was able to execute Dio's unfulfilled design, even Timoleon's success was no more than ephemeral. By the date of the Corinthian elder-statesman's death at Syracuse, Agathocles had already been born at Thermae to become a greater scourge to the Siceliots than either of the Dionysii. The sequel to the career of Sphaerus's pupil Cleomenes was the tyranny of Nabis and the subsequent collapse of the Lacedaemonian body politic. The sequel to the career of Blossius's pupil Tiberius Gracchus was a century of revolution and civil war which tore the Roman body politic to pieces and was only brought to an end at the price of acquiescence in a permanent dictatorship. The sequel to the philosophic eclecticism of Akbar was the religious bigotry of Awrangzīb. The West European enlightenment which seeped through philosophical channels into Central and East European courts in the eighteenth century brought in its trail an infection of the West European political virus of Nationalism which first attacked the *bourgeoisie* and is now ravaging the masses. Bion's pupil Antigonus Gonatas was succeeded in due course by a Philip V, whose personal folly undid the political results of Gonatas' personal self-discipline. Panaetius's pupil Marcus deliberately broke with an admirable custom of adoption, which had been inaugurated by Nerva, in order to bequeath the Principate to his own physical offspring in the person of Commodus! The Babylonian medicine-man's pupil and namesake Julian taught Theodosius how to turn a Neoplatonist emperor's fanaticism to a Christian fanatic's account. The personal holiness of Gautama's pupil Açoka did not save the Mauryan

Empire from collapsing at a blow from the fist of the usurper Pushyamitra. And in the Far Eastern World the eighteenth-century splendour of the reign of Confucius's pupil Ch'ien Lung was followed, within little more than forty years from the death of this second Manchu philosopher-emperor, by an age of disasters and humiliations which was opened by the first salvo of British naval ordnance in 'the Opium War' and which was not yet in sight of its end in a year which was the ninety-eighth anniversary of that sinister date.

Nor is the picture different when we turn from these kings who have been made philosophers by force of example to those who have been born philosophers without requiring mentors. Ikhnaton's vision of peace through fraternity was marred, even before the Egyptiac visionary's death, by the beginning of the break-up of 'the New Empire'; and in the sequel even the homelands of the Egyptiac Society in the Nile Valley were only saved from barbarian clutches by the rude hands of soldier-emperors who unceremoniously thrust their way on to a throne which Ikhnaton and his like were too delicate to hold. As for Alexander's vision of the same ideal goal of human endeavours, it did, as we have seen,[1] continue to haunt the Hellenic World thereafter. But the immediate sequel to Alexander's career was not Augustus's partially successful translation of a Macedonian dream into a Roman reality. The immediate sequel was the warfare of diadochi and epigoni who contended with one another, for two live-long generations, over the spoils of the Achaemenian Empire in campaigns that ravaged the domains of no less than five civilizations.[2] The practical effect of Alexander's career was thus the very opposite of the philosophic war-lord's intentions. So far from living to establish the ideal *Pax Oecumenica* of which he dreamed, he merely lived to destroy an actual *Pax Achaemenia* which he only learnt to appreciate at its proper worth after he had dealt it its death-blow.[3]

Thus an empirical survey which registered a certain amount of

---

[1] In V. C (i) (d) 7, pp. 6–11, above.

[2] The Hellenic, Syriac, Egyptiac, Babylonic, and Indic worlds were all involved in the sordid struggles of the Macedonian *conquistadores*.

[3] For Alexander's tardy appreciation of Persian virtues see V. C (i) (c) 1, vol. v, pp. 51–2, and V. C (i) (c) 7, in the present volume, p. 9, above. This feat of insight bears witness both to the sublimity of Alexander's genius and to the profundity of his failure. In his personal attitude towards an imperial people with whom he had become acquainted only as their conqueror and supplanter, Alexander was able to rise above a Hellenic prejudice which had been part and parcel of the Hellenic tradition throughout the century and a half that had passed since the failure of Xerxes' attempt to conquer European Greece, and which, among the Hellenes of Alexander's own generation and entourage, had merely been confirmed and accentuated as a result of Alexander's military victories. Yet this extraordinary spiritual achievement of Alexander's, which puts all his military glory into the shade, was the Dead-Sea fruit of an act of wanton destruction which it proved impossible for Alexander to repair, just because he was almost the only Hellene of this day who learnt to appreciate the worth of the thing that had been destroyed by Alexander's own military prowess.

success at the first assay now reveals an overwhelming preponderance of failure when the investigation is pursued, beyond the first
chapter, to the end of the story. The philosopher-king—be he a
philosopher born or the receptive pupil of a philosopher-mentor—
turns out, after all, to be incapable of saving his fellow men from
the shipwreck of a disintegrating society. To this extent the facts
speak for themselves; but we have still to ask whether they also
provide their own explanation. And, if we consult them again with
this question in mind, we shall again find that they duly yield an
answer.

This answer is indeed implicit in the passage of *The Republic* in
which Plato introduces on to his stage the figure of the prince who
is a born philosopher. After putting forward his postulate that,
sometime and somewhere, at any rate one such born philosopher-
prince will live to ascend his father's throne and will there make it
his business to translate his own philosophical principles into
political practice,[1] Plato eagerly jumps to the conclusion that
'a single one such ruler would suffice—if he could count on the
consent of the governed (πόλιν ἔχων πειθομένην)—to carry out in
full a programme that looks quite impracticable under existing
conditions'. And the conductor of the argument then goes on to
explain the grounds of his optimism. 'Supposing', he continues,
'that a ruler were to enact our ideal laws and introduce our ideal
social conventions, it would assuredly not be beyond the bounds
of possibility that his subjects should consent to act in accordance
with their ruler's wishes.'[2]

These final propositions are manifestly essential to the success
of Plato's scheme for making a philosopher's Utopia work out 'in
real life'; but they are no less manifestly dependent upon an
enlistment of the faculty of mimesis; and at earlier points in this
Study[3] we have observed that this resort to a kind of social drill—
with the object of bringing and keeping an uncreative rank-and-
file abreast of a creative leader—is a short cut which is apt to bring
those who take it to destruction instead of expediting their journey
towards their goal. The inclusion of any element of coercion—
mental or physical—in the social strategy of the philosopher-king
would therefore perhaps suffice in itself to account for his failure
to bring to pass the salvation which he professes to offer; and, if
we examine his strategy more closely from this standpoint, we
shall find that his use of coercion is particularly gross. For, though
Plato is at pains to give the philosopher-king's government the

---

[1] For this postulate of Plato's see the present chapter, p. 245, above.
[2] Plato: *Respublica*, 502 A–B.
[3] In III. C (ii) (a), vol. iii, pp. 245–8, and IV. C (iii) (a), vol. iv, pp. 119–33, above.

benefit of the consent of the governed, it is evident that there would be no purpose in the philosopher's surprising personal union with a potentate who is to be an absolute monarch unless the despot's power of physical coercion is to be held in readiness for use in case of necessity; and the case in point is as likely to arise as it is obvious to foresee.

'The nature of the peoples is inconstant, and it is easy to persuade them of a thing, but difficult to hold them to that persuasion. Accordingly it is expedient to be so equipped that, when their belief gives out, one will have it in one's power to make them believe by force.'[1]

In these wholesomely brutal words Machiavelli brings out a sinister feature in the strategy of the philosopher-king which Plato almost disingenuously slurs over. If ever the philosopher-king finds himself at a point at which he is no longer able to gain his end by the exercise of charm or bluff, he will throw away his copy-book of moral maxims and proceed to enforce his will by laying about him with a sword which he took care not to lay aside when he exchanged his royal robe for a philosopher's mantle. Even a Marcus reluctantly resorted to this *ultima ratio regum*, and that not only against Parthian and Marcomannian fighting-men beyond the frontier, but also against unarmed and unresisting Christians in the interior.[2] Such a denouement is a scandal which brings the philosopher-king's whole profession into disrepute; for the mantle is an even more deceitful cloak than the robe for concealing a lethal weapon. Once again we are presented with the shocking spectacle of Orpheus changing into a drill-sergeant;[3] and in this case the simile is a literal description of the fact; for the king who drops the philosopher's mask is a drill-sergeant whose instruments are not the psychological devices of 'personal magnetism' and 'the confidence trick', but the physical weapons of the cat-o'-nine-tails and the firing-squad.

If a flagrant resort to coercion thus turns out to be the false step that explains the failure of the philosopher-king when he is a philosopher born, the same explanation holds good *a fortiori* when the philosopher-king is merely the royal pupil of an academic mentor. In proof of this it will be sufficient to take note of Plato's analysis of his own motives for accepting the invitation to revisit Sicily which he received, on Dio's initiative, from the Younger Dionysius after the accession of that prince to his father's throne at Syracuse.

'After [the death of the Elder Dionysius] Dio came to think that perhaps he might not for ever remain solitary in holding the views which

---

[1] Machiavelli, Niccolò: *Il Principe*, chap. 6, quoted already in V. C (i) (*d*) 1, vol. v, p. 389, footnote 3, above.   [2] See p. 202, footnote 1, above.
[3] For this simile see IV. C (iii) (*a*), vol. iv, p. 123, above.

he himself had acquired as a result of the proper instruction [imparted to him by Plato during the Athenian philosopher's earlier visit to Syracuse]. He noticed, from observation, that the same views were taking root in other minds too—not in many, but any way in some; he thought that, with Heaven's help, [the Younger] Dionysius might perhaps come to be numbered among these converts; and, if anything like that did happen, this in turn, as Dio saw it, would raise his own life, and the life of the whole Syracusan community, to a hardly imaginable degree of felicity. Further, Dio thought it essential that at all costs I should come to Syracuse post-haste to collaborate with him in all this. He had not forgotten our previous intercourse with one another and how effectively this had stimulated in him a passion to live the life that was finest and best. If he could now achieve the same result in Dionysius, which was what he had set himself to do, then he had great hopes of being able to make the life of happiness and truth into a general and permanent institution of the country, without the bloodshed and the loss of life and the other evils that have come to pass in the event.

'Having come to these conclusions—which were right—Dio persuaded Dionysius to send me an invitation, and at the same time he sent a personal message of his own, begging me to come post-haste at all costs, before others would have time to gain Dionysius's ear and divert him into some other way of life than the best way. At the risk of prolixity I shall recapitulate the considerations with which Dio supported his plea. "What opportunities", he asked, "are we to wait for that could be more favourable than those which have now been presented by a heaven-sent piece of good fortune?" And he went on to dwell, in detail, upon the extent of the Dionysian dominions in Italy and Sicily, and upon his (Dio's) own power in the state; upon Dionysius's youth and the intensity of his passion for an education in philosophy; upon the ripeness of his (Dio's) own nephews and other intimate friends for conversion to the doctrine and the way of life which I consistently preached; and upon the strength of the influence which they would have on Dionysius, in helping to convert him along with them. "And so (he concluded) now, if ever, is the moment for a realization of all our hopes of a personal union between philosophy and political power[1] in a state of large calibre."

'These—with many others in the same strain—were the arguments with which Dio sought to prevail upon me. As regards my own opinion, it was divided between an anxiety on the score of how things might go with the young people—considering how volatile are the passions of youth and how often they react by "going into reverse"—and a confidence in the character of Dio, which was, I knew, stable by nature and was now also fortified by the comparative maturity of his age. So I long debated and hesitated whether I should go, as I was asked, or what I should do, till in the end I inclined to the opinion that, if ever a philosopher was to set himself to realize his ideas about legislation and government,

[1] See the passage from *The Republic*, 473 C–D, that has been quoted in Part III. A, vol. iii, p. 93, and again in the present chapter and volume, p. 242, above.—A.J.T.

this was just the occasion for making that experiment, since I now had only to convince one person thoroughly and at this one stroke I should have achieved a whole world of good.

'These were the considerations that led me to take the bolder course and set out from home, not at all in the spirit with which some people have credited me, but under a most powerful moral compulsion not to lose my own self-respect, as I was in danger of losing it if I were to be convicted, in my own judgement, of being simply nothing but a mere voice—a fellow who would never take action, not even a hand's turn, if he could help it. I was also afraid of waking up to find that I had proved false, among other things, to my friendship with my former host, Dio, and this at a time when he was really in no little danger. Suppose that some misfortune were to overtake him and he were to be banished by Dionysius and his other enemies and then arrive at my door as a fugitive and interrogate me like this: "Plato, I come to you as an exile, not asking for, or wanting, foot and horse for fighting my enemies, but wanting and asking for those persuasive arguments with which you, of all men, as I know, have the ability to arouse in young men an enthusiasm for goodness and righteousness and, in the same act, to bring them into friendship and good-fellowship with one another, whenever occasion arises. It is because I have been left in want of this assistance on your part that I have now had to leave Syracuse and appear here and now on your door-step. But it is not this plight of mine that is the worst reproach to you; for what about your obligations to Philosophy? Are you not always singing her praises and complaining that she is without honour among the rest of Mankind? Yet hasn't she, like me, now been betrayed as far as it has lain with you? If we had happened to be living at Megara, no doubt you would have come to my aid in the cause in which I was invoking your help, on pain, if you had hung back, of feeling yourself the vilest creature on Earth. And now, [when I have called you to Syracuse,] do you really think that you could plead the length of the journey and the immensity of the voyage and the fatigue as a valid defence against an imputation of cowardice? You know very well that you would not have a leg to stand on!"

'If I had had to meet this attack, what plausible answer would there have been for me to make? Just none at all. And so I came for the most unimpeachable of reasons that mortal man could ever have. And on this account I left my own occupations, which were by no means despicable, and put myself under a tyranny which might well be thought unbecoming both to my teaching and to myself. In coming in spite of all this, I acquitted myself of my duty to Zeus Xenios and cleared myself of all reproach on the part of Philosophy—who would have been put to shame in my person if, through defect of hardihood and courage, I had got myself into real disgrace.'[1]

If this analytical reminiscence is a true account of the workings of Plato's mind at the time when Dionysius's invitation was awaiting

---

[1] Plato, Letter No. 7, 327 B–329 B.

Plato's answer, it tells us that Plato's mission was doomed *a priori* to failure; for neither of the two principal considerations that he here attributes to himself can bear examination. We here see the philosopher not only yielding to the temptation to exploit the use of the despot's material power as a short cut to the translation of a Utopia into 'real life', but even being influenced by a self-regarding feeling which looks less like a genuine prick of conscience than like a twinge of the scholar's painful sense of inferiority to the man of action; and, whether we adopt the more or the less charitable of these two alternative interpretations, we are bound to discern in either of them a latent lack of confidence in the policy of Detachment on which, *ex hypothesi*, the philosopher has staked his personal hope of salvation.

In fact, the philosopher-king is doomed to fail because he is attempting to unite two contradictory natures in a single person. The philosopher stultifies himself by trespassing on the king's field of ruthless action, while conversely the king stultifies himself by trespassing on the philosopher's field of loveless and pitiless contemplation.[1] Like the saviour with the 'time-machine', the philosopher-king is driven, sooner or later, into proclaiming his own failure by drawing a weapon which convicts him of being a saviour with the sword in disguise. If the sword spells self-defeat and the 'time-machine' self-deception, the philosopher's mantle and the prince's mask are emblems of hypocrisy; and, since 'hypocrite' and 'saviour' are incompatible roles, our search for a genuine saviour must be carried further.

The God Incarnate in a Man.

We have now examined three different epiphanies of the creative genius who is born into a disintegrating society and who bends his powers and energies to the task of coping with the challenge of social disintegration by finding and making some effective response. We have reviewed in turn the would-be saviour *of* Society who puts his trust in the sword, and the would-be saviours *from* Society whose respective instruments are the 'time-machine' and the philosopher-king. And in each case we have found that the vaunted way of salvation leads nowhere but to the brow of a precipice. There is no salvation in the sword. It proves impossible after all, as might have been expected *a priori*, to make a deadly weapon do the very opposite of the work for which it has been designedly forged. However cunning the hand that wields it, and

---

[1] For this attitude of mind, which in Greek is called θεωρία, see III. C (ii) (b), vol. iii, p. 253, and V. C (i) (d) 10, in the present volume, pp. 144–8, above.

however well-meaning the will that governs the hand, the sword can neither be compelled to bring salvation nor prevented from dealing the destruction which it is its nature to bring to pass. The would-be saviour with the sword is self-condemned to self-defeat; and in exposing him for the failure that he is we have also exposed his two competitors; for we have found that both the would-be saviour with the 'time-machine' and the sage who operates as the mentor of a philosopher-king are apt, at the critical moment, to drop their pretentious instruments and take to the old-fashioned killing-tool. We have thus reduced our three ostensibly diverse types of would-be saviour to the single figure of a man with a sword. Whether the weapon happens at the moment to be drawn or sheathed or cloaked, it is the only means of salvation which the man has to offer in the last resort.

What conclusion are we to draw from this series of disillusionments? Do they signify that any and every attempt to find and bring salvation is doomed to end in destruction if the would-be saviour is merely a human being? Let us remind ourselves of the context of the classic statement of the truth which we have been verifying empirically in this chapter. 'All they that take the sword shall perish with the sword' are the words of a saviour who gives this as his reason for commanding one of his followers to sheathe again a sword which this henchman has just drawn and used. In thus taking to the sword at the critical moment, the henchman has done his best according to his present lights.[1] He has taken his own life in his hands for the sake of playing the man on his Master's behalf. But the Master swiftly and sternly rejects an offer of self-sacrifice that is made in this militant form. So far from following up this first blow with a general counter-offensive in the fashion of Judas Maccabaeus[2] or Ismā'īl Shāh Safawī[3] or Guru Govind Singh,[4] Jesus of Nazareth first heals the wound that Peter's sword has already inflicted,[5] and then delivers his own person up to suffer the last extremes of insult and torment.

Nor is Jesus moved to choose this agonizing alternative by any fear that, if he did take to the sword, he might be courting a military defeat. 'Thinkest thou', he says to Peter, 'that I cannot now pray to my Father, and he shall presently give me more than twelve legions of angels?'[6] And to Pilate he says: 'If my kingdom were

---

[1] For Peter's conversion from a futurist's militancy to the gentleness of a soul which has grasped the meaning of the Transfiguration see V. C (i) (d) 1, vol. v, pp. 392–3, above.
[2] See V. C (i) (c) 2, vol. v, p. 68, and V. C (i) (d) 6 (δ), Annex, vol. v, pp. 657–9, above.
[3] See I. C (i) (b), Annex I, vol. i, pp. 366–88, and V. C (i) (d) 6 (δ), Annex, vol. v, pp. 661–5, above.
[4] See V. C (i) (d) 6 (δ), Annex, vol. v, pp. 665–8, above.
[5] Luke xxii. 51.
[6] Matt. xxvi. 53.

of this world, then would my servants fight, that I should not be delivered to the Jews; but now is my kingdom not from hence.'[1] Jesus's motive for refusing to take to the sword is thus not any practical calculation that, in the particular circumstances, his own force is no match for his adversaries'. He believes that, if he did take to the sword, he could be certain of winning all the victory that swordsmanship can procure. Yet, believing this, he still refuses to use the weapon. Rather than conquer with the sword he will die on the Cross.

In choosing this alternative in the hour of crisis, Jesus is breaking right away from the conventional line of action which has been taken by the other would-be saviours whose conduct we have studied. What inspires the Nazarene saviour to take this tremendous new departure? We may answer this question by asking, in turn, what distinguishes him from the saviours who have refuted their own pretensions by turning into swordsmen. The answer is that these were men who knew themselves to be no more than human, whereas Jesus was a man who believed himself to be the Son of God.[2] Are we to conclude that 'salvation belongeth unto the Lord',[3] and that, without being in some sense divine, a would-be saviour of Mankind will always be impotent to execute his mission in act and deed?[4] Now that we have weighed and found wanting those *soi-disant* saviours who have avowedly been mere men, let us turn, as our last recourse, to the saviours who have presented themselves as gods.

To pass in review a procession of saviour-gods, with an eye to appraising their claims to be what they profess to be and to do what they profess to do, is perhaps an unprecedentedly presumptuous application of our habitual method of empirical study. And, if we are to venture upon the attempt, it may be easiest to begin with those claimants whose performance of the saviour-god's part has been the most perfunctory. Let us start with the *deus ex machina* and try to ascend from this possibly infra-human level towards the ineffable height of the *deus cruci fixus*. If dying on the Cross is the utmost extreme to which it is possible for a man to go in testifying to the truth of his claim to divinity, appearing upon the stage is perhaps the least trouble that an acknowledged god can decently take in support of a claim to be also a saviour.

On the Attic stage in the century which saw the breakdown of

---

[1] John xviii. 36.
[2] For the association between the revelation of Jesus's divinity and the announcement of his Passion see V. C (i) (*d*) 11, p. 165, with footnote 3, above.   [3] Ps. iii. 8.
[4] In V. C (i) (*d*) 9 (*γ*), pp. 124–32, above, we have already observed how this conclusion forces itself upon would-be saviours of the futurist school as the insistent lesson of their own repeated and cumulatively disastrous failures to achieve their aim by their own method.

the Hellenic Civilization the *deus ex machina* was a veritable god-send to embarrassed playwrights who, in an already enlightened age, were still constrained by a tenacious convention to take their plots from the traditional corpus of Hellenic Mythology. If the action of the play had in consequence become caught, before its natural close, in some, humanly speaking, insoluble tangle of moral enormities or practical improbabilities, the author could extricate himself from the toils in which he had been involved on account of one of the conventions of his art by resorting to another of them. He could appeal to his stage-manager for help, and that obliging and resourceful technician would promptly wheel or hoist on to the stage a god out of the blue to effect a denouement. This is the role of Artemis in Euripides' *Hippolytus* and of Athena in the same poet's *Ion* and *Iphigeneia in Tauris*; and this trick of an Attic dramatist's trade has given scandal to scholars. The solutions of human problems that are propounded by these Olympian inter-ventionists neither convince the human mind nor appeal to the human heart. Was Euripides simply making use of a traditional convention of his art without troubling to question or criticize it? That can hardly be believed of a 'high-brow' who was patently a born sceptic, and whose natural scepticism had been vehemently stimulated by a catastrophic social experience in which it had been his fortune to participate. Or was he perhaps just professionally incompetent? Was he driven to resort to this clumsy trick by finding that he had tied himself into knots from which he could see no other way of escape? No, it is impossible to attribute such silliness to an intelligence which in all else is so dazzlingly clever. The puzzle seems to admit of only one solution. If our fifth-century Attic dramatist was not a 'low-brow' and not a fool, must he not have been a knave?

It has, in fact, been seriously suggested by one modern Western scholar that Euripides never brings on a *deus ex machina* without having his tongue in his cheek. According to Verrall, the sly Athenian rationalist has made this quaint traditional convention serve his own purposes by using it as a screen for sallies of irony and blasphemy upon which he could hardly have ventured with impunity if he had come out into the open. This screen is ideal in texture, since it is impervious to the hostile shafts of the poet's 'low-brow' adversaries while it is transparent to the knowing eyes of his sophisticated brother sceptics. In fact, the Euripidean use of the *deus ex machina* is an artistic *tour de force* which is a con-summate artist's *chef d'œuvre*.

'It is not too much to say that on the Euripidean stage whatever is said by a divinity is to be regarded, in general, as *ipso facto* discredited.

It is in all cases objectionable from the author's point of view, and almost always a lie. "By representing the deities he persuaded men that they did not exist."[1] . . . This character of mere theatrical and conventional pretence, contradictory to the sense of the part and transparent to the instructed reader, which Lucian[2] rightly attributes to the machine-gods of Euripides, is nowhere better illustrated than by the Athena of the [*Iphigeneia in Tauris*].'[3]

In this play the goddess ostensibly intervenes in order to stop a barbarian tyrant from catching and killing some distinguished Hellenic fugitives. In Verrall's opinion this 'happy ending' is not meant to be taken seriously. The spectator of the performance—or reader of the text—is intended to understand that the play is after all a tragedy. The fugitives are not really going to escape their persecutor's clutches; it is made perfectly clear, all along, that they have not a dog's chance; and, what is more, they do not morally deserve any miraculous reprieve; for it cannot be denied that they have brought this fate upon themselves by trying to practise a fraud upon their barbarian captor. Well, but is not Thoas a savage in fighting whom all is fair? Yes, but are not his captives Hellenes who should scruple to retort even to savagery with deceit?[4] And how did these representatives of Civilization come to place themselves in the false position for which they are going to pay so tragic a penalty? Were they not 'let in' by the very divinities who are now 'letting them down'? What possessed Orestes to think of stealing the holy image of the Tauric Artemis? Was it not Apollo who sped him on this knavish errand with the promise that, if he brought the stolen statue to Athens, he might hope to win as his reward a breathing-space from the cruel malady which had descended upon him as the penalty for the commission of a greater crime in obedience to a previous behest of the same divinity?[5]

The same scholar applies the same *apparatus criticus* to the interpretation of Euripides' *Ion*. Just as, according to Verrall, Iphigeneia and Orestes and Pylades and the chorus of Attic women are not miraculously reprieved by Athena but are tragically put to death—in the sight and hearing of any audience that

---

[1] Aristophanes: *Thesmophoriazusae*, ll. 450–1, apropos of Euripides.
[2] Lucian: *Zeus Tragœdus*, § 41.
[3] Verrall, A. W.: *Euripides the Rationalist* (Cambridge 1895, University Press), pp. 138 and 201.
[4] A modern Western reader who finds Euripides' *Iphigeneia in Tauris* too alien in its atmosphere for him to appreciate its point can see this 'ancient' drama replayed in 'modern' dress if he will attend a performance of William Archer's *The Green Goddess*. The colloquy between the Rajah and the *parlementaire ex machina* from the rescue squadron of the R.A.F. raises an issue—'What is Civilization?'—which is precisely the issue that arises (undeclared) between Thoas and Athena.
[5] Euripides: *Iphigeneia in Tauris*, ll. 85–92 and 1438–41 b.

has ears to hear and eyes to see—so, according to the same interpreter, the illegitimacy of Ion's birth and the unchastity of Creusa's
life before her marriage are tragically exposed through the thread-
bareness of the veil which Athena makes a pretence of throwing
over this pair of scandals.[1]

If there is any substance in Verrall's interpretation of Euripides'
plays, it would seem to be the practice of the Euripidean gods
first malevolently to inveigle the human *dramatis personae* into
putting themselves in the wrong, and then heartlessly to abandon
their dupes to a doom which ought in justice to overtake the
divine mischief-makers and not their human victims. But who,
'in the last analysis', are these odious divinities? Have they really
any independent existence in themselves? Are they not, rather,
the mythical 'externalizations' of psychological forces that 'in real
life' are immanent in the souls of the human actors? And is not
Euripides' esoteric theme the moral frailty of his own enlightened
countrymen and contemporaries?

On this showing, the *deus ex machina* is nothing but a caricature
of the human saviour with the 'time-machine', whose trick we have
seen through already.[2] In bringing this mountebank on to his
stage in the mask of a god and not of a mortal the playwright is
hinting to his audience that he intends this character to be taken
satirically in the spirit of Lewis Carroll, and not seriously in the
spirit of Mr. Wells.[3] The *deus ex machina* thus turns out to be a
joke—and that a bitter one. And the Olympians would hardly
be able to rehabilitate themselves even if they could convince us
that Verrall's theory is moonshine and that the Euripidean Artemis
and Athena are genuinely doing all that they are professing to do.
Morally it makes little difference whether a miraculously 'happy
ending' is a genuine miracle or a fake; for it cannot in either case
save a tragedy from being anything but what it is. What are we
to think of divine shepherds who neglect their duty towards their
human flocks until the wretched sheep have fallen into the deepest
moral errors and suffered the utmost spiritual agonies of which
their nature is capable? Are we to acquit them of blame just
because, at the thirteenth hour, they are kind enough to avert—
by an exercise of magical power which costs them no exertion—

[1] See A. W. Verrall's reconstruction of the epilogue to the *Ion*—as the author (according to the scholar) intends us to read it between the lines of the play—on pp. xx-xliii
of his edition and translation of *The Ion of Euripides* (Cambridge 1890, University
Press).

[2] In the present chapter, pp. 213-42, above.

[3] This moral depreciation of traditional divinities in the Hellenic World has its
analogue in the Indic World in the intellectual depreciation of the members of a kindred
pantheon (see V. C (i) (d) 7, pp. 19-20, above). In either case a human enlightenment
has taken the shine out of the gods to a degree at which their once radiant colours have
faded to a positively infra-human drabness.

some of the material consequences of moral disasters which, owing to their neglect, are now beyond repair? Divinities who behave like this cannot defend themselves by pleading that they are practising what has been preached to them by human philosophers;[1] for Epicurus, as we have seen,[2] had not the heart, when it came to the point, to lower his own conduct to the level of his doctrine; and, if a human sage knew better than to take a heartless philosophy seriously, even when he had invented it himself, his divine disciples, too, ought to know better *a fortiori*. Nor is the practice of tempering a habitual neglect with an occasional intervention morally salvaged by expanding the field of the *deus ex machina's* perfunctory performance from the stage of the theatre at Athens to the sum-total of the Universe, as Plato expands it in a myth which we have already quoted in another context.[3] The *deus ex machina* is indefensible in any field and on any hypothesis. And yet we need not be discouraged by this outcome of our first essay towards a survey of saviour-gods; for a train of ideas that starts with a conceit may end in a revelation. If 'Cloudcuckooland' can open human eyes to the Kingdom of Heaven,[4] it is not impossible that the *deus ex machina* may put us, if we persevere, on the track of another epiphany of God which 'unto the Greeks' was likewise 'foolishness'[5]—the figure of Christ on the Cross.

If putting in an appearance as a *deus ex machina* is the cheapest of all the ways in which a god can present himself to Man as his saviour, the next cheapest kind of epiphany is an avatar. At first sight, perhaps, it might seem to imply a considerably greater expenditure of divine time and trouble when a god condescends to exchange his proper form for a tenement of human flesh and to linger in this shape on Earth for the length of a human lifetime, instead of just for the duration of the last act of a play. On closer scrutiny, however, the apparent generosity dwindles. In point of time those three score years and ten must count for much the same as three minutes in the consciousness of an immortal who has Eternity to play with; and in point of trouble the divinity who is living through an avatar is apt, we shall find, to avail himself of his latent supernatural powers as soon as things look nasty. In Euripides' *Bacchae* Dionysus does not dream of allowing a deluded Pentheus to have his way with this divinity in human disguise. When it comes to the crisis the camouflaged god, with one wave of his magic wand, causes Pentheus' own womenkind to tear

[1] See V. C (i) (*d*) 10, pp. 144–6, above.
[2] See the present chapter, pp. 244–5, above.
[3] See the passages from Plato's *Politicus* that have been quoted in IV. C (i), vol. iv, pp. 26–7, above.
[4] See V. C (i) (*d*) 11, Annex I, below.   [5] 1 Cor. i. 23.

the wretched man to pieces in the blind frenzy of their orgiastic religious exaltation.

> The god recovered from the bout;
> The man it was that died.

In thus meanly drawing upon his reserves of superhuman potency, Dionysus is breaking the rules of his own game, like the human saviour with the 'time-machine' and the human philosopher-king when they drop their pretences and take to their swords. But the god is behaving more detestably than his human counterparts; for the crisis that moves him to make use of his hidden weapon is one that he himself has deliberately provoked. This god incarnate has kept his human assailant in ignorance of his superhuman bugbear's true nature in order to lure the silly fellow into a cruel trap. The show of patience and humility with which the mysterious stranger replies to the headstrong prince's ill-usage of him in the first act of the play is neither sincere nor disinterested. It is not Dionysus's intention to put Pentheus out of countenance, and so win him to repentance, by eventually revealing his own identity. His plan is to catch him out, and his temper is malicious.

Nor does Dionysus, in his sojourn among men, always make even so much as a pretence of being other than an Olympian. The best part of Dionysus's earthly career is devoted to a campaign of world-conquest in which the divine aggressor takes advantage of his supernatural powers in order to anticipate (or emulate), at his ease, the human exploits of Sesostris and Alexander. And woe betide the human potentate who ventures to offer resistance to the conqueror-god's triumphal progress. For the crime of successfully repelling this Olympian invader, Lycurgus King of the Êdônes pays the same dreadful penalty that is exacted from Pentheus King of Thebes for his refusal to acknowledge Dionysus's divinity. But the principal theatre of Dionysus's military prowess lies neither in Boeotia nor in Thrace. Dionysus, like Alexander, glories chiefly in being the conqueror of India; and on this Indian soil the Hellenic deity's brutal epiphany has its analogues in the avatars of Shiva and Vishnu.[1] As for Shiva, he is nothing but Destructiveness personified. And even Shiva's divine antithesis is capable of sinking to Dionysus's level when Vishnu goes on the war-path in the guise of a Krishna or a Rama.

If the avatar thus turns out to be morally almost as repulsive as the epiphany *ex machina*, the demigod, who presents himself next, is a decidedly more sympathetic figure. We have only to

---

[1] For certain likenesses and differences between these two Hindu worships and Christianity see V. C (i) (c) 2, vol. v, p. 138, and V. C (i) (d) 7, in the present volume, pp. 47–9, above.

cast our eye over the goodly company of these heroes: a Sumeric Gilgamesh; a Hellenic Hêraklês and Asklêpios and Castor and Pollux and Perseus and Achilles and Orpheus; and a Sinic contingent that includes, among others, the 'culture-heroes' Yu and Yi and Yao and Shwen.[1] These half-divine beings in human flesh live out their lives on Earth without benefit of that privilege of arbitrarily contracting out of the game which the full-blown gods, in their avatars, retain and abuse. The labours of Hêraklês are at least as serviceable to Mankind as Dionysus's escapades; yet the sufferings which such labours must entail for the labourer in the natural human course of events are suffered by Hêraklês as genuinely as though he were no more than an ordinary mortal. The divinity of the demigods is housed in common clay; and they have to contend with all the challenges which present themselves to 'Man that is born of a woman'.[2] The demigod, too, 'is of few days, and full of trouble'; and he is not even exempted from having to do battle with Man's 'last enemy'.[3] The demigod—and this is his glory—is subject, like Man, to Death.

Still less remote from our common humanity are the authentic human beings who have been credited by their fellows with the half-divine parentage that is the demigods' birthright. The divine paternity which in Euripides' play is ascribed by Athena to Ion has also been attributed to princes and sages that are no legendary figures but are well-known historical characters who have unquestionably lived in the flesh, and whose acts and thoughts are on record in documents that must rank as unimpeachable evidence. In the Hellenic tradition not only Ion and Asklêpios, but also Pythagoras and Plato and Augustus, have been reckoned among the sons of Apollo; and not only Hêraklês and the Dioscuri and Perseus, but also Alexander, among the sons of Zeus, while Apollonius of Tyana has been reckoned alternatively as a son of Zeus or as either a son of Zeus or a son of Proteus.[4] The common form of the tale is that the human hero's human mother is visited by a superhuman mate who usurps the place of her lawful human husband.[5] Apollo ousts Mnesarchus and Ariston and Octavius;

---

[1] See Maspéro, H.: *La Chine Antique* (Paris 1927, Boccard), pp. 26–32.
[2] Job xiv. 1.   [3] 1 Cor. xv. 26.
[4] 'When Apollonius's mother was pregnant with him she was visited by an apparition (φάσμα) of an Egyptian divinity (δαίμονος)—it was the Proteus who keeps on changing shape in Homer. The woman was not afraid, and asked him what kind of a child she was going to bear. "Me" was the apparition's reply; "Who are you?" she asked; "I am Proteus, the Egyptian god," said he.... The local belief [in Apollonius's home country, the Tyanitis] is that Apollonius was a son of Zeus; but Apollonius himself calls himself the son of [his mother's human husband] Apollonius.'—Philostratus: *Apollonius of Tyana*, Book I, chaps. 4 and 6. For the common features in the stories of Apollonius and of Jesus see Seeck, O.: *Geschichte des Untergangs der Antiken Welt*, vol. iii, 2nd ed. (Stuttgart 1921, Metzler), pp. 183–4.
[5] When the tale is told of historical characters whose official parents are both of them

Zeus-Amon ousts Philip. Sometimes the divine visitor presents himself in the form of a man, sometimes in the form of an animal, and sometimes in the form of a thunderbolt or a ray of light. Zeus-Amon is fabled to have visited Alexander's mother Olympias in the form either of a thunderbolt or of a snake,[1] and in the course of ages this fable has travelled far and wide. In Italy it was transferred in the third century B.C. from Alexander to Scipio Africanus Major[2] and in the last century B.C. to Augustus;[3] in Central Asia by the fifteenth century of the Christian Era it had come to be transferred to a legendary common ancestor of Chingis Khan and Timur Lenk.[4] In an etherial version the same story is also told of a man of the people who has outshone every one of these kings and statesmen and philosophers.

'These tales have their counterpart in the Christian legends of the birth of Jesus; and the version followed by Matthew exhibits the direct influence of the Hellenic *motif*.[5] This influence has not, of course, been

perfectly well known, it is, of course, easier to deny the paternity of the human father than the maternity of the human mother. It would probably be difficult to cite a genuinely historical personage who has been credited, like Orpheus and Achilles, with a mother who was a goddess.

[1] Both fables are recounted, side by side, in Plutarch's *Life of Alexander*, chaps. 2–3.
[2] See Livy, Book XXVI, chap. 19. The Roman historian, who retells the tale with a sneer, does not inform us whether Scipio's, as well as Alexander's, snake-father was identified with Zeus, or whether his identity was left in doubt.
[3] 'In Asclepiadis Mendetis *Theologumenôn* libris lego.'—Suetonius: *Life of Augustus*, chap. 94.
[4] See Herzfeld, E.: 'Alongoa' in *Der Islam*, vol. vi (Strassburg 1916, Trübner), pp. 317–27. This legendary Mongol hero Budhuntchar is fabled to have had no human father, but to have been conceived in the womb of his mother Alongoa through the incidence of a ray of light. The legend is recited in the inscription on the tomb of Alongoa's reputed descendant Timur Lenk at Samarqand, and in this context it is brought into connexion with the story of the Annunciation to Mary, as this is told in the Qur'ān xix. 20 and xix. 17 (Herzfeld, op. cit., p. 318). The same legend, with the same comparison between Alongoa's miraculous experience and Mary's according to the Qur'ān, figures (ibid., pp. 318–19) in the *Zafarnāmah* of Timur's biographer Sharaf-ad-Dīn 'Alī Yazdī (for whom see II. D (v), vol. ii, p. 149, above). It is not, however, through the Qur'ān that the tale has attached itself to Timur's and Chingis' legendary common ancestress Alongoa. The tale, as it is told in this context, has come direct from the Alexander Romance (Herzfeld, ibid., p. 326), as is attested by the heroine's name; for 'Alongoa' is a transparent travesty of Olympias (in the inscription on Timur's tomb the name is written, in the Perso-Arabic Alphabet, الــنوا; and, if we may assume that the ambiguous letter ٯ has been pointed ڧ [qāf] in mistake for ڢ [fā] at some weak link in a long chain of literary transmission, we arrive at an earlier form 'Alanfoa' which is very near indeed to the original Greek).
[5] 'The view that the Messiah has to be born of a virgin is notoriously quite unknown to the Jews; it is a purely Christian (pagan) myth' (Meyer, E.: *Ursprung und Anfänge des Christentums*, vol. i (Stuttgart and Berlin 1921, Cotta), p. 60, footnote 2), which attaches, not to the Jewish Messiah, but to the Zoroastrian Saošyant (Meyer, op. cit., vol. ii (1921), p. 68; von Gall, A.: Βασιλεία τοῦ Θεοῦ (Heidelberg 1926, Winter), pp. 418–19). In the Jewish view the Messiah is a man with nothing superhuman, and *a fortiori* nothing divine, about him (on this point see V. C (i) (d) 11, p. 163, footnote 1, above). To a Jewish mind the Christian attribution of a divine paternity to Jesus seems like a lapse from the slowly and painfully attained monotheism of the Chosen People of the One True God into one of the grossest and most unedifying superstitions of a Hellenic paganism. This Jewish reproach against Christianity is forcefully expressed in a passage placed in the mouth of the Jewish disputant in the *Dialogus cum Tryphone Judaeo*, chap. 67 (Migne, J.-P.: *Patrologia Graeca*, vol. vi, col. 629) of the Christian philosopher, saint, and martyr Justin (*vivebat aevi Christiani saeculo secundo*):
'Trypho replied: "The Scripture [Isa. vii. 14] does not read *Behold a virgin shall*

transmitted through any literary channel; what has happened is that the popular ideas that have been diffused far and wide through all peoples and all religions have been laid under contribution for the benefit of the Christian myth. Be that as it may, the correspondence between Matthew and the legend of the birth of Plato is as exact as it could possibly be. Before Mary's marriage with Joseph has been consummated, she becomes with child ἐκ πνεύματος ἁγίου = φάσμα Ἀπολλωνιακὸν συνεγένετο τῇ Περικτιόνῃ (Olympiodorus). Joseph proposes to put her away when the Angel of the Lord (the mal'ak Yahweh, the representative of the Godhead, as so often in the Old Testament) appears to him in a dream and reveals to him what has come to pass and what is his son's future. In obedience to this revelation Joseph "did as the Angel of the Lord had bidden him and took unto him his wife and knew her not till she had brought forth her first-born son"—the exact instructions that are given to Plato's father.[1]

conceive, and bear a son, but Behold a young woman shall conceive, and bear a son—and so on to the end of the passage that you have just quoted. And the whole prophecy refers to Hezekiah—in whose life events in consonance with this prophecy can be shown to have taken place. There is, however, in the mythology of the so-called Hellenes, a story of how Perseus was gotten upon Danae, when she was a virgin, by the streaming upon her, in the form of gold, of the [demon] whom the Hellenes called Zeus. You [Christians] ought to be ashamed of reproducing this Hellenic tale, and ought to admit that this Jesus is a human being of human parentage. And, if you want to prove from the Scriptures that he is the Christ, your thesis ought to be that he was accounted worthy to be singled out for being the Christ because he led a perfect life in conformity with the Law. But beware of telling tall stories (τερατολογεῖν) if you do not want to be convicted of being as silly as the Hellenes are."

Justin, however, is not ashamed of finding himself in the Hellenes' company. In his First Apologia on behalf of the Christians, which is addressed to the Emperor Antoninus Pius, he submits, in chap. 22 (Migne, J.-P.: Patrologia Graeca, vol. vi, col. 361), that 'if we [Christians] say that [Jesus] was born of a virgin, this too has a Hellenic parallel in what you say of Perseus'.—A.J.T.

[1] Meyer, E.: Ursprung und Anfänge des Christentums, vol. i (Stuttgart and Berlin 1921, Cotta), pp. 56–7. This modern Western scholar has not, of course, been the first to point out the parallelism between these two stories. As he himself mentions in the same context (op. cit., p. 55, footnote 4), the Christian father Origen (in his Contra Celsum, Book I, chap. 37) 'cites the story of the birth of Plato as a parallel to the birth of Jesus, with the object of making it clear to the Hellenes that what is related in the Gospels is by no means incompatible with Hellenic ideas'. ('In an argument with Hellenes it is quite in place to bring in Hellenic tales in order to show that we [Christians] are not unique in telling this extraordinary tale [of the virgin birth and divine paternity of Jesus]. There are Hellenic authors who have deliberately recorded, as a thing within the bounds of possibility—and this with reference, not to Ancient History or to "the Heroic Age", but to what happened only yesterday or the day before—that Plato was born of Amphictionē when Ariston had been debarred from having sexual relations with her until she should have given birth to the child begotten by Apollo.'—Migne, J.-P.: Patrologia Graeca, vol. xi, col. 732.) How is this parallel to be explained? Are we to suppose that the story of the birth of Jesus was adapted from that of the birth of Plato or Pythagoras or Alexander or Scipio Africanus or Augustus? It is true that the stories attributing a divine paternity to these pagan Hellenic heroes must all have been in circulation by the time when the sources of the Gospels began to take shape. Yet, although the hypothesis of a direct mimesis is thus tenable in point of chronology, it is improbable in itself. It seems more likely that the parallel between the birth-stories of Jesus on the one hand and of our five pagan Hellenic heroes on the other is due, not to an adaptation of the later story from one or other of the earlier stories, but to an independent derivation of each of the six stories from a common source. The essence of each of the six stories is that it ascribes to an historical character the semi-divine parentage that is the birthright of a demigod. And, if we compare the birth-story of Jesus with that of Hêraklês, we shall find a still greater number of points of correspondence than Meyer has pointed out in his comparison of the birth-story of Jesus with that of Plato. The parallel between the birth-stories of Jesus and Hêraklês is set out in Pfister, Fr.: 'Hêraklês und Christus' in Archiv für Religionswissenschaft, XXXIV, Heft 1/2 (Berlin and Leipzig 1937, Teubner),

This divine paternity of a saviour born of a woman is a form of epiphany which brings the saviour-god into a perfect intimacy with human kind. But how is the nature of fatherhood to be conceived of if God is the subject of it? Can God's fatherhood really be supposed to take the form of an act of physical procreation? It would be hard to say whether the suggestion is the more shocking when the divinity is pictured as masquerading in the body of a human seducer or when this sordid realism is evaded by the childishly grotesque device of turning a god into a beast and a myth[1] into a fairy-tale. In whatever physical shape the god may be portrayed, a literal paternity cannot be attributed to him without making blasphemous nonsense of his fatherhood in the judgement of any human soul that is morally sensitive and intellectually critical. If the hero's divine father was really behaving like a human rake, there is no reason why the hero should have turned out better than any other child that has been born out of lawful wedlock. On the other hand, if it be accepted that the hero has displayed an unmistakably superhuman prowess, and if it be granted that a spiritual endowment which cannot be of human origin can only be accounted for as the gift of a divine parent, then the nature of the divine paternity with which the hero must be credited will have to be conceived of in the non-corporeal terms in which it is in fact presented in our Christian version of the Hellenic myth.[2] If God has begotten a Son, the divine act must be an eternal truth and not an occurrence in Time. And if God can create the Universe by uttering a word,[3] then assuredly he can

pp. 46-7. Amphitryon, the husband of Hêraklês' mother Alcmena, refrains, like both Joseph and Ariston, from having sexual intercourse with his newly wedded wife until she has conceived and born a child whose paternity is not human but divine. But between the birth-stories of Jesus and Hêraklês there is a further point of resemblance that is not to be found in the birth-story of Plato. Before the birth of the divine child the child's mother and her husband change their residence—Alcmena and Amphitryon from Mycenae (Alcmena's native city) to Thebes; Mary and Joseph from Nazareth to Bethlehem—so that the child has a birth-place (a Judaean Bethlehem or a Boeotian Thebes) which is not his parents' home (in a Galilaean Nazareth or an Argive Mycenae). We may conjecture that the birth-story of Hêraklês is the archetype of the birth-stories of all our six historical Hellenic heroes (see further V. C (ii) (a), Annex II, p. 469, below).

[1] For the view that the story or drama of the encounter between the Virgin and the Father of her Child is a mythological image of the mystery of Creation, see II. C (ii) (b) 1, vol. i, p. 272, above.

[2] In expounding the parallelism between the Christian and the Hellenic Mythology, Saint Justin Martyr (*First Apology*, chap. 21, in Migne: *Patrologia Graeca*, vol. vi, col. 360) implicitly absolves the Hellenic *motif* of divine paternity from the imputation of grossness which is usually read into it. 'When we say that the Logos, which is the first offspring of God, has been begotten without sexual intercourse—the Logos who is Jesus Christ our Master—and that this [Jesus Christ] has been crucified and has died and has risen again and has ascended into Heaven, we are saying nothing novel, for we are saying nothing that is not to be found in the stories of the sons that are attributed, in your Hellenic Mythology, to Zeus.'

[3] The Jewish conception of a creative 'Word' ('Memra') of God may be either an independent discovery of the Jewish religious genius or else a Jewish adaptation of the Hellenic conception of the 'Logos' (see Meyer, E.: *Ursprung und Anfänge des Christen-*

send his Son into the World by making an Annunciation.[1] This is the common foundation of all varieties of Christian belief concerning the manner in which the saviour-god has made his historical epiphany. But this primary common ground leaves some critical secondary questions outstanding. To whom, and at what moment, and in what circumstances, will the creative Annunciation be made?

If it be agreed that God's way of revealing himself as a father is to speak with the voice of the Spirit to a human soul, it may still be debated whether the Father is to be expected to announce His divine intention to the human mother of His Son at the moment when her child is physically conceived. May it not be more god-like to confer the grace of this divine paternity upon a soul which has already reached the threshold of its human maturity and has already proved its worthiness of sonship by offering itself to God without blemish or reserve? 'God is the common father of all men, but he makes the best ones peculiarly his own.'[2] This adoptive kind of fatherhood is not unknown even among men. Even in the gross economy of a purely mundane society the physical act of procreation is not the only means by which a man can acquire a son. As an alternative to the begetting of a child whose character is *ex hypothesi* an unknown quantity, the would-be father may adopt a grown man who has already shown himself capable of taking over the heritage which his adoptive parent has to hand on. And, if this heritage be one that carries heavy responsibilities and imposes exacting tasks involving many people's welfare, then a conscientious man of affairs—be he householder or prince—may well find greater comfort in a son of his choice than in a son of his loins. In such a spirit the second Scipio Africanus[3] adopted Scipio Aemilianus; Divus Julius adopted Octavian; and Nerva initiated a succession of imperial adoptions which ran through Trajan and Hadrian and Pius to Marcus. In the Age of the Antonines it had come to be almost a constitutional convention of the Roman Empire that the Principate should be transmitted by adopting a successor and not by begetting one. Did Marcus do well when he broke Nerva's 'Golden Chain' for the benefit of his own child

---

tums, vol. ii (Stuttgart and Berlin 1921, Cotta), pp. 103–4, and the present Study, V. C (i) (d) 6 (δ), vol. v, p. 539, with footnote 4, above).

[1] Had this idea already struck the mind of a Hellenic poet-prophet in a generation that was born before the breakdown of the Hellenic Civilization?

λαβοῦσα δ' ἔρμα Δῖον ἀψευδεῖ λόγῳ
γείνατο παῖδ' ἀμεμφῆ,
δι' αἰῶνος μακροῦ πάνολβον.

Aeschylus: *Supplices*, ll. 580–2.

[2] This 'logion', attributed to Alexander the Great, has been quoted already in V. C (i) (d) 7, p. 9, above.

[3] This physical son of Scipio Africanus Major was himself prevented by ill-health from carrying on his father's work.

Commodus? And, if adoption works better than procreation when the father is a human prince and the heritage a mundane empire, may it not be better, *a fortiori*, when the father is God himself and when the business on hand is Man's salvation?

The belief that a Son of Man may in this way become a Son of God has declared itself, in the first instance, in the deification of oecumenical monarchs.[1] In some oecumenical empires the adoption of the prince by the god has been conceived of as taking place at the moment of the prince's accession, and in others as being deferred until after his death. Posthumous apotheosis appears to have been the rule among the Hittites and in Japan; adoption-upon-accession in the Egyptiac and Sumeric and Sinic and Andean worlds; while in the Hellenic World the two practices came into currency side by side[2]—with the strange consequence that a Hellenic ruler in the Age of Disintegration might find himself already an object of worship in his own lifetime in certain parts of his dominions or among certain classes of his subjects, while elsewhere he must be content with the knowledge that he would receive— or at any rate become a candidate for receiving—the same honours as soon as he had ceased to be present in the flesh.[3] This belief in divine paternity by adoption has had the same social history as the cruder belief in divine paternity by procreation. While it likewise makes its first appearance as an expression of the awe in which an oecumenical ruler is held by his subjects, it also likewise breaks these original bounds and comes to be extended to commoners instead of remaining a monopoly of kings. In the history of the disintegration of the Hellenic Society the earliest example of the deification of a man of the people is to be found in a comedy. In the closing verses of Aristophanes' *Birds* the chorus hail Peithe-taerus as 'God of Gods' (δαιμόνων ὑπέρτατε) when, in reward for the feats of having founded 'Cloudcuckooland' and blockaded Olympus into an abject surrender, the Athenian cockney makes a triumphal epiphany with the sceptre of Zeus in his hand and with

[1] For Caesar-worship and its limitations see IV. C (iii) (c) 2 (β), vol. iv, pp. 348–9, and V. C (i) (d) 6 (δ), Annex, pp. 648–57, above.

[2] This seems also to have happened in certain overseas domains of the Hindu World —Java, Camboja, Champa—where we have evidence for a deification of monarchs of which there are only slight traces in the main body of the Hindu Society in Continental India (Eliot, Sir Ch.: *Hinduism and Buddhism* (London 1921, Arnold, 3 vols.), vol. iii, pp. 115–20, already cited in V. C (i) (d) 6 (δ), Annex, p. 653, footnote 4, above.

[3] This was the situation of the Roman Emperors in the Age of the Principate. In Rome itself, and in those parts of the Ager Romanus that were peopled by communities of Roman citizens, a princeps was in no circumstances accorded divine honours till after his death, and even then his apotheosis was not a matter of course, but was a special recognition of merit which could only be conferred by act of the Senate. On the other hand the Emperors were worshipped as gods in their lifetime at many places in the Greek and Oriental provinces and protectorates of the Empire, while in Egypt a Roman Emperor automatically became an adopted son of Re upon his accession, in virtue of his recognized status of being a legitimate Pharaoh.

'the Queen' on his arm as his heavenly bride.[1] But a scene which, in the first generation of the Hellenic 'Time of Troubles', had thus been played in the theatre of Dionysus at Athens as the crowning extravaganza of a fantastic farce was replayed four and a half centuries later on the banks of the Jordan in an amazingly different setting and spirit. In the story of the Gospels the designation of a Nazarene carpenter as the Son of God is presented as the opening revelation of a mystery which was to culminate in the Crucifixion and which was nothing less than God's scheme for Man's salvation.

In all four Gospels[2] it is told of Jesus that he was designated as the Son of God after his baptism in Jordan by John, as he was coming up out of the water.[3] And in the earliest, as well as in the latest, of the four the whole story begins with this act of adoption, and not with any account of the saviour-god's conception or birth or infancy or upbringing.[4] There is, of course, an apparent

[1] For this extraordinary finale of the *Birds* see further V. C (i) (d) 11, Annex I, below.

[2] Matt. iii. 16–17; Mark i. 10–11; Luke iii. 21–2; John i. 32–4.

[3] In all the three Synoptic Gospels this designation of Jesus as the Son of God is represented as having been both visual and aural. The Spirit of God is seen descending upon Jesus in the likeness of a dove, and simultaneously the voice of God is heard from Heaven proclaiming Jesus to be God's beloved Son in whom God is well pleased. In the Gospel according to Saint Mark the story is told in words which seem to imply that the vision was seen and the voice heard by Jesus alone in a flash of spiritual enlightenment. The words used in Matthew would seem to imply that the vision was seen by Jesus alone, but that the voice was addressed to—and therefore, presumably, heard by—the spectators. Inversely, the words used in Luke would seem to imply that Jesus alone heard the voice, but that the spectators saw the vision. In the Gospel according to Saint John no mention is made of the voice, while, in regard to the vision, it is explicitly stated that this was seen by John, and is implicitly suggested that it was not seen by any one else—not even by Jesus himself.

[4] It is noteworthy that this story of the Designation of Jesus, at his baptism, as the Son of God is not omitted in either of the two Gospels which preface this story with an account of Jesus's birth and which represent him as having acquired his divine paternity at the moment of his physical conception and therefore, by implication, not at the moment of his baptism, when, according to Luke iii. 23, he was about thirty years old. The internal evidence can hardly fail to produce on the mind of the literary critic an impression that the form of the story in which this begins with the baptism and Designation of Jesus in his prime is the original form, and that the Lucan and Matthaean prologues represent a later accretion. The discrepancy between an 'adoptionist' gospel and its 'conceptionist' preface is particularly conspicuous in Luke. In the first place Luke iii. 22 reads, in one set of manuscripts (D, a, b, c, ff, &c., with the support of Clement of Alexandria): 'Thou art my beloved Son; *this day have I begotten thee*', in place of the standard reading: 'Thou art my beloved Son; *in thee I am well pleased*'; and it is not impossible that this discarded reading may be the authentic original text (Streeter, B. H.: *The Four Gospels* (London 1924, Macmillan), p. 143; cf. pp. 188 and 276). In the second place the vagueness of the estimate of Jesus's age at the moment of the Designation seems to imply (in contradiction to what is told in chapters i and ii) that little or nothing was known about his life before this event, which is represented as having occurred at his first public appearance. In the third place the genealogy of Jesus's human ancestry (which, curiously enough, is introduced into the story in both Luke and Matthew, while it is not to be found in Mark, where there is nothing with which it would be incompatible) is placed in Luke immediately after the account of the Designation, which would be the natural place for it if this were the beginning of the story, whereas in Matthew it is placed, less awkwardly, at the opening of the preface, before the account of the Annunciation. In the fourth place the genealogy—and this not only in Luke but also in Matthew—is traced through Joseph, with the implication that Jesus was in the physical sense Joseph's son, and not through Mary, though Mary is the sole physical parent of Jesus according to the story told in both these Gospels in their

discrepancy between this account, in all the Gospels, of the adoption of Jesus as the Son of God in the prime of his manhood and the account of his conception by the Holy Ghost which precedes the account of the adoption in the Gospels according to Saint Matthew and Saint Luke. And this raises difficult problems of literary criticism and theological exegesis which have exercised scholars and have divided Christians.[1] Is 'adoption' or 'conception' the proper description of a humanly ineffable utterance of the Creative Word that gave God a man for his son and Mankind a god for their saviour? At what moment in Jesus's human life on Earth did a divine wave of salvation break upon the shoals of Time in the course of its everlasting passage over the boundless ocean of Eternity?[2] Instead of attempting to answer a question that is humanly unanswerable, it may perhaps be more useful to suggest that the two words 'adoption' and 'conception', which bear their literal meaning in the crude Hellenic embryo of the myth, have in our Christian version acquired a new connotation which is neither legal in the one case nor physical in the other, but is in both cases metaphorical. The essence of the Christian mystery lies in a belief that God has made himself, by means that have been spiritual and not corporeal, the father of a son who has lived and died on Earth as a man in the flesh. This belief in an incarnation of Divinity postulates in its turn the further belief that the human vehicle of the Godhead has been a physical reality with a physiological origin; and, on every Christian interpretation of the story, Jesus the Son of God is deemed to have been born, in the literal physical sense of the word, by a human mother. The issue on which the 'adoptionists' and 'conceptionists' part company is not either the question whether God made himself the father of a man by a

prologues (in the Lucan genealogy (Luke iii. 38), in contrast to the Lucan prologue; it is not Jesus, but Jesus's first human forefather Adam, who is the Son of God). With this we may compare the double paternity that is ascribed to both Alexander and Hêraklês. Plutarch, *Life of Alexander*, chap. 2, records that Alexander was believed to be a Heracleid on his father's (i.e. Philip's) side, and an Aeacid on his mother's, besides recounting the story of his father's being, not Philip at all, but Zeus-Amon (the story of Alexander's divine paternity, as recounted by Plutarch, comes closer to the Matthaean than to the Lucan prologue to the story of the Gospels: Herzfeld, op. cit., pp. 326–7). Similarly Hêraklês is represented as being both the son of Amphitryon and the son of Zeus (Pfister, op. cit., p. 47).

[1] For the traces of an 'adoptionist' Christian Church which appears to have been overwhelmed, without having been completely obliterated, by a following wave of the 'conceptionist' Christianity which now prevails, see IV. C (iii) (c) 2 (β), Annex III, vol. iv, pp. 624–34, above. The 'adoptionist' type of Christianity has manifestly a closer affinity than the 'conceptionist' type has with the Mahayanian cult of the Bodhisattva Amitābha (Amida). 'In the oldest documents he is a man who becomes a Buddha in the traditional manner. The fundamental idea is not that God is Love but rather that Love is God: lovingkindness raised Amida to a place which may be called divine' (Eliot, Sir Ch.: *Japanese Buddhism* (London 1935, Arnold), p. 394).

[2] 'History is the result of a deep interaction between Eternity and Time; it is the incessant eruption of Eternity into Time.'—Berdyaev, N.: *The Meaning of History* (London 1936, Bles), p. 67.

non-corporeal act or again the question whether the man of flesh and blood had a physical origin. The two schools agree in answering both these questions in the affirmative. They are divided on the question whether the physical procreation of Jesus was normal or miraculous; and it may be neither uncharitable nor unreasonable to suggest that this point of discord—sharp though it be—is minute by comparison with the expanse of the encompassing field of harmony.

In any case a theophany can never avail in itself to fulfil the promise of salvation. Whether *machina* or avatar or conception or adoption be the means that God elects for making his divine intervention in a human tragedy, an epiphany must lead on to a Passion if God Manifest is to become Man's Saviour by proving himself 'a very present help in trouble'.[1] Suffering is the key to salvation, as well as to understanding;[2] and a saviour's suffering must fathom the uttermost depths of agony. Even a Hellenic philosopher whose idea of salvation was Detachment has demanded an extremity of suffering from the sage who is to testify to his fellow men that Justice is an end in itself which is to be ensued at any cost for the sake of its own absolute and infinite value. The testimony, as Plato perceives, will only carry conviction if the just man bears it out by submitting to be scourged and racked and shackled, to have his eyes seared with red-hot irons, and finally to be impaled after having gone through every lesser torture.[3] In imagining this extremity of suffering for an utterly unselfish object, Plato assuredly had in mind the historic martyrdom of his own master Socratès.[4] And this human martyr who gave his witness at Athens in the year 399 B.C. was following the example of super-human prototypes whose labours and tribulations—undergone for the sake of Mankind—were the themes of the holiest legends in the Hellenic cultural heritage. Even the hero Achilles had deliberately cut short his brief allotted span of life on Earth for the sake of avenging the death of a comrade. Hêraklês had toiled, and Prometheus endured,[5] and Orpheus died, for all men. And even the death of this dying demigod was not the acme of divine suffering in the panorama of the Hellenic *Weltanschauung*. For, though no living being can pay a greater price than life itself, the life of a demigod is not so precious as the life of a god of unalloyed divinity;

[1] Ps. xlvi. 1.
[2] For the Aeschylean πάθει μάθος see I. C (iii) (*b*), vol. i, p. 169, footnote 1; II. C (ii) (*b*) 1, vol. i, p. 298; IV. C (iii) (*b*) 11, vol. iv, p. 218; IV. C (iii) (*c*) 3 (β), vol. iv, p. 584; V. C (i) (*c*) 2, vol. v, p. 78; and V. C (i) (*d*) 4, vol. v, p. 416, footnote 3, above.
[3] Plato: *Respublica*, 360 E–362 C, quoted again in V. C (ii) (*a*), Annex II, p. 494, below.
[4] Some analogies between the theophany and Passion of Socrates and the theophany and Passion of Jesus are examined in V. C (ii) (*a*), Annex II, pp. 486–95, below.
[5] For the Passion of Prometheus see III. B, vol. iii, pp. 112–27, above.

and behind the figure of the dying demigod Orpheus there looms the greater figure of a very god who dies for different worlds under diverse names—for a Minoan World as Zagreus,[1] for a Sumeric World as Tammuz,[2] for a Hittite World as Attis,[3] for a Scandinavian World as Balder,[4] for a Syriac World as Adonis ('Our Lord'),[5] for an Egyptiac World as Osiris,[6] for a Shī'ī World as Husayn, for a Christian World as Christ.

Who is this god of many epiphanies but only one Passion? Though he makes his appearance on our mundane stage under a dozen diverse masks, his identity is invariably revealed in the last act of the tragedy by his suffering unto death. And if we take up the anthropologist's divining-rod we can trace this never varying drama back to its historical origins. 'He shall grow up before him as a tender plant, and as a root out of a dry ground.'[7] The Dying God's oldest appearance is in the role of the ἐνιαυτὸς δαίμων, the spirit of the vegetation that is born for Man in the spring to die for Man in the autumn.[8] And both the epiphany and the Passion of this nature-god bring material benefits to Mankind that are plainly indispensable for the physical salvation of the race. If the grass were not clothed in glorious raiment to-day in order to be cast into the oven to-morrow,[9] the fire on the householder's hearth would go out for lack of fuel; and, if the wheat did not ripen for the sickle, the husbandman would harvest no grain-store for the impending winter and no seed-corn for the following spring. Man profits by the nature-god's death, and would perish if his benefactor did not

---

1 See I. C (i) (b), vol. i, pp. 98–9, and V. C (i) (c) 2, vol. v, p. 85, above.
2 See I. C (i) (b), vol. i, p. 115, footnote 1, and V. C (i) (c) 2, vol. v, pp. 148–9, above.
3 See V. C (i) (c) 2, vol. v, p. 149, above.
4 See ibid., p. 150, above.
5 See ibid., p. 149, above. In the Syriac Mythology the theme has a variation (see V. C (i) (d) 11, p. 162, above) which is reproduced in the Christian Theology. Side by side with the figure of a god who dies for the World in his own person there is the figure of a god who so loves the World that he gives his only begotten son to save it (John iii. 16). The original Syriac myth, in its Phoenician version, is preserved in a passage from Philo of Byblus's Greek translation of the work of the Phoenician author Sanchuniathôn which is quoted by Eusebius of Caesarea in his *Praeparatio Evangelica*, Book I, chap. 10 (Migne, J.-P.: *Patrologia Graeca*, vol. xxi, col. 85): 'Cronos, whom the Phoenicians call Israel [in cap. cit., col. 81, above, his name is given as Il]—a king of Phoenicia who, after his departure from this life, was consecrated into Cronos' Star—had an only begotten son (υἱὸν μονογενῆ) by a local nymph called Anôbret (they called him Ieûd, which is still the word for "only begotten" in Phoenician). When Phoenicia was overtaken by immense dangers arising from war, Cronos arrayed his son in royal insignia, set up an altar, and sacrificed his son upon it.' In the Israelitish version of the same Syriac myth the fatal consummation of the sacrifice of Isaac is averted at the last moment; the son and the father are ordinary human beings and not demigods; and the sacrifice of the son is undertaken by the father on the initiative, not of the father himself, but of the father's god (Gen. xxii). In the saga of Jephthah (Judges xi) the only child is transposed from a son into a virgin daughter who is a Syriac counterpart of the Hellenic Iphigeneia.
6 See V. C (i) (c) 2, vol. v, pp. 150–2, as well as I. C (ii), vol. i, pp. 137 and 140–5, above.
7 Isa. liii. 2.
8 For the annual tragedy of the ἐνιαυτὸς δαίμων as a prototype of the movement of Withdrawal-and-Return see III. C (ii) (b), vol. iii, pp. 256–9, above.
9 Matt. vi. 30.

die for him perpetually. 'He was wounded for our transgressions, he was bruised for our iniquities, the chastisement of our peace was upon him and with his stripes we are healed.'[1] That is one aspect of the salvation which the Dying God's epiphany and Passion bring to Man. But an outward achievement—however imposing and however dearly paid for—cannot reveal the mystery at the heart of a tragedy. If we are to read the secret, we must look beyond the human beneficiary's material profit and the divine protagonist's material loss. The god's death and the man's gain are not the whole story. We cannot know the meaning of the play without also knowing the protagonist's circumstances and feelings and motives. Does the Dying God die by compulsion or by choice? With generosity or with bitterness? Out of love or in despair? Till we have learnt the answers to these questions about the saviour-god's spirit, we can hardly judge the value of the salvation that Man will derive from his death. We cannot tell whether this salvation will be merely a profit for a man through a god's equivalent loss, or whether it will be a spiritual communion in which Man will repay, by acquiring ('like a light caught from a leaping flame'),[2] a divine love and pity that have been shown to Man by God in an act of pure self-sacrifice.

In what spirit, then, does the Dying God go to his death? If we address ourselves once more to our array of tragic masks and adjure the hidden actor to reply to our challenging question, we shall see the goats being separated from the sheep, and the tragedy[3] being transfigured into a mystery, under this searching test. Even in Calliope's melodious lamentation for the death of Orpheus there is a jarring note of bitterness which strikes, and shocks, a Christian ear when it rings out of one of the most beautiful poems in Greek.

$$\tau i\ \phi\theta\iota\mu\acute{\epsilon}\nu o\iota\varsigma\ \sigma\tau o\nu\alpha\chi\epsilon\hat{\upsilon}\mu\epsilon\nu\ \acute{\epsilon}\phi'\ \upsilon\iota\acute{\alpha}\sigma\iota\nu,\ \acute{\alpha}\nu\acute{\iota}\kappa'\ \acute{\alpha}\lambda\alpha\lambda\kappa\epsilon\hat{\iota}\nu$$
$$\tau\hat{\omega}\nu\ \pi\alpha\acute{\iota}\delta\omega\nu\ \H{A}\iota\delta\eta\nu\ o\upsilon\delta\grave{\epsilon}\ \theta\epsilon o\hat{\iota}\varsigma\ \delta\acute{\upsilon}\nu\alpha\mu\iota\varsigma;[4]$$

'Why do we mortals make lament over the deaths of our sons, seeing that the Gods themselves have not power to keep Death from laying his hand upon their children?' What a moral to read into the Dying God's story! So the goddess who was Orpheus' mother would never have let Orpheus die if she could have helped it; and *ergo*, if even the Gods are thus impotent to satisfy their dearest wishes, then the only reasonable attitude for feebler beings to adopt when the same pangs of bereavement come upon them is

[1] Isa. liii. 5.
[2] Plato's Letters, No. 7, 341 C–D, quoted already in III. C (ii) (a), vol. iii, p. 245, and in V. C (i) (d) 11, in the present volume, p. 165, footnote 6, above.
[3] The word 'tragedy' means literally what the performance was originally: a 'goat-chant'.
[4] Elegy on the death of Orpheus by Antipater of Sidon (*floruit circa* 90 B.C.).

a posture of dull resignation—barely relieved by the faintest thrill of malicious pleasure at the greater discomfiture of the mightier Olympians. Like a cloud that veils the Sun, the Hellenic poet's thought takes the light out of Orpheus' death. But Antipater's poem is answered in another masterpiece which responds to it like antistrophe to strophe, though it was written at least two hundred years later, and that in a Judaic Greek which would have grated on the aesthetic sensibilities of the exquisite Sidonian Hellenist.

'For God so loved the World that he gave his only begotten Son, that whosoever believeth in him should not perish but have everlasting life. For God sent not his Son into the World to condemn the World, but that the World through him might be saved.'[1]

When the Gospel thus answers the elegy, it delivers an oracle. Οἷος πέπνυται, τοὶ δὲ σκιαὶ ἀΐσσουσιν.[2] 'The one remains, the many change and pass.'[3] And this is in truth the final result of our survey of saviours. When we first set out on this quest we found ourselves moving in the midst of a mighty marching host; but, as we have pressed forward on our way, the marchers, company by company, have been falling out of the race. The first to fail were the swordsmen, the next the archaists, the next the futurists, the next the philosophers, until at length there were no more human competitors left in the running. In the last stage of all, our motley host of would-be saviours, human and divine, has dwindled to a single company of none but gods; and now the strain has been testing the staying-power of these last remaining runners, notwithstanding their superhuman strength. At the final ordeal of death, few, even of these would-be saviour-gods, have dared to put their title to the test by plunging into the icy river. And now, as we stand and gaze with our eyes fixed upon the farther shore, a single figure rises from the flood and straightway fills the whole horizon. There is the Saviour; 'and the pleasure of the Lord shall prosper in his hand; he shall see of the travail of his soul and shall be satisfied.'[4]

(b) THE INTERACTION BETWEEN INDIVIDUALS IN DISINTEGRATING CIVILIZATIONS

The Rhythm of Disintegration.

In the last chapter we have studied the effect of the disintegration of a society upon the individuals who are born into it in this unhappy phase of its history. We have seen that in a disintegrating body social the 'member' who has in him the spark of creative

[1] John iii. 16–17.
[2] *Odyssey*, Book X, l. 495, quoted in V. C (i) (d) 7, p. 44, above.
[3] Shelley: *Adonais*, l. 460.   [4] Isa. liii. vv. 10–11.

genius finds his field of social action in the role of a saviour. We have passed in review the diverse types of would-be saviours who arise in response to the challenge that social disintegration presents. And we have found that the only claimant to the title who makes his claim good is the saviour *from* Society who does not allow himself to be deflected from his aim. The would-be saviour *from* Society who lapses into the role of a would-be saviour *of* Society is condemning himself to the failure that is in store for his comrade who has cast himself for this role deliberately. It is only in so far as he succeeds in finding, and showing, the way into an Other World, out of range of the City of Destruction, that the would-be saviour is able to accomplish his mission. And this conclusion, to which we have just been led as the result of an empirical survey, will confine the present chapter, *a priori*, within a narrower compass than its predecessor. For in this chapter we are not concerned with the destinies of the pilgrims who are moved by the awful prospect of impending catastrophe to break out of the doomed city and shake off the dust of their feet.[1] If the leader whom they are following in their exodus is a saviour indeed, he will lead them into the Kingdom of God and there build them a New Jerusalem. 'And he led them forth by the right way, that they might go to a city of habitation'[2]—but that is another story.[3] In the present chapter our business is with these pilgrims' unhappy fellow citizens who remain sitting in darkness and in the shadow of death,[4] whether through lack of the imagination to foresee their city's doom or through lack of the courage to forestall it by making their escape. Our business now is with the interaction between individuals *in* disintegrating civilizations; and this means that we shall not be so much concerned with the relations of the uncreative rank-and-file with creative personalities or minorities, since, *ex hypothesi*, the creators are being moved, *ex officio creativitatis*, to leave the doomed city at the head of the departing bands of pilgrims.

> Excessere omnes, adytis arisque relictis
> di quibus imperium hoc steterat.[5]

We shall therefore mainly be studying the relations between an uncreative rank-and-file and a minority that in most of its activities is not creative either, but is merely dominant.[6]

[1] Matt. x. 14.   [2] Ps. cvii. 7.
[3] The question whether the New Jerusalem can be brought down to Earth in the shape of a universal church is discussed in Part VII, below.
[4] Ps. cvii. 10.
[5] Virgil: *Aeneid*, Book II, ll. 351–2, quoted already in this Study in I. C (i) (*a*), vol. i, p. 57, footnote 1; in II. D (vi), vol. ii, p. 216; and in IV. C (iii) (*c*) 2 (*β*), vol. iv, p. 349, above.
[6] See V. C (i) (*b*), vol. v, pp. 23–35, above. The Dominant Minority deserves its name, since it relies on force, and not on charm, for the maintenance of its hold. At the

This means in turn that we shall not find our key this time in that movement of Withdrawal-and-Return which is the key to the interaction between individuals in civilizations that are still in the growth-stage.[1] All the same, we shall not find the rhythm of social disintegration altogether unfamiliar, for we shall recognize in it several other movements which we have learnt to know in studying the processes of genesis and growth. Indeed, we have observed already at an earlier point in this Part that the disintegration of a civilization, like its growth, is a process that is both continuous and cumulative;[2] that the process has a rhythm which is repetitive;[3] that each beat of the music follows from the last and leads on to the next;[4] and that the basis of this periodic rhythm is the principle of Challenge-and-Response.[5] In the same context, however, we have also noted[6] a point of difference between the rhythm of disintegration and the rhythm of growth which is clearly of capital importance.

In the growth-rhythm each successive beat is introduced by the presentation of a new challenge which arises out of a successful response to a previous challenge, and which is met, in its turn, by a successful response to itself out of which, again, another new challenge arises. This is the nature of the growth-rhythm *ex hypothesi*, since on the one hand the movement could not be continuous if a successful response were the end of the whole story, while on the other hand the movement could not be one of growth if any of the responses to any of the challenges were to prove, not successes, but failures. A failure to respond to a challenge successfully is the essence of the catastrophe of social breakdown which cuts short a process of growth and gives rise, in its place, to a process of disintegration. A disintegrating society is failing *ex hypothesi* to respond to a challenge that is presented to it; and so long as a challenge remains unanswered it will continue to hold the field. This means that a disintegrating society is confronted all the time by a single challenge—the particular challenge over which it has broken down—instead of being called upon, like a growing society, to deal with a series of challenges which are severally different from one another. And this means, in turn, that the periodicity which is one of the features that the process of disintegration has in common with the process of growth cannot be accounted for by the same explanation. While the growth-beats

same time—as we have observed in cap. cit., pp. 33–4—the Dominant Minority cannot be entirely lacking in creative power, since the schools of philosophy and the universal states are the Dominant Minority's handiwork, and both these works bear witness to the creativity of the hands that have made them.

[1] See III. C (ii) (*b*), vol. iii, pp. 248–377, above.
[2] See Part V. B, vol. v, pp. 12–13, above. [3] Ibid., p. 12, above.
[4] Ibid., p. 12, above. [5] Ibid., pp. 11–12, above. [6] Ibid., pp. 12–13, above.

arise out of a series of successes in responding to a series of different challenges, the disintegration-beats arise out of a series of failures to respond to a single challenge; and, if the disintegration-process, like the growth-process, is continuous, this must be because each successive failure sows, in failing, the seeds of a fresh attempt. This must be the nature of the disintegration-rhythm because, if any one of the failures to respond to the unanswered but inexorable challenge were to prove so conclusive as absolutely to close the door upon all possibility of making any further endeavours, that would mean that, in this particular beat, the process had come to a stop and the disintegration-movement had thus ended—as of course, it must end sooner or later—in the *rigor mortis*.

Thus, while the disintegration-movement resembles the growth-movement in having Challenge-and-Response for its basis, it does not turn this basis to the same account in building its periodicity-structure. In the growth-movement each beat of the rhythm consists in a new performance of the drama of Challenge-and-Response which is at the same time a new rendering; in the dis-integration-movement the beats are merely repetitive performances of one rendering of the play that never varies so long as this run of the play lasts; and, if we were to try to formulate the two series of beats as though they were mathematical progressions, we should find that we had to describe them in different terms. Our formula for the growth-progression would be 'a challenge evoking a suc-cessful response generating a fresh challenge evoking another successful response and so on, pending a breakdown'; our formula for the disintegration-progression would be 'a challenge evoking an unsuccessful response generating another attempt resulting in another failure and so on, pending dissolution'. Rout-rally-relapse is the form of the disintegration-process that any failure to respond to a challenge sets in train. And this is the pattern of the dance that the individual 'members' of a disintegrating society lead one another.

This interaction between individuals in a disintegrating society may be described in a military simile.

The failure of a response results in a retreat in which ground is lost and discipline is relaxed; but the débâcle is neither complete nor final, because the very danger and disgrace of it call out latent powers of leadership and latent habits of obedience. On some line, at some moment, some officer will temporarily succeed in checking the fugitives' flight and re-forming their ranks; the shaken army will then once more face the enemy and allow itself to be led into another attack upon the objective that it has failed to capture in the previous engagement; and for a time it will almost look as though the fortunes of the battle might be retrieved. But these reviving hopes soon prove delusive; for the recovery of *moral* upon which the leaders are counting in their hope for better success at a second attempt is no more than a fair-weather courage. The rally has only been achieved after the discomfited army has succeeded in breaking contact with a victorious enemy by shamefully taking to its heels, and it only lasts so long as the troops are not led back into action. Their recovery is more than offset by the shock of finding themselves once again under fire; and the result is another débâcle which is more serious than its predecessor.

In the sphere of human activity from which our simile is taken we have seen a tragic illustration of this process in our own world and generation. On the East European front in the General War of 1914-18 the Russians suffered in 1915 a military disaster which resulted in the first place in a great military retreat and in the second place in a great political revolution. In 1917 the Tsardom was overthrown and was replaced by a Liberal parliamentary government. This change of political régime was followed by a moral rally; and thereupon pressure was brought to bear upon the new Government of Russia—partly by its nationalist supporters at home and partly by its West European allies—to turn this moral rally to military account by launching a new offensive. Against their better judgement the new Russian Government reluctantly consented to do what was being so insistently demanded of them, and the consequences were ruinous beyond their worst forebodings. After an indecisive initial success the new offensive broke down; and the disaster of 1917 quite eclipsed that of 1915. In 1917 the Russian army did not simply retreat: this time it melted away. And the political revolution in which the military disaster was reflected once again was this time far more violent and more destructive than it had been on the former occasion. The Liberal régime which had momentarily taken the place of the old autocracy was now swept away by Bolshevism; and one of the first acts of the Bolshevik Government of Russia was to make peace at Brest-Litovsk on the enemy's terms.

This illustration brings out the grim truth that the process of social disintegration is a galloping consumption. The rider's desperate efforts to rein in the runaway horse do not avail to bring the frantic animal to a halt. They merely stampede him into plunging on again, with a demonic impetus, along his breakneck course.

If Rout-and-Rally is thus the rhythm in which the individual 'members' of a disintegrating civilization are prone to interact with one another, does this rhythm assert itself on the large scale as well as on the small? Can we discern it in the broad lines of the historical process of social disintegration with which we have now made ourselves familiar?

If, with this question in mind, we now cast our eye over the conspicuous features of the disintegration-process, we shall find an unmistakable example of a rally in the foundation of a universal state, and an equally unmistakable example of a rout in the foregoing 'Time of Troubles'; and we shall also find that the process does not exhaust itself in this single beat of the rhythm; for the establishment of the universal state is not the end of the story. For a time it may look as though this were something better than a rally from a rout. Is not the universal state a genuinely, even if belatedly, successful response to the challenge that has remained unanswered since the original breakdown? This challenge usually seems to take the form of a warfare between parochial sovereign states which threatens to become deadly unless the institution of parochial sovereignty can be transcended. Is not this condition for salvation fulfilled in the establishment of a unitary state of oecumenical range? And does not this justify the creators and preservers of a universal state in expecting that their handiwork will endure for ever? The answer seems to be that the establishment of a universal state is a response which falls short of success because it has been achieved both too late and at too great a cost. The stable door has been bolted only after the steed has fled. The cease-fire has been sounded only after the soldier has been dealt a mortal wound. The sword has been sheathed only after it has drunk so deep of blood that its thirst for bloodshed can never now be slaked until it has stolen out of its scabbard again and buried its blade up to the hilt in the body of the blood-guilty swordsman.[1] And, whatever the explanation, there is at any rate no doubt about the fact; for the march of events proves incontrovertibly that the universal state has an Achilles' heel, and that its belief in its own immortality is nothing but an illusion.[2] Sooner or later the universal state passes away; and its passing brings the disintegrating society to its dissolution. In the terms of our formula the rally that is represented by the foundation of a universal state is followed by a relapse when the society *in extremis* is either attacked and devoured by some aggressive contemporary or else dissolves in an interregnum out of which an affiliated civilization eventually emerges.[3]

[1] The truth of the saying that 'they that take the sword shall perish with the sword' is impressively demonstrated by the transitoriness of a universal state's *Pax Oecumenica* (see V. C (ii) (a), pp. 191–206, above).
[2] For this belief, and its ironical nemesis, see Part VI, below.
[3] For these two alternative endings to the life of a disintegrating civilization see IV. C (ii) (b) 1 and 2, vol. iv, pp. 56–114, above.

Thus in the disintegration-phase of the history of any civilization we can trace a movement of the disintegration-rhythm through at least one beat and a half. A rout which begins at the breakdown of the civilization is eventually followed by a rally which begins at the foundation of its universal state and which is eventually followed in its turn by the breakdown of this universal state's *Pax Oecumenica*. This latter breakdown marks the beginning of another rout which, instead of being followed by another rally, runs on unchecked until it results in annihilation.

On this grand scale the pattern is conspicuous; but, if we look into the movement of disintegration more closely, we shall perceive that the beats which catch our attention first are not the whole of the tune: they are major beats that are interspersed with at least as many minor ones.

While it is true, for example, that the foundation of a universal state marks the beginning of a rally, and its breakdown the beginning of a rout, it is not true that the rally maintains itself continuously, without flagging, from the first until the second of these two moments. In our survey of saviours with the sword we have passed in review the company of the 'Illyrians',[1] whose mission is to re-establish the *Pax Oecumenica* of a universal state after the society has suffered a relapse into anarchy; and this is as much as to say that, 'in the last analysis', the reign of the *Pax Oecumenica* proves not to be a single continuous régime, but to resolve itself, under the analyst's lens, into a couple of minor reigns with a minor interregnum in between them. On this showing, the periodicity-formula for a universal state is not a single beat of Rally-and-Relapse but a double one; and, if we employ a more powerful microscope, we may be able to carry our analysis farther.

For example, if we focus upon the Roman Empire, which was the Hellenic universal state, we shall easily discern the minor interregnum—beginning after the death of Marcus in A.D. 180 and ending at the accession of Diocletian in A.D. 284[2]—which splits the total span of the *Pax Romana* into two discontinuous bouts: the first bout ending in the year of the death of Marcus and beginning in the year of the Battle of Actium (*commissum* 31 B.C.), while the second bout begins in the year of the accession of Diocletian and ends in the year of the Battle of Adrianople (*commissum* A.D. 378). But, if we now take the first of these two bouts of the *Pax Romana* (*durabat* 31 B.C.–A.D. 180) and analyse this in its turn, we shall find that even this bout did not run quite continuously from beginning

---

[1] See V. C (ii) (*a*), pp. 207–8, above.
[2] This temporary collapse of the Roman Empire *post Marcum* has already been noticed in IV. C (i), vol. iv, p. 8; V. C (i) (*c*) 3, vol. v, p. 219; V. C (i) (*d*) 6 (δ), Annex, vol. v, p. 649; and V. C (ii) (*a*), in the present volume, p. 207, above.

to end of its own relatively short span. Even within this sub-period we can put our finger, at the year A.D. 69, 'the Year of the Four Emperors', on a sub-interregnum which is undoubtedly a genuine example of its kind, however mild a case we may pronounce it to be—judging by the length of its duration and the degree of its anarchy—in comparison even with the minor interregnum of A.D. 180–284 and *a fortiori* with the major interregnum which began in A.D. 378 and which was never retrieved.

If we now turn from the Roman Empire to the Tokugawa Shogunate, which was the universal state of the Far Eastern Society in Japan, we may be able to carry our analysis to yet a further degree of refinement. The *Pax Tokugawica* (*durabat* A.D. 1600–1868) did not last out its natural term, because it was overtaken and overwhelmed by the impact on Japan of the alien civilization of the West; yet, even within this exceptionally short Time-span, a modern Western scholar has detected three sub-relapses and two sub-rallies between the foundation of the Tokugawa Shogunate in the year of the Battle of Sekigehara (*commissum* A.D. 1600) and its abrupt end in the year of the Meiji Revolution (*actum* 1868).[1]

Again, in the major interregnum that follows the decisive breakdown of a *Pax Oecumenica*, it is possible in some cases to discern a sub-rally punctuating a débâcle which at first glance appears to run on and out, without any check at all, into a never-retrieved annihilation. In the major interregnum that followed the decisive breakdown of the *Pax Romana* in A.D. 378, we can espy a sub-rally of this kind in the reign of Justinian (*imperabat* A.D. 527–65).[2] In Indic history Justinian has a counterpart in Harsha (*imperabat* A.D. 606–47),[3] who temporarily arrested the ebb of a tide which, by the time when Harsha came to the throne, had been running out, unchecked, for no less than four generations since the decisive breakdown of the *Pax Guptica* in the eighth decade of the fifth century of the Christian Era. And, if Harsha is an Indic Justinian, the 'Abbasid Caliph Nāsir[4]—who for a moment successfully reasserted the temporal authority of his office more than three hundred years after its eclipse in the ninth century of the Christian Era—may be called a Syriac Heraclius. In Sinic history the major interregnum that followed the decisive breakdown of the

---

[1] See Murdoch, J.: *A History of Japan*, vol. iii (London 1926, Kegan Paul), p. 427. According to Murdoch, the initial rally, which began with Ieyasu's great victory in A.D. 1600, did not continue for more than seventy years without flagging, and from first to last the Bakufu régime experienced the following vicissitudes: 1600–70: rally; 1670–1709: relapse; 1709–51: rally; 1751–86: relapse; 1786–93: rally; 1793–1868: relapse.
[2] For Justinian as an example of a 'Second Solomon', see V. C (ii) (*a*), pp. 209–10, above. For the disastrous effects of Justinian's Archaism see cap. cit., pp. 223–5, above.
[3] See V. C (ii) (*a*), p. 209, footnote 3, above.   [4] See ibid., p. 212, above.

Pax Hanica in the last quarter of the second century of the Christian Era was momentarily interrupted—in this case after an interval of about a hundred years—when the political unity of the territories which had formerly been embraced in the Sinic universal state was temporarily restored under the dynasty of the United Tsin (*imperabant* A.D. 280–317).[1] This Sinic sub-rally in the course of a major interregnum was impressive so long as it lasted; but in the sequel it proved as costly a luxury as Justinian's blaze of magnificence. In the Sinic, as in the Hellenic, case the dissolving society was harrowed by more cruel tribulations after the abortive rally than it had ever undergone before it. For example, the 'successor-states' of the Sinic universal state in the first bout of the interregnum, which had followed immediately upon the break-up of the empire of the Posterior Han at the turn of the second and third centuries of the Christian Era, had been the indigenous Sinic principalities that still live on in the realm of romance under the name of 'the Three Kingdoms'. On the other hand the 'successor-states' by which the empire of the United Tsin was supplanted in its turn were carved out of the flesh of the Sinic body social by barbarian invaders.[2]

If we turn, in the third place, from the major interregnum which follows the decisive breakdown of a *Pax Oecumenica* to the 'Time of Troubles' that precedes its establishment, we shall find that this phase, too, in the disintegration of a civilization is not really uniform in colour or seamless in texture. The rout that is precipitated by the breakdown of a civilization does not run quite unchecked until the moment of the rally that is marked by the foundation of a universal state. Just as the *Pax Oecumenica* of a universal state is punctuated by a minor interregnum which splits its reign into two discontinuous bouts, so the anarchy of a 'Time of Troubles' is punctuated by a minor recovery which breaks the seizure up into two distinct paroxysms.

If, in the light of these considerations, we now try to strike a mean between an over-simple and an over-subtle analysis, we may be inclined to concentrate our attention upon a run of the disintegration-rhythm in which it takes three and a half beats of the movement of Rout-and-Rally to cover the journey from the breakdown of a civilization to its dissolution. Let us test our periodicity-pattern, as it presents itself on this scale, by our usual empirical method. Do the histories of the disintegrations of the civilizations whose histories are known to us fall naturally into this shape? Our survey will necessarily be confined to cases in

---

[1] See I. C (i) (*b*), vol. i, p. 88; IV. C (ii) (*b*) 1, vol. iv, p. 65, footnote 3; and V. C (i) (*c*) 3, vol. v, p. 272, above. [2] See V. C (i) (*c*) 3, vol. v, p. 273, above.

which our evidence is sufficient and in which, at the same time, the normal course of events has not been distorted out of all recognition by the disturbing impact of external forces. These conditions are fulfilled in the histories of the Hellenic and Sinic and Sumeric civilizations, and again in the history of the main body of the Orthodox Christian Society. The history of the Hindu Civilization has likewise followed a normal course which in our day is all but complete. And we shall also find it worth while to look at the histories of the Syriac Civilization, the Far Eastern Society both in Japan and in China, the Babylonic Civilization, the Orthodox Christian Society in Russia, and the Minoan Civilization—in spite of the irregularities which deform the first five of these six histories in their later chapters.

The Rhythm in Hellenic History.

The Hellenic example may be convenient to take first, because the challenge that worsted the Hellenic Civilization is one which has been the common bane of most of the civilizations whose breakdowns and disintegrations are on record, and at the same time one which is nowhere more easy to identify than it is in the Hellenic case in point. The challenge under which the Hellenic Civilization broke down was manifestly the problem of creating some kind of political world order that would transcend the institution of Parochial Sovereignty. And this problem, which defeated the generation that stumbled into the Atheno-Peloponnesian War of 431–404 B.C., never disappeared from the Hellenic Society's agenda so long as such a thing as Hellenism survived in any recognizable form.[1]

The moment of the breakdown of the Hellenic Society is not difficult to date; it can be equated with the outbreak of the Atheno-Peloponnesian War in 431 B.C.; and we can be equally confident in dating the establishment of the *Pax Romana*, which served as the Hellenic *Pax Oecumenica*, from Octavian's victory at Actium in 31 B.C. Can we also discern a movement of Rally-and-Relapse in the course of the 'Time of Troubles' that extends between these two dates? If we scan the history of the Hellenic World during the four centuries ending in 31 B.C., the vestiges of an abortive pre-Augustan rally are unmistakable.

One symptom is the social gospel of Homonoia or Concord[2] which was preached by Timoleon (*ducebat* 344–337 B.C.) in Sicily and by Alexander (*imperabat* 336–323 B.C.) in a vaster field east of

[1] See IV. C (iii) (b) 10, vol. iv, pp. 206–14; IV. C (iii) (c) 2 (β), vol. iv, pp. 303–15; and V. B, vol. v, p. 12, above.
[2] See V. C (i) (d) 7, pp. 6–8, above.

the Adriatic.[1] Another symptom of a rally is the subsequent prescription by two philosophers, Zeno and Epicurus, of a way of life for citizens of a commonwealth which was not any parochial city-state but was nothing less than the *Cosmopolis*.[2] A third symptom is a crop of constitutional experiments—the Seleucid Empire, the Aetolian and Achaean Confederacies, the Roman Commonwealth—which were all of them attempts to transcend the traditional sovereignty of the individual city-state by building up political communities on a supra-city-state scale out of city-states which had been persuaded or coerced into playing the part of constituent cells of a larger body politic.[3] A fourth symptom is the endeavour to put new life into a dead-alive 'patrios politeia' which was made by certain high-minded sons of the Hellenic dominant minority—the two Heracleidae at Sparta and the two Gracchi at Rome[4]—who idealistically overrated the blessings which their country had derived in times past from its traditional constitution when this had been 'a going concern', and who were naïvely blind to the dangers of attempting to reinstate an obsolete institution which had now become an anachronism as well as a dead letter.[5] A fifth symptom is a certain considerateness towards civilian life and property which appears to have been shown by the belligerents in the wars of Alexander's successors.[6] A sixth symptom is the social re-enfranchisement, *post Alexandrum*, of the women and slaves.[7] It will be observed that these symptoms of a rally in the course of the Hellenic 'Time of Troubles' extend over four or five generations, reckoning from Timoleon's to Cleomenes',[8] so that it is not easy to pin this rally down between definite dates; but, if we try to determine the period in which all this promise seemed nearest to being translated into performance, we may be inclined to single out the breathing-space of half a century between the death of Pyrrhus in 272 B.C.—an event that marked the end of

1 For the respective missions of Timoleon and Alexander as a philosopher-statesman and a philosopher-king see V. C (ii) (*a*), pp. 248, 251, and 253, and pp. 246 and 254, above.
2 For the Hellenic conception of the *Cosmopolis* see V. C (i) (*d*) 7, Annex, pp. 332–8, below.
3 For this crop of constitutional experiments in the third century B.C. see IV. C (iii) (*c*) 2 (β), vol. iv, pp. 309–13, above.
4 The two Gracchi are 'philosophically contemporary with' the two Heracleidae, though in chronological time they lived and worked a hundred years later. For the concept of 'philosophical contemporaneity' see I. C (iii) (*c*), vol. i, pp. 172–4, above. For the chronological Time-lag of the history of Rome, in the Pre-Imperial Age, behind the histories of the states at the heart of the Hellenic World see IV. C (iii) (*b*) 9, vol. iv, p. 205, above, and also Part XI, below.
5 For the Archaism of the Heracleidae and the Gracchi, and its disastrous outcome, see V. C (ii) (*a*), pp. 219–20, above.
6 On this convention see the passage quoted in IV. C (iii) (*b*) 3, vol. iv, p. 147, footnote 1, above, from Polybius, who gives to Alexander himself the credit of having been the first Hellenic captain to set this example of humanitarianism.
7 See IV. C (iii) (*b*) 14, vol. iv, pp. 239–40, above.
8 And leaving the generation of the Gracchi out of the reckoning, for the reason given in footnote 4, above.

the strife over the division of the heritage of Alexander the Great
—and the outbreak of the Hannibalic War in 218 B.C. This relatively prosperous spell of Hellenic history in the third century B.C.
is not incomparable with the earlier spell of rather greater prosperity and almost equal length which in the fifth century had
intervened between the repulse of Xerxes and the outbreak of the
Atheno-Peloponnesian War; and the two general wars which
respectively cut the two breathing-spaces short were disasters of
an approximately equal magnitude. It will be seen that, if the
third century B.C. witnessed a rally which almost looked like a
return of the Periclean Age, this rally was followed by a relapse
which was at least as serious a débâcle as the breakdown in which
the Periclean Age had found its tragic end.[1]

Can we diagnose the weak point in the rally that accounts for its
ultimate defeat? The weakness arose out of a sudden great increase
in the material scale of Hellenic life that had been a by-product
of the first paroxysm of the Hellenic 'Time of Troubles'. Hellenic
arms which had been exercised and sharpened in a hundred years
of internecine warfare were turned against non-Hellenic targets
towards the end of the fourth century B.C.; and, in practised
Macedonian and Roman hands, these formidable weapons then
conquered, and in conquering annexed to the Hellenic World, the
domains of four alien civilizations[2] as well as vast tracts of Barbarism.[3] This sudden change of material scale seriously—and, as it
turned out, fatally—aggravated the difficulty of solving the unsolved problem on the solution of which the fate of the Hellenic
Civilization hung. The problem, as we have seen, was that of
creating some kind of political world order that would transcend
the traditional sovereignty of the individual city-state; and, while
the change of material scale did promise to serve this end in one
negative way by making the maintenance of City-State Sovereignty
impossible, the same change also had a positive consequence
which militated—and this with far greater effect—against the.
endeavour to bring a world order into being.

Experiments in overcoming a traditional parochialism which
were unprecedentedly successful in themselves were now turned

---

[1] On a first view of Hellenic history we were content to trace the disintegration of
the Hellenic Society back to the Hannibalic War and to let our investigations rest at that
point for the time being (see I. B (iv), vol. i, pp. 40–2, above). It was not till we had
come to grips with the problem of the breakdowns of civilizations that we took this
inquiry up again and this time traced the story farther back, through an earlier chapter,
from the Hannibalic War of 218–201 B.C. to the Atheno-Peloponnesian War of 431–404
B.C. (See IV. C (ii) (b) 1, vol. iv, pp. 61–3, and V. C (i) (c) 3, vol. v, p. 213, above.)

[2] The Syriac, Egyptiac, Babylonic, and Indic.

[3] For this sudden territorial expansion of the Hellenic World at this time see III. C
(i) (a), vol. iii, pp. 140 and 150–1; III. C (i) (d), vol. iii, p. 197; IV. C (iii) (c) 2 (α), vol.
iv, p. 265; IV. C (iii) (c) 2 (β), vol. iv, pp. 305–6; and V. C (i) (c) 3, vol. v, p. 214, above.

to account, not for the large and vital purpose of creating an all-embracing Hellenic world order, but for the petty and perverse purpose of forging new-fangled Great Powers of a supra-city-state calibre which would be capable of continuing, on the new scale of Hellenic affairs, the internecine warfare that had been waged on the old scale by a Sparta and an Athens and a Thebes with such disastrous effects upon the life of the society in which all these parochial communities had their being. Thus the political shape which the Hellenic Society assumed in the new chapter of Hellenic history that had been opened by Alexander's passage of the Helles-pont[1] was something that was at the opposite pole from a political world order. When the epigoni of the diadochi of Alexander had fought one another to a standstill and the dust of battle had had time to settle down, the political landscape that became visible in the fourth decade of the third century B.C. revealed a cluster of pygmy states at the heart of the Hellenic World compassed about by a ring of giant Powers whose ambitions were set, and energies bent, upon the perilous game of contending with one another in the central arena for the prize of a hegemony over its puny and defenceless denizens.[2] Both the geographical expansion of the Hellenic World that had been achieved by Macedonian and Roman military prowess and the constitutional progress in transcending city-state sovereignty that had been accomplished by Aetolian and Achaean and Seleucid and Roman statesmanship had been seized upon, and successfully misapplied, for the purpose of recruiting the strength of the new competitors for a military ascendancy. And these giants' only notion of how to employ their huge physical powers was to refight the battles of Athens and Sparta with a titanic violence that had never come within those old-fashioned belligerents' capacity.

The inevitable consequence was a repetition in the third century of the catastrophe which the Hellenic Society had brought upon itself once already in the fifth century. In that earlier age the city-states which had indulged in 'temperate contests' with one another during the half-century following the repulse of Xerxes had eventually fallen into the internecine conflict of 431–404 B.C. And now, in the third century, the new Great Powers of supra-city-state calibre which had taken Athens' and Sparta's place proved likewise unable to contend with one another for longer than half a century without stumbling, in their turn, into a disaster. The respite that had begun after the death of Pyrrhus ended in the

---

[1] For this 'new era' of Hellenic history see V. C (i) (d) 9 (β), Annex, p. 340, below.
[2] For this constellation of Hellenic political forces in this age see III. C (ii) (b), vol. iii, pp. 310–13 and 339–41, and IV. C (iii) (c) 2 (α), vol. iv, pp. 265 and 268–9, above.

Hannibalic War of 218–201 B.C. And this time the havoc was proportionate to the unprecedented material 'drive' of the conflicting forces. The overthrow of Athens in 404 B.C. had been followed by nothing worse—bad enough though this might be—than a series of indecisive epilogues to the Great War which had ended at Aegospotami. Sparta, Thebes, and Macedonia in turn had won and lost an originally Athenian hegemony. On the other hand the overthrow of Carthage in 201 B.C. was followed by the destruction or subjugation of three other Great Powers in a series of decisive conflicts from which Rome emerged as the sole surviving combatant. Zama was followed by Cynoscephalae and Magnesia and Pydna; and the cumulative effect of half a century of catastrophic warfare (218–168 B.C.) upon the stamina of the Hellenic Society of the day was so devastating that the victor's triumph was immediately followed by a series of social convulsions which racked the victor himself quite as cruelly as his victims and which left the whole Hellenic body social mortally enfeebled by the time when this second paroxysm of the Hellenic 'Time of Troubles' was brought to an end at last through the tardy conversion of a Roman Anarchy into a Roman Peace.[1]

In the history of the disintegration of the Hellenic Society we have now verified the occurrence of one perceptible rally and one flagrant relapse between the original breakdown of the Hellenic Civilization in 431 B.C. and the establishment of a Hellenic *Pax Oecumenica* in 31 B.C.; and, since we have already taken note[2] of the subsequent relapse and rally that intervened between the first establishment of the *Pax Romana* in 31 B.C. and its final breakdown in A.D. 378, we can now report that the disintegration of one historic society, at any rate, does in fact present itself in the pattern of a run of three and a half beats of a recurrent movement of Rout-and-Rally. Let us see whether this finding is confirmed in other cases.

The Rhythm in Sinic History.

If we turn to the Sinic case next we shall identify the moment of the breakdown of the Sinic Civilization with the date of the disastrous collision between the two Powers Tsin and Ch'u in 634 B.C.,[3] and the moment of the establishment of a Sinic *Pax*

[1] Saint Augustine, in *De Civitate Dei*, Book III, chaps. 18–28, surveys the evils of this second paroxysm of the Hellenic 'Time of Troubles', from the outbreak of the Hannibalic War to the establishment of the *Pax Augusta*; and in chaps. 29–30 he submits that at any rate the climax of this paroxysm—i.e. the Roman *stasis* and civil wars of 133–31 B.C.—had been more dreadful than any of the experiences of his own generation, not excluding Alaric's sack of Rome in A.D. 410.
[2] In IV. C (i), vol. iv, p. 8; V. C (i) (c) 3, vol. v, p. 219; V. C (i) (d) 6 (δ), Annex, vol. v, p. 649; V. C (ii) (a), in the present volume, p. 207; and the present chapter, p. 284, above.
[3] See IV. C (ii) (b) 1, vol. iv, p. 66, above.

Oecumenica with the overthrow, in 221 B.C., of Ts'i by Ts'in—a 'knock-out blow' which left Ts'in alone alive as the solitary survivor in an arena now littered with the corpses of all the other Great Powers of the Sinic World.[1] If these are the two terminal dates of the Sinic 'Time of Troubles', are there any traces of a movement of Rally-and-Relapse within the intervening period? In the Sinic, as in the Hellenic, case the answer to this question is in the affirmative.

There is a perceptible rally in the course of the Sinic 'Time of Troubles' round about the generation of Confucius (*vivebat circa* 551–479 B.C.); and this rally may be taken to have been inaugurated by the disarmament conference of 546 B.C.,[2] in which a serious attempt was made to grapple with the fundamental problem of Sinic international politics.

In the Sinic World the dangerous political constellation into which the Hellenic World fell *post Alexandrum*[3]—that is to say, not until half-way through the Hellenic 'Time of Troubles'—had already taken shape in the last phase of the growth of the Sinic Society, before its breakdown. Even as early as that, the geographical expansion of the Sinic culture had produced the political effect of encircling the older states in the cradle of the Sinic Civilization with a ring of younger states which outclassed their elders in material calibre as decidedly as these surpassed the *parvenues* in every other respect.[4] The catastrophe of 634 B.C. can perhaps be traced back to the failure of a previous attempt to deal with this awkward situation by international co-operation. In 681–680 B.C. the pygmy states in the heart of the Sinic World had organized themselves into a Central Confederacy under the presidency of the eastern Great Power, Ts'i, with the object of opposing a collective resistance to the pressure of the preponderant and aggressive southern Great Power, Ch'u. But, although this Central Confederacy was equipped with a permanent constitution which provided for recurrent assemblies of the heads of states with the Prince of Ts'i as their convener,[5] its existence did not avail to prevent 'power politics' from becoming the dominant factor in Sinic international relations; and the conference of 546 B.C. represented a fresh attempt[6] to rescue the Sinic World from a chronic

---

[1] For the significance of this event see I. C (i) (*b*), vol. i, p. 89, above.

[2] See cap. cit., vol. cit., pag. cit.

[3] See the present chapter, pp. 289–91, above.

[4] See III. C (ii) (*b*), vol. iii, p. 303, footnote 2, and p. 313, footnote 3, above, as well as Maspéro, H.: *La Chine Antique* (Paris 1927, Boccard), pp. 286 and 336–7.

[5] For the foundation, organization, and history of this Sinic Central Confederacy see ibid., pp. 299–301. The Assembly was convened annually for the first four years of the Central Confederacy's existence, but thereafter only at longer intervals which were of no fixed length.

[6] Between the foundation of the Central Confederacy in 681–680 B.C. and the calling

warfare which, in and after the Tsin-Ch'u War of 634–628 B.C., had ceased to be temperate and had become internecine. This time the two Great Powers which for eighty-eight years past had been struggling inconclusively for the prize of hegemony were implored by Sung—which was one of the most ancient and most respectable of the pygmy states at the centre—to lay aside their mutually incompatible ambitions and to assume a joint presidency of the Central Confederacy on a footing of equality with one another; and this statesmanlike diplomacy did secure a breathing-space for an already grievously self-lacerated Sinic body social.

What the Sung Government accomplished in 546 B.C. gave an opportunity in the next generation for a sage who had been born in the neighbouring central state of Lu about five years before the date of the conference. Confucius was able to devote his life to the self-imposed mission of saving the Sinic Society from suicide by converting its princes to a philosophically archaistic way of living and ruling.[1] But Confucius's personal experience gives the measure of the rally which the conference of 546 B.C. had inaugurated, for Confucius is perhaps the supreme example of a prophet who has been not without honour save in his own time. A sage who was to be honoured superlatively by Posterity after the Sinic World had been tragically overtaken by the catastrophe from which the posthumous hero had hoped to save it, found himself unable to gain the ear of any contemporary ruler. And, if Posterity has been right in recognizing in Confucius's prescription the sovereign cure for Sinic troubles, then it is not to be wondered at that the generation who refused to take this healing medicine when the cup was brought to their lips should have fallen into a relapse which was to prove to be still graver than the seizure that had almost been the death of their fathers.

The first warnings of fresh trouble had already declared themselves quite early in Confucius's own lifetime. For example, the Covenant of 546 B.C. had been broken by Ch'u in 538 after one renewal in 541.[2] But a disturbing factor to which the relapse of the Sinic Society *post Confucium* can be traced back more directly is the decline and fall of the principality of Tsin. This northern

of the conference of 546 B.C. the Central Confederacy had one conspicuous success when, in the successive assemblies of 655 and 652 B.C., it succeeded in regulating the succession to the throne of the Imperial Dynasty of the Chou. At the second of these two meetings the Governments there represented appear to have subscribed to a Covenant of five articles, in which they pledged themselves to act upon certain rather vaguely formulated principles of political and social behaviour. (See Hirth, F.: *The Ancient History of China* (New York 1908, Columbia University Press), pp. 209–10.)
[1] Confucius's career has been taken as an illustration of the *motif* of Withdrawal-and-Return in III. C (ii) (*b*), vol. iii, pp. 328–30, above, and as an illustration of the sage's endeavour to save souls by proxy in V. C (ii) (*a*), in the present volume, p. 252, above.
[2] See Maspéro, op. cit., p. 348.

Great Power, which had been the first Sinic state to militarize itself,[1] was also the first to go to pieces.[2] Since about 573 B.C. there had been signs that the central government of Tsin was losing its hold over its feudatories; from 497 B.C. onwards this weakening of the central authority in the state began to be reflected in a process of internal disintegration; in the course of the fifth century the principality virtually dissolved into a mere congeries of fiefs; and this anarchy was only overcome at the cost of the life of the principality itself. About the year 424 B.C. Tsin broke up into three 'successor-states'—Chao, Han, and Wei—which secured diplomatic recognition in 403. This was the signal for a fresh outbreak of internecine warfare in the Sinic World; and that warfare was now waged in a larger arena and with a greater intensity than the pre-Confucian bout.

The increase in the extent of the arena was directly due to the break-up of Tsin; for the three 'successor-states' of the defunct principality were none of them of a calibre to play the part of a Great Power effectively; and their individual weakness was enhanced by the interlacement of their territories and by the mutual hostility of their governments; so that the effect of the change was to add three new members to the cluster of pygmy states at the heart of the Sinic World. On the other hand the ring of giants on the periphery was not broken, but was merely expanded, by the transference of the territories of the *ci-devant* northern Great Power from the outer circle to the inner; for all this time the Sinic World as a whole had continued steadily to expand; and by the time when Tsin collapsed a younger Power, Yen, which had latterly come into existence to the north of Tsin, was ready to step into the defunct northern Power's place. As for the increase in intensity that accompanied this increase in the scale of the warfare between the Sinic Great Powers, it is commemorated in the trivial yet significant fact that the name *Chan Kwo*—'the [period of] contending states'—which is properly applicable to the whole of the period between the outbreak of war between Tsin and Ch'u in 634 B.C. and the conquest of Ts'i by Ts'in in 221 B.C., has actually been confined, in the usage of Sinic historiography, to the second of the two paroxysms[3] into which the Sinic 'Time of Troubles' is divided by the respite which began at the conference of 546 B.C.

---

[1] See Maspéro, op. cit., p. 322.

[2] See ibid., pp. 345, 353, 362–3, and 367–8, for the principal stages in a decay which was a gradual process.

[3] The beginning of the *Chan Kwo* period seems to have been sometimes reckoned from 403 B.C. (the date of the diplomatic recognition of the three 'successor-states' of Tsin) and sometimes from 479 B.C. (the supposed date of the death of Confucius); but the usage of the term does not seem ever to have been stretched to include either Confucius's lifetime or, *a fortiori*, the bout of internecine warfare before Confucius's birth.

The second paroxysm engraved so much more harrowing an impression upon Sinic minds that it came to be thought of as the 'Time of Troubles' *par excellence*.

'Avec la chute du Tsin, ce n'est pas seulement un des grands états qui avait disparu, c'était aussi tout un idéal d'organisation politique sous la forme d'une sorte de confédération respectant dans une certaine mesure les droits des princes locaux: à partir du Vᵉ siècle, le vieux système des hégémonies était bien mort, et ce n'est pas pour le ressusciter à leur profit que les grands états luttèrent, ce fut pour s'agrandir directement aux dépens de leurs voisins plus faibles, jusqu'à ce que le triomphe définitif d'un seul réalisât pour la première fois l'unité absolue du monde chinois entier.'[1]

Thus in Sinic, as in Hellenic, history we can verify the occurrence of one perceptible rally and one flagrant relapse between the original breakdown of the society and the establishment of its *Pax Oecumenica*; and, if we go on to inquire whether the Sinic, like the Hellenic, *Pax Oecumenica* was punctuated by a relapse and a rally, we shall find this question easy to answer in the affirmative. The break in the continuity of the *Pax Hanica* is marked by a literal interregnum (*durabat* A.D. 9–25) which intervened between the fall of the dynasty of the Prior Han and the establishment of a new dynasty which had no genuine connexion with the House of Liu Pang, though it assumed the name of 'the Posterior Han' in a barefaced endeavour to gloze over its lack of any legitimate title to the Imperial Throne. The historical fact of the interregnum disposes of this fiction of continuity, and the bout of anarchy was longer *de facto* than *de jure*; for the Prior Han had let the reins of government fall from their hands about half a century before they lost the throne itself to the usurper Wang Mang.[2] It will be seen that the subsequent decisive breakdown of the *Pax Hanica* towards the close of the second century of the Christian Era, when the Posterior Han collapsed in their turn, was the fourth débâcle, reckoning from the initial disaster of 634–628 B.C., in the history of the disintegration of the Sinic Society; and, since this fourth débâcle was not successfully retrieved by the abortive rally in the time of the United Tsin,[3] the number of standard beats of the movement of Rout-and-Rally that can be counted in the course of the disintegration-process from first to last turns out in Sinic, as in Hellenic, history to be three and a half.

---

[1] Maspéro, op. cit., pp. 390–1.
[2] This collapse of the Prior Han is perhaps to be explained, at least in part, as an effect of the strain of the great wars of conquest on the Eurasian Steppe which had been launched by the Emperor Wuti (see V. C (i) (c) 3, vol. v, p. 271, above).
[3] See pp. 285–6, above.

The Rhythm in Sumeric History.

If we pass from Sinic history to Sumeric we shall register the same reading here again; for in the course of the Sumeric 'Time of Troubles' a beat of Rally-and-Rout is distinctly, even if only faintly, perceptible, while the life-span of the Sumeric universal state is punctuated by a counter-beat of Rout-and-Rally which is unusually emphatic.

If we date the beginning of the 'Time of Troubles'[1] from the career of the Sumerian militarist Lugalzaggisi of Erech (Uruk) and Umma (*dominabatur circa* 2677–2653 B.C.)[2] and equate its end with the foundation of a Sumeric universal state by Ur-Engur of Ur (*imperabat circa* 2298–2281 B.C.),[3] we may detect, in the life-time of the Akkadian militarist Naramsin (*dominabatur circa* 2572–2517 B.C.), at least one symptom of a rally in a sudden notable advance in the field of visual art which had been achieved between the generation of Naramsin and that of his predecessor Sargon (*dominabatur circa* 2652–2597 B.C.).[4] At the same time this very increase, in this age, of the Sumeric Society's powers of visual representation has served to testify that this successful cultivation of the arts of peace was not accompanied by any renunciation of Militarism. The scene portrayed on Naramsin's celebrated stele cries out for a nemesis that duly overtook the hero's successors.[5] Within a quarter of a century of Naramsin's death the Akkadian power had been shaken by disputes over the succession to the throne;[6] within sixty-two years the sceptre had passed back from Akkad to Erech; and within eighty-eight years the Gutaean bar-barians who had been brought to bay and slaughtered by Naramsin in their native mountain fastnesses had taken their revenge by descending upon the plains of Shinar and imposing their own rule on both Akkad and Sumer.[7] This interlude of barbarian domina-tion—which marked the acme of the second paroxysm of the Sumeric 'Time of Troubles'—lasted for 124 years (*circa* 2429–

---

[1] The dates given in the following paragraphs for events in Sumeric history are all taken, except where other references are given, from Meyer, E.: *Die Aeltere Chronologie Babyloniens, Assyriens und Aegyptens* (Stuttgart and Berlin 1925, Cotta).

[2] See I. C (i) (*b*), vol. i, p. 109, above.

[3] See I. C (i) (*b*), vol. i, p. 106; V. C (i) (*d*) 6 (γ), vol. v, p. 497; V. C (i) (*d*) 6 (δ), Annex, vol. v, pp. 650–1; and V. C (ii) (*a*), in the present volume, p. 190, above.

[4] For this advance—for which one of the most striking pieces of evidence is afforded by the stele on which Naramsin has commemorated his aggression against the high-landers of Gutium—see Meyer, E.: *Geschichte des Altertums*, vol. i, part (2), 3rd ed. (Stuttgart and Berlin 1913, Cotta), p. 533.

[5] For Naramsin's militarism and its nemesis see also I. C (i) (*b*), vol. i, p. 109; V. C (i) (*c*) 3, vol. v, pp. 203 and 262; and V. C (ii) (*a*), in the present volume, p. 184, above.

[6] The triennium, *circa* 2491–2489 B.C., which saw no less than four successors of Naramsin come and go may be compared with the Roman 'Year of the Four Emperors'.

[7] See V. C (i) (*c*) 3, vol. v, p. 262, above.

2306 B.C.) before Utuchegal of Erech (*militabat circa* 2305–2299 B.C.) made his abortive, and Ur-Engur of Ur (*imperabat circa* 2298–2281 B.C.) his successful, attempt to establish a *Pax Sumerica*.[1]

The Time-span of this *Pax Sumerica* extends between Ur-Engur's accession *circa* 2298 B.C. and Hammurabi's death *circa* 1905 B.C.; but when we look into the course of Sumeric history between these two dates we find that in this case the 'Peace' is a thin shell encasing a wide welter of anarchy.[2] The peace which Ur-Engur succeeded in establishing did not remain unbroken for more than 118 years. It was suddenly and violently interrupted when in 2180 B.C. Ur-Engur's fourth successor, the Emperor Ibisin, was defeated and taken prisoner by a host of Elamite rebels. Thereupon 'the Empire of the Four Quarters' broke into fragments. The triumphantly insurgent province of Elam not only recovered its own independence: it also imposed its rule upon a portion of the metropolitan territory of the Sumeric universal state in Shinar, which was now organized into a client-state of Elam with its capital at Larsa and with an Elamite prince installed there as the vassal of an Elamite suzerain who was the King of Elam itself. In other parts of Shinar the tradition of the Empire of Ur was carried on by a 'Realm of the Two Lands'[3] with its capital at Isin; but this relic of the Sumeric universal state was not strong enough to hold together the provinces on which the Elamites had not laid hands. This or that city-state (*imprimis* Erech) was perpetually asserting its independence here and there; and 130 years after Ibisin's catastrophe a new 'successor-state' with a greater future was carved out of the former domain of the Empire of Ur by Amorite marchmen who made themselves masters of Babylon in 2049 B.C. From first to last the tide of anarchy that had broken loose in 2180 B.C. went on flowing for more than 200 years. The first sign of a recoil from disruption towards consolidation was the conquest and annexation of the Empire of Isin by the Elamite client-state of Larsa *circa* 1954–1948 B.C. The work of re-union was completed in 1918 B.C. when Rimsin of Larsa, the Elamite conqueror of Isin, was overthrown in his turn by Hammurabi, the Amorite prince of Babylon. In virtue of this feat

---

[1] See I. C (i) (*b*), vol. i, p. 106; V. C (i) (*d*) 6 (γ), vol. v, p. 497; V. C (i) (*d*) 6 (δ), Annex, vol. v, pp. 650–1; and V. C (ii) (*a*), in the present volume, p. 190, above.

[2] The following facts and dates in the history of this recrudescence of the Sumeric 'Time of Troubles' are taken from Meyer, E.: *Geschichte des Altertums*, vol. i, part (2), 3rd ed. (Stuttgart and Berlin 1913, Cotta), pp. 559–69, as corrected by the same scholar in his *Die Aeltere Chronologie Babyloniens, Assyriens und Aegyptens* (Stuttgart and Berlin 1925, Cotta), pp. 26–31.

[3] i.e. Sumer and Akkad. After the catastrophe of 2180 B.C. the demi-emperors at Isin reverted to this original style and title of the Emperor Ur-Engur and abandoned the more ambitious style and title of 'the Empire of the Four Quarters' which had been introduced by Ur-Engur's successor Dungi (see V. C (i) (*d*) 6 (δ), Annex, vol. v, p. 651, above).

Hammurabi justly regarded himself as the successor of Ur-Engur and Dungi;[1] and there was a moment when he was effectively master of the whole of Dungi's 'Empire of the Four Quarters', Elam included. But Hammurabi's restoration of the *Pax Sumerica* was as ephemeral as it was far-reaching. For the author of it was hardly in his grave before the Sumeric Society was swept off its feet again in a fourth and final débâcle from which it never rallied.[2]

The Rhythm in the History of the Main Body of Orthodox Christendom.

The now familiar pattern reappears, just complete, in the disintegration of the main body of Orthodox Christendom, and again —this time all but complete—in the disintegration of the Hindu Society.

We have identified the breakdown of the Orthodox Christian Society with the outbreak of the great Romano-Bulgarian War of A.D. 977–1019;[3] and the eventual establishment of a peace which was oecumenical for the main body of Orthodox Christendom— though it did not extend to the offshoot of this civilization on Russian soil—may be dated from the Ottoman conquest of Macedonia in A.D. 1371–2.[4] In between these two termini of an Orthodox Christian 'Time of Troubles' we can discern a rally led by the East Roman Emperor Alexius Comnenus (*imperabat* A.D. 1081–1118),[5] a consequent respite which lasted through the reigns of the next two sovereigns of the Comnenian Dynasty, and a relapse into which the society fell in the ninth decade of the twelfth century.[6] The subsequent tribulations of Orthodox Christendom, which were only ended by the establishment of a *Pax Ottomanica*,[7] were still more grievous than the earlier troubles

---

[1] See Meyer, E.: *Geschichte des Altertums*, vol. i, part (2), 3rd ed. (Stuttgart and Berlin 1913, Cotta), p. 633.

[2] See I. C (i) (*b*), vol. i, pp. 106 and 110, and IV. C (ii) (*b*) 1, vol. iv, pp. 63–4, above.

[3] See IV. C (ii) (*b*) 1, vol. iv, p. 72, and IV. C (iii) (*c*) 2 (*β*), vol. iv, pp. 390–1, above.

[4] See Part III. A, vol. iii, p. 27, and V. C (ii) (*a*), in the present volume, p. 191, footnote 1, above.

[5] See IV. C (iii) (*c*) 2 (*β*), Annex II, vol. iv, pp. 619–20, and V. C (ii) (*a*), in the present volume, p. 184, above.

[6] This relapse at this date was the penalty that Orthodox Christendom had to pay for the fault of a dynasty which had forgotten its founder's mission of bringing salvation to a disintegrating society. The successors of Alexius I Comnenus succumbed to a fatal spirit of military adventure which had first taken possession of the East Roman Government in the tenth century of the Christian Era (see IV. C (iii) (*c*) 2 (*β*), vol. iv, pp. 399–404, above).

[7] This second paroxysm of the Orthodox Christian 'Time of Troubles' was faintly relieved in the middle decades of the thirteenth century by the success of the Nicene Greek 'successor-state' of the East Roman Empire in putting together again some of the fragments into which the Empire had broken up between A.D. 1186 and A.D. 1204. In other contexts (Part III. A, vol. iii, p. 27, and V. C (ii) (*a*), in the present volume, p. 184, above) these Nicene Greek achievements have been taken as symptoms of a turn in the tide of disruption, and as portents of the later and greater achievements of the

which had been momentarily overcome by the prowess of Alexius Comnenus.

The *Pax Ottomanica* which was inaugurated by the Ottoman conquest of Macedonia in A.D. 1371–2 eventually collapsed under the shock of defeat in the great Russo-Turkish War of 1768–74; but, while this collapse marked the decisive breakdown of a régime that had been first established four hundred years earlier, the Ottoman annals of the intervening centuries present plain evidence of an anticipatory relapse that was retrieved by a temporary rally. The relapse is to be discerned in the rapid decay of the Pādishāh's Slave-Household after the death of Suleymān the Magnificent in A.D. 1566.[1] The rally is heralded in the subsequent experiment of compensating for the demoralization of the *qullar* by taking the Pādishāh's Orthodox Christian *ra'īyeh* into partnership with the free Muslim citizens of the Ottoman commonwealth—who had now seized the reins of power—without any longer insisting that the *ra'īyeh* should become renegades as the price of their admission to a share in the government of the state.[2]

This almost revolutionary innovation, which was introduced in the seventeenth century by the statesmanship of the vezīrs of the House of Köprülü,[3] won for the Ottoman Empire in the eighteenth century a breathing-space which is still wistfully remembered by the 'Osmanlis of a later day as 'the Tulip Period'. During this brief spell (*circa* A.D. 1718–36) the ruling class of an empire that was already standing on the defensive against the Franks and the Russians was still able for a moment to rest from the toils of war and to forget the cares of state in the recreation of cultivating a flower.[4] The breathing-space, however, was as short as it was pleasant; for, even before it began, the statesmanlike salvage-work of the Köprülüs had been fatally sabotaged by the reckless

'Osmanlis. Yet, if the Nicene Greek attempt at political reconstruction is to be regarded as a sub-rally, it must also be written off as an abortive one; for the Principality of Nicaea did not enlarge its dominions, but merely shifted its centre of gravity, when it conquered Adrianople in A.D. 1235 and Macedonia in A.D. 1246 and Constantinople itself in A.D. 1261. As fast as these Greek princes of Nicaea acquired territories in Europe from Greek or Latin rivals, they lost territories in Asia to the Turks. For the subsequent flashes of religious and artistic light in Orthodox Christendom in the fourteenth century see IV. C (iii) (*c*) 2 (β), vol. iv, pp. 359–61, above.

[1] For this decay see Part III. A, vol. iii, pp. 44–7, above.

[2] For this experiment see II. D (vi), vol. ii, pp. 223–5, and Part III. A, vol. iii, pp. 47–8, above.

[3] See V. C (ii) (*a*), pp. 208–9, above. These Albanian statesmen performed the same service for the Ottoman Empire in the seventeenth century of the Christian Era as the Illyrian soldiers had performed for the Roman Empire in the third century.

[4] For this interlude of dilettantism in the grim history of the Ottoman governing class see von Hammer, J.: *Histoire de l'Empire Ottoman*, French translation (18 vols.+ atlas), vol. xiv (Paris 1839, Bellizard, Barthès, Dufour et Lowell), pp. 61–70. 'La passion des fleurs devint le goût dominant du peuple, à tel point qu'elle surpassa bientôt celle qu'un grand nombre d'individus avaient à cette époque en France et dans les Pays-Bas, pour la culture des tulipes' (p. 65). See also Jorga, N.: *Geschichte des Osmanischen Reichs* (5 vols.), vol. iv (Gotha 1911, Perthes), Book II, chap. 4, pp. 361–99.

militarism of Mehmed Köprülü's unluckily chosen protégé Qāra
Mustafā.[1] This megalomaniac had wasted the precious strength
which the Köprülüs had been nursing back into the Ottoman body
politic on a new attempt to conquer Western Christendom—a
military task which had proved to be beyond the Ottoman Empire's power when this had been still at its height in Suleymān the
Magnificent's lifetime. Qāra Mustafā's folly had precipitated the
great war of 1682–99, in which the ascendancy had passed once
for all from the Ottoman to the Frankish side.[2] And, although the
Köprülüs' work did avail to stave off disaster for three-quarters
of a century—from A.D. 1699 to A.D. 1774—the nemesis of Qāra
Mustafā's wanton stroke was merely postponed and was not
averted. The military disaster of A.D. 1768–74 proved irretrievable
because, by that time, the ra'īyeh whose support the Köprülüs had
enlisted were ceasing to be content with a partnership in the
government of a declining Ottoman Empire and were being captivated by the ambition of carving up the decrepit Ottoman body
politic into young national states of their own in the fashion of the
rising peoples of the West.[3] The sequel to the decisive breakdown
of the *Pax Ottomanica*—which was Orthodox Christendom's *Pax
Oecumenica*—in the last quarter of the eighteenth century was not
a rally: it was a merger of the main body of Orthodox Christendom in a 'Great Society' of a Western complexion.[4] And thus we
see that in Orthodox Christian history, too, the process of disintegration has run through three and a half beats of the movement of Rout-and-Rally from first to last.

The Rhythm in Hindu History.

In the history of the disintegration of the Hindu Society the
final half-beat is not yet quite due, since the second instalment of
the *Pax Oecumenica*—which in the Hindu World has been provided by the British Rāj—is not yet quite over.[5] On the other

---

[1] See V. C (ii) (a), p. 208, footnote 3, above.
[2] See Part III. A, vol. iii, pp. 46–7, above.
[3] For the Westernization of the 'Osmanlis' Orthodox Christian ra'īyeh, and for the political consequences of their cultural conversion, see II. D (v), vol. ii, pp. 181–6; II. D (vi), vol. ii, pp. 226–8; and IV. C (ii) (b) 2, vol. iv, pp. 76–8, above.
[4] See ibid.
[5] Since the usual span of a *Pax Oecumenica*—including both its two instalments and the bout of anarchy in between them—seems to be round about four hundred years, and since the original establishment of the present *Pax Oecumenica* in the Hindu World may be equated (if there is any virtue in a conventional date) with the conquest of Gujerat by Akbar in A.D. 1572—as being the event which, perhaps more than any other, marked the elevation of the Mughal Rāj from a parochial to an oecumenical status—the break-up of the British Rāj was to be expected, on this showing, within thirty or forty years of the time of writing in A.D. 1938. At that moment, however, it seemed rather more probable that the history of India would take a different turn; for the establishment and collapse and re-establishment of a 'sub-continental' *Pax Oecumenica* was not the only experience of first-rate historical importance which India had undergone by then since Akbar's day. In the meantime the contact between India and the Western World,

hand the three earlier beats of Rout-and-Rally have all left some trace on the record of Hindu history. The third beat of the three has been particularly emphatic; for in this beat the 'rout' is represented by the collapse of the Mughal Rāj in the eighteenth century of the Christian Era and the 'rally' by the establishment of the British Rāj in the nineteenth century;[1] and these two instalments of peace—which are separated from one another in Time by no less than a hundred years of virulent anarchy—have been the work of two gangs of empire-builders who are as alien from one another as they both are from their Hindu *ra'īyeh*.[2] The rally-stroke of the second beat of the rhythm is equally clear. It is represented by the establishment of the Mughal Rāj in the reign of Akbar (*imperabat* A.D. 1556–1602). The foregoing rout-stroke is not so conspicuous. But, if we peer into the history of the Hindu 'Time of Troubles', which ends in the reign of Akbar and begins in the latter part of the twelfth century of the Christian Era with an outbreak of internecine warfare among the Hindu Powers of the age,[3] we shall notice—in between the tribulations of India under the heel of the Ghaznawīs and Ghūrīs and Slave-Kings in the eleventh and twelfth centuries of the Christian Era and the similar tribulations that were inflicted upon her in the fifteenth and sixteenth centuries by the Lōdī Afghans and by Akbar's own ancestor Bābur—some signs of a temporary relief in an intervening period which begins with the accession of 'Alā-ad-Dīn in A.D. 1296 and ends with the death of Fīrūz in A.D. 1388.[4] If the second beat of Rout-and-Rally in Hindu history, which ends in the establishment of the *Pax Mogulica*, may be taken as beginning with the collapse of Fīrūz's régime after its author's death, we may see in the preceding establishment of 'Alā-ad-Dīn's régime the end of a first beat of Rout-and-Rally which begins with the original breakdown of the Hindu Civilization in the twelfth century of the Christian Era.

The Rhythm in Syriac History.

These cases in which a run of three and a half beats of the disintegration-rhythm can be traced throughout—or almost through-

---

which Akbar himself had done much to promote, had increased to a degree of intimacy at which India had ceased to be a world in herself and had become, instead, one of the members of a new 'Great Society' of a Western complexion. At the time of writing it seemed likely that the British Rāj—which had served at first as a second instalment of a Hindu *Pax Oecumenica*—would now transform itself, without any violent break, into an Indian national state-member of a world-wide political society.

[1] See V. C (ii) (*a*), pp. 189 and 191, above.   [2] *Angiicè* 'ryot'.
[3] See IV. C (ii) (*b*) 2, vol. iv, pp. 99–100, above.
[4] The slave-households that were maintained by these two Turkish empire-builders in Hindustan have been brought into comparison with the Ottoman Pādishāh's Slave-Household in Part III. A, vol. iii, p. 31, footnote 1, above.

out—its entire course may be supplemented by a glance at several other cases in which the same pattern can be made out, beyond mistake, in a run that is incomplete.

In Syriac history, for example, the disintegration-process was interrupted immediately after the third rally by a militant irruption of Hellenism into the Syriac World in the train of Alexander the Great; but down to that point, which in this case was as far as the process went, it followed the regular course which we have learnt to recognize in other instances. The third rally of the Syriac Society had been achieved, on the eve of Alexander's epiphany, by the Achaemenian Emperor Artaxerxes Ochus (*imperabat* 358–338 B.C.),[1] who had crushed a coalition of rebellious satraps and had followed up that victory by the reconquest of Egypt.[2] The rout which Ochus was stemming had set in about the turn of the fifth and fourth centuries B.C. (the first portent had been the secession of Egypt from the Achaemenian Empire in 404 B.C.; and the impunity with which the Egyptians had repudiated their allegiance to the Great King had nerved other rebels, less remote from Susa, to follow this Egyptian example). But the *dégringolade* of the Achaemenian power in the reigns of Darius II and Artaxerxes II was not, of course, the first chapter of Achaemenian history. It marked the collapse of an effective *Pax Achaemenia* which had first been established by the successive labours of Cyrus and Darius the Great[3] and which had not been more than locally disturbed by Xerxes' fiasco in the hinterland of the North-West Frontier.[4] And that first establishment of the *Pax Achaemenia* in the sixth century B.C. had been the second rally of the Syriac Society in the course of its disintegration. The Achaemenian Empire was the universal state which had put an end to the Syriac 'Time of Troubles'; and in another context[5] we have identified the original breakdown of the Syriac Society, which had brought the Syriac 'Time of Troubles' on, with an outbreak of internecine warfare among the parochial states of the Syriac World which had occurred towards the end of the tenth century B.C. after the death of Solomon. Between Solomon's generation and Cyrus's, can we observe any symptoms of a first rally and a second rout? One

---

[1] This grim Achaemenid 'saviour' has been inspected, in company with the Ottoman Pādishāh Murād IV, in V. C (ii) (*a*), p. 207, above.

[2] See V. C (i) (*c*) 2, vol. v, p. 94, and V. C (i) (*c*) 3, vol. v, p. 245, footnote 4, above, and V. C (ii) (*a*), Annex II, in the present volume, p. 442, below.

[3] For the respective contributions of these two empire-builders see V. C (ii) (*a*), pp. 187–8 and 190, above.

[4] The Achaemenian Rāj in South-Western Asia was no more seriously shaken by the disastrous failure of the Persian invasion of European Greece in 480–479 B.C. than the British Rāj in India was by the even more disastrous failure of the British invasion of Afghanistan in A.D. 1838–42.

[5] In IV. C (ii) (*b*) 1, vol. iv, pp. 67–8, above.

plain token of a rally in the course of the intervening age is a coalition of Syriac forces which defeated an Assyrian aggressor at the Battle of Qarqar in 853 B.C.[1] Conversely, we may diagnose a rout in the subsequent relapse of the Syriac states into a fratricidal strife that made it easy for Tiglath-Pileser III and Sargon to conquer piecemeal in the eighth century B.C. a cosmos of Syriac city-states which had not found it difficult in the ninth century to keep Shalmaneser III at bay by making common cause against a common alien enemy.

The Rhythm in the History of the Far Eastern Civilization in Japan.

In the disintegration of the Far Eastern Society in Japan the duration of the *Pax Tokugawica* has been cut short, as we have seen, by the collision of Japan with the West; and the observable fluctuations in the fortunes of the Tokugawa Shogunate, so long as it lasted, are of a shorter wave-length than the normal run of the disintegration-rhythm which we are investigating at the moment.[2] On the other hand the first two beats of this standard run of rhythm can be detected in the preceding chapter of Japanese history[3] which ends with the establishment of a *Pax Oecumenica* by Hideyoshi (*dominabatur* A.D. 1582–98)[4] and which begins in the latter part of the twelfth century of the Christian Era with the overthrow of the régime of 'the Cloistered Emperors' in the military revolutions of A.D. 1156 and 1160 and 1183–5.[5]

A first rally, in reaction to this original breakdown, can be discerned in an attempt to re-establish a civilian government which was made immediately after the downfall, in A.D. 1333, of the military regency which had been ruling Japan from Kamakura since A.D. 1184.[6] This rally, however, was abortive.[7] Within five years the restored civilian régime had been superseded by a new military regency[8] which was not the less true to type because it made the conciliatory gesture of establishing its official headquarters at Kyoto—the ancient Imperial Capital—instead of simply entrenching itself in the north-eastern stronghold from which

---

[1] For the Battle of Qarqar see ibid., p. 67, and IV. C (iii) (c) 3 (α), vol. v, pp. 468, footnote 1, 473, footnote 3, and 475, above.
[2] For Murdoch's analysis of the rhythm of the Tokugawa Shogunate see the present chapter, p. 285, footnote 1, above.
[3] For Nichiren's designation of this period as the Age of Mappō ('the Destruction of the Law') see V. C (i) (c) 2, vol. v, p. 96, footnote 6, above.
[4] For Hideyoshi's role in Japanese history see V. C (ii) (a), pp. 188–9, above.
[5] For this revolutionary change of régime in Japan see IV. C (ii) (b) 2, vol. iv, p. 94, above. For the antecedent and underlying differentiation between the êthos of Yamato and the êthos of the Kwanto see II. D (v), vol. ii, pp. 158–9, above.
[6] See Sansom, G. B.: *Japan, A Short Cultural History* (London 1932, Cresset Press), p. 319; Murdoch, J.: *A History of Japan*, vol. i (London 1910, Kegan Paul), p. 539. The civilian Imperial Government at Kyoto had made one previous attempt, as early as A.D. 1221, to overthrow the Kamakura Bakufu (ibid., p. 442).
[7] Ibid., p. 554.   [8] Ibid., p. 569.

Japan had been ruled for 150 years by Minamoto Yoritomo and his successors. This swift reversion to Militarism was the first symptom of a fresh rout. In the days of the Shoguns of the Ashikaga Dynasty who succeeded one another at Kyoto from A.D. 1338 until the last of the line was hustled off the stage by Hideyoshi in A.D. 1597, Japan suffered worse tribulations than she had known in the days of the previous line of Shoguns who had succeeded one another at Kamakura from 1184 to 1333.[1]

The immediate sequel to the establishment of the Ashikaga Shogunate was the unprecedented scandal of a schism of the Imperial House itself into two rival courts. This enormity, which was a sin against religious ritual as well as a breach of political etiquette, had to be atoned for by fifty-five years of civil war (gerebatur A.D. 1337–92);[2] and, even when the Ashikaga Shogunate—acting in the name of the court which was its puppet—eventually succeeded in suppressing the rival court which had refused to acknowledge its title, the tale of calamities did not cease.[3] In the fifteenth century of the Christian Era a feudal anarchy which the Shoguns were impotent to reduce to order goaded an intolerably oppressed peasantry into a chronic state of revolt and stimulated the monasteries to militarize themselves—in flat defiance of all precepts of both the Greater and the Lesser Vehicle—as the only alternative to becoming the lay militarists' victims.[4] In the War

---

[1] Sansom, op. cit., p. 342. [2] Murdoch, op. cit., vol. cit., pp. 584–6.
[3] Between the end of the War of the Rival Courts in A.D. 1392 and the beginning of the War of Onin in A.D. 1467 there was a minor rally (Sansom, op. cit., pp. 345, 358, and 371).
[4] This militarization of the monasteries during the Japanese 'Time of Troubles' cannot be entirely explained as an unavoidable measure of self-defence which was forced upon the monks by the turbulence of the worldlings among whom their lot had been cast. The metamorphosis, in Japan, of monks into fighting-men which was completed in this age had a long history behind it, and, while it was partly an effect of the breakdown of the Far Eastern Civilization in Japan, it was also one of the antecedents and causes of this catastrophe. The first recorded case of monks taking up arms in Japan occurred in the seventh decade of the tenth century of the Christian Era (see Eliot, Sir Charles: Japanese Buddhism (London 1935, Arnold), p. 246, and the present Study, IV. C (ii) (b) 2, vol. iv, p. 94, footnote 2, above); and in this case the militant monastery was not defending itself against a lay aggressor, but was resorting to war as a method of asserting its claims against a rival religious house. Thus, when the militarization of the monasteries in Japan is traced back to its origins, it becomes apparent that this was one of several symptoms of a relapse into barbarism which was the cause of the breakdown of the Far Eastern Civilization in Japan, and not a consequence of it. In other contexts we have observed that this relapse was the nemesis of a cultural tour de force by which the hot-house plant of Far Eastern culture had been transplanted from its kindly native soil and climate on the Asiatic Continent into the uncongenial environment of the Japanese Archipelago (for this feature of Japanese history see II. D (v), vol. ii, pp. 158–9, and IV. C (ii) (b) 2, vol. iv, p. 94, above). Conversely, one of the labours that had to be performed by Nobunaga and Hideyoshi in order to accomplish their mission of imposing a Pax Oecumenica by force was to break the military power of the monasteries, which in their day was at its apogee.
'During all the latter half of the sixteenth century [of the Christian Era] Buddhism was an important force in Japan, but, strange to say, more conspicuous as a military and political force than in its proper sphere. The principal monasteries appear on the scene from time to time in exactly the same way as the great military houses with armies and forts of their own, with territorial ambitions and designs to crush or annex their rivals.

of Onin (*gerebatur* A.D. 1467–77) the Imperial City of Kyoto was devastated by street-fighting between contending provincial forces who made the capital their arena. In the sixteenth century the Shoguns were overtaken by the ignominious fate which their pre-decessors had inflicted on the Emperors. The Shogun's *de jure* powers were now exercised *de facto* by a Kwanryo; and this travesty of government by the deputy of a deputy was perhaps the one thing worse than no government at all.[1] This was the state of misery to which Japan had been reduced by the second paroxysm of her 'Time of Troubles' before her convulsed and writhing frame was forced into a strait-waistcoat by the successive exertions of Nobu-naga and Hideyoshi and Ieyasu (*militabant* A.D. 1549–1615).[2]

The Rhythm in the History of the Main Body of the Far Eastern Civilization.

In the history of the main body of the Far Eastern Society the process of disintegration took an abnormal turn at an earlier stage than in Japan; for, whereas in Japan the *Pax Oecumenica* which had been imposed by Hideyoshi and had been organized by Ieyasu lasted for more than two and a half centuries before the impact of the West precipitated the Meiji Revolution of A.D. 1868, the *Pax Oecumenica* which was imposed on China by alien Mongol arms between A.D. 1209[3] and A.D. 1280 did not remain unchallenged for more than seventy years before it was shaken off by a Chinese insurrection which began about A.D. 1351 and which persisted until the Mongol intruders had been driven right out of Intramural China into their native wilderness beyond the Great Wall.[4] This Chinese counterstroke was followed in its turn by a back-wash of barbarian invasion in which the Manchus re-established the

---

But the same period witnessed the end of this system and the definite defeat of the Church Militant. There was evidently a danger that the country might be ruled by priests, like Tibet. The leaders of Japan forestalled this danger but were careful to avoid anything like a war against Religion as such' (Eliot, op. cit., p. 301).

[1] The century between the opening of the War of Onin in A.D. 1467 and Nobunaga's assumption of dictatorial powers *de facto* in A.D. 1568 seems to have been the worst phase of the whole of the Japanese 'Time of Troubles' (Sansom, op. cit., pp. 394–5 and 419–20). It was during these hundred years that the four popular Japanese 'higher religions' (see V. C (i) (*c*) 2, vol. v, pp. 96–103, above) were at the height of their influence (Sansom, op. cit., pp. 366–7).

[2] For the respective roles of these three saviours with the sword see V. C (ii) (*a*), pp. 186, 188, and 191, above. Nobunaga and Hideyoshi both died in harness, and Nobunaga literally under arms (though the hand that took his life was his own). Ieyasu died in the year following his last campaign against the castle of Osaka. Hideyoshi and Ieyasu took up arms simultaneously with one another in A.D. 1558.

[3] This seems to have been the date of Chingis Khan's first assault upon the princi-pality of Tangut, which was a north-western barbarian 'successor-state' of the Empire of T'ang and Sung. His attack on the far more important north-eastern barbarian 'successor-state'—the principality of the Kin—was not launched until A.D. 1211.

[4] For the *Pax Mongolica* in the main body of the Far Eastern Society, and for the successful Chinese reaction against it, see II. D (v), vol. ii, pp. 121–2; IV. C (ii) (*b*) 2, vol. iv, pp. 86–7; and V. C (i) (*c*) 4, vol. v, pp. 348–51, above.

empire which the Mongols had won and lost; and this interlude
has been followed by the impact of a Western Civilization which
has collided with China as well as with Japan in the course of its
ubiquitous modern expansion. In a period of Chinese history
which has been dominated by this capricious play of external
forces it is not to be expected that the pulse of the disintegrating
society should register the normal beat. On the other hand, in the
'Time of Troubles' of the disintegrating Far Eastern Society in
China, as in Japan, we can detect two beats of Rout-and-Rally
which are of the standard wave-length.

In the main body of the Far Eastern Society we have identified
the end of the 'Time of Troubles' with the completion of the
Mongol conquest of China in A.D. 1280,[1] and the beginning of it
with the decay of the T'ang Dynasty in the last quarter of the
ninth century of the Christian Era;[2] and in the interval between
these two termini there are clear traces of both a rally and a relapse.

On the political plane this first rally in the history of the disintegration of the main body of the Far Eastern Society declares
itself in the establishment of the Sung Dynasty in A.D. 960. In the
field of technique it declares itself particularly in a remarkable
advance in the art of printing.[3] In the field of visual art it declares
itself in the rise of a school of painting which is the fine flower of
Far Eastern achievement in this line.[4] In the field of abstract
thought it declares itself in the work of the five Neo-Confucian
philosophers (*vivebant* A.D. 1017–1200),[5] who reinterpreted Confucius in the light of the Mahāyāna as, in the contemporary Western
World, the Schoolmen read the philosophy of Aristotle into the
doctrines of Catholic Christianity. In the field of social theory
and practice the same rally is represented by the Neo-Confucians'
bugbear Wang An Shih.[6]

---

[1] See IV. C (ii) (*b*) 2, vol. iv, pp. 86–7, above.
[2] See ibid., pp. 86 and 87–8, above.
[3] See Carter, T. F.: *The Invention of Printing in China and its Spread Westward*,
revised edition (New York 1931, Columbia University Press), chap. 10. 'In invention,
what the T'ang period conceived, the Sung era put to practical use. The magnetic
needle, used in the main in earlier times either as a toy or for the location of graves, was
applied to navigation. Gunpowder, already known and used for fireworks, was during
the Sung Dynasty applied to War. Porcelain was so developed as to become an article
of export to Syria and Egypt. A similar development took place in printing' (p. 55).
According to the same authority, op. cit., p. 32, block printing for the production of
books had been invented as early as the reign of T'ang Ming Hwang (*imperabat* A.D.
712–56).
[4] See Münsterberg, O.: *Chinesische Kunstgeschichte*, vol. i (Esslingen 1910, Neff),
p. 204.
[5] See Part II. B, vol. i, p. 202, above.
[6] See Fitzgerald, C. P.: *China, A Short Cultural History* (London 1935, Cresset
Press), chap. 19; Hackmann, H.: *Chinesische Philosophie* (Munich 1927, Reinhardt),
pp. 313–15; and Williamson, H. R.: *Wang An Shih* (London 1935–7, Probsthain, 2
vols.). The true purpose of Wang An Shih's administrative and social reforms seems
to have been to increase the prosperity of the state by alleviating the burdens of the
peasantry, on whose shoulders the political superstructure rested. His most important

The subsequent relapse declares itself in the tragic career of the connoisseur-emperor Huitsung (*imperabat* A.D. 1101–25).[1] Huitsung's life-work was the making of a collection of works of art, and he lived to publish a catalogue of this, in twenty volumes, in A.D. 1120. But the unfortunate collector lived on to see his collection dispersed when, five years later, the city of Kaifêng, in which it was housed, was attacked and captured by the Kin barbarians from Manchuria—not because these uncultivated invaders coveted the possession of Huitsung's artistic treasures, but because Kaifêng happened also to be the political capital of the Sung Empire. This was a challenge which Huitsung was utterly unprepared to meet; and in the last chapter of his life he had to atone for his neglect of his political duties during a reign of twenty-five years by lingering on for another ten years as a refugee, or prisoner, in the tents of the Kin barbarians' evicted predecessors the Khitan—an asylum in which the unhappy exile could neither exert himself as an emperor nor enjoy himself as a connoisseur.[2] While Huitsung was thus languishing in limbo, the barbarians whom he had so lamentably failed to keep at bay were conquering the northern provinces of the Sung Empire; and this Kin war of conquest, which went on from A.D. 1124 to A.D. 1142 and did not stop until the invaders had reached the line of the River Hwai and the watershed between the Yellow River and the Yangtse, signalized the second rout in the disintegration of the main body of the Far Eastern Society—as the first rout had been signalized by the earlier loss of sixteen frontier districts to the Kin's predecessors the Khitan between the years A.D. 927 and A.D. 937.[3] This second rout was not followed by a rally until the Mongols—supplanting the Kin as the Kin had supplanted the Khitan—completed the barbarian conquest of China by pushing on from the northern watershed of the Yangtse to the southern sea-board of China, which they reached in A.D. 1280. It

measures were aimed at protecting the peasants against the twin scourge of the tax-collector and the money-lender. His success is attested by the increase in the population of the Sung Empire—on the evidence of the census returns—during the period in which Wang An Shih's new laws were in force. And the mass-revolts which his critics prophesied never broke out. The new laws were in force throughout the reign of Wang An Shih's Imperial patron the Emperor Shêntsung (*imperabat* A.D. 1068–85). Upon this emperor's death Wang An Shih's reactionary opponents regained the upper hand, and the new laws were in abeyance during the minority of Shêntsung's successor Chêtsung (*imperabat* A.D. 1086–1100). One of the young emperor's first acts, however, upon coming of age and taking the reins of government into his own hands in A.D. 1093 was to call to office Wang An Shih's disciple Ts'ai Ching (Wang An Shih himself had retired in A.D. 1076, before Shêntsung's death). And Wang An Shih's laws were in force again from the date of this appointment, which was made in A.D. 1094, down to the invasion of Northern China by the Kin, *imperante* Huitsung, in A.D. 1124.

[1] See Münsterberg, op. cit., p. 249.

[2] Huitsung's Babylonic counterpart, the archaeologist-emperor Nabonidus (see V. C (i) (d) 8 (δ), p. 94, above), was *felicior opportunitate mortis*. He was already in his grave when the Neo-Babylonian Empire was overwhelmed by Cyrus.

[3] See II. D (v), vol. ii, p. 121; IV, C (ii) (b) 2, vol. iv, p. 86; and V. C (i) (c) 3, vol. v, p. 308, above.

will be seen that in the main body, as in the Japanese offshoot, of the Far Eastern Society the 'Time of Troubles' falls into two paroxysms which are separated from one another by a perceptible breathing-space.

The Rhythm in Babylonic History.

If we turn from the main body of the Far Eastern World to the Babylonic Society, we shall find that the Neo-Babylonian Empire, which served as a Babylonic universal state, was cut short as prematurely as the Far Eastern universal state that was provided by the Mongols. Indeed, the respective lives of the two régimes were of an almost equal brevity, if we reckon the reign of the *Pax Mongolica* in China as running from A.D. 1280 to A.D. 1351,[1] and that of the *Pax Chaldaica* in Babylonia as beginning with the annihilation of the last Assyrian fighting force at Harran in 610 B.C.[2] and ending with the capture of Babylon by Cyrus in 539 or 538 B.C. At the same time we shall find that, if we cast our eyes back from the prematurely ended universal state to the antecedent 'Time of Troubles', at least a fragment of our disintegration-pattern can be recognized at this stage in Babylonic history, as in Far Eastern. The second paroxysm of the Babylonic 'Time of Troubles', which clearly ends in the holocaust of 610 B.C., no less clearly begins with the act of aggression against Babylonia which was committed by King Tiglath-Pileser III of Assyria in 745 B.C.; for this act sowed the seeds of a hundred years' war between the two principal Powers of the Babylonic World, and that war had the decisive battle of Harran for its grand finale.[3]

The Rhythm in the History of Orthodox Christendom in Russia.

These cases in which a glimpse of our disintegration-pattern can be caught in the earlier, though not in the later, stages of the disintegration-process are balanced by inverse cases in which the pattern is visible in the later stages though not in the earlier. The history of the offshoot of the Orthodox Christian Society in Russia, for example, offers a contrast in this respect to the otherwise analogous history of the offshoot of the Far Eastern Society in Japan.

The Russian 'Time of Troubles' (in the sense in which the term is used in this Study, and not in the original Russian usage of the

---

[1] See II. D (v), vol. ii, p. 121; IV. C (ii) (*b*) 2, vol. iv, pp. 86–7; V. C (ii) (*a*), in the present volume, p. 191; and the present chapter, pp. 305–6, above.

[2] See II. D (v), vol. ii, pp. 135–6; IV. C (ii) (*b*) 2, vol. iv, p. 101, footnote 1; and IV. C (iii) (*c*) 3 (*α*), vol. iv, p. 475, above.

[3] For Tiglath-Pileser III's intervention in Babylonia, and its consequences, see IV. C (ii) (*b*) 2, vol. iv, pp. 101–2, and IV. C (iii) (*c*) 3 (*α*), vol. iv, pp. 473 and 476–84, above.

words)[1] may be taken as having been brought to a close by the
union of Novgorod with Muscovy in A.D. 1478[2]—an act of political
consolidation which marks the establishment of a *Pax Oecumenica*
—and as having been opened by the decay of the principality of
Kiev in the last quarter of the eleventh century,[3] when the political
centre of gravity of the Russian World shifted from the Upper
Dniepr to the Upper Volga.[4] Concomitantly with this politico-
geographical change, the exotic plant of Orthodox Christian culture,
which at Kiev had been kept artificially in the exquisite condition
to which it had been brought by a Byzantine gardener's art, ran
wild and at the same time reverted to a barbaric coarseness as the
price of becoming acclimatized to a natural life in the open air in
this forbidding Russian clime in which it had only managed to
keep alive hitherto on condition of being confined in a hothouse. In
other contexts[5] we have noticed an analogy between this chapter
of Russian history and a corresponding chapter of Japanese history
—and this on both the political and the cultural plane. The north-
eastward shift of the Russian political centre of gravity from
Kiev in the Dniepr Basin to Vladímir in the Volga Basin has its
analogue in the north-eastward shift of the Japanese political
centre of gravity from Kyoto in Yamato to Kamakura in the
Kwanto. In Japan, as in Russia, this geographical movement was
accompanied by a relapse into anarchy and barbarism. And in the
next chapter of the story—again in both cases alike—the back-
woodsmen themselves stepped in to rally the disintegrating society
from a rout which was their own barbaric handiwork. The *Pax
Muscoviana* which was established in A.D. 1478 has its counterpart
in the *Pax Tokugawica* which was established at the turn of the
sixteenth and seventeenth centuries of the Christian Era by the
cumulative labours of Nobunaga, Hideyoshi, and Ieyasu. These
points of likeness between Russian and Japanese history from the
original breakdown until the establishment of the universal state
are so striking that we should expect *a priori* also to find a Russian
parallel to the abortive attempt which was made in the course of
the 'Time of Troubles' in Japan to bring back the political centre
of gravity from the north-east to the south-west, and at the same
time to revert from a military to a civilian régime. Yet, if we look in
Russian history for the equivalent of the Japanese flash-in-the-pan

[1] For this difference between the conventional usage in this Study and the traditional
Russian usage see the references in V. C (ii) (*a*), p. 195, footnote 2, above, and in the
present chapter, p. 311, footnote 4, below.
[2] See IV. C (ii) (*b*) 2, vol. iv, p. 88; V. C (i) (*c*) 3, vol. v, p. 312; and V. C (ii) (*a*),
in the present volume, p. 191, above.
[3] See IV. C (ii) (*b*) 2, vol. iv, p. 96, above, with the authorities there cited in footnote 1.
[4] See II. D (v), vol. ii, p. 154, above.
[5] Ibid., p. 158, and in IV. C (ii) (*b*) 2, vol. iv, pp. 91-6, above.

in the fourth decade of the fourteenth century of the Christian Era,[1] we shall find ourselves drawing blank.[2]

On the other hand, when we come to the next chapter of the story, in which the 'Time of Troubles' has given place to a *Pax Oecumenica*, we shall find, when we look for traces of our disintegration-pattern in the respective histories of the two societies at this stage, that there is again a discrepancy but that this time it is the other way round. In this chapter, too, the analogies between the two histories are striking.[3] In both Russia and Japan a hibernating society has been overtaken by a collision with the alien civilization of the West before it has completed the normal hibernation period; and in both cases the statesmanship of the society whose repose has been thus abruptly and perilously disturbed has shown itself capable of coping with the emergency.[4] In Japan, as in

---

[1] See the present chapter, p. 303, above.

[2] The abortive endeavour in the fourth decade of the fourteenth century of the Christian Era in Japan to bring back the Kingdom, the Power, and the Glory from Kamakura in the Kwanto to Kyoto in Yamato was made about 150 years after the beginning of the Japanese 'Time of Troubles', if we are right in dating the breakdown of the Far Eastern Civilization in Japan in about the last quarter of the twelfth century of the Christian Era. And, if we are also right in dating the breakdown of the Orthodox Christian Civilization in Russia about a hundred years earlier than that, then in the Russian field we ought to focus our attention upon the fourth decade of the thirteenth century of the Christian Era and inquire whether, at or about that time, there was an abortive attempt to bring back the Kingdom, the Power, and the Glory from Vladîmir in the Volga Basin to Kiev on the Dniepr. This inquiry yields a negative answer. So far from recapturing her ancient status of political primacy in that decade, Kiev suffered in A.D. 1240 the supreme disaster of being stormed and sacked by the Mongol host of Bātū Khan; and from this blow she has never fully recovered. At the same time we shall observe that, while the Russian sceptre did not return to Kiev either then or at any later date, it did pass back from the north-eastern principality of Vladîmir, which had likewise been prostrated by Bātū's hammer-stroke, to a south-western principality in whose domain Kiev came to be included—though this not as the capital but only as an outlying dependency. The fortunate Russian principality which thus rose to a position of relative power and prosperity in an age that was one of deep adversity for the Russian World as a whole was Red Russia or Galicia (see V. C (i) (c) 3, vol. v, p. 312, footnote 1, above). During the ninety years that elapsed between Bātū's onslaught upon the Russian World in A.D. 1238–40 and the gravitation of the hegemony over what was left of Russia to the principality of Moscow in A.D. 1328, Galicia was the leading Russian state. One of the reasons for Galicia's primacy among the Russian states in these earlier decades of the period of Tatar domination was the accident of a geographical position which counted for most in the years when the Tatar yoke was at its heaviest. Galicia was ensconced among the foothills of the Carpathians in the hinterland of the western extremity of the Don-to-Carpathians Steppe (see Part III. A, Annex II, vol. iii, p. 401, above), and its capital, Halicz, on the banks of the Upper Dniestr, was more difficult for Tatar raiders and tribute-collectors to reach than either Kiev on the Dniepr (in a district which now came to be known as the Ukraina or 'borderland' *par excellence*) or even Vladîmir in the Upper Basin of the Volga. Thus Galicia's fortune was made by a Mongol conquest of Russia which had overthrown Vladîmir and crushed Kiev; and, in the light of this episode of Russian history, we may speculate on what might have happened in Japan if Qubilay's invasion of Japan in A.D. 1281, instead of being the disastrous failure that it was, had been as brilliantly successful as Bātū's invasion of Russia in A.D. 1238 (for the contrast between the respective outcomes of these two Mongol enterprises see IV. C (ii) (b) 2, vol. iv, pp. 92–4, above). In that hypothetical event, would the hegemony in Japan have passed from Kamakura—not to Kyoto, which would then in all probability have suffered the fate of Kiev, but to one of the remoter islands of the Japanese Archipelago?

[3] See IV. C (ii) (b) 2, vol. iv, pp. 82–3 and 88–91, above.

[4] In the light of the catastrophic sequel to Peter the Great's brilliant attempt to solve 'the Western Question' in Russia, we may hesitate to award him the victor's palm; and,

Russia, a non-Western universal state has been skilfully transformed into a national state member of a 'Great Society' of a
Western complexion. But here, once more, the points of likeness
only throw into sharper relief the discrepancy in the disintegration-
pattern. Whereas the disintegration of the Japanese Society during
the prematurely interrupted currency of the *Pax Tokugawica* ran
in a rhythm with a wave-length that was shorter than the standard,[1]
the normal run of the disintegration-rhythm is conspicuously
visible in the course of the *Pax Muscoviana*—in spite of the fact that
the Russian universal state was overtaken and interrupted at a still
earlier stage than the Japanese by the impact of an alien social
force.[2] Between its foundation in A.D. 1478 and its decay in the
latter part of the nineteenth century[3] the Russian universal state
experienced one notable relapse and one notable rally. The relapse
was the bout of anarchy in the early years of the seventeenth
century which is known as the 'Time of Troubles' in the Russian
historical tradition.[4] The rally was the subsequent recovery,
which was not less astounding than the fall which it retrieved. And
the single beat of Rout-and-Rally which is struck out by this
sequence of a downward followed by an upward movement in so
steep a curve punctuates the history of the *Pax Muscoviana* into
two separate chapters which are sharply divided by an interregnum
that has made up for the shortness of its length by the virulence of
its anarchy. In Russian, as in Sinic, history this punctuation of a
Pax Oecumenica by a short and sharp interregnum is emphasized
by a change of dynasty. The transference of the Sinic Imperial

on this showing, we shall be well advised also to reserve judgement on the Japanese
statesmanship which carried out the Meiji Revolution of A.D. 1868. We have to reckon
with the possibility that the tragic view of the Westernization of Russia which an alien
observer in A.D. 1938 was constrained to take in the light of Russian history since
A.D. 1825 might also be taken with regard to the Westernization of Japan by a Posterity
as far removed in time from the year 1868 as our own generation is removed from the
year 1689. (This point has been touched upon already in IV. C (ii) (*b*) 2, vol. iv, pp. 88–
90, above.)
    [1] See the present chapter, p. 285, above.
    [2] While the Japanese universal state had been in existence for rather longer than two
and a half centuries by the time of the Meiji Revolution, the Russian universal state had
not been in existence for much longer than two centuries before the advent of Peter the
Great (see IV. C (ii) (*b*) 2, vol. iv, p. 88, above).
    [3] The outer shell of the Tsardom was not, of course, broken until A.D. 1917, but the
spirit had departed from the body at least half a century before that; and, if we wish to
identify the end of the *Pax Muscoviana* with some conventional date, the assassination
of the Tsar Alexander II in A.D. 1881 will come nearer the mark than the abdication of
the Tsar Nicholas II in A.D. 1917. On the same principle the end of the *Pax Romana* is
to be identified with the Goths' victory at Adrianople in A.D. 378 and not with their
capture of Rome itself in A.D. 410; the end of the *Pax Hanica* with the palace revolutions
that began *circa* A.D. 172 and not with the final eviction of the Posterior Han Dynasty from
the Imperial Throne in A.D. 221; and the end of the T'ang régime with the great catastrophe of A.D. 878 (see IV. C (ii) (*b*) 2, vol. iv, pp. 87–8, above) and not with the official
abdication of the last of the T'ang emperors in A.D. 907.
    [4] See I. C (i) (*a*), vol. i, p. 53, footnote 2; II. D (v), vol. ii, pp. 157 and 176; IV. C (ii)
(*b*) 2, vol. iv, pp. 90 and 91–2; V. C (i) (*c*) 3, vol. v, p. 311, footnote 2; and V. C (ii)
(*a*), in the present volume, p. 195, footnote 2, above.

Sceptre from the Prior to the Posterior Han[1] has a Russian parallel in the elevation of the parvenu Romanovs to an Imperial Throne left vacant by the extinction of the ancient House of Rurik.

Vestiges in Minoan History.

There is perhaps one other case in which our disintegration-pattern can be detected in the history of a universal state without being discernible in the foregoing 'Time of Troubles', and that is in the disintegration of the Minoan Society. In a field in which our evidence is still exclusively archaeological and also still only frag-mentary—even in this unilluminating medium—our findings can only be tentative. Yet, while the history of the Minoan 'Time of Troubles' is far too obscure to warrant our venturing upon any analysis at all, we may perhaps provisionally interpret the archaeo-logical strata in historical terms when we come to the following chapter. In other contexts[2] we have hazarded the conjecture that the Minoan Society, in the course of its disintegration, lived through a universal state that must have been founded after the first destruction of the Cretan palaces at the break between the two stratigraphically attested periods which our archaeologists have labelled 'Middle Minoan II' and 'Middle Minoan III'; and we have suspected that a violent overthrow of our supposed universal state may be the political event that is commemorated in the second destruction which overtook the same palaces, some centuries later, at the break between 'Late Minoan II' and 'Late Minoan III' circa 1400 B.C. If these two termini give the measure of the total span of the duration of 'the thalassocracy of Minos', does the dim light of the archaeologist-miner's lamp enable us to discern any intervening vestige of a beat of Rout-and-Rally? It is perhaps not altogether too fanciful to read a political punctuation into the change of technique and style which is the basis of the archaeo-logists' distinction between 'Late Minoan I' and 'Late Minoan II'.

Symptoms in Western History.

While a Minoan game of blind-man's-buff may not add much to our knowledge, its very uncertainty may serve to warn us that we are now approaching the limits of the field within which it is possible to pursue with any profit our empirical investigation into the occurrence of the disintegration-rhythm in its standard run of three and a half beats from beginning to end of the process. The results that we have obtained already suffice, however, to show that

---

[1] See the present chapter, p. 295, above.
[2] In I. C (i) (a), vol. i, pp. 92–3; IV. C (ii) (b) 1, vol. iv, pp. 64–5; and V. C (i) (c) 3, vol. v, p. 236, above.

the pattern which we have been studying does occur with a considerable frequency. And this conclusion leads us irresistibly to a final question. If our pattern has proved to be one of the regular features of the disintegration-process in the histories of those civilizations that have unquestionably made the dreadful transit from growth to decay, is it legitimate to argue in the inverse direction? Supposing that we are confronted with the history of a civilization which it is peculiarly difficult for us to see in perspective, shall we be warranted in pronouncing that this society is already in a state of disintegration on the strength of finding in its history the imprint of our now familiar disintegration-pattern?

Our problematical case is, of course, the history of the society into which we happen ourselves to have been born. At the beginning of this Study[1] we took note of the difficulty with which any Western observer will have to contend, *ex officio originis*, if he tries to take, *en voyage*, the bearings of the ship on board which the observer himself is sailing into the uncharted waters of an unknown Future. The position of our Western Society in our age cannot become known with any certainty of knowledge till the voyage has come to an end; and so long as the ship is under way the crew will have no notion whether she is going to founder in mid-ocean through springing a leak or be sent to the bottom by colliding with another vessel or run ashore on the rocks or glide smoothly into a port of which the crew will never have heard before they wake up one fine day to find their ship at rest in dock there. A sailor at sea cannot tell for which, if for any, of these ends the ship is heading as he watches her making headway during the brief period of his own spell of duty. To plot out her course and write up her log from start to finish is a task that can be performed only by observers who are able to wait until the voyage is over, since it will only be then that the unexplored Future, into which the ship is for ever sailing so long as she is in motion at all, will have been converted, without any dubious residue, into a traversed and recorded Past; and such observers must, *ex hypothesi*, be members of some other society that will still be alive when ours has ceased to exist, since their post of observation must, again *ex hypothesi*, lie not on board the ship, but somewhere outside of her gunwales. Yet, granting that the present position of our now still living and moving Western World cannot be ascertained in this accurate and comprehensive way by observers who are handicapped, as we are, by the fact of living and moving and having our being in the society that is the object of observation, may there not be some rough-and-ready means by which even we, here and now, can reckon,

[1] In I. B (iv), vol. i, pp. 36–7, above.

within a margin of error that will be not excessive for practical purposes, approximately where we stand? And may not a clue have been put into our hands by the acquaintance with the standard run of the disintegration-rhythm that we have gained in the present chapter through a comparative study of the histories of other civilizations than our own in which we have the advantage of knowing the whole story? Suppose that the pattern which we have now detected in the histories of so many disintegrating civilizations were to prove to be discernible in our own Western history too. Might that not be regarded as presumptive evidence that our own civilization has already been overtaken by a process of disintegration which is known for certain to have been the fate of so many other representatives of the species?

If we look into our Western history with eyes sharpened by the practice of the survey that we have just been making, do we in fact perceive, here too, the now familiar beats of the movement of Rout-and-Rally?

On this point there is one observation that we can make at once and have in fact made already:[1] our Western Society, whether it be already in disintegration or not, has at any rate certainly not yet arrived at the second rally in the disintegration-process; for this second rally is regularly marked by the establishment of a *Pax Oecumenica*; and a *Pax Oecumenica* is a state to which our Western Society has certainly not yet attained. Why is it, though, that we are—as undoubtedly we are—so acutely aware of this fact? The answer to that question is that, in our generation in the West, we are no longer content, as our forebears were so complacently, to see our society remain partitioned among a number of parochial sovereign states that are apt to assert their sovereignty by going to war with one another. Unlike our forebears, we in our generation feel from the depths of our hearts that a *Pax Oecumenica* is now a crying need. We live in daily dread of a catastrophe which, we fear, may overtake us if the problem of meeting this need is left unsolved much longer.[2] It would hardly be an exaggeration to say that the shadow of this fear that now lies athwart our future is hypnotizing us into a spiritual paralysis that is beginning to affect us even in the trivial avocations of our daily life.[3] And, if we can screw up the courage to look this fear in the face, we shall not be rewarded by finding ourselves able to dismiss it with contempt as nothing but a panic phobia. The sting of this fear lies in the undeniable fact that it springs from a rational root. We are terribly

---

[1] In Part IV. A, vol. iv, p. 3, above.
[2] See IV. C (iii) (c) 2 (β), vol. iv, pp. 318–20 and 405–8, above.
[3] Written in the autumn of 1937.

afraid of the immediate future because we have been through a horrible experience in the recent past. And the lesson which this experience has impressed upon our minds is indeed an appalling one. In our generation we have learnt, through suffering, two home truths. The first truth is that the institution of War is still in full force in our Western Society. The second truth is that, in the Western World under existing technical and social conditions, there can be no warfare that is not internecine. These truths have been driven home by our experience in the General War of A.D. 1914–18; but the most ominous thing about that war is that it was not an isolated or unprecedented calamity. It was one war in a series; and, when we envisage the whole series in a synoptic view, we discover that this is not only a series but also a progression. In our recent Western history war has been following war in an ascending order of intensity; and to-day it is already apparent that the War of 1914–18 was not the climax of this crescendo movement. If the series continues, the progression will indubitably be carried to ever higher terms, until this process of intensifying the horrors of war is one day brought to an end by the self-annihilation of the war-making society.

We may now remind ourselves that this progressive series of Western wars, of which the War of 1914–18 has been the latest but perhaps not the last, is one of two chapters of a story that we have already studied in another context.[1] We have observed that the history of our Western warfare in the so-called 'Modern Age' can be analysed into two bouts which are separated from one another chronologically by an intervening lull and are also distinguished from one another qualitatively by a difference in the object—or at any rate in the pretext—of the hostilities. The first bout consists of the Wars of Religion[2] which began in the sixteenth century and ceased in the seventeenth. The second bout consists of the Wars of Nationality, which began in the eighteenth century and are still the scourge of the twentieth. These ferocious Wars of Religion and ferocious Wars of Nationality have been separated by an interlude of moderate wars that were fought as 'the Sport of Kings'. This interlude manifestly did not begin on the Continent till after the end of the Thirty Years' War in A.D. 1648, and in Great Britain not till after the Restoration of the Monarchy in England in A.D. 1660; and it is equally manifest that the lull did not outlast the outbreak of the French Revolutionary War in A.D. 1792, even if we leave it an open question whether it survived the American

---

[1] In IV. C (iii) (b) 3 and 4, vol. iv, pp. 141–85, above.
[2] See V. C (i) (c) 2, vol. v, pp. 160–1, and V. C (i) (d) 6 (δ), Annex, vol. v, pp. 668–72, above

Revolutionary War of A.D. 1775–83.[1] On a narrower reckoning we might confine the Time-span of the 'Golden Age' of eighteenth-century moderation between the dates A.D. 1732 and A.D. 1755, if the eviction of a Protestant minority from the Catholic ecclesiastical principality of Salzburg in A.D. 1731–2 is to be taken as the last positive act of religious persecution in Western Europe, and the eviction of a French population from Acadia in A.D. 1755 as the first positive act of persecution for Nationality's sake in North America.[2] In any case the interlude is palpable; and, whatever dates we may choose to adopt as the props for a conventional scheme of chronological demarcation, the play will fall into the same three acts in the same sequence, and this sequence of acts will present the same plot. This underlying plot, and not the superficial time-table, is the feature that is of interest for our present purpose. And in the plot of this three-act play, with its couple of bouts of ferocious warfare and an interlude of moderate warfare in between them, can we not discern the familiar pattern of a couple of paroxysms, separated by a breathing-space, which we have learnt to recognize as the hall-mark of a 'Time of Troubles'? If we scrutinize in this light the picture that is presented by the modern history of our Western World, we shall find that the cap does at any rate fit to a nicety.

If the outbreak of the Wars of Religion in the sixteenth century is to be taken as a symptom of social breakdown, then the first rally of a since then disintegrating Western Society is to be seen in the movement in favour of religious toleration which gained the upper hand, and brought the Wars of Religion to an end, in the course of the seventeenth century. This victory of the Principle of Toleration in the religious sphere duly won for several succeeding generations that interlude of moderation which gave an ailing Western World a welcome breathing-space between a first and a second paroxysm of its deadly seizure. And the cap fits again when we observe the fact that the relief was only temporary and not permanent, and when we go on to inquire into the reason. For our empirical study of the rhythm of the disintegration-process has led us to expect to see a rally give way to a relapse; and it has also

---

[1] We have already observed (in IV. C (iii) (b) 3, vol. iv, pp. 147–9, and in IV. C (iii) (b) 4, vol. iv, pp. 163–4 and 165–7, above) that the testimony of the American Revolutionary War is self-contradictory and therefore ambiguous. When we consider the moderateness of the terms which a victorious France imposed upon a defeated Great Britain in A.D. 1783, we shall be inclined to pronounce that in that year Moderation was still reigning. On the other hand, when we consider the treatment of the defeated United Empire Loyalists by the victorious insurgents in the ci-devant British colonies in North America, we shall be no less inclined to pronounce that by that time the reign of a fanatical Nationalism had already set in.

[2] For these two acts of eighteenth-century persecution and their significance see IV. C (iii) (b) 4, vol. iv, pp. 164–5, above.

led us to expect to find that this monotonously repeated tale of failure can be explained in each case by some particular element of weakness by which the abortive rally has been vitiated. Are these expectations fulfilled in the Western case in point? We are bound to reply that, in this case too, the reason for the failure of the rally is as clear as the fact of it is conspicuous. Our modern Western Principle of Toleration has failed to bring salvation after all because (as we must confess) there has been no health in it.[1] The spirits that presided over its conception and birth were Disillusionment, Apprehension, and Cynicism, not Faith, Hope, and Charity; the impulse was negative, not positive; and the soil in which the seeds were sown was arid.

'Some fell upon stony places where they had not much earth, and forthwith they sprung up because they had no deepness of earth; and when the Sun was up they were scorched, and because they had no root they withered away.'[2]

A Principle of Toleration which unexpectedly clothed the stony heart of our modern Western Christendom in a sudden crop of fresh verdure when the fierce sun of religious fanaticism had burnt itself out into dust and ashes, has wilted—no less suddenly and no less unexpectedly—now that the fiercer sun of national fanaticism has burst blazing through the firmament. In the twentieth century we are seeing our seventeenth-century Toleration making an unconditional surrender to a masterful demon whose onslaught it has proved incapable of withstanding. And the cause of this disastrous impotence is manifest.

A Toleration that has no roots in Faith has failed to retain any hold upon the heart of *Homo Occidentalis* because human nature abhors a spiritual vacuum. If the house from which an unclean spirit has gone out is left empty, swept, and garnished, the momentarily banished possessor will sooner or later enter in again with a retinue of other spirits more wicked than himself, and the last state of that man will be worse than the first.[3] The Wars of Nationalism are more wicked than the Wars of Religion because the object—or pretext—of the hostilities is less sublime and less etherial. The moral is that hungry souls which have been given a stone when they have asked for bread[4] cannot be restrained from seeking to satisfy their hunger by devouring the first piece of carrion that comes their way. They will not be deterred by a warning from the giver of the stone that the heaven-sent carrion is

---

[1] The êthos of this modern Western Principle of Toleration has been examined in IV. C (iii) (*b*) 3, vol. iv, pp. 142–3 and 150; in IV. C (iii) (*b*) 4, vol. iv, p. 184; in IV. C (iii) (*b*) 12, vol. iv, pp. 227–8; in IV. C (iii) (*c*) 3 (α), Annex, vol. iv, pp. 643–5; and in V. C (i) (*d*) 6 (δ), Annex, vol. v, pp. 669–71, above.   [2] Matt. xiii. 5–6.
[3] Matt. xii. 43–5; Luke xi. 24–6.   [4] Matt. vii. 9; Luke xi. 11.

poisoned; and, even when the threatened agonies duly begin to
wrack the miserable scavengers' entrails, they will persist in feasting
upon the tainted meat with an unabated appetite until death ex-
tinguishes their greed—as once in Sicily a routed Athenian army
that had gone mad with thirst as it walked through dry places,
seeking rest and finding none, drank heedlessly of the waters of the
River Asinarus while the enemy was shooting them down from
the bank and the stream was running foully red with the blood
of the dying drinkers' already slaughtered comrades.

There is yet another point in which our modern Western history
conforms to the pattern of a disintegrating society's 'Time of
Troubles'; and this is perhaps the most alarming of all these points
of congruence. Our survey has shown us that, as a rule, the
paroxysm which follows the intermediate breathing-space is more
violent than the paroxysm which precedes it; and this rule is certainly exemplified in our Western case if the Wars of Nationality
are to be taken as the second paroxysm of our seizure and the Wars
of Religion as the first.

Our forebears who fought that earlier cycle of ferocious Western
wars may not have been behindhand in the will to work havoc, but
—fortunately for themselves and for their descendants—they
lacked the means which we now have at our command unfortunately for our children and for ourselves. No doubt the Wars of
Religion were much worse—and this in point both of rancour and
of command of resources and of technical ability to turn these
resources to account—than the Western warfare of previous ages
in which our Western Christendom was still unquestionably in
growth. The Wars of Religion had been anticipated by the invention of gunpowder and by voyages of discovery that, at least on the
material plane,[1] had extended the range of the Western Society
from one small corner of the Eurasian Continent to the hinterlands
of all the navigable seas on the face of the planet. The bullion that
had been accumulating in the treasuries at Tenochtitlan and Cuzco
was ultimately expended on paying mercenaries to fight in the
Wars of Religion on European battle-fields, after the discovery,
conquest, and rifling of the Central American and Andean worlds
by the Spanish *conquistadores*—just as, after the corresponding
geographical expansion of the Hellenic World through the exploits
of Alexander, the treasures piled up by Achaemenian policy at
Ecbatana and Susa found their way into the hands of mercenaries
who fought in the wars of Alexander's diadochi and epigoni on

---

[1] For the discrepancy which is apt to reveal itself between the respective extensions
of any society, at any date, on different planes of social life, see I. B (iii), vol. i, pp. 27–36,
and V. C (i) (c) 3, vol. v, pp. 199–202, above.

battle-fields in Greece.[1] And the professional soldiery that was maintained in a sixteenth-century and seventeenth-century Western World out of this sudden huge increase in the Western princes' supplies of the precious metals was not only more numerous than the old feudal militia of Transalpine Western Europe. It was also more formidably armed and, worse still, more ferociously enraged against an enemy who now, as a rule, was not only a military opponent but was also a religious miscreant in the eyes of his adversary. The unprecedented violence with which the Wars of Religion were imbued by the combined operation of these several causes would doubtless have shocked both Saint Louis and the Emperor Frederick II if they could have returned to life to witness the Western warfare of the sixteenth and seventeenth centuries. But we may also as confidently presume that the Duke of Alva and Gustavus Adolphus would have been shocked to an equal degree if they, in their turn, could have returned to life to witness the subsequent Wars of Nationality. This later cycle of ferocious Western wars which began in the eighteenth century, and which has not ceased in the twentieth, has been keyed up to an unprecedented degree of ferocity by the titanic driving-power of two demonic forces—Democracy and Industrialism—which have entered into the institution of War in our Western World[2] in these latter days when that world has now virtually completed its stupendous feat of incorporating the whole face of the Earth and the entire living generation of Mankind into its own body material. Our last state is worse than our first because, in this vastly expanded house, we are possessed to-day by devils more terrible than any that ever tormented even our seventeenth-century and sixteenth-century ancestors.

Are these devils to dwell in our empty and swept and garnished house till they have driven us to suicide? If the analogy between our Western Civilization's modern history and other civilizations' 'Times of Troubles' does extend to points of chronology, then a Western 'Time of Troubles' which appears to have begun sometime in the sixteenth century may be expected to find its end sometime in the twentieth century; and this prospect may well make us tremble; for in other cases the grand finale that has wound up a 'Time of Troubles' and ushered in a universal state has been a self-inflicted 'knock-out blow' from which the self-stricken society

---

[1] See IV. C (iii) (c) 3 (α), vol. iv, p. 485; V. C (i) (c) 2, vol. v, pp. 62–4; V. C (i) (d) 11, in the present volume, p. 155, footnote 3; and the present chapter, pp. 289–90, above.

[2] For this impact of Democracy and Industrialism upon War see IV. C (iii) (b) 3, vol. iv, pp. 141–55, above. For the advent of these two demonic forces see Part I. A, vol. i, pp. 1–2, above.

has never been able to recover. Must we, too, purchase our *Pax Oecumenica* at this deadly price? The question is one which our own lips cannot answer, since the destiny of a live civilization is necessarily as obscure to its living members as the fate of a dead civilization is to scholars when their only clues are undeciphered scripts or dumb artifacts. We cannot say for certain that our doom is at hand; and yet we have no warrant for assuming that it is not; for that would be to assume that we are not as other men are; and any such assumption would be at variance with everything that we know about human nature either by looking around us or by introspection.

This dark doubt is a challenge which we cannot evade; and our destiny depends on our response.

'I dreamed, and behold I saw a man cloathed with rags, standing in a certain place, with his face from his own house, a book in his hand, and a great burden upon his back. I looked, and saw him open the book and read therein; and as he read he wept and trembled; and, not being able longer to contain, he broke out with a lamentable cry saying "What shall I do?"'

It was not without just cause that Christian was so greatly distressed.

'I am for certain informed [said he] that this our city will be burned with fire from Heaven—in which fearful overthrow both myself with thee my wife and you my sweet babes shall miserably come to ruine, except (the which yet I see not) some way of escape can be found, whereby we may be delivered.'

What response to this challenge is Christian going to make? Is he going to look this way and that way as if he would run, yet stand still because he cannot tell which way to go—until the fire from Heaven duly descends upon the City of Destruction and the wretched haverer perishes in a holocaust which he has so dismally foreboded without ever bringing himself to the point of fleeing from the wrath to come? Or will he begin to run—and run on crying 'Life! Life! Eternal Life!'—with his eye set on a shining light and his feet bound for a distant wicket-gate? If the answer to this question depended on nobody but Christian himself, our knowledge of the uniformity of human nature might incline us to predict that Christian's imminent destiny was Death and not Life. But in the classic version of the myth we are told that the human protagonist was not left entirely to his own resources in the hour that was decisive for his fate. According to John Bunyan, Christian was saved by his encounter with Evangelist. And, inasmuch as it cannot be supposed that God's nature is less constant than Man's, we may and must pray that a reprieve which God has granted to our society once will not be refused if we ask for it again in a contrite spirit and with a broken heart.[1]

(III) STANDARDIZATION THROUGH DISINTEGRATION

We have now arrived at the close of our inquiry into the process of the disintegrations of civilizations; but, before we take leave of this subject and turn our attention to other problems, there is one more manœuvre to be performed if we are to carry our present operations to their completion. Now that we find ourselves at last at the end of a road on which we have been travelling for so long, we are in a position to look back with an eye to taking in, at one view, the whole of the ground that we have traversed; and such a retrospect will perhaps throw light on a question which at this stage we can hardly leave unasked. In making a journey that, at least in certain stages, may have seemed, while we were on the march, like an aimless wandering in the wilderness, have we perchance been following a single guiding thread? Now that we have surveyed the whole course of disintegration by going laboriously over the ground, does the process prove to be governed by any master-tendency?

If we address ourselves to this concluding question we may obtain a clue to the answer in the findings that we have reached already in the last chapter before this.[2] In studying the interaction between individuals in disintegrating civilizations we have been led into an examination of the rhythm of the disintegration-process, and in this rhythm we have detected an element of uniformity—a uniform run of three and a half standard beats of the movement of Rout-and-Rally—which is apparently so definite and so constant that, on the strength of its regularity, we have almost ventured to cast the horoscope of one civilization that is still alive and on the move. If, with this clue in our hands, we now cast our eyes backward, we shall find that this tendency towards uniformity is the key-note, not only of the last chapter, but of the whole of the present part of this Study. In that uniform rhythm the principle of uniformity is manifesting itself only in a superficial way. In earlier chapters we have already come across some more significant expressions of uniformity in the uniform schism of disintegrating societies into three sharply divided classes and in the uniform works of creation that are respectively produced by each of these. We have seen dominant minorities uniformly working out philosophies and setting up universal states; internal proletariats

[1] Pss. xxxiv. 18 li. 17.   [2] In V. C (ii) (b), above.

uniformly discovering 'higher religions' which aim at embodying themselves in universal churches; and external proletariats uniformly mustering war-bands which find vent in 'heroic ages'.[1] The uniformity with which these several institutions are generated in the body social of a disintegrating civilization is indeed so perfect that it is possible to display this aspect of the disintegration-process in tabular form.[2] But this is still not the most impressive of the ways in which the tendency towards uniformity declares itself in the histories of disintegrating civilizations. The uniformity of institutions that is revealed by a study of schism in the body social is not so illuminating as the uniformity of ways of behaviour, feeling, and life that is revealed by a study of schism in the Soul.[3]

The conclusion to which this retrospective reconnaissance brings us is that in the histories of civilizations standardization is the master-tendency of the process of disintegration—in antithesis to the differentiation which we have found, at an earlier point,[4] to be the master-tendency of the process of growth. And this conclusion is only what we should expect *a priori*. For, if differentiation is the natural outcome of a succession of successful responses to a series of different challenges, standardization is no less manifestly the natural outcome of a succession of unsuccessful responses to a single challenge which monotonously continues to present itself so long as it thus remains unanswered.[5]

This fundamental difference between the processes of disintegration and of growth is brought home in the simple parable of Penelope's web.

> ἔνθα καὶ ἠματίη μὲν ὑφαίνεσκεν μέγαν ἱστόν,
> νύκτας δ' ἀλλύεσκεν, ἐπεὶ δαΐδας παραθεῖτο.[6]

When the faithful wife of the absent Odysseus had promised her importunate suitors that she would give herself in marriage to one of them so soon as she had finished weaving a winding-sheet for old Laertes, she used to weave away at her loom in the day-time day by day and then spend the night-watches night by night in unpicking her last day's work. If we look into the differences between the heroine's day-work and her night-work we shall perceive that the most obvious difference is not the only one. The most obvious difference is, of course, that in the day-time Penelope was making

---

[1] The three classes into which a disintegrating society splits up, and these classes' respective works, have been examined in V. C (i) (*c*), *passim*, above.

[2] See the tables of universal states, philosophies, higher religions, and barbarian war-bands at the end of this chapter, on pp. 327–31, below.

[3] See V. C (i) (*d*), *passim*, above.   [4] In III. C (iii), vol. iii, pp. 377–90, above.

[5] On this point see Part V. B, vol. v, pp. 12–13, and V. C (ii) (*b*), in the present volume, pp. 280–1, above.

[6] *Odyssey*, Book II, ll. 104–5.

something, whereas at night she was undoing what she had just made. But there is another difference, besides, which is more pertinent to our present purpose. When the webster set up her warp and began to weave her weft each morning she had at her command an unlimited choice of patterns. If she chose she could make it her practice never to weave the same pattern more than once; and she could have kept up this practice without flagging, even if she had succeeded in carrying on her surreptitious game not just for three years but for thirty. The number of possible patterns was infinite; and, since every different pattern would require from the webster a different set of movements of eye and hand and body, it was open to Penelope to allow herself an infinite variety in the execution of her daily task. But, when each night she had the torches brought in, and set to work to unpick what she had woven between morn and eve, her night-work was monotonously uniform; and from this monotony there was no escape; for, when it came to unravelling the web, the pattern made no difference. However complicated the particular set of movements that had been required for the weaving of the pattern of the day, one simple movement, and this one only, was allowed by the nature of the task of undoing the day's work. The simple movement of drawing the threads has an obligatory rhythm upon which it is inherently impossible to ring any changes at all.

For this inevitable monotony of her night-work poor Penelope is assuredly to be pitied. To have to work into the small hours is hard enough anyway; and the toil becomes excruciating if it is not only hard but dull. If its hardness and dullness led nowhere the drudgery would be quite unbearable. What was it, then, that nerved the heroine to endure this self-imposed penance year-in and year-out? What inspired her was a song in her soul that was the unfaltering accompaniment of her repetitive night-work no less than of her varied daily task; and that song was 'ilayhi marji'ī':[1] 'With Him will I be reunited.' In drawing the threads by night after weaving them during the day Penelope was not blindly repeating a meaningless round of ineffectual labour. She was working and living in hope; and her hope was not disappointed; for those three years spent on a drudgery that kept the suitors at bay just enabled her to tide over the latter end of the decade of Odysseus' absence. The hero returned to find the heroine still his; and the *Odyssey* duly ends in the reunion of the devoted wife who has resisted the suitors' importunity with the devoted husband who has been proof against the blandishments of Calypso.[2]

[1] 'Ilayhi marji'ukum': 'To Him is your return': Qur'ān x. 4, quoted in III. C (iii), vol. iii, p. 390, above.   [2] See II. D (i), vol. ii, pp. 23-4, above.

If, then, as it turns out, even Penelope has neither woven nor drawn her threads in vain, what of the mightier weaver whose work is our study and whose song our ears have caught already in an earlier part of this book?

> In Lebensfluten, im Tatensturm
> Wall' ich auf und ab,
> Webe hin und her!
> Geburt und Grab
> Ein ewiges Meer,
> Ein wechselnd Weben,
> Ein glühend Leben,
> So schaff' ich am sausenden Webstuhl der Zeit
> Und wirke der Gottheit lebendiges Kleid.[1]

The work of the Spirit of the Earth, as he weaves and draws his threads on the Loom of Time, is the temporal history of Man as this manifests itself in the geneses and growths and breakdowns and disintegrations of human societies; and in all this welter of life and this tempest of action we can hear the beat of an elemental rhythm whose variations we have learnt to know as Challenge-and-Response and Withdrawal-and-Return and Rout-and-Rally and Apparatation-and-Affiliation and Schism-and-Palingenesia. This elemental rhythm is the alternating beat of Yin and Yang;[2] and in listening to it we have recognized that, though strophe may be answered by antistrophe, victory by defeat, birth by death, creation by destruction, the movement that this rhythm beats out is neither the fluctuation of an indecisive battle nor the cycle of a treadmill.[3] The perpetual turning of a wheel is not a vain repetition if, at each revolution, it is carrying a vehicle that much nearer to its goal; and, if 'palingenesia' signifies the birth of something new, and not just the rebirth of something that has lived and died any number of times already,[4] then the Wheel of Existence is not just a devilish device for inflicting an everlasting torment on a damned Ixion. On this showing, the music that the rhythm of Yin and Yang beats out is the song of creation; and we shall not be misled into fancying ourselves mistaken because, as we give ear, we can catch the note of creation alternating with the note of destruction. So far from convicting the song of being a diabolic counterfeit, this doubleness of note is a warrant of authenticity. If we listen well we shall perceive that, when the two notes collide, they produce not a discord but a harmony. Creation would not be

---

[1] Goethe: *Faust*, ll. 501–9, quoted in Part II. B, vol. i, p. 204, above.
[2] See Part II. B, vol. i, pp. 196–204, above.
[3] See IV. C (i), vol. iv, pp. 23–37, above.
[4] See V. C (i) (*b*), vol. v, p. 27, footnote 2, and V. C (i) (*e*), in the present volume, pp. 172–5, above.

creative if it did not swallow up in itself all things in Heaven and Earth, including its own antithesis.

But what of the living garment that the Earth Spirit weaves? Is it laid up in Heaven as fast as it is woven, or can we, here on Earth, catch glimpses at any rate of patches of its etherial web? What are we to think of those tissues that we see lying at the foot of the loom when the weaver, in the course of his tempestuous activity, has been at work unravelling? In the disintegration of a civilization we have found that, though the pageant may have been insubstantial, it does not fade without leaving a rack behind. When civilizations pass from breakdown through disintegration into dissolution, they regularly leave behind them a deposit of universal states and universal churches and barbarian war-bands. What are we to make of these objects? Are they mere waste-products of the disintegration-process—a tangle of spoiled threads from a piece of tapestry which the weaver, on an impulse of his inscrutable caprice, has willed to unpick before it has been half completed? Or will these debris prove, if we pick them up, to be fresh masterpieces of the weaver's art which he has woven, by an unnoticed sleight of hand, on some more etherial instrument than the roaring loom that has ostensibly been occupying all his attention and energies?

If, with this new question in mind, we cast our thoughts back over the results of our previous inquiries, we shall find reason to believe that these three objects of study are something more than by-products of social disintegration; for we came across them first[1] as tokens of Apparentation-and-Affiliation; and this is a relation between one civilization and another. Evidently, therefore, these three institutions cannot be explained entirely in terms of the history of any single civilization; their existence involves a relation between one civilization and another; and, to this extent at any rate, they must be independent entities with a claim to be studied on their own merits. But how far does their independence carry them? In dealing with universal states[2] we have found already that the peace which they bring is as ephemeral as it is imposing; and in dealing with barbarian war-bands[3] we have found, again, that these maggots in the carcass of a dead civilization cannot hope to live longer than it takes the putrefying corpse to dissolve into its clean elements. Yet, though the war-bands may be foredoomed to the premature death of Achilles, the barbarian hero's short life leaves at least an echo behind it in the poetry that commemorates

[1] In I. C (i) (a), vol. i, pp. 51–63, above.
[2] In V. C (ii) (a), pp. 181–213, and V. C (ii) (b), *passim*, above.
[3] In I. C (i) (a), vol. i, pp. 58–62, above.

an 'heroic age'.[1] And what is the destiny of the universal church in which every higher religion seeks to embody itself?[2]

It will be seen that we are not in a position at present to answer our new question off-hand; and at the same time it is clear that we cannot afford to ignore it; for this question holds the key to the meaning of the weaver's work; and a yearning that *tantus labor non sit cassus* will not allow us to rest without trying to unlock the secret of this mystery. Our Study is not at an end; but we have arrived at the verge of the last of our fields of inquiry.

[1] See I. C (i) (a), vol. i, p. 62; II. D (iii), vol. ii, pp. 94–6; and V. C (i) (c) 3, vol. v, pp. 233–4, above.
[2] We have already asked ourselves this question, without having yet tried to answer it, in V. C (i) (c) 4, vol. v, pp. 371–6, above.

TABLE I. *Universal States*

Civilization	'Time of Troubles'	Universal State	Pax Oecumenica	Provenance of Empire-builders
Sumeric	c. 2677–2298 B.C.	The Empire of Sumer and Akkad ("The Realm of the Four Quarters")	c. 2298–1905 B.C.	Founders metropolitans (from Ur); restorers marchmen (Amorites)
Babylonic	–610 B.C.	The Neo-Babylonic Empire	610–539 B.C.	Founders metropolitans [?][1] (Chaldaeans); successors barbarians (Achaemenidae) and aliens (Seleucidae)
Indic	–332 B.C.	The Mauryan Empire	322–185 B.C.	Founders metropolitans [?][2] (from Magadha)
		The Guptan Empire	A.D. 390–c. 475	Founders metropolitans (from Magadha)
Sinic	634–221 B.C.	The Ts'in and Han Empire	221 B.C.–c. A.D. 172	Founders marchmen (from Ts'in); successors metropolitans (Prior and Posterior Han)
Hellenic	431–31 B.C.	The Roman Empire	31 B.C.–A.D. 378	Founders marchmen (Romans); restorers marchmen (Illyrians)
Egyptiac	c. 2424–2070/60 B.C.	The Middle Empire	c. 2070/60–1660 B.C.	Marchmen (from Thebes)
		The New Empire	c. 1580–1175 B.C.	Marchmen (from Thebes)
Orthodox Christian (in Russia)	A.D. 1075–1478	The Muscovite Empire	A.D. 1478–1881	Marchmen (from Moscow)
Far Eastern (in Japan)	A.D. 1185–1597	Hideyoshi's dictatorship and the Tokugawa Shogunate	A.D. 1597–1868	Marchmen (from the Kwanto)
Western (medieval cosmos of city-states)	c. A.D. 1378–1797	The Napoleonic Empire	A.D. 1797–1814	Marchmen (from France)
Western (carapace against assaults of 'Osmanlis)	c. A.D. 1288[2]–1526	The Danubian Hapsburg Monarchy	A.D. 1526–1918	Marchmen (from Austria)
Andean	–c. A.D. 1430	The Incaic Empire ("The Realm of the Four Quarters")	c. A.D. 1430–1533	Founders marchmen (from Cuzco); successors aliens (Spaniards)
Syriac	c. 937–525 B.C.	The Achaemenian Empire	c. 525–332 B.C.	Barbaro-marchmen (from Iran)
		The Arab Caliphate	c. A.D. 640–969	Barbarians (from Arabia)
Far Eastern (main body)	A.D. 878–1280	The Mongol Empire	A.D. 1280–1351[3]	Barbaro-aliens (Mongols)
		The Manchu Empire	A.D. 1644–1853[4]	Barbaro-marchmen (Manchus)
Central American	–A.D. 1521	The Spanish Viceroyalty of New Spain	A.D. 1521–1821	Forerunners barbaro-marchmen (Aztecs); founders aliens (Spaniards)
Orthodox Christian (main body)	A.D. 977–1372	The Ottoman Empire	A.D. 1372–1768	Aliens ('Osmanlis)
Hindu	c. A.D. 1175–1572	The Mughal Rāj	c. A.D. 1572–1707	Aliens (Mughals)
		The British Rāj	c. A.D. 1818–	Aliens (British)
Minoan	c. 1750 B.C.	'The Thalassocracy of Minos'	c. 1750–1400 B.C.	No evidence
Mayan	c. A.D. 300	'The First Empire' of the Mayas	c. A.D. 300–690	No evidence

[1] The Chaldaeans in Babylonia might be classified either as metropolitans or as marchmen.

[2] Magadha might be regarded either as part of the interior of the Indic World of the Pre-Mauryan and the Mauryan Age or else as the eastern march of the Indic World in those ages.

[3] The date of the outbreak of the first of the wars between Hungary and the 'Osmanlis' East Roman forerunners the Comneni (see IV. C (iii) 2 (β), vol. iv, p. 403, footnote 3, above).

[4] The date of the capture of Nanking by the T'aip'ing insurgents.

TABLE II. *Philosophies*

Civilization	Philosophy
Egyptiac	Atonism (abortive)
Andean	Viracochaism (abortive)
Sinic	Confucianism
	Moism
	Taoism
Syriac	Zervanism (abortive)
Indic	Hinayanian Buddhism
	Jainism
Western	Cartesianism
	Hegelianism[1]
Hellenic	Platonism
	Stoicism
	Epicureanism
	Pyrrhonism
Babylonic	Astrology

[1] Hegelianism confined to the field of social affairs = Marxism; Marxism transplanted from the Western World to Russia = Leninism.

TABLE III. *Higher Religions*

Civilization	Higher Religion	Source of Inspiration
Sumeric	Tammuz-worship	indigenous
Egyptiac	Osiris-worship	alien [?] (Sumeric [?])
Sinic	The Mahāyāna	alien (Indo-Helleno-Syriac)
	Neotaoism	indigenous but imitative (of the Mahāyāna)
Indic	Hinduism	indigenous
Syriac	Islam	indigenous
Hellenic	Christianity	alien (Syriac)
	Mithraism	alien (Syriac)
	Manichaeism	alien (Syriac)
	The Mahāyāna	alien (Indic)
	Isis-worship	alien (Egyptiac)
	Cybele-worship	alien (Hittite)
	Neoplatonism	indigenous (*ci-devant* philosophy)
Babylonic	Judaism	alien (Syriac)
	Zoroastrianism	alien (Syriac)
Western	Bahaism	alien (Iranic)
	The Ahmadīyah	alien (Iranic)
Orthodox Christian (main body)	Imāmī Shi'ism	alien (Iranic)
	Bedreddīnism	semi-alien (Iranic tincture)
Orthodox Christian (in Russia)	Sectarianism	indigenous
	Revivalist Protestantism	alien (Western)
Far Eastern (main body)	Catholicism	alien (Western)
	T'aip'ing	semi-alien (Western tincture)
Far Eastern (in Japan)	Jōdo	semi-alien (from Far Eastern, main body)
	Jōdo Shinshū	indigenous (from Jōdo)
	Nichirenism	indigenous
	Zen	semi-alien (from Far Eastern, main body)
Hindu	Kabirism and Sikhism	semi-alien (Islamic tincture)
	Brahmō Samāj	semi-alien (Western tincture)

TABLE IV. *Barbarian War-Bands*

Civilization	Universal State	Frontier	Barbarians	Poetry	Religion
Sumeric	The Empire of Sumer and Akkad	NE.	Gutaeans		
			Eurasian Nomads (Aryas)	The Sanskrit Epic	The Vedic Pantheon
Babylonic	The Neo-Babylonian Empire	NW.	Kassites		
		NE.	Hittites		The Hittite Pantheon
			Eurasian Nomads (Scyths)		
			Medes and Persians		Zoroastrianism
Indic	The Mauryan Empire / The Guptan Empire	NW.	Sakas	The Sanskrit Epic (recultivated)	
		NW.	Huns		
			Gurjaras		
Sinic	The Ts'in and Han Empire	NW.	Eurasian Nomads {(Hiongnu)(To Pa)(Juan Juan)(Sienpi)}		
Hellenic	The Roman Empire	NE.	Eurasian Nomads {(Sarmatians)(Huns)}		
		NW.	Insular Celts	The Irish Epic	Far Western Christianity
		N.	Continental Teutons	The Teutonic Epic	First the Continental Teutonic Pantheon, then Arianism
Egyptiac	The Middle Empire	SE.	Arabs	The Pre-Islamic Arabic Poetry	Islam
		SW.	Berbers		
		S.	Nubians		
		NE.	Hyksos		Set-worship
	The New Empire	N.	Achaeans	The Homeric Epic	The Olympian Pantheon
		NW.	Libyans		
		E.	Hebrews and Aramaeans		Yahweh-worship
Orthodox Christian (in Russia)		SE.	Eurasian Nomads {(Tatars)(Torgut Calmucks)}		Islam / Lamaistic Mahayanian Buddhism
Far Eastern	The Tokugawa Shogunate	NE.	Ainu		
Western	In Europe	NW.	Insular Celts	The Irish Epic	Far Western Christianity
		N.	Scandinavians	The Icelandic Sagas	The Scandinavian Pantheon
		NE.	Continental Saxons		
			Wends		
		E.	Lithuanians		
			Eurasian Nomads (Magyars)		
		SE.	Bosniaks	The Muslim Jugoslav 'heroic' ballads	First Bogomilism, then Islam
Andean	In North America / The Incaic Empire	W.	Red Indians		
		E.	Amazonians		
		S.	Araucanians		Non-violent 'Zealotism'

(Civilization)	Universal State		External Proletariat	Universal Church / Heroic Poetry	Higher Religion
Syriac	The Achaemenian Empire	NW.	Macedonians	The Alexander Romance	
	The Arab Caliphate	NE.	Parthians	The Iranian Epic	
		NW.	Sakas	The French Epic	Catholicism
		SW.	Franks	The Byzantine Greek Epic	Orthodox Christianity
		SE.	East Roman 'Borderers'		Ismā'īlī Shī'ism
		N.	Berbers		Ismā'īlī Shī'ism
		NE.	Arabs		Judaism
		NE.	Eurasian Nomads (Khazars)		{ Manichaeism
		NW.	Eurasian Nomads { (Turks) (Mongols) }		Nestorianism
Far Eastern (main body)	[Time of Troubles]	NE.	Eurasian Nomads (Khitan) (Kin)		
	The Manchu Empire	NE.	Eurasian Nomads (Mongols)		Lamaistic Mahayanian Buddhism
Central American	The Spanish Viceroyalty of New Spain	NW.	Eurasian Nomads (Zungar Calmucks)		
Orthodox Christian (main body)	The Ottoman Empire	N.	Chichimecs		
		NW.	Serbs	The Orthodox Christian Jugoslav 'heroic' ballads	
			Albanians	The Albanian 'heroic' poetry	Bektāshi Sunnism
			Rumeliot Greeks	The Rumeliot Greek Armatole and Klephtic ballads	
		NE.	Lazes		
		SE.	Kurds		
		S.	Arabs		Najdi Wahhabism
		NW.	Arabs		Kordofāni Mahdism
Hindu	The Mughal Rāj	NW.	Uzbegs		
		N.	Afghans		
	The British Rāj	E.	Afghans		
Minoan	"The thalassocracy of Minos"	NE.	Achaeans and Aramaeans	The Homeric Epic	The Olympian Pantheon
		NE.	Hebrews and Aramaeans		Yahweh-worship
Iranic	[Time of Troubles]	SW.	Uzbegs		
		NW.	Afghans		
Hittite		E.	Gasgas	The Homeric Epic	The Olympian Pantheon
		NW.	Phrygians		
			Achaeans		
			Bastarnae		
Eurasian Nomadism	The Royal Scythian Horde	E.	Sarmatians		
	The Khazar Horde	NW.	Varangians	The Russian 'heroic' ballads	Orthodox Christianity
		E.	Pechenegs		
	The Golden Horde	NW.	Cossacks		
		NE.	Kirghiz Qāzāqs	The Kirghiz Qāzāq 'heroic' ballads	

ANNEXES

ANNEX TO V. C (i) (*d*) 7

THE HELLENIC CONCEPTION OF THE 'COSMOPOLIS'

THE Hellenic conception of the *Cosmopolis* may be illustrated by a cento of quotations from Latin and Greek authors. Of the four who are drawn upon below, the first, Cicero, lived on the eve of the foundation of a Roman Empire which provided the Hellenic World with a universal state and Hellenic minds with a terrestrial image of the constitution of the vaster commonwealth of the Universe. The other three—Seneca, Epictetus, and Marcus—lived and worked in the social environment of an established Roman Empire at dates which all fall within the first two centuries of the Roman Peace. Both Marcus and Seneca were called upon to govern the Empire; and they both of them drew from their ideal of the *Cosmopolis* the moral strength to perform a burdensome and thankless mundane task for the sake of which Marcus sacrificed his happiness and Seneca forfeited his life—though Seneca's death at Nero's hands was not so ironical a tragedy as Cicero's death at the hands of a Triumvirate which included the future Augustus.[1]

The first concern of these Hellenic philosophers in their disquisitions on the *Cosmopolis* was to demonstrate its existence; and the following proofs, on closely parallel lines, are offered by Cicero and by Marcus. Cicero's argument runs thus:

'Man has a primary social bond with God in their common possession of Reason—seeing that there is nothing higher than Reason, and that this highest of all faculties is to be found in Man and in God alike. Those, however, who have Reason in common have Right Reason in common as well; and, since Right Reason is another name for Law (*lex*), we human beings must be regarded as being associated with the Gods through the bond of Law likewise. But those who share the same law are living under the same juridical dispensation (*ius*), and this implies that they are members of the same commonwealth. If, however, they are subject to the same authorities and powers, then they are also subject, *a fortiori*, to the heavenly ordinance and to the Divine Intelligence

---

[1] In retrospect Augustus seems to have recognized that the eloquent voice which he had allowed Mark Antony to silence with the sword had been one of the heralds of Augustus's own life-work. At any rate this seems a legitimate reading of the following anecdote in Plutarch's *Life of Cicero*, chap. 49:

'I have heard that, many years later, Augustus once came into a room where one of his grandchildren (a child of his daughter's) was sitting reading one of Cicero's works. The boy was horrified and tried to hide the book under his coat; but his grandfather saw what he was doing, took the book, started to read it, and stood there reading on and on until he had been through a considerable part of the volume. Then he handed it back to the child with the words: "A great writer, my boy, a great writer and a great patriot."'

and to Almighty God. And so the whole of this Universe is to be regarded as one single commonwealth of gods and men.'[1]

Marcus's argument follows much the same course:

'If we have Intelligence in common, we must also have in common the
Reason (λόγος) in virtue of which we are reasonable creatures; and from
this it would follow that we have in common, again, the Reason that
tells us what to do and to leave undone. From this it would follow that
we have Law (νόμος) in common; from this that we are citizens; and
from that, again, that we are members of some kind of polity (πολίτευμα).
If so, the Universe is like a commonwealth (πόλις); for what other polity
can any one think of which has a membership comprising the entire
Human Race? And is not this all-embracing commonwealth the only
conceivable source of the intelligent and reasonable and law-abiding
veins in our own human nature?'[2]

The conception of the Universe as a commonwealth, at which
Marcus and Cicero have arrived by this road, is worked out as
follows by Epictetus:

'This Universe is one commonwealth, and the substance out of which
it has been fashioned is likewise one; and there is in its economy an
inevitable periodicity which makes things give place to one another—
one thing dissolving as another comes on into existence, and some
things remaining unmoved while others are in motion. And everything
is full of friends: in the first place gods but also human beings, who are
likewise natural friends because they have been designed by Nature for
living as members of one human family. In the natural course of this
family life some have to keep each other company and others have to
part company; and while we may rejoice in the companionship we must
not grieve at the separation.'[3]

One of the excellences of the constitution of the *Cosmopolis* is
the harmonious solution of the problem of the distribution of
allegiance between the cosmic commonwealth and the terrestrial
parish—and this is a topic on which we shall obtain the clearest
light from those Hellenic philosophers who were at the same time
Roman citizens; since Rome, as we have seen,[4] had been more successful than any other terrestrial community in the Hellenic World
in reconciling Cicero the citizen of the municipality of Arpinum
with Cicero the citizen of an oecumenical Roman State. The
analogous reconciliation of allegiances on the cosmic scale is propounded as follows by Seneca:

'We have to envisage two commonwealths. There is a great one—

---

[1] Cicero: *De Legibus*, Book I, chap. 7.
[2] Marcus Aurelius Antoninus: *Meditations*, Book IV, chap. 4.
[3] Epictetus: *Dissertationes*, Book III, chap. 24, §§ 10–11.
[4] In III. C (ii) (*b*), Annex IV, vol. iii, p. 481; IV. C (iii) (*b*) 10, vol. iv, pp. 208–14;
and IV. C (iii) (*c*) 2 (β), vol. iv, pp. 310–13, above. See also V. C (ii) (*b*), in the present
volume, p. 291, above.

truly deserving of the name—which embraces both gods and m^n and
in which we do not let our eyes dwell on some insignificant corner but
include in the bounds of our polity all that is under the Sun. And then
there is that other commonwealth in which we have been enrolled by
the accident of birth—an Athens or a Carthage or some other state with
a citizenship that is not oecumenical but is merely parochial. Some
people work for both commonwealths—the greater and the lesser—
simultaneously; others exclusively for the lesser; and others, again,
exclusively for the greater. It is in our power to serve this greater
commonwealth in retirement as well as in active life; and indeed I am
inclined to think that in retirement we can actually serve it better.'[1]

The points here made by Seneca are put more pithily by Marcus:

'*Qua* Antoninus I have Rome for my commonwealth and country;
qua human being I have the Universe. The public interest of these two
commonwealths gives the whole measure of my own private good.'[2]

If an apparent conflict of duties does arise, the philosopher may
take it for granted that his duty to the Universe takes precedence.
As Seneca sees it,

'When we have given the sage a commonwealth that is worthy of him
by giving him the Universe, he will not be cutting himself off from the
common weal by going into retirement. On the contrary, he will perhaps be leaving a hole in the corner in order to pass out into a greater
and more spacious life, and to realize—when he finds himself on the
heights of Heaven—the lowliness of the seat on which he sat when he
used to take the chair or mount the tribunal. Let it sink into your mind
that the sage is never so active as when he has brought within his purview the sum of things human and divine.'[3]

The same answer is given to the same question by Epictetus in
his dissertation on the perfect practitioner of the Cynic discipline:

'I suppose you want to ask me whether the Cynic sage will go into
politics? You blockhead! What greater field of political activity do you
propose to give him than the field in which he is actually at work? Is
he to take the floor at Athens and make a speech on revenue or supply
when his role is to address the whole World—Athens and Corinth and
Rome in the same world-wide audience—and to take for his subject, not
supply or revenue or peace or war, but the Soul's prosperity and adversity, good fortune and bad fortune, slavery and freedom? You see
a man working in a field of political activity of that titanic scope, and
you ask me whether he will be going into politics? Suppose you go on
to ask me whether he will take office, and once more I shall say to you:
You fool! What greater office could he conceivably hold than the office
that he is exercising already?'[4]

---

[1] Seneca, L. A.: *Ad Serenum de Otio*, chap. 4.
[2] Marcus, op. cit., Book VI, chap. 44.
[3] Seneca, L. A.: *Epistolae*, Book VII, Ep. lxviii, § 2.
[4] Epictetus: *Dissertationes*, Book III, chap. 22, §§ 83–5.

In the last resort the Commonwealth of the Universe has a claim
upon the sage's allegiance to which the parochial commonwealth
must give way; for

'Man [is] a citizen of the supreme commonwealth, in which the other
commonwealths are no more than houses;'[1]

and this simile reappears in the Stoic philosopher-emperor's confession of faith:

'Everything that is in harmony for thee, O Universe, is harmonious
for me likewise. Nothing that is in season for thee is for me either
premature or tardy. All is fruit for me that is brought by thy seasons, O
Nature. From thee all things proceed; in thee all things subsist; to thee
all things return. The worldling says "O beloved City of Cecrops", and
shalt *thou* not say "O beloved City of Zeus"?'[2]

The philosopher may even rise to a height at which the parochial
commonwealth fades out of view and leaves the Soul free to live
the life of the 'City of Zeus' without any other claim on her attention.

'If there is truth in what the philosophers say about the kinship
between God and men, is not the moral of this, for us men, that one
should do like Socrates and never say, when asked one's nationality, that
one is an Athenian or a Corinthian, but always answer that one is a
native of the Universe ($\kappa\acute{o}\sigma\mu\iota os$)? Why is it that you call yourself an
Athenian, instead of calling yourself simply by the name of the corner
in which your vile body happened to be deposited at birth? Isn't it
obvious that you call yourself an Athenian or a Corinthian because the
area that is denoted by the name of Athens or Corinth is intrinsically
more important and at the same time comprehends not merely the
corner in which you were actually born, but also the whole of your
house and, in short, the roots of your family tree? Well, any one who
has studied the economy of the Universe will have learnt that the
greatest and most important and most comprehensive of all things is
this combine of men and God ($\sigma\acute{v}\sigma\tau\eta\mu\alpha$ $\tau\grave{o}$ $\dot{\epsilon}\xi$ $\dot{\alpha}\nu\theta\rho\acute{\omega}\pi\omega\nu$ $\kappa\alpha\grave{\iota}$ $\Theta\epsilon o\hat{v}$), and
he will also have learnt that God has been the source of life not only for
my father and for my grandfather, but for everything that comes to life
and grows upon the face of the Earth, and particularly for creatures
endowed with Reason, since these alone are capable of enjoying a true
intercourse with God thanks to the links by which Reason binds them
to Him. A man who has learnt this may properly be called a native of
the Universe and a son of God.'[3]

These words of the philosopher-slave Epictetus are echoed by
a fellow Stoic who had to reconcile his freedom of the City of

[1] Marcus, op. cit., Book III, chap. 11, quoted already in V. C (i) (*d*) 11, p. 158, above.
[2] Ibid., Book IV, chap. 23, quoted already in V. C (i) (*d*) 1, vol. v, pp. 384 and 395,
above.
[3] Epictetus: *Dissertationes*, Book I, chap. 9, §§ 1–6.

Zeus with the slavery of being the sovereign of the Roman Empire.

'Live as though you were on a mountain; for it makes no difference being here or there if, wherever one is, the Universe is one's commonwealth. . . . [And] if, when you find yourself approaching your end, you concentrate upon caring for nothing but your higher self and the spark of divinity that is in you . . . then you will be a man who is worthy of the Universe that has begotten you and at least you will no longer be a stranger in your own true native country.'[1]

The Hellenic sage whose citizenship of the Universe thus swallowed up his citizenship of Rome or Athens did not make the mistake of imagining that he was thereby being translated from a harder to an easier state of existence.

'All this that you see—this sum of things human and divine—is a unity. It is a vast body of which we are the members. Nature brought us into the World already bound to one another by the ties of kinship, when she fashioned us from the same elements and placed us in the same environment. It was she who planted a mutual love in our hearts and made us social animals. It was she who created Right and Justice. It is by her enactment that it is more painful to inflict injury than to suffer it. Let us obey her command by holding out our hands to those who need our succour. Let us have on our lips and in our heart the line "I am a child of man and there is nothing human which does not touch me".[2] Let us hold in common what we have, for we have been born [to a common lot]. Our human society is like nothing so much as an arch—which would fall if the stones did not mutually support one another, whereas it actually remains in position just because they do.'[3]

This exhortation of Seneca's is capped by Epictetus:

'You are a citizen of the Universe and a member of it—and not one of the menial members either, but one of those in authority; for you have the intelligence to follow the divine economy and to work out its sequence. What, then, is the citizen's vocation? It is to have no private interests of his own and to take no action *in vacuo*, but rather to act as one's hand or foot would act if they were reasonable beings with the intelligence to follow the laws of Physiology—for we may be sure that, if they *were* endowed with Reason, these members would yield to no impulse and entertain no desire without reference to the welfare of the whole organism. On this showing, the philosophers are profoundly right in saying that if the man of honour could foresee the future he would be a consenting party to his own sickness and death and disablement, because he would perceive that his personal lot was an integral part of the order of the Universe, and that the whole was more important than the part, and the commonwealth than the citizen.'[4]

This duty of self-surrender to the operation of the laws of the

---

[1] Marcus, op. cit., Book X, chap. 15, and Book XII, chap. 1.
[2] This line has already been quoted in this Study in V. C (i) (*d*) 7, on p. 8, above.—A.J.T.   [3] Seneca, L. A.: *Epistolae*, Book XV, Ep. xcv, §§ 52–3.
[4] Epictetus: *Dissertationes*, Book II, chap. 9, §§ 3–5.

Commonwealth of the Universe has received a sublime expression
in the following adjuration with which Marcus concludes his
colloquy with himself:

'Man, you have enjoyed the franchise of this mighty commonwealth;
what difference does it make to you whether your term has been five
years or three? To be treated in accordance with the law is equitable
treatment, however it may work out for the individual. So where is the
hardship if you are removed from the commonwealth by the action, not
of a tyrant or of an unjust judge, but of Nature herself by whom you
were originally introduced. Isn't it just like the actor being given his
dismissal from the stage by the public authority that has engaged him?
—"But I haven't played my five acts; I have only played three of them!"
—Quite true; but then Life happens to be a three-act play. And what
constitutes a complete play is a matter for the decision of the power who
was once the author of your composition and is now the author of your
dissolution—and in neither of these events have *you* any say. So take
your departure with a good grace; for he who dismisses you is gracious.'[1]

In this passage the Stoic sovereign of the Roman Empire submits himself to the Olympian sovereign of the *Cosmopolis* with the
absolute devotion that is doubtless due to the supreme authority
in a truly 'totalitarian' state; yet there is an earlier passage in
Marcus's meditations in which the philosopher's faith in the existence of a constitution of the Universe seems to falter and throw
him back upon a bleak reliance on the self-respect of a self that can
look for no support in the Macrocosm.

'The cyclic movements of the Universe repeat themselves, up and
down, from aeon to aeon; and one of two alternatives must be the truth.
Either the All-Pervading Intelligence takes a fresh initiative each time—
and, if that is the truth, it is for you to acquiesce in it—or else It took
one primal initiative once for all, and everything else is a consequence
of that—in which case, why extenuate yourself? For this would imply
a sort of unbroken continuum. It amounts to this, that if God exists
all's well with the world, while, if the ultimate reality is something without rhyme or reason, that is no excuse for you to take this chaos for your
own standard of behaviour.'[2]

In these tragic cries we seem to hear the voice of a devoted
citizen of the *Cosmopolis* who has suddenly awoken to find that
Zeus has absconded from his presidential post and has left his
faithful servant to bear the burden of Atlas on his solitary human
shoulders. Marcus himself could never have been guilty of such a
betrayal. He bore the terrestrial burden of the Roman Principate
till he dropped dead under its weight. But Marcus's Christian
readers ought not to be too hard on Marcus's Zeus; for Zeus, after

---

[1] Marcus, op. cit., Book XII, chap. 36.   [2] Ibid., Book IX, chap. 28.

all, had never asked to be elected president of a cosmic republic; he had started life as the disreputable war-lord of a barbarian war-band; and all that we know about him goes to show that this was the life that he enjoyed. If a Zeus whom the philosophers had belatedly caught and caged was unable to endure an eternity of enforced respectability as the senior inmate of a Stoic reformatory, have we the heart to blame the poor old fellow for proving incorrigible?

NEW ERAS

ONE of the simplest and most natural ways of celebrating an attempt to make a breach with the Present by taking a flying leap into the Future is to inaugurate a 'new era'.

This may be done in formal terms, as when the authors of a new political régime decree that all documents and events are to be dated officially by their subjects as from the Year One of the reigning Government's accession to power. On the other hand a new era may obtain a wide currency, and exert a profound influence upon the *Weltanschauung* of people who have come to think in terms of it, through being adopted by a free consensus without the intervention of any political authority—as, for example, the new era of Hellenic history *post Alexandrum* came to be adopted as the principal landmark in the historical retrospect of most of the post-Alexandrine Greek historians.

Apart from this superficial distinction between an official and a spontaneous origin, new eras can be classified in a more significant way according to the nature of the breach which they commemorate. This breach may be merely the transition from one chapter to the next in the unbroken history of a single society; or it may be one of those sharper and deeper interruptions of continuity that are produced by the impact of one society upon another.[1] In this sphere the inauguration of a new era may celebrate either the experience of conversion to an alien civilization or the still greater spiritual travail of conversion to an alien religion. It may be convenient to consider each of these different kinds of new era separately in an ascending scale measured by the extent of the breach which they celebrate.

The most notorious Western example of the official inauguration of a new era to mark the advent of a new political régime is the substitution, in Revolutionary France, of Years of the Revolution for Years of Our Lord. In our own day this Revolutionary French conceit has been followed by the Fascist Régime in Italy, in curious contradiction with the Fascists' vociferous repudiation of 'the Ideas of 1789', and with an even more curious disregard for the obvious consideration that a French era which remained in currency for so short a span of time is an inauspicious precedent for an Italian régime which boasts itself to be building for Eternity. The experience of an independent nationhood which has not only maintained

---

[1] The Contact of Civilizations with one another is dealt with in Parts IX and X below.

itself for more than 150 years but has gone in the meantime from strength to strength would give a greater justification to the Government of the United States if it were to decide to-day to date its own official transactions from the year of the Declaration of Independence; and it is a not impossible *tour de force* for a North American historian to begin his unofficial story with the landing of the Pilgrim Fathers—or at any rate with the voyages of Cabot and Columbus—as an Alexandrian or an Antiochene historian, in his place and day, might have begun with the crossing of the Helles-pont by Alexander. In Hellenic historiography the new era which starts from Alexander's passage into Asia and destruction of the Achaemenian Empire has its counterpart in another new era which starts from the foundation of a New Rome on the Bosphorus by the Emperor Constantine; and this latter-day Hellenic era *post Constantinopolim conditam*, which remained a landmark for the affiliated Orthodox Christian Society after the Hellenic Society itself had gone into dissolution, has its analogue in a latter-day Sumeric era, *post primam regum Babylonis dynastiam institutam*, which the affiliated Babylonic Society likewise continued to take as its chronological starting-point.

To return to our own society, we shall find that almost any modern Western economic historian—even if he has been born and brought up, not in the New World overseas, but in the European homeland of our civilization—is capable of producing in a medieval quadrangle and under the shadow of a Gothic spire a history pur-porting to record the economic achievements of Man which will begin with the Industrial Revolution and will ignore all that hap-pened, either in the Western World or elsewhere, before the advent of the so-called 'Machine Age'.[1] In the same futurist spirit a student of the history of modern Western science—or even of modern Western philosophy—may sometimes yield to the tempta-tion to start with the radiation of the North Italian culture into Transalpine Europe at the turn of the fifteenth and sixteenth cen-turies of the Christian Era.

The unofficial new era, starting *circa* A.D. 1500, which is com-monly taken to mark the beginning of the so-called Modern Age of Western history, is on the borderline between the kind of new era which signalizes merely the beginning of a new chapter in the domestic history of a single society and the other, more profoundly 'epoch-making', kind which signalizes the impact of one civiliza-tion upon another. The conventionally accepted signal of the

---

[1] The contrary view that Man's greatest technical triumphs have been his earliest, and not his most recent, has been put forward in this Study in III. C (i) (*b*), vol. iii, pp. 158–9, above.

beginning of our Modern Age has affinities in two respects with
the eras that signalize an impact. In the first place the North
Italian culture which radiated out over the Transalpine parts of the
Western World at that time was a variation of the Western culture
which had differentiated itself on Italian ground—during a period
of political insulation which had lasted for some two centuries—to
a degree at which the Italians felt and called their Transalpine
fellow Westerners 'barbarians', while the Transalpine peoples
made a silent but eloquent acknowledgement of the Italians' accomplished superiority in an imitation of Italian ways which in this
case was unquestionably the sincerest form of flattery.[1] In the
second place this Italian version of the Western culture, which had
already surpassed the Transalpine version by its own efforts, was
enriching itself still further, by the time when it was radiating
abroad, by drawing upon the treasures of the Hellenic culture
which had been brought within its reach by a renaissance of
classical Latin and Greek letters.[2] Thus, for Italy herself, the
Quattrocento introduced a new era which was marked by a contact
in the Time-dimension with the defunct Hellenic Society, while,
for Transalpine Western Europe, the *Cinquecento* introduced in its
turn a new era in which this Italian contact in Time with Hellenism
was transmitted to the Transalpine countries through the agency
of a contact in the Space-dimension between this Transalpine ruck
of Western Christendom and the now superior Western Civilization of contemporary Italy.

Another new era that is likewise on the borderline between a
mere beginning of a new chapter of domestic history and a collision
between two different civilizations is the Seleucid Era which runs
from the October of the year 312 B.C. In the minds of the Seleucidae themselves this era simply commemorated the definitive
establishment of the authority of the Dynasty through the triumphal re-entry of Seleucus Nicator into Babylon on the day that
was taken as the initial date; and in this aspect the Seleucid Era is
comparable to our modern Western eras of the French Revolution
or of the Fascist Régime, while it is precisely analogous to the
Gupta Era, running from the 26th February, A.D. 320,[3] which
commemorates the definitive inauguration of the authority of the
Gupta Dynasty that eventually re-established the Indic universal
state after an interlude of Hellenic and Nomadic intrusion which

---

[1] See I. B (i), vol. i, p. 19; III. C (ii) (*b*), vol. iii, pp. 299–305 and 341–57; and IV. C
(iii) (*c*) 2 (α), vol. iv, pp. 274–5, above.
[2] For the correct usage and the popular misuse of the term 'Renaissance' see IV. C
(iii) (*c*) 2 (α), vol. iv, p. 275, footnote 1, above.
[3] See Smith, V. A.: *The Early History of India*, 3rd ed. (Oxford 1914, Clarendon
Press), p. 280.

had followed the premature fall of the Mauryas.[1] In the minds of the Hellenic contemporaries of the Seleucidae, both inside and beyond the frontiers of the Seleucid Empire, the official Seleucid Era probably stood for much the same thing as the unofficial era which ran from Alexander's passage of the Hellespont some twenty-two years before Seleucus Nicator's re-entry into Babylon. Alexander had destroyed the Achaemenian Empire; Seleucus had founded the principal Hellenic 'successor-state' of the Achaemenian Empire in Asia; and either event would serve to mark the sudden vast territorial expansion of the Hellenic World in that generation. For the Hellenes this expansion was a domestic event, though this an outstanding one, in their own Hellenic history. The expansion, however, had been achieved at the Syriac World's expense; and the sudden violent interruption of the continuity of Syriac history through the irruption of an alien Hellenism was the event for which the Seleucid Era stood in the minds of Syriac peoples who continued to reckon by it long after the Seleucid Dynasty itself had passed away.[2]

This diverse significance of the Seleucid Era in different eyes has an analogue in the history of the Far Eastern Civilization in Japan, where the Meiji Era, which runs from the year A.D. 1868 of the Christian Era, commemorates two events that are distinct from one another notwithstanding their close historical association. On the one hand the new Japanese Era commemorates the domestic event of the restoration of the Imperial Dynasty to a position of authority which it had certainly not enjoyed since A.D. 1192,[3] and perhaps not since A.D. 858.[4] On the other hand it commemorates the deliberate 'reception' of the alien civilization of the West—a landmark in the history of the contact between the Far Eastern and the Western culture which eclipses in importance the domestic Japanese political revolution that was one of its corollaries.

The corresponding 'reception' of the Western Civilization in the Russian province of the Orthodox Christian World at a date about

---

[1] For the role of the Guptas in Indic history see I. C (i) (b), vol. i, p. 85, above. The inaugural date of the Gupta Era anticipates the actual foundation of the Gupta Empire (as distinct from the embryonic Gupta principality) by about thirty years, and the expansion of this empire to the dimensions of a universal state by about seventy years (see V. C (ii) (a), pp. 189–90, above).

[2] The Seleucid Era was not only widely adopted but was also widely imitated by dynasties and commonwealths which, instead of taking over the Seleucid Era itself, preferred to institute rival eras of their own (see Meyer, E.: Geschichte des Altertums, vol. i, part (1), 4th ed. (Stuttgart and Berlin 1921, Cotta), p. 241; Tarn, W. W.: The Greeks in Bactria and India (Cambridge 1938, University Press), p. 359).

[3] The date of Yoritomo's formal appointment to the new office of Shogun after his substitution of a Minamoto for a Taira military ascendancy in the Revolution of A.D. 1183–5 and his simultaneous removal of the seat of the de facto government of Japan from Kyoto to Kamakura.

[4] The date of the establishment of the ascendancy of the House of Fujiwara over the Imperial Government at Kyoto.

two centuries and three-quarters in advance of its 'reception' in
Japan is not commemorated in any official era; yet the reign of the
Emperor Meiji is not a more epoch-making period in the history
of Japan than the reign of the Tsar Peter the Great in the history
of Russia; and, if we wish to date the beginning of the new age of
Westernization in Russia from some particular year, we have
several choices at our disposal.[1] We can choose the year A.D. 1689,
which is the date, not of the official beginning of Peter's reign, but
of his actual advent to power; or we can choose the 16th May,
1703, which is the date of the beginning of the building of St.
Petersburg. The foundation of St. Petersburg by Peter was a
symbolic act of the same significance as the foundation of Constantinople by Constantine. The Roman Emperor who had made
it his mission to convert the Hellenic World to Christianity built
himself a new capital which was to be Christian from the start;[2]
and a new capital which was to be Western from the start was built,
in pursuance of corresponding considerations of statecraft, by the
Muscovite Tsar who had made it his mission to westernize all the
Russias.

The conversion of a society to an alien religion is the third type
of epoch-making event that is apt to find expression in the inauguration of a new era. A new era commemorating the conversion
of the Hellenic World to Christianity would most naturally be
dated from some event in the career of Constantine the Great—
though it might be difficult to select one single event for the purpose, since Constantine's establishment of Christianity as the—or
an—official religion of the Roman state was (like the Emperor's
own personal adoption of Christianity) a gradual and perhaps never
quite completed process and not either an abrupt or a 'totalitarian'
act.[3] Constantine's career was indeed regarded, as Alexander's had
been regarded, by later generations as a landmark in Hellenic history which virtually amounted to a new beginning. But this unofficial consensus of feeling was not given expression in the
establishment of a Constantinian Era; and after the break-up of the
Roman Empire and the concomitant dissolution of the Hellenic

[1] We should be less in doubt if we had to choose a date for the inauguration of the
Communist régime under which, in our own day, the process of Westernization, begun
by Peter the Great, is being carried forward with incomparably greater intensity in the
territories inherited from the defunct Muscovite Empire by the Union of Soviet Socialist Republics. We should have little hesitation in dating our Bolshevik Era from the
seizure of power in Petrograd by Peter's authentic successor Lenin on the 7th November
(New Style, which is the 25th October, Old Style), 1917.

[2] On this point Constantine's purpose was only partially achieved; for the newly laid
out city that was officially dedicated by its Imperial founder to Christ admitted into its
precincts the pagan worship of the Goddess Tychê (see V. C (i) (d) 4, vol. v, p. 413,
footnote 6, above).

[3] This is clearly brought out by Professor N. H. Baynes in *Constantine the Great and
the Christian Church* (London 1929, Milford).

Society the event that stood out the most prominently in retrospect to Christians belonging to new societies that were Christian from the start was not the conversion of the Hellenic World to Christianity in the reign of the Roman Emperor Constantine but the revelation of Christianity itself through the Incarnation of Christ. Accordingly, the era which gained currency in Western Christendom from the post-Hellenic interregnum onwards was an era which took for its initial date the supposed year of the birth of Jesus; but it is noteworthy that this practice of reckoning by years of the Christian Era has prevailed only in Western Christendom, where the evocation of a ghost of the Roman Empire has been a fiasco and the renaissance of Hellenic letters has been tardy. In Orthodox Christendom, where a ghost of the Roman Empire was effectively evoked and Hellenic learning effectively reborn in the eighth century of the Christian Era,[1] civil servants continued to date by fiscal 'Indictions'[2] and historians by 'Years of the World'. In the Orthodox and the other non-Western Christendoms the reckoning by Years of the Christian Era has eventually been introduced as an automatic—and ironical—consequence of their capitulation to the culture of a Western Society which has itself ceased to be intrinsically Christian[3] without having taken the trouble to remove the traditional Christian imprint from its official calendar.

We have still to mention a new era which purports to signalize a greater new departure in the way of life on Earth than any of those that we have passed in review so far, and that is the Advent— or, in the Christian version of the belief, the Second Coming[4]— of a supernatural saviour who is to inaugurate a Millennium of life which will still be a life on this Earth and in the flesh, but a life to be lived under unprecedented and unimaginable conditions of righteousness and felicity. This belief, in which the beginning of the new age is not equated with some already accomplished event[5]

---

[1] For this momentous divergence between the respective courses of events in Western and in Orthodox Christendom from the eighth century onwards see IV. C (iii) (c) 2 (β), vol. iv, pp. 320–408, with Annexes II and III, above.

[2] i.e. periodical tax-assessments.

[3] For the metamorphosis of a once Western Christian Society into a merely Western Society at the beginning of the Modern Age of our Western history see I. B (iii), vol. i, p. 34, above, and Part VII, below. The neutral word 'metamorphosis' can be interpreted to mean either purification or sterilization according to the interpreter's 'ideological' bias; but it can hardly be denied that the process has been, whether for better or for worse, some kind of 'boiling-down' or 'Bowdlerization' which has had the effect of turning thick soup into thin.

[4] This concept of a Second Coming has been examined in III. C (ii) (b), Annex I, vol. iii, pp. 462–5, above.

[5] In another context (V. C (i) (d) 9 (γ), in the present volume, pp. 129–32, above) it has been suggested that the expectation of a Millennium is apt, in the historical sequence of ideas, to arise as a middle term between the expectation of an entirely mundane futurist kingdom and the expectation of the Civitas Dei. In the history of Judaism, at a stage when Jewry was still tempted to follow the will-o'-the-wisp of a mundane Messiah, the year 142 B.C., in which the Hasmonaean anti-Seleucid insurgent Simon

but is discerned in the future by the eye of Faith, seems to be a
Zoroastrian idea which Judaism has borrowed and handed on to
Christianity.[1] We need not attempt to analyse it in this place,
since we have examined it already in another context.[2]

Maccabaeus succeeded in establishing the ephemeral Hasmonaean 'successor-state' of
the Seleucid Empire, was taken as the initial date for a new era in which Jewry was to
reckon by the years of the Messianic Kingdom which the Hasmonaean principality was
blindly assumed by its partisans to be (see von Gall, A.: Βασιλεία τοῦ Θεοῦ (Heidelberg
1926, Winter), pp. 388–9).

  [1] See V. C (i) (d) 7, p. 43, footnote 4, above.
  [2] In V. C (i) (d) 9 (γ), in the present volume, pp. 129–32, above.

'ARISTOPHANES' FANTASY OF CLOUDCUCKOOLAND'

IN the chapters[1] to which this Annex attaches, we have studied in succession four alternative ways of trying to escape from the Present which suggest themselves to souls that are being excruciated by the agonizing experience of living in a society that is in process of disintegration. In these chapters we have concerned ourselves mainly with the points of difference between these diverse inward reactions to a single supreme social challenge. We have observed the contrast between the two ways—Archaism and Futurism—which are attempts to escape from the Present without abandoning the plane of mundane life, and the other two—Detachment and Transfiguration—which recognize and act upon the truth that the only possibility of genuinely escaping from the Present lies in renouncing This World altogether and migrating into a different spiritual clime.[2] Again, we have observed the contrast between the three ways—Archaism, Futurism, and Detachment—which are so many variations upon an act of sheer withdrawal, and the fourth way—Transfiguration—which is an act of withdrawal-and-return.[3] There is, however, one feature, common to all four ways, which we have so far taken for granted, and this is that all four are apt to be pursued (to judge by our survey up to this point) with a uniform earnestness which is as tragically intense as the challenge of social disintegration is pitilessly importunate. This last feature perhaps demands further consideration; for, as a matter of historical fact, the importunity of the challenge is not of one constant degree from beginning to end of the process. The long descent that leads from the first breakdown of a society to its final dissolution is not only gradual but is not even continuous; the routs are punctuated by rallies;[4] and a spiritual pressure which in the end becomes intolerable is not imposed upon the Soul in its full force at the outset, but is the cumulative product of successive turns of a social screw. On this showing, we might expect *a priori* to find that the earnestness of the reaction which the pressure evokes in its victims takes time, like the pressure itself, to arrive at its maximum; and this expectation seems to be borne out by the actual history—which has been reserved for examination in this Annex—of one particular idea,

[1] V. C (i) (*d*) 8–11, above.
[2] For this contrast see V. C (i) (*d*) 1, vol. v, p. 394, and V. C (i) (*e*), in the present volume, pp. 169–70, above. [3] See V. C (i) (*d*) 11, p. 149, and V. C (i) (*e*), pp. 170–2, above.
[4] The movement of Rout-and-Rally in the disintegrations of civilizations has been examined in V. C (ii) (*b*), *passim*, above.

expressing the will to escape, which eventually came to inspire a
grimly earnest political movement and a raptly earnest religious
one, but which made its first recorded appearance on the stage of
history as a *jeu d'esprit*.

When Saint Paul exclaimed that the Christ Crucified whom he
was preaching was foolishness in the sight of the Greeks who seek
after wisdom,[1] he was almost certainly not aware of the literalness
of the sense in which these words were true, for he was almost certainly unconscious of the historical chain of associated ideas which
linked the Tarsian Apostle's own faith with a fantasy that had
germinated in the fertile imagination of the Athenian dramatist
Aristophanes more than four hundred and fifty years back—in the
first generation of the Hellenic 'Time of Troubles'. The links of
this chain hang together, nevertheless, without a break; for Christ
Crucified is the King of the Kingdom of God; the Kingdom of
God is more commonly known in the New Testament by the name
of the Kingdom of Heaven; and the Kingdom of Heaven was
introduced by Aristophanes to his Attic audience in the guise of
'Nephelococcygia' or 'Cloudcuckooland'—a city of refuge in which
the citizens are neither gods nor men but birds.

Aristophanes' *Birds* was produced at the Great Dionysia in the
spring of the year 414 B.C.; and this was a critical moment in Hellenic history; for the breakdown of the Hellenic Civilization,
which had been heralded by the outbreak of the Atheno-Peloponn-
nesian War in 431 B.C., and had then seemed for a moment to have
been averted after all by the patching-up of a peace in 421 B.C.,
had been made irretrievable by the sailing of an Athenian armada
to Sicily in the summer of 415 B.C., just before the play was composed. The atmosphere in which the *Birds* was written and produced was therefore tense; and at the same time the tension was
not yet of the agonizing degree to which it afterwards swiftly rose
when the Peloponnesians occupied Decelea in the following spring
and when the Athenian expeditionary force in Sicily was annihilated in the following autumn. In the spring of 414 B.C. the
malaise in Athenian souls was already sufficiently uncomfortable to
give topical interest to 'a play of escape', but not yet sufficiently
disturbing to warrant any suggestion that there could be anything
in this idea of an escape except an entertaining fantasy. The play
appears to be innocent of any direct allusion to current military and
political events;[2] but it is studded with words and phrases and

---

[1] 1 Cor. i. 22–3, quoted in V. C (i) (d) 11, p. 150, above.
[2] This feature of the *Birds* is commented upon as follows by a modern Western
connoisseur of the Attic drama:

'It does seem strange that the poet should have had this successful pursuit of a great
kingdom in the clouds staged just at the time when, as Thucydides and Plutarch tell us,
Athens was going mad after a kingdom in the west almost as cloudy, and yet should have

incidents that have an historical significance and a consequent
emotional timbre for latter-day readers which they cannot have
had for a playwright and an audience who were deliberately playing
the fool and who were able to enjoy themselves with an unfeigned
light-heartedness in that spring of 414 B.C. because they were
mercifully unaware of the calamities that were in store for their
own generation next year and for succeeding generations throughout the next four centuries. In echoing down the steeps of a Hellenic 'Time of Troubles' these incidents and phrases and words
that were contrived and coined by Aristophanes and were received
by his Athenian countrymen and contemporaries as a delectable
piece of deliberate foolishness have called forth unintended and
portentous reverberations; and, if we look and listen, we may hear
Aristophanes' nonsensical phrases turn into political and religious
watchwords, and see his farcical incidents reproduce themselves
as acts of high tragedy played out on the stage of 'real life'.

If we wish to assist at a dramatic performance that lasted four
or five hundred years instead of the few hours that it took to play
the *Birds* in 414 B.C., we may find it convenient first to remind ourselves of Aristophanes' plot and then to follow out its traces along
two of the historic lines of escape from the Hellenic 'Time of
Troubles'—in one direction along the violent political line of
Futurism, and in another direction along the non-political and
non-violent line of approach to a spiritual Transfiguration of This
World through its irradiation with the light of the Kingdom of
God.

The plot of Aristophanes' play is the recapture by the Birds,
under the leadership of a human being, of 'the Kingdom' of the
Universe which had belonged to the Birds originally before the
Gods usurped it.

The Birds' sharp-witted human leader in this brilliantly successful *coup d'état* is a truant citizen of Athens, Peithetaerus ('Mr.
Plausible'); and the opening of the play discovers him, in the
company of his compatriot Euelpides ('Mr. Hopefulson'), making

intended no particular political reference. Nevertheless it is impossible to discover any
direct allusion, or even any clear attitude towards the schemes for the conquest of Sicily
and Carthage. It cannot be an intentional encouragement of them, yet on the other hand
it does not read like satire. It seems to be just an "escape" from worry and the sordidness of life, away into the land of sky and clouds and poetry. If people want a cloud
empire, here is a better one!' (Murray, Gilbert: *Aristophanes: A Study* (Oxford 1933,
Clarendon Press), chap. 6: 'The Plays of Escape' (*Birds*), pp. 155–6).

In the Athenian mood of the year and the day (which was a holiday in a year of
anxiety but not of disaster) a direct allusion to the hazardous military adventure on
which Athens was at that moment staking her political fortunes might have been irritat-
ingly unwelcome to Aristophanes' audience. And we may perhaps discern in the playwright's choice of subject for the Great Dionysia of 414 B.C. the same tact which he
afterwards showed in taking the even more pointedly non-political theme of the *Frogs*
for a play that was to be produced at the Lenaea of 405 B.C., on the gloomy morrow of
Arginusae and eve of Aegospotami.

tracks from an Athens which is not that tragic City of Destruction
from which Christian flees at the outset of the Pilgrim's Progress,
but a ridiculous City of Botheration in which a fellow never has a
moment's peace from summonses and demand-notes. The trek-
kers are looking for a new home on some soft spot where they can
be sure of a quiet life (ll. 27–48 and 121–2); they apply to the
hoopoe on the chance that he may happen to know of such a place
(ll. 114–22); and, when he fails to make any helpful suggestion,
Peithetaerus himself is struck by a bright idea. Why should not
the Birds exploit their air-power as the Athenians have exploited
their sea-power? The Birds are masters of the clouds and heaven,
and this area is the strategic key to the command of the Universe.
If the Birds now found and fortify a city here they will have Mankind at their mercy—'like insects' (l. 185)—and will be able to 'do
in' the Gods; for they will be able to intercept the sweet savour of
sacrifice on its way from Earth to Olympus and so to starve the
Olympians into surrender as the Melians had been starved out in
416 B.C. by an Athenian naval blockade (ll. 162–93 and 550–637).
No sooner said than done. The heavenly city—for which Peithetaerus invents (ll. 809–25) the name of 'Cloudcuckooland' ('Nephelococcygia')—is duly built (ll. 1122–63);[1] the air-lines along which
the savour of sacrifice has been wont to ascend from Earth to
Olympus are duly cut (ll. 1514–24); and the Gods are quickly
forced into a capitulation by this hostile exercise of a veritable
'power of the air'.[2] In return for the raising of the aerial blockade
they have to agree to hand back to the Birds the sceptre which
Zeus has usurped, and also to hand over 'the Queen' ($Ba\sigma\iota\lambda\epsilon\iota\tilde{a}$)[3] to
the Birds' *ci-devant* human leader Peithetaerus. In implementa-
tion of the terms Peithetaerus ascends to Olympus and returns to
'Cloudcuckooland' with Zeus' thunderbolt in his hand and 'the
Queen' on his arm in the shape of a buxom bride (ll. 1535–41 and
1713–14). The closing scene is a marriage-feast, and in the last
two lines of the play the chorus hails the happy bridegroom as a
conquering hero and a God of Gods.

$$T\acute{\eta}\nu\epsilon\lambda\lambda\alpha\ \kappa\alpha\lambda\lambda\acute{\iota}\nu\iota\kappa\sigma\varsigma,\ \tilde{\omega}$$
$$\delta\alpha\iota\mu\acute{\sigma}\nu\omega\nu\ \acute{\upsilon}\pi\acute{\epsilon}\rho\tau\alpha\tau\epsilon.$$

'Who is the Queen?' Peithetaerus asks when Prometheus gives
him the 'tip' to insist on the surrender not only of Zeus' sceptre but

---

[1] Unlike the never-to-be-completed lines of circumvallation with which an Athenian
expeditionary force in Sicily was trying to cut the land-communications of Syracuse at
the very moment when the *Birds* was being acted under the lee of the Acropolis of
Athens.

[2] . . . $\tau\tilde{\eta}\varsigma\ \acute{\epsilon}\xi\sigma\upsilon\sigma\acute{\iota}\alpha\varsigma\ \tauο\tilde{\upsilon}\ \acute{\alpha}\acute{\epsilon}\rho\sigma\varsigma$—Eph. ii. 2.

[3] *Sic* (as the scansion shows): $Ba\sigma\iota\lambda\epsilon\iota\tilde{a}$, not $Ba\sigma\iota\lambda\epsilon\acute{\iota}\tilde{a}$, and therefore 'Queen', not
'Sovereignty' or 'Kingdom' (Sheppard, T. J., in *Fasciculus Joanni Willis Clark Dicatus*
(Cambridge 1909, University Press), p. 532).

of 'the Queen' as well. Prometheus' answer is that she is 'a lovely girl who keeps in her store-cupboard Zeus' thunderbolt and the rest of his bag of tricks: statesmanship, law-and-order, discretion, naval bases, vituperation, tithe-collector, and dole' (ll. 1537–41). And, though this answer may leave us still guessing,[1] we can at any rate identify the kingdom over which this Queen from Heaven has come down to reign. This Aristophanic caricature is the first appearance in Hellenic dress of a kingdom that is not of This World. If we follow the fortunes of the idea through the subsequent chapters of the Hellenic 'Time of Troubles', we shall find it assuming two forms—one political and the other religious—which both agree in taking Aristophanes' jest in earnest but otherwise differ from one another *toto caelo*.

In the political line of evolution the first step—which took rather more than a century—was the metamorphosis of the 'Cloud-cuckooland' which had been a poet's conceit into a 'Kingdom of Heaven' which was the Utopia of a pair of scholars. One of these scholars, Euhemerus, was the protégé, and the other, Alexarchus, was the brother, of the post-Alexandrine war-lord Cassander (*in Macedonia dominabatur* 316–298 B.C.). Cassander's protégé had to be content with describing his Utopia in a book in which Heaven (Uranus) figured as the first founder of an oecumenical empire.[2] Cassander's brother was able to command the means of bringing the Kingdom of Heaven down to Earth by setting up in real life an oecumenical empire on a miniature scale. On a patch of ground, given to him by Cassander, at the neck of the Athos Peninsula,[3] Alexarchus built and peopled—for all the world like Peithetaerus in the play—a model city-state which was to be a practical sample

---

[1] Mr. Sheppard, op. cit., pp. 533–4, points out that the festival of the Great Dionysia, at which the *Birds* was produced, followed only a few weeks after the festival of the Anthesteria, in which the principal rite was a sacred marriage between the god Dionysus himself and a mortal woman who was 'the Queen' (in this case not Βασίλεια but Βασίλισσα) in virtue of being the wife of the King Archon (a ghost of a long since vanished authentic kingship which lingered on to perform the ritual functions of a Rex Sacrificulus). Mr. Sheppard further points out that the Anthesteria, in their turn, were preceded by a festival in which the principal rite was a sacred marriage between Zeus and Hera. Thus, at the season of the Great Dionysia, sacred marriages were in the air. Mr. Sheppard's conclusion (op. cit., p. 540) is that 'Peithetairos . . . recalls to the audience Zeus, with a touch of Dionysus. Basileia recalls the Basilissa, not without a touch of Hera. The whole scene is at once a reminder of two brilliant functions of Athenian ritual, and, in itself, to the superstitious an effectual ceremony for the prosperity of Athens and the fertilizing of the crops'.

[2] Tarn, W. W.: *Alexander the Great and the Unity of Mankind* (London 1933, Milford), p. 24.

[3] The site bore traces of a ship-canal which had been dug, some two hundred years back, at the command of the Achaemenid Emperor Xerxes in order to give passage to his fleet in a campaign which was to make the Achaemenian Empire literally oecumenical by bringing the Hellenic World under the dominion to which the Syriac and Babylonic worlds and portions of the Egyptiac and Indic worlds were already subject. In the immediate neighbourhood the tangle of sea-girt, tree-clad hills between the isthmus and the mountain was one day to harbour a confederation of Christian monasteries of the Basilian Order in which Alexarchus's experiment was to be practised upon the *Civitas Dei*.

of the ideal world-commonwealth; and he called this city 'Urano-
polis' ('the Heavenly City') and its citizens 'Uranidae' ('the Children of Heaven').[1]

Iam nova progenies caelo demittitur alto![2]

The title which Alexarchus conferred upon himself in his role
of ruler of this Heavenly City was not 'Heaven' but 'the Sun';[3] and
the constitution of the Solar City was set out—in a Utopia-on-
Paper which became only less famous than Euhemerus's work—
by Iambulus, a social theorist who may have been a younger contemporary of Euhemerus and Alexarchus, though we know no
more than that he wrote at some date between 290 and 132 B.C.[4] In
Iambulus's hands the Kingdom-not-of-this-World was dragged
out of the scholar's study into the arena of political controversy;
for Iambulus's 'Heliopolis' was a Utopia that was classless and
communistic.[5] The last step was to translate this egalitarian ideal
into real life; and the experiment was duly made. The reason why
we know that Iambulus's book must have been written before the
year 132 B.C. is that this was the date of the desperately serious
attempt of Aristonicus of Pergamum to set up in Western Anatolia
a revolutionary proletarian commonwealth which its would-be
founder inaugurated under the name of 'Heliopolis' and doubtless
intended to build up on the pattern of the imaginary Solar City of
Iambulus.[6] Thus the Heavenly Kingdom which had been staged
as a joke by Aristophanes at Athens in 414 B.C. was fought for to
the death in Asia, 282 years later, by the last of the Attalids. In
Aristonicus's hands, however, blood and iron did not show themselves to be such efficacious materials for empire-building as they
were one day to prove in Bismarck's; for in 132 B.C. the 'strong man
armed' was quickly overcome by 'a stronger than he'.[7] Aristonicus's
callow Pergamene 'Heliopolis' succumbed to the overwhelming
power of Rome;[8] and that was the miserable end of 'Cloudcuckooland's' audacious descent into the arena of futurist politics.

[1] Tarn, op. cit., pp. 21–2. Alexarchus's experiment on the Athos Peninsula must
have been a 'going concern' at the moment when it gave birth to a daughter city-state
of the same name in Pamphylia (Tarn, W. W.: *The Greeks in Bactria and India* (Cambridge 1938, University Press), p. 12).   [2] Virgil: *Eclogues*, No. IV, l. 7.
[3] Tarn, *Alexander the Great and the Unity of Mankind*, pp. 22–3. According to
Bidez, J.: *La Cité du Monde et la Cité du Soleil chez les Stoïciens* (Paris 1932, Les Belles
Lettres), pp. 32–4, this role of the Sun-God was of Oriental provenance, and was imported
into the Hellenic *Weltanschauung* by Zeno of Citium's disciple Cleanthes of Assos.
[4] Tarn, op. cit., pp. 9–10.
[5] See Tarn, op. cit., loc. cit.; Bidez, op. cit., pp. 37–9; and the present Study, V. C
(i) (c) 2, vol. v, pp. 69, 70, 82, footnote 4, and 180; V. C (i) (d) 1, vol. v, p. 384; and
V. C (i) (d) 6 (δ), Annex, vol. v, p. 692, footnote 2, above.
[6] Tarn, op. cit., pp. 9–10. Tarn dates the outbreak of Aristonicus's insurrection
133 B.C., not 132 B.C.   [7] Luke xi. 21–2.
[8] See IV. C (iii) (c) 3 (β), vol. iv, p. 507; V. C (i) (c) 2, vol. v, pp. 69–70 and 179–
82; V. C (i) (d) 1, vol. v, p. 384; V. C (i) (d) 6 (δ), Annex, vol. v, p. 692, footnote 2; and
V. C (i) (d) 9 (γ), in the present volume, p. 126, above.

When we turn from Politics to Religion we shall be struck by certain correspondences between the *Birds* and the New Testament which are perhaps sufficiently numerous and remarkable to raise the question whether they are fortuitous assonances or the vestiges of a chain of literary tradition of which nothing now happens to survive except the beginning and the end.[1]

The point of correspondence which we may do well to examine first, because it is the point which is of the greatest intrinsic importance, is the assertion—made in both these contexts—that a man is God. In the *Birds*, as we have seen,[2] this claim is made for Peithetaerus by the chorus; in the Gospels it is made for Jesus both by Peter[3] and by Jesus himself;[4] and, if Aristophanes gives this piece of 'foolishness' a place of honour as the crowning joke of his play, that is no doubt because his Attic audience agreed with the Jewish High Priest in feeling such a claim to be the last word in blasphemy.[5] Thus the formal elements of the incident in the Gospels and in the *Birds* are the same—however profound the difference in spirit and meaning and outcome between the comic scene in the theatre at Athens, where the blasphemously deified protagonist is carried off the stage in mock triumph, and the tragic trial in the High Priest's palace at Jerusalem, in which the prisoner who declares himself to be the Son of God is condemned to death and led away to execution.[6]

The imagery in which Jesus is represented in the Gospels as making his claim to divinity is taken, of course, from the thirteenth

---

[1] The possibility that such a tradition may have propagated itself—without being uninterruptedly conscious and uniformly deliberate—by allowing itself, at some stage, to drift, for part of its way, down the primitive mental stream of 'folk-memory', is examined in V. C (ii) (a), Annex II, pp. 438–64, below. Whatever the channel or the means of conveyance, it is at any rate certain that, somehow or other, the *motifs* of Attic works of literature written before the end of the fifth century B.C. did sometimes find their way, *post Alexandrum*, into works of Oriental literature and did thereby succeed in giving a new Hellenic turn to old Oriental tales. A conspicuous case in point is the infusion of the Hippolytus-and-Phaedra *motif* into the traditional Jewish story of Joseph and Potiphar's wife as this is retold in *The Testaments of the Twelve Patriarchs* and in the *Antiquities* of Josephus (see Braun, Martin: *Griechischer Roman und Hellenistische Geschichtschreibung* (Frankfurt a. M. 1934, Klostermann), pp. 23–117, and eundem: *History and Romance in Graeco-Oriental Literature* (Oxford 1938, Blackwell), pp. 44–95).

[2] See p. 349, above.

[3] Matt. xvi. 16 = John vi. 69: 'Thou art the/that Christ, the Son of the Living God.' In the corresponding passages in the other two Gospels the claim is not to divinity but only to Messiahhood (Mark viii. 29 = Luke ix. 20); and, according to the orthodox Jewish belief, the concepts of Messiahhood and divinity are mutually exclusive (see V. C (i) (d) 9 (γ), *passim*, and V. C (i) (d) 11, p. 163, footnote 1, above).

[4] Matt. xxvi. 63–4 (anticipated in xxiv. 30, and in xvi. 28); Mark xiv. 61–2 (anticipated in xiii. 26, and in ix. 1); Luke xxii. 69–70 (anticipated in ix. 26–7).

[5] At the time when the *Birds* was produced at Athens there were still ten more years (*sed quales!*) to run before Lysander (an unknown name in 414 B.C.) was to enjoy at Samos the distinction of being the first of the Hellenes to be given divine honours (see V. C (i) (d) 6 (δ), Annex, vol. v, p. 648, above).

[6] The *motif* of mock-acceptance of a claim which the mockery stigmatizes as preposterous does, of course, occur in the story of the Passion. But the claim which is burlesqued in the crown of thorns and the purple robe is not the claim to be God but the claim to be the Lord's Anointed King.

and fourteenth verses of the seventh chapter of the Book of Daniel, in which the Zoroastrian conception of the coming of the Saošyant —the saviour whose superhuman yet also less than divine status is indicated in his title of 'the Son of Man'[1]—has been seized upon by a Jewish poet-publicist, writing *circa* 166–164 B.C., as a vehicle for the expression of Jewry's hopes of mundane salvation in its desperate resistance to the high-handed Hellenism of Antiochus Epiphanes.[2] Yet, although the idea by which Jesus's claim is inspired may thus be of Zoroastrian origin, the key words both of the imagery in the Book of Daniel and of the narrative in the Gospels are words which are also to be found in a cento of quotations from the *Birds*.

The passage in the Book of Daniel (vii. 13–14) runs as follows:

'Behold, one like the Son of Man came with the clouds of heaven (ἐπὶ τῶν νεφελῶν τοῦ οὐρανοῦ) and came to the Ancient of Days, and they brought him near before him. And there was given him dominion (ἐξουσία).'

The passage in the Gospel according to Saint Mark (xiv. 61–4) runs as follows:

'The High Priest asked him and said unto him: "Art thou the Christ, the Son of the Blessed?" And Jesus said: "I am—and ye shall see the Son of Man sitting on the right hand of power (τῆς δυνάμεως) and coming in the clouds of heaven (μετὰ τῶν νεφελῶν τοῦ οὐρανοῦ)." Then the High Priest rent his clothes and saith: "What need we any further witnesses? Ye have heard the blasphemy".'[3]

The passages in the *Birds* which this passage in the Gospel calls to mind are the following:

Peithetaerus: 'I spy a great *coup* which the Birds can bring off, and a way of getting power (δύναμιν), if only you do what I tell you.' (ll. 162–3.)

Peithetaerus: 'Did you see anything?'—*Hoopoe*: 'Just the clouds and heaven (τὰς νεφέλας γε καὶ τὸν οὐρανόν).'—*Peithetaerus*: 'Well, isn't that the fairway of the Birds?' (ll. 178–9.)

Peithetaerus: 'Well, what name shall we give our city then?'—*Chorus*: 'Some utterly vacuous name which we will take from the clouds and from the supernal regions.'—*Peithetaerus*: 'Will "Cloudcuckooland" do for you? . . . It is the same as the Phlegraean Plain—the place where the

---

[1] See V. C (i) (d) 9 (γ), pp. 126 and 130–1, and V. C (i) (d) 11, p. 163, footnote 1, above.

[2] For Antiochus Epiphanes' policy of forcible Hellenization see V. C (i) (d) 9 (β), pp. 103–5, above.

[3] In the corresponding passage according to Saint Matthew (xxvi. 63–5) the Marcan text is reproduced in substance (including, in particular, all the words that have been quoted above in the original Greek, except that the Marcan μετά is here replaced by the Danielic ἐπί). In the corresponding passage according to Saint Luke (xxii. 66–71) 'the right hand of the power of God' has been retained but the 'coming in the clouds of heaven' has been omitted.

Gods took on the Giants, and walked away from them, in a competition in false pretences.' (ll. 817–19 and 824–5.)

    Chorus (*to Peithetaerus*): 'O God of Gods!' (ll. 1764–5.)

If these correspondences are not to be dismissed as a fortuitous concourse of accidents, but are to be taken as evidence for some chain of literary reminiscence which runs (through however many missing links and altered meanings) from Aristophanes' *Birds* to the Book of Daniel and thence to the Gospels, then we may see in the change of connotation that has come over the word 'power' *en route*[1] an example of the working of the principle of 'etherialization'.[2] And this may recall a passage from the Gospel according to Saint Matthew (vi. 26) which we have quoted already in our examination of that principle at an earlier point in this Study.[3]

'Behold the fowls of the air: for they sow not, neither do they reap nor gather into barns (ἀποθήκας); yet your heavenly father feedeth them. Are ye not much better than they?'

The first of the three points that are made in this passage of the Gospel—namely, the point that a bird's life is happy in being care-free—is also made in the following passage of Aristophanes' play:

    Euelpides: 'And what is life like here—this life that one leads among the Birds?'—*Hoopoe*: 'It is not without charm when you come to try it. Well, first you have to live without a purse.'—*Euelpides*: 'And that at one stroke takes half the falsity out of life.'—*Hoopoe*: 'And then we browse in gardens on white sesame-grains and myrtle-berries and poppy-seed and cress.'—*Euelpides*: 'You seem to live like a bridal pair on honeymoon.' (ll. 155–61.)

A comparison of the two passages shows that, while an identical idea is the theme of both of them, this idea is not expressed in identical words or even in identical illustrations; and in this case, as in the other which we have just examined, it is possible to point out passages of Jewish literature which are older than the Gospel—though not older than *Birds*[4]—from which the Gospel may have

---

    [1] This change in the meaning of the Greek word δύναμις from the sense of 'military power' to that of 'divine power' is recorded not only in the vocabulary of Christianity but also in that of the abortive contemporary religion of the Samaritan Simon Magus (see V. C (i) (*d*) 6 (δ), Annex, vol. v, p. 685, footnote 3, above), of whom it was asserted by his worshippers that οὗτός ἐστιν ἡ δύναμις τοῦ Θεοῦ ἡ μεγάλη (Acts viii. 10).

    [2] For this principle see III. C (i) (*c*), vol. iii, pp. 174–92, above.

    [3] In III. C (i) (*c*), vol. iii, p. 191. In that place the chapter of the Gospel has been wrongly cited as vii instead of vi.

    [4] The Book of Job is at any rate not older than the *Birds*, though its date of composition is on any hypothesis sufficiently early to make it unlikely that any Hellenic influences should have found their way into it. On the other hand, as far as the question of date goes, there would not be the same *a priori* unlikelihood of Hellenic influences being traceable in the Psalms.

been borrowing. The variant of the same parable in the Gospel according to Saint Luke (xii. 24) runs:

'Consider the ravens; for they neither sow nor reap—which neither have storehouse (ταμεῖον) nor barn (ἀποθήκη); and God feedeth them. How much more are ye better than the fowls?'

And this version, in which the theme is enunciated with reference, not to birds in general, but to birds of one particular kind, has at least two antecedents in the Jewish scriptures:

'He giveth to the beast his food, and to the young ravens which cry' (Psalm cxlvii, verse 9);

and

'Who provideth for the raven his food? When his young ones cry unto God, they wander for lack of meat' (Job xxxviii. 41).

These two passages not only agree with the passage in Luke, and differ from the passage in the *Birds*, in speaking of ravens in particular and not of birds in general; they further differ from the *Birds*, while agreeing this time not only with Luke but with Matthew as well, in the point that they make. They do not remark, as both Aristophanes and the Gospels do, that the birds obtain their livelihood without having to practise the rational and provident but, by the same token, anxious economy which is Man's characteristic way of earning his living; but they do declare, as the Gospels do but Aristophanes does not, that this enviable insouciance is practicable for the birds because their food is provided for them by God. On this showing, the passage in the Gospels can be at least partially accounted for as a derivative from Jewish sources; and, if this were all, the point of correspondence between the Gospels and the *Birds* which has no counterpart in the Old Testament might conceivably be dismissed as a freak of Chance. We have, however, to take into account another passage of pagan Hellenic literature which is unmistakably related to the passage in the Gospels by a literary kinship which is distinctly closer than that which links the Gospels in this instance to the Book of Job and to the Hundred and Forty-Seventh Psalm; and that is a passage from one of the works of Gaius Musonius Rufus, a Stoic philosopher who was a contemporary of the authors of the two Gospels here in question.[1]

This passage of Musonius is a fragment of a dialogue between a Stoic sage and a lay inquirer. The layman is putting the difficulties

[1] On the assumption that the Gospels according to Saint Matthew and Saint Luke were written (as is argued by Eduard Meyer in his *Ursprung und Anfänge des Christentums*, vol. i (Stuttgart and Berlin 1921, Cotta), p. 239) at some date after the destruction of Jerusalem in A.D. 70 and before the persecution of the Church, *imperante Domitiano*, in A.D. 95.

that deter him from responding to the philosopher's serious call to a detached and blissful life, and the philosopher is trying to resolve the layman's doubts.

Layman: 'That is all very well; but I am a poor man—financially destitute—and I have a swarm of children. Where am I going to find the means to bring them up?'—*Philosopher*: 'Well, how do these little birds that are much more destitute than you are—the swallows and nightingales and larks and blackbirds—manage to bring up *their* young? Homer, too, has something to say about that: "And as a bird proffers a morsel, when at last she gets one, to her unfledged young, though she is sore an hungred herself . . . ."[1] Are these creatures superior to Man in intelligence? The question can only be answered in the negative. Well, are they superior in physical strength? The answer is in the negative *a fortiori*. Well, do the birds store (ἀποτίθεται) food and hoard it?'[2]

It will be seen that, in contrast to Aristophanes, Musonius not only propounds the same theme as the Gospels, but also propounds it in the self-same words and images (e.g. Musonius's ἀποτίθεται corresponds to the ἀποθήκη of both Gospels, and his φυλάσσει to the ταμεῖον of the Gospel according to Saint Luke). And a still more striking proof of literary kinship is the fact that the text of Musonius contains two of the three points that are made in the Gospels, whereas the passage in the *Birds* and the pair of passages from the Book of Job and from the Hundred and Forty-Seventh Psalm only contain one of these points apiece. The three points are as follows: (α) the Birds manage to live without practising a human economy;[3] (β) they manage this because their food is given them by God; (γ) if the birds can manage it, then we human beings, who are so much their superiors, can certainly manage it *a fortiori*. Of these three points, (α) is common to the Gospels and the *Birds* and Musonius; (β) is common to the Gospels and

---

[1] *Iliad*, Book IX, ll. 323-4.—A.J.T.

[2] This passage of Musonius will be found in *The Rendel Harris Papyri* of Woodbrooke College, Birmingham, edited by Powell, J. E. (Cambridge 1936, University Press), Part I, No. i, pp. 4-5. Before the discovery of the papyrus containing this text, the whole of that portion of the fragment which has been quoted above, save for the opening words 'That is all very well', was unknown to modern Western scholarship; for these words were the last in the extract that had been handed down by a continuous literary tradition. The text of the fragment in this already known shorter form, in which the parable of the birds is not included, will be found in O. Hense's edition of Musonius (Leipzig 1905, Teubner), Fragment No. XVA, pp. 78-9. The identity of this already known fragment with the papyrus text, in which the name of the author was missing, was first pointed out by Mr. M. P. Charlesworth; and it was also he who drew the attention of the writer of this Study to the Jewish pedigree of the ravens in Luke xii. 24.

[3] This point (α) is also made—apropos, not of the birds of the air, but of the beasts of the field—in Lucretius: *De Rerum Natura*, Book V, ll. 228-34; but the Epicurean poet uses this *locus communis* as an argument *against* points (β) and (γ) and *not* in favour of them. The ability of the animals to grow up and live their lives without apparatus, in contrast to the helplessness of the puling human babe, proves the thesis (enunciated ibid., ll. 198-9):

> nequaquam nobis divinitus esse paratam
> naturam rerum: tanta stat praedita culpa.

the pair of passages from the Old Testament; (γ) is common to the Gospels and Musonius. Thus Musonius not only has one point in common with the Gospels that is not to be found in either Aristophanes or the Old Testament: he also has a second point in common with the Gospels which is not to be found in the Old Testament but *is* to be found in Aristophanes (though it is to be noticed that in this point Musonius comes less close to Aristophanes than he comes to the Gospels, since there is some community of imagery and vocabulary between him and the Gospels, but not between him and Aristophanes).

The exact literary relation between these several passages of Christian and Hellenic and Jewish literature is perhaps impossible to trace out with any certainty. Since Musonius and the authors of the Gospels appear to have been contemporaries, it is theoretically conceivable—in the absence of evidence for determining the exact dates of publication of their respective works—that Musonius may have borrowed direct from the Evangelists, and equally conceivable, vice versa, that the Evangelists may have borrowed from Musonius. But neither of these theoretical possibilities will seem very probable when we consider the greatness of the gulf which in that generation still divided the cultivated circles of the Hellenic dominant minority, to which Musonius belonged, from the Syriac section of the Hellenic internal proletariat which was the cradle of the Christian Church. On the whole it seems more probable that Musonius and the authors of the Gospels were each drawing independently on some common source to which Aristophanes and the Jewish scriptures had each made some contribution (though, as likely as not, an indirect one).[1]

---

[1] There is a parallel to this rather baffling three-cornered literary relation between Aristophanes, the New Testament, and Musonius in another three-cornered relation between the New Testament and a pair of pagan authors of whom, in this second case likewise, one was pre-Christian while the other lived and wrote in the Christian Era. In this second case the piece of imagery in the Gospels that is matched by this pair of correspondences in pagan Greek literature is found in Matthew and Mark, and there is a vestige of it in Luke as well. The pre-Christian Greek author in this case is not Aristophanes but Aeschylus. The post-Christian author is Philostratus (*vivebat circa* A.D. 170–250).

The passage of Philostratus that is reminiscent of both Aeschylus and the Gospels occurs in Philostratus's work on the Hellenic philosopher-thaumaturge Apollonius of Tyana, whose long life was approximately conterminous with the first century of the Christian Era. Near the beginning of his own book Philostratus recounts the following story of Damis—a previous biographer of Apollonius who was his subject's contemporary and disciple.

'On one occasion he [Damis] was being harried by a critic with a loose tongue and a malicious mind who made the point that it was all very well for Damis to put on record important things like Apollonius's maxim˄ and speculations, but that when he went on to pick up tiny trivialities he was doing like the dogs who feed on the scraps that fall from the feast. At this point Damis cut in with the retort that "If there are feasts of the Gods at which it is gods that are feeding, then as a matter of course there will be servants in attendance who will see to it that even the scraps shall not be lost—when these are scraps of ambrosia!"' (Philostratus: *Apollonius of Tyana*, Book I, chap. 19).

There is patently some literary connexion between this passage of Philostratus and

There are two more assonances between the *Birds* and the
Gospels which perhaps deserve notice here—in spite of their both
being trivial in themselves—for the possible bearing that they may
have upon the more important correspondences that have been
examined above. The Informer's plaintive question—'What else
would you have me do? For I do not know how to dig'[1]—is echoed
in the Unjust Steward's discreet reflexion: 'What shall I do?
For . . . I cannot dig.'[2] And Jesus's enigmatic saying that 'the
Kingdom of Heaven suffereth violence, and the violent take it by
force'[3] is anticipated by Euelpides' satirical remark that at Athens
'aliens are pushing their way in by violence'[4] at the very time when
he and Peithetaerus, who are native-born Athenian citizens, are
leaping out of their native land with both feet in the air. 'I cannot
dig' sounds as though it must have been a proverbial apologia for
the practice of any easy but discreditable trade; and, if it was a
mot that passed from mouth to mouth wherever the Attic κοινή
was spoken, it might find its way into works of literature at wide
intervals of time and place without there being any literary kinship
between the diverse works in which it made its appearance. On
the other hand, the *motif* of outsiders making a forcible entry into
a commonwealth which has won prestige abroad is perhaps too

Mark vii. 27–8 (with its counterpart in Matt. xv. 26–7, and its vestige in Luke xvi. 21,
where 'crumbs falling from the table' are also mentioned in juxtaposition with 'dogs',
though in this context it is not the dogs that eat the crumbs, but the beggar Lazarus).
If Philostratus has taken his story about Damis from Damis himself, who was a contemporary of the authors of the Synoptic Gospels, then the literary problem here is
precisely parallel to that of the relation between the Gospels and Musonius. And the
echo of Aristophanes in Musonius likewise has its parallel in an echo, in Philostratus,
of Aeschylus's saying (quoted already in this Study in I. C (iii) (e), Annex, vol. i, p. 449,
and in III. C (ii) (b), vol. iii, p. 339, above) that his tragedies were 'slices from the great
banquets of Homer (τεμάχη τῶν Ὁμήρου μεγάλων δείπνων)'. Philostratus's relation to
Aeschylus would appear to be independent of his relation to the New Testament; for
Damis's word 'feasts' (δαῖτες), as reported by Philostratus, comes nearer to Aeschylus's
word 'banquets' (δείπνων), as reported by Athenaeus, than it comes to the word 'table'
in Matthew, Mark, and Luke. On the other hand the Aeschylean epigram lacks the
feature, which is common to Philostratus and the Gospels, of scraps of human food
falling and being eaten by dogs; and it also stands *in vacuo*, whereas the corresponding
sayings that are attributed to Damis and to the Syro-phoenician woman are both introduced, in the contexts in which they respectively occur, as disarming retorts to a provo-
cation. The points that are common to all the three contexts are: (α) some one gives an
arrestingly humble estimate of his own worth in a simile taken from the dinner-table;
(β) the parable consists in a depreciation of the part by comparison with the whole—
whether the part be a crumb falling from the table or a slice carved from the joint.
We may also notice a correspondence between the Gospels and a passage in the work
of a Stoic philosopher of a later generation than that of Musonius and Damis. 'Can I
really fear somebody to whom I am able to abandon my body?' (Epictetus: *Dissertationes*,
Book I, chap. 23, § 13) sounds to a Christian ear like an echo of Matt. x. 28, and Luke
xii. 4, though the master whom Epictetus here believes himself to be following is not
Jesus but Diogenes.

[1] τί γὰρ πάθω; σκάπτειν γὰρ οὐκ ἐπίσταμαι (*Birds*, l. 1432).
[2] τί ποιήσω, ὅτι . . . σκάπτειν οὐκ ἰσχύω (Luke xvi. 3).
[3] ἡ βασιλεία τῶν οὐρανῶν βιάζεται, καὶ βιασταὶ ἁρπάζουσιν αὐτήν (Matt. xi. 12; cf. Luke
xvi. 16). For a further assonance between this pair of sayings in the Gospels and the
Birds and a saying that is attributed to King Cleomenes III of Sparta see V. C (ii) (a),
Annex II, p. 415, below.
[4] ὁ μὲν γὰρ ὢν οὐκ ἀστὸς ἐσβιάζεται (*Birds*, l. 32).

complicated an image to pass, like 'I cannot dig', into popular currency; and, if this *motif* first appears in a context where it does explain itself, and then reappears—and this with a clear verbal echo[1]—in a different context where its meaning is obscure, it would be a not unreasonable inference to suppose that the later context in which the *motif* occurs is related to the earlier by a literary tradition in which a *motif* that originally served a purpose has been mechanically preserved after it has ceased to have a point and even ceased to be intelligible.

There is one more question that may conveniently be discussed in this Annex because it arises out of topics that have just been examined in the present context; and this final question may be put in the following way. One of the most prominent of the *motifs* that are common to the *Birds* and the Gospels is a claim to divinity that is made either by or on behalf of beings who are not gods—at any rate not according to the current convention of the time and place at which the claim has been put forward. Whether this claim is treated as a joke (as it is by Aristophanes) or as a supremely serious and momentous revelation of ultimate truth (as it is in the Gospels), there is one common feature in the treatment of it in both contexts: in both it is treated as something unexpected to the point of being startling. Now the beings who are not gods in the ordinarily accepted sense, but in respect of whom this claim to divinity is nevertheless made, are beings of two different kinds. Some of them are men; some of them are birds. And our question is this: To Hellenic minds in 414 B.C., which claim to divinity would seem the more preposterous? A bird's claim or a man's? There is reason to believe that, in the mind of a Hellene of Aristophanes' day, it required a greater effort of imagination to deify a man than to deify a bird.

The ground for this opinion lies in the probability that, even off the comic stage, the birds of the air were invested with a certain aura of divinity in the eyes of the generation of Hellenes who were Aristophanes' contemporaries. Aristophanes himself has devoted an appreciable part of his play (e.g. ll. 467–538 and 685–736) to a presentation of the thesis that the Birds were the original and legitimate lords of the Universe; that the present lordship of the Gods is a usurpation at the Birds' expense; and that even now there are tell-tale traces of the Birds' lost status which the Gods have either neglected or failed to efface. There are two particular traces that the playwright calls in evidence. One is that some of the reigning gods who are represented by statues in human form are also regularly accompanied in Hellenic works of art by

---

[1] i.e. with βιάζεται echoing ἐσβιάζεται.

representations of birds that are regarded as being their respective familiars or emblems. Zeus, for example, has his eagle,
Athena her owl,[1] Apollo his hawk (*Birds*, ll. 514–16). The second
piece of evidence that Aristophanes cites is the role still played by
birds in the magic arts of omen-taking and fortune-telling (*Birds*,
ll. 716–22). This thesis that the Birds are *ci-devant* gods[2] is presented by Aristophanes in the tone of mock-earnestness that is
proper to the Old Comedy; and, if the evidence that Aristophanes
offers us were all that we had at our command, we might be at
a loss to know whether it was to be taken at all seriously or whether
it was to be written off, from alpha to omega, as a sheer prank of
the poet's riotous imagination. Fortunately, however, we have, as
it happens, a good deal of independent evidence; and the conclusion to which this leads us is that Aristophanes' thesis was not
really such arrant nonsense as the author himself would ostensibly
have us believe.

On the one hand we find the Birds figuring as quasi-super-
natural beings—and this particularly in virtue of a supposed fore-
knowledge of impending events—in Modern Greek folklore; and
on the other hand it seems (though here the evidence is scantier)
that the Birds were objects of religious veneration in the Minoan
World.[3] If the birds of the air have had this divine, or at any rate
semi-divine, status in the eyes of both the pre-Hellenic and the
post-Hellenic inhabitants of the region which was Hellas in an
intervening age, there would be a presumption in favour of the
hypothesis of there being an historical connexion between two cults
of birds which are so similar in character and which have been
practised in one and the same area, albeit in two different ages that
are separated from each other by a chronological gap. On this
hypothesis we should expect to find our bird-cult in existence
under the surface during the intervening reign of Hellenism—even
though, in that age, the dominant religion were anthropomorphic
and not theriomorphic. And this is, of course, what we do find;
for Aristophanes' thesis that the Birds had a touch of divinity

---

[1] The owl was Athena's bird in the city that bore her name (or rather the plural name
of the multitude of images of her that were to be found there). In the *Odyssey*, however,
which was not written on Attic soil, there are two passages in which Athena is depicted,
not as being merely accompanied by a bird, but as herself assuming the form of one;
and this Homeric bird-shape of Athena is not an owl's in either case. In one passage
(*Odyssey*, Book XXII, l. 240) the bird whose form Athena assumes is a swallow; in the
other passage (*Odyssey*, Book I, l. 320) it is a sea-eagle, if that is really the meaning of
the mysterious word ἀνοπαῖα.

[2] This notion of *ci-devant* gods who have been deposed and suppressed was of course
familiar to the Hellenic minds of Aristophanes' age in the legend of the Titans. The
complementary conception of the reigning Olympians as usurpers who have won and
kept their dominion by force is inherent in the picture of Zeus and his fellow divinities
as a war-lord and his war-band (for this picture see I. C (i) (*b*), vol. i, pp. 96–7, and V. C
(i) (*c*) 3, vol. v, pp. 231–3, above).

[3] On this point see Murray, op. cit., pp. 147–8.

about them in the eyes of the Hellenes of his own day is borne out by a wealth of other evidence that comes not only from literary but also from archaeological sources.

On this showing, Aristophanes has exercised the professional skill that we should have expected of him in taking the thesis of the Birds being gods as a theme for one of his dramatic *jeux d'esprit*. He has here put his hand upon a joke which, for an audience accustomed to the Hellenic *Weltanschauung* of the day, was preposterous enough to be amusing without being quite so preposterous as to defeat itself by altogether passing the bounds of imagination. The fantasy was not unimaginably fantastic and the blasphemy not scandalously blasphemous because the foolery had in it an ingredient which 'unto the Greeks' was not sheer 'foolishness', but was something that most of the people who were assembled in the theatre at Athens for the Great Dionysia of 414 B.C. would unconsciously take for granted and might even, if pressed, acknowledge to be truth[1]—however difficult it might be to reconcile a traditional belief in the semi-divinity of birds with the 'wisdom' after which the Greeks were by this time already beginning to seek along the paths of Reason.[2]

In Aristophanes' catalogue of Olympian Gods who had birds for their familiars or their emblems[3] there is one name which is conspicuous by its absence, and that is Aphrodite's; for the Olympian Goddess of Love was popularly associated with birds, and these of many kinds: the iynx, the swan, the swallow, the sparrow, the dove. None of these bird-familiars of Aphrodite is mentioned by Aristophanes in the play.[4] The playwright himself, however, figures as a participant in one of Plato's imaginary dialogues—the

[1] For the alloy of 'fact' (whether actual or merely reputed) which is an indispensable ingredient in so-called 'works of fiction', see I. C (iii) (e), Annex, vol. i, pp. 449–50, above.

[2] Has the poet likewise tempered, by another touch of the same deft art, his salutation of his human hero as 'God of Gods' (l. 1765, cited in this Annex on pp. 349, 352, and 354, above)? We have suggested (on pp. 352 and 359) that, in a generation of Hellenic rationalists who had not yet lived to see divine honours conferred upon Lysander, the deification of a man might appear even more preposterous than the deification of a bird to the minds of an Attic playwright's audience. In the growth-stage of the Hellenic Civilization the distinction between human and superhuman beings was clearly maintained as a rule. There was, however, one exception; for a human being who had successfully performed the supremely creative social act of founding a new city-state was customarily worshipped—not indeed as a god, but as a hero—by the community of which he had made himself the historical ἀρχηγέτης. Now Aristophanes, in the middle act of the *Birds*, almost goes out of his way to show us Peithetaerus painstakingly performing the ritual which would be incumbent upon a founder. He sets to work to inaugurate his aviary by solemnly giving it a name and then clinching the ceremony by offering sacrifice (ll. 809–11), and, in spite of successive interruptions, he succeeds in accomplishing both these duties (ll. 1118–20) before a messenger arrives to announce that the city has been constructed *de facto* (ll. 1122–67) besides having been inaugurated *de jure*. In the minds of Aristophanes' audience, would these transactions imply that Peithetaerus had now qualified himself to rank as an ἀρχηγέτης? And would this perhaps partially prepare them for a *finale* in which the cockney *in excelsis* is saluted not merely as a hero but as a god?   [3] See pp. 359–60, above.

[4] The pairing of the coot with Aphrodite in line 565 is shown by the context to imply that this was *not* a bird that was popularly associated with this goddess in current folklore.

Symposium—in which the topic of discussion is that faculty of
Love which was recognized as being Aphrodite's province before
it was revealed in a new light as the heart of Christianity; and in
the *Symposium* itself a first step is taken on the long journey towards the Christian view of Love from the traditional Hellenic
attitude towards it when one of the speakers declares that there is
not one Aphrodite but two Aphrodites and therefore not one kind
of Love but two likewise.[1] Besides Aphrodite the Vulgar (Pandêmus) there is an Aphrodite the Heavenly (Urania), says Plato's
Pausanias.[2] And this Platonic clue may encourage us to look for
traces of the passage of the Heavenly Love, of which this Heavenly
Aphrodite was the Hellenic image, from the bleak spiritual clime
of the Hellenic 'Time of Troubles' to a Christian haven. In the
story told in the Gospels[3] the supernatural designation of Jesus as
the Son of God is not only proclaimed orally by a voice from
Heaven but is also visually revealed by an opening of the Heavens
and a descent of the Spirit upon Jesus in the shape of a dove; and
on the strength of this incident in the New Testament the dove
has become the emblem of the Holy Ghost in Christian art; but
this is not the first case in which the dove has figured as an emblem
of divinity; for in Hellenic art, as we have already noticed, the dove
is an emblem of Aphrodite. May we venture to infer that the
visual image in which the Spirit of God is depicted in the Gospels
has been derived from a Hellenic source? Such imagery cannot
be of native Jewish origin; for the second of the ten Commandments forbids the visual representation of any object whatsoever,
and to portray God Himself in the shape of a living creature that
was not even human would be the most shocking violation of the
Second Commandment that a Jewish mind could conceive. But
if it is thus evident that the image of a dove, even if it should
prove to have been inherited by Christianity from Judaism, must
previously have made its way into Judaea from elsewhere, then we
must look for the nearest possible antecedent provenance; and, as
soon as we look, we cannot fail to observe how short a flight it is
to the banks of Jordan from the coasts of Paphos.

To return for the last time to the *Birds*, we may notice, in the
present connexion, that the descent of a winged harbinger of peace
is also one of the incidents in Aristophanes' play,[4] and that the

---

[1] The distinction between the two kinds of Love which was thus drawn by Plato was
afterwards emphasized, in the Greek vocabulary of the New Testament, by a difference
of name. The new word ἀγάπη was coined to denote the etherial Love that, in Plato's
terms, was the spirit of the Heavenly Aphrodite, in contrast to the grosser Love, patron-
ized by Aphrodite Pandêmus, with which the word Erôs was too deeply compromised
to be acceptable to a Christian ear.
[2] Pausanias in Plato's *Symposium*, 180 D–E.
[3] Matt. iii. 16; Mark i. 10; Luke iii. 22; John i. 32–3.
[4] Aristophanes: *Birds*, ll. 1196–1261.

Olympian goddess Iris, whom the Athenian playwright casts for
this part, is described by him in an earlier passage[1]—in language
borrowed from a Homeric simile—as 'like unto a gentle dove'.[2]

This brings us to the end of an argument which points to a paradoxical conclusion. If our argument has any force, the conclusion
can only be that Aristophanes' lightly uttered foolishness is somehow less remote than Zeno's scrupulously pondered wisdom from
a Gospel that, in Christian belief, is God's revelation of His Truth.
This verdict would no doubt have astonished the Athenian playwright as greatly as it would have incensed the Cypriot sage; and,
if the English reader is inclined, in his turn, to exclaim, with
Horatio, that 'this is wondrous strange', the writer must answer,
with Hamlet, that

> 'There are more things in Heaven and Earth, Horatio,
> Than are dreamt of in your philosophy.'

In the comedy which the Muses moved Aristophanes to write for
performance in the holy place of Dionysus on the flank of the
Acropolis of Athens in the year 414 B.C., the goddesses seem to
have been doing their best to exercise the second of two powers
of which they had boasted, centuries before, to shepherds 'abiding
in the field'[3] on the flank of holy Helicon:

> ἴδμεν ψεύδεα πολλὰ λέγειν ἐτύμοισιν ὁμοῖα,
> ἴδμεν δ', εὖτ' ἐθέλωμεν, ἀληθέα γηρύσασθαι.[4]

The monument of the Muses' other boasted power—to wit, the
knack of telling specious lies[5]—is presumably the theogony which
they recited to one of those shepherds of Ascra whom they had
greeted with such an insulting form of address;[6] but, when the
time was to come for another theogony, which might prove to be
the truth, to be announced to other shepherds,[7] the scene of the

---

[1] l. 575.
[2] The simile is applied to Iris and Eileithyia in the Homeric Hymn to Apollo, l. 114,
and to Hera and Athena in *Iliad*, Book V, l. 778.
[3] The word used by Hesiod of himself and his fellow shepherds in *Theogony*, l. 26, is
ἀγραυλοι; the word used of the shepherds in Luke ii. 8, is ἀγραυλοῦντες. (This assonance
was pointed out to the writer of this Study by Professor H. T. Wade-Gery.)
[4] Hesiod: *Theogony*, ll. 27–8.
[5] This knack is commended by Aristotle as one of the important weapons in a poet's
armoury (see I. C (iii) (e), Annex, vol. i, p. 450, footnote 1, above).
[6] κάκ' ἐλέγχεα, γαστέρες οἶον (Hesiod: *Theogony*, l. 26). It is curious to find a variation
on this form of insult turning up in the Cretan prophet Epimenides' poem *Minos* and
being quoted with approbation by a missionary of Christianity (Titus i. 12); for the
Cretan 'lie' against which Epimenides was inveighing was the belief that a god had died
and risen again from the dead! (see I. C (i) (b), vol. i, p. 99, footnote 2, above).
[7] Why are 'shepherds abiding in the field' chosen, out of all Mankind, to be the
recipients of theogonies? This trait is not only common to the Hellenic and the Christian Mythology: it is also one of the more striking of the details in which these two
mythologies agree in painting the same mysterious picture. Some light is perhaps
thrown on this particular point of agreement by a passage in the mythical colloquy
between Solon and the Saïte priest in Plato's *Timaeus*. The gist of the passage (which
has been quoted above in IV. C (i), vol. iv, pp. 24–5) is that Egypt has been exempted

revelation was to be the countryside of Judaea and not of Boeotia, and the glad tidings were to be delivered by the tongues, not of Muses, but of Angels. It would almost seem as though all that the Muses themselves were able to do by way of demonstrating their power to tell the truth when they chose, as well as to counterfeit it as a rule, was to instil here and there a darkly anticipatory meaning into some of the winged words of an *insouciant* Athenian poet on the brink of a Hellenic 'Time of Troubles' that was to close, after unspeakable tribulations, in the Angels' proclamation of 'glory to God in the highest and peace on Earth to men of good will'.[1]

by Nature from the incidence of recurrent physical catastrophes which visit the rest of the Earth, including Hellas, and which account for the frequent breaches of continuity —everywhere save in Egypt—in the transmission of culture. When the oecumenical catastrophe takes the form of a deluge, 'the shepherds and herdsmen on the mountains survive, while the inhabitants of your towns in Hellas are swept away by the rivers'— and with them perishes, each time, their barely achieved sophistication. 'When the waters that are above the firmament descend upon you like a recurrent malady' they 'only permit the illiterate and uncultivated members of your society to survive, with the result that you become as little children and start again from the beginning with no knowledge whatever of Ancient History.' This drastic destruction of a cultural heritage is assumed by the Saïte priest to be a grievous loss; but the contrast between the respective states of the Egyptiac and Hellenic worlds in either Solon's day or Plato's suggests that there may be another side to the story. The possession of old knowledge may be an impediment to the acquisition of new knowledge; and, if so, the heritage may be a burden from which it is a blessing to be even forcibly relieved. 'Except ye be converted and become as little children ye shall not enter into the Kingdom of Heaven' (Matt. xviii. 3). The guileless shepherds who have survived the flood have hearts that are ready to receive a new revelation.

[1] Luke ii. 14.

SAINT AUGUSTINE'S CONCEPTION OF THE RELATIONS BETWEEN THE MUNDANE AND THE SUPRA-MUNDANE COMMONWEALTH

THE problem of the relations between the Kingdom of God and the Society of This World—a society which, for Saint Augustine, is embodied in the oecumenical empire of Rome—is a thread that runs right through the texture of the *De Civitate Dei*; and it would be impossible even to attempt to follow out consecutively the course of Saint Augustine's thought on this question without being drawn into making a systematic analysis of his *magnum opus*. In this place we cannot do more than quote a few passages that illustrate certain crucial points.

One crucial point with which Saint Augustine deals is the question of what is the essential difference between the two commonwealths; and in making this spiritual assay Saint Augustine takes Love as his touchstone.

'The great distinction which differentiates the two commonwealths— the society of the religious and the society of the irreligious—is this: in the one the love of God comes first, in the other the love of Self. . . . Indeed, the two commonwealths have been created by the two loves—the earthly commonwealth by a love of Self that goes to the length of contemning God; the heavenly commonwealth by a love of God that goes to the length of contemning Self. The one glories in itself, the other in the Lord. The one seeks glory from men; the other finds its greatest glory in God as the witness to its own good conscience. The one lifts up its head in its own glory; the other says to its God: *My glory and the lifter up of mine head.*[1] The one is dominated by a thirst for domination in its princes and in the nations which it subdues; in the other those in authority and those under authority serve one another mutually and lovingly by taking counsel and by following it. The earthly commonwealth loves its own strength as displayed in its own mighty men; the heavenly commonwealth says to its God: *I will love thee, O Lord my strength.*[2] And so in the earthly commonwealth its wise men, living on the human level, pursued the interests of the body or the mind or both, while those among them who succeeded in knowing God *glorified Him not as God, neither were thankful, but became vain in their imaginations, and their foolish heart was darkened. Professing themselves to be wise* (that is, extolling themselves for their own wisdom under the dominion of pride), *they became fools and changed the glory of the uncorruptible God into an image made like to corruptible Man and to birds and four-footed beasts and creeping things* (for the leaders of the peoples, or their followers, were given over to the adoration of images of this kind) *and worshipped and served the creature more than the Creator, who is blessed for ever.*[3] On the

[1] Ps. iii. 3.   [2] Ps. xviii. 1.   [3] Rom. i. 21-3 and 25.

other hand, in the heavenly commonwealth there is no wisdom of Man save the devotion with which the True God is properly worshipped—a devotion which He expects to receive as His guerdon in a society of saints (not only human beings, but also angels), *that God may be all in all*[1].'[2]

It may be noted that in this passage Saint Augustine starts from a premiss which is common to him and to the philosophers, but that he arrives at a conclusion which is the opposite of theirs. The philosophers, too, condemn and reject the love of mundane things; but they infer, from their unfavourable experience of Love when it is directed towards one particular kind of object, that Love itself is a spiritual infirmity which the sage must make up his mind to pluck out and cast from him—on the reckoning that it is profitable for him to be without the faculty of Love rather than to renounce the possibility of attaining that absolute Detachment which, in the judgement of a philosophically enlightened understanding, is the only complete cure for a spiritual malady that consists in the very fact of being alive. The philosopher arrives at this radical conclusion because he does not take the precaution, which Saint Augustine does take, of looking into his premiss before proceeding to argue from it; and the philosopher therefore overlooks the capital point that Love *in vacuo* is a logical abstraction which is morally neutral (ἀδιάφορον in the Stoic terminology), while the moral character of real Love in action is determined by the nature of the object towards which it is directed. On this criterion the condemnation of the love of the creature is a right moral judgement; but the correct inference from it is not that Love itself is bad, but that the proper object of Love is not the creature but the Creator.

Another crucial point that is discussed in the *De Civitate Dei* is the question of the attitude which the citizen of the supra-mundane commonwealth ought to take up, in his pilgrimage through This World, towards the institutions of the mundane commonwealth which he will find in force around him.

'It is written of Cain that he founded a commonwealth; but Abel— true to the type of the pilgrim and sojourner that he was—did not do the like. For the commonwealth of the Saints is not of This World, though it does give birth to citizens here in whose persons it performs its pilgrimage until the time of its kingdom shall come—the time when it will gather them all together. . . . And then the promised kingdom will be given to them, and they will reign there with their prince, the King of the Ages, world without end. . . .

'The household of those who do not live by faith seeks to win an earthly peace out of the properties and amenities of this temporal life;

---

[1] 1 Cor. xv. 28.   [2] Saint Augustine, *De Civitate Dei*, Book XIV, chaps. 13 and 28.

but the household of those who do live by faith awaits the blessings which are promised for an eternal future; and so it makes use of earthly and temporal things as a pilgrim would use them—as things which must not be allowed to captivate it and deflect it from its goal (which is God), but on which it may perhaps lean in order to ease and reduce to a minimum the burdens of a corruptible body that weighs upon the Soul. Accordingly, things necessary for this mortal life are made use of by both kinds of person and by both households alike; but, in using them, each has his own distinctive purpose, and these purposes differ profoundly. Even the earthly commonwealth, which does not live by faith, ensues an earthly peace and bases the social harmony of its citizens, in their relations as rulers and ruled, upon some kind of mutual adjustment of human wills in regard to the things that pertain to this mortal life. At the same time the heavenly commonwealth—or, rather, that part of it which is making its pilgrimage in this state of mortality, and which lives by faith—must perforce make use of that earthly peace until the state of mortality, for which that kind of peace is a necessity, has passed away; and on this account, so long as it is leading its pilgrim's life in this earthly commonwealth—and leading it in a virtual captivity, though it has already received the promise of redemption and the gift of the spirit as a pledge [of ultimate release]—it does not hesitate to submit to the laws of the earthly commonwealth by which this mortal life is regulated in the ways most conducive to its maintenance. Mortality itself being common to both commonwealths [in this temporal environment], it is desirable that, in things pertaining to this mortal state, a harmony should be preserved between the two. . . .

'While the heavenly commonwealth is making its pilgrimage on Earth it recruits citizens from all the tribes of Man and gathers its society of pilgrims from people of every tongue—not minding the diversity of manners, laws, and institutions (the instruments by which the earthly peace is earned and secured), and not rescinding or destroying any of these institutions, but on the contrary preserving them and falling in with them, because, underlying this diversity of institutions in different nations, there is the single identic purpose of earthly peace. The sole limiting condition of this conformity is that it must not interfere with Religion—in the sense of the inculcation of the worship of the One Supreme True God. So the heavenly commonwealth too, in its pilgrimage here, makes use of the earthly peace; and (as far as may be possible without conflicting with the duties of Religion) it cherishes and ensues that mutual adjustment of human wills in regard to things pertaining to Man's mortal nature; but it orients this earthly peace towards the heavenly peace which really is peace—the only peace worthy of being regarded as such, and of being called by the name, for creatures endowed with Reason. This heavenly peace is a perfectly organized and perfectly harmonious common participation in the enjoyment of God and of one another in God.[1] And, when we reach that state, our life

---

[1] This definition is also given, in the same words, in the passage quoted in V. C (i) (*d*) 11, p. 166, above.—A.J.T.

will not be mortal, but will be unmistakably vital; and our body will not be an animal body that weighs down the soul as it decays, but will be a spiritual body that has no wants and that is wholly subject to the will. The earthly peace is possessed by the heavenly commonwealth while it is making its pilgrimage in faith; and by this faith it genuinely lives when it orients towards the winning of the heavenly peace whatever good actions it performs in relation to God and also in relation to human neighbours—the life of a commonwealth being a social life *ex hypothesi*. . . .

'Thus the highest good of God's commonwealth is a peace which is eternal and perfect—not just a peace for mortals to travel through between birth and death, but a peace for immortals to abide in without any shadow of adversity. If this be granted, who can deny that that life is blessedly happy, and who refuse to pronounce that, by comparison, this life which we lead here is wretchedly miserable—filled though it may be, to overflowing, with amenities mental, bodily, and external? Any one, however, who lives this earthly life in such a way as to orient his use of it towards an end which is the end of the heavenly life—loving the heavenly life ardently, and loyally hoping for it—any one who lives like that can without absurdity be called blessedly happy even now: happy in the heavenly hope rather than in the earthly reality. On the other hand this earthly reality, divorced from the heavenly hope, is a false happiness which is nothing but the deepest misery. It is false because it does not command the true treasures of the spirit. For wisdom is no true wisdom when it exercises its virtues of discernment, resoluteness, restraint, and justice without directing its intention, in all that it does, to that end where God will be all in all in an eternity that is sure and in a peace that is perfect.'[1]

It will be seen that, in Saint Augustine's view, the duty—and it is, of course, an obvious one—of avoiding the snares of This World can be conscientiously and effectively carried out by the pilgrim-citizen of the supra-mundane commonwealth without his being required to adopt the radical precautionary policy of non-co-operation and non-intercourse. There is a legitimate use which the pilgrim can make of the institutions of the mundane commonwealth as a matter of practical convenience. But Saint Augustine goes farther than that. He tells the pilgrim that he will find that the pagan heroes of the mundane commonwealth have moral lessons to teach which the pilgrim may profitably learn and take to heart for their bearing upon his own duty as a citizen of the *Civitas Dei*.

'The [Christian] martyrs . . . outdid the Scaevolae and Curtii and Decii in bearing ordeals inflicted upon them, instead of inflicting ordeals upon themselves; and they also outdid them in that true religion which is true virtue—not to speak of their immense superiority in numbers. But the Roman heroes were citizens of the earthly commonwealth

---

[1] Saint Augustine, *De Civitate Dei*, Book XV, chap. 1, and Book XIX, chaps. 17 and 20.

(*terrenae civitatis*); and the object set before them in all the duties which they performed on their commonwealth's behalf was the security of that commonwealth and a dominion that was not in Heaven but on Earth— not in a life eternal, but in a perpetual decease of the dying and succes- sion of generations born to die in their turn—and so what else was there for these Roman heroes to love except a glory through which they hoped to live, even after death, a life of sorts in the mouth of an applauding Posterity?

'To these Roman heroes God was not going to give eternal life with his holy angels in his heavenly commonwealth (*caelesti civitate*)—for that is a society to which the only entrance lies in the true religion which does not pay worship to any but the One True God—and so, if God had not granted to those Romans this earthly glory either (the glory of a magnificent empire), they would have been cheated of the reward that was due to their good qualities, or in other words to the virtues by which they were striving to attain this pinnacle of glory. For God himself has something to say of heroes such as these who perform fine actions with the evident motive of gaining glory among men. *Verily I say unto you*, He says, *They have their reward.*[1] And in fact those Romans spurned their own private interests for the sake of the common—that is to say, the public—good. . . . As eagerly as though they had been on the true road, they strove, with every faculty that they possessed, to win honours, power and glory; and they did win an honour which was almost world- wide, they succeeded in imposing upon many peoples the laws in which their empire expressed itself, and to-day they enjoy a literary and his- torical fame that is almost universal. Thus they have no case for im- pugning the justice of the Supreme and True God: *They have their reward.*

'Vastly different, even in This World, is the reward of the Saints who have to endure contumely for the sake of the truth of God—a truth which is hateful to those for whom This World is all in all. The Saints' commonwealth is everlasting: there, none comes into existence, because none dies; there we find that true and full felicity which is not a goddess but is a gift of God; from there we have received the pledge of faith for the duration of our pilgrimage, while we are longing for that heavenly commonwealth's beauty; there the *Sun* does not *rise on the evil and on the good*,[2] but the Sun of Justice protects the good alone. . . . And so God's purpose, in allowing the Roman Empire to expand to the extreme of human glory, has not been solely to render to earthly heroes their due reward; God has also meant to afford an example to the citizens of that eternal commonwealth during their pilgrimage here—an example to which He wills them to pay close and careful heed, in order that they may realize the greatness of the love which they manifestly owe to their heavenly country for the sake of the life eternal, if an earthly country has been so greatly loved by its citizens for the sake of glory among men.'[3]

---

[1] Matt. vi. 2.   [2] Matt. v. 45.
[3] Saint Augustine. *De Civitate Dei*. Book V. chaps. 14, 15, and 16.

THE HELLENIC PORTRAIT OF THE SAVIOUR WITH THE SWORD

OUR presentment of the Saviour with the Sword in the diverse postures of a Hêraklês and a Zeus is one of the political common-places of the Imperial Age of the Hellenic Society from whose mythology these two types are taken; and the surviving records of that age of Hellenic history provide a wealth of illustrations of this piece of political imagery. The monuments that are instructive for our purpose are of several kinds. There are the unofficial and semi-official literary works of philosophers and publicists; and there are the official inscriptions on public buildings and legends on coins. The pair of types was given an explicitly official currency when the Emperor Diocletian proclaimed the fulfilment of his task of salvaging the Empire from the bout of anarchy that had preceded his own advent to power by taking the title 'Jovius' for himself and conferring the title 'Herculius' upon his comrade and colleague Maximian. But this was merely the last step in a gradual process of crystallizing the portrait of the Saviour with the Sword in this dual form. It may be convenient to take a glance at this process in the literary medium first, and then to scan the corre-sponding series of titles on coins and in inscriptions.

In the early days of 'the Indian Summer' of Hellenic history, which began with the accession of the Emperor Nerva in A.D. 96 and ended with the death of the Emperor Marcus Aurelius in A.D. 180,[1] we find the attributes of Hêraklês and Zeus in turn being ascribed to the Emperor Trajan, who had to complete the task of slaying the hydra of tyranny before he could inaugurate the new era of philanthropic government. Trajan was hailed as Hêraklês by the Greek publicist Dio Chrysostom (*vivebat circa* A.D. 45–115),[2] and as both Hercules and Juppiter in successive passages of a single laudatory address from the mouth of the Roman Senator Gaius Plinius the Younger (*vivebat circa* A.D. 60–110).[3] And the activi-ties of the Emperor which entitled him in Pliny's opinion to be regarded as Juppiter's vicegerent on Earth are described by the panegyrist in the following terms:

'These are cares worthy of a prince, and even of a god—to reconcile

---

[1] The view that this epoch of Hellenic history is to be regarded as an 'Indian Summer' rather than as a 'Golden Age' has been put forward in IV. C (ii) (*b*) 1, vol. iv, pp. 58–61, above.

[2] Dio Chrysostom: *Oratio* I, §§ 49–84 (cited again in V. C (ii) (*a*), Annex II, pp. 470, 471, and 478, below).

[3] In Pliny's *Panegyricus* Trajan is praised in the similitude of Hercules in chaps. 14, §5, and 15, § 4, and in the similitude of Juppiter in chap. 80.

rival cities and to restrain arrogant peoples by reason as much as by
authority; to prevent unfairness on the part of magistrates; to reverse
anything done amiss; and lastly like some swift star to visit all places,
to hear all things, and wheresoever your aid is invoked to appear and
stand by like a god.'[1]

This passage could be matched by many others in the same vein,
but we must content ourselves here with a single quotation from
a laudatory address to Rome which was delivered by another
Greek publicist, Aelius Aristeides (*vivebat circa* A.D. 120–80), at a
time when the Hellenic 'Indian Summer' was verging towards its
close. In reviewing Rome's gifts to the Hellenic World, Aristeides
extols, as one of the most signal of them, the institution of the
Principate:

'In the last instance there is a supreme judge of appeal, whose eye for
Justice nothing ever escapes; and at the bar of his tribunal there is the
most complete and magnificent equality between the small and the
great, the obscure and the distinguished, the poor and the rich, the low-
born and the high-born. This emperor-judge is one who, in the words
of Hesiod, *hath but to stretch forth his hand, and, lo, the weak receiveth
strength and the strong man chastisement.*[2] He is a judge who suffers
Justice to direct him like the wind in the sails of a ship—the wind which
shows no favour to the rich man over the poor man in wafting him on
his course, but bestows its beneficent service impartially on every man
who comes in its way.'[3]

These words were written in a generation when they still rang
true; but the term of this 'Indian Summer', during which a
Serene Majesty could rule the Hellenic World 'by reason as much
as by authority', and could maintain the balance of justice by the
touch of an outstretched finger, was shorter than a century. The
sword that had been auspiciously returned to its sheath had to be
ominously drawn again. While Trajan had been able to exchange
the role of Hercules for that of Juppiter, Marcus found himself
compelled to descend from his happier predecessors' Olympian
throne in order to enter again upon the temporarily suspended
round of Hercules' labours;[4] and, in the age of anarchy that
followed, this treadmill had to be trodden by a succession of

---

[1] Pliny: *Panegyricus*, chap. 80, translated by Charlesworth, M. P., in *The Virtues of
a Roman Emperor* (London 1937, Milford), p. 15. The writer of this Study is also indebted to this lecture of Mr. Charlesworth's for the references in the two preceding
footnotes.

[2] ‘Ρέα μὲν γὰρ βριάει, ῥέα δὲ βριάοντα χαλέπτε.—Hesiod: *Works and Days*, l. 5. In
its original context the line refers to Zeus.—A.J.T.

[3] Aristeides, P. Aelius: *In Romam*, p. 363.

[4] There is a bitter irony in the fact that this role of Hercules, which was reluctantly
assumed by Marcus as a grievously burdensome duty, was lightly fancied as a frivolous
pose by Marcus's son Commodus, who did his worst to undo his father's work and to
provide urgent labours for a long series of Herculean emperors after him (for Commodus's pose as Hercules see V. C (i) (d) 6 (α), vol. v, pp. 454–5, above).

soldier-emperors—a Decius and a Claudius and an Aurelian and a Probus and a Carus—before it became possible for a Diocletian to slough off the role of Hercules on to a Maximian's uncouth shoulders and to reassume for himself the role of Jove.

If we now pass from the literary to the epigraphical and numismatical evidence[1] we shall find that the official titles and mottoes of the rulers of the Hellenic World in the Imperial Age are apt to strike an attitude which reproduces one or other of our two postures in some epigrammatic phrase—though the posture that an emperor elects to assume by no means necessarily corresponds to, and may even be deliberately intended to dissimulate, the part that has been forced upon him in fact by an inexorable march of events.

This last point is illustrated by the formulae that date from the recurrent 'Time of Troubles' through which the Hellenic World passed between the death of Marcus in A.D. 180 and the accession of Diocletian in A.D. 284.[2] There are some formulae of this age that breathe the authentic spirit of it. For example, the *Vota Orbis* on coins of Valerian and Gallienus vividly express the agonized suspense of a world that is hanging breathlessly on the issue of the struggle between a single-handed Hêraklês and a hydra

---

[1] The specimens, here cited, of titles and mottoes in inscriptions and on coins of the Hellenic World in the Imperial Age are taken from Vogt, J.: *Orbis Romanus* (Tübingen 1929, Mohr), pp. 18–22; from Hahn, L.: *Rom und Romanismus im Griechisch-Römischen Osten* (Leipzig 1906, Dieterich), p. 140, footnote 4; and from Homo, L.: *Essai sur le Règne de l'Empereur Aurélien (270–275)* (Paris 1904, Fontemoing), pp. 362–4.

[2] The cause of this terrible relapse into anarchy was analysed long beforehand, with a prophetic insight, by the Stoic sage and Roman statesman Seneca (*vivebat circa* 5 B.C.–A.D. 65) in a passage of his *De Clementia* (Book I, chap. 4, §§ 1–2) in which the author gives his view of the social function of a prince.

'He is the bond that holds the Commonwealth together; he is the breath of life that is breathed by subjects, in their thousands, who in themselves would be nothing but a burden and a prey if they were left to their own devices through the removal of a presence which is the soul of the Empire.

> Their king is safe? One mind informs them all;
> Lost? They break troth straightway.

'If this calamity [which Virgil (*Georgics*, IV, ll. 212–13) imagines as overtaking the bees] were to overtake us, it would be the destruction of the *Pax Romana* and the ruin of a great people. This people will be safe from that particular danger for just so long as it has the sense to put up with the curb; but, if ever it snaps the reins—or refuses to allow itself to be bridled again if the bridle has been accidentally shaken off—then the texture of this mighty empire will be rent, and its present unity will fly apart into a hundred shreds. Rome will cease to bear rule at the moment at which she ceases to render obedience.'

A foretaste of the fulfilment of this prophecy that had been made in a treatise addressed to the Emperor Nero was inflicted upon the Hellenic World in A.D. 69 as an immediate consequence of Nero's tyranny; but this touch of calamity acted as a stimulus. 'The Year of the Four Emperors' was followed by the principate of Vespasian; and, when the Neronian reign of terror was reinaugurated by the son of an emperor who had earned the title of 'Saviour and Benefactor of All Men', this tyranny of Domitian in its turn was followed by the philanthropic régime of a series of philosopher-emperors who succeeded one another without a break from Nerva to Marcus. It was only after the death of Marcus that the new 'Time of Troubles' set in; and even then the tyranny of Commodus was followed by the principate of Septimius Severus, who repeated Vespasian's work—albeit with a rougher hand. It was not till after the death of Alexander Severus that the storm broke with an uncontrollable and shattering violence.

with a hundred heads.[1] And there are other contemporary formulae which implicitly confess that the Roman Peace has been
broken and the structure of the Hellenic universal state been
destroyed—or at any rate gravely damaged. These unwelcome
truths are admitted in the title *Pacator Orbis* which is taken by
Septimius Severus and Caracalla and Valerian and Gallienus and
Postumus and Aurelian and Tacitus and Florian and Probus and
Numerian.[2] And the same admission is made in the title *Reparator
Orbis* or *Restitutor Orbis*[3] or *Restitutor Generis Humani* or *Restitutor
Saeculi* which is taken by Gordianus III and the two Philips, by
Otacilia Severa (the wife of the first Philip and the mother of the
second), by Valerian, by Gallienus, by Postumus, by Claudius, by
Aurelian, by Tacitus, by Probus, by Carus, by Carinus, and there-
after by Constantius II and by Julian. The common characteristic
of these titles is their note of frankness. On the other hand it is
the wish, and not the fact, that is father to the thought in the
motto *Securitas Orbis* which is displayed on the coins, not of any
emperor whose reign falls within the Hadrianic and Antonine
'Indian Summer', but of a series which begins with Commodus
and continues through Caracalla and Geta and the first Philip and
Philip's wife Otacilia Severa and Decius's wife Etruscilla and
Gallienus and Probus until it closes in the generation of Diocletian
with the great man himself and with his lieutenants Maximian and
Galerius and with his opponent Carausius. This catalogue suggests that the men who were responsible for the welfare of the
Empire did not find it necessary to boast of the performance of
their elementary duty of keeping order except in times when the
boast was unwarrantable.

There is another group of formulae which proclaim the metamorphosis of a Hercules into a Juppiter: for example, the specious
Pax Orbis Terrarum which was a false claim on coins of Otho but
a true one on coins of the Flavians; the well-earned *Fortuna*

---

[1] The *Vota Orbis et Urbis* on coins of Constantine the Great and Licinius perhaps
express the recurrence of this anxious atmosphere during the further bout of anarchy
between the abdication of Diocletian in A.D. 305 and the overthrow of Licinius by
Constantine in A.D. 323.

[2] There is evidence in the legends on coins for the assumption of this title by all
these ten emperors except Tacitus. In Tacitus's case the evidence is epigraphical—and
there is also epigraphical as well as numismatical evidence in the case of Caracalla.

[3] The evidence for *Restitutor Orbis* is both numismatical and epigraphical, while that
for *Reparator Orbis* appears to be epigraphical only. It is noteworthy that the title
Restitutor Orbis Terrarum appears to have been invented by Hadrian—an emperor who
was able to sheathe the sword which Trajan had drawn and to rule thereafter without
drawing it again (save for the suppression of Bar Kōkabā). Hadrian was not constrained
to emulate Hêraklês in his labours, though he chose to emulate him in his travels. The
work which Hadrian made his special business was more aptly described in his other
title of *Locupletator Orbis Terrarum*; for Hadrian was able to devote more of his energy
to improving and completing what his predecessors had left unfinished than to merely
repairing what they had wrecked or had allowed to fall into ruin.

Redux on coins of Aurelian[1] and *Gloria Orbis* on coins of Probus;
the controversial *Liberator Orbis* on inscriptions of Constantine,
Magnentius, and Julian; and the audacious *Toto Orbe Victor* which
may pass muster in the inscriptions of a Constantius II and a
Valentinian and a Theodosius, but which takes our breath away
when we find the self-same title in the inscriptions of a Valens or
an Arcadius.

Finally we may glance at the group of formulae in which the
Saviour of Society displays himself—now serenely at rest, with
sword no longer naked but in scabbard—in the posture of a
Zeus with Olympus for his throne and with the prostrate Titans
for his footstool. There are inscriptions in which Divus Julius is
hailed as Σωτὴρ τοῦ Κόσμου and as Σωτὴρ τῆς Οἰκουμένης;[2] Augus-
tus as *Custos Imperi Romani Totiusque Orbis Terrarum*; Tiberius as
Κοινὸς τῆς Οἰκουμένης Εὐεργέτης; Claudius as Σωτὴρ τῆς Οἰκουμένης;
Nero (!) as Ὁ Ἀγαθὸς Δαίμων τῆς Οἰκουμένης; Vespasian as Ὁ
Πάντων Ἀνθρώπων Σωτὴρ καὶ Εὐεργέτης; Trajan as Σωτὴρ τῆς
Οἰκουμένης and as *Conservator Generis Humani*.[3] There are coins of

---

[1] Aurelian's *Fortuna Redux* may pass, but his *Felicitas Saeculi* and *Felicitas Temporum*
must have drawn wry smiles from the faces of his subjects as they fingered the coins on
which these two mottoes were displayed.

[2] Pauly-Wissowa: *Real-Encyclopädie der Klassischen Altertumswissenschaft*, 2nd ed.,
2nd ser., Halbband v, col. 1214. The former of these two variants of a single title was
affected by a number of Caesar's successors, especially by Hadrian; the latter was affected
(see below) by Claudius and by Trajan. This title for a ruler of the Hellenic universal
state has a remarkably close Andean parallel in the title 'Pachacutec' which was borne
by the Inca who has the best claim to be regarded as the founder of the Andean universal state (see I. C (i) (b), vol. i, p. 121, and II. D (iv), vol. ii, p. 103, above). According
to Baudin, L.: *L'Empire Socialiste des Inka* (Paris 1928, Institut d'Ethnologie), p. 114,
'Pachacutec' is a compound of the Quichuan substantive 'Pacha', meaning 'World', with
a past participle passive 'cutec', meaning 'changed'—i.e., in this context, 'changed for
the better'. The grammatical equivalent of 'Pachacutec' would thus be a motto which
might appear on a Roman Imperial coin in some such Latin legend as *Orbis [in Statum
Meliorem] Conversus*. If this Latin sentence had to be transposed into a Greek epithet,
Σωτὴρ τῆς Οἰκουμένης would provide as good a translation as could be wished for; and,
conversely, the statement, in a Greek inscription of 9–8 B.C. (O.G.I. 458, quoted in Gall,
A. von: Βασιλεία τοῦ Θεοῦ (Heidelberg 1926, Winter), p. 453) that Augustus ἑτέραν ἔδωκε
παντὶ τῷ κόσμῳ ὄψιν could be rendered as 'pacha cutec' in Quichuan.

[3] For this Latin version of Trajan's title see Pauly-Wissowa, op. cit., col. 1219.
Aurelian rings changes on it—*Conservator Orbis* and *Conservator Semper Vitae*—but
it reappears in its original form in Arnobius: *Adversus Nationes*, Book II, chap. 64,
where it is applied, not, of course, to Trajan, but to Christ. *Conservator* had come to
be accepted as the regular Latin rendering of the Greek word σωτήρ in the pagan Latin
usage of the Imperial Age (though Cicero had resorted to the periphrasis 'Is est . . .
σωτήρ qui salutem dedit', on the plea that the Greek title meant something 'ita magnum
ut Latine uno verbo exprimi non possit' (*In Verrem*, Actio II, Book II, chap. 63, § 154)).
The Christian Latin rendering *Salvator* originated in a solecism, since it is based on a
non-classical verb *salvare* which was coined in a Christian mint from the classical adjec-
tive *salvus* (Pauly-Wissowa, vol. cit., col. 1220). This solecism makes its first appearance
in Latin literature in the works of the African Tertullian; and nearly two hundred years
later a greater African father and man-of-letters still shows some discomfort in making
use of it. 'Christus inquit, Iesus, id est Christus Salvator [Matt. i. 21] . . . nec quaerant
grammatici quam sit Latinum, sed christiani quam verum . . . "salvare" et "salvator"
non fuerunt haec Latina antequam veniret Salvator; quando ad Latinos venit, et haec
Latina fecit' (Saint Augustine: *Sermo* CCXCIX, chap. 6). 'Verbum ['salvator'] Latina
lingua antequam non habebat, sed habere poterat, sicut potuit, quando voluit' (idem:
De Trinitate, Book XIII, chap. [10] 14).

Galba, Trajan, Commodus, and Caracalla which bear the motto *Salus Generis Humani*; and others on which Didius Julianus (!) and Septimius Severus and Caracalla and Constantine are depicted, holding the globe, with the legend *Rector Orbis*. And there are inscriptions, again, in which the title *Dominus Orbis* is given to Florian (!) and Diocletian and Julian.

In this array of Hellenic Imperial titles the truth is evidently blended with an alloy of make-believe. The debasement was not so gross as to prevent the coin from being accepted at its face value by contemporaries who managed to live through the collapse of the Empire without ever being aware of the tremendous event which they were witnessing and were perhaps even helping to bring to pass. But for our eyes, which can see it in perspective, this Hellenic portrait of the Saviour with the Sword brings out, with all the force of dramatic irony, the truth that mundane weapons, whether naked or sheathed, cannot be converted into effective instruments of even a mundane salvation.

CHRISTUS PATIENS

The Problem

IN the chapter to which this annex attaches we have found that in a disintegrating society the creative genius assumes the role of a saviour; and an empirical survey of would-be saviours has led us to distinguish four types: the saviour with the sword, the saviour with 'the Time-Machine', the philosopher masked by a king, and the god incarnate in a man. Our purpose in making this tentative classification was to discover which of the alternative ways of seeking salvation is the true road and which are the aberrations; and accordingly, in following out the main thread of our argument, we have paid more attention to points of difference and contrast between our four types of saviour than to points of resemblance and connexion.[1] Yet, *ex hypothesi*, these different types have something in common, or it would have been impossible to apply the same name—'saviour'—to all of them. What is this common element? How far does it extend? And what is its significance?

Perhaps the most promising approach to these questions will be to look for the answer in a concrete case. If we concentrate upon the history of the Hellenic Society in the age of its disintegration, we shall become aware of certain correspondences between the accounts that have come down to us of divers saviours who arose in the Hellenic World in this chapter of its story; and we shall find that these correspondences override our classification of types; for the subjects of them are on the one hand Jesus—the saviour who made his epiphany as God incarnate in a man—and on the other hand a number of the pagan Hellenic saviours with the 'time-machine'. These partial counterparts of Jesus fall, for their part, into two sub-groups. Some of them—i.e. Aristonicus, Eunus, Salvius, Catiline—are leaders of the Hellenic internal proletariat who either were born into it, as Jesus was, or were adopted into it as deserters from the ranks of the Hellenic dominant minority. The saviours in this sub-group, both born proletarians and renegades, differ from Jesus in being futurists. The other sub-group —which includes the two Heracleidae, Agis and Cleomenes; the two Gracchi, Tiberius and Gaius; a companion of the Gracchi,

---

[1] One point of resemblance has, however, been touched upon in V. C (i) (*d*) 11, Annex I, p. 346, above.

Marcus Fulvius Flaccus; and also Cato Minor—consists entirely of members of the dominant minority who lived and died as archaists (though some of them came to be adopted, in the teeth of their own aims and desires, as heroes of an internal proletariat that was marching militantly along a futuristic war-path).[1] It will be evident at once that there is one fundamental difference in aim and outlook between Jesus and all these other saviours. The futurists and the archaists alike were seeking to establish a kingdom in This World, and their quest of Utopia was foredoomed to take to violence and to end in failure, whereas Jesus was seeking to establish a kingdom which was not of This World, he refused to take the sword, and in submitting, without resistance, to an unjust judgement and a painful death he accepted a material defeat which was in itself a supreme spiritual victory. This difference between Jesus and the pagan saviours who are his partial counterparts involves and expresses an element in Christianity which is of its essence, and, by comparison with this deep diversity, the correspondences with which we are now concerned are obviously superficial and trivial. Nevertheless they may still be worth examining for the light which they throw in the first place upon the passage of ideas and feelings across the gulf between the Hellenic dominant minority and the Hellenic internal proletariat, and in the second place upon the scope, and the limits, of the possibility of using old bottles to hold new wine.[2] If we keep our present *caveat* in mind throughout the following inquiry, we may perhaps be able to reap some of the fruits of what is called 'the Higher Criticism' without losing our sense of spiritual proportion. With this proviso let us now set out the correspondences between the accounts of these saviours of different kinds, and then see whether we can explain them.[3]

Correspondences between the story of Jesus and the Stories of certain Hellenic Saviours with the 'Time-Machine'

Since the story of Jesus enters into all the correspondences in question, it will be best to tabulate the points in the order in which they occur in the Gospels, after noticing several correspondences of a general nature which have no exact place in a chronological series.

---

[1] On this point see V. C (i) (a), pp. 236–41, above.

[2] Matt. ix. 17 = Mark ii. 22, quoted in IV. C (iii) (b) 1, vol. iv, p. 133, above.

[3] The writer's purpose is, not to make a case for or against this or that explanation, but to put before his readers all the materials within the writer's knowledge that are relevant to a study of the problem. In the following survey he has therefore included many correspondences which, in his opinion, are certainly slight and almost certainly fortuitous, and has omitted only such as are demonstrably fortuitous (e.g. the example examined on pp. 418–19, below).

1. *There is a pair of heroes who are distinguished from one another by the double difference—of age and of êthos—between a gentle predecessor and a violent successor.*

Since Gentleness and Futurism are incompatible,[1] this correspondence is limited *a priori* to Jesus and the archaists. The double difference comes out most clearly in the contrast between Agis and Cleomenes, and it also appears in the relation between Tiberius and Gaius Gracchus. But in the Gracchan story Gaius does not play the role of the violent hero consistently. At the crisis—when the Government are trying to provoke him into resorting to force—he changes over from the violent to the gentle hero's part, while the part that he discards is taken on by Marcus Fulvius Flaccus, who in this last act of the tragedy plays Cleomenes to Gaius's Agis (see Plutarch: *Lives of the Gracchi*, chaps. 34-8).[2] At the corresponding crisis in the career of Jesus, Jesus himself reacts with the gentleness of Gaius, and Peter with the violence of Fulvius. But there are also traces in the Gospels (e.g. the description of Jesus's mission that is given in Matt. x. 34-9 = Luke xii. 49-53; the description of the nature of the contrast between the new and the old dispensation that is given in Matt. xi. 11-12 = Luke xvi. 16; the incident of the cleansing of the Temple (Matt. xxi. 12-13 = Mark xi. 15-17 = Luke xix. 45-6 = John ii. 13-17); and the hint, in Luke xxii. 35-8, of at least an impulse in Jesus's mind, on the eve of the Passion, to take to the sword) of a different distribution of roles in which Jesus plays the violent hero's part;[3] and if, in the light of this, we ask ourselves who it is that plays Tiberius Gracchus to Jesus's Gaius, the answer will be: John the Baptist.[4]

2. *The hero is of royal lineage.*

Jesus is a son of David according to the Synoptic Gospels (e.g. Matt. ix. 27; xv. 22; xx. 30-1; Mark x. 47-8; Luke xviii. 38-9);[5] Agis and Cleomenes are Heracleidae; Aristonicus is an Attalid. The Gracchi are not themselves of royal birth, though they are

---

[1] See V. C (i) (d) 1, vol. v, pp. 385-7, above.

[2] Plutarch's *Lives of the Gracchi* and *Lives of Agis and Cleomenes* are cited and quoted here from K. Ziegler's edition (Leipzig 1915, Teubner).

[3] This vein of Violence also shows itself here and there in other parts of the New Testament: e.g. in James v. 1-6 (though a violent preamble is here followed by a gentle sequel) and, above all, in the Book of Revelation. See V. C (i) (c) 2, Annex III, vol. v, pp. 589-90, above.

[4] The writer is indebted to Dr. Martin Braun for having pointed out to him that both Gaius Gracchus and Jesus appear in both the two roles, and that in both cases the violent role is played first, while the change over from Violence to Gentleness is made in the last act, in which the tragedy reaches its crisis. He also owes to the same scholar the equation Tiberius : Gaius = John the Baptist : Jesus.

[5] On the other hand, John i. 43-51, and vii. 40-53, might be read as implicit rejections of a story that Jesus was of Davidic lineage.

aristocrats; but their mother moves in royal society (Plut., chap. 40) and has, in King Ptolemy, a royal wooer (Plut., chap. 1) who is a counterpart of Jesus's mother's royal husband;[1] and Tiberius is eventually assassinated by his enemies on the ground that he is asking for a crown (Plut., chap. 19).

3. The hero's genealogy is recited.

Jesus's genealogy in Matthew i. 1–17, and in Luke iii. 23–38;[2] Agis' genealogy in Plutarch, chap. 3.

4. The hero's genealogy has a flaw in it.

According to the 'conceptionist' (though not according to the 'adoptionist') version of Christianity, Jesus's claim to be a son of David is disputable, inasmuch as it is derived from a descendant of David who is the husband of Jesus's mother but who—in this version of the story—is not, himself, Jesus's father.[3] There is a comparable doubt about Aristonicus's claim to be an Attalid (δοκῶν τοῦ γένους εἶναι τοῦ τῶν βασιλέων καὶ διανοούμενος εἰς ἑαυτὸν ποιεῖσθαι τὴν ἀρχήν—Strabo: *Geographica*, Book XIV, chap. 38 = Kramer, p. 646); and, even if he is acknowledged to be King Eumenes' son, the legitimacy of his birth is contested ('Erat ex Eumene Aristonicus, non iusto matrimonio, sed ex paelice Ephesia, citharistae cuiusdam filia, genitus—qui post mortem Attali velut paternum regnum Asiam invasit.'—Justin, Book XXXVI, chap. 4, § 6).

5. The hero's mother believes in him and encourages him.

This is the attitude of Jesus's mother towards Jesus in the Gospel according to Saint John (e.g. in John ii. 3–5 and 12; xix. 25–7); and it is also the attitude of Cleomenes' mother towards Cleomenes (Plutarch: *Lives of Agis and Cleomenes*, chap. 27) and of the mother of the Gracchi towards both Tiberius (Plutarch: *Lives of the Gracchi*, chap. 8) and Gaius (chap. 34). Again, it is the eventual attitude of the mother of Agis towards her son (Plut., chap. 7).

N.B. On this point the Gospel according to Saint John is in

[1] This equation Joseph : Mary : Jesus = Ptolemy : Cornelia : the Gracchi holds good only for the 'conceptionist' Christianity according to which Jesus's claim to be a son of David is derived from a husband of the hero's mother who is not, himself, the hero's father. If we assume the, perhaps older, 'adoptionist' position, according to which Jesus is really Joseph's son, the analogy breaks down; for in the Roman story there is no possibility of a version in which the Gracchi turn out to have been really the sons of Ptolemy. Cornelia is not wooed by Ptolemy till after her children are born and the husband to whom she has borne them is dead; and then she does not accept Ptolemy, but rejects him! For the distinction between 'conceptionist' and 'adoptionist' Christianity see IV. C (iii) 2 (β), Annex III, vol. iv, and V. C (ii) (a), in the present volume, pp. 271–5, above.
[2] See ibid., p. 273, footnote 4, above.
[3] See the passage of Eduard Meyer that is quoted ibid., pp. 268–9, and also the same chapter, p. 267, footnote 5, above.

apparently deliberate contradiction with the Synoptic Gospels.
In all three of these it would appear to be implied that Jesus and
his mother are out of sympathy with each other (Matt. xii. 46–50
= Mark iii. 31–5 = Luke viii. 19–21); and his mother is not mentioned among the women who are present at the Crucifixion (see
Point 80, below). The two apparently contradictory accounts of the
attitude of the hero's mother which are given in this apparently
irreconcilable form in two different versions of the story of Jesus
are reconciled in the story of Agis, in which the hero's mother
starts as a sceptic but ends as a convert (Plut., chap. 7).

6. *The hero is recognized and accepted by a forerunner as the
latter's successor and superior.*

Jesus by John the Baptist (Matt. iii. 11–17; Mark i. 7–11; Luke
iii. 15–22; John i. 15–17 and 25–37, and iii. 22–36); Eunus by
Cleon (Diodorus, Books XXXIV–XXXV, chap. 2, § 17); Salvius
by Athenio (Diodorus, Book XXXVI, chap. 7, § 2).

7. *The hero inveighs against the powers that be, on the ground that
they are usurpers who have driven out or slain without trial the
legitimate authorities and have perverted the ancient law.*

Jesus's denunciations of the Scribes and Pharisees (e.g. Matt.
xxiii, *passim*; Mark xii. 38–40; Luke xx. 45–7); Cleomenes' denunciation of the Ephors (Plut., chap. 31).

8. *The hero proclaims that the right of membership in the society
that is the field of his mission is not a privilege of birth, but is a reward
of merit.*[1]

This is one of the principal *motifs* in the Gospels:[2] 'Many that
are first shall be last, and the last shall be first' (Matt. xix. 30, and
xx. 16 = Mark x. 31 = Luke xiii. 30); it is expressed in the
miracle of the healing of the centurion's servant (Matt. viii. 5–13
= Luke vii. 1–10) and in the parables of the Wicked Husbandmen (Matt. xxi. 33–44 = Mark xii. 1–11 = Luke xx. 9–18), the
Labourers in the Vineyard (Matt. xx. 1–16), the Father and his
Two Sons (Matt. xxi. 28–32), the King's Son's Marriage (Matt.
xxii. 1–14 = Luke xiv. 15–24), the Good Samaritan (Luke x.
25–37), Dives and Lazarus (Luke xvi. 19–31), the Pharisee and the
Publican (Luke xviii. 9–14). Publicans and harlots who believe are

---

[1] This truth is, of course, one of the facts that account for the phenomenon of *Peripeteia* (see IV. C (iii) (c) 1, vol. iv, pp. 245–61, above).
[2] The clearest enunciation of it is: 'Think not to say within yourselves: "We have
Abraham to our father"; for I say unto you that God is able of these stones to raise up
children unto Abraham' (Matt. iii. 9). But this saying is attributed, not to Jesus himself, but to his forerunner John the Baptist. It is only in the Gospel according to Saint
John (viii. 31–59) that it is put—in an elaborated version—into Jesus's mouth.

preferred to Scribes and Pharisees who do not repent (Matt. xxi. 31–2). Similarly, the enfranchisement of non-citizens who are worthy of the franchise is of the essence of the programme of the Spartan and Roman archaists: Agis and Cleomenes enfranchise not only select perioeci but also select aliens (Plut., chaps. 8–10 and 31–2).

9. *The hero denounces a state of affairs in which there are human beings who are so utterly destitute of any part or lot in the inheritance of the Earth that in this respect, at any rate, they are worse off than wild animals.*

Jesus makes this invidious comparison apropos of himself and his followers (Matt. viii. 19–20 = Luke ix. 57–8); Tiberius Gracchus makes it apropos of a *ci-devant* peasantry that has been turned into a landless proletariat (Plut., chap. 9);[1] Aristonicus makes it apropos of his followers implicitly in calling them 'Heliopolitae' (i.e. human beings who, if they can be held to possess civic rights in any commonwealth at all, are certainly not in enjoyment of these in any commonwealth that is to be found on the face of the Earth)[2] (Strabo: *Geographica*, Book XIV, chap. 38 = Kramer, p. 646).

10. *The hero calls on all who are within hearing to win the reward of merit for themselves by following him through an ordeal.*

Jesus calls to the Cross (Matt. x. 16–42, and xvi. 24–8 = Mark viii. 34–8 = Luke ix. 23–7, and xiv. 25–33); Cleomenes (Plut., chap. 58) and Aristonicus (Strabo: *Geographica*, Book XVI, chap. 38 = Kramer, p. 646) call to liberty. Cleomenes calls upon the people of Alexandria to take up arms and risk their lives under his leadership for the sake of winning their political liberty by over-throwing the autocratic government of the Ptolemies;[3] Aristonicus calls upon the proletarian freemen and the slaves in Asia Minor to join his standard for the sake of winning their economic and social liberty by making 'Heliopolis', instead of Rome, into the heir of the Kingdom of the Attalids.

11. *The crowds that flock round the hero are so great that any one who is determined to approach him, or even to see or hear him, has to take extraordinary steps.*

In the picture given in the Gospels the multitude tread on one another as they surge round Jesus (Luke xii. 1); the four men

---

[1] This correspondence between a saying attributed to Tiberius Gracchus and a saying attributed to Jesus has been touched upon, by anticipation, in IV. C (iii) (c) 3 (β), vol. iv, pp. 508 and 510; in V. C (i) (c) 2, vol. v, pp. 70–1; and in V. C (i) (c) 1, Annex, vol. v, p. 574, above.
[2] For the implications of the term 'Heliopolitae' see V. C (iii) (c) 2, vol. v, pp. 69, 70, 82, footnote 4, and 180; V. C (i) (d) 1, vol. v, p. 384; V. C (i) (d) 6 (δ), Annex, vol. v, p. 692, footnote 2; and V. C (i) (d) 11, Annex I, in the present volume, p. 351, above.
[3] See V. C (ii) (a), p. 217, above.

bearing the man sick of the palsy have to take the tiles off the roof of the house where Jesus is and then let the bed down through the hole, because it is impossible to get in by the door (Mark ii. 1–4); Zacchaeus has to climb a tree if he is to gain even a sight of Jesus (Luke xix. 1–6). When Gaius Gracchus is standing for election to the Tribunate of the Plebs, the crowd that flocks to Rome to vote is so great that many fail to find lodgings, and on polling day they have to climb on to the roofs because the campus will not hold them all (Plut., chap. 24).

12. The hero's programme obtains an extraordinary publicity.

'That which ye have spoken in the ear in closets shall be proclaimed upon the house-tops' (Luke xii. 3).[1] The acclamations with which Gaius Gracchus was hailed on the campus 'were echoed from the roofs and the tiles' (Plut., chap. 24).

13. In his domestic life the hero avoids ostentation by deliberately taking a middle course between asceticism and luxuriousness.

Jesus's attitude towards the Sabbath (Matt. xii. 1–8 = Mark ii. 23–8 = Luke vi. 1–5); Cleomenes' attitude towards the 'Lycurgean' *agôgê* (Plut., chap. 34).[2]

14. By his refusal to go to extremes of asceticism—which he combines with a readiness to keep company with people of all sorts and conditions—the hero causes scandal.

Jesus's avoidance of an extreme asceticism scandalizes the disciples of John the Baptist (Matt. ix. 14–15 = Mark ii. 18–20 = Luke v. 33–5, and vii. 31–5); his keeping company with publicans and sinners scandalizes the Pharisees (Matt. ix. 10–13 = Mark ii 14–17 = Luke v. 27–32; vii. 36–50; and xv. 1–2). Tiberius Gracchus was censured by Quintus Metellus for allowing himself to be lighted home at night by 'the most offensive and most poverty-stricken people in Rome'—in contrast to the behaviour of Tiberius's father, who had made his countrymen live in such awe of him that during his censorship, whenever he went home after dining out, the householders used to put out their lights for fear that he might think them immoderately addicted to parties and to drink (Plut., chap. 14).

N.B. Cleomenes, too, made himself accessible; but in his case this affability, so far from causing scandal, was decidedly popular (Plut., chap. 34).

---

[1] Cf. Luke iv. 14–15, quoted in this connexion on p. 471, below.
[2] This passage of Plutarch is evidently derived from Phylarchus *apud* Athenaeum *Deipnosophistae*, Book IV, pp. 141 F–142 F (see the present Annex, p. 436, below).

15. *The hero makes a sensational claim to kingship, which he supports by the further claim that he has been commissioned by God (by a god or by certain gods or by the Gods).*

Jesus claims to be the Messiah: i.e. the saviour-king, anointed (i.e. commissioned) by God, whose advent is expected by Jewry (Matt. xvi. 13–20 = Mark viii. 27–30 = Luke ix. 18–21); correspondingly, three leaders of slave-insurrections in Sicily claim, on divine authority, that they are destined to win a victory which will be rewarded with a royal crown. Eunus declares, before he rises in insurrection, that the Dea Syra has appeared to him and has told him that he is to become a king (Diodorus, Books XXXIV–XXXV, chap. 2, §§ 5–7).[1] Salvius, who is elected king by the insurgents in the second Sicilian slave-insurrection, is an expert in divination by interpreting the meaning of the entrails of sacrificial victims, and he is also a devotee of 'the feminine gods' (Diodorus, Book XXXVI, chap. 4, § 4); Athenio is an expert in astromancy, and he maintains that the Gods have signified to him through the stars that he is destined to become king of the whole of Sicily (Diodorus, Book XXXVI, chap. 5, §§ 1 and 3).

N.B. According to the traditional Jewish conception of the Messiah's mission, the Messiah was to do for Jewry exactly what the Sicilian slave-kings did momentarily succeed in doing for their insurgent followers. By an act of human physical force which was to acquire an irresistible impetus from the divine auspices under which it was being put into action, the Messiah was to achieve, on the mundane plane of life, a reversal of political roles. The subject people of to-day was to be the imperial people of to-morrow; the Messiah was to transfer the sceptre to Jerusalem from Susa or Antioch or Rome, and, as a result of his victory, the Jews were to step into the shoes of the Persians or the Macedonians or the Romans.[2] In the Gospels, however, the accounts of Jesus's claim to be the Messiah are associated with a departure, in two important respects, from the traditional Jewish conception of the Messiah's mission and nature; and, on both counts, this departure diminishes the closeness of the correspondence between the claims to kingship that are made respectively by Jesus and by the Sicilian slave-leaders. In the first place Jesus perplexes his disciples' minds and devastates their hopes by telling them at once that his Messiahship spells, not military victory and political triumph, but being put to death (Matt. xvi. 21–3 = Mark viii. 31–3 = Luke

---

[1] See V. C (i) (d) 7, p. 34, footnote 5, and V. C (i) (d) 9 (γ), pp. 124–5, above.
[2] See IV. C (iii) (b) 12, vol. iv, pp. 224–5; V. C (i) (c) 2, vol. v, pp. 68–9; V. C (i) (d) 6 (δ), Annex, vol. v, pp. 657–9; and V. C (i) (d) 9 (γ), in the present volume, pp. 120–3, above.

ix. 22);[1] in the second place, according to Matthew (xvi. 16)[2]—though not according to Mark (viii. 29) or to Luke (ix. 20)—Peter hails Jesus as the Son of God as a corollary of his acknowledgement of Jesus's Messiahship—in contradiction with the traditional Jewish view, which expected the Messiah to be, not the divine Son of God, but a human son of David.[3]

N.B. In the Gospel according to Saint John the incident is transformed to a degree which makes its correspondence with the analogous Sicilian incidents barely recognizable. In this Gospel Peter's declaration—'We believe and are sure that thou art Christ, the Son of the living God' (John vi. 69)—is overshadowed by a preamble (John vi. 22–68) in which Jesus, instead of evoking an acknowledgement of his Messiahship by asking a question, propounds in his own words a claim to have been sent down from Heaven by God to perform, for all men who accept his claim, a service that is analogous to, though infinitely more valuable and more wonderful than, the service that is performed for Mankind by the Spirit of the Vegetation.[4] The Vegetation Spirit provides material bread for a single year; Jesus is spiritual bread that confers eternal life.

16. *A tableau of a rider riding through the streets of a capital city on a mount which has been commandeered for him by his companions on the spur of the moment without opposition from the owner.*

Jesus riding into Jerusalem on an ass, accompanied by his followers on foot (Matt. xxi. 1–7 = Mark xi. 1–7 = Luke xix. 29–35 = John xii. 14–15); Hippitas, a lame companion of Cleomenes, riding through the streets of Alexandria on a horse—that has been commandeered from a passer-by—in company with Cleomenes himself and with the rest of the king's companions, who are all on foot (Plut., chap. 58).

17. *The hero in person forcibly clears a public place from trespassers who have unlawfully encroached upon it for their private profit.*

Jesus overthrows the tables of the money-changers and the seats of the poulterers (who are selling doves for sacrifice) in the precincts of the Temple at Jerusalem (Matt. xxi. 12–13 = Mark

---

1 This new association of ideas has been touched upon in V. C (i) (d) 1, vol. v, pp. 392–3, above.

2 Matt. xvi. 16 is echoed in John vi. 69, and xi. 27.

3 See V. C (i) (d) 11, p. 163, footnote 1, above. For the association between Jesus's claim to divinity and his premonition of his death see V. C (i) (c) 2, vol. v, p. 74; V. C (i) (d) 1, vol. v, pp. 392–3; and V. C (i) (d) 11, in the present volume, p. 165, above.

4 For the myth of the ἐνιαυτὸς δαίμων see III. C (iii) (b), vol. iii, pp. 256–9, and V. C (ii) (a), in the present volume, pp. 276–7, above.

xi. 15–17 = Luke xix. 45–6 = John ii. 13–17); Gaius Gracchus
pulls down the seats which his fellow magistrates, by an abuse of
privilege, have erected round the Forum at Rome in order to let
them, for money, to sightseers on the day of a show (Plut.,
chap. 33).

18. *The authorities want to compass the hero's ruin, but are at
a loss how to proceed against him because of his popularity.*

Jesus at Jerusalem (Matt. xxi. 46, and xxvi. 3–5 = Mark xi. 18,
and xiv. 1–2 = Luke xxii. 2); Cleomenes at Alexandria (Plut.,
chap. 54 = Polybius, Book V, chap. 35); Tiberius Gracchus at
Rome (Plut., chap. 10).

19. *The authorities try to catch the hero out by asking him awkward questions, but his answers recoil upon the questioners.*

The Pharisees and Herodians ask Jesus whether it is lawful to
pay tribute to Caesar; the Sadducees set him a trap over the
doctrine of the Resurrection; and a doctor of the Law asks him
which is the greatest of the Commandments (Matt. xxii. 15–40 =
Mark xii. 13–34 = Luke xx. 20–40); but Jesus silences them all.
Similarly, Agis silences Leonidas when he asks him whether
Lycurgus had cancelled debts or enfranchised aliens, as Agis was
proposing to do (Plut., chap 10).
N.B. On the other hand Tiberius Gracchus is put out of
countenance by a question from Titus Annius (Plut., chap. 14).

20. *At a meal the hero is offered a special luxury by an admirer
(by admirers) from outside his most intimate circle.*

The alabaster box of precious ointment that is offered by a
woman to Jesus in the house of Simon at Bethany (Matt. xxvi.
6–13 = Mark xiv. 3–9 = Luke vii. 37–50[1] = John xi. 2,[2] and xii.
1–8); the dinner and gifts that are sent in to Cleomenes, in the
prison at Alexandria, by his friends outside (Plut., chap. 58).

21. *The authorities are at a loss how to proceed against the hero
because he has a safe retreat.*

Jesus at Jerusalem spends only the daytime in the city and
sleeps at night outside the walls at Bethany;[3] Agis at Sparta takes
sanctuary in the temple of Athena Chalcioecus (Plut., chap 16);

---

[1] In this Gospel the incident is placed in a different context.
[2] In this verse the woman—who in the Synoptic Gospels is anonymous—is identified
with Mary the sister of Lazarus.
[3] This is recounted in all four Gospels, but in the Gospel according to Saint John the
retreat at Bethany has a doublet in a retreat in Ephraim (John xi. 53–4).

Gaius Gracchus at Rome moves house from a fashionable quarter on the Palatine to a working-class quarter in the neighbourhood of the Forum (Plut., chap. 33).

22. *One of the hero's companions undertakes to betray him to the authorities by giving them an opportunity to arrest him at a moment when he is out of shelter.*

Judas undertakes to betray Jesus (Matt. xxvi. 14–16 = Mark xiv. 10–11 = Luke xxii. 3–6); Amphares undertakes to betray Agis (Plut., chap. 18).

23. *The traitor perpetrates his treachery for a trifling consideration.*

Judas for thirty pieces of silver (Matt. xxvi. 15); Amphares in the hope of being able to retain possession of some clothes and plate that he has recently borrowed from Agis' mother Agesistrata (Plut., chap. 18).

24. *The hero's Last Supper.*

Jesus's (Matt. xxvi. 17–29 = Mark xiv. 12–25 = Luke xxii. 7–38 = John xiii–xvii); Cleomenes' (Plut., chap. 58); Fulvius's (Plut., chap. 35); Cato Minor's (Plutarch: *Life of Cato Minor*, chap. 67).

N.B. The atmosphere at Fulvius's Last Supper is at the opposite extreme from the atmosphere at Cato's or Jesus's. In the stories of Jesus's and Cato's Passions the supper is eaten in a mood of sublime tension and with a sense of tragic foreboding, whereas Fulvius and his companions seek to drown care and banish any thought of the morrow by turning the meal into a drunken orgy. This scene of sordid debauchery serves as a foil to an agonizing vigil which, in the Roman story, is not subsequent to the supper but is contemporaneous with it and, by the same token, has a different protagonist. Fulvius and his companions carouse while Gaius Gracchus and his companions watch and pray (for Fulvius's role as the violent foil to Gaius Gracchus when Gaius himself is playing the gentle instead of the violent hero's part, see p. 378, above). Yet, although Fulvius's Last Supper may seem to present as great a contrast to Jesus's and Cato's Last Suppers as it does present, and is intended to present, to Gaius Gracchus's vigil, there is nevertheless a link between these two antithetical presentations of the Last Supper, and this is to be found in the account of Cleomenes' Last Supper. In this scene (Plut., chap. 58) the hero and his companions at table are really in the mood of Jesus and his disciples and of Cato and his circle; but they pretend to be in the mood of Fulvius and his companions in order to deceive the warders. In the scene in Cleomenes' prison, as in the scene in

Fulvius's house, there is a tableau of one (or some) of the carousers lying in a drunken sleep after the carouse is over (see Point 38, below); but, whereas in the Roman scene the drunken sleeper is the hero (in this case Fulvius) himself, in the Alexandrian scene it is the prison warders who are lying drunk and asleep; Cleomenes has deliberately reduced them to this condition in order to be able to effect his escape; and it has been in order to lure the warders into getting drunk that Cleomenes and his companions have pretended to be carousing, when really they have been steeling themselves for facing the ordeal of a forlorn hope.

25. *There are thirteen at table.*

At Jesus's last supper (Matt. xxvi. 20 = Mark xiv. 17 = Luke xxii. 14); at Cleomenes' Last Supper (Plut., chap. 58).

26. *The traitor is denounced (is suspected) at the supper.*

The denunciation of Judas (Matt. xxvi. 21–5 = Mark xiv. 18–21 = Luke xxii. 21–3 = John xiii. 18–22); the suspicion falling on Cleomenes' slave (Plut., chap. 58).

27. *The traitor goes (has gone) out.*

Judas (John xiii. 27–30); Cleomenes' slave (Plut., chap. 58).

28. *A tableau of a favourite companion lying on the hero's breast.*

John on Jesus's breast (John xiii. 23–6); Panteus on Cleomenes' breast (Plut., chap. 58); Philocrates on Gaius Gracchus's breast (Plut., chap. 38).

29. *A religious rite at which the hero gives the participants to eat of the flesh and drink of the blood of a human sacrificial victim.*[1]

Jesus at his Last Supper institutes the Communion-Rite of the Christian Church by giving his companions bread to eat and wine to drink as symbols of a metaphorical eating of his own flesh and drinking of his own blood (Matt. xxvi. 26–9 = Mark xiv. 22–5 = Luke xxii. 15–20); Catiline, at the secret meeting which he has convened in order to broach his conspiracy, sacrificially kills a slave and gives this human victim's flesh to eat (Plutarch: *Life of Cicero*, chap. 10; Dio Cassius: *History of Rome*, Book XXXVII, chap. 30) and his blood—mixed with wine—to drink (Sallust: *De Coniuratione Catilinae*, chap. 22) to those present before taking them into his confidence.

N.B. Cleomenes and his companions in prison at Alexandria

---

[1] The writer owes this point to Dr. Martin Braun.

revolt at the idea of waiting while they are fattened for slaughter 'like sacrificial victims' (Plut., chap. 57).[1]

30. *The hero declares to his companions at table his conviction that the death which now stares him in the face will prove a triumph.*

Jesus (John xiii. 31–2, and xvii); Cato Minor (Plutarch: *Life of Cato Minor*, chap. 67).

31. *The hero assures those at table who are his friends that in the hour of his triumph he will reward them for their friendship towards him.*

Jesus at his Last Supper (Luke xxii. 28–30; John xiv–xvi); Eunus at the supper-parties of his master Antigenes (Diodorus, Books XXXIV–XXXV, chap. 2, § 8).

32. *When the Last Supper is over, the hero calls for swords (for his sword).*

Jesus (Luke xxii. 35–8); Cato Minor (Plutarch: *Life of Cato Minor*, chap. 68). Fulvius and his companions equip themselves with arms that are hanging in Fulvius's house as spoils of war (Plut., chap. 36).

N.B. Tiberius Gracchus takes to wearing a dagger under his clothes when he finds, in the middle of his conflict with Octavius, that the Senatorial dominant minority are plotting to kill him (Plut., chap 10); Gaius Gracchus orders all his companions to carry swords under their togas (Diodorus, Books XXXIV–XXXV, chap. 28[a]).

33. *A tableau of the hero and his party going out into the open.*

Jesus and his companions going out on to the Mount of Olives (Matt. xxvi. 30 = Mark xiv. 26 = Luke xxii. 39 = John xviii. 1); Fulvius and his companions going out on to the Aventine (Plut., chap. 36); Cleomenes and his companions going out into the streets of Alexandria (Plut., chap. 58).

N.B. There is, however, a sharp discrepancy in respect of the time of day: Jesus and his companions go out at night (Matt. xxvi. 31 = Mark xiv. 27), Fulvius and his companions at dawn (Plut., chap. 36), Cleomenes and his companions at midday (Plut., chap. 58).

---

[1] Dr. Martin Braun brings into comparison the cock-and-bull story of the alleged Jewish practice of ritual murder, as recounted by Apion and quoted from this source by Josephus: *Contra Apionem*, Book II, §§ 91–6: 'The practice was repeated annually at a fixed season. They would kidnap a Greek foreigner, fatten him up for a year, and then convey him to a wood, where they slew him, sacrificed his body with their customary ritual, partook of his flesh, and, while immolating the Greek, swore an oath of hostility to the Greeks' (§ 95).

34. *An enthusiastic companion of the hero boasts that he will never desert his leader; but the hero disapproves of the boast and prophesies that it will not be lived up to when it comes to the point.*

Peter and Jesus (Matt. xxvi. 31–5 = Mark xiv. 27–31 = Luke xxii. 31–4 = John xiii. 36–8);[1] Statilius and Cato Minor (Plutarch: *Life of Cato Minor*, chaps. 55–6).

N.B. In the corresponding scene between Therycion and Cleomenes (Plut., chap. 52) Cleomenes disapproves of Therycion's proposal that the party of fugitives should commit suicide instead of leaving Laconian ground as refugees and seeking asylum in the dominions of Ptolemy; but in the sequel the parts are reversed. Therycion lives up to his proposal by duly committing suicide on the beach of Aegialia; Cleomenes does not follow his example on the spot, but does follow it at Alexandria after his disillusionment with his experience of exile (see further Points 54 and 84, below).

35. *The hero singles out three companions (one companion) for a task that demands special endurance.*

Jesus singles out Peter, James, and John to keep watch during his agony (Matt. xxvi. 37 = Mark xiv. 33); Cleomenes—having decided that he and his companions shall die by their own hands —singles out Panteus to wait till the last and make sure that all the rest are dead before putting an end to himself (Plut., chap. 58).

36. *A tableau of the hero in spiritual agony during the night before his dying day.*[2]

Jesus's agony of prayer to his Father at Gethsemane (Matt. xxvi. 36–46 = Mark xiv. 32–42 = Luke xxii. 40–6); Gaius Gracchus's agony of silent contemplation of his father's statue (Plut., chap. 35; cf. Diodorus, Books XXXIV–XXXV, chap. 28ª).[3]

N.B. In the picture of Jesus's agony in the Gospel according to Saint Luke the visual correspondence with the picture of Gaius Gracchus's agony is accentuated by the introduction of a feature that does not appear in the other two Synoptic Gospels: according to Saint Luke, Jesus's prayer is answered by the vision of an angel. It may be noted, as a curious though perhaps trivial detail, that, in Mantegna's picture of the agony of Jesus, which follows Luke on this point, the figures of the angels are distinctly statuesque.

---

[1] In the Gospels according to Saint Matthew and Saint Mark this incident is placed after the exit, on the road to the Mount of Olives; in the Gospels according to Saint Luke and Saint John it is placed before the exit, as a sequel to the denunciation of Judas.

[2] The correspondence between Jesus's and Gaius Gracchus's foreboding of his fate is noticed by Meyer, E.: *Ursprung und Anfänge des Christentums*, vol. i (Stuttgart and Berlin 1921, Cotta), p. 166.

[3] In Diodorus's narrative Gaius's agony is placed immediately before the murder of Antullus, and not in the night after it.

37. *Tableaux of a bodyguard* (α) *keeping watch* (β) *asleep.*

Jesus takes three of the eleven—Peter, James, and John—and asks them to keep watch while he prays, but three times over they fall asleep (Matt. xxvi. 37–46 = Mark xiv. 33–42 = Luke xxii. 45–6);[1] a number of Gaius Gracchus's supporters, seeing him in agony at his father's statue, accompany him home and spend the night at the door, where they organize themselves into watches which are on and off duty by turns (Plut., chap. 35). Similarly, on the night before the death of Tiberius Gracchus, a number of his supporters camp round Tiberius's house and keep watch (Plut., chap. 16).

38. *A tableau of watchers caught asleep at the moment of crisis.*

In Jesus's Passion Peter, James, and John are caught asleep at the moment when the officers of the Sanhedrin, guided by Judas, take them by surprise (Matt. xxvi. 45–6 = Mark xiv. 41–2); in Cleomenes' Passion the prison warders are caught asleep at the moment when Cleomenes and his companions break out (Plut., chap. 58); in Gaius Gracchus's Passion Fulvius is caught asleep when the return of daylight exposes the Gracchans to the danger of being attacked at any moment by the Government forces (Plut., chap. 36).

39. *The traitor fulfils his undertaking to give the authorities an opportunity of arresting the hero when he is out of shelter.*

Judas guides the officers of the Sanhedrin to the spot where Jesus is praying in Gethsemane (Matt. xxvi. 47 = Mark xiv. 43 = Luke xxii. 47 = John xviii. 2–3); Amphares (aided by Damochares and Arcesilaus) kidnaps Agis on the road back from a bath-house, outside the precincts of Athena Chalcioecus, which Agis has been visiting according to his practice, and drags him off, with the help of accomplices, to a prison which Leonidas then surrounds with a cordon of foreign professional soldiers (Plut., chap. 19).

40. *The traitor tries to put the hero off his guard by a heartlessly deceitful show of affection.*

Judas betrays Jesus with a kiss (Matt. xxvi. 48–9 = Mark xiv. 44–5 = Luke xxii. 47–8); Amphares and his two confederates waylay Agis [on his way back from the bath-house], give him a cordial greeting, and then go along with him—keeping up all the

---

[1] The Gospel according to Saint Luke does not record that three out of the eleven were picked out to keep watch, and does not represent the disciples as having fallen asleep more than once.

time a patter of talk and chaff, as one would with a young fellow
with whom one was on terms of familiarity (Plut., chap. 19).

41. *A tableau of a crowd in a hubbub, with lights.*

In the Passion of Jesus at the moment of the arrest (John xviii.
3); in the Passion of Agis between the passing of the death-
sentence and its execution (Plut., chap. 19).

N.B. Whereas in the story of Jesus the crowd is hostile to the
hero and intends to arrest him, in the story of Agis it is friendly
to the hero and intends to rescue him.

42. *The men who take violent action against the hero and his companions are armed with staves.*

The officers of the Sanhedrin who arrest Jesus (Matt. xxvi. 47
= Mark xiv. 43); the Senators who assault Tiberius Gracchus
(Plut., chap. 19).

N.B. In the Gospels according to Saint Matthew and Saint
Mark the phrase is μετὰ μαχαιρῶν καὶ ξύλων (which is telescoped
into μετὰ . . . ὅπλων in John xviii. 3); in Plutarch it runs περὶ αὐτοὺς
ῥόπαλα καὶ σκυτάλας ἐκόμιζον. In the story of the killing of Tiberius
Gracchus the point is made that, while there were more than 300
fatal casualties, not one of the victims was killed with cold steel.
The casualties were all inflicted with sticks and stones. Gracchus
himself was killed by being hit over the head with the leg of a
broken chair.

43. *The officers of the law are overcome by a momentary psychological inhibition.*

The officers of the Sanhedrin flinch from arresting Jesus (John
xviii. 6); the officers of the Ephors flinch from carrying out the
order to put Agis to death—and so do Leonidas' foreign professional soldiers (Plut., chap. 19).

44. *The hero's party sheds blood.*

One of Jesus's disciples draws his sword and strikes off the ear
of a servant of the High Priest (Matt. xxvi. 51 = Mark xiv. 47 =
Luke xxii. 50 = John xviii. 10);[1] Cleomenes and his companions
draw their swords, as they spring from table and rush into the
street, and cut down King Ptolemy's minister Ptolemy son of
Chrysermus and also another Ptolemy who is Chief of Police in
Alexandria (Plut., chap. 58); Tiberius Gracchus's partisans blind

---

[1] In the three Synoptic Gospels both the swordsman and his victim are anonymous.
It is only in the Gospel according to Saint John that the swordsman is identified with
Peter, and the victim's name is given as Malchus.

a slave of Octavius (Plut., chap. 12); Fulvius's companions stab to
death with stilettos an officer of the Consuls called Quintus
Antullus (Plut., chap. 34).

45. *The hero commands his followers to cease fighting.*

Jesus (Matt. xxvi. 52 = Luke xxii. 51 = John xviii. 11); Cleomenes (Plut., chap. 58); Tiberius Gracchus (Plut., chap. 12);
Gaius Gracchus (Plut., *Gracchi*, chap. 34, and *Comparison of Agis
and Cleomenes with the Gracchi*, chap. 5).

46. *The hero himself refrains on principle from resorting to force.*

Jesus (Matt. xxvi. 52–4, and John xviii. 36); Agis, of whom his
mother Agesistrata testifies, as she embraces his corpse: 'My child,
it is your immense moderation and gentleness and humanity that
have been your ruin—and ours' (Plut., chap. 20);[1] Tiberius
Gracchus (Plut., *Gracchi*, chap. 19, and *Comparison*, chap. 4);
Gaius Gracchus (Plut., *Gracchi*, chaps. 33, 34, and 36–8, and
Comparison, chaps. 4 and 5).[2]

N.B. This gentleness of Jesus, Agis, and both the Gracchi is
in contradiction with the violence that is exhibited by Cleomenes,
by all the futurist heroes, and also by Jesus and Gaius Gracchus
themselves in certain passages of their careers, before they arrive
at the crisis (see Point 1, above). Plutarch (*Agis and Cleomenes*,
chap. 22, and *Comparison*, chaps. 4–5) regretfully stigmatizes
Cleomenes—in contrast to Agis and the two Gracchi—as a man
of blood.

47. *The hero's companions take to flight and leave him to his fate.*

Jesus's (Matt. xxvi. 56 = Mark xiv. 50); Tiberius Gracchus's
(Plut., chap. 19).

48. *A tableau of a young man in flight leaving a wrap, which is
a badge of rank, in the clutches of (one of) his pursuers.*

In the flight of Jesus's companions an anonymous young man
leaves in the hands of the officers of the Sanhedrin a wrap of fine
linen (σινδών) and continues his flight naked (Mark xiv. 51–2); in
the flight of Tiberius Gracchus's partisans Tiberius himself leaves

---

[1] Compare the same author: *Comparison of Agis and Cleomenes with the Gracchi*
chap. 3: 'Rather than cause the death of a single one of his countrymen, Agis met his
own death almost voluntarily.'

[2] According to Diodorus, Books XXXIV–XXXV, chap. 28ᵃ, Gaius himself knocked
Antullus down and told his followers to kill him; but this story is rejected by Plutarch
(*Comparison*, chap. 5). According to Plutarch (*Gracchi*, chap. 34), the crime was committed by Fulvius's men, and Gracchus, so far from wanting it, was deeply upset by it
and indignantly upbraided the perpetrators. Plutarch's version of the incident is supported by Appian (*Studies in Roman History: The Civil Wars*, Book I, chap. 25).

his toga in the hands of one of the assailants and continues his flight in his shirt (Plut., chap. 19).

49. *The hero is arrested and is then immediately brought to an impromptu trial during the night.*

Jesus is brought to trial in the High Priest's palace before the Chief Priests and the Sanhedrin (Matt. xxvi. 57 = Mark xiv. 53 = Luke xxii. 54 = John xviii. 13 and 24);[1] Agis is brought to trial in the prison before the Ephors and some members of the Gerusia (Plut., chap. 19).

50. *A true saying of the hero's is dishonestly twisted by his enemies into a misrepresentation which is extremely damaging to him.*

Jesus has said that the Temple at Jerusalem is going to be destroyed (Matt. xxiv. 1–2 = Mark xiii. 1–2 = Luke xxi. 5–6);[2] on an earlier occasion he has also said that he himself is greater than the Temple (Matt. xii. 6); at his trial the false witnesses represent him as having said that he is able to destroy (or will destroy) the Temple and is able to build (or will build) another in three days (without having to use the ordinary physical means of construction) (Matt. xxvi. 60–1 = Mark xiv. 57–8).[3]

Similarly Tiberius Gracchus, in a public apologia for his high-handed and unconstitutional act of deposing his colleague Octavius, argues that a Tribune of the Plebs is sacrosanct only in virtue of having been consecrated to the service of the Plebs, and that he therefore automatically deposes himself from office if he misuses his power in order to do the opposite of what is his proper function. 'A Tribune of the Plebs who demolished the Capitol and set fire to the naval dockyard would have to be left in office; for if he committed these crimes he would still be a Tribune of the Plebs, however bad a one; but, if he set out to bring the Plebs to ruin, then he would no longer be a Tribune. . . . Again, nothing can be so sacrosanct as votive offerings (ἀναθήματα)[4] to the Gods; yet nobody has ever thought of estopping the Plebs from using and moving and transferring such offerings as it thinks fit. On this

---

[1] In the Gospel according to Saint John the impromptu trial is resolved into two hearings in different places and before different judges—the first before Annas and the second before Caiaphas.

[2] In Luke xix. 44 the same phrase is applied to the whole city of Jerusalem.

[3] This alleged saying of Jesus that is placed in the mouths of the false witnesses at the trial in the Gospels according to Saint Matthew and Saint Mark is placed in Jesus's own mouth, in quite a different context, in the Gospel according to Saint John (ii. 18–22), where it is accepted as being authentic and is then interpreted as being metaphorical (i.e. as an enigmatic prophecy of the Resurrection).

[4] Cf. Luke xxi. 5–6, *cit. supra*: 'And as some spake of the Temple, how it was adorned with goodly stones and gifts (ἀναθήμασι), he said: "As for these things which ye behold, the days will come in the which there shall not be left one stone upon another that shall not be thrown down." '

showing, the Plebs is entitled to transfer the Tribunate of the Plebs—which is a votive offering to the Plebs itself—from one incumbent to another' (Plut., chap. 15). On the strength of this speech of Tiberius's, his companion Blossius, in a judicial examination before the Consuls to which he is subjected after Tiberius's death, is asked by Nasica: 'What would you have done if Tiberius had ordered you to set fire to the Capitol?'

Again, when Cleomenes' enemy Nicagoras of Messene wants to compromise Cleomenes in the eyes of King Ptolemy Philopator, he first reports to Ptolemy's minister Sosibius a satirical remark about the King which Cleomenes has really made to Nicagoras. Since, however, the genuine saying of Cleomenes is just personally offensive without being also politically treasonable, Sosibius persuades Nicagoras to write him a letter alleging—what is a sheer fabrication—that Cleomenes has made up his mind to seize Cyrene if Nicagoras will find him the necessary ships and men (Plut., chap. 56).

51. *The hero on trial is reproved by the authorities for contempt of court.*

Jesus is reproved by the High Priest for making no answer to the witnesses' charges against him (Matt. xxvi. 62–3 = Mark xiv. 60–1). Alternatively, he is struck by one of the officers of the court for replying to a question from Annas—not Caiaphas—about his disciples and his doctrine with the answer that all this is a matter of public knowledge (John xviii. 19–23).[1] Similarly Agis at his trial is reproved by Amphares for having burst out laughing at his judges' hypocrisy (Plut., chap. 19).

52. *When a question is put to the hero which offers him a possible line of retreat, the hero does not take the opening, but gives, instead, an answer that is calculated to exasperate the Court more than anything else that he could conceivably have said.*

When the High Priest asks Jesus whether he is (α) the Messiah (β) the Son of God, Jesus, instead of recanting, answers both questions in the affirmative in the most emphatic terms possible (Matt. xxvi. 63–4 = Mark xiv. 61–2 = Luke xxii. 66–70).[2] Simi-

---

[1] The saying that is presented in the Gospel according to Saint John as Jesus's answer to Annas is presented in the Synoptic Gospels (Matt. xxvi. 55 = Mark xiv. 48–9 = Luke xxii. 52–3) as being said at Gethsemane to the officers of the Sanhedrin between the moment when, at Jesus's command, the disciples cease fighting, and the moment when the officers place Jesus under arrest.

[2] In the Gospels according to Saint Matthew and Saint Mark the two questions are telescoped into one and the two claims are treated as though they were synonymous. On the other hand in the Gospel according to Saint Luke the Court first asks Jesus whether he is the Messiah, and it is the terms of his answer to this question—an answer

larly, when one of the Ephors (not Amphares) asks Agis (α) whether he has been acting under pressure from Lysander and Agesilaus and (β) whether he repents of what he has done, Agis replies to the first question that he has been acting as an entirely free agent and that his source of inspiration has been Lycurgus, while to the second question he replies that he does not repent of what he has done because his policy has been the best that could be conceived (Plut., chap. 19).

53. *On the strength of the hero's answers to the two test questions the Court immediately passes sentence of death upon him.*

Upon Jesus (Matt. xxvi. 65–6 = Mark xiv. 63–4 = Luke xxii. 71);[1] upon Agis (Plut., chap. 19).

54. *The hero's prophecy regarding his enthusiastic companion's boast [see Point 34, above] is fulfilled by the failure of the boaster to live up to it when it comes to the point.*

Peter does not live up to his resolution never to desert Jesus (Matt. xxvi. 69–75 = Mark xiv. 66–72 = Luke xxii. 54–62 = John xviii. 15–18 and 25–7); Statilius does not live up to his resolution of following suit to Cato Minor in committing suicide (Plutarch: *Life of Cato Minor*, chap. 73). (See further Point 84, below.)

55. *The authorities seek to enlist the aid of a foreign potentate for the accomplishment of their purpose of bringing the hero to destruction.*

The Jews bring their fellow countryman Jesus before the Roman Procurator, Pontius Pilate, because the power of life and death is in his hands and not in theirs, so that the sentence of death which they have passed on Jesus cannot be executed unless Pilate endorses it (Matt. xxvii. 1–2 = Mark xv. 1 = Luke xxiii. 1 = John xviii. 28 and 31). The Achaeans make a military alliance against their fellow Peloponnesian, Cleomenes, with the Macedonian King Antigonus Dôsôn, because they realize that, without the support of Macedon, they will be unable to crush a Sparta which enjoys the support of Egypt.

in which Jesus claims to be the Son of Man (see V. C (i) (*d*) 11, vol. v, p. 163, footnote 1, above)—that then move the Court to ask, in horror and indignation, 'Art thou then the Son of God?' Of these two versions of the incident the Lucan account alone is in consonance with Jewish beliefs; for according to Jewish doctrine the Messiah is to be, not a son of God, but a son of David (see V. C (i) (*d*) 11, vol. v, p. 163, footnote 1, and V. C (ii) (*a*), in the present volume, p. 268, footnote 5, above); and the suggestion that God has any son at all—and *a fortiori* a son incarnate in a man—is the greatest conceivable blasphemy against God's unity and majesty. It is attributing to the One True God a *bassesse* that is attributed to the false gods of Olympus by the Hellenes.

[1] Cf. John xix. 7.

56. *The animus of the hero's enemies in his own household is so intense that they are willing to purchase the foreign potentate's aid at the price of sacrificing one of their own most cherished principles.*

In order to force Pilate to put Jesus to death, the Jews accuse Jesus of having committed high treason against the Roman Imperial Government by declaring himself to be a king—though this indictment involves the Jews themselves in an admission of the legality of the Roman jurisdiction (Luke xxiii. 2, and John xix. 12–15). In order to induce Antigonus to throw his weight into the scales against Cleomenes, the Achaeans submit again to the hegemony of Macedon—which they have made it their mission to throw off—and re-admit a Macedonian garrison into the Acrocorinthus, though this fortress is the strategic key to the military command of the Peloponnese, and the greatest achievement in the past career of the Achaeans' leader Aratus has been his feat of wresting the Acrocorinthus out of Macedonian clutches some twenty years back.

57. *The hero maintains his claim to kingship before the face of a foreign potentate in whose power he finds himself.*

Jesus before Pilate (Matt. xxvii. 11–14 = Mark xv. 2–5 = Luke xxiii. 3 = John xviii. 33–8);[1] Cleomenes before Ptolemy Euergetes (Plut., chap. 53); the Syrian slave Eunus before his Sicilian master Antigenes (Diodorus, Books XXXIV–XXXV, chap. 2, § 8).

58. *The hero will not accept the good offices of the representative of a potentate who is all-powerful.*

Jesus will not accept Pilate's invitation to reply to the charges against him which the Jewish authorities have repeated in Pilate's presence (Matt. xxvii. 12–14 = Mark xv. 3–5); Cato Minor will not accept Lucius Caesar's offer to intercede on his behalf with Lucius's victorious kinsman Gaius (Plutarch: *Life of Cato Minor*, chap. 66).

59. *The impression which the hero makes on a foreign potentate is a favourable one.*

Pilate is favourably impressed by Jesus (Matt. xxvii. 23 = Mark xv. 14 = Luke xxiii. 22; Luke xxiii. 4 and 14–15 = John xviii. 38,

---

[1] The maintenance of the claim to kingship is implied in all four Gospels alike, but they differ from one another in their account of the way in which Jesus conveys his meaning. According to Saint Matthew and Saint Mark he conveys it by a bare assent to Pilate's proposition, followed by silence in face of the charges that are repeated against him, in Pilate's presence, by the Jewish authorities; according to Saint Luke by a bare assent to Pilate's proposition; according to Saint John by an exposition of the 'Other-worldly' nature of his kingdom.

and xix. 4 and 6); Ptolemy Euergetes is favourably impressed by Cleomenes (Plut., chap. 53).[1]

60. *The hero's fate is affected by an official custom relating to the release of a prisoner.*

At Jerusalem there is a custom that, at the Feast of the Passover, the Roman procurator releases one prisoner, at the people's choice; but, when Pilate offers them the choice between Jesus and Barabbas, they choose Barabbas (Matt. xxvii. 15–26 = Mark xv. 6–15 = Luke xxiii. 16–25 = John xviii. 39–40). At Alexandria there is a custom that a dinner and gifts are sent on the King's behalf to a prisoner who is going to be released; and Cleomenes takes advantage of this custom in order to make his warders believe that his own release has been decreed (Plut., chap. 58).

61. *A potentate who has the hero's fate in his hands allows himself, out of cowardice, in consideration of an embarrassing incidental consequence of the hero's claim to kingship, to be persuaded, against his own conscience, into condemning the hero to an undeserved penalty.*

Pilate condemns Jesus to be crucified for fear that, if he acquits him, his claim to kingship—even though Pilate himself may be aware that the kingship claimed by Jesus is not of the literal mundane kind—may be represented by the Jews to the Emperor as a treasonable pretension which Pilate has culpably neglected to repress (John xviii. 28–40, and xix. 1–16; a hint of the consideration which has prevailed with Pilate is also given in Luke xxiii. 23, when this is read together with Luke xxiii. 2). Ptolemy Philopator condemns Cleomenes to be interned[2] because he fears that, if he lets him go, he may become a public danger to the Ptolemaic state owing to his popularity with the Peloponnesian mercenaries in the Ptolemaic service and his first-hand acquaintance with the weakness of the Ptolemaic régime (Plut., chaps. 54–6).

[1] Euergetes gave his admiration for Cleomenes the g *A History of Egypt under the* erecting a statue of Cleomenes at Olympia (see Bevan, E.: *Ptolemaic Dynasty* (London 1927, Methuen), p. 221).

[2] If internment be thought too mild a penalty to be compared with crucifixion, it may be recalled that, whereas Pilate had no obligation towards Jesus except that (on which he, like Philopator, defaulted) of doing justice, Cleomenes was Philopator's guest; that Cleomenes was, moreover, a political refugee towards whom the Ptolemaic Government had obligations of honour; that no formal charges had been brought against him; that, while the penalty of internment may have been mild in itself, its infliction did in fact bring about Cleomenes' death; and, last but not least, that Philopator's ministers had never intended to allow Cleomenes to come out of prison alive (see Plut., chap. 57), though they had not calculated upon getting rid of Cleomenes by way of the heroic and spectacular death which their prisoner succeeded in winning for himself in despite of their cat-and-mouse tactics.

62. *The potentate is subject to a feminine influence which inclines him to be superstitious.*

Pilate under the influence of his wife (Matt. xxvii. 19); Ptolemy Philopator under the influence of his mistress Agathoclea and her mother Oenanthe (Plut., chaps. 54 and 60).

63. *After having, out of cowardice, sent the hero to an undeserved death, the potentate attempts to salve the pricks of conscience by performing a ritual of purification.*

Pilate (Matt. xxvii. 24–5); Ptolemy Philopator (Plut., chap. 60).

64. *A tableau of a Roman ostentatiously washing his hands in public (immediately after he has been instrumental in bringing upon a fellow human being a death by protracted torture).*[1]

Pilate washing his hands, in front of his own tribunal, after having sentenced Jesus to crucifixion (Matt. xxvii. 24); Catiline washing his hands, in front of Sulla's tribunal, in the holy water basin at the door of a temple of Apollo, after having brought to Sulla the head of Marcus Marius (Plutarch: *Life of Sulla*, chap. 32), upon whom Catiline has just inflicted 'the death of a thousand cuts' (Seneca: *De Ira*, Book III, chap. 18).

65. *The hero's claim to kingship is callously turned to ridicule.*

Jesus's claim is ridiculed, after Pilate has condemned him to death, by Pilate's soldiers (Matt. xxvii. 27–31 = Mark xv. 16–20), or, alternatively,[2] by Herod's soldiers before Pilate has condemned him to death (Luke xxiii. 11); Eunus's claim is ridiculed by the guests of his master Antigenes: 'The thing [i.e. the slave Eunus's prophecy that one day he would be a king] was taken as a joke and Antigenes, who was entertained by the hocus-pocus, took to producing Eunus at his dinner-parties and cross-questioning him about his kingship.' Eunus's answers used to cause merriment among the guests (Diodorus, Books XXXIV–XXXV, chap. 2, § 8).

N.B. The Lucan story of the mocking of Jesus before the Crucifixion corresponds more closely than the alternative story with the episode in the history of Eunus: in the first place Herod as tetrarch of Galilee, is in the political sense Jesus's master, and it is expressly on this account that Pilate remits Jesus to him (Luke xxiii. 5–7); in the second place Jesus is an object of curiosity as well as of amusement (Luke xxiii. 8); in the third place the way

---

[1] The writer owes this point to Dr. Martin Braun.
[2] The version according to Saint John (xix. 2–3) stands midway between the two main variants of the story. According to Saint John the mocking is done by Pilate's soldiers and not by Herod's, but this before, and not after, Pilate has passed the sentence of crucifixion.

in which Herod and his soldiers turn Jesus's claim to ridicule is heartless without being physically cruel (as the Roman soldiers' mockery is cruel in the alternative version of the story).

66. *A tableau of the hero being invested in private with a royal crown (diadem) and robe to which he is not entitled.*

Jesus (Matt. xxvii. 28–9 = Mark xv. 17–18 = Luke xxii. 11 = John xix. 2–3);[1] Tiberius Gracchus: 'Pompeius rose in the Senate in order to depose that he was a neighbour of Tiberius's and that in this way it had come to his knowledge that Tiberius had been presented with a diadem and a purple robe, belonging to the Pergamene regalia, by the Pergamene envoy Eudêmus, in anticipation of Tiberius's becoming King in Rome' (Plut., chap. 14).

67. *A tableau of the hero being exhibited in public as a claimant to kingship.*

'Pilate therefore went forth again and saith unto them: "Behold, I bring him forth to you that ye may know that I find no fault in him." Then came Jesus forth, wearing the crown of thorns and the purple robe. And Pilate saith unto them: "Behold the man!" ' (John xix. 4–5). 'The people who were farther off were puzzled about what was going on and were trying to find out; so Tiberius touched his head with his hand as a visual signal—for the benefit of those to whom his voice did not carry—of the danger in which he found himself. When his enemies saw him do this they ran to the Senate to report that Tiberius was asking for a diadem and that this was the significance of his gesture of touching his head' (Plut., chap. 19).

68. *On the hero's way to his execution, people (a person) accompanying him are (is) in tears, whereupon the hero declares that, notwithstanding his present plight, his own lot is nevertheless relatively enviable.*

'And there followed him a great company of people and of women, which also bewailed and lamented him. But Jesus, turning unto them, said: "Daughters of Jerusalem, weep not for me, but weep for yourselves and for your children" ' (Luke xxiii. 27–8). 'On his way to the gallows Agis saw one of the officers of the law

[1] In the Lucan story of the mockery of Jesus by Herod and his men, only the robe is mentioned, and not the crown. (N.B. This follows from the omission of the element of physical cruelty, since the crown in the alternative story is a crown of thorns.) In the Johannine version of the story of the mockery of Jesus by Pilate's soldiers the crown is mentioned as well as the robe, but there is no mention of the reed which figures in the Marcan and Matthaean versions of the same story. According to Mark (xv. 19) they smote him on the head with a reed; according to Matthew (xxvii. 29–30) they first put the reed into his right hand to simulate a sceptre; according to John (xix. 3) they smote him with their hands.

crying and showing other signs of deep distress, whereupon he said to him: "My friend, stop weeping for me. When I am being put to death as illegally and unjustly as I am, I have the moral advantage over my murderers" ' (Plut., chap. 20).

69. *The hero is crucified.*

Jesus (Matt. xxvii. 35 = Mark xv. 24 = Luke xxiii. 33 = John xix. 18); Cleomenes (Plut., chaps. 59 and 60).

N.B. Whereas Jesus is put to death by crucifixion, Cleomenes dies by his own hand (Plut., chap. 58), and it is only his corpse that is crucified. Agis—who, like Jesus, is put to death, instead of committing suicide like Cleomenes[1]—is not crucified but is hanged (Plut., chaps. 19 and 20).

70. *Two other persons are put to death at the same time as the hero and in the same fashion.*

The two thieves are crucified with Jesus (Matt. xxvii. 38 = Mark xv. 27 = Luke xxiii. 32–3 = John xix. 18); Agis's grandmother Archidamia and his mother Agesistrata are hanged with Agis (Plut., chap. 20).

N.B. In the Spartan story the three victims are hanged, not on separate gallows side by side, but on the same gallows one after another; but the three corpses are brought out together (Plut., chap. 21).

71. *The shirt (χιτών) in which the hero has gone to his death is made of a single piece of stuff without a seam.*

Jesus's shirt (John xix. 23); Cleomenes' shirt (Plut., chap. 58).

N.B. The two shirts are, however, seamless for different reasons: Jesus's because it has been originally so woven; Cleomenes' because, at the moment before he rushes out into the street, he rips open the original seam down the right sleeve in order to give free play to his sword-arm.

72. *On an occasion on which the hero's claim to kingship is being turned to ridicule by most of those present, one person (some people) accords (accord) recognition to his claim and asks (ask) to be remembered by him when he enters into his kingdom. The hero grants his (their) petition by giving him (them) a dazzling reward for his (their) act of homage.*

While Jesus on the Cross is being mocked by the people, by the rulers, by the soldiers, and by the Impenitent Thief, the Penitent

---

[1] The suicide of Cleomenes and his companions in the streets of Alexandria has a correspondence in the suicide of the Sicilian insurgent-slave-leader Satyrus and his companions on the public altars in the amphitheatre at Rome (Diodorus, Book XXXVI, chap. 10, §§ 2–3).

Thief 'said unto Jesus: "Lord, remember me when thou comest into thy kingdom." And Jesus said unto him: "Verily I say unto thee, to-day shalt thou be with me in Paradise" ' (Luke xxiii. 35–43).[1] When Eunus's master, at his dinner-parties, used to cross-question Eunus about his kingdom [see Point 65, above], one of the questions that he used to ask was 'how he would behave, when king, to each member of the present company. Eunus used to go through his story without turning a hair, explain how kind he would be to the masters, and in fact perform his hocus-pocus so extravagantly as to move the guests to laughter. Some of the guests used to take handsome portions from the table and present them to him with the request that he would remember the favour when he came into his kingdom—and actually, as it turned out, the hocus-pocus ended in Eunus's becoming king in truth and deed, and in his recompensing in sober earnest the favours that had been shown him by those who, at the dinner-parties, had paid him a mock-deference. . . . After his proclamation as king, Eunus put all [the slave-owners] to death with the sole exception of those who, under the *ancien régime*, had welcomed him at dinner-parties or at his spiritualist *séances* when he went out into society with his master, and who had shown their good will in presenting him with portions from the table. These old friends he now surreptitiously set at liberty' (Diodorus, Books XXXIV–XXXV, chap. 2, §§ 8–9 and 41).

73. *The hero's mother is supported in her ordeal by the hero's favourite companion (by the favourite companion's wife).*

Jesus's mother by John (John xix. 25–7); Cleomenes' mother by Panteus' wife (Plut., chap. 59).

74. *The end of an ordeal.*

'He said: "It is finished"; and he bowed his head and gave up the ghost' (John xix. 30). 'When it [i.e. Cleomenes' death-agony] was finished, he [Panteus] . . . slew himself' (Plut., chap. 58).

75. *The hero, hanging dead on the Cross, is hailed as the Son of God (a child of the Gods) under the impression of a portent that is witnessed by the soldiers on duty at the foot of the Cross.*

'Now when the centurion and they that were with him, watching Jesus, saw the earthquake and those things that were done, they feared greatly, saying: "Truly this was the Son of God" ' (Matt.

[1] The mocking of Jesus on the Cross is narrated also in the two other Synoptic Gospels (though not in the Gospel according to Saint John); but according to both Saint Matthew (xxvii. 39–44) and Saint Mark (xv. 29–32) *both* the thieves that are being crucified with Jesus join in abusing him.

xxvii. 54).[1] 'The soldiers who were on guard by Cleomenes' crucified corpse saw a large snake wound round the head and covering the face,[2] with the result that no carrion-eating bird alighted on it. This portent threw the King into a state of superstitious fear—which gave his women an excuse for starting a fresh bout of purifications—in case the man whom he had put to death might have been peculiarly dear to God and not of any common clay. The populace of Alexandria went farther. They showed their respect by making pilgrimages to the spot and hailing Cleomenes as a hero[3] and a child of the Gods' (Plut., chap. 60).

76. *After the hero's death there is a revulsion of public feeling in his favour.*

While Jesus was still hanging alive on the Cross, 'the people stood beholding, and the rulers also with them derided him' (Luke xxiii. 35); but, as soon as he had expired, 'all the people that came together to that sight, beholding the things that were done, smote their breasts and returned' (Luke xxiii. 48). Similarly the Alexandrians, who had not moved a foot to follow Cleomenes, or lifted a finger to help him, when he was calling to them, in their streets, to join him in a fight for freedom (Plut., chap. 58), afterwards paid his crucified corpse a semi-religious veneration (Plut., chap. 60, quoted under Point 75, above). And the Roman Plebs, after allowing the Gracchi to be done to death by the Senatorial dominant minority, afterwards demonstrated their love and their sorrow for them by paying them religious honours (Plut., chap. 39).[4]

---

[1] According to Saint Mark (xv. 39) the centurion utters the words attributed to him according to Saint Matthew, but here it is not stated that he is speaking under the impression of the experience of a miracle. According to Saint Luke the centurion is neither speaking under the impression of a miracle, nor does he hail Jesus as the Son of God ('Now when the centurion saw what was done, he glorified God, saying: "Certainly this was a righteous man" ' (Luke xxiii. 47)).

[2] The same portent was related of Spartacus—not, however, after death, but in sleep, when his career still lay, unsuspected, before him—and his wife, who was a fortune-teller, interpreted the portent (as Ptolemy Philopator did when it happened to Cleomenes' corpse) as a sign of greatness ('It is said that, when he was first brought to Rome to be sold, a snake was seen wound round his face as he slept. His wife, who was of the same tribe and who had the gift of divination, besides being a Bacchanal, interpreted the portent as a sign that he was going to rise to something very great and formidable, but with an unlucky ending' (Plutarch: *Life of Crassus*, chap. 8, adopting Reiske's conjecture ἀτυχές for εὐτυχές). A similar portent was related of Bar Kōkabā. His corpse, in contrast to that of Jesus and that of Cleomenes, was not preserved intact (see Point 78, below), but was mutilated; and thereafter a snake was found coiled, not round his head, but round his severed privy parts (see Lagrange, M.-J.: *Le Messianisme chez les Juifs* (Paris 1909, Gabalda), p. 320). Again, Tiberius Gracchus took it as a bad omen when snakes hatched out their eggs in his helmet (Plutarch: *Gracchi*, chap. 17).—A.J.T.

[3] In its original, and technical, Hellenic sense the word hero has a connotation which is a cross between those of our two Western words 'demigod' and 'saint'.—A.J.T.

[4] The judicial murders of Agis and his mother and his grandmother likewise aroused indignation among the public at Sparta (Plut., chap. 21); but here the correspondence is imperfect, because in this case the public, so far from having been hostile or even indifferent, had made a move to rescue the hero, and this move had only been foiled by a *fait accompli* (Plut., chap. 19).

77. *The two other persons who are put to death at the same time as the hero do not die till after he is dead.*

The two thieves not till after Jesus (John xix. 32–3); Archidamia and Agesistrata not till after Agis (Plut., chap. 20).

78. *Contrary to what usually happens to a crucified corpse,[1] the hero's corpse remains physically intact.*

Jesus dies so unexpectedly soon (Mark xv. 44–5) that, when the soldiers come with the intention of breaking the legs of the bodies on the crosses in order to hasten their deaths, they find it unnecessary to break Jesus's legs, because he is already dead, so they only break the legs of the two thieves (John xix. 31–3). Cleomenes' corpse is protected from being eaten by carrion-birds through the portent of the snake that winds itself round the head and covers the face (see Point 75, above).

79. *When a soldier pricks the hero's body with the point of a weapon, in order to test whether life is completely extinct, the body gives an unexpected sign of life.*

When a Roman soldier pierces Jesus's side with a spear, blood flows (John xix. 34); when Panteus pricks Cleomenes' ankle with a dagger, Cleomenes' face twitches (Plut., chap. 58).

80. *While the hero is being put to death, some women, with whom he is in an intimate relation, are in the vicinity, though not actually on the spot.*

The Crucifixion of Jesus is witnessed from a distance by Galilaean women whose link with Jesus is not one of kinship but one of personal devotion, and who have shown this devotion by coming to Jerusalem in his entourage; among them are Mary Magdalene, Mary the mother of James and Joses, and the mother of Zebedee's children or (? *alias*) Salome (Matt. xxvii. 55–6 = Mark xv. 40–1 = Luke xxiii. 49).[2] While Agis is being hanged inside the building

---

[1] When Polycrates the despot of Samos received a tempting invitation from Oroetes the Achaemenian satrap of Sardis, he suspected a trap but felt inclined to take the risk. While he was still in two minds whether to accept or to refuse, his daughter had a dream in which she saw her father aloft in the air, being washed by Zeus and anointed by the Sun. In consideration of this dream, she begged her father not to go; and, when he did go all the same, her worst forebodings were fulfilled; for the invitation *was* a trap, and Oroetes, after putting Polycrates to death by tortures too horrible to describe, inflicted on his victim the last indignity of crucifying his corpse. 'So, hanging on the cross, Polycrates fulfilled every particular of his daughter's vision. He was washed by Zeus when it rained, and he was anointed by the Sun when the corpse itself exuded liquid matter' (Herodotus, Book III, chaps. 122–5, already quoted in IV. C (iii) (c) 1, vol. iv, pp. 252–3, above).

[2] Though the Gospel according to Saint Luke mentions no names, it agrees with the other two Synoptic Gospels in describing the women as Galilaeans and stating that they witnessed the Crucifixion from a distance. On the other hand the Gospel according to Saint John (xix. 25), which does mention names, is in implicit, and perhaps deliberate,

called the Dechas, his mother Agesistrata and his grandmother Archidamia are outside, making an outcry (Plut., chap. 19–20).

81. *A tableau of the descent from the Cross (or gallows).*

The dead body of Jesus being lowered from the Cross by men who are being assisted by the women of Jesus's entourage (there is no text in the Gospels describing this event;[1] yet, all the same, the scene is one of the favourite subjects of the traditional iconography of the Christian Church); the dead body of Agis' grandmother, Archidamia, being lowered from the gallows by officers of the law who are being assisted by Agis' mother—who is Archidamia's daughter—Agesistrata (Plut., chap. 20).

82. *A tableau of the Pietà.*

The dead body of Jesus at the foot of the Cross being tended by Joseph of Arimathaea (with the women's assistance)[2] (Matt. xxvii. 59 = Mark xv. 46 = Luke xxiii. 53 = John xix. 39–40); the dead bodies of Agis and Archidamia, at the foot of the gallows, being tended by Agesistrata (Plut., chap. 20).

N.B. The dead body of Tiberius Gracchus is refused to the dead man's brother by the Government, even when he offers to bury it unobtrusively by night (Plut., chap. 20).

83. *The hero, after his death, comes to receive religious worship.*

Jesus from the Christian Church; the Gracchi from the Roman Plebs: 'They dedicated to them statues, which they erected in public places; they consecrated the spots that had been the scenes of their deaths; and they offered there the first-fruits of all the produce of the seasons, while many people actually made it a daily

---

[1] contradiction with the Synoptic Gospels on two points. In the first place it names, as having been present, Mary Magdalene, Mary the wife of Cleophas (? *alias* Mary the mother of James and Joses) and—in place of the mother of Zebedee's children (? *alias* Salome)—Mary the mother of Jesus, whose name does not occur in the other Gospels in this context. In the second place the women are standing, according to Saint John, not at a distance, but close to the Cross (xix. 25), within speaking distance (xix. 26–7). In this second feature the version of the incident according to Saint John has a correspondence in the epilogue to the Passion of Cleomenes, in which (not the hero but) the hero's children are put to death in the immediate presence of the hero's mother (Plut., chap. 59).

[1] The only hint of it is to be found in the adverbial prefix 'down', which is attached to the verb 'take' in Luke xxiii. 53; but the Lucan word καθελών is manifestly an unwarrantable amplification of the Matthaean word λαβών. What is being recorded here is not the physical descent of the body from the Cross, but the legal delivery of it to Joseph of Arimathaea by Pilate.

[2] The participation of the women, which is given such prominence in the traditional treatment of the subject in the iconography of the Christian Church, is not mentioned in the Gospels. In the Gospel according to Saint John (xix. 39–40), which is the only Gospel in which Joseph of Arimathaea is represented as having assistance, he is assisted, not by the women, but by Nicodemus. In the Synoptic Gospels (Matt. xxvii. 61 = Mark xv. 47 = Luke xxiii. 55) the women are represented as following at a distance in order to mark the place where the body is being buried.

practice to visit these spots in order to offer sacrifice and to pay
their devotions—just as if they were visiting temples of gods'
(Plut., chap. 39).

84. *The hero's enthusiastic companion makes good, after the hero's
death, the boast to which he has failed to live up during the hero's
Passion* [*see Points* 34 *and* 54, *above*].

Peter in the Acts; Statilius at Philippi (Plutarch: *Life of Cato
Minor*, chap. 73).

N.B. As between Therycion and Cleomenes, the parts are
reversed (see Point 34, above). Therycion lives up to Spartan
ideals by practising at once the suicide that he preaches, while it
is Cleomenes who does belatedly at Alexandria what Therycion
had done betimes at Aegialia.

85. *The villain perishes miserably.*

Judas commits suicide (Matt. xxvii. 3–10, and Acts i. 16–20);
Nasica has to flee the country, and he dies a premature death
abroad after roaming disconsolately (like Cain or the Wandering
Jew) (Plut., chap. 21); Opimius is convicted of having taken
bribes from Jugurtha, and he dies in disgrace (Plut., chap. 39).

86. *The most effective executor of the hero's purpose, after the
hero's death, is a convert of a younger generation who has never been
in personal relations with the hero, has been brought up as a fanatical
opponent of his cause, and is indirectly tainted with the blood-guiltiness for the hero's death.*

Jesus's executor Paul; Agis' executor Cleomenes, who is the son
of Agis' deadly enemy King Leonidas.

87. *The executor's conversion is partly due to the twofold influence
of a martyr who is devoted to the dead hero's person and of a sage who
is sympathetic to the dead hero's ideas.*

Paul is influenced by (α) his victim Stephen (Acts vii. 58–60, and
viii. 1) and (β) his mentor Gamaliel (Paul's early studies under
Gamaliel are mentioned in Acts xxii. 3, and Gamaliel's plea, in the
Sanhedrin, for toleration of the Apostles is recorded in Acts v.
33–40). Cleomenes is influenced by (α) Agis' widow Agiatis, who
has been forcibly married to the young Cleomenes through the
tyranny of Cleomenes' father King Leonidas (Plut., chap. 22) and
(β) his mentor Sphaerus of Borysthenes, under whom he has
studied as a child (Plut., chap. 23).[1]

---

[1] For the question whether Sphaerus had been Agis' mentor as well see V. C (ii) (a),
p. 249, footnote 2, above.

A Synopsis of Results

Our survey of correspondences between the Gospels and the stories of certain pagan heroes of the Hellenic internal proletariat and dominant minority has now yielded us a considerable harvest; but in order to make some effective use of these abundant materials for study we must first sift them out and arrange them in order. Our first need is to make a concordance of the literary authorities from which our evidence has been drawn (Table I). This will give us a basis for submitting the correspondences to a numerical analysis (Tables II and III), and after that we shall find ourselves able to pass from a purely quantitative to a partly qualitative treatment of our materials by singling out, for separate study, several different kinds of common features which our set of correspondences will be found to display. The correspondences work themselves out into an identical drama which appears, at least in essence and outline, to underly the whole of this group of hero-stories, pagan and Christian alike. And this drama has certain common characters (Table IV) common scenes (Tables V and VI), common properties (Table VII), and even common words (Tables VIII and IX).

The synopsis has been reduced as far as possible to tabular form in order to enable the reader to take in at a glance its bearing upon what follows.

[*Tables I–IX, pp.* 407–17.]

TABLE I. *Concordance of the Literary Authorities*

Point	Matthew	Mark	Luke and Acts	John	Agis	Cleomenes	Spartans taken together	Tiberius Gracchus	Gaius Gracchus	Fulvius	Cato Minor	Romans taken together	Aristonicus	Eunus	Salvius	Athenio	Catiline	Futurists taken together	Total of pagan correspondences to points in the Gospels
	Jesus				*The Spartan Archaists*			*The Roman Archaists*					*The Futurists*						
I*	×	×	×	×	×	×	1		×		×	1							2
IA†	×	×	×	×	×	×	1	×	×			1							2
2	×	×	×		×	×	2						×					1	3
3	×		×		×		1												1
4	×		×										×					1	1
5	o	o	o	o	×	×	2	×	×			2							4
6	×	×	×	×										×	×			2	2
7	×	×	×			×	1												1
8	×	×	×	×	×	×	2	×	×			2							4
9	×		×					×				1	[×]					1	2
10	×	×	×	×		×	1						×					1	2
11		×	×						×			1							1
12			×						×			1							1
13	×	×	×			×	1												1
14	×	×	×			o		×				1							1
15	×	×	×	×	[×]									×	×	×		3	3
16	×	×	×	×		×	1												1
17	×	×	×	×					×			1							1
18	×	×	×			×	1	×				1							2
19	×	×	×		×		1	o											1
20	×	×	×	×	×		1												1
21	×	×	×	×	×		1	×				1							2
22	×	×	×		×		1												1
23	×				×		1												1
24	×	×	×	×		×	1			×	×	2							3
25	×	×	×			×	1												1
26	×	×	×	×		×	1												1
27			×	×		×	1												1
28			×	×		×	.1	×				1							2
29	×	×	×			o										×		1	1
30		×									×	1							1
31		×	×											×				1	1
32		×	×							×	×	2							2
33	×	×	×	×		×	1		×			1							2
34	×	×	×	×		o					×	1							1
35	×	×			×	×	1												1
36	×	×	×						×			1							1
37	×	×	×						×			1							1
38	×	×				×	1			×		1							2
39	×	×	×	×	×		1												1
40	×	×	×		×		1												1
41				×	×		1												1
42	×	×						×				1							1
43			×		×		1												1
44	×	×	×	×		×	1	×			×	2							3
45	×		×	×		×	1	×	×			2							3

Note: × means a correspondence, o means a contradiction.
* Jesus as the gentle predecessor and Peter as the violent successor.
† John the Baptist as the gentle predecessor and Jesus as the violent successor

TABLE I. *Concordance of the Literary Authorities—continued.*

Point	Jesus — Matthew	Mark	Luke and Acts	John	Spartan Archaists — Agis	Cleomenes	Spartans taken together	Roman Archaists — Tiberius Gracchus	Gaius Gracchus	Fulvius	Cato Minor	Romans taken together	Futurists — Aristonicus	Eunus	Salvius	Athenio	Catiline	Futurists taken together	Total of pagan correspondences to points in the Gospels
46	×			×	×	o	1	×	×			2							3
47	×	×						×	×			1							1
48	×	×										1							1
49	×	×	×	×	×		1												1
50	×	×	×	o		×	1	×				1							2
51	×	×		×	×		1												1
52	×	×	×		×		1												1
53	×	×	×		×		1												1
54	×	×	×	×		o					×	1							1
55	×	×	×	×		×	1												1
56			×	×		×	1												1
57	×	×	×	×		×	1							×				1	2
58	×	×									×	1							1
59	×	×	×	×		×	1												1
60	×	×	×	×		×	1												1
61			[×]	×		×	1												1
62	×					×	1												1
63	×					×	1												1
64	×																×	1	1
65	×	×	×											×				1	1
66	×	×	×	×				×				1							1
67				×				×				1							1
68			×		×		1												1
69	×	×	×	×		×	1												1
70	×	×	×	×	×		1												1
71				×		×	1												1
72			×											×				1	1
73				×		×	1												1
74				×		×	1												1
75	×	[×]	o			×	1												1
76				×		×	1	×	×			2							3
77				×	×		1												1
78		[×]		×		×	1												1
79				×		×	1												1
80*	×	×	×		×		1												1
80A†				×		×	1												1
81			[×]		×		1												1
82	×	×	×	×	×		1	o											1
83								×	×			2							2
84			×			o		×	×		×	2							2
85	×		×					×	×			2							2
86			×		×		1												1
87			×		×		1												1
	60	53	61	45	26‡	38‡	64‡	17‡	16	5‡	7	45‡	4	6	2	1	2	15	124‡

* The women are not akin to the hero, and they remain at a distance.

† One of the women is the hero's mother, and she witnesses, from close at hand, the execution of the hero (of the hero's children).

‡ Reckoning the 'pairs' in Points 1 and 1A as one and not two correspondences each.

TABLE II. *Analysis of Correspondences between the Gospels and the Stories of Pagan Heroes*

	In one or more of the Synoptic Gospels only	In John only	In both one or more of the Synoptic Gospels and John as well	In one or more of the Synoptic Gospels, not exclusively	In John, not exclusively	In at least one of the four Gospels
Total number of points in the Gospels	43	13	32	75	45	88*
Correspondences in the story of Agis	13	4	9	22	13	26
,, ,, ,, Cleomenes	13	8	17	30	25	38
,, ,, ,, at least one Spartan archaist	25	11	25	50	36	61
,, ,, ,, Tiberius Gracchus	9	2	5	14	7	16
,, ,, ,, Gaius Gracchus	6	2	7	13	9	15
,, ,, ,, Fulvius	2	0	3	5	3	5
,, ,, ,, Cato Minor	3	1	3	6	4	7
,, ,, ,, at least one Roman archaist	17	4	13	30	17	34
,, ,, ,, Aristonicus	4	0	0	4	0	4
,, ,, ,, Eunus	2	0	4	6	4	6
,, ,, ,, Salvius	0	0	2	2	2	2
,, ,, ,, Athenio	0	0	1	1	1	1
,, ,, ,, Catiline	2	0	0	2	0	2
,, ,, ,, at least one futurist	8	0	4	12	4	12
Total number of individual pagan correspondences	54	17	51	105	68	122

* Omitting Point 83, but reckoning Points 1A and 80A as separate points.

TABLE III. *Analysis of Correspondences between the Stories of the Spartan Archaists and those of the Other Heroes*

	With the story of Agis only	With the story of Cleomenes only	With both the story of Agis and the story of Cleomenes	With the story of Agis, not exclusively	With the story of Cleomenes, not exclusively	With at least one of the two Spartan stories
Correspondences in the story of Jesus	23	35	3	26	38	61
,, ,, ,, Tiberius Gracchus	2	5	2	4	7	9
,, ,, ,, Gaius Gracchus	3	4	2	5	6	9
,, ,, ,, Fulvius	0	5	0	0	5	5
,, ,, ,, Cato Minor	0	1	0	0	1	1
,, ,, ,, at least one Roman archaist	3	10	2	5	11	15
,, ,, ,, Aristonicus	0	1	1	1	2	2
,, ,, ,, Eunus	0	1	0	0	1	1
,, ,, ,, Salvius	0	0	0	0	0	0
,, ,, ,, Athenio	0	0	0	0	0	0
,, ,, ,, Satyrus	0	1*	0	0	1	1
,, ,, ,, Catiline	0	0	0	0	0	0
,, ,, ,, at least one futurist	0	3	1	1	4	4
Total number of individual correspondences	28	53	8	36	61	89

* See p. 400, footnote 1, above, referring to Point 69.

TABLE IV. *Common Characters*

Characters	Point(s)	Jesus		The Spartan Archaists			The Roman Archaists					The Futurists						Total of pagan correspondences to characters in the Gospels
		At least one Synoptic Gospel	John	Agis	Cleomenes	Spartans taken together	Tiberius Gracchus	Gaius Gracchus	Fulvius	Cato Minor	Romans taken together	Aristonicus	Eunus	Salvius	Athenio	Catiline	Futurists taken together	
The pair of heroes (a gentle predecessor and a violent successor)	1*	×	×	×—×		1	×—×				1							2
	1A†	×	×	×—×		1	×—×				1							2
The hero's mother	5+73+80A	o	×	×	×	2	×	×			2							4
The forerunner .	6	×	×										×	×				2
The traitor .	22+23+39+40	×	×	×		1												1
The hero's twelve companions	25	×				×	1											1
The bosom friend	28		×			×	1		×			1						2
The boaster .	34+54+48	×	×			×	1‡				×	1§						2
The chosen companion(s) .	35	×				×	1											1
The enemy victim(s) .	44	×	×			×	1	×		×		2						3
The false witness(es) .	50	×				×	1	×				1						2
The foreign potentate .	55–63	×	×			×	1											1
The mockers .	65+72	×	×											×				1
The hero's two fellow victims .	70	×	×	×		1												1
The convert-executor .	86	×			×	1												1
The convert's martyr .	87	×			×	1												1
The convert's mentor . .	87	×			×	1												1

* Jesus as the gentle predecessor and Peter as the violent successor.

† John the Baptist as the gentle predecessor and Jesus as the violent successor.

‡ Therycion was 'a man who was high-souled in deed and high-falutin and boastful in word' (Plutarch: *Lives of Agis and Cleomenes*, chap. 52).

§ Statilius was 'a young man who affected a resoluteness beyond his years and who studied in all respects to appear to be, like Cato, the master of his feelings' (Plutarch: *Life of Cato Minor*, chap. 65).

TABLE V. Common Scenes

Scene	Point(s)	Jesus — At least one Synoptic Gospel	Jesus — John	Spartan Archaists — Agis	Spartan Archaists — Cleomenes	Spartans taken together	Roman Archaists — Tiberius Gracchus	Roman Archaists — Gaius Gracchus	Roman Archaists — Fulvius	Roman Archaists — Cato Minor	Romans taken together	Futurists — Aristonicus	Futurists — Eunus	Futurists — Salvius	Futurists — Athenio	Futurists — Catiline	Futurists taken together	Total of pagan correspondences to scenes in the Gospels
A crowd mounting on to the roof(s) in order to get within range of the hero	11	×			×	1		×			1							1
A rider, with companions on foot, making a progress through the streets of a city	16	×	×		×	1		×			1							1
The hero forcibly clearing a public place of trespassers	17	×	×		×	1							×				1	1
A supper	20+24+	×	×		×	1	×	×	×		2							4
	65+72	×			×	1					1							2
A bosom friend leaning on the hero's breast	28	×	×		×	1	×	×			2							2
A party going out of doors	33	×			×	1												1
The Agony	36	×		×		1	×				1							1
A bodyguard watching and sleeping by turns	37	×					×				1							1
Watchers (a watcher) caught napping	38	×		×		1		×			1							2
A hubbub at night-time with lights	41	×	×						×		1							1
A posse of officers of the law abashed in the hero's presence	43		×				×		×		2							1
A fight	44	×	×		×	1	×	×	×		2							3
A young male fugitive leaving his wrap in the hands of his pursuer(s)	48	×			×	1												1
A trial at night-time	49	×	×													×	1	1
A Roman washing his hands in a basin in public	64	×	×		×	1												1
The hero arrayed in a royal robe and crown	66	×	×		×	1												1
'Ecce homo!'	67	×		×		1												1
The Via Dolorosa	68	×	×		×	1												1
The Crucifixion	69	×	×	×		1												1
The acclamation of a crucified man as the Son of God (a child of the Gods)	75	×		×		1												1
The pricking of the hero's body with a stabbing weapon	79	×		×		1												1
The women in the background	80	×	×		×	1												1
The women in the foreground	80A	[×]		×		1												1
The Descent from the Cross (or gallows)	81	×	×		×	1												1
The Pietà	82	×	×	×		1												1

VI   O

TABLE VI. *Analysis of Visual Correspondences between the Gospels and the Stories of Pagan Heroes*

	In one or more of the Synoptic Gospels only	In John only	In both one or more of the Synoptic Gospels and John as well	In one or more of the Synoptic Gospels, not exclusively	In John, not exclusively	In at least one of the four Gospels
Total number of points in the Gospels	10	6	9	19	15	25
Correspondences in the story of Agis	3	2	2	5	4	7
,, ,, ,, Cleomenes	2	3	5	7	8	10
,, ,, ,, at least one Spartan archaist	5	5	7	12	12	17
,, ,, ,, Tiberius Gracchus	1	1	2	3	3	4
,, ,, ,, Gaius Gracchus	3	1	1	4	2	5
,, ,, ,, Fulvius	1	0	3	4	3	4
,, ,, ,, Cato Minor	0	0	1	1	1	1
,, ,, ,, at least one Roman archaist	5	2	5	10	7	12
,, ,, ,, Aristonicus	0	0	0	0	0	0
,, ,, ,, Eunus	0	0	1	1	1	1
,, ,, ,, Salvius	0	0	0	0	0	0
,, ,, ,, Athenio	0	0	0	0	0	0
,, ,, ,, Catiline	1	0	0	1	0	1
,, ,, ,, at least one futurist	1	0	1	2	1	2
Total number of individual pagan correspondences	11	7	15	26	22	33

TABLE VII. *Common Properties*

Property	Point(s)	At least one Synoptic Gospel	John	Agis	Cleomenes	Spartans taken together	Tiberius Gracchus	Gaius Gracchus	Fulvius	Cato Minor	Romans taken together	Aristonicus	Eunus	Salvius	Athenio	Catiline	Futurists taken together	Total of pagan correspondences to properties in the Gospels
		Jesus		The Spartan Archaists			The Roman Archaists					The Futurists						
A genealogy .	3	×	—	×		1												1
A tiled roof (roofs).	11+12	×						×										1
A commandeered mount .	16	×	×		×	1												1
A precious gift (gifts)	20	×	×		×	1												1
A traitor's trifling reward .	23	×		×		1												1
Sacramental flesh and blood . .	29	×			o											×	1	1
Swords (a sword) .	32+44	×	×		×	1	×	×	×	×	4							5
Staves . . .	42	×					×											1
An official custom relating to the release of a prisoner	60	×	×		×	1												1
A basin of water .	64	×														×	1	1
A royal crown (diadem) and robe .	66+67	×	×				×											1
A cross (gallows) .	69	×	×	×	×	2												2
A seamless shirt .	71		×		×	1												1
A stabbing weapon	79		×		×	1												1
A consecrated site of a martyrdom .	83	(cal-vary)					×	×										2

TABLE VIII. *Common Words*

Words*	Point	Matthew	Mark	Luke	John	Paul	Agis	Cleomenes	Spartans taken together	Tiberius Gracchus	Gaius Gracchus	Fulvius	Cato Minor	Romans taken together	Aristonicus	Eunus	Salvius	Athenio	Catiline	Futurists taken together	Total of pagan correspondences to words in the New Testament
(α)†	9	×		×						×				I	[×]					I	2
(β)†	–	×		×				×	I												I
(γ)†	–	×		×				×	I												I
(δ)‡	12			×							×			I							I
(ε)§	36	×	×	×							×			I							I
(ζ)‡	37	×	×								×			I							I
(η)†	50			×						×				I							I
(θ)†	68			×			×		I												I
(ι)§	71				×			×	I								×			I	I
(κ)†	72			×																	I
(λ)‡	74				×			×	I												I
(μ)‡	75	×	×	o				×	I												I
(ν)†	–					×		×	I												I

* The letters of the Greek Alphabet in this column refer to the passages quoted at the foot of the present table.

† In the correspondences marked thus the corresponding words in *both* the New Testament *and* the pagan text occur, not in the narrative, but in the mouth of one or more of the characters, as a quotation either from a speech (α, β, γ, η) or from a dialogue (θ, κ, ν).

‡ In the correspondences marked thus the corresponding words are placed in Jesus's mouth (δ, ζ, λ) and in a centurion's mouth (μ) in the New Testament, but occur in the narrative in the pagan text.

§ In the correspondences (ε, ι) marked thus the corresponding words in *both* the New Testament *and* the pagan text occur in the narrative only, and not in the mouth of any of the characters.

(α) 'The foxes have holes (φωλεούς) and the birds of the air have nests (κατασκηνώσεις), but the Son of Man hath not where to lay his head' (Matt. viii. 20 = Luke ix. 58). 'The wild animals that range over Italy have a hole (φωλεόν), and each of them has its lair (κοιταῖον) and nest (κατάδυσις), but the men who fight and die for Italy have no part or lot in anything but the air and the sunlight.[1] Without home or domicile, they wander over the face of the Earth with their children and their wives; and the generals are cheating them when they exhort them, in action, to fight for the sake of their cemeteries and sanctuaries. Of all these thousands of Romans not one has either an ancestral altar or a family tomb. It is for the sake of other men's wealth and luxury that these go to the wars and give their lives. They are called the lords of the World, and they have not a single clod of earth to call their own' (Plutarch: *Gracchi*, chap. 9).[2]

[1] In this passage of his speech Tiberius Gracchus is making the same point as Aristonicus makes by calling his followers 'Citizens of the City of the Sun' (see the references on p. 381, footnote 1, above).—A.J.T.   [2] Quoting from a speech by Tiberius Gracchus.

(β) 'The Kingdom of Heaven suffereth violence, and the violent take it by force' (ἡ βασιλεία τῶν οὐρανῶν βιάζεται, καὶ βιασταὶ ἁρπάζουσιν αὐτήν) (Matt. xi. 12); 'The Kingdom of God is preached, and every man presseth into it' (ἡ βασιλεία τοῦ Θεοῦ εὐαγγελίζεται, καὶ πᾶς εἰς αὐτὴν βιάζεται) (Luke xvi. 16). 'To change a political régime without violence and intimidation is not easy' (πολιτείαν μεταβαλεῖν ἄνευ βίας καὶ φόβου χαλεπόν ἐστιν) (Plutarch: *Agis and Cleomenes*, chap. 31).[1]

(γ) 'Some of them ye shall kill and crucify' (ἐξ αὐτῶν ἀποκτενεῖτε καὶ σταυρώσετε) (Matt. xxiii. 34); 'Some of them they shall slay and persecute' (ἐξ αὐτῶν ἀποκτενοῦσι καὶ ἐκδιώξουσιν) (Luke xi. 49). 'To the point of persecuting some of them and slaying others' (ὥστε . . . τοὺς μὲν ἐξελαύνειν, τοὺς δ' ἀποκτιννύειν) (Plutarch: *Agis and Cleomenes*, chap. 31).[2]

(δ) 'That which ye have spoken in the ear in closets shall be proclaimed upon the housetops' (ὃ πρὸς τὸ οὖς ἐλαλήσατε ἐν τοῖς ταμείοις, κηρυχθήσεται ἐπὶ τῶν δωμάτων) (Luke xii. 3). '. . . that many failed to find lodgings, and the acclamations were echoed from the roofs and the tiles because the campus could not contain the multitude' (ὡς πολλοῖς μὲν οἰκήσεις ἐπιλιπεῖν, τοῦ δὲ πεδίου μὴ δεξαμένου τὸ πλῆθος ἀπὸ τῶν τεγῶν καὶ τῶν κεράμων τὰς φωνὰς συνηχεῖν) (Plutarch: *Gracchi*, chap. 24).

(ε) 'He . . . began to be sorrowful and very heavy' (ἤρξατο λυπεῖσθαι καὶ ἀδημονεῖν) (Matt. xxvi. 37); 'He . . . began to be sore amazed and to be very heavy' (ἤρξατο ἐκθαμβεῖσθαι καὶ ἀδημονεῖν) (Mark xiv. 33); 'Being in agony he prayed more earnestly; and his sweat was as it were great drops of blood falling down to the ground' (γενόμενος ἐν ἀγωνίᾳ ἐκτενέστερον προσηύχετο· ἐγένετο δὲ ὁ ἱδρὼς αὐτοῦ ὡσεὶ θρόμβοι αἵματος καταβαίνοντες ἐπὶ τὴν γῆν) (Luke xxii. 44). 'Gaius Gracchus became more and more depressed and unaccountably upset until it ended in his falling into a sort of frenzy in which he was virtually out of his mind. . . . He went off . . . very heavy, like a man who is fey. In this state of mental excruciation. . . .' (ἀεὶ καὶ μᾶλλον ταπεινούμενος καὶ παρὰ προσδοκίαν ἀποπίπτων εἰς λύτταν τινὰ καὶ μανιώδη διάθεσιν ἐνέπιπτε. . . . ἀπεχώρησεν . . . ἀδημονῶν καὶ ποινηλατούμενος. οὕτω δ' αὐτοῦ παροιστρηκότος . . .) (Diodorus, Books XXXIV–XXXV, chap. 28ᵃ); 'On his way back from the Forum, Gaius stopped in front of the statue of his father, gazed at it in silence a long while, and finally went off after bursting into tears and lamentations' (ὁ δὲ Γάϊος ἐκ τῆς ἀγορᾶς ἀπερχόμενος ἔστη κατὰ τὸν τοῦ πατρὸς ἀνδριάντα, καὶ πολὺν χρόνον

[1] Quoting from a speech by Cleomenes. In another context (V. C (i) (d) 11, Annex I, p. 358, above) it has already been noticed that there is also a correspondence between Matt. xi. 12 and Aristophanes: *Birds*, l. 32.
[2] Quoting from a speech by Cleomenes.

ἐμβλέψας εἰς αὐτὸν οὐδὲν ἐφθέγξατο, δακρύσας δὲ καὶ στενάξας ἀπῄει)
(Plutarch: *Gracchi*, chap. 35).

(ζ) 'Sleep on now and take your rest' (καθεύδετε τὸ λοιπὸν καὶ
ἀναπαύεσθε) (Matt. xxvi. 45 = Mark xiv. 41). 'They passed the
time watching and taking their rest by turns' (ἐν μέρει φυλάττοντες
καὶ ἀναπαυόμενοι διῆγον) (Plutarch: *Gracchi*, chap. 35).

(η) 'And as some spake of the Temple, how it was adorned
with goodly stones and gifts (ἀναθήμασι), he said: "As for these
things which ye behold, the days will come in the which there
shall not be left one stone upon another that shall not be thrown
down (καταλυθήσεται)" ¹ (Luke xxi. 5–6). 'Nothing can be so
sacrosanct as votive offerings (ἀναθήματα) to the Gods; yet nobody has ever thought of estopping the Plebs from using and
moving (κινεῖν) and transferring (μεταφέρειν) such offerings as it
thinks fit' (Plutarch: *Gracchi*, chap. 15).²

(θ) 'Weep not for me' (μὴ κλαίετε ἐπ' ἐμέ) (Luke xxiii. 28).
'Stop weeping for me' (παῦσαί με κλαίων) (Plutarch: *Agis and
Cleomenes*, chap. 20).

(ι) 'The coat (shirt) was without seam' (ἦν δὲ ὁ χιτὼν ἄρραφος)
(John xix. 23). 'He put on his coat (shirt) and ripped open the
seam across the right shoulder' (ἐνδυσάμενος τὸν χιτῶνα καὶ τὴν
ῥαφὴν ἐκ τοῦ δεξιοῦ παραλυσάμενος ὤμου) (Plutarch: *Agis and
Cleomenes*, chap. 58).

(κ) 'Lord, remember me when thou comest into thy kingdom'
(μνήσθητί μου, κύριε, ὅταν ἔλθῃς ἐν τῇ βασιλείᾳ σου) (Luke xxiii.
42). 'With the request that he would remember the favour when
he came into his kingdom' (ἐπιλέγοντες ὅπως, ὅταν γένηται βασιλεύς,
τῆς χάριτος μνημονεύοι) (Diodorus, Books XXXIV–XXXV, chap. 2, § 8).

(λ) 'It is finished' (τετέλεσται) (John xix. 30). 'When it was
finished at last' (τέλος ἔχοντος ἤδη) (Plutarch: *Agis and Cleomenes*,
chap. 58).

(μ) 'Truly this was the Son of God' (ἀληθῶς Θεοῦ Υἱὸς ἦν οὗτος)
(Matt. xxvii. 54 = Mark xv. 39). '. . . hailing Cleomenes as a
hero and a child of the Gods' (ἥρωα τὸν Κλεομένη καὶ Θεῶν παῖδα
προσαγορεύοντες) (Plutarch: *Agis and Cleomenes*, chap. 60).

(ν) 'For none of us liveth to himself, and no man dieth to himself' (οὐδεὶς γὰρ ἡμῶν ἑαυτῷ ζῇ, καὶ οὐδεὶς ἑαυτῷ ἀποθνῄσκει) (Saint
Paul: *Epistle to the Romans*, xiv. 7). 'It is base for people to live
to themselves, and base for them to die to themselves' (αἰσχρὸν γὰρ
⟨καὶ⟩ ζῆν μόνοις ἑαυτοῖς καὶ ἀποθνῄσκειν) (Plutarch: *Agis and
Cleomenes*, chap. 52).³

---

¹ In the corresponding passage, quoted below, from a speech by Tiberius Gracchus,
this same verb (κατελύθη) occurs, a few sentences earlier, with reference to the fall of the
monarchy at Rome.   ² Quoting from a speech by Tiberius Gracchus.
³ Quoting from a dialogue between Cleomenes and Therycion.

TABLE IX. *Analysis of Verbal Correspondences between the Gospels and the Stories of Pagan Heroes*

	In one or more of the Synoptic Gospels only	In John only	In Paul only	In both one or more of the Synoptic Gospels and John as well	In one or more of the Synoptic Gospels, not exclusively	In John, not exclusively	In at least one book of the New Testament
Total number of points in the Gospels	10	2	1	0	10	2	13
Correspondences in the story of Agis	1	0	0	0	1	0	1
" " " Cleomenes	3	2	1	0	3	2	6
" " " at least one Spartan archaist	4	2	1	0	4	2	7
" " " Tiberius Gracchus	2	0	0	0	2	0	2
" " " Gaius Gracchus	3	0	0	0	3	0	3
" " " Fulvius	0	0	0	0	0	0	0
" " " Cato Minor	0	0	0	0	0	0	0
" " " at least one Roman archaist	5	0	0	0	5	0	5
" " " Aristonicus	1	0	0	0	1	0	1
" " " Eunus	1	0	0	0	1	0	1
" " " Salvius	0	0	0	0	0	0	0
" " " Athenio	0	0	0	0	0	0	0
" " " at least one futurist	2	0	0	0	2	0	2
Total number of individual pagan correspondences	11	2	1	0	11	2	14

Alternative Possible Explanations

How are our eighty-nine correspondences to be accounted for? Evidently there will be a number of alternative possible explanations; but it is equally evident that the first of these that should be taken into consideration is the play of chance. It is safe to assume *a priori* that at any rate some of these correspondences—it is idle to guess how many—are fortuitous; and there is at least one clear case (which, for this reason, has been excluded from our collection) in which the fortuitousness of the correspondence is demonstrable.

In all four Gospels (Matt. iii. 3 = Mark i. 3 = Luke iii. 4–5 = John i. 23) John the Baptist is quoted as saying, when he starts to preach:

'The voice of one crying in the wilderness: "Prepare ye the way of the Lord; make his paths straight (εὐθέίας). Every valley shall be filled (πᾶσα φάραγξ πληρωθήσεται), and every mountain and hill shall be brought low; and the crooked shall be made straight, and the rough ways shall be made smooth (λείας)." '[1]

This passage in the Gospels has a correspondence—which is particularly striking because it extends here and there to an actual identity of words—in the following passage in Plutarch's *Lives of the Gracchi* (chap. 28):

'[Gaius Gracchus] was especially keen on road-building, and in this work he had an eye for elegance and beauty as well as for sheer utility. His roads were carried through the countryside dead straight (εὐθεῖαι . . . ἀτρεμεῖς). . . . The hollows were filled (πιμπλαμένων) with embankments; the clefts carved by torrents or ravines (φάραγγες) were spanned with bridges; the road was graded to the same level on both sides; and as a result of all this care the work displayed a beautiful symmetry (ὁμαλὴν κὰι καλὴν ὄψιν εἶχε) throughout its length.'

The closeness of this correspondence might seem at first sight to rule the hypothesis of accident out; and it might appear probable that in this case the Gospels (or their source) were drawing upon Plutarch (or his source), either directly or indirectly, rather than vice versa. We might conjecture that the Roman art and practice of road-building had made a profound impression on the minds of the Romans' Oriental subjects; that these Oriental admirers of a Roman achievement had concentrated their admiration upon the figure of one of the first great road-builders in Roman history; and that the record of this Roman hero's road-building

---

[1] This is according to Saint Luke. The Gospels according to Saint Matthew and Saint Mark give the first sentence only, without the second. The Gospel according to Saint John gives the first sentence only, and that in a paraphrase.

feats had been turned to allegorical account by a Jewish prophet who had grown up under the Roman régime without losing hold upon the Jewish tradition of seeing life in terms of the spirit rather than in terms of matter. Such a theory of the origin of this passage in the New Testament would be as pretty as the Ptolemaic theory of the movements of the heavenly bodies; but it would suffer from the same single but fatal defect of being demonstrably untrue. Its falsity can be verified at a glance; for in each of the four Gospels the passage is ascribed to the Prophet Isaiah; and the ascription is correct. If the Greek text of Luke iii. 4–5 is compared with the Septuagint Greek version of Isa. xl. 3–4, the quotation will be found to reproduce the original with only trifling inaccuracies which do not affect either the general sense of the passage or any of the verbal coincidences with the corresponding passage of Plutarch. The proof of the fortuitousness of the correspondence is decisive; for the Septuagint translation of the Old Testament into Greek was made *circa* 170–132 B.C.;[1] and that is not only long before the earliest possible date of the writing of Plutarch's *Lives of the Gracchi* or the composition of Plutarch's sources; it is, at latest, at least nine years before the earliest possible date at which Plutarch's hero Gaius Gracchus himself can have begun to build his roads after entering upon his first term of office as Tribune of the Plebs in 123 B.C.

On this showing, are we to dismiss as fortuitous every correspondence between the New Testament and pagan Greek literature in which the New Testament passage contains either a quotation (express or tacit) from the Old Testament or a reminiscence of it? It might be rash to accept so sweeping a generalization as that without examining on their merits the actual cases in point.

One instance of a feature in the New Testament which can be traced back to the Old Testament with almost as great a certainty as the passage quoted by John the Baptist from Isaiah is the figure given in Matt. xxvi. 15 for the price paid by the Chief Priests to Judas (Point 23). Matthew's 'thirty pieces of silver' can hardly be explained except as an echo of Zechariah's (xi. 12). In this case sheer accident is clearly a less probable explanation than plagiarism; and, while Matthew makes no express reference to Zechariah in this place, he does refer to the Old Testament—though he names the prophet incorrectly and misquotes the words[2]—when he gives the sequel to the story of the betrayal (in xxvii. 9–10). This instance, however, is hardly relevant, because the exact figure of the price of the betrayal is not the feature in our Point 23 in

---

[1] See Tarn, W. W.: *Hellenistic Civilization* (London 1927, Arnold), p. 178.
[2] On this see further the present Annex, p. 424, below.

which we have detected a correspondence between the respective stories of the betrayal of Jesus and the betrayal of Agis.

We may notice next a pair of cases in which a narrative that has been incorporated into the New Testament seems to have been cut to fit a passage from the Old Testament that is quoted with reference to it.

In the tableau of the rider riding through the streets of a city (Point 16), Mark (xi. 1–7) and Luke (xix. 29–35) mention *one* riding animal only—'a colt'—and make no reference to the Old Testament in connexion with it. John, again, mentions (xii. 12–15) one riding animal only, and quotes, in connexion with it, a passage from Zechariah—introduced anonymously as 'the prophet'—in a shortened form in which there can be no question of more than one animal being intended. The original (Zech. ix. 9) runs:

'Behold, thy king cometh unto thee . . . lowly and riding upon an ass, and upon a colt the foal of an ass.'

And, in the version of the incident in Matthew, Zechariah—introduced anonymously as 'the prophet' here too—is quoted in this fuller form (Matt. xxi. 5). In the Matthaean version of the incident in the story of Jesus on which the quotation from Zechariah bears, there are also two animals—'an ass, and a colt with her' (Matt. xxi. 2)—and *both* of these are brought by the disciples to Jesus and are saddled for his use. Now, since a rider cannot bestride two mounts at once, Matthew's divergence from the other three Gospels in the matter of the number of the animals introduces an anomaly into his account of the incident from which the other versions are free. And this may prompt us to conjecture that Matthew has altered the narrative—in defiance of the probabilities—in order to bring it into line with the full text of Zechariah, which Matthew appears to have read as referring to two animals, though it seems much more likely that only one animal is really intended, and that Zechariah is merely indulging in the conceit—which is one of the characteristic ornaments of Hebrew poetry—of saying the same thing twice over in different words.

In the second case (Point 71) in which a narrative incorporated into the New Testament seems to have been cut to fit a quotation from the Old Testament the probable explanation is the same: the literary artifice of repetition in periphrasis has been mistaken for a pair of references to two separate things. Ps. xxii. 18—'They part my garments among them, and cast lots upon my vesture'—is quoted in Matt. xxvii. 35, and in John xix. 24 (with respective references to 'the prophet' and to 'the scripture') in connexion with a statement—that is also made (though here without any reference to the Old

Testament) in Mark xv. 24, and in Luke xxiii. 34—that the soldiers 'parted his garments, casting lots'. In the Synoptic Gospels, Matthew included, it is assumed that there was a single procedure in which lots were cast in order to determine how the clothes were to be distributed among the claimants. According to John (xix. 23–4), however, all the clothes except a seamless 'coat' or shirt (χιτὼν ἄρραφος) are parted without any casting of lots—presumably in the literal sense of pulling them to pieces at the seams—and the casting of the lots is a special device for dealing with the seamless coat, which the soldiers are loath to spoil by tearing it. We may conjecture that the writer of the Gospel according to Saint John has altered the narrative in order to bring it into line with the text of Ps. xxii. 18, and that he has been moved to make this alteration because he has interpreted the Psalm as describing, not one act, but two acts.

Again, the betrayal of Jesus by Judas with a kiss (Point 40) may be thought to have been suggested by the incident, narrated in 2 Sam. xx. 8–10, of Joab taking Amasa by the beard with his right hand to kiss him, in order to put him off his guard while he treacherously smites him in the fifth rib with his sword. And, if the incident, as it appears in the New Testament, is really a literary echo of this corresponding incident in the Old Testament (to which it does not make any reference), then we might have to dismiss as a mere effect of chance the correspondence which we have descried, in this point, between the betrayal of Jesus and the betrayal of Agis.

There are two other cases in which it is possible, though not convincingly probable, that a feature in the New Testament has been derived from a feature in the Old Testament to which the relevant passages of the New Testament make no reference. The silence of Jesus, first before the Sanhedrin (Point 51) and then before Pilate (Point 58), *may* have been derived from Isa. liii. 7. Similarly, the picture in the Synoptic Gospels of the women standing afar off to watch the Crucifixion (Point 80) *may* have been derived from Ps. xxxviii. 11.

There is an unmistakable, though again unacknowledged, quotation from Ps. xxii in the Matthaean and Marcan versions of the mocking of Jesus on the Cross (Point 72). Matt. xxvii. 39 and Mark xv. 29 both reproduce Ps. xxii. 7, and Matt. xxvii. 43 goes on to reproduce Ps. xxii. 8. Moreover in Matt. xxvii. 40 (= Mark xv. 29–30) and 43 there are almost certainly reminiscences of a passage in the Book of Wisdom.[1] Since it is hardly credible that

---

[1] Wisd. of Sol. ii. 12–20, quoted in this Annex on pp. 494–5, below. In this passage 'the ungodly' are represented as plotting to inflict a horrible death upon a righteous man who claims to be the Son of God, in order to see whether his Divine Father will deliver him in his extremity.

'in real life' the Jews would have chosen to quote or paraphrase, in mockery, passages of Scripture in which the sympathy is (as it is in both these contexts) on the side, not of the mockers, but of their victim, we may conjecture that these particular taunts in Matthew and Mark are merely echoes, in the evangelist's own mind, of the corresponding verses of the Book of Wisdom and the Twenty-second Psalm, and we might even go so far as to dismiss the whole of this incident in the New Testament as unhistorical on the same ground if it did not include other taunts—e.g. 'he saved others; himself he cannot save' (Matt. xxvii. 42 = Mark xv. 31; cf. Luke xxiii. 35)[1]—which do not appear to be reminiscences of anything either in Ps. xxii or in the Book of Wisdom or in any other piece of the Old Testament.

Are we then to explain away, as a mere effect of chance, every correspondence between a point in the Gospels and a point in the story of some pagan Hellenic hero wherever the passage in the New Testament can be shown to contain some reminiscence of a passage in the Old Testament? Such a procedure can best be tested by observing how it works in another set of circumstances. The writer of this Study had an uncle, the late Dr. Paget Toynbee, who in the course of his life contributed a considerable number of letters to *The Times* quoting either Dante or else Horace Walpole with reference to some current piece of news in that newspaper. The subjects were extremely diverse and the quotations were usually apt; and, if one were to slip a file of these letters of Dr. Paget Toynbee's into the hands of a New Testament scholar when he was in an unguardedly 'higher critical' mood, one can imagine the unhappy victim of our practical joke being inveigled into fathering the theory that the passages from two ancient authors which Dr. Toynbee was in the habit of quoting were manifestly the sources of the old-wives' tales about current events which the Editor of *The Times* had palmed off upon his readers as authentic news. The theory is plausible because news is notoriously expensive. It means paying toll to telegraph companies and salaries to correspondents. A frugal editor might surely yield to the temptation to save his purse by coining counterfeit news out of passages of ancient authors with which an assiduous scholar was kind

---

[1] There are other taunts, again, which are manifestly not derived from the Old Testament, since they are echoes of statements or avowals which are attributed to Jesus in the New Testament itself in the preceding chapter of the story of the Passion: e.g. 'Thou that destroyest the Temple and buildest it in three days, save thyself' (Matt. xxvii. 40 = Mark xv. 29–30, echoing Matt. xxvi. 61 = Mark xiv. 58). Similarly, 'if he be the King of Israel, let him now come down from the cross, and we will believe him' (Matt. xxvii. 42 = Mark xv. 32) may be an echo of Matt. xxvi. 63–4 = Mark xiv. 61–2 = Luke xxii. 67–9. On this showing, the reminiscences of the Book of Wisdom in Matt. xxvii. 40 (= Mark xv. 29–30) and 43, may be at second hand, through Matt. xxvi. 63–4 (= Mark xiv. 61–2).

enough to supply him. The theory is so attractive that its present inventor could hardly have resisted adopting it himself if there were not one flaw in it that is fatal to it. This flaw is a chronological one—for investigation will show that Dr. Toynbee's letters containing the quotations from Dante and Horace Walpole never appeared in *The Times* in advance of the news with reference to which they purported to be written: they always appeared after an interval of at least twenty-four hours!

This imaginary parallel reveals the weak point in the argument with which we have been playing. The fact of an ancient work of literature being quoted, either expressly or tacitly, with reference to an alleged current event is, of course, no proof whatever that the alleged event is a piece of fiction which has been fabricated out of the quotation. The event need not be fictitious just because the quotation is apt. For, if the work that is quoted is of a certain size and has a certain variety of content, and if the scholar who quotes it has a retentive memory, then an appropriate quotation may spring to the scholar's mind in almost any conceivable circumstances. And, if our scholar is a *hāfiz* whose study is the Holy Writ of Islam or Jewry and who has learnt his Qur'ān or his Law and Prophets by heart, then the fact that his narrative of current events contains telling quotations from Scripture will throw little or no light upon the question whether the incidents to which these quotations refer are fictitious or authentic.

In the set of passages from the New Testament with which we are at present concerned there is at least one clear case of a quotation from the Old Testament which certainly cannot be the origin of the incident in the Gospels with reference to which it is quoted. This case occurs in the account of Judas' miserable end (Point 85).

We may begin by taking note of a correspondence between the Gospels and the story of Cleomenes which we have not included in our list. In both stories the question of the payment of the price of a field is introduced in connexion with the machinations of the villain who brings the hero to ruin. In Plutarch's *Lives of Agis and Cleomenes*, chap. 56, Nicagoras' animosity against Cleomenes is put down to his resentment at not having received payment for a field which Cleomenes has bought from him. In the story of Judas a field is bought—according to the Matthaean version (Matt. xxvii. 7) by the chief priests when the thirty pieces of silver have been flung back by Judas in their faces, and according to the Lucan version (Acts i. 18) by Judas himself—out of the blood-money. This particular correspondence is so tenuous that it would be prudent to ignore it in any case—as, in fact, we have ignored it in this Study—but in the present context we may take note of it to the extent of observing that the question of its significance is not affected one way or the other by the fact that Matthew (xxvii. 9–10) hails the miserable end of Judas as the fulfilment of an Old Testament prophecy.

'Then was fulfilled that which was spoken by Jeremy the prophet, saying: "And they took the thirty pieces of silver, the price of him that was valued, whom they of the children of Israel did value, and gave them for the potter's field, as the Lord appointed me."'

This alleged fulfilment of scripture proves nothing, because in this case the *hāfiz*'s memory has played its owner false. The prophet in question is really not Jeremiah but Zechariah, and the passage (Zech. xi. 13) is misquoted. According to the Septuagint it ought to run:

'And the Lord said unto me: "Drop them into the smelting-furnace (χωνευτήριον) and see if it is genuine, in the manner in which my genuineness was tested on their behalf." And I took the thirty pieces of silver and cast them into the house of the Lord—into the smelting-furnace.'

How has the memory of the writer of the Gospel come to play on its owner the trick of substituting a 'potter's field' for the 'smelting-furnace' of the passage in the Old Testament which this *hāfiz*-caught-napping is trying to recall? The explanation is given, not by anything in Zechariah, but by the context in the New Testament. To the knowledge of the writer of the Gospel according to Saint Matthew there was, on the outskirts of Jerusalem, a burial-ground for strangers which went by the name of 'the Field of Blood' in the writer's (or his source's) own day, and which was remembered to have been a potter's field before it had been acquired for this other use by the Jewish public authorities. The context in the Gospel according to Saint Matthew informs us that, in the tradition of the Christian community at Jerusalem, the current name of 'the Field of Blood' had come to be associated with the last chapter in the story of the treachery of Judas; and for our present purpose we need not raise the question whether that story was an authentic piece of history of which the name of the field was a monument or whether the story was a legend that had arisen as an explanation of a name of which the true origin had been forgotten.[1] Whatever may lie behind the traditional association of the name of the field with Judas' end, it is apparent

---

[1] The hypothesis that the story of Judas' miserable end is an *aition* (in the technical sense in which that Greek word is used by Hellenic antiquaries) is perhaps favoured by the fact that the person from whose blood the field is alleged to have taken its name is not the same person in the Matthaean as in the Lucan version of the story. According to Matthew (xxvii. 3–8) the field has acquired its name because it has been bought by the chief priests with the blood-money paid to Judas for the betrayal of Jesus. According to the Lucan version (Acts i. 18–19) the blood is not Jesus's but Judas' own—the field having been the scene of Judas' miraculously horrible death.

that the subsidiary tradition of the field having been originally a potter's field has suggested, in the mind of the evangelist or his source, an echo of something in the Old Testament, and that in this case the *hāfiz*'s memory has been at fault. This rules out all possibility of the story of Judas' end being derived from the misquoted text of Zechariah; and our conclusion will be confirmed if we go on to compare the Matthaean version of the story of Judas' end with the Lucan; for in the Lucan version (Acts i. 18–19) there is no mention of 'the Field of Blood' having been originally a potter's field; and while, here too, the story is capped by a quotation from the Old Testament, the texts cited in this Lucan variant of the story (Acts i. 20) are not Zech. xi. 12–13, but Ps. lxix. 25 and cix. 8, which have nothing in common with the passage from the prophet either in its authentic original form or in Matthew's misquotation of it. It is evident that the story associating 'the Field of Blood' with Judas' end cannot have arisen either out of the verses from Zechariah or out of the verses from the Book of Psalms which are respectively quoted in connexion with the story in Matthew and in the Acts, but which have no other connexion whatsoever with one another.

Even if there had not been the alternative—and incorrect—quotation from Zechariah in Matthew, the two verses quoted from the Psalms in the Acts could not in any case have been seriously supposed to be the origin of the story that has evoked the memory of them in the author's mind—and this for the simple reason that, though they are apposite as far as they go, their appositeness is only of the vaguest and most general order. There are at least three other reminiscences of the Old Testament in our present collection of passages from the New Testament which are in the same case.

One such reminiscence is the combination of a passage of Trito-Isaiah—'Mine house shall be called an house of prayer for all people' (Isa. lvi. 7)—with a passage of Jeremiah—'Is this house, which is called by my name, become a den of robbers in your eyes?' (Jer. vii. 11)—which is cited in all three Synoptic Gospels (Matt. xxi. 13 = Mark xi. 17 = Luke xix. 46) with reference to the incident of the cleansing of the Temple (Point 17). This combination of two passages from the Old Testament cannot have generated the incident with which it is associated in the New Testament; for the text of Isaiah, though not inapposite, is exceedingly vague in its application, while the text of Jeremiah refers, not to people who have had the effrontery to do unlawful business in the Temple, but to people who have had the effrontery to come and worship in the Temple after having done unlawful business outside its precincts. We shall conclude that these two quotations from the Prophets have not generated, but have been evoked by, the incident in the story of Jesus to which they are attached in the Synoptic Gospels; and this conclusion will be confirmed when we observe that, in the Gospel according to Saint John (ii. 17), the same incident is capped by quite a different quotation—'The zeal of thine house hath eaten me up'—which comes from Ps. lxix. 9.

The record of Jesus being crucified with a malefactor on either side of him is followed in the Gospel according to Saint Mark (xv. 28)—alone of the four—by the quotation of a verse from Deutero-Isaiah (referred to as 'the scripture'): 'And he was numbered with the transgressors' (Isa. liii. 12). This verse from the Old Testament can hardly be the origin of the incident in the New Testament with which it is associated in one Gospel out of four, since it does not itself comprise any of this incident's distinctive features. There is no mention in it of the transgressors being two in number; no hint of the 'numbering' taking the tragically practical form of being put to death together; and *a fortiori* no inkling of the three victims' simultaneous and identical death being a death by crucifixion. In fact, the bearing of the quotation upon the incident with which it is associated is so vague that we shall be inclined to dismiss it as a reminiscence which throws no light whatever on the incident's origin; and our last hesitation will disappear when we find the same verse of Isaiah being quoted in the Lucan account of the Passion (Luke xxii. 37) in quite a different place, namely in the story of the hero sending, after the Last Supper, for swords (i.e. in connexion with our Point 32 instead of with our Point 70).

Similarly, the text of Zechariah (xii. 10)—'and they shall look upon me whom they have pierced'—cannot seriously be supposed to be the origin of the incident of the piercing of Jesus's side with a spear (Point 79), in reference to which it is quoted (as 'another scripture') in John xix. 37.

The piercing of Jesus's side is related in the Gospel according to Saint John in connexion with the story (xix. 32-3) that the soldiers, after they had broken the legs of the two malefactors, refrained from breaking Jesus's legs because they saw that he was dead already; and with reference to this (Point 78) the evangelist (John xix. 36) quotes, or rather paraphrases, a pair of texts from the Old Testament—Exodus xii. 46 and Numbers ix. 12—in the form: 'A bone of him shall not be broken.' Now, in the two passages thus cited, the prescription refers to the paschal lamb; and the Crucifixion of Jesus was identified with the sacrifice of the paschal lamb at an early stage in the Christian tradition. In Saint Paul's First Epistle to the Corinthians, v. 7, for example, the identification is made explicitly; and it is made tacitly in the Synoptic Gospels, inasmuch as they identify the Last Supper with the Passover meal. Are we to conclude that the same identification of Jesus with the paschal lamb has generated, in the Gospel according to Saint John, the story of Jesus's bones being preserved unbroken on the Cross?

The Fourth Gospel, in contradiction with all the other three, places the Crucifixion—and not the Last Supper—on the day of the preparation of the Passover (John xviii. 28 and xix. 14 and 31; cf. Matt. xxvii. 62);[1] and this was the day on which the Passover lamb was slain and eaten. But this difference of dating, which might seem at first sight to support the hypothesis of the story in John being derived from the identification of Jesus with the paschal lamb, in point of fact rules that hypothesis out of court; for in the Christian tradition the identification is proclaimed in the symbolic act of the consecration by Jesus, at the Passover meal, of bread and wine as his own body and blood; and the author of the Gospel according to Saint John has found himself unable to reconcile this vitally important point in the tradition with his own chronology —according to which, Jesus was already dead, and perhaps already in the tomb, by the hour on the day of preparation at which the Passover meal would have been eaten. Accordingly the author of the Fourth Gospel of necessity refrains from identifying the Last Supper with the Passover meal, and, consistently with this, he omits to mention the institution of the Holy Communion, which is recorded in this context in all the Synoptic Gospels. On this showing, it is evidently improbable that the author of the Fourth Gospel will have been so eager, after all, to identify Jesus with the paschal lamb that he will have invented for this purpose an epilogue of his own to the story of the Crucifixion. Whatever may be the origin of the incident of the soldiers refraining from breaking Jesus's legs, it seems probable that the reference to the ritual prescription concerning the paschal lamb has not generated the incident but has merely been evoked by it.

We shall arrive at a similar conclusion with regard to the relation between Matt. xxvii. 24 (Point 64) and Deut. xxi. 6–7. The correspondence which we have noted between Pilate's hand-washing and Catiline's may seem at first sight to be proved fortuitous when we observe, first, that the outwardly identical act is not inspired by an identical motive, and, secondly, that Pilate's motive has no known ground in Roman, while it has a clear ground in Jewish, religious custom and belief. Catiline washes his hands in order to

---

[1] For this question of dates see Meyer, E.: *Ursprung und Anfänge des Christentums*, vol. i (Stuttgart and Berlin 1921, Cotta), pp. 167–72.

cleanse them literally from the physical blood of a victim whom Catiline has just killed with his own hand; Pilate washes his in order to cleanse them ritually from blood-guiltiness for the death of a victim whom he has condemned to death but whose blood has not yet been shed. And in this procedure Pilate, as Origen points out,[1] 'Iudaico usus est more . . . faciens non secundum aliquam consuetudinem Romanorum'.[2] Though the relevant passage in Deuteronomy is not expressly cited in Matthew, there can be no doubt that it was in the evangelist's mind. Are we then to conclude that the incident of Pilate's hand-washing has been generated, not by the visually corresponding incident in the story of Catiline, but by a ritually corresponding prescription of the Jewish Law? This hypothesis may be attractive at first sight, but its probability dwindles as soon as we examine the relevant passage in the Book of Deuteronomy (xxi. 1–9). No doubt this passage has suggested both the *explanation* that is given of the act and the *words* that Pilate utters while he is performing it; but the differences between the two contexts are not less striking than the resemblances. In Deuteronomy the ritual of hand-washing is prescribed as an expiation for the death of a victim who, instead of being about to be slain, has been slain already, and the case envisaged is that of a person who, instead of having been publicly condemned to death, has been found slain without its being known who is the slayer. These circumstances are so different, and the differences touch the essence of the situation so closely, that we are led to the conclusion that the passage in Deuteronomy has merely coloured the incident in Matthew but has not generated it.

Finally we may ask whether the tableau of the fugitive leaving his wrap in the hands of his pursuers (Point 48) may have been derived from an at first sight analogous incident in the Old Testament story of Joseph and Potiphar's Wife (Gen. xxxix. 12), and may therefore, after all, bear no more than a fortuitous resemblance to the last scene in the Passion of Tiberius Gracchus. Here again we shall find that the superficial resemblance between the respective incidents in the New Testament and in the Old Testament will not stand the test of closer examination. The wrap which, in both the story of Jesus and the story of Tiberius Gracchus, is left in the hands of an unknown male pursuer, is left, in the story of Joseph, in the hands of a woman who is the villainess of the piece in which the fugitive is the hero. Moreover in the story of Joseph and Potiphar's Wife the incident of the seizure

---

[1] Origen: *In Matthaeum Commentariorum Series, Vetus Interpretatio*, cap. 124, in Migne, J.-P.: *Patrologia Graeca*, vol. xiii, col. 1774.
[2] The writer's attention has been drawn to this passage of Origen by Dr. Martin Braun.

of the wrap is not isolated, as it is in both the other two contexts, but is merely the prelude to a more important incident in which the abandoned wrap is put by its captor to a fraudulent use as a piece of material evidence for lending apparent credibility to a false accusation of which the owner of the wrap is the victim. On this showing, we may hesitate to pronounce that Gen. xxxix. 12 has even coloured Mark xiv. 51–2.

The results of the foregoing examination of quotations from, and allusions to, and reminiscences of, the Old Testament in the collection of passages from the New Testament with which we are here concerned seem to indicate that while the play of chance may, and indeed must, be taken into consideration as one possible explanation of our correspondences between the Gospels and the stories of certain pagan Hellenic heroes, this explanation cannot be pressed to extremes and will not offer us a complete solution of our problem.

An alternative possible explanation is the production of identical results by identical causes.

One obvious general identical cause is the element of uniformity in human nature. Since every human being is brought into the World by a physical process of conception and birth, every hero, like every one else, is bound to have had a mother, and the hero's mother is as likely as anybody else's mother to play an important part in the life of her son. This would dispose of our Point 5. Again, every human being is eventually removed from the World by death; and therefore any enterprise which cannot be accomplished by a single hero in a single lifetime is bound—if it does not die prematurely by dying with its originator—to be handed on from a predecessor to a successor. This would dispose of one of the elements in our Points 1 and 1 A and 86 and 87. In the third place we may observe that, without possessing the intrinsic universality of the figures of a mother or a predecessor or a successor, the figures of a traitor[1] and a bosom friend and a boaster and a mocker—and perhaps even those of a false witness and a convert—are all of them stock characters in the tragi-comedy of human life. It will be seen that the principle of the uniformity of human nature suffices to account for a majority of the common characters set out above in Table IV.

A more precise identical cause which is likewise capable of producing identical results is to be found in a social environment which is the common setting of all the stories of all the heroes

---

[1] In the story of Dio, for instance (see V. C (ii) (*a*), pp. 248 and 253, above), Callippus plays Judas to Dio's Jesus, as is pointed out by Eduard Meyer: *Ursprung und Anfänge des Christentums*, vol. i (Stuttgart and Berlin 1921, Cotta), p. 173.

whom we have brought into comparison with one another in our present inquiry. Their lives are all lived in a society that is in course of disintegration; disintegration, as we have seen,[1] brings standardization in its train; and, if the disintegration-process produces a certain measure of uniformity as between the histories of different disintegrating civilizations, it may be expected to produce the same effect in a still higher degree as between the lives of individuals who are all of them children of one and the same disintegrating civilization. The naturalness of this expectation is pertinent to our present subject, since Jesus and the pagan heroes with whom we are bringing him into comparison are, all alike, children of the Hellenic Society in an age—beginning in the latter part of the Hellenic 'Time of Troubles' and running over into the early days of the Hellenic universal state —which is all comprised within a span of not more than three centuries from first to last. This identity of social environment would account, in Points 1 and 1 A, for the change from the predecessor's gentleness to the successor's violence, since we have seen[2] that both Archaism and Futurism—that is, two out of four alternative ways of life that are followed by would-be saviours in times of social disintegration—are doomed *a priori* to explode into violence sooner or later. The same cause would also account for the hero's addressing himself to the Proletariat and denouncing the Dominant Minority (Points 7–10), and likewise for his pretension to kingship (Point 15). In this connexion we may remind ourselves[3] that, in this group of points, the superficial likeness is trivial by comparison with the profound dissimilarity between the respective attitudes and actions of our pagan heroes and of Jesus. While the people to whom they appeal and the people whom they denounce are respectively much the same, there is an extreme difference between the heroes' own respective responses to an identical challenge. The pagan heroes—even those who set out with the gentlest intentions—all end sooner or later by meeting force with force and by attempting to substitute a new mundane régime of their own for the existing mundane régime against which they are up in arms, whereas Jesus not only parts company with all his pagan counterparts but actually breaks right away from the Jewish tradition in which he has been brought up when he persists in retorting to violence with gentleness; in accepting death with resignation instead of with defiance; and in proclaiming that his kingdom is not of This World (Points 45 and 46).

It now looks as though the operation of identical causes and the

---

[1] In V. C (iii), above.   [2] In V. C (i) (d) 8 and 9, *passim*, above.
[3] See V. C (i) (d) 9 (γ), pp. 128–32, and V. C (i) (d) 11, pp. 155–6, above.

play of chance were capable of accounting between them for a majority of our points of correspondence in those chapters of the story that precede the hero's Passion; but this conclusion does not take us very far on our road in search of explanations; for a glance at Table I will show that the points which fall within these earlier chapters amount to no more than 16[1] out of a total of 89,[2] so that the last chapter, of which the Passion is the theme, accounts for nearly five-sixths of the total number (i.e. for 73 points out of 89). No doubt, in this last chapter too the two causes which we have taken into consideration so far will account for an appreciable number of our correspondences; but in this chapter these correspondences come thronging in such numbers and are also in many cases so remarkably close that we cannot reasonably attribute them all either to the play of chance or to the operation of some identical cause. We must seek farther before we can conscientiously declare ourselves quit of the investigation that we have undertaken. We have still to examine a third possible alternative explanation; and that is the possibility of mimesis.

If mimesis has in fact played a part in producing the correspondences that we are seeking to explain, it is evident that this faculty may have been brought into play in either or both of two quite distinct sets of relations. On the one hand there is the possibility that some of the characters on our historical stage who have made their appearance there at a relatively early date have been taken as objects of mimesis by other characters who have made their appearance later. On the other hand there is the possibility that the mimesis may have been the work, not of our characters themselves, but of the authors who have recorded—and who, in recording, may perhaps have taken liberties with—the heroes' histories.

Is it likely that any of the later characters have modelled their lives and actions to any appreciable extent upon those of other characters that have anticipated them in making their appearance upon the stage of Hellenic history? There is certainly a strong *a priori* probability that the two Gracchi may have consciously and deliberately taken the two Heracleidae as their pattern. In the first place the Roman aristocracy as a whole had already, in the Post-Hannibalic Age, become so deeply imbued with Hellenic culture that the entire Hellenic heritage of memories and ideals had by this time come to be virtually an integral part of the Roman tradition. In the second place we know that the mother of the Gracchi, Cornelia—who was solely responsible for the upbringing of the two heroes, since their father died while they were both

---

[1] Reckoning 1 A as a separate point.
[2] Reckoning 1 A and 80 A as separate points.

still quite young[1]—moved, with a markedly greater intimacy than most Roman aristocrats of her generation, in the Greek-speaking circles of Hellenic Society. Cornelia was intimate alike with Macedonian Greek royalties and with men-of-letters and philosophers of all Greek nationalities.[2]

'Gracchus's mother Cornelia saw to it that her son should receive a liberal Hellenic education, and should be thoroughly grounded in Greek literature, from boyhood (*Fuit Gracchus diligentia Corneliae matris a puero doctus et Graecis litteris eruditus*). He always had tutors from Greece who were picked men; and one of these—who had the teaching of Gracchus when he was on the verge of manhood—was Diophanes of Mitylene, who was the greatest master of language in his day in all Greece.'[3]

This Mitylenaean rhetor Diophanes, as well as the Cumaean philosopher Blossius,[4] is said still to have been Tiberius Gracchus's mentor at the moment when he entered upon his term of office as Tribune of the Plebs and launched his social reforms.[5] Blossius himself may be reckoned as a semi-Greek in nationality, since Cumae was an Italian city-state of Greek origin which had obtained its charter of Latinization from the Roman Government as recently as the year 180 B.C.[6] To both Blossius and Diophanes, Agis and Cleomenes would be familiar figures; and their story would be bound to make a deep impression on Tiberius Gracchus as soon as his attention was drawn to it. As aristocrats, as archaists, and as reformers who had made it their first business to grapple with an acute agrarian problem, these two Spartan Heracleidae could hardly fail to suggest themselves to the young Roman statesman as patterns for him to follow.

There is also a certain *a priori* probability that the examples of the Heracleidae or of the Gracchi or of both the Spartan and the Roman pair of heroes may have influenced the leaders of the Hellenic internal proletariat whose stories we have embraced in our comparative view. We have seen[7] that, in being driven willy-nilly out of the path of gentleness into the path of violence, the would-be archaist reformer is often driven into becoming, in spite of his original intentions, a champion of the Proletariat, and further that, if and when his almost inevitable quarrel with his own kin and kind comes to a climax at which they positively dis-

---

[1] Plutarch: *Gracchi*, chap. 1.   [2] Plutarch: *Gracchi*, chaps. 1 and 40.
[3] Cicero: *Brutus*, chap. 27, § 104.
[4] For Blossius of Cumae and his relation to Tiberius Gracchus and to Aristonicu see V. C (i) (c) 2, vol. v, p. 179, and V. C (ii) (a), in the present volume, p. 249, above.
[5] Plutarch: *Gracchi*, chap. 8.
[6] 'Cumanis eo anno petentibus permissum ut publice Latine loquerentur et prae conibus vendendi Latine ius esset.'—Livy, Book XL, chap. 42.
[7] In V. C (ii) (a), pp. 236–41, above.

own him, he sometimes seeks and finds a new social habitation and a new political career by turning from an archaist into a futurist and putting himself at the Proletariat's head. One such social migrant is included among our present group of pagan heroes in the person of Catiline. It is evident that a Catiline might bring with him an admiration for a Gaius Gracchus which he might then transmit to the proletarian-born leaders of the Proletariat with whom he had now thrown in his lot.

On this showing, it seems reasonable to make a considerable allowance for the possibility of the direct imitation of one character by another in attempting to account for the correspondences between the stories of our pagan heroes; but this explanation does not carry us very much farther, as will be shown by a glance at Table III above; for, out of 89 instances of correspondences between the stories of one or other of the two Heracleidae and those of the rest of the heroes in our group, only 28 instances are contributed by the stories of other pagan heroes, while no less than 61 are contributed by the story of Jesus. It is these 61 instances from the story of Jesus, and not the 23 from the stories of the Gracchi or the one from the story of Cato Minor or the 4 from the stories of the futurists, that cry out for explanation; and the suggestion that Jesus may have been consciously following in the footsteps of the Heracleidae has only to be formulated in order to refute itself. The Gospels and Josephus alike make it clear that in the first century of the Christian Era the Jews and Hellenes who in that age were living cheek-by-jowl in Palestine lived lives as separate as the Arabs and the Jews are living in the same country to-day. It is improbable that Jesus of Nazareth had ever heard even of his fellow proletarian and fellow Syrian Eunus of Apamea, or of the two Cilician slave-kings, Cleon and Athenio; for, though Coele Syria, and even Cilicia, was not very far from Galilee, these three Oriental futurists only rose to fame in their distant place of exile overseas in Sicily. *A fortiori* it is improbable that Jesus had ever heard of the Gracchi or of Agis and Cleomenes. Accordingly, if we are to believe that the faculty of mimesis has played a part in producing any of the 89 correspondences between the story of Jesus and the stories of our eleven pagan Hellenic heroes, and if we want to discover the field in which mimesis has operated in this case, we must concentrate our attention, not upon the relations between the heroes themselves, but upon the relations between the literary authorities in whose works the heroes' respective stories have been recorded.

In setting out to discover, if we can, whether some of these literary authorities have been influenced by others, our first step must be to ascertain, as nearly as possible, their respective dates; and our first findings will be—in chronological order—as follows:

Diodorus (*vivebat circa* 70–1 B.C.).

The Gospel according to Saint Mark (*scriptum circa* A.D. 65).[1]

Plutarch (*vivebat circa* A.D. 45–120).

The Gospels according to Saint Matthew and Saint Luke (*scripta inter* A.D. 70 *et* 95).[2]

The Gospel according to Saint John (*scriptum circa* A.D. 100).[3]

It will be seen that, while Diodorus's *Library of Universal History* was written at least sixty-five years earlier than any of the other works here in question, the chronological relation of Plutarch's *Lives* to the Gospels cannot be ascertained precisely. We can only say that probably the *Lives* were published later than the Gospel according to Saint Mark, at about the same time as the other two Synoptic Gospels, and earlier than the Gospel according to Saint John.

These results, however, even as far as they go, still leave us on the threshold of our chronological problem; for these works of literature which we have just tentatively arranged in a chronological order all have pedigrees; and, if we now try to grope our way back from the works themselves to their sources, we shall arrive at a different chronological sequence.

To take the Gospels first: Matthew and Luke have one common source in the collection of sayings of Jesus which New Testament scholars call 'Q',[4] and another common source in Mark; and, while the relative dates of Mark and 'Q' are matters of controversy between scholars, it seems to be generally agreed that both works must have been written before A.D. 70.[5] The date of Mark is of particular importance for the purpose of our present inquiry, because Matthew, at any rate, is almost entirely dependent on Mark for his account of the Passion.[6] And, if we proceed to an

---

[1] 'About half-way through the sixties' according to Meyer, E.: *Ursprung und Anfänge des Christentums*, vol. i (Stuttgart and Berlin 1921, Cotta), p. 237; *circa* A.D. 65 (i.e. *after* the Neronian persecution of the Christians, but *before* the destruction of the Temple at Jerusalem) according to Streeter, B. H.: *The Four Gospels* (London 1924, Macmillan), p. 495.

[2] Meyer, op. cit., vol. i, p. 239. Streeter dates Luke *circa* A.D. 80 (op. cit., p. 540) and Matthew *circa* A.D. 85 (op. cit., p. 524).

[3] *Circa* A.D. 100–20, according to Meyer, E.: *Ursprung und Anfänge des Christentums*, vol. iii (Stuttgart and Berlin 1923, Cotta), p. 647. Streeter, on the other hand, dates John *circa* A.D. 90–5 (op. cit., pp. 456–7).

[4] For a tentative reconstruction of 'Q' see Streeter, op. cit., p. 291.

[5] Meyer, E.: *Ursprung und Anfänge des Christentums*, vol. i, pp. 234–6, dates 'Q', on internal evidence, between A.D. 67 and A.D. 70, and therefore slightly later than Mark, which the same scholar, as we have seen (footnote 1, above), dates *circa* A.D. 65. Streeter, on the other hand, who dates Mark between A.D. 64 and A.D. 70, inclines (op. cit., pp. 150 and 191) to date 'Q' earlier than Mark—perhaps as early as A.D. 50.

[6] Meyer, op. cit., vol. i, p. 212, holds that Luke's, as well as Matthew's, account of the Passion is mainly based on Mark. Streeter, on the other hand, op. cit., p. 202, holds 'that Luke is in the main reproducing an account of the Passion parallel to, but independent of, Mark, and enriching it with occasional insertions from Mark'.

analysis of Mark, we can distinguish one source—'the Twelve-source'—which must have been written later than the martyrdom of the son of Zebedee in A.D. 44, and another, embodying the recollections of Peter, which appears to be of an earlier date than 'the Twelve-source'.[1] *Ex hypothesi*, however, the very earliest sources of the Gospels cannot be anterior in date to the fourth decade of the first century of the Christian Era, and the sources of our pagan authorities for the stories of our pagan heroes can all be traced back to earlier dates than that. For example, the books of Diodorus's work that deal with the history of the Hellenic World during the half century beginning, where Polybius left off, in 146 B.C. are believed to reproduce a continuation of Polybius's history from the hand of Poseidonius (*vivebat circa* 135–51 B.C.).[2] Plutarch's *Lives of the Gracchi* appears to be derived immediately from a Greek source[3] written from the point of view of the philosophic and aristocratic school of Roman republicans whose proto-martyr and fount of inspiration was Cato Minor.[4] But this immediate source of Plutarch's work appears in turn to have been derived in large measure from Latin biographies of the Gracchi[5] which were themselves derived from the *Annals* of Gaius Fannius —a statesman-historian who was approximately Tiberius Gracchus's contemporary.[6] Fannius scaled the walls of Carthage at Gracchus's heels in 146 B.C.,[7] and he was consul in 122 B.C., which was the year of Gaius Gracchus's second tribunate. We may take it that Fannius's life falls within the dates 166–96 B.C. In the third place Plutarch's *Lives of Agis and Cleomenes* appears to have been derived—again not immediately, but ultimately—in part from the history of Polybius (*vivebat circa* 206–128 B.C.), who must have been born rather less than half a century after Cleomenes himself, and in part from the works of two of Cleomenes' senior contemporaries: his political opponent Aratus of Sicyon (*vivebat* 271–213 B.C.) and his panegyrist Phylarchus (*vivebat circa* 270–210 B.C.).

[1] For the sources of Mark see Meyer, op. cit., vol. i, pp. 236–7. For the grounds for supposing that John was put to death at the same time as James, see ibid., vol. i, pp. 144–5, and vol. iii, pp. 174–7 and 420.

[2] It is to this source that we may trace the surprisingly humane and sympathetic attitude towards the insurgent slaves in Sicily which comes out in Diodorus's narrative. While Diodorus of Agyrium might perhaps have been inclined, for his own part, to see the story from the point of view of his own compatriots, Poseidonius of Apamea sees it through the eyes of the slaves from Syria and Cilicia who had started life, like Poseidonius himself, as subjects of the Seleucid Monarchy. Poseidonius and Eunus actually came from the same city).

[3] See Kornemann, E.: *Zur Geschichte der Gracchenzeit: Quellenkritische Untersuchungen* (Leipzig 1903, Dieterich), pp. 41–2.

[4] For this school see V. C (i) (d) 1, vol. v, pp. 390 and 392; V. C (ii) (a) 3, vol. v, p. 405; and V. C (ii) (a), in the present volume, p. 250, above.

[5] Kornemann, op. cit., p. 42.

[6] For Fannius's work and life see Kornemann, op. cit., pp. 20–37.

[7] Fannius himself is cited as the authority for this anecdote in Plutarch: *Gracchi*, chap. 4.

What is Plutarch's relation to these literary authorities whose works were written perhaps 250 or even 300 years before Plutarch's own? So far from drawing directly upon these original sources, Plutarch seems to have been content to take over his stories in the shape which they had assumed as the result of a long and complicated literary history.

'The foundation of the narrative, which comes from the historians, the piecing together of this with the biographical matter which had to be imported from elsewhere, the arrangement of the whole round the person of the hero—all this was found by Plutarch ready made. . . . His authorities come from here, there, and everywhere. . . . This variegated tissue is part and parcel of the genre of literature of which Plutarch is for us the representative. . . . Plutarch does not dream of claiming to have woven it himself; his achievement is simply to have produced a work that has on it a sheen of newness. . . . Plutarch's *Lives* constitute, through their existence, a proof that, before Plutarch's day, there was a bio-graphical literature of the Plutarchan kind with a history extending over many generations.'[1]

If Plutarch's work is so remote from the original sources as this, it would seem at first sight improbable that his text would repro-duce the original texts at all closely; yet, surprising though this may be, we have evidence that, at least in one passage, Plutarch's *Lives of Agis and Cleomenes* does reproduce Phylarchus's *Histories*[2] with a closeness that here and there approximates to identity. This may be verified by comparing Plutarch's chap. 34 (our Point 13) with the passage that is expressly quoted from Phylarchus by Athenaeus in *Deipnosophistae*, Book IV, pp. 141 F–142 F.[3] And the equally close verbal correspondence between a passage of Plutarch's chapter 50 and a passage of Book XXVIII, chap. 4, of Justin's epitome of Pompeius Trogus's *Historiae Philippicae* is probably to be explained likewise as an effect of the preservation, in both, of Phylarchus's *ipsissima verba*. When we further consider that the style, tone, and colour of these two passages in the *Lives of Agis and Cleomenes* also prevail through the greater part of this piece of Plutarch's work, and that they exactly tally[4] with the account of Phylarchus's work that is given by Polybius,[5] we may feel war-ranted in concluding that a substantial portion, and perhaps even the greater part, of Plutarch's text consists of *résumés* of the text

[1] Leo, F.: *Die Griechisch-Römische Biographie nach ihrer Literarischen Form* (Leipzig 1901, Teubner), p. 155. The whole of chapter 8, 'Plutarch', and chapter 9, 'Die Form der plutarchischen Biographie', is pertinent to our present inquiry.

[2] According to Suidas, Phylarchus's work covered the history of the Hellenic World from the death of Pyrrhus in 272 B.C. to the death of Cleomenes in 220 B.C.

[3] See Bux, E.: 'Zwei sozialistische Novellen bei Plutarch' in *Klio*, vol. xix (1925), pp. 426–9. It is the latter part of this passage quoted in Athenaeus, i.e. 142 C–142 F, that actually overlaps with the chapter of Plutarch.

[4] This point is made by Bux, op. cit., p. 428.   [5] See pp. 457–9, below.

of Phylarchus[1] which survived, with remarkably little defacement, all their temporary lifts in the successive literary conveyances in which they made their long and broken journey from Phylarchus's manuscript to Plutarch's.

This excursion into the realm of *Quellenkritik* gives us the following chronological sequence for our original authorities,[2] in so far as we can identify these with any certainty:

Aratus (*vivebat* 271–213 B.C.).
Phylarchus (*vivebat circa* 270–210 B.C.).
Polybius (*vivebat circa* 206–128 B.C.).
Fannius (*vivebat circa* 166–96 B.C.).
Poseidonius (*vivebat circa* 135–51 B.C.).
Peter (*testimonium prompsit post* A.D. 30).
'The Twelve-source' (*scriptum post* A.D. 44).
A source peculiar to the Gospel according to Saint Luke[3] (*scriptum prae* 'Q', if Meyer is right in dating 'Q' *post* A.D. 67).
'Q' (*scriptum inter* A.D. 67 *et* A.D. 70).
A source peculiar to the Gospel according to Saint Matthew (*scriptum post* 'Q').[4]
The Gospel according to Saint John (*scriptum post* A.D. 100).

Now that we have arrived at this sequence of the earliest authorities which we are able to identify in each case, what are we to make of it? How do our findings bear upon our problem of literary apparentation-and-affiliation? If we are to believe that some, at least, of our correspondences are to be credited to the account of a practice of literary mimesis, then the most obvious conclusion to draw would be that, wherever we have detected a point of

---

[1] Leo observes in op. cit., p. 175, that Plutarch's *'Lives of Agis and Cleomenes* are reminiscent of his *Life of Aratus*, except that the *Aratus* has been constructed by working the historians into Aratus's *Memoirs*, while the *Agis and Cleomenes* has been constructed by working Aratus and Polybius into the narrative of Phylarchus'. This high estimate of Plutarch's debt to Phylarchus is not impugned by the fact that in the *Lives of Agis and Cleomenes* Phylarchus is cited by name only three times (in chaps. 9, 26, and 49). It is more pertinent to observe that Phylarchus is *not* cited as Plutarch's authority in either of the two passages (in chaps. 34 and 50) which are known, almost for certain, to be of Phylarchan origin. There is a far greater number of other passages in this particular piece of Plutarch's work that can be traced back with certainty to Polybius, and yet Plutarch here cites Polybius as an authority not even three times but only once (in chap. 48). It will be seen that, in Plutarch, the number of express references to an authority gives no indication whatsoever of the extent to which that authority has actually been drawn upon as a source.

[2] The sequence here given for the sources of the Gospels follows Meyer, op. cit., vol. i, pp. 236–7.

[3] See Meyer, op. cit., vol. i, pp. 216–24. Streeter, op. cit., p. 218, suggests that this document, which he calls 'L', was the work of Luke himself, and was written by him *circa* A.D. 60, during his two years' sojourn at Caesarea in attendance upon Saint Paul. He further suggests that Luke subsequently combined 'L', first with 'Q' into a 'Proto-Luke', and then, through this intermediate stage, with Mark, to make the Gospel according to Saint Luke as we now have it (op. cit., p. 219).

[4] See Meyer, op. cit., vol. i, pp. 213–16, and Streeter, op. cit., p. 231. Streeter, op. cit., p. 150, dates 'M' *circa* A.D. 65. This would make 'M', as well as 'L', anterior to 'Q' if Meyer's date for 'Q' is right. On the other hand, 'Q' is anterior to both 'M' and 'L' if Streeter is right in dating 'Q' perhaps as early as A.D. 50 (see p. 434, footnote 5, above).

correspondence between one literary authority and another, the incident as recorded by the earlier or the earliest of two or more authorities is an authentic matter of fact, but that, when the same incident reappears in some later authority or authorities, it is in this context a piece of fiction which has been fraudulently fabricated out of the genuine fact which the earlier authority has honestly put on record. This conclusion may be obvious, but it involves at least three assumptions: first that the earlier authority in each case is reporting, if not the whole truth, at any rate nothing but the truth; second that the later authority has been guilty of a deliberate act of fabrication; and third that the point in common between the two or more authorities that are in question in any given case has ultimately been derived by the later authority or authorities from the earlier or the earliest, even if only at second or at tenth hand—to the exclusion of the alternative possible hypothesis that all the authorities in question, the earlier and the later alike, have derived the point which is common to them from some source that is not identical with any of them and that is earlier than them all. Not one of these three assumptions can properly be taken for granted; and to look into all three of them closely may be the most profitable step for us to take next.

Dichtung und Wahrheit

Is the apparent case of literary mimesis with which we are now concerned a clear case of plagiarism? The concept of plagiarism pre-supposes the existence of a series of works of literature which have been successively published at definite dates in a chronological sequence and which, each and all, can be attributed respectively to the pens of particular individual authors. In any sophisticated social milieu authorship is the normal way of literary creation, and in such milieux it eclipses every alternative way so completely that it becomes easy to forget that works of literature can be brought into existence in any other way than through being deliberately planned in the mind, and as deliberately written by the pen, of somebody who in consequence will be recognized on all hands as the sole and unquestionable author of 'his' book. Nevertheless this sophisticated way of literary creation ought not to be taken for granted, without inquiry, in any and every case; for, while every act of creation is, no doubt, the travail of some individual soul,[1] it does not follow that every creator will think of setting his stamp upon his handiwork in order to apprise the World that it has come from his workshop. This assertion of authorship implies

---

[1] On this point see III. C (ii) (*a*), vol. iii, pp. 230–1, above.

some touch of a self-consciousness and egotism which are in-grained on the seamy side of Civilization but which are conspicu-ous by their absence on the primitive level of human life; and in human history hitherto Civilization has been the exception and primitiveness the rule. In other contexts we have not only ob-served that the number of human societies of the primitive species that have come into existence up to date is vastly greater than the present muster-roll of civilizations:[1] we have also observed that within the bosom of any civilization of which we know—and this at any stage of its history in regard to which we have at our com-mand the necessary evidence for making the observation—the individual 'members' of the society who still remain at or near the primitive level will always be found to outnumber, and this over-whelmingly, the handful of higher personalities who create and sustain the civilization by projecting a shadow of their own inner life into social institutions which govern the outward lives of the primitive majority of their fellows.[2] On this showing, it is evident that the primitive êthos does not cease to count just because it may have been pushed momentarily into the background; it has to be reckoned with always and everywhere; and this consideration applies to the study of literature no less than to that of any other human activity.

What, then, is the normal means of literary creation—and trans-mission—in a primitive social milieu? The question can be answered in negative terms which may have a bearing upon our present inquiry. On the primitive level there is no consciousness of authorship, no desire to claim copyright, and consequently no such thing as plagiarism. There is also, in such milieux, no sense of a distinction between 'fact' and 'fiction'. In a primitive social circle the tale of life is taken, by teller and listener alike, in the way in which a child takes a fairy story.[3] And in the telling of a fairy story everybody and everything is anonymous—'the author' as well as his audience, and the heroes and heroines as well as the author. Fairy-tales are, in fact, 'folk-tales' which have lingered on in the nursery after they have been swept out of the parlour; for the anonymity of the characters is the hall-mark which distin-guishes 'folk-tales' from other forms of literature.[4]

Such anonymous 'folk-tales' are the native voice of a 'folk-memory' which is at work all the time behind the scenes even in those sophisticated theatres of life in which audience and actors

---

[1] See I. C (iii) (a), vol. i, pp. 147–8, above.
[2] See III. C (ii) (a), vol. iii, pp. 239–44, above.
[3] See I. C (iii) (e), Annex, vol. i, p. 442, above.
[4] See Chadwick, H. M.: *The Heroic Age* (Cambridge 1912, University Press), pp. 110–111.

virtually conspire to draw a veil over this telltale relic of a simpler past; and in primitive milieux this ancient way of distilling the quintessence of experience and transmitting the elixir from one generation to another holds the field without a rival. 'Folk-memory' performs, for people who are still content to rely on it, substantially the same service as is performed for the sophisticated by the writing and reading of books. It serves as a channel for the passage of a mental current from mind to mind *in saecula saeculorum*; but the waters that flow along this primitive bed have quite a different effect upon the mental works of Man according to whether these works themselves happen to be primitive or sophisticated. For the works of primitive minds the waters of this subterranean mental stream serve as waters of Memory; but on the works of sophisticated minds they act as waters of Lethe. It seems that this current cannot carry along with it the experiences that fall into its stream without reducing them, all alike, to an anonymity which is native to the works of primitive minds, but which for the works of sophisticated minds is tantamount to a loss of identity. As a literal torrent of water tools the rocks and pulps the tree-trunks that cross its path until at length it casts them up again, far down stream, high and dry in the unrecognizable shape of smooth-faced boulders and water-logged driftwood, so the mighty current of 'folk-memory' is perpetually engulfing foreign objects—fragments of historical events, glimpses of historical personages, and sometimes even scraps of sophisticated literature (where a primitive social milieu is in contact with a sophisticated one)—and the flotsam fares as hardly in the mental as in the physical stream. Here too it is battered out of all recognition before it is cast up again as jetsam on a distant strand.[1]

In other contexts we have already watched the waters of Lethe at their work of weathering away the authentic original features of historical events and historical personages which have fallen into their bed. We have seen how some barbarian war-lord, whose historical career can be traced, and his historical importance assessed, from the archives of the civilization on which he has preyed, may, as a hero of epic, assume an importance and acquire a career in the realm of poetic imagination which bear little or no relation to his authentic standing in the realm of prosaic fact.[2] Nor is it only the External Proletariat that displays this imagina-

---

[1] For example, in the Ahiqar Romance the characters of Sennacherib and Esarhaddon have been transformed to a degree at which they no longer betray any recognizable affinity with their historical originals (Meyer, E.: *Der Papyrusfund von Elephantine*, 2nd ed. (Leipzig 1912, Hinrichs), pp. 120–1).

[2] See V. C (i) (c) 3, Annex III, 'Historical Fact and Heroic Tradition', in vol. v, pp. 607–14, above.

tive power of transmuting 'fact' into 'fiction' by an alchemy which
is at once destructive and creative. We have also watched the
history of Alexander the Great being transmuted into the Alexander Romance at the very time when an authentic record was being
made, out of an ample dossier, by conscientious and scientific-
minded Hellenic historians.[1] How came the figure of the Macedonian war-lord to be kidnapped and carried off bodily into
Fairyland[2] in the broad daylight of Hellenic rationalism? And
whose were the impudent hands that stole the body? The answer
is that Alexander's body was snatched by Orientals whom the
conqueror himself, in his historical career, had forcibly conscripted
into the ranks of the Hellenic internal proletariat.[3] And this
sensational capture, which was effected almost on the morrow of
Alexander's death, was the first successful stroke in an Oriental
counter-attack which was to culminate, more than nine centuries
later, in the eviction of Alexander's Roman successors from their
last foothold on Oriental ground by the prowess of the Primitive
Muslim Arabs. A millennial war of *revanche* which was carried
to its conclusion on the military plane in the days of the Caliph
'Umar had been opened on the literary plane as early as the days
of Alexander's own diadochi.

Why was it that the Orientals, in their long-drawn-out encounter
with Hellenism, were able to score this precocious and premoni-
tory success in the field of literature so long before they were able
to follow it up in the fields of war and politics? The answer seems
to be that, at the time when Alexander suddenly annexed the
domain of the Achaemenian Empire to the Hellenic World by the
superficial method of military conquest, the ground—or, rather,
the river-bed—was already prepared for a rapid transmutation of
an episode of Hellenic history into a theme of Oriental romance.

[1] See V. C (i) (c) 3, vol. v, p. 252, and V. C (i) (c) 3, Annex III, vol. v, p. 608, above.
'Pseudo-Callisthenes should be regarded as the narrator and formulator of an historical
myth. . . . That he used historical sources is no argument against this, for in the era of
Alexandrian scholarship even myths were built upon a foundation of scholarship, as
"the Myth of the Twentieth Century" is based upon an interpretation of anthropology
and history. It is from the dregs and lower strata of historiography that the Alexander
Romance has drawn its "erudition" ' (Braun, M.: *History and Romance in Graeco-
Oriental Literature* (Oxford 1938, Blackwell), p. 32).
[2] 'One may be sure that the common people, to whom it belonged spiritually and
socially, believed in the truth of the account as implicitly as a child believes a fairy-
tale. . . . The Alexander Romance belongs spiritually and socially to the common people
who cannot clearly and consciously differentiate between truth (ἀλήθεια), lies (ψεῦδος), and
literary fiction (πλάσμα) and therefore willingly accept the myth, especially the written
myth, above all when this myth appeals to their wishes and ideals, as members of a
particular social group. In the Alexander Romance truth and fiction are inextricably
interwoven. The categories ψεῦδος and πλάσμα cannot be applied at all to the mass of
untrue and fantastic statements. To apply them would be unjust to the anonymous
author and his readers, because the standards and categories of the historian are not
applicable to their intellectual capacities' (ibid., pp. 33–4).
[3] For this social effect of Alexander's conquests see III. C (i) (a), vol. iii, pp. 140 and
149–51; III. C (i) (d), vol. iii, pp. 197–9; and V. C (i) (c) 2, vol. v, pp. 64–5, above.

The 'sea-change' which the historical Hellenic figure of Alexander was now to undergo in the imagination of the Oriental subjects of the Achaemenian Empire's Macedonian 'successor-states'
had already been undergone by other historical figures who once
upon a time had played an authentic part in the histories of two
non-Hellenic civilizations—the Babylonic and the Egyptiac. By
the time when Hellenism imposed itself, by force of Macedonian
arms, upon the Syriac, Egyptiac, Babylonic, and Indic worlds, the
Babylonic and Egyptiac worlds had already been subjugated, by
force of Achaemenian arms, to the Syriac. In other contexts we
have noticed how vehemently and persistently these two subjugated societies kicked against the pricks, and how warmly they
welcomed Alexander as a deliverer from the Syriac yoke.[1] But,
while they had been fighting a losing battle against the aggression
which the Syriac Society was committing against them on the
military and political plane in the shape of an Achaemenian
imperialism, the Egyptiac and Babylonic societies had all the time
been taking their Syriac conquerors captive on the plane of 'folk-
lore'. They had both of them succeeded in instilling a memorial
of their own past greatness into the 'folk-memory' of their latter-
day masters. And this memorial had taken the form of 'folk-tales'
in which certain authentic characters and events of Egyptiac and
Babylonic history had been transmuted into subjects of romance.
The past greatness of the Babylonic World had been embalmed
in the romance of 'Ninus and Semiramis'; the past greatness of
the Egyptiac World in the romances of 'Sesostris' and 'Nectanebos'.
And the historical materials out of which these three romances are
woven can be identified. The name of the legendary Queen
'Semiramis of Babylon' is taken from that of an historical queen of
Assyria, Sammu-ramat, who was the wife of King Shamshiadad V
(*regnabat* 824–810 B.C.) and the mother of King Adadnirari III
(*regnabat* 809–782 B.C.).[2] 'Ninus', who plays the hero to Semiramis' heroine, is an abstraction that stands for the prowess of all
the kings that ever went forth to war from Nineveh.[3] In a similar
way 'Sesostris' seems to stand for the prowess of all the emperors
of the Twelfth Egyptiac Dynasty who were the life and soul of the
Egyptiac universal state,[4] while Nectanebos stands for the prowess
of all the patriot-kings who ever led Egyptiac forlorn hopes against
any of the Asiatic oppressors of the Egyptiac World from the days
of Esarhaddon to the days of Artaxerxes Ochus.[5]

[1] See IV. C (ii) (*b*) 2, vol. iv, p. 100, footnote 4; V. C (i) (*c*) 2, vol. v, pp. 94 and 123,
with footnote 2; V. C (i) (*c*) 4, vol. v, pp. 347–8; and V. C (ii) (*a*), in the present
volume, p. 203, above.
[2] Braun, Martin: *History and Romance in Graeco-Oriental Literature* (Oxford 1938,
Blackwell), p. 7.   [3] Ibid., p. 8.   [4] Ibid., p. 13.
[5] In these romances the Babylonic and Egyptiac imagination found 'compensation'

Thus, by the time when the Hellenes broke in upon the Oriental scene, the Egyptiac and Babylonic 'folk-tales' had already travelled far from the historical facts which had been their starting-point; and in this situation the Egyptiac and Babylonic civilizations presented themselves for inspection by Hellenic eyes in two distinct guises.[1] In both societies there was a sophisticated upper stratum which wanted, and tried, to set before its Hellenic liberators the authentic history of the venerable civilization for which the constituents of this still surviving upper social stratum felt themselves to be trustees. The monuments of this effort are the learned works of the Egyptiac scholar Manetho and the Babylonic scholar Berossus; and the fragments of the two works that have come down to us are enough to show that both these scholars were at pains to exclude all 'folk-lore' from treatises that were intended to be scientific. Manetho boycotts the legend of 'Sesostris', Berossus the legend of 'Semiramis'.[2] This scholarly conscientiousness, however, was ultimately of no avail; for the sophisticated Hellenic public to which these treatises were intended to appeal was inevitably a small one; and the picture of the Egyptiac and Babylonic civilizations that eventually impressed itself on Hellenic minds was not the authentic portrait which the two scholars had presented: it was a fancy picture in the gorgeous colours of the legends which Manetho and Berossus had sought, without success, to suppress. In the matter of Nectanebos the extant literature enables us to catch a glimpse of the stages by which 'fiction' gained the upper hand over 'fact'.[3] The historical tradition, in which the motives, as well as the actions, that are attributed to Nectanebos are soberly realistic, has been preserved in Diodorus's *Library of Universal History*.[4] In the next stage—which appears to be represented by a story, preserved by Josephus, in which the hero's name has been changed from Nectanebos to Amenophis[5]—the actions are still historical, but the motives are already fictitious.[6] In the third and last stage, which is represented by the Nectanebos Prologue to the Alexander Romance,[7] the actions as well as the motives have passed out of the realm of History into that of Legend.

It will be seen that, by the time when Alexander burst into view

(in the psycho-analyst's technical sense of the term) for the brute fact of Achaemenian supremacy. The apocryphal conquests of the legendary 'Sesostris' are carefully made to surpass those of the historical Achaemenidae: e.g. Sesostris succeeds where Cambyses had failed when he conquers the Arabs and Ethiopians, and where Darius the Great had failed when he conquers the Scyths (ibid., pp. 15–17).
[1] Ibid., pp. 3–5.   [2] Ibid., pp. 14–15.
[3] See ibid., pp. 19–25.
[4] Diodorus, Book XVI, chap. 48, § 6; chap. 51, § 3 (see Braun, op. cit., pp. 21–2).
[5] Josephus: *Contra Apionem*, Book I, §§ 243–77, citing Manetho (see Braun, op. cit., loc. cit.).   [6] Ibid., ~. 22.   [7] Ibid., pp. 21–2.

over the horizon of the Oriental World, the flood of Lethe was
already flowing strong and the waters were waiting to swallow the
audacious intruder up. *Patet immane et vasto respectat hiatu!*[1] The
alchemy which had done such wonders with the historical Sammu-
ramat and with the historical Nectanebos and with all the Senwosrets was promptly applied to Alexander in his turn. On the magic
soil of Egypt the son of Philip became a son of Amon; his Hellenic
human head sprouted his Egyptiac father's ram's-horns;[2] and, in
this shape of Dhu'l-Qarnayn, Alexander soon went the way of
Nectanebos.[3] The Alexander Romance is presented from an
Egyptiac standpoint.[4] It pictures the Egyptiac and Hellenic
worlds as in league with one another against the Syriac World.[5]
We may infer that the Alexander Romance was conceived in the
womb of a Graeco-Egyptian underworld in the purlieus of the
City of Alexandria;[6] for this Alexandrian fraction of a now vastly
expanded Hellenic internal proletariat was the sole remaining
beneficiary of Alexander's vision of a universal human fellowship[7]
in an Egyptiac World in which Alexander's Lagid successors had
elsewhere substituted a cold-blooded policy of exploitation[8] for
Alexander's own generous dream of fraternization.[9]

Here we see Hellenic history being transmuted into Oriental
'folk-lore'; but this process of transmutation was not a 'one-way'
movement. We can also see Oriental 'folk-tales' being transmuted
—not, of course, into authentic history but into the sophisticated,
instead of the primitive, kind of literature, through being suffused
with Hellenic *motifs* that are palpably alien from the native Oriental êthos. For example, the Hellenic *motif* of eroticism has made
its way into a piece of Jewish literature—*The Testaments of the
Twelve Patriarchs*—which appears to have been written towards
the end of the second century B.C.;[10] for in *The Testament of Joseph*
the Old Testament story of Potiphar's Wife has demonstrably been
recast under the influence of the Hellenic story of Phaedra.[11] There

---

[1] Lucretius: *De Rerum Natura*, Book V, l. 375.
[2] These horns found their way on to Alexander's head even on the otherwise Hellenic
coins that were designed by Greek artists for the mints of Alexander's Greek successors.
[3] For the relation of the Alexander Romance to the Nectanebos Romance see Braun,
op. cit., pp. 23–4.   [4] Ibid., pp. 32 and 36–43.
[5] Ibid., pp. 38–9.
[6] Ibid., pp. 32 and 36–7.
[7] For this vision of Alexander's see V. C (i) (d) 7, pp. 6–10, and V. C (ii) (a),
pp. 246–7, above.
[8] For this aspect of the Lagid régime see V. C (i) (c) 2, vol. v, p. 65, above.
[9] For this local Alexandrian realization of Alexander's oecumenical ideal see Braun,
op. cit., pp. 37–8 and 40–1.   [10] Ibid., p. 46.
[11] For the influence of the Hellenic story of Phaedra and Hippolytus upon the Jewish
story of Potiphar's Wife and Joseph see ibid., pp. 46–95, and eundem: *Griechischer
Roman und Hellenistische Geschichtschreibung* (Frankfurt am Main 1934, Klostermann),
pp. 23–117. Dr. Braun's thesis is summed up in the last paragraph on p. 114 of the
latter monograph. For what follows on this subject in the present Study the writer
is wholly indebted to the results of Dr. Braun's researches.

is even a verbal correspondence between *The Testament of Joseph*, v, 2, and Euripides' *Hippolytus*, ll. 656–8.[1] And we can observe how the cumulative effect of the Hellenic influence upon Jewish literature told during the two hundred years or so that elapsed between the lifetime of the author of *The Testaments of the Twelve Patriarchs* and the lifetime of Josephus (*vivebat circa* A.D. 38–108). *The Testament of Joseph* has adopted the *motif* of the Hellenic story of Phaedra without abandoning the native Jewish style, spirit, or ethical standards; and 'the Haggadoth narrator judaizes alien elements' in the same fashion. On the other hand 'Josephus hellenizes Biblical and Haggadic tales, so that they become something completely new and different'.[2]

In Josephus's sophisticated pages the Hebrew patriarch Joseph has been disguised out of all recognition by being dressed up in the Hellenic habiliments of an invulnerable Stoic sage who is τύχῃ δοῦλος, φύσει ἐλεύθερος.[3] In this Josephan Hellenized version of the story of Joseph and Potiphar's Wife there are a number of points of correspondence not only with the story of Hippolytus and Phaedra, but also with the story of Lucretia, as these two Hellenic stories are recounted in the works of five different Greek and Latin authors;[4] and some of the correspondences between Josephus's *Antiquities* and Seneca's *Phaedra* extend to an identity of words.[5] How are these correspondences to be explained? It seems unlikely that Josephus has been borrowing directly from the Hellenic authors in whose works the points of correspondence are to be found. Three out of the five—Livy, Ovid, and Seneca—write in Latin; and it seems most improbable that Latin literature was an open book to Josephus, considering the imperfectness of his mastery even of Greek. Of the two Greek authors—Dionysius of Halicarnassus and Heliodorus of Emesa—Dionysius, again, seems unlikely to have been studied by Josephus, while Heliodorus is ruled out of account by the fact that he was Josephus's junior by perhaps not less than 200 years. We are left with the alternative of explaining the correspondences between Josephus and the five pagan Hellenic authors here in question on the hypothesis that they have all of them been borrowing—though not necessarily any of them at first hand—from some common source;

---

[1] Braun, *History and Romance*, p. 57.
[2] Ibid., p. 93. Compare *Roman und Geschichtschreibung*, pp. 41 and 113.
[3] Ibid., pp. 30–4.
[4] See the table of nine correspondences between Josephus, on the one hand, and Dionysius, Heliodorus, Livy, Ovid, and Seneca, on the other hand, ibid., p. 96.
[5] e.g. Josephus: *Antiquities*, Book II, § 43 (Joseph's first speech) ‖ Seneca: *Phaedra*, ll. 131–5 (Braun: *Roman und Geschichtschreibung*, pp. 41–2); Josephus: *Antiquities*, Book II, §§ 51–2 (Joseph's second speech) ‖ Seneca: *Phaedra*, ll. 145–64 (Braun, op. cit., pp. 82–7). The second of these two verbal correspondences also extends to a passage of Philo (ibid., pp. 82–4).

and the scholar who has brought this set of correspondences to light has put his finger on a possible common source for them all in the shape of a no longer extant first version of Euripides' *Hippolytus*.[1]

Thus, by the time of Josephus, who was an approximate contemporary of Plutarch's, the volatile waters of Lethe had made considerable play with the Hellenic and Oriental flotsam that had been jostling in the current since the time, by then some four hundred years back, when Alexander had troubled the waters in his momentous act of crossing the Hellespont. On the one hand the historical figure of the Hellenic conqueror had been transmuted into the legendary figure of a hero of Egyptiac romance; and on the other hand the mythical figure of the Syriac patriarch Joseph —who was the eponym of a pair of Israelitish tribes—had been dressed up in an outfit of Hellenic stage properties borrowed partly from Euripides and partly from Zeno.

These proven facts of Hellenico-Oriental literary history during the first four centuries *post Alexandrum* throw at least three beams of light on the problem which we are studying in this Annex. In the first place these facts make it clear that 'folk-memory' is a highly conductive medium within the limits of its operation. We have observed above that these limits are narrowly drawn. A large part—perhaps the greater part—of the conventional furniture of sophisticated minds will not float in these waters at all; and a piece of this precious furniture that falls into the river is apt to sink like a stone to the bottom of the river-bed, where it may remain stuck in the mud for good and all, without any prospect of being rolled along with the current and so eventually being cast up again on shore. On the other hand we can see now that any foreign bodies that the current of 'folk-memory' is capable of carrying along with it have a prospect of travelling far and fast; and in the second place we can read the secret of this mobility. The characters and events that travel in Lethe's stream become mobile thanks to becoming anonymous. In reducing them to anonymity the alchemy of these waters fines them down to a degree of tenuity at which they are almost capable of passing through a needle's eye.[2] In this medium

---

[1] For this possible common source see Braun: *Roman und Geschichtschreibung*, pp. 87 and 97; *History and Romance*, pp. 49–50. On this point Professor Gilbert Murray observes: 'I have always had a difficulty about the First Hippolytus. Normally a second version outbids the first, but here the first goes beyond the second, and the second has more sophrosyne. I think the explanation is that Euripides was putting on the stage a story, an Egyptian 'novelle', and first made the mistake of putting the incidents of the story straight on to the stage: e.g. Phaedra's appeal to Hippolytus. Afterwards he made the technical improvements required for the stage.'

[2] e.g., 'concepts and figures belonging to the religion of Zarathustra found their way [into Judaism] above all in the lower strata of the [Jewish] people—even though those concerned were perhaps entirely unaware that these elements were of foreign origin'

of 'folk-memory' 'what is associated with the story of one figure is soon attributed to another'.[1] In the third place—and this point is of particular importance for our main inquiry—we can see that, in the shape of 'folk-lore', elements native to one culture can make their way into the life of another culture even at times when, on the sophisticated surface of life, the two cultures which are thus in effective communication with one another at a lower level are consciously antipathetic and are even each doing their utmost to hold the other at arm's length. The 'folk-tales' of 'Ninus and Semiramis' and 'Sesostris' and 'Nectanebos' made their way into the Syriac culture out of the Babylonic and Egyptiac cultures at a time when the upper social stratum of the two transmitting societies was in revolt against the recipient society. The *motif* of the Hellenic story of Hippolytus and Phaedra began to make its way into the Jewish story of Joseph and Potiphar's Wife after the breach between Jewry and Hellenism in the second quarter of the second century B.C.;[2] and this literary commerce reached its climax, about two hundred years later, in a generation which also saw the climax of the conflict between Jewry and Hellenism on every plane of conscious life. It looks as though the stream of 'folk-memory' flows at some level in the psyche at which the consciousness of cultural and national differences does not interfere with the primitive sense of a common humanity. And here we have an underground channel of intercourse between one culture and another which cannot easily be blocked by conscious and deliberate mental inhibitions. When once a piece of mental furniture that is the product of one culture has succeeded—at whatever price in the way of transmutation and attenuation—in keeping afloat in the stream of 'folk-memory', it will have acquired—at this price—a prospect of being carried past obstacles, and under barriers, which would almost certainly have availed to prevent its passage from one culture to another if it had been travelling in its original form on the sophisticated surface of life instead of having sunk to the primitive depths and there changed almost out of recognition.

These lights from other examples of literary intercourse across, or underneath, the superficial barriers between mutually hostile cultures prompt us to ask whether 'folk-memory' may be perchance the medium through which the story of Jesus and those

---

(Meyer, E.: *Ursprung und Anfänge des Christentums*, vol. ii (Stuttgart and Berlin 1921, Cotta), p. 95). If for 'even though' (*auch wenn*) we were to substitute 'just because' (*gerade weil*), we might be approaching nearer to the truth.
[1] Braun: *History and Romance*, p. 4.
[2] See V. C (i) (c) 2, vol. v, p. 68, and V. C (i) (d) 9 (β), in the present volume, pp. 103–5, above.

stories of pagan Hellenic heroes with which it displays our 89 points of correspondence have come into contact with one another. If the answer to this question is found to be in the affirmative, we shall still have to inquire whether this contact has been direct or whether—as seems the more probable explanation of the correspondences between the story of Joseph and the story of Hippolytus —the two stories, or sets of stories, have acquired their common features through having respectively and independently come into contact with some older piece of jetsam which has been travelling in the stream of Lethe side by side with both of them. It is idle, however, to enter upon these other inquiries until we have answered the prior question whether the story of Jesus on the one hand, and the stories of our eleven pagan Hellenic heroes on the other hand, do contain any elements of 'folk-lore'. A physiographer can tell, by the evidence of shape and patina, that a boulder or a log has at some stage of its history been water-borne. It may perhaps be practicable for a student of history to tell by analogous signs that a character or event which lies embedded to-day in some work of sophisticated or semi-sophisticated literature has travelled in the stream of 'folk-memory' once upon a time.

In the Gospels—to take them first—we shall not be surprised to find elements of this sort; for the Gospels can be properly described as the epic cycle of the Hellenic internal proletariat;[1] and epic poetry is a kind of *Zwischenreich* between the two mental realms of 'folk-lore' and history.

We have already taken note[2] of one piece of 'folk-lore' which the Gospel according to Saint Luke has in common with a work of the pagan Hellenic poet Hesiod. Shepherds abiding in the field are startled by an epiphany of the Heavenly Host, who have singled them out to be the recipients of the announcement of a theogony. We may now observe that not only the song of the Heavenly Host (Luke ii. 8–14) but also the song of the seer Simeon, which comes in the same chapter of Luke (ii. 25–35), has a counterpart in one of the Pālī scriptures of the Hinayanian Buddhist school of philosophy (Suttanipāta III, ii, 679–700) in the vision and the song of the seer Asita. This Indic seer has a vision of the Gods singing and dancing for joy, and is told that they are rejoicing over the birth of the Buddha in the form of a man child in the village of the Sakyas. Thereupon Asita goes to Kapilavastu, takes the infant Gautama in his arms, and prophesies his future greatness, with the further prophecy that the seer himself will not live to witness it. On this last point Asita's feeling is different from Simeon's;

---

[1] For this description of them see I. C (iii) (e), Annex, vol. i, p. 449, above.
[2] In V. C (i) (e), pp. 174–5, and in V. C (i) (d) 11, Annex I, pp. 363–4, above.

instead of being content to depart in peace after one glimpse of the
saviour in his infancy, he regrets that he will not live long enough
to hear the doctrine that the saviour will preach when he has grown
to manhood; but this single point of difference is outweighed by
the several points of similarity between the respective passages of
the Suttanipāta and the Gospel according to Saint Luke; and
these resemblances are cumulatively too close to be dismissed as
fortuitous.[1]

[1] This correspondence between a point in the Gospels and a point in the legend of
the Buddha is taken—as are also all the other correspondences between the Gospels and
the legend of the Buddha that are cited in the following pages—from Aufhauser, J. B.:
Buddha und Jesus in ihren Paralleltexten (Bonn 1926, Weber).

How are we to account for the presence of these common elements, which all bear
the marks of having either originated in, or travelled down, the stream of 'folk-lore', in
the stories of an Indic saviour who lived in Bihar and a Syriac saviour who lived in
Palestine? The common source may, of course, be some stratum of 'folk-lore' that was
so ancient and widespread that it was inherited by both the Indic and the Syriac culture,
independently of one another, from the cultural common stock of Primitive Mankind.
This explanation is simple, but it is not very convincing, considering that neither the
Indic nor the Syriac Society was one of those primary civilizations that arose directly
out of primitive life, and also considering the closeness of the correspondences even in
points of detail. It seems unlikely that these correspondences would have remained as
close as this if the legends had been travelling down two separate streams of 'folk-
memory' since, at latest, the fourth millennium B.C. It seems more probable that these
common elements in the stories of Jesus and Gautama have originated either in a
specifically Syriac or in a specifically Indic cycle of 'folk-lore' and that they have
travelled from the Syriac to the Indic World, or alternatively from the Indic World to
the Syriac, at some date not long anterior to that of the latest, and perhaps considerably
posterior to that of the earliest, of the Christian and Buddhist scriptures in which they
are now embedded.

While the Gospels all appear to date from the second half of the first century
of the Christian Era, the Buddhist scriptures here in question have a much wider
chronological range. The Suttanipāta appears to have been written *circa* 300 B.C., while
the date of the Padhānasutta and Samyutta-Nikāya appears to be at any rate anterior to
the beginning of the Christian Era (ibid., p. 7); but on the Buddhist side the correspondences are not confined to these relatively early Pāli scriptures of the Hinayanian
Buddhist philosophy. Some of them occur in the scriptures of the Mahayanian Buddhist
Church which are younger—and this in some cases perhaps by several centuries—than
the Christian Gospels, though their sources may be almost as old as the Pāli scriptures
of the Hīnayāna (ibid., loc. cit.). The correspondences between the Gospels and
these Mahayanian scriptures may, of course, be due to elements in the latter which
only found their way into them in the latest phase of their literary history; and in
that case these particular correspondences might be explicable as the result of an in-
filtration of Syriac 'folk-tales', which had already made their way into the Gospels, into
the Mahayanian legend of the Buddha in an age (*circa* A.D. 78–123, in the reign of the
Kushan King Kanishka) when the Mahāyāna was the prevailing religion in a Kushan
Empire which bestrode the Hindu Kush and embraced the north-eastern corner of the
Syriac World as well as the north-western corner of the Indic World (see II. D (vii),
vol. ii, pp. 372–3, and V. C (i) (c) 2, vol. v, pp. 132–6 and 139–40, above). This explanation, however, would not in any case cover the correspondences between the Gospels
and the Pāli scriptures which are anterior to the Christian Era; and these will have to be
accounted for in one or other of two possible ways. If the common elements are of Syriac
origin, we must suppose that they found their way out of the Syriac into the Indic World
during the period—beginning before the close of the sixth century B.C. and ending at
some date unknown before the invasion of India by Alexander the Great—when the
Indus Valley was politically united with the Syriac World under the aegis of a common
Pax Achaemenia. On the other hand, if the common elements are of Indic origin, we
must suppose that they found their way from India to Palestine, at some date between
Alexander's incursion into Northern India and the middle of the first century of the
Christian Era, either by the overland route from Pataliputra via Seleucia-on-Tigris and
Antioch-on-Orontes or by the maritime route from the South Indian ports to Egypt.
The overland route seems to have been opened after the approximately simultaneous
establishment of the Mauryan Empire in India and the Seleucid Empire in South-Western
Asia; the trade along this route received a great stimulus from the conquest of the now

We have also already come across another unmistakable deposit of 'folk-lore' in the Matthaean and Lucan prologues to the Gospel story of Jesus's life and preaching; and this tale of the conception and birth of a child who is not the son of his mother's husband is told, as we have seen, not only of Jesus but also of several pagan Hellenic men of mark—Plato, Alexander, Scipio Africanus Major, Augustus—who all of them likewise in some sense played the part of saviours, besides being told of several pagan Hellenic demigods or heroes: Ion, Perseus, Hêraklês.[1] Another story which hangs together with the miraculous-birth story, and which is found in the Gospels in the same context, is that of the miraculous—or, at any rate, extraordinary—escape of the child from a mortal danger which threatens him in his infancy. In another context[2] we have already noticed one widespread version of this story in which the babe is a foundling; and in this connexion we have observed that the Lucan account of the infancy of Jesus preserves at least one vestige of the foundling *motif* in representing the new-born babe as being laid in a manger. We may now observe that the Matthaean account preserves a variation on this theme which is also included in the legend of one of those pagan men of mark who are credited with a divine paternity. In the legend of the infancy of Augustus,[3] as in the prologue to the Gospel according to Saint Matthew, the villain does not confine his villainy—as he does in the more usual

derelict domain of the Mauryan Empire by the Euthydemid Bactrian Greek prince Demetrius in the second decade of the second century B.C.; it survived the collapse of the Euthydemid and Seleucid Empires; and it revived in the last century B.C., when Pompey imposed a *Pax Romana* upon Syria and when the Palmyrenes (see II. D (i), vol. ii, p. 11, above) opened up a short cut from Dura to Damascus across the northern corner of the North Arabian Desert (see Tarn, W. W.: *The Greeks in Bactria and India* (Cambridge 1938, University Press), pp. 61–2, 260–1, 361–3, 366–7). As for the maritime route, the trade along it was commanded by South Arabian middlemen until the first through-voyage from Egypt to India was made by Eudoxus of Cyzicus *circa* 120 B.C. Eudoxus's Greek successors gradually shortened the voyage—which in Eudoxus's day was still made coastwise all the way—by cutting more and more adventurously across the open sea with the aid of the monsoons; and this process of shortening, which began *circa* 100–80 B.C., was completed *circa* A.D. 40–50 (i.e. on the eve of the precipitation of the story of Jesus in the Gospels), when the Greek navigators of the Indian Ocean ventured at last to sail straight across the open sea from the Somali coast to the southern tip of India, without approaching Arabia at all. As a result of this Greek conquest of the Indian Ocean, pepper was obtainable in abundance at Athens in 88 B.C., and a Buddhist gravestone, erected before the end of the Ptolemaic Age, has been discovered by Sir Flinders Petrie at Alexandria (Tarn, op. cit., pp. 367–75, superseding eundem: *Hellenistic Civilization* (London 1927, Arnold), pp. 196–9). It will be seen that the means of communication between India and the Levant steadily improved in the course of the three and a half centuries between the writing of the Suttanipāta in India *circa* 300 B.C. and the writing of the Gospels in the Levant in the second half of the first century of the Christian Era.

[1] See IV. C (iii) (c) 2 (α), vol. iv, p. 263, and V. C (ii) (a), in the present volume, pp. 266–9, above. [2] In III. C (ii) (b), vol. iii, pp. 259–61, above.

[3] Recounted, on the authority of one of Augustus's freedmen, Julius Marathus, by Suetonius: *Life of Augustus*, chap. 94 (see Meyer, E.: *Ursprung und Anfänge des Christentums*, vol. i (Stuttgart and Berlin 1921, Cotta), pp. 57–8). A massacre of innocents, as an expiation for the appearance of a comet, is also ascribed to Nero (Suetonius: *Life of Nero*, chap. 36), but in this case it is not suggested that the villain's motive is a fear that one of his victims may be destined to supplant him on his throne.

version of the tale[1]—to an attempt upon the life of a single babe who (he fears) may be destined to supplant him; in order to make sure that his destined supplanter shall not survive, he gives orders for the destruction of all the infant life of an entire community. Herod, made aware by the Magi that a Messiah has been born in Jewry, and informed by the doctors of the Jewish Law that the Messiah's birth-place is to be Bethlehem, decrees the slaughter of all children in Bethlehem from two years old and under.[2] The Senate, being warned by a prodigy that Nature is pregnant with the future King of the Roman People, decrees that no child born in that year is to be reared.[3]

If we pass from the Matthaean and Lucan accounts of Jesus's birth and infancy and childhood to the episode of the Baptism in Jordan by John and the simultaneous Designation of Jesus as the Son of God, we may remind ourselves that, in another context,[4] we have found Hellenic affinities for the figure of a dove as an emblem and emissary of a godhead. And if we pass on from the Designation to the Temptation, which is placed immediately after it in all three Synoptic Gospels[5] and is recounted in detail in both Matthew and Luke, we shall observe that the Tempter's invitation to Jesus to cast himself down from a pinnacle of the Temple[6] is one version of a 'folk-tale' which makes its appearance in pagan Hellenic literature in the forms of the challenge to Theseus to cast himself overboard into 'his father's house' in the depths of the sea,[7] and the invitation to Psyche to cast herself down from the brow of a crag into the arms of Zephyr.[8]

An analogous Temptation of Gautama by Māra (the Indic

[1] e.g. in the legends of Oedipus, Perseus, Jason, Orestes, Zeus, Horus, Cyrus (a single babe), and in the legend of Romulus and Remus (twins).   [2] Matt. ii. 1–18.
[3] The tale, in Exod. i–ii, of Pharaoh's instruction to the midwives to kill all the male children borne by the Hebrew women agrees with the Matthaean and Marathan tale in representing the villain as making an attempt upon the lives of all the (male) children of a community, and not merely upon the life of a single child; but the motive ascribed to Pharaoh is not the same as that ascribed to Herod and to the Senate. In the Matthaean and Marathan tale the villain's reason for deciding to massacre the children wholesale is not because he wishes to exterminate an entire generation, but simply to make sure that a single child, whom he cannot identify, shall not escape. On the other hand Pharaoh's design against the lives of all the (male) children of the Hebrews is not incidental to another aim, but is an end in itself. What Pharaoh fears is not that some particular Hebrew child is going to usurp Pharaoh's throne, but that the Hebrew community as a whole is going to become more than a match for the Egyptiac Society as a whole. In this matter of motive the Matthaean and Marathan tale follows, not the tale of Pharaoh's atrocity in Exodus, but the myths of Uranus's and Cronos' atrocities in the *Theogony* of Hesiod. Uranus buries *all* (his own) children alive (ll. 154–60) and Cronos swallows *all* (his own) children (ll. 459–67), for fear (implicitly in the case of Uranus and explicitly in the case of Cronos) of being supplanted one day by *one* of them.
[4] In V. C (i) (d) 11, Annex I, pp. 361–2, above.
[5] Matt. iv. 1–11; Mark i. 12–13; Luke iv. 1–13.
[6] Matt. iv. 5–6 = Luke iv. 9–11.
[7] This parallel in Bacchylides, *Dithyramb* xvi [xvii] (F. Blass' edition (Leipzig 1898, Teubner), pp. 121–33), has been pointed out to the writer of this Study by Professor Gilbert Murray.
[8] This parallel has been pointed out by Braun, *History and Romance*, pp. 66–70. The

counterpart of Ahriman and Satan) is a theme which occurs in several passages in the Pālī scriptures of the Hinayanian Buddhist school of Indic philosophy. In a passage of the Padhānasutta Māra exhorts Gautama not to push his self-mortification to the point of severing the last thread that still binds the philosopher-ascetic to physical life on Earth; in a passage of the Samyutta-Nikāya Māra exhorts Gautama to assume the sovereignty of a mundane kingdom; and these two incidents look like counterparts in the one case of the Devil's suggestion to Jesus to turn stones into bread and in the other case of his suggestion to him to accept a mundane oecumenical sovereignty. The hypothesis of a fortuitous coincidence between these respective legends of the Temptation of Gautama and the Temptation of Jesus would appear to be ruled out by the fact that, in each of the two correspondences here cited, certain details that are to be found in the Gospels are likewise to be found in the Pālī scriptures, though this not in exactly the same relation to the incident as a whole. For instance, the conceit of a superficial resemblance between a stone and a piece of food, which in the Gospels is crystallized into a suggestion for turning a stone into a loaf of bread, turns up in the corresponding passage of the Padhānasutta as a simile of Gautama's impregnability to Māra's assaults. 'A crow,' says Māra, 'was once disappointed at finding that an object which looked like a lump of fat was only a stone after all. The crow had to fly away hungry; and now I, Māra, have to give up Gautama as a bad job—as the crow gave up the stone!' Similarly, in the Samyutta-Nikāya, Māra exhorts Gautama to turn, not a stone into bread, but a mountain into gold as a sequel to his exhortation to him to assume sovereignty over a mundane kingdom. The mountain which Māra names is the Himalaya—and we are left wondering whether, in some common source of the Buddhist and the Christian Temptation-story, this may not have been the 'exceeding high mountain' from the summit of which the Devil showed Jesus all the kingdoms of the World.[1]

We may next notice two miracles—the Walking on the Water (Matt. xiv. 22–33 = Mark vi. 45–51 = John vi. 15–21) and the Feeding of the Multitudes (Matt. xiv. 15–21 = Mark vi. 35–44 = Luke ix. 12–17 = John vi. 5–13, and Matt. xv. 32–8 = Mark viii. 1–9)—which are embedded not only in the Gospels but also in

challenge which in the Gospels is represented as a temptation that Jesus resists is represented in the stories of Theseus and Psyche as a test of faith from which the hero (heroine) does not flinch. But the ordeal (and also the tableau in which it is visualized) is the same in all three stories; and in all three, again, the hero (heroine) responds to this identical challenge victoriously, though in the one case the victory is won by a refusal and in the other two cases by an acceptance.

[1] Matt. iv. 8 = Luke iv. 5. Compare the setting of Lucian's dialogue between Hermes and Charon, from which a passage has been quoted in V. C (i) (d) 10, pp. 133–4, above.

Mahayanian Buddhist scriptures (the Jātaka and the still younger Vimalakīrtinirdeśasutra)[1] which, at least in their present form, are all of them considerably later than the Gospels in date. Again, there is a tale—'the Widow's Mite'—which is found not only in the Gospels according to Saint Mark (xii. 41–4) and Saint Luke (xxi. 1–4) but also in the Sutrālamkāra, IV, 22, which is a work from the pen of one of the early fathers of the Mahayanian Buddhist Church, Aśvaghosa (*floruit circa* A.D. 100).[2] And there are two similes—'the Birds of the Air' and 'Dogs and Crumbs'—which, as we have already observed in another context,[3] are each of them to be found on the one hand in the Gospels and on the other hand in two pieces of pagan Hellenic literature, one of which appears to be approximately contemporary with the Gospels, while the other is at least five hundred years older. There is another simile of two roads—representing respectively the ways of Vice and Virtue—which is to be found not only in the Gospel according to Saint Matthew (vii. 13–14) but also in Xenophon's *Memorabilia* (Book II, chap. 1, § 21)[4] and in Hesiod's *Works and Days* (ll. 287–92). There is also a 'folk-tale'—recounting the disappointment that is the inevitable consequence of looking for figs out of season—which can be detected as the common source of the incident of the Cursing of the Barren Fig Tree (Matt. xxi. 18–19 = Mark xi. 12–14) and of a passage in one of the lectures of the Stoic philosopher Epictetus (*Dissertationes*, Book III, chap. 24, §§ 85–8) which we have quoted already[5] in another connexion. We may also here recall two apparently proverbial sayings—'I cannot dig' and 'the city is being taken by storm'—which are to be found on the one hand in the Gospels and on the other hand in Aristophanes' *Birds*,[6] and add another saying of the same character—'Many are called, but few are chosen'—which is to be found on the one hand in the Gospel according to Saint Matthew[7] and on the other hand in the scriptures of the Orphic Church.[8]

---

[1] The Walking on the Water is to be found in the introduction to Jātaka 190; the Feeding of the Multitudes in the introduction to Jātaka 78, and in Vimalakīrtinirdeśasutra, chap. 10 (a Chinese translation of a Sanskrit scripture of the Mahayanian Church). It will be noticed that in the Mahayanian Buddhist scriptures the two miracles occur in quite different contexts, whereas they are placed in immediate juxtaposition with one another in the Gospels.

[2] Aśvaghosa appears to have been a contemporary of the Kushan King Kanishka, who reigned *circa* A.D. 78–123 (see Smith, V. A.: *The Early History of India*, 3rd ed. (Oxford 1914, Clarendon Press), pp. 260–1; Eliot, Sir Ch.: *Hinduism and Buddhism* (London 1921, Arnold, 3 vols.), vol. ii, pp. 82–4).

[3] In V. C (i) (d) 11, Annex I, pp. 354–7 and 357, footnote 1, above.

[4] See p. 470, below.   [5] In V. C (i) (d) 10, p. 147, footnote 1, above.

[6] See V. C (i) (d) 11, Annex I, p. 358, above.

[7] Πολλοὶ γάρ εἰσι κλητοί, ὀλίγοι δὲ ἐκλεκτοί (Matt. xxii. 14).

[8] Πολλοὶ μὲν ναρθηκοφόροι, παῦροι δέ τε βάκχοι (*Orphicorum Fragmenta*, Collegit Otto Kern (Berlin 1922, Weidmann), fragments 5 and 235, preserved by Plato in *Phaedo* 69 c).

Most of the topics that we have cited up to this point—as examples of what appears to be the jetsam of 'folk-lore' which has been washed up on to the shores of the river of 'folk-memory' and has there come to be imbedded in more or less sophisticated works of literature—are topics which not only bear marks of having drifted, at some stage of their literary history, in the current of Lethe's stream, but which, to all appearance, are native to these waters and display no trace of ever having known any other mental environment than this before they finally came to rest in their present literary context. Miracles and parables and similes and proverbs are the very stuff of which 'folk-lore' consists; and if, when we find specimens of any of these primitive genres incongruously embedded in sophisticated works of literature, we can legitimately account for them as being the jetsam of 'folk-lore', we need seek no farther than that for an explanation of their origin. There is, however, one set of verbal correspondences[1] between an incident in the Gospels and a cento of passages from the *Birds* which may be explicable on the hypothesis of a subterranean contact on the level of psychic life at which the waters of 'folk-memory' flow, but which at the same time cannot be interpreted as a seepage, into the *Birds* on the one hand and into the Gospels on the other, of an element which has not merely travelled for a season in the current of 'folk-memory' but has also actually originated at this primitive level of psychic life. The Aristophanic phrases here in question bear no obvious marks of an extraneous origin in 'folk-lore'; there is no reason to doubt that they are the original work of the Attic playwright himself; and, if so, then in this case we are confronted with a process that is different from, and more complex than, the process that we have been studying so far. We are here apparently in the presence of a group of mental images or ideas which have started life on the plane of sophisticated literature; have percolated down from this starting place to the level of 'folk-lore'; have travelled at this level from Attica to Palestine in the subterranean stream of 'folk-memory'; and, after having eventually been washed ashore in a barely recognizable shape, have become embedded in a semi-sophisticated work of literature, the Gospels.[2] This reconstruction of the literary history of these Aristophanic phrases is supported by the unquestionable occurrence of Menandrean phrases in the New Testament; for we need have no hesitation in accepting as the original work of Aristophanes' fellow countryman and successor Menander one fragment from this later Attic playwright's lost plays which recurs *verbatim* in one of Saint Paul's

---

[1] See V. C (i) (d) 11, Annex I, pp. 353–4, above.
[2] This is perhaps also the history of the proverbial saying about 'the city being taken by storm' (see V. C (i) (d) 11, Annex I, pp. 358–9, above).

Epistles,[1] and another fragment which juxtaposes two *motifs* that both recur in the Gospels, though here in different contexts.[2] The common source of the manifestly kindred pictures of the Primitive Christian and the Primitive Pythagorean communal life, in the Acts of the Apostles and in Iamblichus's *Life of Pythagoras*,[3] can also hardly have been other than a sophisticated piece of literature; and there are two passages in the New Testament—one in the Epistle to Titus[4] and the other in the speech on the Areopagus which is placed in the mouth of Saint Paul by the author of the Acts[5]—in which a tag of Greek poetry not only reappears *verbatim* but is quoted by the Christian writer with an express acknowledgement of the pagan Hellenic literary source.

We have, indeed, already had occasion to observe that the jetsam on the strand of the stream of 'folk-memory' by no means exclusively consists of matter that has originated in those waters, and that some of the objects which the current deposits high and dry are flotsam which has stood on dry land already once before, at an earlier stage of its existence, before ever it was engulfed by the stream which has now disgorged it. We have noticed, for example, a number of heroes and heroines of romance—'Ninus' and 'Semiramis' and 'Sesostris', 'Nectanebos' and 'Dhu'l-Qarnayn'—whose 'fictitious' shapes have been fashioned out of the authentic portraits of historical personages. And this phenomenon can perhaps also be illustrated from the Gospels. Is it conceivable, for instance, that the parable of the husbandmen who did the dastardly deed of putting to death the son of the owner of the vineyard when his father had sent him to them as his emissary (Matt. xxi. 33–41 = Mark xii. 1–9 = Luke xx. 9–16) is an echo of the historic crime of Opimius, who arrested and executed Fulvius's son when the boy was sent across no-man's-land, under flag of truce, to parley with his father's adversaries (Plutarch: *Gracchi*, chaps. 37–8)? And is it conceivable, again, that the episode of the

---

[1] Φθείρουσιν ἤθη χρήσθ' ὁμιλίαι κακαί: 'Evil communications corrupt good manners.' —Menander, T. Kock's edition, vol. iii, p. 62, No. 218 = 1 Cor. xv. 33.

[2]
Μειράκιον, οὔ μοι κατανοεῖν δοκεῖς ὅτι
ὑπὸ τῆς ἰδίας ἕκαστα κακίας σήπεται,
καὶ πᾶν τὸ λυμαινόμενόν ἐστιν ἔνδοθεν.
οἷον ὁ μὲν ἰός, ἂν σκοπῇς, τὸ σιδήριον,
τὸ δ' ἱμάτιον οἱ σῆτες, ὁ δὲ θρὶψ τὸν ξύλον.
ὁ δὲ τὸ κάκιστον τῶν κακῶν πάντων, φθόνος
φθισικὸν πεπόηκε καὶ ποήσει καὶ ποεῖ,
ψυχῆς πονηρᾶς δυσσεβὴς παράστασις.

Of this fragment of Menander (Kock, vol. iii, p. 162, No. 540) the first three lines are echoed in Matt. xv. 10–20 (the two passages have already been quoted together in IV. C (iii) (a), vol. iv, p. 120, above), while the rest are echoed in Matt. vi. 19 (ὅπου σὴς καὶ βρῶσις ἀφανίζει) = Luke xii. 33.

[3] See V. C (i) (c) 2, Annex II, vol. v, p. 583, footnote 1, above.

[4] Titus i. 12, quoting Epimenides' poem *Minos* (see I. C (i) (b), vol. i, p. 99, footnote 2, and V. C (i) (d) 11, Annex I, in the present volume, p. 363, footnote 6, above).

[5] See V. C (i) (d) 7, p. 11, footnote 2, above.

pilgrimage of the Magi, which is recounted in the Matthaean prologue (chap. ii) to the Gospels, has been precipitated by an impact
which may have been made on the imagination of the internal
proletariat of the Hellenic World by an historic visit of a party of
Magi, not to the infant Jesus at Bethlehem, but to the adult
Emperor Nero at Rome, in the suite of Tiridates, when the Arsacid
King of Armenia came to pay his respects to his Roman suzerain
in A.D. 66 (Pliny: *Historia Naturalis*, Book XXX, chap. 2; cf.
Suetonius: *Life of Nero*, chap. 13)?

Whatever judgement we may pass on these two last-suggested
possibilities,[1] we shall probably agree that historical events and
literary phrases are not the only kinds of foreign matter that can
find their way into the stream of 'folk-memory'. How, for example,
are we to account for a striking correspondence between two
passages in the exordium of the Gospel according to Saint John
(i. 16 and 18)—'And of his fullness have we all received' (καὶ ἐκ
τοῦ πληρώματος αὐτοῦ ἡμεῖς πάντες ἐλάβομεν); and 'No man
hath seen God at any time; the only begotten Son, which is in the
bosom of the Father, he hath declared him' (Θεὸν οὐδεὶς ἑώρακε
πώποτε· ὁ μονογενὴς υἱός, ὁ ὢν εἰς τὸν κόλπον τοῦ πατρός, ἐκεῖνος
ἐξηγήσατο)—and the last words of Plato's *Timaeus* (92 C): 'Having
thus received, and been filled full with, living creatures, mortal and
immortal, the Cosmos—a living creature that contains the things
that are seen, being such a thing itself, a god that is a sensible
image of the intelligible [godhead]—has become superlatively
great and good and beautiful and perfect, being this unique and
only begotten Heaven' (Θνητὰ γὰρ καὶ ἀθάνατα ζῷα λαβὼν καὶ
συμπληρωθεὶς ὅδε ὁ κόσμος οὕτω, ζῷον ὁρατὸν τὰ ὁρατὰ περιέχον,
εἰκὼν τοῦ νοητοῦ θεὸς αἰσθητός, μέγιστος καὶ ἄριστος κάλλιστός τε
καὶ τελεώτατος γέγονεν εἷς οὐρανὸς ὅδε μονογενὴς ὤν)? Does it not
seem probable that the stream of 'folk-memory' has provided a
channel along which the imagery, and even the vocabulary, of the
Timaeus has flowed into a semi-philosophical work of Christian
literature which, in all probability, was composed not much less
than five hundred years after the last sentence of the *Timaeus* had
taken shape in Plato's mind?

'In Christianity there are echoes of Stoic or Platonic ideas; but in
saying this we do not mean to imply that the Apostles, and certainly not
that Jesus Himself, had frequented the schools of the philosophers or
had read their books. It is true that the Logos in the opening sentences
of the Gospel according to Saint John can be traced back with certainty

---

[1] Eduard Meyer (*Ursprung und Anfänge des Christentums*, vol. i (Stuttgart and Berlin
1921, Cotta), p. 59, footnote 1) rejects, as unconvincing, this explanation of the appearance of the Magi in the Gospel according to Saint Matthew. For another possible source
of the episode of the Magi see p. 524, footnote 2, below.

to Philo; and nothing stands in the way of the supposition that the author of the Gospel may have been acquainted with some of Philo's writings or even have been in personal contact with Philo himself. These, however, are isolated exceptions; and in general the New Testament is very remote from the cultivated life, and, by the same token, from the philosophy, of the age. Yet in similar conditions to-day one often hears people in a humble walk of life reproducing ideas originally put into currency by Schopenhauer or Darwin, although the plagiarist has never read one word of these thinkers' works. The fact is that ideas which suit the times spread rapidly from mouth to mouth, and sometimes turn up in different places simultaneously, without their exponents being necessarily dependent on one another. Whether Christianity is really indebted for its Platonic or Stoic content to the disciples of Plato and Zeno, or whether it is merely a case of the same ideas being evoked in Christianity too by the same *Zeitgeist*, is thus a question which cannot be answered with certainty in any particular instance. The one point that is impregnably established is that the teachings of Christianity are not entirely new and original, but are for the most part rooted in the spiritual life of the age.'[1]

From the foregoing survey it would appear that the Gospels contain, embedded in them, a considerable number and variety of elements which have been conveyed to them by the stream of 'folk-memory', and which have originated partly in these waters but partly also on stretches of once dry ground which the shifting subterranean currents of a perennially flowing primitive psychic life have subsequently undermined and swept away. On this showing, it would seem that the Gospels contain elements which are not 'historical' in the conventional usage of that word. We shall find, however, if we carry our inquiry farther, that in this respect the Gospels are not unique among the works of literature which are our sources for the hero-stories of which we are here trying to make a comparative study. For example, if we now apply to the work of the pagan Hellenic historian Phylarchus the analytical treatment that we have just been applying to the Gospels, we shall see the 'historicity' of this sophisticated Hellenic author's narrative dissolve, almost melodramatically, before our eyes. We have only to turn to the masterly and devastating analysis that has already been made by a genuinely scientific Hellenic historian of the post-Phylarchan generation: to wit, Polybius (Book II, chap. 56, §§ 1–6 and 7–12):

'Among the historians who are Aratus's contemporaries, Phylarchus is one who enjoys a high reputation in some circles; and, as Phylarchus is perpetually breaking out into polemics against Aratus and into con-

---

[1] Seeck, O.: *Geschichte des Untergangs der Antiken Welt*, vol. iii, 2nd ed. (Stuttgart 1921, Metzler), pp. 203–4, referred to, by anticipation, in V. C (i) (d) 6 (α), vol. v, p. 456, footnote 1, above.

tradictions of what Aratus says, it would seem useful, or rather unavoidable, for the present writer, who has deliberately elected to follow Aratus in his account of Cleomenes and all that pertains to him, to take up this issue. If we were to pass it over without looking into it, we might be exposing ourselves to the reproach of leaving Falsehood to take her stand in the field of historiography on a footing of equality with Truth.

'We may begin with the general criticism that the whole of this historian's treatment of his subject bristles with examples of carelessness and slovenliness. In the present place, however, we may perhaps allow ourselves to confine our censure on points of detail to that portion of Phylarchus's work that overlaps with our own: that is to say, the part that deals with the Cleomenic War. This much of his work we cannot avoid subjecting to the lens of criticism. And that will certainly be sufficient to bring to light the *penchant* and the *forte* that Phylarchus displays in his treatment of the whole of his subject. . . .

'In his eagerness to move his readers to pity and to win their sympathy for his story he introduces scenes of women locked in one anothers' arms, with hair dishevelled and breasts exposed, and throws in, as further ingredients, the tears and lamentations of persons of both sexes, all cluttered up with aged parents and tiny children, on their way to the gallows. He plays this game all through his history, and his perpetual aim in every episode is always to give a visual impression of the horrors. His vein is an ignoble and effeminate one; but we may let that pass and may proceed to examine his work from the standpoint of what is strictly relevant and useful for the professional historian. From this standpoint we may lay it down that the business of a writer of history is not to use his subject as an instrument for making a shattering impression on his public by hocus-pocus (τερατευόμενον),[1] and not to invent oratory that may be appropriate to the occasion or to elaborate the subsidiary details that may be implicit in the facts.[2] These are the tricks of the playwrights.[3] The historian's business is to give an exact record of

---

[1] N.B.—This is the word that is used of the conjuring tricks that were performed by Eunus (Points 65 and 72).—A.J.T.

[2] Polybius lives up to these principles when his own turn comes for recording Cleomenes' end. Phylarchus's excruciatingly circumstantial account of the suicide of the hero and his twelve companions (if we may take this to be substantially reproduced in Plutarch, chap. 58, §§ 13–16) is replaced in Polybius's narrative (Book V, chap. 39, § 5) by the unadorned statement: 'They took their own lives with a characteristically Spartan fortitude' (προσήνεγκαν αὐτοῖς τὰς χεῖρας εὐψύχως πάνυ καὶ Λακωνικῶς).—A.J.T.

[3] While Polybius has manifestly kept his own work free from Phylarchus's vice of draping his narrative of historical events in the trappings of melodrama, he has been accused of, no doubt unintentionally, falsifying the true history of at least one episode by mistakenly dramatizing, not the details of the story, but the plot itself. The episode in question is that of the unhappy last phase of the life and reign of King Philip V of Macedon. According to Walbank, F. W.: 'Φίλιππος Τραγῳδούμενος: A Polybian Experiment' in *The Journal of Hellenic Studies*, vol. lviii, 1938, part i, pp. 55–68, 'The tragic version in Polybius is of his own construction and does not spring from the uncritical use of tragedies or historical novels (if indeed such a thing as an historical novel existed in the Greek literature of Polybius's time). Polybius's strictures on Phylarchus make it at least extremely unlikely that he could have fallen into such a crude error in a matter of source-selection. . . . Polybius's mistake—either his own or perhaps one prompted by his Macedonian informant, who may have retailed popular gossip and superstition then current in Macedon—was to interpret Philip's last years as a career of infatuation induced by Tyche and showing itself in an unreasoned programme of planned aggression against Rome' (p. 67).—A.J.T.

the things that were actually done and the words that were actually uttered, even if these happen to be rather tame. The purposes of History and of the Drama are not identical: they are antithetical. The dramatist's business is momentarily to make a shattering impression on his audience and to carry them away by putting into the mouths of his characters whatever words will make the strongest appeal. The historian's business is for all eternity to instruct and convince scholars by presenting them with the truth, both of act and of word. On the stage, where the object is to take the audience in, the first necessity is to say what will appeal, no matter whether it be a falsehood; in the writing of history, where the object is to be of service to scholars, the first necessity is to tell the truth.'

This Polybian criticism of Phylarchus's manner and method exactly applies to Plutarch's *Lives of Agis and Cleomenes*, in which (as we have seen reason to believe)[1] long *résumés* of Phylarchus's history are reproduced with a closeness that in places approximates to identity. Indeed, if we may take Plutarch, in this piece of his work, as being tantamount to Phylarchus himself, there are indications that Phylarchus positively gloried in the vices that Polybius attributes to him. The opening sentence of his peroration, for instance, runs (Plutarch, chap. 60):

'Thus Lacedaemon staged a female drama which could hold its own against the male drama that had preceded it. In her last hour of life Sparta showed the World that hers was a virtue that was proof against all the slings and arrows of outrageous Fortune.'

And in an earlier passage (chap. 24) he writes of Xenares as 'reciting the myth' ($\mu\upsilon\theta o\lambda o\gamma\hat{\omega}\nu$) of Agis to Cleomenes, as a way of saying that he told him the story of Agis' life. In fact, it looks as though in Phylarchus's imagination the authentic history of his heroes has already undergone a histrionic and sentimental transmutation which has carried it a long distance away from the original. In other words, Phylarchus's treatment of the lives of Agis and Cleomenes is another example of that mental process which has spun the stuff of romance out of the originally authentic histories of a likewise Hellenic Alexander the Great, as well as an Egyptiac Nectanebos and a Babylonic Sammu-ramat; and this clue, which Polybius's strictures on Phylarchus have placed in our hands, has been followed out to its logical conclusion by a modern Western scholar.[2]

'There can be no doubt that in both these two of Plutarch's lives there is a workmanship which, for short, we can describe as being "artistic". The mere material is about all that this method of work has in common with the strict laws of our science of historical research; and I can see no

[1] See pp. 435–7, above.
[2] Bux, E.: 'Zwei Sozialistische Novellen bei Plutarch' in *Klio*, vol. xix (1925).

ground for our continuing to count it as serious history. . . . It would be far better to describe these lives, without beating about the bush, as historical novels, in which everything is centred round the hero himself.'[1]

Now that we have followed the story of Agis and Cleomenes out of the realm of history into that of romance, can we carry our pursuit of it into the domain of 'folk-lore'? If a piece of sophisticated literature is to win its way into 'folk-lore', the first necessity is that it should have achieved popularity; and the popularity of Phylarchus's treatment of his subject is attested by the first sentence in the passage which we have quoted from Polybius.[2] This general presumption is supported by at least one piece of positive evidence. In the Plutarchan reproduction of the Phylarchan romance the Passion of Cleomenes is followed by an epilogue which Polybius boycotts as completely as he boycotts the Phylarchan embroideries on the episode of Cleomenes' death; and this epilogue has a heroine who is brought on to the stage at this late hour in the day in the role of Panteus' wife, but who incongruously preserves that anonymity which, as we have seen,[3] is the hall-mark of a character in a 'folk-tale'.

In this anonymous heroine of the Cleomenes Romance a modern Western scholar[4] detects the lineaments of a heroine who appears —at first anonymously, and later under the name of Pantheia[5]— in Xenophon's romance, the *Cyropaedia*, in the role of the wife of Abradatas. Like Panteus' wife, Abradatas' wife is separated from her husband by a military disaster that overtakes a cause to which the husband has devoted himself. Like Panteus' wife, she never rests till she has secured a reunion. Like Panteus' wife, she achieves this reunion with her husband only to suffer a second separation which is worse than the first, since this time the barrier which interposes itself between man and wife is not just an ordinary sea or continent but is the river of Death. And, like Panteus' wife, she reunites herself with her lost husband for the second time by the only means now left to her: that is to say, by committing suicide. In this last scene the two tragedies coincide even in

---

[1] Bux, op. cit., p. 423. This verdict is based by its author (pp. 417–22) upon certain episodes in particular: e.g. upon Chilonis' intercession with her father Leonidas for her husband Cleombrotus (Plutarch, chaps. 17–18); the Passion of Agis (Plutarch, chaps. 18–21); and the post-Sellasian act of the tragedy of Cleomenes (Plutarch, chaps. 49–60).
[2] This point is made by Bux in op. cit., p. 430.
[3] On p. 439, above. [4] Dr. Martin Braun, in a letter to the writer of this Study.
[5] The tale of Pantheia is told, in instalments that are separated from one another by other matter, in Xenophon: *Cyropaedia*, IV. 6, § 11; V. 1, §§ 1–18; VI. 1, §§ 31–49; VI. 4, §§ 2–11; VII. 3, §§ 2–16. It is not till VI. 1, § 41, that she is called by her name. In the preceding passages she is referred to as 'the woman from Susa who is said to have been the loveliest woman in Asia'; 'the wife of Abradatas of Susa'; 'the lovely woman'. Similarly, in the epilogue to the Cleomenes Romance, the heroine is introduced as 'the wife of Panteus, a woman with a most lovely and noble presence' (Plutarch, chap. 59).

detail. As Panteus' wife, when she is on the point of taking her life, makes all spectators withdraw with the sole exception of the sheriff's officer (Plutarch, chap. 59), so Abradatas' wife makes all spectators withdraw except her old nurse (Xenophon vii. 3, § 14). In this last gesture, it is true, Phylarchus's heroine goes one degree farther than her Xenophontean precursor; for, whereas Abradatas' wife instructs the nurse to drape her corpse and her husband's in one and the same pall, Panteus' wife has 'need of none to lay her body out or drape it in a pall after she is dead'. But this variation is explained by the fact that in the Phylarchan romance the heroine does not slay herself over her husband's dead body; and this antecedent variation is explained in its turn by the fact that in the Phylarchan romance the 'business' (in the theatrical meaning of the term) which in the Xenophontean romance is assigned to the wife alone is distributed between wife and husband.

In the Xenophontean romance Abradatas' wife, when she has struck herself her death-stroke, 'lays her head on her husband's breast and dies in this posture'. In the Phylarchan romance this tableau is not omitted (it constitutes our Point of Correspondence No. 28 between the stories of certain pagan Hellenic heroes and the story of Jesus), but the figure that leans on the hero's breast is not that of a woman but that of a bosom friend who is of the hero's own sex, and the man who is cast by Phylarchus for this part in the last scene of the main drama is the man who figures posthumously as the husband of the anonymous heroine of the epilogue. Nor is this the only tableau belonging to the Xenophontean romance which Phylarchus has thus transferred from his epilogue to his main drama. At the opening of the last act of the tragedy of Pantheia in the *Cyropaedia*, Pantheia is discovered (VII, 3, §§ 5 and 8) with her dead husband's head on her knees in the posture of the *Pietà* (our Point 82);[1] and in the Phylarchan romance this tableau likewise is, not omitted, but lifted out of the epilogue to the Passion of Cleomenes in order to provide an epilogue for the Passion of Agis.

This transference of theatrical 'business' from Panteus' anony-

[1] The resemblance between this Xenophontean *Pietà* and the traditional Christian representation of the same tableau is very close; for, while Pantheia and her attendants are the counterparts of the women in the Christian tableau, Cyrus, who enters after the curtain has risen, corresponds to Joseph of Arimathaea. Like Joseph, Cyrus (by proxy through Gadatas and Gobryas) brings costly materials for laying out the corpse. The same tableau, followed by an entry of male characters, constitutes the second scene of the first act of Heliodorus's melodramatic romance, the *Aethiopica* (Book I). A lovely girl (Chariclea) is discovered by pirates sitting motionless on a rock and gazing at the motionless body of a youth (Theagenes). Happily the young man is not dead and the young woman does not commit suicide. In these capital points Heliodorus is bound to part company with Xenophon, because otherwise—since he has introduced the *Pietà* in his first act—his melodrama would be brought to an abrupt and premature end at the outset.

mous wife in the likeness of Xenophon's Pantheia to Panteus
himself perhaps offers a clue for finding the answer to the at first
sight puzzling question of why the Pantheia-*motif* should have
been dragged into the Cleomenes Romance at all. May we venture
upon the guess that Panteus annexed to himself certain appropriate incidents from the Pantheia Romance on the strength of an
accidental and superficial resemblance between the two proper
names?[1] And that Phylarchus, having first plundered the Pantheia
Romance of everything in it that was conveniently transferable
to the male deuteragonist in his own melodrama,[2] packed the rest
of the booty into an epilogue because he could not bear not to
make some use of such admirable material?

On this showing, Xenophon's heroine has provided Phylarchus
with the whole substance for one character that is perhaps entirely

---

[1] 'Panteus' has a look of being the masculine counterpart of the feminine name
'Pantheia', but this appearance is, of course, deceptive. The correct counterpart of
'Pantheia' is 'Pantheios' and, while this masculine form might perhaps legitimately be
contracted by substituting the termination '-eus' for as large a portion as possible of the
second member of the compound word, the result, even then, would be not 'Panteus' but
'Pantheus'. The actual form 'Panteus' may itself, no doubt, be a contraction of a compound word; but, if so, then the original form will have been of the order, not of
'Pan-[th—]', but of 'Panta-[—]' or 'Panto-[—]' (e.g. 'Pantaclês', 'Pantaenus', 'Panta-
leon', 'Pantauchus').

[2] If we were in an aggressively 'higher critical' mood and had confined our attention
to Plutarch's *Lives of Agis and Cleomenes* without taking the precaution of comparing
this reproduction of Phylarchus's romance with the overlapping portions of the historical
narrative of Polybius, we might be tempted into hazarding the further conjecture that
the Panteus who plays his part as Cleomenes' bosom friend is not in fact an historical
personage who has been posthumously decked out by Phylarchus in borrowed plumes
of romance that have been plucked out of Xenophon's *Cyropaedia*. We might go the
length of suggesting that 'Panteus' is a fictitious character through and through, with no
substance in him whatsoever beyond the spoils which a third-century Greek historical
novelist has pillaged from the work of a fourth-century predecessor. Is 'Panteus' really
nothing but Pantheia transformed from a woman into a man? We might seem to have
here in our grasp a second anonymous character that has drifted into Phylarchus's
romance out of the stream of 'folk-lore'. But we shall abandon this particular path of
exploration if we happen to open our copy of Polybius at Book V, chap. 37, § 8; for here
we shall find Polybius (whose veracity is above suspicion) showing us a snapshot of
Cleomenes prowling up and down the quayside at Alexandria attended by—Panteus
and Hippitas! So Panteus turns out after all to be a man of flesh and blood, and likewise
Hippitas into the bargain. Polybius has done us a good turn in pulling us up short; for,
if, in our 'higher critical' mood, we had taken a synoptic view of this pair of proper
names, the comparison might have clinched our conviction that we were here in the
presence of the stuff of 'folk-lore'. Hippitas means 'the horseman'; and, when we come to
the Plutarchan (i.e. Phylarchan) account of Cleomenes' last sortie at the head of his
twelve companions, we find, sure enough, that 'Hippitas' is put up on horseback! If
we did not know from Polybius that Hippitas was an historical personage who genuinely
bore that name, we might have let ourselves be inveigled into imagining that 'the horseman' in the last scene was an anonymous character from a folk-tale whose 'business' in
a scene in which he plays a conspicuous part has been laid under contribution in order
to furnish him with a proper name when he is being lifted out of the sump of 'folk-lore'
and being interpolated into a chapter of authentic history. The testimony of Polybius
proves that, as a matter of fact, we should have no warrant at all for rejecting either
Hippitas' or Panteus' claim to historicity on the ground that their respective names
were too exquisitely appropriate to be accepted as genuine. On the same line of argument we should be compelled to disbelieve that, a hundred years before Hippitas' and
Panteus' day, the cause of Athenian democracy was really upheld against the assaults
of Macedonian autocracy by a man bearing the name of Demosthenes! These awful
warnings throw horrifying spots of light upon the pitfalls that everywhere beset an
inquiry of the present kind.

fictitious and with some heavy embroideries for another character that demonstrably cloaks a genuinely historical personage under these adventitious trappings. There is a wealth of romance in the figure of Pantheia from which Phylarchus has known how to draw profit; and the spectacle of these riches naturally whets our curiosity. By whose hands has Pantheia been endowed with them? Has Xenophon created his heroine *de toutes pièces*? Or has Xenophon anticipated Phylarchus in plundering somebody else's treasure-house? Who is Pantheia? Is she a new woman, or is she one whose countenance is familiar to us already? In the opinion of one modern Western scholar,[1]

'Behind the form of Xenophon's Pantheia I suspect a presence which is none other than that of Semiramis. Both women, Pantheia and Semiramis, are "the loveliest in Asia" (Xenophon: *Cyropaedia*, IV, 6, § 11, and V, 1, § 7; Diodorus, Book II, chap. 4, § 1); both of them are desired by a number of different men; both of them are as heroic as they are lovely. Again, both of them are married to a vassal of the King of Assyria (Xenophon: *Cyropaedia*, V, 1, § 3; Diodorus, Book II, chap. 5, §§ 1–2), and in both cases the King desires the woman for himself and wants to take her away from his vassal (Xenophon: *Cyropaedia*, VI, 1, § 45; Diodorus, Book II, chap. 6, §§ 9–10). The husbands of both women are abroad temporarily—but this at a critical moment—in Bactria (Xenophon: *Cyropaedia*, V, 1, § 3; Diodorus, Book II, chap. 6, § 5). The one substantial difference is that Xenophon's Pantheia—and in this she is a forerunner of the heroines of later [Hellenic] romance—has been purged of the "non-moral" elements, proper to Ishtar, which still inhere in the Oriental figure of Semiramis.'[2]

Perhaps we have now followed out our immediate line of investigation far enough to have convinced ourselves that the *soi-disant* 'history' of Phylarchus, as well as the fourfold picture of the life and preaching of Jesus that is presented in the Gospels, does in fact reveal in itself the presence of elements which have all the appearance of being the jetsam of 'folk-lore' that has become embedded in a stratum of sophisticated or semi-sophisticated literature without having lost the characteristic marks that bear witness to its passage through the waters of 'folk-memory' at some stage before it came to rest in its present setting. We are perhaps

[1] Dr. Martin Braun, in a letter to the writer of this Study.
[2] Semiramis, in one of her adventures, masquerades in a costume which makes it impossible to tell her sex (Diodorus, chap. 6, § 6). If Pantheia is an emanation of Semiramis, this masquerade perhaps throws light on the process by which tableaux that originally depicted the heroine's exploits have apparently come to be attributed to a character of the other sex (see p. 461, above). In Xenophon's romance (*Cyropaedia*, VI. 4, § 2) Pantheia equips her husband with effeminate accoutrements, including just such a dress as Semiramis dons according to Diodorus (in loc. cit. supra). This anecdote of Semiramis' masquerade would appear, from the context in the passage of Diodorus, to be an *aition* to account for the origin of the so-called Median, but originally Assyrian, male costume, which was effeminate in Hellenic eyes.

also warranted in coming to the further conclusion that the quantity of the foreign bodies, bearing marks of this history, in the works of literature that we have been scrutinizing, is abundant enough to justify us in adopting the view that the medium of 'folk-memory'—which we have found to be a highly conductive one—has in fact been one medium of communication between these works. And this conclusion leads on to yet another. We may conclude that this medium of 'folk-memory' has been instrumental in producing that residue of our observed correspondences which has to be attributed to the operation of mimesis after we have made all possible allowance for the several effects of a common social environment and of the uniformity of human nature and of the play of chance. If mimesis has indeed also played its part, then it seems probable that its principal channel of operation has been the 'folk-memory', and that the practice of plagiarism, in the sense of a conscious and deliberate spoliation of one 'author' by another, has been a minor factor.[1] If we are able to accept these results of our inquiry up to this point, we shall now be in a position to address ourselves to the ulterior question which we have raised, by anticipation, already,[2] and that is: In which of two alternative possible ways has this operation of mimesis through the channel of the 'folk-memory' taken place? Has the stream of 'folk-memory' carried certain elements out of the pages of Phylarchus (or out of those of any of the other pagan Hellenic authors here in question) into the pages of the Gospels? Or has it carried these same elements into the pages of Phylarchus and of the Gospels alike out of some other piece or province of literature which is independent of, and anterior to, both of them? Let us first try to take a survey of possible common sources, before we proceed to examine the possibility of a direct conveyance into the Gospels of elements from those older books that set forth the stories of our eleven pagan Hellenic heroes.

---

[1] 'The resemblances [between Philostratus's *Apollonius of Tyana* and the Gospels] have evoked the hypothesis that Apollonius's biographer Philostratus has been seeking to create, in his Apollonius, a counterpart of Christ, and, with this in mind, has freely invented many of the details of his biography. Yet any one who reads Philostratus's work with an open mind will reject this hypothesis unhesitatingly; for there is nothing that points to the author's having had any close acquaintance with Christianity. The common features can, no doubt, be detected by a scholar versed in the comparative method of research, but they do not by any means force themselves upon the attention of the casual reader. The explanation of them lies simply in the fact that the Gospels, as well as the sources used by Philostratus, have painted the portrait of the immaculate God-Man in the typical form in which this was conceived by the imagination of that age, and have each invested their own hero with this God-Man's characteristic traits, whether these traits were actually to be found [in the historical hero] or not.'—Seeck, O.: *Geschichte des Untergangs der Antiken Welt*, vol. iii, 2nd ed. (Stuttgart 1921, Metzler), pp. 184–5. (For the emergence of the figure of the God-Man, to which Seeck alludes in this passage, see Bieler, L.: Θεῖος Ἀνήρ: *Das Bild des 'Göttlichen Menschen' in Spätantike und Frühchristentum* (Vienna 1935–6, Höfel, 2 vols.))

[2] On p. 448, above.

The Legend of Hêraklês

There is one obvious possible common source from which the stories of our pagan historical heroes on the one hand and the story of Jesus on the other hand may have acquired independently of one another—along two distinct channels of the stream of 'folk-memory'—at least some of those common features which can only be accounted for on the hypothesis that they are in some sense the consequence of mimesis; and this source is the legend of Hêraklês.

The picture in Hellenic minds of the life and character of this Hellenic demigod would presumably have, *a priori*, a better opportunity than any other piece of Hellenic mythology for colouring the traditional portraits of eminent representatives of Hêraklês' reputed offspring, the historical Heracleidae of Sparta. At the same time the Hêraklês Legend would have at any rate as good an opportunity of affecting the story of Jesus as the Phaedra Legend would have of affecting the story of Joseph; and there is evidence, as we have seen,[1] that, in this latter case, a Jewish story has in fact been perceptibly influenced by a Hellenic myth. If Phaedra has thus found her way into one province of the domain of Jewish literature, there is no reason *a priori* why, in another province, Phaedra's fellow Hellene Hêraklês should not have gained at least as much ground—especially considering that in the Oriental World *post Alexandrum* Hêraklês had acquired a number of local *points d'appui*, while Phaedra, so far as we know, never possessed *in partibus Orientalium* any foothold of this kind to assist her in the dissemination of her legend.

When a veneer of Hellenic culture was imposed upon the surface of Oriental life as a consequence of the military triumph of Macedonian over Achaemenian arms, one of the formal means by which the Orientals symbolically signified their deliberate 'reception' of the Hellenic way of life consisted in the official identification of their own gods with approximately equivalent members of the Hellenic Pantheon; and in this expansion of the Hellenic divinities' respective spheres of influence[2] Hêraklês was one of the principal beneficiaries. At Tarsus, for example, Hêraklês now lent his name to the ancient *genius loci* Sandan, and at Tyre to the ancient *genius loci* Melkart.[3] In the first chapter of the story of the contact between Hellenism and the four non-Hellenic cultures which were

---

[1] On pp. 444–6, above.

[2] For this expansion in this way see the passage quoted from Turgot in V. C (i) (d) 7, p. 32, footnote 1, above.

[3] The identification of Melkart of Tyre with Hêraklês did not have to wait for Alexander's destructive passage in 332 B.C. It was already an accomplished fact in the time of Herodotus, whom it confronted with some difficult problems of both theology and chronology (see Herodotus, Book II, chap. 42).

brought into collision with it through the destruction of the Achaemenian Empire by Alexander, these identifications of Oriental with Hellenic divinities were merely nominal; but with the passage of time a contact which had begun as a mere collision began to grow into an interpenetration; and one of the ways in which this fruitful change took place was through a progressive fusion of the cults and the myths of those Oriental and Hellenic divinities who, to begin with, had been identified with one another in name only. In this second chapter of the story the native Oriental worships, as they pursued their competition with one another for the allegiance of Mankind,[1] would tend to radiate out not only their own native elements but also some of the elements of the Hellenic worships with which they had come respectively to be identified; and by this means Hêraklês, among other Hellenic divinities, would come to exert by proxy—here in virtue of his identification with Melkart, and there in virtue of his identification with Sandan—an influence upon Oriental hearts and minds which might have remained for ever beyond his power if he had presented himself in his alien Hellenic shape and not in the familiar forms of his numerous Oriental 'opposite numbers'. Conversely, the once purely Hellenic legend of Hêraklês, in the course of its transmission from its Hellenic homeland into Oriental hinterlands through the prowess of a Hêraklês-Sandan and a Hêraklês-Melkart, would gradually acquire an alloy of Oriental gold to ennoble its native Hellenic metal.

As a matter of fact, it is hardly credible that Hêraklês, of all Hellenic figures, would have been chosen out so frequently for identification with well-established and deeply revered Oriental divinities if, at and after the time of Alexander, the native Hellenic idea of him had still been the gross traditional portrait that is caricatured in the figure of fun—compounded of glutton and blockhead—which Aristophanes brought on to the stage of the Dionysiac Theatre at Athens in 414 B.C. in the penultimate scene of the *Birds*.

This year was indeed perhaps the latest date at which it was still possible to present Hêraklês to a Hellenic public in this lighthearted vein; for the swiftly following disaster to Athenian arms in Sicily and the consequent resumption of the Atheno-Peloponnesian War made the breakdown of the Hellenic Civilization unmistakably plain; this vision of material disaster precipitated a spiritual crisis which affected every element in the Hellenic cul-

---

[1] For the expansion of the field of the various Oriental divinities' operation from a parochial to an oecumenical range in the Achaemenian and Post-Achaemenian Age see V. C (i) (*d*) 7, pp. 29–33, above.

tural tradition; and one particularly striking effect was the transfiguration, at this late hour of the Hellenic day, of an invincible
peasant-demigod who had obstinately declined either to put on the
armour of a warrior in 'the Heroic Age' or to enrol himself, in the
next chapter of Hellenic history, as the citizen of a city-state.[1]
Hêraklês was now confronted with a choice of allowing himself
either to be shown up as a monster or to be 'made over' into a
saint; and both these alternative ways of dealing with an uncouth
traditional figure which could no longer be taken for granted had
been tried already, before the production of the *Birds,* by Attic
tragedians who were Aristophanes' contemporaries. Euripides had
done his best to salvage the peasant-demigod by putting a touch
of something heroic into the character in his *Alcestis* (*actum* 438
B.C.) and afterwards raising it to a completely heroic stature in the
last act of his *Hercules Furens* (*actum circa* 423 B.C.),[2] whereas
Sophocles had done his best to jettison Hêraklês by presenting the
traditional figure in the *Trachiniae* as the brute that this Hêraklês
must be felt to be by the sensibilities of any contemporary Athenian
who was willing to let the scales of traditional acquiescence be
stripped away from his eyes.[3] In the end the Euripidean solution
of this Hêraklês-problem prevailed because the Hellenes could not
bring themselves, after all, to jettison a figure which by this time
had made so deep a mark upon the Hellenic imagination; and,
finding that they could not do without their Hêraklês, they went
the necessary lengths in idealizing him.

Hêraklês' choice was decided for him by Prodicus in a fable[4] in
which the bastard son of Zeus was exposed to the competing
solicitations of Virtue and Vice, and was firmly guided, by the
Cean wit who had taken the rustic demigod's education in hand,
into reversing the Judgement of Paris. Thereafter Antisthenes
shaped Hêraklês into a prototype of the future Cynic sage;[5] and
the boor's education was virtually finished by Diogenes.[6] When
Diogenes in his boyhood had expressed a wish to attend Antisthenes' lectures and had thereby drawn down upon himself an
inquiry into his own purpose in life, he had replied that he intended
'to restamp the coinage' (παραχαράττειν τὸ νόμισμα); and this

---

[1] These points are made by Professor Gilbert Murray in an unpublished paper entitled Ἄριστος Ἀνδρῶν, sheet 6.   [2] Ibid., sheet 8.
[3] Murray, ibid., sheets 11–12, points out that, in their respective treatments of the
traditional character of Hêraklês, Euripides and Sophocles have each tried his hand at
the other's usual *modus operandi.*
[4] See the résumé in Xenophon: *Memorabilia,* Book II, chap. i, §§ 21–34.
[5] See Pfister, Fr.: 'Hêraklês und Christus' in *Archiv für Religionswissenschaft,*
vol. xxxiv, Heft 1/2 (Leipzig 1937, Teubner), p. 43.
[6] Diogenes, and not his forerunner Antisthenes, was the founder of the Cynic school
of Hellenic philosophy (Tarn, W. W.: 'Alexander, Cynics and Stoics' in *American
Journal of Philology,* vol. lx, 1, Whole Number 237 (Baltimore, January 1939, Johns
Hopkins University Press), pp. 47–8).

audacity (for which the truculent boy's father happened at that time to be serving a sentence in jail) was duly perpetrated by the son in his turn as soon as he came of age[1]—though the currency on which Diogenes practised was not of the metallic but of the mental kind, and the house of correction—to which the criminal this time condemned himself—was not the conventional jail but a sensational tub. Hêraklês was one of the mental coins that Diogenes restamped; and this process of 'recharacterization', which Prodicus had begun and which Diogenes thus completed, has been summed up in one sentence by a modern Western scholar:

'The Hêraklês Saga is one of the crudest of all Greek myths, and perhaps for that very reason became in the hands of allegorizing philosophers, from Herodorus in the fifth century on to the Stoics and Neoplatonists, the most ideal and edifying of all.'[2]

The unrecognizable shape in which the antique peasant-demigod was at length allowed to rest from his thirteenth and greatest labour of metamorphosis is sharply printed in the opening words of the article on Hêraklês in an encyclopaedia of Hellenic culture from the hand of one of the pioneers of a renaissance of Hellenism in Orthodox Christendom:[3]

'*Hêraklês*: the son of Alcmena: History reveals him as a philosopher. . . .'

This retrospective glimpse of a *Hercules Philosophus* shows how well the Hellenic genius succeeded, before its own eclipse, in solving the awkward Hêraklês-problem with which it had been plagued in the tragic generation of Sophocles and Euripides and Aristophanes and Prodicus. How keep in circulation a treasured mental coin on which the image and the superscription no longer seemed to tally? That was the problem of an image which was Caliban's and a superscription which read ἄριστος ἀνδρῶν—'the finest specimen of manhood'. Sophocles had proposed to remove a no longer tolerable contradiction by sharpening the image and chiselling the superscription off. Diogenes had eventually removed it by the contrary device of retaining the superscription and restamping the image to suit a new idea—revealed by insight won from suffering—of what the traditional legend ought to imply.[4] And it was the coin as it came from Diogenes' masterful hands that set the standard for a Hêraklês-type which began *post Alexan-*

---

[1] The story is told by Murray in op. cit., sheet 1. According to Dudley, D. R.: *A History of Cynicism* (London 1937, Methuen), pp. 20–1 and 54–5, following C. T. Seltman, παραχαράττειν means, not 'restamp', but 'deface', and there is numismatic evidence that Diogenes' father did, in fact, as the magistrate responsible for the mint of Sinope, deface, in order to put out of circulation, imitations of the Sinopic coinage that had been counterfeited by a neighbouring satrap.   [2] Ibid., sheet 5.
[3] Suidas, s.v. *Hêraklês*, quoted by Murray, op. cit., sheet 29.
[4] Murray, op. cit., sheets 29–30.

drum to pass into circulation in the Oriental World and to be accepted there as interchangeable with the familiar local types of the Melkarts and the Sandans.

Let us scrutinize the portrait of *Hercules Philosophus* which thus gained currency in the former domain of the Achaemenian Empire after having been repainted by the Hellenic genius in the throes of a 'Time of Troubles'. We shall find in it a number of points which correspond with the portrait of Jesus in the Gospels; and we shall also find that many of these correspondences between Jesus and Hêraklês coincide with points of correspondence, that have been noted in this inquiry already, between Jesus and some of those historical pagan Hellenic heroes with whose stories we have been attempting to bring the Gospels into comparison.

(α) *There is a pair of heroes who are distinguished from one another by a double difference of age and of êthos* (= Point 1).

Hêraklês has a half-brother, Îphiklês, who plays Tiberius Gracchus to Hêraklês' Gaius. The contrast of character between the two brothers comes out when Hera sends the snakes to destroy the infant Hêraklês in his cradle (see Point (δ) below). While Hêraklês strangles the snakes, Îphiklês runs away (Apollodorus: *Bibliotheca*, Book II, chap. 62, on the authority of Pherecydes).

(β) *The hero is of royal lineage* (= Point 2).

Hêraklês' reputed father Amphitryon is a son of the Perseid King Alcaeus of Tiryns.

(γ) *The hero's genealogy has a flaw in it* (= Point 4).

Hêraklês' claim to be a scion of the Perseid royal house of Tiryns is disputable, inasmuch as it is derived from a Tirynthian Perseid who is the husband of Hêraklês' mother but who is not, himself, Hêraklês' father.[1]

N.B. Hêraklês' claim to be of the royal Perseid blood is, however, salvaged thanks to the fact that his mother Alcmena is a Perseid as well as his reputed father Amphitryon. Alcmena is the daughter of the Perseid King Electryon of Mycenae, who is Amphitryon's uncle. It is noteworthy that one of the means by which the Christian commentators on the Gospels have sought to reconcile Jesus's claim to descent from David with his claim to be the Son of God to the exclusion of his being a son of Joseph has

---

[1] This correspondence of the birth-stories of Hêraklês and Jesus, not only with one another but also with those of a number of other Hellenic heroes, some legendary and others historical, has been noticed already in V. C (ii) (a), p. 269, footnote 1, above. While Hêraklês is a son of Alcmena by Zeus, his half-brother Îphiklês (see Point (α) above), who is his junior by one night, is a son of Alcmena by her husband Amphitryon—as Jesus's half-brothers are sons of Mary by Joseph.

been by supposing that Mary was related to Joseph as Alcmena was related to Amphitryon.

(δ) *The hero has a miraculous escape from a mortal danger which threatens him in infancy.*[1]

Hera plays towards Hêraklês the persecutor's part that Herod plays towards Jesus. The babe is placed in hiding (Diodorus, Book IV, chap. 9, § 6),[2] as Jesus (Matt. ii. 13–21) is taken by Joseph to Egypt, in order to save his life from Hera's murderous designs (compare the stories of Jason, Orestes, Zeus, Zagreus, Horus, Moses, Cyrus).[3] Hera afterwards sends a pair of snakes to kill the babe in his cradle; but Hêraklês strangles the creatures by a miraculously precocious exertion of his superhuman physical strength (Diodorus, Book IV, chap. 10, § 1).

(ε) *The Temptation in the Wilderness* (= the correspondence between the Temptations of Jesus and of Gautama which has been examined in this Annex on pp. 451–2, above).

On reaching the age of discretion at which the young become masters of their own fate and give an indication whether they are going to take the path of virtue or the path of vice as their approach to adult life, Hêraklês goes out to a quiet spot and sits debating within himself which path to take;[4] and then and there Virtue and Vice make their epiphany to him in the form of two women who compete for his affections (Xenophon: *Memorabilia*, Book II, chap. i, §§ 21–34).[5] This fable of Hêraklês' choice has a later variant, according to which the hero is led into the wilderness by Hermes, acting under Zeus' orders, and is taken up by his divine guide into an exceeding high mountain with two peaks, on one of which Kingship is enthroned and on the other Despotism. Hêraklês, of course, makes the appropriate choice between the two (Dio Chrysostom: *Oratio* I, §§ 58–84).[6]

(ζ) *The hero's career is an ordeal* (|| Point 10).

'Hêraklês who has borne so much' (Euripides: *Hercules Furens*, l. 1250). 'When thou hast worked thy way through labours such as these, then, Hêraklês, thou child of worthy parents, the possession of the most blissful felicity is within thy grasp' (*Virtus loquitur apud Prodicum, referente Xenophonte: Memorabilia*, Book II, chap. i, § 33). 'Who, save Hêraklês the son of Zeus, would have been willing, when he was of divine origin, to toil through such peri-

---

[1] For this *motif* see the present Annex, pp. 450–1, above.
[2] See Pfister, op. cit., p. 47.   [3] See III. C (ii) (b), vol. iii, p. 260, above.
[4] For this simile of the two roads see p. 453, above.   [5] Pfister, op. cit., p. 43.
[6] Ibid., p. 48 (the passage from Dio has been cited already in V. C (ii) (a), Annex I, p. 370, above).

lous and grievous and painful labours?' (Plutarch: *De Alexandri Fortitudine*, ii. 11).[1]

(η) *The hero's work obtains an extraordinary publicity* (= Point 12).

'The affair became celebrated through all Hellas (καθ' ὅλην τὴν Ἑλλάδα) and all were amazed at the extraordinariness of it' (πάντων θαυμαζόντων τὸ παράδοξον) (Diodorus, Book IV, chap. 10, § 6). 'And there went out a fame of him through all the region round about (καθ' ὅλης τῆς περιχώρου), and he taught in their synagogues, being glorified of all' (δοξαζόμενος ὑπὸ πάντων) (Luke iv. 14–15).[2]

(θ) *The hero is commissioned by God to exercise a beneficent royal authority over all Mankind* (‖ Point 15).

'Zeus commissioned him to reign over the whole human race . . . and . . . to be the saviour of the whole Earth and of all Mankind' (Dio Chrysostom: *Oratio* I, § 84).[3] 'Thou sayest that I am a king' (John xviii. 37). 'The Father sent the Son to be the saviour of the World' (1 John iv. 14). 'Zeus sent (Ζεὺς μὲν ἀπέστειλε) orders to him to work for Eurystheus' (Diodorus, Book IV, chap. 10, § 7). 'I must preach the Kingdom of God to other cities also; for therefore am I sent' (εἰς τοῦτο ἀπέσταλμαι) (Luke iv. 43).[4]

(ι) *A tableau of the hero in spiritual agony in face of a supreme challenge* (= Point 36).[5]

'Hêraklês made a journey to Delphi and questioned the god [about the orders that he had received from Zeus to work for Eurystheus]. He received an oracle signifying that it was the will of the Gods that he should accomplish (τελέσαι)[6] twelve labours at the bidding of Eurystheus, and that in reward he should gain immortality. Thereupon Hêraklês fell into an extraordinary despondency (ἐνέπεσεν εἰς ἀθυμίαν οὐ τὴν τυχοῦσαν). On the one hand he considered it quite unworthy of his own prowess to serve some one of less distinction,[7] and on the other hand it seemed to him unsuitable, and indeed impossible, not to obey a Zeus who was at the same time his own father.[8] This threw him into a distressing spiritual quandary (εἰς πολλὴν οὖν ἀμηχανίαν ἐμπίπτοντος αὐτοῦ) in which Hera seized the opportunity of casting a frenzy upon him ("Ηρα μὲν ἔπεμψεν αὐτῷ λύτταν). Hêraklês became so sick

---

[1] Ibid., p. 50.
[2] Ibid., pp. 48–9.
[3] Ibid., p. 45.
[4] Ibid., p. 49.
[5] See also Table VIII—Common Words: (ε), on pp. 414 and 415–16, above.
[6] See Point 74 above = Table VIII—Common Words: (λ) = Point (ξ) below in the present series relating to Hêraklês.
[7] Compare: 'The servant is not greater than his lord, neither he that is sent greater than him that sent him' (John xiii. 16).
[8] 'Nevertheless, not as I will but as thou wilt' (Matt. xxvi. 39 = Mark xiv. 36 = Luke xxii. 42 (cf. John v. 30, and vi. 38).

in soul that he went out of his mind (ὁ δὲ τῇ ψυχῇ δυσφορῶν εἰς μανίαν ἐνέπεσε); and the malady grew upon him to a point at which he took leave of his senses and . . .' (Diodorus, Book IV, chap. 10, § 7, and chap. 11, § 1).[1]

(κ) *The hero resigns himself to the will of his heavenly father.*

'On the other hand it seemed to him unsuitable, and indeed impossible, not to obey a Zeus who was at the same time his own father' (Diodorus, loc. cit. in (ι), above). 'Nevertheless, not as I will but as thou wilt' (the Gospels, locc. citt. in footnote 7 on p. 471, above).[2]

(λ) *A shirt (χιτών) in which the hero goes to his death* (‖ Point 71).

The shirt plays, of course, a far more important part in the Passion of Hêraklês than in the Passion of Jesus; for the death of Hêraklês is actually caused by his putting on the poisoned shirt of Nessus.

(μ) *When other passers-by refuse to perform a friendly office for the hero, one person responds to his request and receives a notable reward for his act of friendship* (‖ Point 72).

'Hêraklês went to the pyre and then began to beg everybody who approached, one after another, to set light to it. No one ventured to do his bidding until at last Philoctetes agreed. He received as a reward for his services the gift of Hêraklês' bow and arrows' (Diodorus, Book IV, chap. 38, § 4).

(ν) *The hero's mother is supported in her ordeal by a young man of the hero's entourage* (= Points 73 and 80A).

Alcmena is present at the Passion of Hêraklês (according to Seneca in his *Hercules Oetaeus*, though not according to Sophocles in his *Trachiniae*). The part of the favourite companion is played by Philoctetes, who is described as ἐρώμενος Ἡρακλέους in the scholia to Apollonius Rhodius: *Argonautica*, Book I, l. 1207; but the young man who supports Alcmena (according to the Senecan version of the passion-play) is not Philoctetes but Hyllus, who is Hêraklês' son and therefore Alcmena's own grandson.[3]

N.B. Philoctetes' friendly office to Hêraklês (see Point (μ),

---

[1] Pfister, op. cit., p. 49. In the legend of Hêraklês according to Diodorus the hero's spiritual agony discharges itself in a murderous assault upon the hero's faithful companion Iolaus and upon the hero's own children. This was, of course, the common form of this chapter of the Hêraklês Story. May we infer that the attraction exercised by it is responsible for the Diodoran version of the corresponding chapter in the story of Gaius Gracchus, in which the guilt for the murder of Antullus is laid upon Gaius Gracchus and not upon Marcus Fulvius, and the murder itself is placed after Gaius's agony and not before it? (See p. 389, footnote 3, and p. 392, footnote 2, above.)

[2] Ibid., p. 49.　　　　　　　　　　　　　　[3] Ibid., p. 53.

above) corresponds to Panteus' friendly office to Cleomenes (see Point 79).

(ξ) *The end of an ordeal* (= Point 74).[1]

'It is finished' (*peractum est*) (Seneca: *Hercules Oetaeus*, ll. 1340, 1457, 1472).[2]

N.B. The same phrase is repeated twice in the Gospel according to Saint John (xix. 28 and 30).

(o) *The hero commends his spirit to his heavenly father.*

'Quacumque parte prospicis natum, pater, . . . spiritum admitte hunc, precor, in astra' (Seneca: *Hercules Oetaeus*, ll. 1696 and 1703–4).

'Father, into thy hands I commend my spirit' (Luke xxiii. 46).[3]

(π) *Three portents* (‖ Point 75).

Hercules prays to the Sun to cease to shine on this day of the hero's death (Seneca: *Hercules Oetaeus*, ll. 1131–4). He prays to his father Juppiter to rend the Earth from pole to pole (ll. 1134–6). He prophesies that the buried giants will break out from under the mountains that cover them, and that Pluto will throw open the gates of Hades (ll. 1138–43). All these three portents are mentioned in the Gospels as having occurred at the time of Jesus's death: the darkness in all three Synoptic Gospels (Matt. xxvii. 45 = Mark xv. 33 = Luke xxiii. 44); the earthquake and the opening of the graves in Matt. xxvii. 51–3.

N.B. According to Diodorus, Book IV, chap. 38, § 4, Hêraklês' pyre is miraculously consumed by incendiary thunderbolts. A portent of thunder is mentioned by Apollodorus: *Bibliotheca*, Book II, chap. 160; a portent of darkness by Festus: *De Verborum Significatu*, Book VIII, s.v. *Hercules*.[4]

(ρ) *When the hero is being burnt to death, Iolaus and other intimate companions of his are in the vicinity, though not actually on the spot* (= Point 80).

'Iolaus and the rest waited beholding from a distance to see what would happen' (ἐκ διαστήματος ἀποθεωρούντων τὸ ἀποβησόμενον) (Diodorus, Book IV, chap. 38, § 4). 'And many women were there beholding afar off' (ἀπὸ μακρόθεν θεωροῦσαι) (Matt. xxvii. 55 = Mark xv. 40; cf. Luke xxiii. 49).

---

[1] See also Table VIII—Common Words: (λ), on pp. 414 and 416, above.
[2] Pfister, op. cit., pag. cit.   [3] Ibid.
[4] Ibid., pp. 53–4. According to Festus: 'Hercules astrologus dictus quod eo die se flammis iniecit quo futura erat obscuratio Solis.' For the association of the Hêraklês *motif* of an eclipse with the death of Caesar, as well as with the death of Jesus, see Virgil: *Georgics*, I, ll. 467–8, quoted in V. C (i) (d) 5, vol. v, p. 436, above.

N.B. In the tableau of the Crucifixion of Jesus these onlookers from a distance are a chorus of Galilaean women corresponding to the chorus of Trachinian women who are present at the cremation of Hêraklês in Sophocles' play. In Seneca's play Iolaus and the rest have followed Hêraklês from his and their home in Trachis to the scene of his death on Oeta, just as the Galilaean women have followed Jesus from his and their home in Galilee to the scene of his death at Jerusalem.

(σ) *The hero, after his death, comes to receive religious worship* (= Point 83).

Diodorus, Book IV, chap. 39, § 1.

(τ) *The villain perishes miserably* (= Point 85).

'Deïaneira was prostrated at the greatness of the disaster that had befallen Hêraklês, and, being conscience-stricken by the conviction that the sin was hers, she put an end to her life by hanging herself' (συνειδυῖα ἑαυτῇ τὴν ἁμαρτίαν, ἀγχόνῃ τὸν βίον κατέστρεψεν) (Diodorus, Book IV, chap. 38, § 3). 'Then Judas . . ., when he saw that he was condemned, repented himself (μεταμεληθείς) . . . saying "I have sinned (ἥμαρτον) . . ." . . . and went and hanged himself' (καὶ ἀπελθὼν ἀπήγξατο) (Matt. xxvii. 3–5).[1]

N.B. Deïaneira's tragedy resembles Judas' in the further point that she, too, has been a tool in hands more villainous than her own.

(υ) *The disappearance of the hero's mortal remains.*

'After [the miraculous conflagration of the pyre by thunderbolts] Iolaus and the rest went to collect the bones; but not one bone was to be found—from which they inferred that, in accordance with the oracles, Hêraklês had been translated from the world of men to the world of the Gods' (Diodorus, Book IV, chap. 38, § 5). After the burial of Jesus, when the women return to visit the Sepulchre, they find it open and empty (Matt. xxviii. 1–8 = Mark xvi. 1–8 = Luke xxiv. 1–9 = John xx. 1); and their extraordinary discovery is confirmed by Peter (Luke xxiv. 10–12) or by John and Peter (John xx. 2–10).[2]

(φ) *The hero has conquered Death and harrowed Hell.*

Hêraklês' twelfth labour is a descent into Hades to seize and bring back Cerberus. He successfully accomplishes this task, and on another occasion—and this time, too, with success—he

---

[1] Pfister, op. cit., p. 53. [2] Ibid., p. 55.

descends into Hades to rescue and bring back Alcestis. (Compare Seneca: *Hercules Furens*, ll. 604–12 and 889–93, and *Hercules Oetaeus*, ll. 1943–62, with Rom. vi. 9, and 2 Tim. i. 10.)[1]

(χ) *The hero, after his death, appears to one (or to two) of the women of his entourage.*

Hêraklês appears to his mother Alcmena (Seneca: *Hercules Oetaeus*, ll. 1940–82); Jesus appears to Mary Magdalene and 'the other Mary'[2] (Matt. xxviii. 9) or to Mary Magdalene alone (Mark xvi. 9–11 and John xx. 11–18).[3]

(ψ) *The hero's disciples return to his and their home.*

Iolaus and his companions from Oeta to Trachis (Diodorus, Book IV, chap. 39, § 1); Peter and his companions from Jerusalem to Galilee (Matt. xxviii. 10 and 16; John xxi).

(ω) *The hero ascends to Heaven in a cloud.*

Hêraklês (Apollodorus: *Bibliotheca*, Book II, chap. 160); Jesus (Acts i. 9).

This completes our survey of correspondences between the legend of Hêraklês on the one hand and the stories of Jesus, and of the pagan historical heroes whom we have brought into comparison with Jesus, on the other hand. If we glance at the analysis of our results which is set out in Table X we shall see that the correspondences that we have observed are not only numerous but are also representative of the several different kinds of elements that are common to the Gospels and to the stories of the pagan historical heroes. This finding suggests that the legend of Hêraklês may be an important common source from which the story of Jesus on the one side and the stories of the pagan historical heroes on the other side may have derived some of their common features, independently of one another, through separate channels of the stream of 'folk-memory'.[4]

---

[1] Ibid., p. 51.

[2] i.e. Mary the mother of James and Joses (Matt. xxvii. 56), not Mary the mother of Jesus.

[3] Jesus's salutation to Mary Magdalene at the Sepulchre—'Woman, why weepest thou?' (John xx. 15)—has a correspondence in Hêraklês' adjuration *post mortem* to his mother Alcmena: 'Quid me . . . planctu iubes/sentire fatum?' (Seneca: *Hercules Oetaeus*, ll. 1940–2). There is a closer verbal coincidence in l. 1507: 'Parce iam lacrimis, parens' (Pfister, op. cit., p. 55); but these words are spoken by the hero before his death and not after it. The next line (1508) of Seneca's play—'Superba matres inter Argolicas eris' —corresponds verbally with the salutation—'Blessed art thou among women'—with which Mary the mother of Jesus is greeted first by Gabriel (Luke i. 28) and then by Elisabeth (Luke i. 42).

[4] This suggestion has already been made apropos of the birth-stories in V. C (ii) (a), p. 269, footnote 1, above.

TABLE X. *Concordance of Correspondences between the Legend of Héraklês and the Stories of Jesus and the Pagan Historical Heroes*

Hēraklês	Point in Table I	At least one Synoptic Gospel	John	A Pauline Epistle	At least one part of the New Testament	Agis	Cleomenes	At least one Spartan hero	Tiberius Gracchus	Gaius Gracchus	At east one Roman hero	Aristonicus	Eunus	At least one futurist	Siddhārtha Gautama	Common Element
(α)	1	×	×		2	×—	××	1	×—	××	1					A pair of common characters
(β)	2	×			1	×	×	2					×	1	×	
(γ)	4	×			1								×	1		
(δ)		×			1											
(ε)		×			1										×	
(ζ)	10	×			1		×	1					×	1		
(η)	12	×			1					×	1					
(θ)	15	×	×		2							×		1		
(ι)	36	×			1					×	1					A common scene
(κ)	36	×			1											A common word
(λ)	71		×		1		×	1								A common property
(μ)	72	×			1								×	1		
(ν)	73 + 80A		×		1		×	1								Two common characters
(ξ)	74		×		1		×	1								A common word
(ο)		×			1											
(π)	75	×			1		×	1								
(ρ)	80	×			1	×		1								A common scene
(σ)	83								×	×	2					A common property
(τ)	85	×			1				×	×	2					A common character
(υ)		×	×		2											
(φ)				×	1											
(χ)		×	×		2											
(ψ)		×	×		2											
(ω)		×			1											

The Ritual Murder of an Incarnate God

Legend, however, is not the only kind of foreign matter that may fall into Lethe's stream and be carried along by it. According to the anthropologists a myth usually proves, when we are able to trace its history back to its origins, to be the verbal echo of some ritual act;[1] and the deed is anterior to the word[2] logically as well as historically; for a society that performs some act for its own sake without being moved to seek for any explanation is manifestly in a more primitive mental state than one which is led by a disinterested curiosity into trying to explain the reason for what is

[1] In an aesthetically gifted primitive society or nascent civilization the ritual act is apt to blossom into a religious drama and the myth into Epic or Saga (see II. D (iii), vol. ii, pp. 92–6, above).

[2] 'Im Anfang war die Tat.'—Goethe: *Faust*, l. 1237.

done when this indulgence of the speculative intellect cannot be supposed to add in any way to the practical efficacy of the customary magical or religious performance. If, therefore, we have found evidence which suggests that a myth may make its way into the stream of 'folk-memory' and may be deposited by these waters in fields of sophisticated literature that happen to adjoin the river banks, then we may expect *a priori* to see pieces of ritual being carried along the same channels to the same eventual resting-places; and, to verify this hypothesis, we need not for the moment look beyond the figure of the demigod who has been engaging our attention in the immediately preceding pages.

We have already come to the conclusion that the legend of Hêraklês would have been unlikely—even in the etherialized form to which it had been refined by the cumulative labours of three successive generations of Hellenic philosophers—to make the headway that it did make in the Oriental World *post Alexandrum* if the Hellenic demigod himself had not first been officially identified with local divinities who were ancient, familiar, and popular. And, if we now look into the reasons why Hêraklês was taken to be the Hellenic equivalent of this or that Oriental god, we shall find that the decisive factor was apt to be some striking point of similarity, not in myth, but in ritual. Sandan the god of Tarsus, for example, was identified with Hêraklês because an effigy—inanimate or living—of the Tarsian god was annually cremated on a pyre.[1] This explanation of Hêraklês-Sandan is hardly open to doubt; and it would likewise seem probable that the Tyrian god Melkart was identified with Hêraklês because the Tyrians celebrated an annual festival of the resurrection of Melkart which recalled to Hellenic minds the triumph of Hêraklês over Death. This Tyrian festival is referred to as that of 'the Resurrection of Hêraklês' ($Ηρακλέους$ $έγερσις$) in a Greek work from the pen of a half-Hellenized Jewish scholar who lived and wrote in the first century of the Christian Era.[2] Did the Tyrians, we may wonder, look eastward, when the season of this festival came round, to catch sight of, and salute, their lord god as he rose, with the Sun, above the mountains of Galilee? And did some such lingering local custom also direct the steps of certain sons of 'Galilee of the

---

[1] See Frazer, J. G.: *The Scapegoat = The Golden Bough*, 3rd ed., Part VI (London 1913, Macmillan), pp. 388–90.

[2] Josephus: *Antiquities*, Book VIII, chap. 5, § 3, cited by Pfister, op. cit., pp. 58–9. The foundation of this festival of the Resurrection of Hêraklês in the month of Peritius is attributed to Solomon's Tyrian contemporary King Hiram by Josephus, loc. cit., on the authority of 'Menander the translator of the archives of Tyre out of the original Phoenician into Greek'. Peritius was the fourth month of a Macedonian calendar which took the autumnal equinox for its New Year's Day, so that, if the Tyrian festival of the Resurrection of Hêraklês was celebrated on the *first* day of the month, its date would be identical with that of the Birthday of the Sun and Christmas Day.

Gentiles'[1]—whose grandfathers had been numbered among the heathen before Alexander Jannaeus (*regnabat* 102–76 B.C.) converted them to Judaism by the sword—when, in their agony of sorrow and despair on the morrow of their Master's death, they 'went away into Galilee, into a mountain where Jesus had appointed them', and 'worshipped him when they saw him'?[2] In an equally speculative vein we may ask ourselves whether the annual ritual at Tarsus, in which Hêraklês-Sandan died a cruel death in order to enjoy a glorious resurrection, may not have made on the imagination and emotions of Saint Paul as a boy an impression which we can trace in the grown man's Christology.[3] The Hêraklês who was the universally acknowledged saviour ($\sigma\omega\tau\eta\rho$) of all Mankind[4] was also, at Tarsus, the local prince ($\dot{\alpha}\rho\chi\eta\gamma\acute{o}s$) of a community that worshipped him as Hêraklês-Sandan.[5] Is it sheer chance that the same two titles of 'prince' and 'saviour' are applied to Jesus in a passage of the Acts of the Apostles in virtue of the prodigy of a resurrection[6] which is ascribed to Jesus as well as to Hêraklês-Melkart?

'The God of our fathers raised up ($\eta\gamma\epsilon\iota\rho\epsilon\nu$) Jesus, whom ye slew and hanged on a tree. Him hath God exalted with his right hand to be a prince ($\dot{\alpha}\rho\chi\eta\gamma\acute{o}\nu$) and a saviour ($\sigma\omega\tau\eta\rho\alpha$).'[7]

Does it not seem probable that these three almost technical terms have been inherited by Christianity from the Tyrian worship of Hêraklês-Melkart and from the Tarsian worship of Hêraklês-Sandan? And, if this probability is entertained, does it not seem also probable that ritual, rather than myth, was the vehicle in which the three terms were conveyed from one religion to another?

The likelihood that ritual, as well as myth, may have contributed to the production of the correspondences between the story of Jesus and the stories of our eleven pagan historical heroes will not appear less when we remind ourselves that Jesus was not the only

---

[1] Matt. iv. 15, quoted already in II. D (iii), vol. ii, p. 73, above. See further the present Annex, in the present volume, p. 499, below. [2] Matt. xxviii. 16–17.

[3] In later years Paul still spoke of his Tarsian birth with pride ('I am a man which am a Jew of Tarsus, a city in Cilicia, a citizen of no mean city.'—Acts xxi. 39). If Tarsus retained this lasting hold over Paul's affections, it seems likely that the impressions of his childhood in Tarsus will likewise have made a lasting imprint upon his imagination. These suppositions are quite compatible with Paul's own account of the next stage of his life, when he was receiving an education in the Jewish Law at Jerusalem ('My manner of life from my youth ($\dot{\epsilon}\kappa$ $\nu\epsilon\acute{o}\tau\eta\tau\sigma s$, not $\dot{\epsilon}\kappa$ $\pi\alpha\iota\delta\acute{o}s$), which was at the first among mine own nation at Jerusalem, know all the Jews—which knew me from the beginning, if they would testify, that after the most straitest sect of our religion I lived a Pharisee.'—Acts xxvi. 4–5).

[4] See the phrase quoted on p. 471, above, from Dio Chrysostom: *Oratio* I, § 84.

[5] 'Your prince Hêraklês' ($\dot{o}$ $\dot{\alpha}\rho\chi\eta\gamma\grave{o}s$ $\dot{\upsilon}\mu\hat{\omega}\nu$ $'H\rho\alpha\kappa\lambda\hat{\eta}s$).—Dio Chrysostom: *Oratio* XXXIII (*Tarsica Prior*), § 47.

[6] The ritual of the cremation of Hêraklês-Sandan is similarly mentioned, in association with his title of 'prince', by Dio Chrysostom in loc. cit.

[7] Acts v. 30–1. The three verbal correspondences are pointed out by Pfister, op. cit., p. 59.

one of these twelve to become a recipient of worship after his death. The Gracchi, as we have seen (Point 83), are reported by Plutarch's authorities to have been worshipped—and this with a regular ritual which was comparable to the services in the temples of the Gods—at the spots that had been hallowed by these two Roman heroes' deaths. And at Alexandria the spot where the crucified corpse of Cleomenes had been miraculously preserved intact (Points 75, 76, and 78) became a place of pilgrimage where the dead Spartan exile was hailed 'as a hero and a child of the Gods' by the populace of Alexandria.

In the same passage (*Lives of Agis and Cleomenes*, chap. 60, *ad fin.*) Plutarch (or is it really Phylarchus?) goes on, it is true, to narrate how this nascent worship of Cleomenes was nipped in the bud by the intervention of 'educated people' (οἱ σοφώτεροι), who threw cold water on the rising religious ardour of the Alexandrians by explaining to them that the apparently miraculous portent which had made such an impression on their hearts via their intellects was scientifically explicable as a commonplace effect of certain wholly natural causes. If there is any truth in this tale, it is easy to guess that these zealous rationalists were not exerting themselves *proprio motu*. Behind their propaganda we can discern the policy of the Ministers of King Ptolemy Philopator. While Cleomenes was still alive, the Ptolemaic Government had been seriously concerned at the alarming evidences of their Spartan guest's popularity among King Ptolemy's soldiers and subjects. It was on this account that they had taken the precaution of interning him; and now the romantic fool had turned the tables on these prudent statesmen by managing, in their despite, to die a heroic death and to cap it with a sensational miracle to the credit of his dead body. It was not to be borne that the tiresome fellow should defeat their calculations by now making himself even more popular as a naturalized ghost than he had ever been as a living alien refugee. The blossoming worship of Cleomenes must be sterilized at once by vigorous counter-measures; and we may well believe that, partly by propaganda and partly by intimidation, Sosibius and his colleagues did succeed in driving this pestilent worship of Cleomenes underground. But who shall say what the fortunes of the cult may have been after it had gone to earth? Not even the Ptolemaic security police could certify that this *Schwärmerei* was completely extinct; and not even the Ptolemaic customs cordon could prevent it, if it did manage to survive in an Alexandrian underworld, from being shipped far and wide out of a port which in that age was the central mart and clearing-house of three continents and five civilizations.

The possible social means of conveyance by which a never quite extinguished worship of Cleomenes might have been carried from Alexandria to the Palestinian glacis of the Ptolemaic Empire are examined at a later point in this Annex.[1] In the present context we may pass on to observe that, while the survival of the worship of Cleomenes is non-proven, and while the institution of a worship of the Gracchi is only vouched for by the unsupported testimony of one of Plutarch's sources, there is no doubt at all about the worship of three other historical Hellenic heroes—Plato, Alexander, and Augustus—who have come into the purview of our present inquiry because they are credited with the divine paternity and the miraculous birth that are likewise attributed to Jesus in the Matthaean and Lucan prologues to the story of the Gospels.[2]

We may also presume that in cases such as these, in which a religious worship came to be paid to the *manes* of mortal men, the ritual with which these were honoured would be modelled, with a minimum of innovation, on some familiar traditional ritual which was in current use in the worship of superhuman heroes and gods. In Plutarch's source, for example, the Gracchi are visualized in the likeness of the Dioscuri.[3] And we may hazard the guess that the pair of historical Roman heroes were thus thought of as counterparts of the pair of Lacedaemonian demigods because the modern statues of them that were dedicated and erected in a conspicuous place[4] were carved in something like the traditional shapes of Castor and Pollux and were honoured with something like the observances to which these statues of Castor and Pollux had a traditional claim. There is, however, no reason to suppose that the rituals in vogue in the worships of the Dioscuri and of Hêraklês were the only pieces of existing religious or magical practice that were laid under contribution in the process of instituting the worships and shaping the legends of Plato and Alexander and Cleomenes and the Gracchi and Augustus and Jesus. There is no obvious limit to the extent of the field of traditional observance from which some common element may, here and there, have found its way independently into the worships, and thence into the legends, of some or all of the historical heroes whose stories reveal those correspondences that we are seeking to trace back to their origins; and, if we make a reconnaissance into some of the tracts that Sir James Frazer has mapped out in the relevant parts of his vast survey,[5] we shall come across at least two rites which

---

[1] On pp. 496–500, below.
[2] See V. C (ii) (a), pp. 267–9, and the present Annex, pp. 379 and 469, above.
[3] Plutarch: *Lives of the Gracchi*, chap. 2.   [4] Ibid., chap. 39.
[5] See Frazer, Sir J. G.: *The Golden Bough*, 3rd ed., Part III: *The Dying God* (London 1911, Macmillan), and Part VI: *The Scapegoat* (London 1913, Macmillan).

look as though they may have been the ultimate sources of certain of the correspondences between the stories of our pagan historical heroes and the story of the Gospels.

(α) 'The Ride of the Beardless One.'[1]

There is a Persian rite in which a naked rider, mounted on a horse, ass, or mule, rides through the city at the head of a cortège (Point 16)—apparently for the magical purpose of bringing warmth back to the Earth in spring.[2] As his reward for playing the part, this human impersonator of the power that annually rejuvenates the face of Nature is allowed to levy contributions on the shop-keepers; and, if they are hesitant about complying with his de-mands, he is entitled to confiscate the whole of their stock (Point 17). Is this Persian rite the ultimate source of two of our common scenes? The conjecture may be fortified by two apparently corro-borative pieces of evidence. On the one hand the rite appears to have precipitated itself, in the shape of a myth, in the incident of Mordecai's ride in the Book of Esther[3]—a post-exilic work of Jewish literature which was undoubtedly generated by a desire to account retrospectively for the origin of the annual festival of Purim,[4] which the Jews had adopted, or at any rate adapted, from the practice of the heathen among whom they had been constrained to dwell during their Babylonish captivity. On the other hand the same spring-rite would seem to have played some part in suggest-ing the idea of an historical piece of horse-play.

(β) 'The Reign of the Mock King.'

The Jewish Hellenist scholar Philo of Alexandria (*vivebat circa* 20 B.C.–A.D. 50) records[5] that at Alexandria in A.D. 38, when Herod Agrippa I, the grandson of Herod the Great, was passing through the city on his way home to Palestine from Rome—where he had just been raised to royal rank and been invested with his uncle Philip's former appanage by the Emperor Caligula—the Alexan-drian populace, who in this age were violently Anti-Semitic,[6] gave

---

[1] See Frazer: *The Scapegoat*, pp. 402–5.
[2] This interpretation of the rite depends on a combination of points—the season at which it is performed, the nakedness of the rider, and the bystanders' practice of douch-ing him with hot water—which are irrelevant for our present purpose.
[3] Esther vi. 7–11.
[4] At the feast of Purim the Jews—even in Western Europe in the Modern Age—used to act a play which had for its subject the story that is told as a tale in the Book of Esther (see Frazer, op. cit., pp. 414–16).
[5] Philo: *In Flaccum*, chap. (6), §§ 36–9 (in *Philonis Alexandrini Opera quae supersunt*, edited by Cohn, L., and Wendland, P., vol. vi, edited by Cohn, L., and Reiter, S. (Berlin 1915, Reimer), p. 127), cited by Frazer, op. cit., p. 418, following Wendland, P.: 'Jesus als Saturnalienkönig' (= Hermes, vol. xxxiii (1898), pp. 175–9).
[6] For this Alexandrian Anti-Semitism and its causes see V. C (ii) (a), pp. 217–19, above.

expression to their chagrin at the aggrandizement of a Jewish prince by burlesquing Agrippa's investiture in a kind of charade, which they improvised in the streets of Alexandria while their unwelcome royal guest was in their midst. To show what they thought of a Jewish kingship of Roman manufacture, the Alexandrians, according to Philo's story, rounded up a naked beggar named Carabas; chevied him into the public gymnasium; set a papyrus-leaf crown on his head, a rug robe on his shoulders, and a papyrus-stalk sceptre in his hand; paid him mock court (Points 65[1] and 66); and exhibited him in these burlesque regalia to the crowd (Point 67), who hailed him with satirical acclamations of 'Marin! Marin!'[2]

In this elaborately offensive piece of fooling[3] the Alexandrians appear to have combined a vague parody of 'the Ride of the Beardless One' with a close parody of another rite which has, perhaps, a certain affinity with 'the Ride' in respect of its magical purpose and which may also, perhaps, have been combined with 'the Ride' in practice when the two rites were being performed in earnest.[4] The sceptre and robe and crown with which the historical victim

---

[1] It will be seen that Philo's story comes closer to the Lucan account of the mocking of Jesus by Herod Agrippa's uncle and brother-in-law Herod Antipas and his men than it comes to the Matthaean and Marcan account of the mocking of Jesus by Pilate's Roman soldiers.

[2] 'Marin! Marin!' seems to be a garbled version of the Hebrew 'Marna! Marna!' ('Our Lord! Our Lord!'). Compare Matt. xxi. 9 = Mark xi. 9–10 = Luke xix. 38 = John xii. 13.

[3] The elaborateness of it will be apparent in the following translation of the whole passage of Philo from Cohn and Reiter's Greek text:
'There was a madman called Carabas whose madness was not of the savage ferocious kind—a kind which shows no more consideration [reading ἄσκεπτος for the ἀσκήπτος of the MSS.] for those who come within range than for those who are possessed by it [cf. Matt. viii. 28 = Mark v. 3–4 = Luke viii. 29]—but was of the kind that is relaxed and milder. This man lived all day long, and all night long as well [Mark v. 5], stark naked [Luke viii. 27] in the streets, exposing himself heedlessly to extremes of heat and cold and to the pranks that were played on him by infants and children who had nothing better to do. They [i.e. the Alexandrian mob] chevied this poor creature to the public gymnasium; stood him on a platform where he would be visible to all eyes; flattened out a papyrus-leaf and set it on his head to do for a diadem, and draped the rest of his body in a rug to do for a robe [χλαμύς, which is the word used in Matt. xxvii. 28], while, to do for a sceptre, some one handed up a short section of papyrus-stalk (the native Egyptian plant) which he had seen lying in the street where it had been thrown away. When Carabas had thus received the insignia of royalty and been tricked out as a king with all the parade of a pantomime, some young fellows took their stand on either side of him with sloped rods, to do for sloped pikes, like a burlesque bodyguard; and then other people made their approach—some as though they were going to pay him their respects, some as though they were going to lay a suit before him, and some as though they were going to consult him on public affairs. And then, from the crowd standing round in a circle, there thundered out the strange cry of 'Marin', which is said to be the Syrian for 'Lord'—for they knew that Agrippa was a Syrian by race and that a large slice of Syria constituted his [newly conferred] kingdom.'

[4] The combination of 'the Ride of the Beardless One' with 'the Reign of the Mock King' may have been an established practice in the realm of serious observance before the two rites were combined in the Alexandrian burlesque of A.D. 38. This possibility is suggested by the fact that Philo's account of this Alexandrian practical joke is not the only context in which we find the two rites associated with one another. There are also traces of both of them in the myth of Esther and Mordecai, which has been precipitated by the ritual of the post-exilic Jewish festival of Purim.

of a heartless practical joke was tricked out at Alexandria in A.D. 38 are properties which seem to have belonged, not to 'the Ride of the Beardless One', but to the different rite of 'the Reign of the Mock King',[1] which was apparently intended, not to conjure back the warmth of spring, but to fulfil the antecedent purpose of ushering the Old Year out and the New Year in.

The main features of this second rite present themselves with an astonishing uniformity[2] in the Babylonian festival of the Sacaea[3] and in the Roman festival of the Saturnalia.[4] In the first place the turn of the calendar year was celebrated in this festival by a temporary abrogation of the workaday social system. At both Babylon and Rome[5] the masters and the slaves temporarily exchanged their usual roles; and the deliberate topsy-turvyness of this brief holiday régime was symbolized in the enthronement of a mock king who was honoured and pampered, for the period of his burlesque reign, as though he were a king in very deed. He was dressed up in the proper regalia (Points 65, 66, and 67) and was allowed to exercise a far-reaching royal licence.[6] But—in some, at any rate, of the many variant versions of the rite—this short-lived pomp and indulgence[7] had to be paid for by the mock king with his life as soon as his ephemeral reign was over.[8] After

---

[1] A survey of diverse local variants of a rite which was in vogue, at the time of the disintegration of the Hellenic Society, over an area that embraced both Babylonia and Roman Italy, will be found in Frazer, op. cit., chap. 8: 'The Saturnalia and Kindred Festivals' (= *The Golden Bough*, 3rd ed., Part VI, pp. 306–411).

[2] We may conjecture that the rite was of Babylonic, or perhaps rather of Sumeric, origin, and that it was gradually propagated from the Land of Shinar into the regions round about. If we ask who brought it from the western shores of Asia to the western shores of Italy, it is tempting to answer: 'The Etruscans'.

[3] See Frazer, op. cit., cap. cit., § 5 (= vol. cit., pp. 354–407).

[4] Ibid., § 1 (= vol. cit., pp. 306–12).   [5] Frazer, vol. cit., p. 355.

[6] This first act in the ritual drama of 'the Reign of the Mock King' appears to have precipitated itself, in the shape of a myth, in the tableau (Point 67) of Mordecai coming out of the King's palace into the city arrayed in royal apparel, including a crown and a purple robe (Esther viii. 15).

[7] The reign of the Roman Saturnalia-king lasted thirty days (Frazer, vol. cit., pp. 414–16), and that of the Babylonian Sacaea-king five days according to the account of the Sacaea in Athenaeus: *Deipnosophistae*, Book XIV, chap. 44, p. 639 C (Athenaeus's authority is Berossus).

[8] The putting to death of the mock king as soon as his reign is over is mentioned as an integral part of the rite by Dio Chrysostom (*vivebat circa* A.D. 45–115) in his account of the Sacaea (*Oratio*, IV, § 67). In the Saturnalia, as celebrated in Rome and in Roman Italy, the mock king was not put to death in any period in regard to which we have any historical record of the nature of the celebrations; and our authorities do not even give us any hint that the Saturnalia-king had been customarily put to death once upon a time in ages past. We have, however, one apparently authentic account of a celebration of the Saturnalia by the troops of a Roman garrison on a remote frontier of the Empire at a late date in which the rite includes the eventual putting to death, as well as the preliminary honouring and pampering, of the mock king, and is thus in conformity with the Sacaea in all respects. At Durostorum in Lower Moesia on the 20th November, A.D. 303, a Christian Roman soldier named Dasius was beheaded as a penalty for having refused to play the part of Saturnalia-king when this had fallen to him by lot; and in this context it is mentioned that, after his brief burlesque reign, Dasius's life would have been fòrfeit to the god if he had accepted his allotted role of the mock kingship instead of rejecting it. The Greek text of Dasius's *acta* has been published by Cumont, Franz: 'Les Actes de Saint Dasius' in *Analecta Bollandiana*, vol. xvi (1897), pp. 5–16. The bones of Saint

having honoured him and pampered him (Points 65, 66, and 67)
'they stripped him and scourged him and crucified (or hanged)
him' (μετὰ δὲ ταῦτα ἀποδύσαντες καὶ μαστιγώσαντες ἐκρέμασαν).[1]
Crucifixion or hanging is, as we have seen, the common fate of
Jesus and the two Heracleidae (Point 70),[2] while the preliminary
stripping[3] and scourging[4] are also mentioned in the Gospels,
though not in the account of the Passion of either of the Spartan
heroes. The correspondence between the extant narratives of these
historical Passions and the surviving accounts of the annual celebration of 'the Reign of the Mock King' in the Babylonian festival
of the Sacaea is so close that it can hardly be fortuitous.[5] In what
direction are we to look for an explanation of it?

Are we to suppose that Jesus was crucified in the role of the
mock king? And, if we entertain that supposition, towards which
of two possible alternative variants of it are we to incline? Is it
likely that Jesus was cast for the role in earnest, and was literally
the victim of a ritual murder at one of the annual celebrations of
the rite in one or other of its diverse regional forms?[6] Or is it more

Dasius now repose under the High Altar of the Church of Saint Pellegrino at Ancona,
and the white marble sarcophagus in which they once rested is to be seen in the crypt
of the Cathedral of the same Italian city (see Frazer, vol. cit., pp. 308–12). The rite
celebrated at Durostorum at the beginning of the fourth century of the Christian Era
may, of course, have been called Saturnalia by analogy, without having been derived
from the genuine Roman Saturnalia as a matter of historical fact.

[1] Dio Chrysostom, op. cit., loc. cit., with reference to the Sacaea. The Greek word
ἐκρέμασαν is ambiguous, since it might equally well mean either 'crucified' or 'hanged'.
This murderous last act in the ritual of the Sacaea appears to have precipitated itself, in
the shape of a myth, in the incident of the hanging of Haman in the Book of Esther.

[2] Agis is hanged; Cleomenes' corpse is crucified.

[3] Matt. xxvii. 31 = Mark xv. 20 (ἐξέδυσαν).

[4] Matt. xxvii. 26 = Mark xv. 15 (φραγελλώσας παρέδωκεν ἵνα σταυρωθῇ).

[5] We may notice a further point of correspondence which is not recorded in our extant
accounts of the ritual of the Sacaea, but which comes out in the myth of Esther and
Mordecai. In the tragedy of Haman, as in the tragedies of Jesus and Cleomenes, the
protagonist partakes of a banquet immediately before he meets his violent death
(Esther v–vii).

[6] The conjecture that Jesus may have been the victim of a ritual murder at some
celebration of the rite of 'the Reign of the Mock King' is considered by Frazer in a note
on 'the Crucifixion of Christ' in vol. cit., pp. 412–23; and the suggestion is not impugned,
but is rather fortified, by the fact—of which there can be no question—that Jesus was
condemned to death on religious and political grounds which, in themselves, had
nothing to do with any such traditional observance. Dio Chrysostom (Oratio IV, § 67)
tells us that, at the celebration of the Sacaea, they took, for Mock King, some prisoner
who had been condemned to death already; and it is indeed evident that the doom of
being conscripted to play a part that was to end so grimly in so near a future could not
easily be made to fall on any man whose life was not already forfeit. In this connexion
Frazer suggests (loc. cit., pp. 418–20) that the word 'Carabas', which according to Philo
was the name of the gentle madman who was paraded as Mock King in the Alexandrian
charade of A.D. 38, is a corruption of 'Barabbas', and that 'Barabbas' is not a name but a
title. This suggestion is philologically attractive, since 'Carabas' is neither Greek nor
Hebrew nor Aramaic, whereas 'Barabbas' means in Hebrew 'the Son of the Father'.
On this showing, the 'Barabbas' of the Gospels (Matt. xxvii. 16 = Mark xv. 7 = Luke
xxiii. 18–19 = John xviii. 40) would be a criminal of unknown name who, having
already been convicted and sentenced to death, had subsequently been cast to play the
ritual role of 'the Son of the Father' which, on this hypothesis, would be the traditional
title of the annually sacrificed Mock King. (Frazer suggests that this title is a relic of an
earlier phase in the history of the ritual in which the human victim was, not a condemned criminal, but the first-born son of the authentic king of the land, who sacrificed

probable that, if Jesus was really robed and crowned and stripped and scourged and crucified in accordance with the customary ritual of 'the Reign of the Mock King', this was not a genuine celebration of the rite but merely a parody of it, like the robing and crowning of the victim of the practical joke at Alexandria in A.D. 38?[1] Or are we to reject altogether the supposition that any of our historical heroes were authentically put to death—or crucified posthumously[2]—in the role of the Mock King, either in earnest or in burlesque, and to explain the apparent correspondences between the narratives of the historical Passions and the accounts of the ritual of the Sacaea by the hypothesis that the rite has precipitated itself in the shape of a myth (as, for example, in the Book of Esther) and that this myth has made its way into the narratives of the historical Passions at some stage in the literary history of these narratives when they were floating, in a plastically receptive state, in the solvent waters of the stream of 'folk-memory'?[3] It will be seen that the problem is not a simple one; and in the present state of our knowledge it would be rash to attempt

his offspring to the god as a ransom for himself until a change of custom—which is perhaps commemorated in the myth of the substitution of the ram for Isaac (Gen. xxii)—reprieved the authentic king's son by substituting a less precious victim; alternatively, the title might mean 'the Son of [God] the Father', and this alternative rendering is perhaps favoured by Points 52 and 75.) According to Frazer's theory the Jews prevailed upon Pilate to release the criminal of unknown name who had thus already been cast for the part of the 'Barabbas' in the forthcoming celebration of an annual ritual murder, and to condemn Jesus to play the part in the reprieved malefactor's stead. If Jesus did die in this role, that would explain the exclamation that is attributed to the centurion in the Gospels according to Saint Matthew and Saint Mark (Point 75).

In a critique of Frazer's theory Monsieur Salamon Reinach has pointed out (*Cultes, Mythes et Religions*, vol. i (Paris 1905, Leroux), Essay xxviii, 'Le Roi Supplicié', pp. 339-40) that in the Armenian, the Syriac, and some of the cursive Greek versions of the Gospels 'Jesus Barabbas' appears instead of 'Barabbas' in the text of Matt. xxvii. 16-17. If this reading (which was already known to Origen) is a survival and not a corruption of the original text, it seems to hint at a vanished variant of the Gospel story in which Jesus was condemned to be put to death as 'the Barabbas' without there being any question of his being substituted for another prisoner who had previously been cast for the part.

[1] One ground for supposing that, if Jesus was put to death in the role of the Mock King, this was done in parody and not in earnest, lies in the date of the Crucifixion; for the Crucifixion took place at the time of the Jewish feast of the Passover, which is celebrated in the spring; and the date of the Passover does not coincide with that of either the Jewish or the Roman celebration of 'the Reign of the Mock King'. If Jesus was mocked by the soldiers of Herod (see Point 65), he was presumably cast by them for the role of Mock King in the Jewish festival of Purim, which falls a month earlier than the Passover (Frazer, loc. cit., pp. 414-16). On the other hand, if the mocking was perpetrated by the soldiers of Pilate (see Point 65), then Jesus was presumably cast for the role of Mock King in the Roman festival of the Saturnalia; and the Saturnalia had been celebrated in December (Frazer, loc. cit., p. 413) since the shifting of the Roman New Year's day from the 1st March to the 1st January in the year 45 B.C. The dates thus tell in favour of the view that the treatment to which Jesus was subjected after his condemnation to death was not part of a genuine celebration of 'the Reign of the Mock King', but was a parody of a familiar ritual which the soldiers improvised, on the spur of the moment, as a sinister practical joke, in allusion to the fact that the offence for which Jesus had been condemned to death by the Jewish ecclesiastical court was his claim—to which he had pleaded guilty (Point 52)—to be the Son of God. It will be seen that in this variant of Frazer's theory there is nothing that is inconsistent with the story of the Passion as this is told in the Gospels.

[2] As was done with the corpse of Cleomenes.

[3] 'This third alternative seems the most likely.'—Professor Gilbert Murray.

to decide between the several alternative possible solutions of it. In this place we may be content with a general conclusion that has a bearing upon our present inquiry; and this is that ritual, as well as myth, is in all probability one of the common sources from which identical elements have flowed, along separate channels of 'folk-memory', into the story of Jesus on the one hand and the stories of our pagan historical heroes on the other.

The Life and Death of Socrates

Ritual and myth would appear to embrace, between them, almost all the possible common sources of which we have to take account. And, if we have thus disposed of the first of our two categories of explanation, we may now turn to the other. We have still to consider whether at least some residue of the correspondences that we are studying may be traceable, not to the influence of some common mythical or ritual source upon each and all of the stories in which our correspondences appear, but rather to the influence of one story upon another.

Is the hypothesis that the story of one historical hero may have influenced the story of another a promising explanation *a priori*? This question appears to be answered in the affirmative by the presence, in the story of Jesus, of a number of elements that wear the appearance of being derived from the story of Socrates; for our extant accounts of the life and death of the Athenian sage are the work of Athenian men-of-letters who were Socrates' contemporaries and associates; they were written from first-hand acquaintance by sophisticated authors at a time and in a place and about a person that were all clearly lit up by the dry light of a mental atmosphere of rationalism; and although, no doubt, it might be imprudent to accept as authentic, *a priori*, all the acts, and *a fortiori* all the words, that are attributed to Socrates by Xenophon and Plato, it would on the other hand be reasonable to suppose that the element of fiction—if such there should prove to be—in the Platonic and Xenophontean picture of the two Athenian writers' common Master is the personal invention of the artists by whom the picture has been painted, and is not a deposit of traditional myth or ritual which might have found its way into the picture of Jesus likewise along some independent channel. If, therefore, certain features of the Platonic and Xenophontean picture of Socrates do reappear in the Gospels, we may reasonably infer that the portrait painted in Attica in the fifth century B.C. is the original which, in these points, has inspired the portrait painted in Palestine in the first century of the Christian Era.

This inference will not, of course, commit us to making the

highly improbable assumption that the authors of the Gospels were copying directly either from Plato or Xenophon themselves or from any later works of Hellenic literature in which the original contemporary Athenian picture of Socrates may have been reproduced at second hand. While the authors of the Gospels were manifestly familiar with the Jewish Scriptures, there is no evidence that any of them were acquainted with the pagan literature of the circumambient Hellenic World; and, when Socratic or other pagan Hellenic literary *motifs* do make their appearance in the Evangelists' work, we must suppose that these have not been copied direct from any literary source but have seeped in through the subterranean channel of 'folk-lore' after having first percolated down from the sophisticated upper mental stratum of the Dominant Minority to the more primitive lower mental level of the Proletariat. In other words, any historical extraneous elements that may have found their way into the Gospels are likely to have come in through the same door as any extraneous elements of a ritual or mythical origin, though this common entrance may be the only thing in common between these different kinds of intrusive foreign matter.[1]

Let us try to make a survey of the features in the portrait of Jesus that also appear in the portrait of Socrates, before attempting to estimate whether some, at least, of the correspondences between the portrait of Jesus and the portraits of our eleven Spartan and Roman and futurist heroes may be attributable—as the Socratic elements in the Gospels would appear to be—to the influence of the story of one historical hero upon the story of another historical hero of a later date.

(α) *Before reaching the age of manhood the hero wins his spurs in a disputation with some of the foremost living wits of an older generation.*

Socrates' disputation with Parmenides and Zeno (Plato: *Parmenides*), like Jesus's disputation with the doctors of the Jewish Law in the Temple at Jerusalem (Luke ii. 40–52), gives a foretaste of the hero's future spiritual prowess. Socrates is described (Plato: *Parmenides*, 127 c) as being 'extremely young' (σφόδρα νέον) at the time, and Jesus as being twelve years old (Luke ii. 42). Parmenides

---

[1] There is a certain *a priori* probability that the story of Jesus may have attracted to itself elements of 'folk-lore' that have been derived from the story of Socrates, because there is a real and deep affinity between the respective roles of Socrates and Jesus in the spiritual history of the Hellenic World, so that Socratic traits would readily harmonize with the character of the protagonist in the drama of the Gospels. The parallelism between the spiritual movements that were originated by Socrates and by Jesus respectively is strikingly displayed in tabular form by P. E. More in *The Greek Tradition from the Death of Socrates to the Council of Chalcedon: 399 B.C.–451 A.D.*, vol. iv: *Christ the Word* (Princeton 1927, University Press), p. 138.

and Zeno are represented (Plato: *Parmenides*, 130 A) as being delighted at Socrates' intellectual eagerness, as Jesus's interlocutors in the Temple are represented as being 'astonished at his understanding and answers' (Luke ii. 47).[1]

(β) *The hero is recognized and accepted by a forerunner as the latter's successor and superior* (= Point 6).

The recognition of Jesus by John the Baptist has a Socratic analogue in the recognition of Socrates by Protagoras. 'There is something about you', says Protagoras to Socrates, 'that I have mentioned to quite a number of people. I have told them that, of all the people whom I come across, I admire you far the most and far and away the most among the people of your own age. And I go farther than that. I tell them that I should not be surprised if you were to become one of the World's famous sages' (Plato: *Protagoras*, 361 E; compare *Parmenides*, 130 A and 135 D).

(γ) *The hero is proclaimed by the voice of God to be unique among Mankind.*

The designation of Jesus as the Son of God by a voice from Heaven immediately after his baptism by John (Matt. iii. 17 =

---

[1] Dr. Martin Braun has drawn the writer's attention to the fact that this Socratic trait of an intellectual precocity which is instantly recognized, and generously acknowledged, by the intellectual leaders of the older generation reappears not only in the Gospel according to Saint Luke but also in Josephus's *Autobiography*, §§ 8–9. 'I made great and fruitful progress in my education and gained a reputation for pre-eminence in power of memory and in understanding [συνέσει, the word applied in Luke ii. 47 to the boy Jesus, and in Josephus's own *Ancient History of the Jewish People*, Book II, § 230, to the boy Moses]. While I was still only an adolescent (ἀντίπαις), about fourteen years old, I was praised by everybody for my devotion to sound learning, and the chief priests and notables of the city were constantly meeting to consult me on some fine point of the Law.'

Dr. Braun goes on to point out two other correspondences between Josephus's *Autobiography* and the story of the Gospels:

The hero's genealogy is recited [= Point 3] with intent to vindicate for the hero a royal lineage [= Point 2] (*Autobiography*, §§ 1–6).

The hero goes into temporary retreat in the Wilderness, as the disciple of an ascetic anchorite who seeks purity through ablutions of cold water [|| Point 6, with the part played by John the Baptist towards Jesus being played towards Josephus by Baunus] (*Autobiography*, § 11, cited in this Study already in III. C (ii) (b), vol. iii, p. 294, footnote 3, above; see further Rasp, H.: 'Josephus und die jüdischen Religionsparteien' in *Zeitschrift für die neutestamentliche Wissenschaft*, vol. xxiii (1924), pp. 34–5).

In regard to these three correspondences between the story of Jesus and the *Autobiography* of Josephus, Dr. Braun observes: 'Josephus was born at about the time of Jesus's death. His *Autobiography*—that is to say, his 'auto-myth'—thus falls within the period in which the Jesus-myth of the primitive Christian community crystallized. It is a striking fact that the Jesus-biography (or myth) coincides with the Josephus-biography in certain characteristic features. This points to a common pattern (*Grundmodell*), either in the psychological or in the literary sense, to which the 'genius' of the religious, or of any other, order had to conform. Two, at any rate, out of the three points of correspondence here in question [i.e. the encounter with the doctors when the hero is still a boy, and the visit to the anchorite when he is on the threshold of maturity] belong to the realm of romance, legend, myth. It is highly significant that the underlying *motif* of [the 'precocity' point of correspondence between the story of Jesus and the *Autobiography* of Josephus] should also make its appearance again in the Josephan legend of Moses.'

Mark i. 11 = Luke iii. 22) has a Socratic analogue in the Pythia's answer in the negative to Chaerephon's question whether there is anybody who is wiser than Socrates[1] (Plato: *Apology*, 21 A; Xenophon: *Apology*, §§ 14–15).

N.B. According to Xenophon, loc. cit., Socrates, when he told the story of Chaerephon's question and the Pythia's answer in court, did not fail to point out that the Delphic Apollo was reputed to have paid a much higher tribute to Lycurgus. 'As Lycurgus was entering the temple, the god is said to have addressed him with the words: "I am wondering whether to call you god or man", whereas he did not liken *me* to a god, though he did single me out as being head and shoulders above my fellow men.' For a fuller version of the story of Apollo and Lycurgus, in which the oracle is rendered in verse, see Herodotus, Book I, chap. 65.

(δ) *The hero inveighs against the powers that be* (= Point 7).

Jesus's denunciations of the Scribes and Pharisees have a Socratic analogue in Socrates' exposure of the sophistry of the Sophists.

(ε) *In his domestic life the hero takes hardship and good cheer as they come, and shows himself capable of standing extremes of either of them without turning a hair* (‖ Point 13).

During the Athenian siege of Potidaea, Socrates goes barefoot in the frost and snow of a Thracian winter (Plato: *Symposium*, 219 E–220 D); at Agathon's drinking-party he sits the night out and keeps a clear head, after every one else—including the host and even Aristophanes—has succumbed (Plato: *Symposium*, 223 B–D).

(ζ) *By his refusal to go to extremes of asceticism—which he combines with a readiness to keep company with people of all sorts and conditions—the hero causes scandal* (= Point 14).

As Jesus scandalizes the Pharisees by keeping company with Publicans and Sinners, so Socrates scandalizes the Democrats by having kept company with Oligarchs: that is to say, with well-connected or well-to-do young men who have eventually come out as Oligarchs when the débâcle of Athens at the end of the Atheno-Peloponnesian War of 431–404 B.C. has opened the way for the establishment of the terroristic régime of 'the Thirty Tyrants'.

---

[1] The parliamentary formula—'the answer is in the negative'—in which the Pythia's response is couched according to Plato, has been transposed into a positive form and been put into verse—ἀνδρῶν ἁπάντων Σωκράτης σοφώτατος—in the later version of the story as this appears in Diogenes Laertius: *De Vitis Philosophorum*, Book II, § 37. This versification of the oracle is also found in the expanded form:

σοφὸς Σοφοκλῆς, σοφώτερος δ' Εὐριπίδης,
ἀνδρῶν δὲ παντῶν Σωκράτης σοφώτατος.

(η) *The hero is publicly declared by one of his disciples to have within him something divine* (= Point 15).

Peter's acclamation of Jesus as the Son of the Living God (Matt. xvi. 16, echoed in John vi. 69, and xi. 27) has a Socratic analogue in Alcibiades' acclamation of Socrates:

'You may take it from me that not one of you knows Socrates, so I am going to reveal him to you. . . . Doesn't he look like a regular Silenus? Of course he is the very image of one; but that is the outer shell, just as it is with your Silenus when he is a work of the sculptor's art. Open this Socrates-Silenus and look inside, and you will find that he is packed with saintliness (σωφροσύνη). . . . He regards all mundane values as valueless and ourselves—let me tell you—as naught. In his intercourse with his fellow men he wears this perpetual mask of simplicity and whimsicality (εἰρωνευόμενος καὶ παίζων . . . διατελεῖ). But sometimes he turns serious and comes open; and I wonder if any of you have seen the figures [of the Gods] inside him which become visible then. I *have* had some glimpses of them, and the effulgence of their divine glory was so amazingly beautiful that I found—to put it in a word —that I had to do just whatever Socrates told me' (Plato: *Symposium*, 216 D–E).

(θ) *The hero claims to be divinely inspired.*

The 'inner voice' which Socrates attributes to a supernatural mentor (δαιμόνιον) is comparable to the Holy Spirit with which Jesus is possessed (Matt. iv. 1 = Mark i. 12 = Luke iv. 1).

(ι) *The hero refrains on principle from trying to evade the operation of the Law of the Land* (= Point 46).[1]

As Jesus refrains from attempting to resist arrest, so Socrates declines to make his escape from prison by flight (Plato: *Crito, passim*; cf. Xenophon: *Apology*, § 23), or from life by suicide (Plato: *Phaedo*, 61 C–62 E).

(κ) *The hero is brought to trial* (= Point 49).

Socrates is brought to trial before a regular Athenian jury, Jesus before an improvised Jewish ecclesiastical court.

(λ) *A true saying of the hero's is dishonestly twisted by his enemies into a misrepresentation which is extremely damaging to him* (= Point 50).

Socrates has averred that a god's voice speaks to him and signifies to him what he ought to do (θεοῦ μοι φωνὴ φαίνεται σημαίνουσα ὅ τι χρὴ ποιεῖν); Melêtus indicts Socrates on a charge of being guilty of not recognizing the gods that are recognized by the

---

[1] See also V. C (i) (d) 3, vol. v, p. 404, above.

state while introducing new-fangled divinities and corrupting the
younger generation (ὡς οὓς μὲν ἡ πόλις νομίζει θεοὺς οὐ νομίζοι,
ἕτερα δὲ καινὰ δαιμόνια εἰσφέροι καὶ τοὺς νεοὺς διαφθείροι) (Xenophon:
Apology, §§ 10–13; compare Plato: *Apology*, 24 B–27 E).

(μ) *The hero on trial is reproved by the jurors for contempt of court*
(= Point 51).[1]

In one passage of his defence Socrates tells the jury that he
intends to obey the dictates of his conscience even at the cost of
his life, and that, if they were to offer to acquit him on condition
that he should renounce the pursuit of philosophy, he would
answer, with all respect, that he proposed to obey God rather than
them[2] and that he would never give his philosophy up so long as
any life and strength were left in him. 'Gentlemen of the jury,'
he would say, 'you may do what you will. You may find in favour
of Anytus or against him; you may acquit me or convict me; but
you may as well know that I am not going to mend my ways—no,
not even if I am to die a thousand deaths.' At this point Socrates'
speech was interrupted by an uproar among the jurors (Plato:
Apology, 28 B–30 C).

(ν) *When a question is put to the hero which offers him a possible
line of retreat, the hero does not take the opening, but gives, instead,
an answer that is calculated to exasperate the Court more than anything else that he could conceivably have said* (= Point 52).

The law at Athens was that, when a prisoner on trial had been
found guilty by the Court, the prosecutor should table an assess-
ment of the penalty and the prisoner a counter-assessment, and
that the Court should then opt between the two assessments.
After the Court had found Socrates guilty, Melêtus proposed the
death penalty; and in this situation the politic course for Socrates,
if he were bent upon saving his life, was to make some counter-
proposal which, while falling short of the death penalty, would be
sufficiently drastic to have a chance of being accepted by the Court
as a suitable alternative. So far from taking this line, Socrates
virtually ensured that the Court should opt for Melêtus's assess-
ment—i.e. for the death penalty—by telling them that, if he was
to make a counter-assessment that corresponded to his true
deserts, he must assess himself to the penalty of being maintained
at the public expense as a veteran benefactor of the community
(Plato: *Apology*, 36 B–E; cf. Xenophon: *Apology*, § 23).

[1] See also V. C (i) (d) 3, vol. v, p. 404, above.
[2] πείσομαι ... μᾶλλον τῷ Θεῷ ἢ ὑμῖν (Plato: *Apology*, 29 D). Compare Acts v. 29: 'We
ought to obey God rather than men' (πειθαρχεῖν δεῖ Θεῷ μᾶλλον ἢ ἀνθρώποις). For this
verbal correspondence see further p. 534, below.

(ξ) *On the strength of the hero's answer the Court immediately passes sentence of death upon him* (= Point 53).

The Athenian Court sentences Socrates to death; the Jewish Court, Jesus.

(o) *A tableau of the hero holding a death-cup, with a small party*[1] *of intimate companions grouped round him.*

Socrates literally drank his death out of a cup (Plato: *Phaedo*, 116 C–117 C), because at Athens in Socrates' day the statutory way of inflicting the death penalty was to administer a cup of deadly poison;[2] and in Plato's *Phaedo* (loc. cit.) this act is commemorated visually in a tableau of the hero holding the poison-cup in his hand in a room in which he is surrounded by his intimate friends. In the Ager Romanus in Jesus's day the statutory way of inflicting the death penalty upon malefactors who were not Roman citizens was not by poisoning but by crucifixion; and this was the death that Jesus actually died according to the Gospels. The tableau of the hero holding the cup in the midst of his friends does, however, occur in the Synoptic Gospels in the scene of the institution of the Communion-Rite of the Christian Church (Point 29 = Matt. xxvi. 27–9 = Mark xiv. 23–5 = Luke xxii. 19–20); and in the Passion of Jesus, as in that of Socrates, this scene is placed just before the hero's death. Moreover there is a connexion between the hero's death and the hero's cup in the story of Jesus as well as in the story of Socrates; for, though Jesus does not meet his death, as Socrates meets his, by drinking the cup, which in Jesus's hands contains not poison but wine, this wine is presented by Jesus to his companions as his own sacrificial blood. There are, of course, two signal differences between the Communion Chalice and the Hemlock Cup. While the Hemlock Cup is drunk by the hero himself, the Chalice is administered by the hero to his companions;[3]

[1] In the picture given by Plato fifteen of those present, including Phaedo, are named (*Phaedo*, 59 B–C), and it is mentioned that there were also several others; in the picture in the Gospels the party consists of the Twelve Apostles.

[2] The poison was hemlock, and the poisonous herb was grated up in a cup of water and was administered to the victim in this liquid form.

[3] In the Gospels the death-cup that is drunk by the hero himself does occur more than once, but each time metaphorically and not 'in real life'. Jesus uses this simile first in his answer to the petition of the mother of the Sons of Zebedee (Matt. xx. 22–3 = Mark x. 38–40), and for the second time during the Agony (Point 36 = Matt. xxvi. 39 = Mark xiv. 36 = Luke xxii. 42). The simile is also placed in Jesus's mouth in the narrative of the Passion in the Gospel according to Saint John (xviii. 11), but here not in the context of the Agony (Point 36) but in the adjuration with which he commands Peter to stop fighting (Point 45). This image of drinking a cup in the meta-phorical sense of having an experience is presumably part of the legacy to the New Testament from the Old Testament, which the Evangelists knew by heart, and in which the use of the image is common. In the Old Testament, however, the simile does not appear ever to be used with reference to the particular experience of dying, and not even invariably with reference to experiences that are unpleasant. There is, of course, the obvious metaphor of draining a cup to the bitter dregs (Isa. li. 17; Ps. lxxiii. 10; Ps. lxxv.

and, while both cups are fraught with death for the hero himself, the Chalice imparts the sacrificial victim's spiritual life to those who are given to drink of it. Here we have a conspicuous example of one significant feature in our collection of correspondences that has been pointed out at the beginning of this Annex.[1] The old bottles of Hellenism are made use of by Christianity for holding its new wine. A *motif* or incident or tableau or saying is taken over into the story of Jesus out of one of the stories of the pagan Hellenic heroes, but, in the act of being taken over, it is given a new meaning —almost as though the old pagan form were being employed deliberately as a foil to bring out the newness of the Christian content.

(π) *When the hero is* in articulo mortis, *the friends who are with him weep—not for the hero, but for themselves because they are losing him—and then the hero tells them to restrain their tears* (= Point 68).

'Up to this point, most of us had been fairly successful in stopping ourselves from crying; but, when we saw him drinking and then holding the empty cup, we could no longer bear it; and for my part my utmost efforts could not prevent the tears from flowing in floods. So I buried my face in my coat and wept for—myself, for it was certainly not for Socrates that I was weeping (ἀπέκλαον —ἐμαυτόν, οὐ γὰρ δὴ ἐκεῖνόν γε [compare Xenophon: *Hellenica*, Book II, chap. 2, § 3: οὐ μόνον τοὺς ἀπολωλότας πενθοῦντες, ἀλλὰ πολὺ μᾶλλον ἔτι αὐτοὶ ἑαυτούς (referring to the reception, by the people of Athens, of the news of the disaster at Aegospotami) and Luke xxiii. 28: μὴ κλαίετε ἐπ' ἐμέ, πλὴν ἐφ' ἑαυτὰς κλαίετε]). I was bewailing my own cruel fate in losing a man who was such an incomparable friend. Crito broke down even before I did, and, when he found that he could not stop his tears from flowing, he got up and went out. And then there was Apollodôrus, who had never stopped crying, even before, and who now burst out into a veritable roar of weeping and lamentation which overcame everybody else in the room except Socrates himself, who now remonstrated with us. 'My dear good people,' he exclaimed, 'what a dreadful exhibition! Why, this was one of my reasons for sending

8); and we also find 'the cup of fury' (Isa. li. 17 (cf. Zech. xii. 2); Jer. xxv. 15) and 'the cup of astonishment and desolation' (Ezek. xxiii. 31–4). No doubt this usage of the simile in the Old Testament accounts for 'the wine of the wrath of God' and 'the cup of his indignation' and 'the cup of the wine of the fierceness of his wrath' in the Book of Revelation (xiv. 10, and xvi. 19). At the same time the 'portion of their cup' in the Old Testament is not invariably 'snares, fire and brimstone, and an horrible tempest' (Ps. xi. 6). While the dregs may be the punishment of the wicked, the wine itself may be the reward of the good (Ps. lxxv. 8). And when 'my cup runneth over' (Ps. xxiii. 5), this is manifestly 'the cup of consolation' (Jer. xvi. 7) or 'the cup of salvation' (Ps. cxvi. 13).

[1] On p. 377, above.

the women away; I was afraid of their misbehaving just like this. I fancy I have heard that one ought to be allowed to die in peace. Do, please, keep quiet and control yourselves' (Plato: *Phaedo*, 117 C–E).

(ρ) *In laying down his life, the hero demonstrates, by a triumphant response to the severest possible ordeal, that Righteousness has a supreme intrinsic value.*

It is commonly supposed that Plato had in mind his Master Socrates' life and death when—in the course of an essay (*Respublica*, 360 E–362 C) in distilling Righteousness and Unrighteousness, for purposes of comparison, in their pure and undiluted essence —he puts into the mouth of 'those who commend Unrighteousness as preferable to Righteousness' a famous prognostic[1] of the Righteous Man's end:

'They will say this: that the Righteous Man (ὁ δίκαιος), being what he is, will be scourged and racked and shackled and will have his eyes seared out with red-hot irons and finally will be impaled after having gone through every lesser torture—to discover, on the stake, that the right aim to set oneself is not to *be* righteous but to *pretend* to be' (Plato: *Respublica*, 361 E).

An echo of this passage of Plato may be caught, by an attentive ear, in a tirade against the Righteous Man which is put into the mouth of 'the ungodly in deed and word' in a post-Alexandrine work of Jewish literature (Wisdom ii. 12–20):[2]

'Let us set an ambush for the Righteous Man (ἐνεδρεύσωμεν τὸν δίκαιον) because he is a nuisance to us. . . . He claims to possess the knowledge of God (γνῶσιν ἔχειν Θεοῦ) and calls himself the Child of the Lord (Παῖδα Κυρίου).[3] He has shown up the thoughts of our hearts (ἐγένετο ἡμῖν εἰς ἔλεγχον ἐννοιῶν ἡμῶν).[4] The very sight of him is tiresome to us, because his life is unlike other lives and his tracks are out of the ordinary run. In his estimation we are counterfeit, and he shuns our paths as though they were dirt. He extols a hyperbole of Righteousness and pretends to have God for his father (ἀλαζονεύεται[5] πατέρα Θεόν). Let

---

[1] Cited already in this Study in V. C (ii) (a), p. 275, above.

[2] Eduard Meyer's observations, in *Ursprung und Anfänge des Christentums*, vol. ii (Stuttgart and Berlin 1921, Cotta), pp. 39–40, on the way in which the Jewish philosophical literature of the Post-Alexandrine Age was affected by Hellenism, are pertinent to the case of the Book of Wisdom, though they are made apropos of the Book of Ecclesiastes.

[3] See Point 75, and compare Plato: *Apology*, 27 C–D: Εἰ δαιμόνια νομίζω, καὶ δαίμονας δήπου . . . τοὺς δὲ δαίμονας οὐχὶ ἤτοι θεούς γε ἡγούμεθα ἢ θεῶν παῖδας; Since Socrates himself used the term δαιμόνιον to describe his supernatura! mentor (Point (θ) above), it would almost seem to follow that Socrates accepted Alcibiades' declaration (Point (η) above) that there was something divine inside him.—A.J.T.

[4] Cf. Plato: *Apology*, 21 B–23 B, especially 23 A: οἴονται γάρ με ἑκάστοτε οἱ παρόντες ταῦτα αὐτὸν εἶναι σοφὸν ἃ ἂν ἄλλον ἐξελέγξω.—A.J.T.

[5] Cf. Aristophanes: *Birds*, ll. 824–5—οἱ θεοὶ τοὺς γηγενεῖς / ἀλαζονευόμενοι καθυπερηκόντισαν—quoted in V. C (i) (d) 11, Annex I, pp. 353–4, above.—A.J.T.

us see if his doctrines are true, and let us experiment with his exit. If the Righteous Man really *is* the Son of God (Υἱὸς Θεοῦ), then God will take his part and will deliver him from the hands of opponents.[1] So let us test him with contumely and torture, that we may know his goodness and may verify his long-sufferingness. Let us sentence him to a sordid death. According to his own doctrines, he will be looked after [by God].'

This passage of the Book of Wisdom has a near relationship with another work of Jewish literature of the same age, the Twenty-Second Psalm. Indeed, the affinity is so close that this Psalm could almost be inserted into the text of the Book of Wisdom—as the Righteous Man's cry of agony when his ungodly adversaries carry out their nefarious design—without the reader's being aware that this piece was an interpolation. And it is manifest that both passages have coloured the description, in the Synoptic Gospels, of the mocking of Jesus on the Cross (Point 72 = Matt. xxvii. 39–44 = Mark xv. 29–32 = Luke xxiii. 35–7 and 39).[2] In this connexion we may recall the incident of the hailing of Jesus by the centurion when Jesus is hanging dead on the Cross (Point 75); for the Lucan variant on the Marcan and Matthaean formula—'Certainly this was a righteous man' (ὄντως ὁ ἄνθρωπος οὗτος δίκαιος ἦν) in place of 'Truly this was the Son of God' (ἀληθῶς Θεοῦ Υἱὸς ἦν οὗτος) —reproduces, as we now see, the title under which the hero is introduced in the passage that we have quoted from the Republic as well as in the corresponding passage of the Book of Wisdom, while in the Book of Wisdom the Marcan and Matthaean formula —'the Son of God'—is also to be found as a description of a status to which the Righteous Man lays claim. The same status is perhaps implicitly claimed by Socrates, too, according to the Platonic version of his *Apology*,[3] not indeed for himself, but for the supernatural mentor who speaks to him through an 'inner voice'.

(σ) *The hero is better appreciated by foreigners than by his own countrymen.*

As Christianity takes root outside Jewry, among the Gentiles, so the teaching of the Attic philosopher Socrates is propagated by Theban and Phliasian Pythagoreans and by Megarian Eleatics. Of the fifteen disciples of Socrates who are mentioned by name as having been present at his death,[4] no less than seven are non-Athenians.[5]

---

[1] Cf. Matt. xxvii. 43 (see p. 421, above).—A.J.T.
[2] For the influence of Ps. xxii, as well as the Book of Wisdom, on the account of this incident in the Synoptic Gospels see the present Annex, pp. 421–2, above.
[3] See p. 494, footnote 3, above.   [4] See p. 492, footnote 1, above.
[5] See Burnet, J.: *Greek Philosophy: Thales to Plato* (London 1914, Macmillan), pp. 151–3.

An Egyptian Bridge between Laconia and Galilee

If a memory of the life and death of Socrates has coloured the story of Jesus to the extent that appears to be indicated by the foregoing survey, we may infer that there is no *a priori* impossibility, or even improbability, in the hypothesis that the same story may also have been coloured in some degree by memories of the lives and deaths of other Hellenic heroes who lived and died in the period intervening between the date of the judicial murder of Socrates in 399 B.C. and the date of the Crucifixion. If we have succeeded in showing that this hypothesis is not ruled out in advance by any insuperable objections, our next step will be to explore the possible ways and means through which the impression made by the careers of our Spartan and Roman and futurist heroes upon the minds of contemporaries of their own kin and kind may have been transmitted to the minds in which—in a different social milieu and in a later age—the story of Jesus took the shape of the four Gospels.

Let us begin by reconnoitring one possible 'geopolitical' way along which the memories of the two Heracleidae, at any rate, may have travelled to Galilee from Laconia, and then examine two possible cultural means, one in a verbal medium and the other in a visual.

If we begin by asking ourselves what was the principal meeting place of Jews and Greeks at all times within the long Time-span during which the Syriac and Hellenic worlds were in contact with one another, we shall not hesitate to answer 'Egypt'. On Egyptian soil Greek and Jewish soldiers of fortune had begun to rub shoulders in the common service of the lords of the land as early as the seventh century B.C.; and a Graeco-Jewish intercourse which had thus begun in Egyptian cantonments under the régime of an indigenous Egyptiac dynasty whose home and capital was at Sais was still going on, four hundred years later, under the régime of an alien dynasty, of Macedonian Greek origin, which had installed itself at Alexandria. In the third century B.C. the structure of the Ptolemaic Empire with its metropolitan territory in Egypt and its outlying dependencies round the eastern and northern coasts of the Levant embraced both the Jewish temple-state of Jerusalem, which formed part of the Ptolemaic province of Coele Syria, and the Greek kingdom of Lacedaemon, which was one of the Ptolemaic Government's dependent allies in Continental European Greece; and there is some evidence that in this age Jerusalem and Sparta were already in direct diplomatic relations with one another.[1]

[1] When the by then independent prince of Judaea, Jonathan Maccabaeus, sent an

The next chapter in this story opens with the refugee Spartan king Cleomenes' arrival at Alexandria in 222 B.C. One of the reasons why Cleomenes was eventually interned by the Ministers of Ptolemy IV Philopator was because of Cleomenes' prestige and influence among the mercenaries of Peloponnesian and Cretan origin in the Ptolemaic service who were stationed at Alexandria. The perhaps dangerously powerful hold which the Spartan exile possessed over these important troops had been brought to the Prime Minister Sosibius's notice by Cleomenes himself when—in a political crisis in which Cleomenes had been taken into the Ptolemaic Government's confidence—Cleomenes had offered to go bail to Sosibius for the loyalty of these troops.

' "Don't you see", Cleomenes had said, "that there are nearly 3,000 mercenaries from the Peloponnese and about a thousand Cretans, and that I have only to nod to them in order to make them spring forward to do their duty like one man? And, with these troops solidly supporting you, what other troops are you terrified of? It must be the soldiers from Syria and Caria that are giving you bad dreams!" '[1]

There is no reason to question the authenticity of this incident, which is credible in itself and is reported on the good authority of Polybius; but if it is authentic it is illuminating; for the Spartan hero who already enjoyed this prestige among these troops at a time when he was nothing more than a romantic exile must have completed his conquest of their hearts and minds in the tragic act of his death. And, even if the Ptolemaic Government did succeed, by a deft combination of repression and propaganda, in driving underground an incipient worship of the dead Cleomenes among the populace of Alexandria,[2] we may guess that the dead Spartan hero's admirers among the Peloponnesian and Cretan soldiery

embassy to Sparta in 145 B.C., he appended to the note which was to be presented to the Lacedaemonian Government by his envoys a document which purported to be a copy of a letter written by King Areus of Sparta (*regnabat* 309/8–265/4 B.C.) to his contemporary the High Priest Onias of Jerusalem. This letter alluded to an alleged historical discovery of a blood-brotherhood between the Spartans and the Jews in virtue of a common descent from Abraham; and, on the strength of this, it proposed a political and economic *entente* between the Lacedaemonian and Hierosolymitan states. This 'letter from Areus' is to be found in the account of Jonathan Maccabaeus's embassy to Sparta in the First Book of Maccabees xii. 21–3, and it has been incorporated, from this source, by Josephus into his *Antiquities*, Book XII, chap. 4, § 10, where the same text will be found transposed into a more elegant style of Greek. As it stands, the document can hardly be genuine, but there is probably some historical fact behind it (on this question see Meyer, E.: *Ursprung und Anfänge des Christentums*, vol. ii (Stuttgart and Berlin 1921, Cotta), pp. 30–1). The legend of the common ancestry of the two peoples turns up again in the Second Book of Maccabees v. 9, apropos of an appeal for support which the High Priest Jason made to Sparta, among other states, after his fall in 170 B.C. (Meyer, op. cit., loc. cit.). It may be noted that King Cleomenes III was King Areus' first cousin once removed (see the genealogical table in Beloch, J.: *Griechische Geschichte*, 2nd ed., vol. iv, part 2 (Berlin and Leipzig 1927, de Gruyter), p. 163).

[1] Polybius, Book V, chap. 36.

[2] For this interpretation of Plutarch: *Lives of Agis and Cleomenes*, chap. 60, see pp. 479–80, above.

silently rendered to him the divine honours which it was their official duty to render to their living paymaster Philopator.

What happened to these 4,000 Greek soldiers of fortune who were stationed in Egypt at the time when the last act of the tragedy of Cleomenes was played at Alexandria in 219 B.C.? We know something of their subsequent history because the year which witnessed Cleomenes' death also saw the launching of a Seleucid war of aggression against the Ptolemaic possessions on the Asiatic mainland; and this formidable threat to Ptolemy Philopator's empire from Antiochus the Great moved Ptolemy's Ministers to take drastic measures for reinforcing and strengthening the Ptolemaic military forces.[1] In the first place they recalled, and concentrated at Alexandria, all the mercenary troops that had previously been stationed in the Ptolemaic Empire's overseas possessions.[2] In the second place they recruited fresh mercenaries —and these in numbers sufficient to bring up to 8,000 men the total force of mercenaries that they were eventually able to put into the field. In the third place they broke up all the existing formations and organized the men in entirely new *cadres*. Finally, after having spent two years on these preparations, they ventured at last, in 217 B.C., to meet Antiochus in the field, and they inflicted on him a signal defeat at Raphia. Antiochus's discomfiture was so decisive that he immediately evacuated all his conquests in Coele Syria, and the liberated territories were promptly reoccupied by Ptolemy and regarrisoned.[3] It is safe to assume that the new Ptolemaic garrisons in Coele Syria were in considerable strength; that they were drawn entirely from the mercenary element in the Ptolemaic Army;[4] and that, in consequence of the thorough-going reorganization of the Ptolemaic forces before the Battle of Raphia, these garrisons must have included some of the 4,000 Peloponnesian and Cretan mercenaries who had been stationed in Egypt in 219 B.C., together with elements from the outlying garrisons which had been recalled to Alexandria in that year, as well as with elements subsequently recruited.

[1] What follows is stated on the authority of Polybius, Book V, chaps. 62–5.
[2] Were these 'the soldiers from Syria and Caria' to whom Cleomenes had referred so scornfully? In itself the phrase is ambiguous. In the light of the context the most natural way of interpreting it is as meaning 'soldiers of Syrian and Carian origin who were stationed in Egypt'; but alternatively it might mean 'soldiers stationed *in* Syria and Caria'.
[3] For this sequel to the Battle of Raphia see Polybius, Book V, chaps. 86–7.
[4] The Ptolemaic Government's practice seems to have been to employ mercenaries for their garrisons outside Egypt, and not to exact garrison duty overseas from the Phalanx, which was a militia recruited originally from military settlers, of Greek origin, in Egypt, and latterly (since the crisis of 219–217 B.C.) from native Egyptians as well. (For the composition of the Ptolemaic garrisons in the outlying dependencies of the Empire see Griffith, G. T.: *The Mercenaries of the Hellenistic World* (Cambridge 1935, University Press), pp. 131–5.)

If these inferences are warranted, two conclusions follow with regard to the history of the cult of Cleomenes between 219 and 217 B.C. The first is that the devotees of Cleomenes among the original 4,000 Peloponnesian and Cretan mercenaries who had been stationed in Egypt would now have every opportunity of imparting their own feeling for the dead hero to their new comrades in arms. The second inference is that the cult of Cleomenes among the troops would now be carried from Alexandria to the garrison-towns in Coele Syria by the new mixed units of mercenary soldiers in the Ptolemaic service which were stationed in these cantonments in and after 217 B.C.

Can we go farther? If 'the soldiers from Syria and Caria' who were recalled to Alexandria in 219 B.C. were native recruits from those regions, and not Greek soldiers who had simply been stationed there, the new Ptolemaic garrisons planted in Coele Syria in 217 B.C. may have included not only some of Cleomenes' Peloponnesian and Cretan devotees but also some soldiers of Syrian nationality (e.g. Judaean Jews and Galilaean Gentiles).[1] And here we see a possible point of cultural contact between the dominant minority and the internal proletariat of the Hellenic Society of the day.[2] Did these mixed Ptolemaic garrisons which lay in Coele Syria in and after 217 B.C. serve as incubators in which a new *motif* of Syriac folk-lore was hatched out of a Hellenic cult of an historical Spartan hero whose recent Passion was still a poignant memory in the souls of fellow soldiers who were also his fellow Greeks?

Farther than this it is hardly possible to go; for we have no record of what happened to the Ptolemaic garrisons in Coele Syria in and after 202 B.C., when Antiochus swooped down upon the coveted province for the second time, avenged his defeat of 217 B.C. at Raphia by an equally decisive victory at Panium,[3] and then annexed the former possessions of the Ptolemaic Empire in Syria to the Seleucid Empire once for all. Did Ptolemy's mercenary garrisons come to terms with the Seleucid invader and purchase his permission to remain in their quarters by going over to his service? Or did they withdraw to Egypt, as their predecessors had

---

[1] The Galilaeans were still Gentiles at this time and were to remain Gentiles for more than a hundred years to come. They only became Jews through their forcible conversion to Judaism by their Maccabaean conqueror Alexander Jannaeus (*regnabat* 102–76 B.C.) (see II. D (iii), vol. ii, pp. 73–4, and the present Annex, in the present volume, p. 478, above). The point is important because the Galilaeans, so long as they remained non-Jews, may be reasonably presumed to have been as receptively inclined towards Hellenic culture as other non-Jewish Syrians demonstrably were.

[2] The Greek soldiers of fortune who played so large a part in the social life of the Hellenic World during the two and a half centuries following the close of the Atheno-Peloponnesian War of 431–404 B.C. were the first contingent of broken men from whom the Hellenic internal proletariat was recruited (see V. C (i) (c) 2, vol. v, pp. 61–4, above).

[3] The Battle of Panium was fought *circa* 200/198 B.C.

withdrawn in 219 B.C.? And, if they withdrew, did they leave any legacy of ritual or myth behind them among the local population with whom they had been living cheek by jowl for the past fifteen years?

These are questions to which we do not know the answers;[1] but the mere fact that we have been able to ask them means that we have stumbled upon a possible road along which the legend of Cleomenes—and, with it, the inseparably associated legend of Agis—may have made its way from Laconia through Alexandria to Galilee of the Gentiles, as the legend of Hêraklês undoubtedly did make its way from its place of incubation in Greece to Galilee's next-door neighbour Tyre.

A Verbal Means of Conveyance

One of the forms in which we meet with the correspondences that we are studying is an assonance of words, and even of whole phrases or sentences, which sometimes amounts to an almost exact identity. Is there any obvious means of conveyance by which these common words might have found their way from one to another of the different contexts in which they are now embedded?

In attempting to answer this question, we may begin by observing that the genres of literary composition that are represented by the Gospels and by their sources—so far as these sources can be reconstructed—are categories which had already become well established in pagan Greek literature long before the Gospels were written, and which are likewise represented in the works of Plutarch, a pagan Hellenic man-of-letters who was approximately a contemporary of the authors of the two Gospels according to Saint Matthew and Saint Luke, if our modern Western scholars have hit the mark in their dating of these two books of the New Testament. The two main categories here in question are 'lives' and 'sayings'. Plutarch's *Lives* are the classical example, among the extant remains of Ancient Greek literature, of a type of composition which Plutarch himself merely inherited from a long line of distinguished predecessors;[2] and there are several collections of 'sayings' in the corpus of Plutarch's miscellaneous essays which is known as the *Moralia*. One such collection is the Ἀποφθέγματα

---

[1] We do know, however, that the Book of Daniel, which was written in Galilee in the fourth decade of the second century B.C., had an Egyptian prototype which would appear to have been written shortly before the end of the third century B.C. (see V. C (i) (c) 2, vol. v, p. 71, footnote 4, above). This is evidence for the existence, at the time in question in our present inquiry, of some channel or channels along which it was possible for an idea to be transmitted from Egypt to Coele Syria in the medium of the literary genre in which this idea had originally found expression. This fact throws at least a side-light on the questions which we are asking ourselves here.

[2] See the passage quoted from Leo on p. 436, above.

Βασιλέων καὶ Στρατηγῶν (*Regum et Imperatorum Apophthegmata*) which Plutarch dedicated to Trajan after the latter's accession to the Principate; another is the Ἀποφθέγματα Λακωνικά (*Apophthegmata Laconica*); and both the Περὶ τῶν Ἀρεσκόντων τοῖς Φιλοσόφοις (*De Placitis Philosophorum*) and the Περὶ Στωϊκῶν Ἐναντιωμάτων (*De Stoicorum Repugnantiis*) really belong to the same class. This latter class of composition is likewise represented by the collection of sayings of Jesus known as 'Q' which is a common source of the two Gospels according to Saint Matthew and Saint Luke.[1] The principal common source of these two Gospels, however, is the Gospel according to Saint Mark; and this, like all the Gospels, is an example of a mixed genre in which a 'life' and a collection of 'sayings' are combined by the artifice of taking the biographical narrative of events as a framework and inserting sayings, or even strings of sayings, at convenient points in the life-story.[2] This mixed genre, however, is not an invention of the Evangelists. It, too, is a well-established form of pagan Hellenic literary composition, of which the classical extant pagan example is the work Περὶ Βίων, Δογμάτων καὶ Ἀποφθεγμάτων τῶν ἐν Φιλοσοφίᾳ Δοκιμησάντων (*The Lives, Doctrines, and Sayings of the Philosophers of Repute*) from the pen of Diogenes Laertius, a pagan Hellenic writer who is believed to have lived in the first half of the third century of the Christian Era.

Did the Evangelists, then, set themselves deliberately to ransack existing works of pagan Hellenic literature—'lives' and collections of 'sayings' and books combining the two genres—in which, *ex hypothesi*, the hero was not Jesus but was Hêraklês or Socrates or possibly the Spartan pair of Heracleidae or the Roman pair of Gracchi? This hypothesis of plagiarism is, as we have seen,[3] not at all a convincing explanation of the verbal correspondences with which we are now concerned. The mere adoption of the pagan Hellenic genres is something that hardly requires explaining; for these well-established categories of composition would be accepted and adopted as a matter of course in the first century of the Christian Era by any one who was writing in Greek; and, as for the recurrence of particular words and phrases, it is much less likely that these were taken direct out of pagan Hellenic books than that they found their way into the Gospels out of a treasure of popular wisdom that was in current circulation by word of mouth. 'Folk-

---

[1] For a tentative reconstruction of 'Q' see Streeter, B. H.: *The Four Gospels* (London 1924, Macmillan), p. 291.

[2] According to Meyer, E.: *Der Papyrusfund von Elephantine*, 2nd ed. (Leipzig 1912, Hinrichs), p. 116, the Ahiqar Romance is another piece of literature of the mixed genre in which the story is merely a setting for the sayings.

[3] In the present Annex, pp. 438–9, above

lore' is, in all probability, the immediate source from which the Evangelists drew the words and phrases, as well as the incidents and characters, that the Gospels have in common with certain works of pagan Hellenic literature; and we have seen reason[1] to believe that the same source was drawn upon, at least in some measure, by certain of the pagan Hellenic authors here in question. At the same time there are a number of common words and phrases that can hardly have found their way into the pagan works of literature in which they occur out of the reservoir of 'folk-lore'. For example, in seven of the thirteen verbal correspondences set out in our Table VIII, the word or phrase or sentence in its pagan context is cited as a quotation from some public speech that is said to have been delivered by the hero or from some dialogue in which he is said to have taken part; and it seems unlikely that any anonymous wisdom that was in oral circulation would have found its way into a context of this kind; for, if a speech or dialogue that is attributed to some celebrated historical character in a sophisticated work of literature is not authentic (as it often is not), it can hardly be anything but a deliberate piece of fiction from a forger's pen. When a pagan work—or the source of a pagan work—in which one of our common words or phrases is ascribed to such an origin as this, is demonstrably anterior to the Gospels in its date of composition, the most natural explanation of the recurrence of the same word or phrase in the Gospels is therefore to suppose that the speech or dialogue (whether genuine or spurious) that is cited by the pagan author is the ultimate source from which the corresponding word or phrase in the Gospels has been derived—even though, in the course of its journey from the pagan to the Christian book, the written word may have temporarily detached itself from the papyrus and have travelled part of its way as one of those winged words (the Homeric ἔπεα πτερόεντα) that flit, like living creatures, from mouth to mouth.[2]

An apparent case in point is the correspondence of a well-known pair of mutually contradictory sayings that are attributed to Jesus in the Synoptic Gospels[3] with a single self-consistent saying that is attributed to Divus Julius by Cicero. In the Gospels according to Saint Matthew (xii. 30) and Saint Luke (xi. 23) Jesus is reported as saying 'He that is not with me is against me', whereas in the Gospel according to Saint Mark (ix. 40) he is reported as saying

---

[1] On pp. 457–63, above.

[2] Nemo me lacrimis decoret nec funera fletu
    faxit. cur? volito vivu' per ora virum.
                                                Ennius.

[3] While the sayings are mutually contradictory, each of them is, of course, in harmony with its own context, and there would be no difficulty about either of them in itself, if it were not for the existence of the other.

'He that is not against us is on our part'. So long as we confine our attention to the Gospels, this pair of sayings is a puzzle, since on the one hand it is impossible to reconcile them, as they stand, with one another, while on the other hand it is difficult to suppose that they are entirely unrelated. Our puzzle appears to be solved by a passage in Cicero's speech *Pro Ligario* (§ 33) in which Cicero attributes *both* sayings to Caesar—just as, in the Gospels, *both* of them are attributed to Jesus—but this in a relation to one another in which, so far from being mutually contradictory, each saying gives point to the other. 'We used to hear you quoted', says the defeated Republican advocate in pleading for mercy upon a Republican political exile at the tribunal of the victorious dictator—'We used to hear you quoted as saying that we (i.e. the Republicans) reckoned as being against us all except those who were with us, whereas you reckoned all who were not against you as being of your party.'[1] It would seem captious to dispute either the authenticity or the originality of the saying that is here attributed to Caesar by Cicero;[2] and, if these two points be granted, then it becomes difficult to resist the conviction that Caesar's saying has passed into popular currency and has suffered, in the process, the twofold mishap of becoming dissociated from the name of its true author and of falling asunder into two separate sayings which seem contradictory instead of complementary when they are torn out of their original Caesarean setting. In this state of fragmentation these two sayings will then have found their way respectively into 'Q' and into Mark as sayings of Jesus which are mutually contradictory because Jesus is represented as uttering *both* of them apropos of himself, whereas the saying that has drifted into 'Q' ought properly to be said by the sayer of it, not apropos of himself, but apropos of his adversaries—in contrast to the antithetical saying which is correctly represented as being said by the sayer apropos of himself in the Gospel according to Saint Mark.

On this showing, we have to reckon with the possibility that, even if an orally circulating treasure of anonymous wisdom may have been the immediate source from which all the common words that we have detected were derived by the authors of the Gospels, some, at least, of these anonymous sayings may have made their way into this popular oral tradition out of sophisticated works of literature in which these same sayings were attributed—whether truthfully or mendaciously—to famous characters of Hellenic

---

[1] 'Te enim dicere audiebamus nos omnes adversarios putare nisi qui nobiscum essent, te omnes, qui contra te non essent, tuos.'

[2] Cicero, loc. cit., introduces the saying that he attributes to Caesar with the words: 'Let that phrase of yours which won you your victory hold good in this present case' ('valeat tua vox illa quae vicit').

history and mythology. If this possibility has to be taken into account, is there any obvious social milieu in which such sayings could have seeped down from a cultural stratum that would be apt to express itself in sophisticated literature to the very different cultural stratum whose natural form of expression would be an orally circulating 'folk-lore'? Is there anything analogous in this field to those mixed battalions of Ptolemaic mercenary troops—part Peloponnesian and part, perhaps, Syrian—which may, as we have seen,[1] have been instrumental in conveying a cult of Cleomenes not only in a vertical direction—from a dominant to a proletarian social stratum—but also in a horizontal direction by transporting this feeling of veneration in human hearts from the tenements and barracks of Alexandria to the cantonments and villages of Galilee? The answer to our question is in the affirmative; for in the Hellenic Society in its disintegration the cultural division between a cultivated and an illiterate class did not coincide with the juridical division between freemen and slaves any more closely than the professional division between soldiers and civilians coincided with the social division between Hellenes and Orientals. While there was a vast herd of freemen-illiterates, there was also an *élite* of slaves who were men of culture; and these cultivated slaves were a highly conductive medium of mental communication between a dominant minority to whom they were culturally akin and an internal proletariat of which they were juridically members.

In the Hellenic 'Time of Troubles' the status of slavery in itself was evidence of nothing except a stroke of Fortune—as cruel as it was common—which had deprived a human being of his freedom either before birth or after it. From the fact that a man was here and now a slave it was impossible to tell whether he had been born into slavery or been kidnapped into it;[2] whether he was illiterate or cultivated; or, supposing that he proved to be cultivated, whether he had acquired his cultivation in a now lost state of freedom or whether he was a born slave who had been given a liberal education—as he might have been trained in the mechanic arts of potting or weaving—by an enterprising owner who had gone to this expense for the improvement of one of his human chattels either because he required a cultivated slave for his own use or because he had speculated that a short-hand calligrapher who knew his way about Greek literature would be likely to fetch so very much higher a price on the slave-market than would be fetched by a potter or a weaver that it would repay the slave-dealer

---

[1] In the present Annex on pp. 496–500, above.
[2] For the diverse sources of recruitment of the slave-force in the latter days of the Hellenic 'Time of Troubles' see II. D (vi), vol. ii, pp. 213–16, above.

to put this particularly brainy piece of man-flesh through the longest and most expensive of the various alternative preparatory processes of improving the article before offering it for sale.

The Hellenic slave-intelligentsia which was recruited in this way—partly from slaves who had been born into slavery and been educated by their owners and partly from free-born members of the dominant minority who had fallen into slavery after having received the liberal education that was customary in their class—was ranged, of course, in several different ranks which were cultivated in different degrees. There were not only slave-amanuenses and slave-secretaries; there were also slave-tutors and slave-physicians and even slave-philosophers who were the pagan equivalents of domestic chaplains. And this cultural *élite* of an enslaved underworld includes names that have left a mark on Hellenic history.

The slave-philosopher Epictetus (*vivebat circa* A.D. 50–130) was the leading exponent of Stoicism in his generation. Epictetus had a younger contemporary in the freedman-scholar Hermippus of Berytus[1] (*floruit imperante Hadriano* A.D. 117–38), who wrote a book on *Slaves who have attained Academic Distinction.*[2] And Hermippus, in turn, had a younger contemporary, as well as fellow countryman, in the Syrian novelist Iamblichus (*floruit circa* A.D. 164), whose mother tongue was Aramaic, and who decorated his *Babyloniaca* with Oriental local colour, though he was writing in Greek for a Hellenic public. According to Suidas, Iamblichus was of servile origin; and, even though this account of Iamblichus's status may lack authority, there can be no doubt about the status of the slave-tutor Mardonius who in a later age weaned his pupil, the young prince Julian, away from a Christianity that was the adopted faith of the Constantian Dynasty to a Hellenism for which the tutor had an enthusiasm that was infectious. In accomplishing this pedagogic feat Mardonius might have given the history of the Hellenic World another turn, if it had been possible for Julian in his prime to succeed in his endeavour to translate into public policy the sentiments that had been inculcated into him in his boyhood (*inde ab* A.D. 339) by his slave-tutor's teaching.[3] Through Julian's failure Mardonius has just missed the fame that was so nearly his; but Tiro (*vivebat ultimo ante Christum saeculo*), who so devotedly served his master Cicero in the more modest roles of

---

[1] According to Suidas, Hermippus was born, not in Bayrūt itself, but in an up-country village.

[2] Περὶ τῶν ἐν παιδείᾳ διαπρεψάντων δούλων—a counterpart, in Greek, of Smiles' *Self Help.*

[3] Julian's failure is discussed in V. C (i) (c) 2, vol. v, p. 147; V. C (i) (d) 6 (δ), vol. v, pp. 565–7; V. C (i) (d) 6 (δ), Annex, vol. v, pp. 680–3; and in V. C (ii) (a), in the present volume, pp. 222–3, above.

secretary and amanuensis, still lives for us in the pages of Cicero's letters—which Tiro preserved by collecting and editing them in a quite disinterested labour of love—as vividly as any other figure of secondary importance, slave or free, whose features happen to be presented to us in the extant remains of a Hellenic portrait gallery that has suffered grievous damage from the ravages of Time. But for a happy accident—contrived by Fortune when, for once in a way, she was in a propitious mood—this goodly company of the Hellenic slave-intelligentsia might have been adorned by the forcible enrolment into it of the greatest intellect to which Hellenism ever gave birth, if there is any truth in the tale that Plato, on his first visit to Sicily, so deeply incensed the Elder Dionysius by the unheard-of freedom of his speech that the Sicilian despot handed over the Athenian sage to the Lacedaemonian Ambassador at the Syracusan Court to dispose of at the Spartan's pleasure. The story goes that Pollis' pleasure was to sell Plato into slavery at Aegina, and that the philosopher only recovered his freedom thanks to the generosity of a Cyrenaean admirer named Annikaris, who bought him up in order to set him at liberty!

It is manifest that the slaves of this cultivated class would be likely to taste both the extreme of happiness and the extreme of misery that would come within the range of a slave's experience under the social system of the Hellenic Society in its disintegration-phase. On the one hand the service of a beloved and considerate master, such as Cicero, might almost charm a Tiro into forgetting the hard fact that, in law, there was a great gulf fixed between himself and this fellow man-of-letters who had never once reminded Tiro, either by deed or by word, of the existence of this juridical enormity. On the other hand a Tiro to whom Fortune had not allotted a master of the Ciceronian stamp might be made more miserable by even a slight failure of tact on his master's part than a slave-herdsman or a slave-gladiator could be made by the most brutal application of the rod or the branding iron. The very sensitiveness that had rendered the slave-intellectual eligible for the comparative amenity of the life that it was his relatively good fortune to live would also expose him to exquisite mental and moral torments. The precariousness of a slave's personal position —even when he was the devoted and valued servant of a high-minded and conscientious master—is illustrated by an incident in the Passion of Cato Minor in which the hero storms at his slaves, and actually draws blood from his own knuckles by striking one slave on the mouth, because, in their fear that their beloved master is meditating suicide, these slaves hesitate to bring back their master's sword which they have surreptitiously removed from its peg in its owner's bedroom while Cato has been at dinner. The sharpness of the shock which this painful scene causes to the sensibilities of a modern Western reader of Plutarch's narrative[1] gives some measure of the suffering to which a cultivated slave would be perpetually exposed in even the most enviable conditions of service. And an exceptionally happy Tiro, who could thank the Gods for having enslaved him to a master at whose hands he had never in his life been repaid for his devotion with the petulance of Cato *in extremis*, might feel his gratitude tempered by the reflection that his own master's humaneness was, after all, unparalleled, and that consequently he, Tiro, was unique in his happiness among the groaning and travailing millions of his unfortunate companions in servitude.

This contrast between his personal devotion to his own master and his social indignation at the general standards of behaviour that were prevalent in the master-class would almost inevitably produce, in a Tiro's sensitive soul, a psychological conflict which would give the patient no peace till he had found some way of resolving it; and a possible resolution of it is not difficult to descry. The slave's first concern would be to dissociate his own beloved master, in his own mind, from a master-class upon which, as a whole, he could never bring himself to look with any feelings except those of abhorrence.[2] And he would achieve this mental dissociation by generalizing the beneficence of which Tiro himself was the beneficiary. In the imagination of his fond heart the grateful slave would idealize his beloved master into the likeness of a benefactor, not merely of the single slave who happened to enjoy his exceptional favour, but of the whole great army of all the slaves in the World, to whom even the most fortunate of their number must always remain bound by indissoluble ties of moral and emotional solidarity. In this mood the souls of Tiro and his like would become spiritual crucibles in which the êthos and outlook of morally eminent members of the Hellenic dominant minority might be transfigured into imaginary shapes that would have astonished the historical originals of the heroes of these slave-romances. An archaistic-minded reformer like Agis or Tiberius Gracchus—whose authentic purpose in urging his reforms upon his peers had been to salvage a social system which he was no less eager to preserve than they were—might be transfigured in the imagination of an adoring slave into a futurist-minded revolutionary

---

[1] Plutarch: *Life of Cato Minor*, chap. 68.
[2] The sharpness of the difference of the respective feelings that were evoked in the hearts of the slaves by good and by bad masters comes out in the passage quoted in Point 72, p. 401, above, from Diodorus's account of the First Sicilian Slave-War. Compare the episode in the same story that is quoted in V. C (i) (c) 2, vol. v, p. 72, footnote 2, above.

on the pattern of the contemporary leaders who were being thrown up out of the ranks of the Hellenic internal proletariat itself. And, when once a Tiberius Gracchus had thus been assimilated to a Eunus in the 'folk-memory' of a proletarian underworld, it would perhaps almost inevitably follow that the actually spoken and accurately remembered words of the imaginarily proletarian-ized reformer in the ranks of the Hellenic dominant minority would be ascribed, in a proletarian epic tradition, to this or that authentically proletarian saviour whose own words, as far as these were still remembered, had been of a somewhat similar tenor.[1]

On this showing the Hellenic slave-intelligentsia—a social ele-ment whose existence in the body social of a disintegrating Hellenic Society is an undoubted matter of historical fact—will suggest itself as a possible means of conveyance of some, at least, of those undoubtedly common words and phrases that occur on the one hand in the extant accounts of heroes who were members of the Hellenic dominant minority while on the other hand they are also to be found in the extant accounts of proletarian revolutionary leaders as well as in the story of Jesus as this is told in the Gospels.

A Visual Means of Conveyance

When, in our consideration of possible means of conveyance, we pass from the verbal to the visual medium, we shall find a clue ready to our hand in the fact, which we have noticed above,[2] that not only Jesus but also some at least of our pagan historical heroes have come, after death, to receive religious worship. There is an historic association between religious worship and visual art. In the history of Christianity it has been one of the traditional prac-tices of the Church to adorn its places of worship with visual works of art expressing the purpose and meaning of the Liturgy performed within the church walls;[3] and the same visual forms of religious expression used to be employed in the temples of both the native and the adopted divinities of the pagan Hellenic World. It is to this Hellenic as well as Christian practice that we owe some of the finest and most famous of the extant remains of pagan Hellenic visual art: for example, the sixth-century frieze, repre-

---

[1] 'Might not the process be simpler and easier than you say? The educated slave would tell his fellow slaves stories of Socrates or Gracchus, or Agamemnon or Odysseus for that matter, and they would forget the names and contexts and have the stories floating in their minds. Compare the Classical traditions among the Norsemen, learnt partly from books, partly (among other sources) from their fellow soldiers at Con-stantinople.'—Professor Gilbert Murray.

[2] On pp. 478–80.

[3] The anti-iconic movements in Orthodox Christendom in the eighth and ninth centuries and in Western Christendom since the sixteenth century (see V. C (i) (d) 9 (β), pp. 116–17, above) have been consciously 'Protestant' in the sense of being deliberate breaches with an established practice.

senting the battle between Gods and Giants, from the Treasury of the Cnidians at Delphi; the third-century representation of the same subject on the frieze from the Altar at Pergamum; and the fifth-century representation of the battle between Lapiths and Centaurs on the metopes from the Parthenon at Athens.

The works of visual art in Hellenic places of worship that have just been mentioned all have two features in common: in the first place they portray only a single scene and not a series, and in the second place this single scene has no special connexion with the ritual or the myth of the particular divinity to whom the temple in question was dedicated; but the Pergamene Altar was also adorned with another frieze which portrays a series of successive scenes in the career of one of the local heroes of Hellenic Mythology, Telephus; and there is at any rate one divinity of Syriac origin whose shrines in the Hellenic World in the Imperial Age were adorned with visual representations which portrayed, not some irrelevant Telephus or Briareus, but the indwelling divinity —Mithras—himself. In a Mithraeum the nature, attributes, functions, and career of Mithras were illustrated in a series of tableaux depicting successive chapters of a continuous story, in the style of the Telephus-frieze from Pergamum or of those pictures of the successive Stations of the Cross by which the last act in the Passion of Jesus is illustrated in the modern Western World on the walls of Catholic Christian Churches.[1]

Such a series of tableaux has been brought to light in a recently excavated Mithraeum at Dieburg, in Germany,[2] which, in the opinion of the archaeologists, was built and consecrated not long before the abandonment, *circa* A.D. 260, of the *limes* of the Roman Empire in the gap between the Rhine and the Danube.[3] In this case—and there is no reason to suppose that it is in any way abnormal or unrepresentative[4]—the bas-relief in which the god is

---

[1] The writer is informed by his sister, Miss J. M. C. Toynbee, that the Stations of the Cross do not appear to have been portrayed—or at any rate not portrayed as prominently as is now customary—until comparatively recent times. The present popularity of the theme seems to be traceable to the influence of the Franciscans. This particular theme, however, is, of course, only one of a number of different applications of a distinctive style of portrayal—the 'continuous style' in which a story is told by the device of presenting a series of successive scenes—and this 'continuous style' is one of the traditional modes of Christian iconography.

[2] More precisely, in Hessen-Darmstadt, at a point, on the road between the present cities of Darmstadt and Aschaffenburg, which lies just inside the former *limes* of the Roman Empire.

[3] See Behn, F.: *Das Mithrasheiligtum zu Dieburg* (Berlin and Leipzig 1928, de Gruyter). For the probable date of the temple see op. cit., pp. 44–5. The excavations which resulted in the discovery were made in June 1926 (op. cit., p. 1). The writer's attention was first drawn to this work by his sister, Miss J. M. C. Toynbee.

[4] The reliefs on the Dieburg *Kultbild* may now be brought into comparison with at least three kindred works of art: a small relief in the Museo Nazionale Romano; a relief representing Mithras Tauroctonus, surrounded by small painted scenes from the life of Mithras, in the Mithraeum at Dura-Europus (see Rostovtzeff, M.: *Dura-Europus and*

presented in visible material form as an object for public worship is set in a square frame which is composed of twelve smaller reliefs representing as many scenes in Mithras' career. The composition can perhaps be set out most briefly and clearly[1] in a simplified diagram:[2]

V	VI	VII	VIII
IV	Principal		IX
	Bas - Relief		
III	Inscription		X
II	I	XII	XI

The subjects of the twelve scenes in the frame round the central relief are as follows:

    I. A pair of horses [? representing the Creation of the Universe in an imagery in which the four elements are symbolized by the four horses of a chariot].

    II. Ahriman lying in wait to fight Mithras [?].

    III. The birth of Mithras from the rock.

    IV. Mithras piercing the clouds to bring rain [?].

    V. Mithras up a tree.

    VI. The steer in his stable.

its Art (Oxford 1938, Clarendon Press), pp. 92 and 96–7); eundem: 'Das Mithraeum von Dura' in *Römische Mitteilungen*, vol. xlix (1934), pp. 180 seqq.); and a painting representing Mithras Tauroctonus, framed on either side by painted scenes from the life of Mithras, in the Mithraeum in the gardens of the Palazzo Barberini at Rome (for this Mithraeum, which was discovered in 1936, see the *Giornale d'Italia*, 1st September, 1936, and the *Archäologisches Jahrbuch*, vol. li (1936), 'Archäologischer Anzeiger', pp. 475 seqq. The writer owes these references to his sister, Miss J. M. C. Toynbee.

  [1] The scholar who has published the results of the excavations at Dieburg describes the composition in the following terms:
  'The margins of the large-scale sculptures of the god that serve as instruments of public worship (*der grossen Kultbilder*) are readily turned to account as fields for the presentation of individual scenes from the Mithras Legend. In the selection of these scenes it is not possible to discern any definite system, but for the most part we find a repetition of uniform types. . . . The Dieburg *Kultbild*, with its twelve sculptured scenes, surpasses all others hitherto discovered, not only in its wealth of *motifs*, but also in the point that, as will appear, a strict chronological order is adhered to in the series of sculptures. The serial order is here completely clear; on the left we find the scene of the birth of the god and on the right, next to the tablet bearing the inscription, his ascension into Heaven—which shows that the series of representations starts, as usual, at the bottom of the left-hand side, and then runs "clockwise". . . . The system that governs this series of scenes, and that is so strictly adhered to, knits them together into what amounts to an extract from the Mithras Legend in the form of a cycle of sculptures; and the order in which the individual sculptures are here placed in the series also throws a good deal of new light on other sculptures that are already well known.'—Behn, op. cit., pp. 10–11.

  [2] This diagram corresponds with the front side of the stone; on the back side there is a different representation of Mithras, here in the guise of Phaethon (Behn, op. cit., pp. 21–2).

VII. Mithras carrying the steer on his back.
VIII Mithras riding on the steer, which is now stampeding.
IX. Mithras again carrying on his back the steer, which is now dead.
X. A tree with three branches and with a Mithras-head on each of them.
XI. Mithras and the steer, now sacrificed; Mithras and Sol drinking to one another, out of horns, over the steer's dead body.
XII. Mithras mounting Sol's chariot, in which he is to ascend to Heaven.

This composition of the sculptured *Kultbild* of the Mithraeum at Dieburg in Hessen reappears, in essentials, in the painted *Kultbild* of the Mithraeum in the gardens of the Palazzo Barberini in Rome.

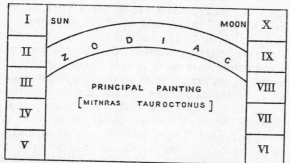

The subjects of the ten paintings flanking the central painting[1] are as follows:

I. Juppiter with his thunderbolt.
II. Terra Mater.
III. The birth of Mithras.
IV. Mithras bringing water out of a rock.
V. Mithras carrying the steer.
VI. Mithras initiating Sol, who kneels.
VII. Mithras kneeling between Heaven and Earth.
VIII. Sol and Mithras sacrificing.
IX. Sol and Mithras ascending to Heaven in Sol's chariot.
X. A heavenly banquet.

Like the series of twelve reliefs at Dieburg, this series of ten paintings in Rome represents in outline the career of the god from its beginning at his birth to its close at his ascension; and the existence of the series of Telephus-reliefs from Pergamum which

[1] It will be seen that here the series starts at the top, instead of the bottom, left-hand corner and runs 'anti-clockwise', in contrast to the arrangement of the Dieburg *Kultbild*, on which the series runs 'clockwise', starting from the bottom left-hand corner.

were carved in the third century B.C. is evidence that the 'continuous style' employed in these Mithraea in Italy and Germany was no recent innovation at the times when their *Kultbilder* were respectively painted and carved, but was a genre that had already been in vogue in the lifetime of King Agis IV of Sparta (*regnabat circa* 244–240 B.C.), who is the earliest in date of the eleven pagan historical heroes whose stories we are here comparing with the story of Jesus. There are also, of course, some conspicuous intervening links—for instance, the series of reliefs which tell a story (or, strictly speaking, act a play) on the Roman victory-columns and triumphal arches of the Imperial Age. Does our archaeological evidence warrant the conjecture that the custom of adorning the temples of the Gods with visual representations in the 'continuous style' dates from an age some five hundred years anterior to the date of the Dieburg Mithraeum? And can we venture further to assume that, if our pair of Heracleidae and our pair of Gracchi did come to receive religious worship, they would be honoured in whatever ways were customary in that age in the current worship of heroes and gods whose title to be worshipped was already well established?[1] If our conjecture and our assumption pass muster, they will lead us to the surmise that, if either Agis or Cleomenes or the Gracchi did have shrines dedicated to them after their deaths, these shrines will have been decorated with visual representations in the 'continuous style', and that the subjects of these series of scenes will have been the lives and Passions of the heroes for whose worship the shrines had been built and adorned. If our imagination will carry us thus far, it will further suggest to us that the scenes included in the series will have been of two different kinds: on the one hand authentically historical scenes commemorating the most celebrated or most critical or most tragic events and moments in the human hero's actual life on Earth; and on the other hand potently traditional scenes which properly belonged to the myth of some god or demigod such as Hêraklês, and which were so indissolubly associated in the popular mind with the temples of this divinity that there will have been an almost irresistible impulse to introduce them into shrines dedicated to human heroes of a similar character, if there was any possibility of co-ordinating these mythical episodes with those authentic events in the human heroes' careers that were notorious matters of public knowledge.

Are there, as a matter of fact, any known examples in the history of Hellenic visual art of series of scenes in the 'continuous style' in which the characters are not gods or demigods but are human

---

[1] For this assumption see p. 480, above.

beings whose lives on Earth are matters of history? The majority
of the figures are, of course, human in the Parthenon frieze, which
is perhaps the most famous surviving work of the Hellenic sculptor's art; but these human figures from the chisel of an Attic
master of the fifth century B.C. are human without being historical;
for they are not individuals with proper names and with ascertain-
able dates of birth and death, but are the timeless and anonymous
typical representatives of a community. Nor, again, do the scenes
of the Parthenon frieze tell a story in the 'continuous style'. We
must descend to the sculptures on the Roman columns and arches
of the Imperial Age to find figures whom we can identify as historical individuals standing out here and there, in the successive
acts of a drama in bas-relief, among the anonymous troops of
Roman soldiers and enemy tribesmen. The pictures in the *salon*
of the Villa dei Misteri at Pompeii, which must have been painted
before the eruption of Vesuvius in A.D. 79, do not quite provide
us with the clue that we are seeking. 'The subject of the paintings
is the initiation of a bride before her marriage into certain mysteries
of Dionysus'; but 'it is not certain whether the pictures represent
several brides being initiated separately by various rites or one
bride going through successive phases in the liturgical act';[1] and,
even if we could be sure that the paintings are to be interpreted
as a unity in the 'continuous style', we should still be in the dark
as to whether or not the series has any personal reference. 'Maiuri
explains the choice of this particular scheme of decoration by
supposing that the mistress of the house was an initiate and priest-
ess of some Dionysiac association, and he suggests that the bride
seated on a couch in the last scene of all is the lady herself and that
the paintings were meant to celebrate her wedding. But this, of
course, cannot be proved.'[2] We shall find ourselves on firmer
ground if, without moving from the point at which we here stand
in the Time-dimension, we make, in Space, the short and easy
journey from Pompeii to Puteoli and at the same time migrate
from the realm of archaeological 'fact' into the realm of literary
'fiction'. For there is one character, located most probably at
Puteoli[3] about the middle of the first century of the Christian Era,
who is not a god or hero and not a deified man and not even a
public personage, but who nevertheless has the crucial scenes of his
life depicted in the 'continuous style' on the walls of his own private
house in which he is still living. And, although this character is a
'fictitious' one, it does not follow that his author's description of

---

[1] Carrington, R. C.: *Pompeii* (Oxford 1936, University Press), p. 164.
[2] Ibid., p. 84.
[3] See L. Friedländer's edition of Petronius Arbiter's *Cena Trimalchionis* (Leipzig
1906, Hirzel), pp. 8–10.

his manners and customs is untrue to the facts of the real life of the age.[1]

In his account of an imaginary dinner-party at the home of a likewise imaginary self-made millionaire-freedman whom he has named Trimalchio, the Roman novelist Petronius Arbiter (*proprio manu obiit* A.D. 66) describes the wall-paintings of which the guests were able to catch a glimpse as they were ushered from the front door to the dining-room.

'On the left as we entered, not far from the porter's cubicle, there was a huge dog (on a chain) painted on the wall, with "Cave canem" written above him in block letters. My companions went into fits of laughter; but for my part, when I had recovered my breath, I was all eyes for what unfolded itself on the rest of the wall. First came a picture of a slave-market, with captions (*cum titulis*),[2] showing Trimalchio himself, with a [child's] head of hair, bearing Mercury's wand in his hand and entering Rome under the guidance of Minerva. Next, the story of how he had learned to keep accounts and had eventually been appointed a cashier had all been rendered indefatigably, with [explanatory] lettering, by the painstaking artist. At the tail-end of the colonnade the hero was being lifted by the chin by Mercury and being towed through the air towards a lofty tribune, where Fortune with her cornucopia and the three Fates spinning golden distaffs were waiting to receive him. . . . I began to ask the major-domo what pictures they had in the interior. "The Iliad and the Odyssey," says he, "and Laenas' show of gladiators." But it was impossible to have eyes for everything.'[3]

In thus depicting the successive stages of his own career, and capping his historical feat of making his pile with the mythical *motif* of an ascension into Heaven, to what lengths of audacity was Trimalchio going? Was he casting himself for a role which the prevailing canons of taste and piety would have reserved exclusively for such superhuman heroes of mythology as Hercules and the Dioscuri? Or was he only committing the rather less flagrant enormity of portraying himself as authentically historical human beings were regularly portrayed, in accordance with an accepted convention of Hellenic religion and art, when these mortal men had become recipients of divine worship? Was it Hêraklês or the Heracleidae, was it the Dioscuri or the Gracchi, that Trimalchio was so impudently aping?

These are questions which it may not be possible to answer conclusively in the present state of our archaeological knowledge;[4]

---

[1] For the indispensable alloy of fact in so-called 'works of fiction' see I. C (iii) (e), Annex, vol. i, pp. 449–50, above.

[2] Compare the Greek transliteration of the Latin *titulum*—τίτλον—which is employed in John xix. 19 to describe the notice which Pilate is said to have affixed to the Cross.—A.J.T. [3] Petronius Arbiter: *Cena Trimalchionis*, chap. 29.

[4] There is, however, one piece of literary evidence (to which the writer's attention has been drawn by Dr. Martin Braun) which suggests that, round about the beginning of

but an inability to determine exactly what may be the historical affiliations of Trimalchio's pictures of himself need not compel us to rule out all probabilities that we are unable to prove; for the always dubious *argumentum ex silentio* is particularly hazardous in the case in point—as is illustrated by one feature of Petronius's description. Trimalchio's visual record of his own career is not in marble, like the twelve scenes from Mithras' career in the Mithraeum at Dieburg; it is in paint, like the ten scenes from Mithras' career in the Mithraeum in the gardens of the Palazzo Barberini; and this touch may serve to remind us of the enormous extent of the lacunae in the array of our extant specimens of Hellenic visual art. The whole of our surviving record of Hellenic art, both visual and verbal, is fragmentary; in the field of sculpture, as in that of literature, what has come down to us is only an arbitrary and accidental excerpt out of a harvest of which by far the greater part has now been lost; and, if so little has survived of those relatively rare Hellenic works of visual art that were deemed worthy of being immortalized by being carved in marble, we possess to-day next to nothing of those no doubt far more numerous works that—like Trimalchio's picture-gallery—were rendered in evanescent paint on perishable plaster.

Trimalchio's wall-paintings, however, were substantial and durable by comparison with the shapes in which the scenes from the lives and deaths of our Heracleidae and our Gracchi are likely to have been handed down. For Trimalchio had a free hand; had it taken his fancy, he could have immortalized himself in marble without getting into trouble with the Imperial police, since, in the eyes of the public authorities of the age, a living freedman-millionaire would be as innocuous as he was contemptible in the eyes of Nero's *arbiter elegantiae*. There would be no such tolerance for visual works of art that were intended to perpetuate and consecrate the memory of notorious social reformers or revolutionaries who were still more dangerous to the established social order as dead martyrs than they had been as living agitators. It seems unlikely

the Christian Era, the visual representation, in the 'continuous style', of the Passions of historical, or supposedly historical, martyrs of recent date was a familiar idea in the Hellenic underworld—even in that Jewish section of it which was inhibited, by a traditional religious tabu, from the practice of the visual arts. In the Fourth Book of Maccabees, which was composed at some date, between 63 B.C. and A.D. 70, which was probably prior to A.D. 38, the account of the martyrdom of the Seven Brethren and their Mother—a possibly fabulous episode in the Jewish tradition of the persecution of Jewry by Antiochus Epiphanes (see V. C (i) (c) 2, vol. v, p. 72, with footnote 3, above)— contains the following passage: 'And had it been lawful for me to paint, as might some artist, the tale of thy piety (τὴν τῆς εὐσεβείας ἱστορίαν), would not the spectators have shuddered at the mother of seven sons suffering for righteousness' sake multitudinous tortures even unto death?' (Fourth Book of Maccabees xvii. 7, in Charles, R. H.: *The Apocrypha and Pseudepigrapha of the Old Testament*, vol. ii (Oxford 1913, Clarendon Press), p. 683).

that any of the régimes that were successively in power at Rome
ever allowed the worship of the Gracchi, that had sprung up spon-
taneously on the spots where these two heroes had met their
deaths (Point 83), to go to the length of housing itself in shrines
with sculptures, or even pictures, on their walls. And it seems still
more unlikely that any public worship of Cleomenes was ever
permitted at Alexandria by a Ptolemaic Government which the
Spartan martyr had incited the Alexandrian bourgeoisie to overthrow. A public worship of Cleomenes, in shrines avowedly dedicated to his memory, could not easily have been instituted even in
the cantonments of the Ptolemaic garrisons in Coele Syria, where
Cleomenes' worshippers would have been less immediately under
the eye of the Ptolemaic police. If religious cults of the Heracleidae
and of the Gracchi did arise and persist, we must think of them
as being carried on underground, in the furtive privacy of an
underworld which had learnt by experience how to evade the
scrutiny of Lynceus; and our conjectural reconstruction of the
visual side of such subterranean cults must be such as will be
compatible with this probable environment. A series of scenes in
the 'continuous style' from the lives of Agis and Cleomenes or
from the lives of the Gracchi could not for long escape detection
if either marble or plaster or boards were the medium in which it
was conveyed. And on this account we must suppose that, while
the plot of the series and the subjects and arrangement of the
scenes might be taken from famous sculptures and wall-paintings
in which the lives and deaths of Hêraklês or the Dioscuri were
publicly exhibited, a clandestine visual record of the Passions of
historical heroes, whose worships were *religiones non licitae*, would
almost certainly be reduced to a miniature scale and reproduced
on less conspicuous materials such as parchment or papyrus.[1]
Popular reproductions of celebrated Hellenic works of art used to
be made on a small scale and in inferior materials for the sake of
cheapness. We know the shape of Pheidias' gold-and-ivory statue
of Athena in the Parthenon thanks to the survival, far afield, of
dwarf reproductions of it in coarser stone that were manufactured
in the Imperial Age; and the author of the Acts of the Apostles

---

[1] This transposition of bas-reliefs into paintings is the more easy to imagine if we
may assume that the Pergamene series of Telephus-reliefs is a typical specimen of the
genre of which it is the earliest extant surviving example; for the Telephus-reliefs display
a twofold innovation by contrast with the older style that is represented by the contemporary *Gigantomachia* that once adorned the same monument. The Telephus-reliefs
are new-fangled not only in telling a story in the 'continuous style' but also in reproducing the painter's effects in relief (on this latter point see, for example, Overbeck, J.:
Geschichte der Griechischen Plastik, 4th ed., vol. ii (Leipzig 1894, Hinrichs), pp. 285–6).
A set of bas-reliefs that had been executed in this *malerische Compositionsweise* would
manifestly be easier to re-translate into paint than a set that had been executed in the
echter Reliefstil.

(xix. 24–5) informs us that one of the industries of Ephesus in the first century of the Christian Era was the mass-production of little silver keepsakes, in the shape of miniature shrines, that were to be bought and taken home by the pilgrims who came to visit the actual shrine of the Ephesian Artemis. We may take it that what was so commonly done for the sake of cheapness would almost certainly be done in cases where the wish for cheapness was reinforced by a need for secrecy.

On this showing, may we venture to imagine sets of pictures—representing scenes of which some would be traditional and others historical—being painted on handy and compact materials and circulating in this form clandestinely, from hand to hand, among members of the Hellenic internal proletariat whose reaction to the oppressiveness of the Hellenic dominant minority was to cherish the memory of reformers and revolutionaries who had died for the people in dying at the hands of the people's rulers? Such sets of pictures might speak for themselves if the mythical scenes were familiar and if the historical scenes were labelled with captions. Alternatively, they might be introduced as illustrations into popular books[1] in which the story of the hero's life and death would also be told in words in the form of either 'lives' or 'sayings' or some combination of the two genres.[2] In either of these two possible alternative formats the pictures would be so perishable that it would not be at all surprising that no specimens of them should have survived and that our only inkling of their existence should come from verbal tableaux into which (according to our conjecture) these visual images were eventually transposed when the pictures were used as sources for works of literature that were semi-popular and semi-sophisticated.

This hypothesis in regard to the origin of the verbal tableaux that occur on the one hand in the Gospels and on the other hand in the stories of certain pagan historical heroes finds some support in an analogous hypothesis which has been put forward by a distinguished modern Western scholar as a possible explanation of some incongruities in a passage of the Sixth Book (ll. 562–627) of the *Aeneid*. This passage purports to be a verbal description, from the mouth of the Sibyl, of the perpetual torments of the damned which it is not lawful for Aeneas to see with his own eyes; but in the opinion of Salamon Reinach the Sibyl's recitative is really a descriptive catalogue of a picture-gallery.

'Les éléments dont elle se compose offrent des détails graphiques qui laissent entrevoir, derrière les sources littéraires, des sources figurées,

---

[1] This notion of illustrated *Volksbücher* has been suggested to the writer by Dr. Martin Braun.   [2] For these genres of Hellenic literature see pp. 500–1, above.

c'est-à-dire des œuvres d'art. C'est comme une galerie de petits tableaux représentant des scènes des Enfers, artificiellement réunies par des formules comme *hic et* (l. 582), *nec non et* (l. 595), *quid memorem* (l. 601). Il importe peu que Virgile ait vu lui-même ces petits tableaux ou qu'il en ait emprunté la description à d'autres poètes; comme nous ne connaissons pas les sources grecques de ce passage, en dehors de l'*Odyssée*, nous pouvons traiter Virgile comme une source et chercher sous ses vers les images dont ils sont la traduction. Un trait comme celui du vers 605 [–6]—*Furiarum maxima iuxta/accubat*—est certainement inspiré d'un modèle graphique; que Virgile ou un autre avant lui s'en soit inspiré, c'est une question insoluble et qui ne nous intéresse pas ici.'[1]

But why should not the verbal means of conveyance by which these tableaux have actually been transmitted to us be accepted at their face value? In reckoning with these we are on sure ground because authentic specimens of them survive. Why should we go out of our way to postulate the existence of visual means of conveyance as well, when we are unable to support this postulate by bringing forward any material evidence in its favour? The answer is that the social stratum with which we are concerned in our present inquiry was one which, to our knowledge, was to a large extent illiterate; for it is well known that, in illiterate social milieux, things that, *ex hypothesi*, cannot be broadcast in writing are apt to be broadcast in pictorial representations instead, in so far as these can be made to do duty for the written word. In the Soviet Union, for example, in the early days of the Bolshevik Revolution, when the new rulers of half a continent set out to win support for themselves by launching an intensive campaign of mass-propaganda among an illiterate population, it is said that they used to send out propaganda-trains in which the rolling stock was plastered with pictorial posters. The Attica of the fifth century B.C. was much more literate than the Russia of the twentieth century of the Christian Era, as is testified by the institution of Ostracism;[2] but even in that enlightened century and country, and *a fortiori* in the vast and only superficially Hellenized Hellenic World *post Alexandrum*, the illiterate element in the population was sufficiently numerous to have to be sedulously catered for by being addressed in picture-language.[3]

The prevalence of a visual habit of mind in fifth-century Attica is attested by at least two passages in the extant masterpieces of the

---

[1] Reinach, S.: *Cultes, Mythes et Religions*, vol. ii (Paris 1906, Leroux), p. 160.

[2] Ostracism involved the taking of a plebiscite in which every adult male citizen had to write on a potsherd the name of a statesman whom he wished to condemn to banishment.

[3] The institution of Ostracism is evidence for literacy being widespread, but not for its being universal—as witness the famous anecdote of the illiterate peasant who, when one of these negative plebiscites was being taken, asked Aristeides, not knowing who he was, to write his (Aristeides') own name on the peasant's voting-sherd.

Attic drama. In Aeschylus's *Agamemnon*, ll. 231–47, the chorus not only depict the sacrifice of Iphigeneia in what reads like a tableau transposed into words, but actually describe the protagonist in this scene as 'looking as she looks in the pictures' (πρέπουσά θ' ὡς ἐν γραφαῖς). In Euripides' *Hippolytus*, ll. 1004–5, the hero, when he is accused of a monstrous crime, protests his innocence in the words: 'I know nothing of this business [i.e. sexual intercourse] except through hearing of it in talk and seeing it in picture' (οὐκ οἶδα πρᾶξιν τήνδε πλὴν λόγῳ κλύων / γραφῇ τε λεύσσων)—without any mention of the possibility of reading about it in the written word. The survival of the same habit of mind in the Hellenized 'Great Society' of the Imperial Age is similarly attested by a passage in Plutarch's *Lives of the Gracchi* (chap. 2), in which the author tries to convey to his readers the likeness-in-difference or difference-in-likeness between the two brothers by putting it to them that

'just as, in statues or pictures of the Dioscuri, the likeness between the two figures is qualified by a difference which is the difference between a boxer and a runner, so the strong resemblance between our two young Romans in the matters of courage and self-discipline and good breeding and eloquence and nobility of character is diversified by some striking points of unlikeness in the actions and policy in which they respectively realized and distinguished themselves.'

If this visual habit of mind is prevalent in both of two societies that have come into contact with one another, it is conceivable that one of them may transmit to the other its ideas and its myths by the visual means of conveyance without these ever being transposed into written, or even into spoken, words at any stage in their journey from the one social milieu to the other. According to one modern Western scholar,[1] 'bien des difficultés que l'on rencontre quand on veut expliquer certaines similitudes entre les fables et les épopées de la Grèce et de l'Inde s'évanouiraient peut-être si l'on admettait moins des emprunts directs, par la parole ou par l'écriture, que des emprunts par voie iconographique'. And Reinach[2] cites other archaeological authorities in support of the view that certain Scandinavian myths—for instance, the tale of Odin hanging on the tree, and the description of this tree itself, which is the World-Tree Yggdrasill—are transpositions into words of the sculptured crosses which met the eyes of the Vikings when they carried their raids into the British Isles.[3]

---

[1] Clermont-Ganneau, cited by Salamon Reinach, ibid., vol. iv (Paris 1912, Leroux), p. 101 (the reference is to an article in the *Revue Critique*, vol. ii, pp. 215 and 232 (1878)).
[2] Ibid., pp. 102–3.
[3] In this context Reinach further suggests that the decorations carved on stone in such works of the Northumbrian sculptor's art as the Bewcastle and Rothwell crosses

The effectiveness of picture-language as a means of communication is brought out vividly in several well-known passages of Greek and Latin literature. In the Hellenic World in all ages of its history that have left us any legacy of literature the normal first step of a stranger who had arrived in a city which he had never visited before was to make the round of the public monuments—statues, colonnades, and temples—and to look at the bas-reliefs and wall-paintings which the public buildings contained.

This, for instance, is the *motif* of the opening scene (Book I, chap. 1) of Achilles Tatius's novel *Cleitopho and Leucippe*. 'As I was wandering', says the imaginary narrator, 'about the city [of Sidon], surveying the votive offerings in the temples, I saw a painting'—and the author straightway plunges into a detailed verbal description of a picture illustrating the myth of Europa. In a later chapter of the same novel (Book III, chap. 6) two ship-wrecked travellers, who are kicking their heels at Pelusium while they are waiting for a passage, spend their time in looking at pictures of Andromeda and of Prometheus—which, again, are described in minute detail—in the temple of Zeus Casius. Nor was it only pagan travellers who condescended to avail themselves of this pleasantly educative means of killing time. 'While Paul waited for' his companions to join him at Athens, 'his spirit was stirred within him when he saw the city full of idols (κατείδωλον οὖσαν τὴν πόλιν)' (Acts xvii. 16); and the Christian apostle took his sightseeing as the text for a missionary sermon: 'For as I passed by and beheld your devotions (διερχόμενος γὰρ καὶ ἀναθεωρῶν τὰ σεβάσματα ὑμῶν), I found an altar with this inscription . . .' (Acts xvii. 23). The urban sightseeing which thus makes its appearance as a *motif* in both the Acts of the Apostles and the romance of *Cleitopho and Leucippe* is translated into a rural setting in the opening scene (Prooemium, chap. 2) of Longus's *Daphnis and Chloe*: 'As I was hunting in Lesbos I saw in a grove of the Nymphs the loveliest sight that I had ever set eyes on, a picture which was a love-story'—and, after describing the subject of the picture, which was a pastoral scene, the author tells his reader that the book which he is about to read is the fruit of a passion, with which the

---

are not original in their design but are translations into sculpture of the miniature paintings in Irish manuscripts which are themselves inspired by Hellenic prototypes of the Imperial and even the Pre-Imperial Post-Alexandrine Age. In this hypothetical translation of small-scale paintings on parchment into large-scale sculptures on stone we have the exact inverse of our hypothetical translation of sculpture and painting on plaster into miniatures painted on parchment or papyrus to illustrate the lives of Jesus and his pagan counterparts (see pp. 515–17, above). Reinach's hypothesis is, however, a matter of controversy. There are some scholars who hold that Northumbrian sculpture owes nothing to Irish inspiration; and there are others who do not admit that even the Northumbrian school of miniature-painting is of Irish origin (see Dawson, Christopher: *The Making of Europe* (London 1932, Sheed & Ward), pp. 206–8).

author was seized, to put some equivalent of the fascinating Lesbian picture into words (πόθος ἔσχεν ἀντιγράψαι τῇ γραφῇ).¹ The fascination exercised by sermons in stones—or on boards or plaster—was indeed so strong that we find even the conscientious Aeneas succumbing to it out of season.² As soon as he steps across the threshold of the temple of Apollo at Cumae, his attention is entirely absorbed by the scenes from the great corpus of Hellenic Mythology that are painted on the walls, and for the moment he becomes oblivious of the quest on which he is bent, though this quest is the serious and formidable one of making a descent into Hell. Aeneas would have lingered there sightseeing until he had taken in everything that there was to be seen, had not the Sibyl hustled him on into performing his religious duties, as Trimalchio's guests were hustled by the major-domo into taking their places at the dinner table.

> quin protinus omnia
> perlegerent oculis, ni iam praemissus Achates
> adforet atque una Phoebi Triviaeque sacerdos,
> Deiphobe Glauci, fatur quae talia regi:
> 'Non hoc ista sibi tempus spectacula poscit.'³

In what did the fascination of this picture-language consist? Perhaps largely in identifying the subjects of the painted or sculptured scenes when these were not provided with captions or when the captions were there but were not intelligible to the sightseer, either because he was illiterate or because they were written in a language and a script which he could not read. This fascinating game of crying τοῦτ' ἐκεῖνο is played competitively by the chorus in Euripides' *Ion* at their first entry (ll. 184–218). This chorus is composed of Athenian women in the service of Queen Creûsa, and the scene is the temple of Apollo at Delphi which these Athenians are now seeing for the first time. In an animated dialogue they call one another's attention to the works of art with which the temple is decorated, as they recognize one mythical scene or figure after another.

' "See this; look; give your eyes to it; it is the Lernaean hydra being slain by Hêraklês."—"Yes, I see it, my dear; and here is Iolaus."—"Well, but just look at this; here is Bellerophon mounted on Pegasus."—"My eyes are being drawn in all directions; don't miss the Giants."—"My dears, we are looking at these."—"Well, do you see her brandishing

---

¹ It will be seen that in this passage Longus professes to have done the very thing that is attributed to Virgil, or to Virgil's source, by Reinach in the passage quoted on pp. 517–8, above. In this connexion it is not without interest to note that Longus betrays some acquaintance with Virgil's work (see J. M. Edmonds in the Loeb edition of *Daphnis and Chloe* (London 1916, Heinemann), p. vii).

² Virgil: *Aeneid*, Book VI, ll. 13–41.   ³ Ibid., ll. 33–7.

her aegis?"—"See Pallas, my own goddess? No mistake!"—"And then Zeus with his thunderbolt?"—"Yes, I see him; he is blasting Mimas." —"And here is Bacchus." [1]

This passage of Euripides' *Ion* bears out Reinach's observation that 'toute image est une énigme qui . . . réclame impérieusement une explication, et les motifs graphiques se transmettent et se perpétuent comme les mots du langage'.[2] Guessing at the answer to riddles is always fun, but it does not always happen that the guesser guesses right; and Reinach's thesis, in the brilliant essay from which we are here quoting, is that the riddles presented in the series of tableaux in *Aeneid* VI, ll. 562–627, are there interpreted in a sense that makes nonsense of the meaning which the hands that originally designed these pictures were intending to convey.

In the *Aeneid*, of course—and not only there but also in every other work of Greek and Latin literature in which they figure— the subjects of these scenes—Salmoneus, Ixion and Sisyphus, Tityos and Tantalus, Theseus and Peirithous, the Danaids, and the rest—are represented as damned souls who are suffering in an Other World eternal punishments for sins which they committed in This World once upon a time. Reinach submits that this is a false interpretation which has been put upon the pictures in order to make them serve as illustrations of a system of theology which was unheard of in the archaic Hellenic World—or was it the pre-Hellenic Minoan World?[3]—in which these pictures had originally taken shape. This system is that of Orphism; and Orphism is a cutting from an exotic plant which was deliberately imported into Hellas no earlier than the sixth century B.C.[4] According to Reinach, the pictures were intended by their original designers to represent their subjects, not as undergoing perpetual tortures in Hell, but as snap-shotted, for the sightseer's information, in either one or other of two alternative postures in which the sightseer would be prone to visualize them. The subject is represented either as engaged in some notoriously characteristic activity of his life or else as *in articulo mortis* if what is notorious about him is, not what he did with his life, but the manner in which he lost it.[5] The

---

[1] This is not, of course, a full translation of the passage but only a sketch of the gist of it.   [2] Reinach, op. cit., vol. ii, pp. 183–4.

[3] It has been brought to the writer's attention by Professor Gilbert Murray that a number of *motifs* which appear in literary form in the Hellenic Mythology—e.g. Odysseus and the Ram; Oedipus and Laius; Orestes killing Clytaemnestra and Aegisthus —are also to be found in visual form engraved on Minoan gems.

[4] Reinach, op. cit., pp. 203–4. For the arguments in favour of the view that Orphism was not the revival of a submerged religious legacy from the Minoan World, but was an artificial product that was manufactured by Hellenic hearts and minds out of contemporary Oriental materials in the sixth century B.C., see V. C (i) (c) 2, vol. v, pp. 84–7, above.

[5] Reinach, op. cit., vol. ii, pp. 166–9.

picture of Salmoneus portrays a successful rain-maker producing
the thunderstorm and lightning-flash in the sky by the sympathetic
magic that he is performing on the ground as he drives a thundering chariot while he waves lightning-torches in his hands. The
proper caption for this picture is 'The storm successfully discharged
by Salmoneus' and not 'Zeus blasting Salmoneus for his impiety
in having attempted to perform a social service which is Zeus'
own exclusive prerogative'.[1] Similarly, Ixion lashed for ever to a
perpetually revolving wheel is not a sinner undergoing eternal
punishment but is the *numen* in the Sun-Disk represented an-
thropomorphically in the style of the Assyrian Asshur and the
Achaemenian Ahuramazda.[2] And Sisyphus, too, in his own way,
is achieving as triumphant a *tour de force* as the divinity that makes
the Sun go round or as the magician who brings the rain. Sisyphus[3]
is not a *forçat* serving a sentence of penal servitude which is as
heart-breakingly futile as it is back-breakingly laborious. He is the
superb technician who built on the heights of the Acrocorinthus
the great white marble structure which was still known as the
Sisypheum in the last century B.C.[4] The stone that he is hoisting
up will never, it is true, quite reach the top of the mountain, but
that is simply because the emplacement of the Sisypheum lies a
little way below the summit![5] The Danaids, again, are not miserably expiating the damnable sin of having murdered their husbands, but are beneficently engaged on their life-work of irrigating
the thirsty plain of Argos.[6] As for Tityos, he is really being eaten,
not excruciatingly alive, but insensitively dead, by his attendant
vultures; for the picture represents, not another of the torments
of the damned, but the corpse of a warrior who has died a glorious
death on the battle-field[7]—just as Tantalus represents, not a sinner
being 'tantalized', but the drowning king of a city that has been
engulfed in a lake as the result of an eruption or an earthquake.[8]

These examples of the misinterpretation of visual riddles are all
taken from the Hellenic cycle of art and mythology, and are all
to be explained (if Reinach's theory is right) as attempts to give
old *motifs* a satisfactory meaning in terms of a new theology. But
this is by no means the only stage on which the same comedy of
errors has been played. There is, for instance, at least one Christian
legend that can be accounted for in a similar way. It is told of a
number of Christian martyrs that, immediately after their de-
capitation, they rose to their feet, picked up their own severed
heads, and walked off head in hand. This legend appears to be a

---

[1] Ibid., pp. 160–6.   [2] Ibid., p. 183.   [3] Ibid., pp. 172–7.
[4] Ibid., p. 174, citing Strabo: *Geographica*, Book VIII, chap. 6, § 21, p. 379, and Diodorus: *A Library of Universal History*, Book XX, chap. 103.   [5] Ibid., p. 176.
[6] Ibid., pp. 193–6.   [7] Ibid., pp. 170–2.   [8] Ibid., pp. 177–81.

transposition into words of statues in which these saints were visually represented in this posture; and these statues themselves can be traced back, as the Bollandist Fathers have shown, to a passage of Saint John Chrysostom[1] in which the writer imagines the martyrs appearing before the throne of God with their heads in their hands, as soldiers address themselves to their commander with confidence when they are able to display to him the wounds that they have received in his service.

Let us now apply these prolegomena to the tableaux, set out in Table V above,[2] that are common to the story of Jesus and the stories of our pagan historical heroes. On a number of points the considerations that we now have in mind may prove illuminating.

In the first place, if we run our eye down the list, we shall see that most of the tableaux in it that do not represent notorious historical scenes in the life of this hero or that can be explained as adaptations of familiar traditional scenes from the myth of some god or demigod.

The tableaux of the Hubbub at Night-time with Lights (Point 41), the Posse of Officers of the Law Abashed in the Hero's Presence (Point 43), and the Trial at Night-time (Point 49), and again those of the Women in the Background (Point 80), the Descent from the Gallows (Point 81), and the *Pietà* (Point 82), would appear to be representations of authentic scenes in the Passion of Agis.[3] The

---

[1] Migne: *Patrologia Graeca*, vols. xlix–l, col. 576: οὕτω καὶ οὗτοι τὰς κεφαλὰς ἃς ἀπε-τμήθησαν ἐπὶ τῶν χειρῶν βαστάζοντες, καὶ εἰς μέσον παράγοντες, εὐκόλως ἅπαντα, ὅσα ἂν θέλωσι, παρὰ τῷ βασιλεῖ τῶν οὐρανῶν ἀνύειν δύνανται.   [2] On p. 411, above.

[3] There is another tableau—not included in our table of eighty-nine points—which may perhaps also have found its way into the story of Jesus out of the authentic history of Agis. When, after the introduction of Agis' social reforms, Agis' partisan Lysander, who was now a member of the governing Board of Overseers, was scheming to remove Agis' colleague and opponent King Leonidas by forcing him into exile, Lysander 'proceeded, in company with his fellow Overseers, to "watch for the sign". This "watching for the sign" is [an ancient Spartan ritual]. Once in every nine years the Overseers choose a clear moonless night and sit through it in silence with their eyes fixed on the sky. If on that night a star shoots across the sky from one quarter to another, they put the Kings on trial on the presumption that they must have committed some offence against Religion, and in the meanwhile they suspend them from office, pending the arrival from Delphi or Olympia of an exculpating oracle. On the occasion in question, Lysander asserted that this "sign" had appeared to him, and on the strength of this he gave notice that there was to be a trial of King Leonidas' (Plutarch: *Lives of Agis and Cleomenes*, chap. 11). This piece of star-gazing was a crucial event in Agis' political career, and a picture of it might well have been one of the regular scenes in a standard pictorial representation of Agis' life and Passion. Is it conceivable that this hypothetical picture in a Spartan picture-book may be the source of the verbal tableau in Matt. ii. 9–11? The original picture would presumably represent a group of magisterial-looking men (the Spartan Board of Overseers) sitting in front of a building (the Brazen House of Athena Chalcioecus) and gazing at a shooting star (the motion of which would perhaps be indicated by a trail of light). A Jewish interpreter of this picture would expect the star-gazers to be magi (especially on the morrow of an historic journey of a party of magi from east to west: see pp. 455–6, above). He might jump to the conclusion that there was a connexion between the star and the house, and might suppose that the star had come to rest over the house in order to draw the star-gazers' attention to it. From this, again, he might infer that the house was the goal of a pilgrimage on which the star-gazers had been led by following the star from their home in the east. We may observe that if, in the original Spartan picture, the house really was the temple of

tableaux of a Party going Out of Doors (Point 33), a Fight (Point 44), the Pricking of the Hero's Body with a Stabbing Weapon (Point 79), and the Women in the Foreground (Point 80 A) would appear to be taken, similarly, from the true history of the Passion of Cleomenes. The tableau of the Young Male Fugitive Leaving his Wrap in the Hands of his Pursuers (Point 48) is a picture of the martyrdom of Tiberius Gracchus.[1] The tableaux of a Crowd Mounting on to the Roofs in order to get within Range of the Hero (Point 11), a Bodyguard Watching and Sleeping by Turns (Point 37), and a Watcher Caught Napping (Point 38) look as though they came from the true history of the life and death of Gaius Gracchus. The Roman Washing his Hands in a Basin in Public (Point 64) is entered, in Clio's register, not as Pontius Pilate but as Catiline.

On the other hand the tableaux of a Rider, with Companions on Foot, Making a Progress through the Streets of a City (Point 16) and the Hero Forcibly Clearing a Public Place of Trespassers (Point 17) would appear to portray two scenes out of the ritual of 'the Ride of the Beardless One'.[2] The tableau of the Bosom Friend Leaning on the Hero's Breast (Point 28) looks like a scene from the romance of Pantheia and Abradatas,[3] which in turn is perhaps a version of the myth of Ishtar and Tammuz; and it is possible that the tableau of the *Pietà* was also generated by this Sumeric myth and that it made its way into the Hellenic story of Agis from an Oriental source. The tableau of the Agony (Point 36) looks like a scene from the tragedy of *Hercules Furens*, and the tableau of the Hero Ripping off his Shirt (Point 71) like a scene from the tragedy of *Hercules Oetaeus* (if we may venture to identify the shirt worn by Cleomenes on his dying day with the deadly Shirt of Nessus).[4] The tableaux of the Hero Arrayed in a Royal Robe and Crown (Point 66) and the Hero being Exhibited in Public as a Claimant to Kingship (Point 67) look like scenes from the ritual of the ephemeral reign of the mock-king of the Saturnalia and the Sacaea;[5] and the tableau of a Crucified Man being Acclaimed as a Son of God (Point 75) may perhaps be traceable to the same origin.

In the next place we may take note of a pair of tableaux—the

Athena Chalcioecus, then, in the next picture in the Spartan series, 'the house' did harbour 'the King'; for the effect of Lysander's prosecution of King Leonidas on the strength of 'the sign' was to frighten Leonidas into taking asylum in Athena's sanctuary (Plutarch, cap. cit.).

[1] Reinach, op. cit., vol. iv, p. 168, suggests that Mark xiv. 51–2 is derived (not from the story of Tiberius Gracchus, but) from Amos ii. 16: 'And he that is courageous among the mighty shall flee away naked in that day.' This suggestion seems far-fetched; for Mark's young man is not represented as being courageous (as is the other anonymous disciple who shows fight in Mark xiv. 47). On the other hand in Amos there is no mention of the fugitive leaving his wrap behind.

[2] See p. 481, above.   [3] See pp. 460–3, above.
[4] See p. 472, above.   [5] See pp. 481–6, above.

Descent from the Gallows or Cross (Point 81) and the *Pietà* (Point 82)—which appear to have passed direct out of the Hellenic into our Christian iconography without having been transposed into words, and then retransposed into visual form again, *en route*. The tableau of the Descent is equally prominent in our Christian iconography and in the word-picture in Plutarch's *Lives of Agis and Cleomenes*; on the other hand there is no corresponding text, describing the event, in the Gospels.[1] The *Pietà* is, of course, depicted in a word-picture in the Gospels as well as in Plutarch; but in its portrayal of the same scene the Christian iconographical tradition differs from the Gospels and agrees with the Passion of Agis in one capital point.[2] In the Christian iconographical tradition, as in the story of Agis, the most prominent actors in this scene are the women of the dead hero's entourage, whereas in the Gospels the women are not mentioned and the laying out of the body for burial is ascribed to a man, namely, Joseph of Arimathaea (who, in the Gospel according to Saint John, is said to have been assisted, not by the women, but by another man, namely Nicodemus). Whatever the ultimate origin of the tableau of the *Pietà*, the assignment of a prominent part in this scene to female characters seems not unlikely to have originated in an authentic feature of the historical Passion of King Agis; for gynaecocracy—'the monstrous regiment of women'—was one of the conspicuous features in the social life of Sparta under the Lycurgean *agôgê*, and this more than ever in the days of Sparta's decadence.[3]

Such direct transmission of tableaux from the Hellenic to the Christian iconography would appear, however, to be exceptional. All the rest of the tableaux under consideration are to be found in verbal form in the Gospels; not all of them have subsequently found their way back into visual form by being adopted as themes of a Christian iconographical tradition; and, in so far as this re-transposition has taken place, the Christian portrayal of these scenes appears to be based upon the text of the Gospels for the most part—though it may have drawn, in addition, upon Hellenic iconographical sources which it is no longer in our power to detect because these have not survived independently.

If we now look into the setting in which our tableaux occur in the Gospels, we may find some corroboration for our conjecture that, at an earlier stage of their history, these tableaux were in circulation in visual form in series which were intended to illustrate the

[1] For the origin of the apparent allusion to the Descent from the Cross in the Gospel according to Saint Luke see p. 404, footnote 1, above.
[2] On this point see p. 404, footnote 2, above.
[3] For the ascendancy of women in 'Lycurgean' Sparta see Part III. A, vol. iii, p. 75, with footnote 4, above.

myths or legends or histories of gods or demigods or human martyrs.

There are, for instance, certain tableaux which in their context in the Gospels seem inconsequent or even incongruous, but which explain and justify themselves in their pagan contexts. This difference in degree of relevancy or congruity suggests that the tableau is native to the context in which it seems to be at home, and that in the other context, in which it does not cohere with its surroundings, it is adventitious. But why should an author have burdened his book with scenes for which he has not succeeded in finding a convenient place or function? The answer may be that the author has been defeated by a problem which he could not solve yet at the same time could not evade. These scenes which he has failed to knit up into the main fabric of his work may have been virtually impossible for him to leave out for the reason that his public may have expected to find them in any *Volksbuch* in which the hero was presented in the role of a saviour. Whether the ultimate origin of these scenes was historical or mythical, they had come, we may surmise, to be regarded as an indispensable part of the credentials of any hero who was a candidate for recognition as being the Saviour *par excellence*. An author whose purpose in writing his book was to present as the Saviour some hero of his own who had not yet won any general acknowledgement could not afford to leave these obligatory scenes out. So in they must go, however difficult it might be to piece them together with the particular story which this particular author was setting out to tell.

Two tableaux which are inconsequent in the Gospels but germane to their other contexts are the Posse Abashed (Point 43) and the Young Man Fleeing (Point 48). The former scene explains itself in the story of Agis, where the men are ordered to put Agis to death and flinch, naturally enough, from executing an order to take the life of a legitimate King of Sparta who has the holy blood of Hêraklês in his veins. The latter scene explains itself in the story of Tiberius Gracchus, where the fugitive is the hero himself, and where the scene is one of supreme dramatic and emotional interest because it portrays the hero at the instant before he meets his death.

Three tableaux which are incongruous in the Gospels but germane to their other contexts are the Presentation of the Two Swords (Point 32), the Fight (Point 44), and the Command to Cease Fighting (Point 45). In the Gospels all three points are incongruous because, at any rate in the version of the story which has prevailed, Jesus is presented as a gentle hero and not as a violent one (Point 1), and his non-resistance is one of the hinges on which the plot of the drama turns. On the other hand the fight followed by a command to cease fighting is of the essence of the story of Cleomenes; for Cleomenes is a man of violence who is attempting to make himself master of Alexandria by a *coup de main* and who will therefore fight like a lion so long as his desperate enterprise seems to have any chance of success, but he is also a man of chivalry who will be prompt to avoid what would now be merely aimless bloodshed as soon as it becomes plain that his stroke has failed. As for the tableau of the Presentation of the Two Swords, we may perhaps hazard the guess that the text in the Gospel according to Saint Luke (xxii. 38)—'And they said: "Lord, behold here are two swords", and he said unto them: "It is enough" '— may be a transposition into words of one of the details in some popular reproduction of the *Necyia*: a panoramic picture of Hades and its denizens, of which the original, from the hand of no lesser a master than Polygnotus, was one of the treasures of Delphi.[1] Among the heroes of Hellenic Mythology with whose figures Polygnotus's picture was thronged were that inseparable pair of friends Theseus and Peirithous; and in Pausanias' description of the picture[2] this particular group of figures is described in the following words: 'Below Odysseus are Theseus and Peirithous sitting on thrones—Theseus holding in both hands the swords, Peirithous's and his own, while Peirithous has his eyes fixed on them.'

We may next return for a moment to the consideration of eight tableaux which, in the Gospels, are all associated with quotations from the Jewish Scriptures and which we have examined in this connexion at an earlier point in our present inquiry.[3] These eight tableaux are the Rider (Point 16), the Harrying of the Hucksters (Point 17), the Presentation of the Two Swords (Point 32), the Roman Washing his Hands (Point 64), the Trio of Victims (Point 70), the Shirt (Point 71), the Corpse Intact on the Cross (Point 78), and the Pricking of the Hero's Body (Point 79). At a first assay we have found ourselves at a loss to understand the relation between these tableaux and the quotations by which they are accompanied in the New Testament. In almost every case the appositeness of the Scriptural text to the tableau is, as we have seen, too slight to warrant the hypothesis that the text may have been the

---

[1] The present writer's attention was drawn to Polygnotus's presentation of Theseus and Peirithous by Reinach's reference to it in op. cit., vol. ii, pp. 184–6. On the other hand Reinach himself, in another place—op. cit., vol. iv, p. 167—suggests that Luke xxii. 38 is derived (not from Polygnotus's picture, but) from Judges vii. 18 and 20: Ῥομφαία τῷ Κυρίῳ καὶ τῷ Γεδεών ('a sword for [sic] the Lord and for Gideon').

[2] Pausanias: *Descriptio Graeciae*, Book X, chap. 29, § 9. The description of the whole picture occupies chaps. 28–31 inclusive. [3] See pp. 420–8, above.

original material out of which the tableau has been made. And this
negative conclusion is borne out by our observation that one of the
texts—Isa. liii. 12—is quoted in the Gospel according to Saint
Mark apropos of Point 70 and in the Gospel according to Saint
Luke apropos of Point 32,[1] while conversely one of the tableaux—
No. 17—is accompanied by a combination of texts from Isaiah and
Jeremiah in the Synoptic Gospels, but in the Gospel according to
Saint John by quite a different text that is taken from one of the
Psalms.[2] How, then, we have still to ask ourselves, have these
tableaux and these texts come to be brought into their present
association with one another? In the light of the results of our
present examination of possible visual means of conveyance we
may at last be able to find the answer to this riddle.

Let us suppose that the eight tableaux here in question had come
to be regarded as obligatory scenes in any portrayal of any saviour's
Passion. Granting this, we may imagine the Evangelists—or the
predecessors who served them as sources—being impelled to
furnish a Hellenic tableau with a Jewish caption by the consciousness of a need to mitigate the inconsequence, or attenuate the incongruity, of a tableau which an exacting popular tradition would
forbid them to leave out, however great might be the difficulty of
bringing this tableau into harmony with a story which possessed a
plot and an atmosphere of its own that were individual and perhaps
unique. The Scriptural caption might not be closely to the point;
it might, indeed, be so irrelevant that an identical caption could be
fitted by different hands to different tableaux, or an identical
tableau be furnished by different hands with different captions. In
a semi-sophisticated work such lapses from the sophisticated
standard of literary competence might cause little heart-searching
either to the author or to his public. On the other hand the author,
for his part, might feel himself considerably fortified by the feat of
having brought the adventitious Hellenic material into even the
loosest relation with the Jewish Canon of Scripture. That feat
might be a *tour de force*, and yet the mere juxtaposition of tableau
and text would go far to consecrate and justify the tableau in eyes
which still saw the Universe through the lens of Judaism. In
bringing such tableaux into even a forced and artificial relation
with Scriptural texts the Evangelist would be taking not only the
first but perhaps actually the decisive step towards capturing from
Hellenism, and annexing to Judaism, certain 'features' (in the
journalistic usage of the word) which it was obligatory for him to
incorporate into his own work because these by now traditional
traits had come to be the hall-marks of a *soi-disant* saviour's

---

[1] See p. 426, above.   [2] See pp. 425–6, above.

authenticity in the eyes of a public which was already being re-cruited from the non-Jewish masses of a promiscuous proletarian underworld.

To furnish a picture with a caption is an attempt to give this old picture a new meaning without actually touching the picture itself; but this is an external treatment which can only be expected to be effective if the reinterpretation that is required is superficial. If the picture has to be reinterpreted in a radical way, this can hardly be achieved without at least some retouching; and we can put our finger upon several tableaux which in fact seem to bear the marks of having been repainted to some extent in order to enable them to carry a new meaning.

There are two cases, for example, in which, to all appearance, a scene has been made to fit into a series to which it did not originally belong by reducing the figure of the original protagonist to the dimensions of a minor character. In this fashion the scene of the Rider (Point 16) seems to have been fitted into the story of Cleo-menes by transferring the Rider's part from the hero to one of his henchmen[1]—in contrast to the treatment of the same scene in the Gospels, where the Rider remains the principal figure that he is in the original rite from which this scene seems to be ultimately derived. In a similar way the scene of the Flight and Pursuit of Tiberius Gracchus on the Day of his Martyrdom (Point 48) seems to have been fitted into the story of Jesus by transferring the Fugi-tive's part from the hero to one of his henchmen whom an em-barrassed adapter leaves anonymous, without attempting to identify this obligatory figure with any of the characters who appear on the stage in earlier acts of the Christian drama.

We may also recall one case in which we have found reason[2] to surmise that a character—'the Bosom Friend'—has undergone a

___

[1] Before we traced the tableau of the Rider back to the rite of 'the Ride of the Beard-less One' (see p. 481, above), we had already rejected the hypothesis that this tableau might have given rise to the name of Cleomenes' companion Hippitas. We took note (on p. 462, footnote 2, above), of the fact that Hippitas was an authentic historical personage whom Polybius displays to us in the act of strolling, in his leader's company, along the quayside at Alexandria. According to Plutarch-Phylarchus, however, Hippitas was a lame man; and this, according to the same authority, was the reason why, on the day of the abortive *coup*, the lame man's companions commandeered a horse and mounted him upon it. No doubt Hippitas may have been too lame to charge at the double when he was not too lame to stroll; or he may have gone lame in the interval between the scene in which he figures on foot in the narrative of Polybius and the scene (which has no counterpart in Polybius's pages) in which he figures on horseback in the narrative of Plutarch-Phylarchus. It seems more likely, however, that Phylarchus has lamed Hippitas with his own hand—or stylus—as an excuse for hoisting his victim into the saddle, and that he has singled out Hippitas for playing the Rider's part on account of his name—if we may assume that Phylarchus had found the inclusion of the Rider Scene obligatory, and that he was in difficulties over conscripting somebody to play a part which even the most audaciously romantic historian could not venture to assign to Cleomenes himself when the whole world was aware that, on that day in Alexandria, Cleomenes had charged and fought on foot.

[2] See pp. 461–3, above.

change of sex.[1] In the tableau of the Favourite Companion Lying on the Hero's Breast (Point 28) the Bosom Friend is of the male sex in the stories of Cleomenes and Gaius Gracchus and Jesus alike. On the other hand in the romance of Pantheia and Abradatas (an older story which is perhaps a version of the myth of Ishtar and Tammuz) the corresponding figure in the same tableau is not male but female. We have already conjectured[2] that this change of sex may have been the work of Phylarchus, and that this romantic historian may have been tempted to take this liberty by the play of his volatile imagination upon the superficial similarity between the names of Pantheia and Panteus.

The necessity of transferring a tableau from a setting in which the hero is violent to one in which he is gentle has, in at least two cases, apparently compelled the authors of the Gospels—or their sources—to make changes that go farther than a transfer of parts or even a change of sex. For example, in the tableau of the Favourite Companion Lying on the Hero's Breast (Point 28)—as this appears in the story of Abradatas (where the favourite companion is the hero's widow Pantheia), as well as in the stories of Cleomenes and Gaius Gracchus (where the favourite companion is a man)—the hero's body is not alive and in peace but is the corpse of a warrior who has died by violence, while the favourite companion is in the act of slaying herself (or himself) upon the hero's dead body. On the other hand in the same tableau, as this appears in the story of Jesus, the hero is lying, not dead on the ground, but alive in the triclinium, and the favourite companion is leaning on his breast, not in order to join him in death, but in order to talk with him privily. It will be seen that in this case (if our explanation is right) the tableau has been reinterpreted as drastically as it well could be without altering the grouping of the figures. It will also be seen that no lesser change would have availed to fit into the Passion of a gentle hero a tableau which is, in origin, a violent hero's death-scene. The same problem has had to be faced in the transfer, from the Passion of Agis to the Passion of Jesus, of the tableau of a Hubbub at Night-time with Lights (Point 41); and here it has been solved by turning a scene which originally portrayed an attempt to rescue the hero into a portrayal of his arrest.

We may also notice two apparent cases of rationalization in the style of Phylarchus's treatment of the Rider Tableau.[3] In the pair of tableaux (Points 66 and 67) in which the hero is arrayed in a royal robe and crown he is dressed (if Frazer's conjecture is right)[4]

---

[1] Compare the metamorphosis of the Bodhisattva Avalokita into the goddess Kwanyin in the course of the migration of the Mahāyāna from India to the Far East.
[2] See pp. 461–3, above.   [3] See p. 530, footnote 1, above.
[4] See pp. 481–6, above.

to fit the part of the mock-king in the ritual of the Saturnalia or the Sacaea. In both the story of Tiberius Gracchus and the story of Jesus, however, this pair of tableaux is given a matter-of-fact explanation which lies quite outside the realm of religious or magical practice. Jesus is represented as being robed and crowned in mockery of the fact that he—an obscure man of the people—has solemnly pleaded guilty to the charge of having claimed to be a king. Tiberius Gracchus is represented as being first robed and crowned in a kind of private dress-rehearsal for a future coronation as King of Rome, and then subsequently denounced to the Senate as asking the People for a diadem. Similarly, when Cleomenes is portrayed as ripping open the seam of his shirt (Point 71), he is represented in the narrative of Plutarch-Phylarchus as performing this trivial action for the matter-of-fact purpose of giving free play to his sword-arm. We may suspect, however, that this ostensibly rational explanation is no more than an ingenious expedient for fitting into the story of Cleomenes a tableau in which, in the original, the Heracleid's ancestor Hêraklês was depicted in the act of trying in vain to tear off from his tormented body the poisoned Shirt of Nessus.

Inversely, there is one case in which an originally matter-of-fact scene appears to have been given a ritualistic meaning in order to fit it into another story. In the original picture the Roman Washing his Hands in a Basin (Point 64) is Catiline; he is washing them because they are literally stained with the blood of a victim whom he has been putting to a lingering death; and the basin that he uses is the nearest one to hand (it happens to be a holy water basin at the door of a temple).[1] In the Gospel according to Saint Matthew, where the Roman's part is transferred from Catiline to Pilate, the blood-stain is not literal but metaphorical; the washing is not a practical or utilitarian act, but a ritualistic and symbolical one; and the water is fetched expressly for the purpose, instead of being casually found at hand. These changes are necessary if the

---

[1] On this point Professor Gilbert Murray queries: 'Would that incident be depicted? Were there pictures of the doings of villains?' No doubt, a character who was a villain in the eyes of the designer of a picture would not be given the *beau rôle*, or even the central part, in the tableau. If he appeared at all (as, e.g., Judas would appear in the scene of the Betrayal) he would figure simply as a necessary foil to the hero. A character, however, who was a villain in one person's eyes might be a hero in another's. We assume that Catiline was a villain because we see him through the eyes of Cicero and Sallust (even though it is possible, and indeed probable, that we should have formed the same opinion of Catiline independently if we had been in a position to pass judgement on him at first hand). At the same time we know that Catiline was not a villain, but a hero, in the eyes of his fellow desperadoes who responded to his call to arms and died fighting under his leadership; and, if Catiline's 'Passion' was pictorially represented in the 'continuous style', it would be in the circle of his followers and admirers that the series of pictures, commemorating his life and death, would originate and circulate. In such circles the atrocity committed by Catiline upon Marcus Marius might count, not as a crime to be buried in oblivion, but as a *beau geste* to be immortalized.

tableau is to be incorporated into the story of a Passion in which the hero suffers his death on the Cross and not under a butcher's knife.

Finally, we may notice that our hypothetical visual means of conveyance might serve to account, not only for all our 'common scenes' (Table V), but also, incidentally, for at any rate more than one of our 'common words' (Table VIII). If we glance back at Petronius's fictitious account of the series of wall-paintings in the 'continuous style', representing scenes from the past life and future apotheosis of Trimalchio, which meet the eyes of the millionaire-freedman's guests, we shall observe that, according to Petronius, every scene in this set is garnished with a number of explanatory captions.[1] We may now observe that this lettering need not necessarily be cast in the form of a statement in the third person nor necessarily be placed outside the picture in the margin either above it or below it. It is just as feasible, and perhaps more neat, to put the explanatory words into the first person and to paint or inscribe them on a scroll issuing out of the mouth or mouths of one or more of the figures in the picture or bas-relief. In Reinach's opinion,[2] one of the lines in the Virgilian word-picture of the eternal punishment of Phlegyas—'Discite iustitiam moniti et non temnere divos' (*Aeneid*, Book VI, l. 620)—reproduces a saying which, in the picture that was Virgil's ultimate source, was painted or inscribed as though it were issuing from the mouth of the figure of Phlegyas.

This hypothesis may not, perhaps, account as a rule for those 'common words' in our list that are quoted as extracts from speeches or dialogues; but it may explain three which are cast in the form of exclamations. These three exclamatory phrases are 'Weep not for me, but weep for yourselves' (Point 68 = Saying (θ)); 'Remember me when thou comest into thy kingdom' (Point 72 = Saying (κ)); and 'It is finished' (Point 74 = Saying (λ)). And we may now perhaps hazard a guess at what was the subject of the original series of tableaux in which two, at any rate, out of our three phrases made their first appearance. 'Weep not for me, but weep for yourselves' are words that might aptly have been put into the mouth of the figure of Socrates by a painter or sculptor who was transposing into visual form the scene in Socrates' prison immediately after Socrates has drained the death-cup (Point (*o*) in the correspondences between the story of Jesus and the story of Socrates), as this scene is described by Plato in his *Phaedo*, 117 C–E (Point (π) in the correspondences between the story of Jesus and the story of Socrates). At any rate, this form of words does

---

[1] See the passage of Petronius's *Cena Trimalchionis* that has been translated on p. 514, above.   [2] Reinach, op. cit., vol. ii, p. 182.

succinctly combine Phaedo's unspoken thoughts and feelings (as analysed, in the Platonic dialogue, by Phaedo himself) with the vocal remonstrance that Plato puts into Socrates' mouth.[1] As for 'It is finished' (τετέλεσται), this sounds like an echo of 'This was the end (ἥδε ἡ τελευτή) of our companion', which is the opening phrase of the last sentence of the *Phaedo*; and we can readily imagine our hypothetical painter taking this phrase for the title of a picture in which Socrates would be depicted lying dead after the poison has taken effect. These would, in fact, almost inevitably be the last two pictures in any series that was intended to tell the story of the Life and Death of Socrates graphically in the 'continuous style'. And we can also guess what must have been the first picture in the portrayal of Socrates' Passion. This first picture would be the trial scene; and here an artist whose theme was *The Apology* might summarize the prisoner's speech in his own defence by inscribing 'One ought to obey God rather than men'[2] on a scroll issuing out of Socrates' mouth.

This last conjecture may conclude our present inquiry.

The Economy of Truth

To what conclusions does this inquiry lead? In the first place it perhaps throws some further light upon the problem of Schism-and-Palingenesia, which has been the chief subject of this part of our Study; and in this light we may be able to see more plainly the bow in the cloud. At first sight it might seem as though the schism that accompanies the breakdown of a civilization were an unmitigated disaster. In this schism a social unity is cleft asunder into a pair of fragments whose ragged edges are divided by an intervening gap, and the stroke of Fate or Fortune that has parted them looks at first like an act of sheer sabotage; but a longer view shows that the shock has not simply shattered the social fabric; it has also set an electric current coursing through its fibres, and in the space where the spark is forced to leap the gap between fragment and fragment it describes, between these severed poles, an arc of light whose glow illuminates the Universe. The vision of salvation as Transfiguration, and of the Saviour as God Incarnate, is attained in a spiritual intercourse, across a social gulf, between souls that have been partially estranged from one another through being confined in the separate prison-houses of a dominant minority and an internal proletariat.

But what of the inquiry itself? The findings of this amateur

---

[1] A translation of this passage of the *Phaedo* has already been given in this Annex on pp. 493–4, above.
[2] Acts v. 29 = Apology 29 D (see p. 491, footnote 2, above).

essay in what is called 'the Higher Criticism' will almost certainly have been felt by some readers to be insufferable if false and desolating if true. Is this bound to be the feeling of the devout soul towards the critical intellect?

If we wish to understand the history of a debate between 'the Higher Critics' and the champions of religious orthodoxy which has been going on in our Western World for the better part of a century, we must look first for the agreed basis—the *compromis* as it is called in the technical terminology of the international lawyers —on which the argument is being conducted; and when we observe what the *compromis* here is we shall perhaps be surprised. The tacit understanding seems to have been that what is at stake in this debate is nothing less than the essence of the Christian Faith: the threefold belief in the love of God, in His incarnation in Jesus Christ, and in His perpetual operation in This World through the Holy Spirit. The champions of orthodoxy appear to have tacitly admitted that these foundations of Christianity will collapse if 'the Higher Critics' succeed in proving their case; and 'the Higher Critics', on their side, have been not loath to accept this construction of the wager. On this tacit understanding 'the Higher Critics' are prone to boast that they have won the match whenever they score even a trifling success; and in the same frame of mind the champions of orthodoxy are no less prone to proclaim that the whole method of 'the Higher Criticism' has been discredited whenever they succeed in forcing their opponents to evacuate some recently occupied advanced post. This common assumption of the possibility of a 'knock-out blow' perhaps accounts for the barrenness that has been characteristic of the debate hitherto. For the assumption is assuredly an untenable one.

On the one hand the champions of orthodoxy are surely deluding themselves if they imagine that they will ever be able to drive 'the Higher Criticism' right out of the religious field. Unquestionably this 'Higher Criticism' has come to stay; and the local counter-attacks which may succeed here and there and now and then in driving it out of this or that advanced post can never seriously threaten its main positions. On the other hand 'the Higher Critics', for their part, are surely deluding themselves no less if they imagine that any of their thrusts have touched the quick. So far they have merely been singeing their opponent's beard and sticking pins into his hide; and these are hits which cause annoyance without endangering life. The rather laborious operations of the present writer in the present inquiry have no doubt been of this superficial kind; and his own expectation, for what it may be worth, is that, at the end of the story, 'the Higher Criticism' will be found to have been, not the bane of Religious Belief, but its useful, though humble, servant.

The 'Higher Critic's' keen-edged blade is not the headsman's but the pruner's; and Religious Belief is a tree whose growth is stimulated by pollarding.[1] The great positive advances in religious insight and saintliness are apt also to have this negative, destructive side; and it was this aspect of both Judaism and Christianity that first struck the imagination of the pagan world on which these two 'higher religions' made their successive impacts. When an Antiochus III and a Pompey forced their way into the Holy of Holies at the Temple in Jerusalem, the one thing that they both of them noticed was that this Jewish sanctum was empty. What an exposure of the hypocrisy of a community that had been making such a fuss about the sacrosanctity of its outlandish religion! So these Jews had not been willing even to go to the expense of providing their Yahweh with the statue that was due to him! On a similar line of reasoning other Hellenes in a later age arrived, bona fide, at the conclusion that the Primitive Christians were atheists because these iconoclasts contested the divinity of the pagan gods.[2] The salutariness of the Jewish and the Christian attack upon idolatry and polytheism escaped the notice of the hostile critics, because they did not apprehend that this negative attitude was ministering to a positive purpose, and that these 'atheists' were sweeping their cloudy pagan pantheon out of the light in order to bring within sight of pagan eyes the beatific vision of the One True God. In the present age it is perhaps not impossible that the same salutary work of unveiling a truth that is divine may be the surprising function of an ostensibly godless 'Higher Criticism'. But an apologist for 'the Higher Critics' cannot file this plea unless he is able to show that, here once again, the pruner's knife is clearing the ground for a more abundant life, and the air for a more penetrating vision.

Perhaps we may plead that our present essay in 'the Higher Criticism' does fulfil this condition in some slight degree. If its negative result has been to call in question the originality of a number of elements in the Gospels, its positive result—which it will have achieved in so far as it has been successful in tracing these apparently adventitious elements back towards their apparently Hellenic origins—will have been to vindicate the claim of Christianity to be a religion in which God has revealed Himself in

---

[1] For the simile of the pollarded tree see I. C (iii) (b), vol. i, pp. 168–9, above.
[2] On this point see IV. C (iii) (c) 2 (β), vol. iv, p. 348; V. C (i) (c) 2, Annex II, vol. v, p. 584; and V. C (i) (d) 7, in the present volume, p. 40, footnote 2, above.

history, while translating this claim into terms which, to traditionally orthodox minds, may seem to empty the claim of just those traditional contents which, for them, give it its supreme significance and value. They will see our investigation as an attack upon the historicity of the story of Jesus Christ as this is presented in the Gospels; and at this price they will not thank us for having perhaps slightly extended, at least in one direction, the traditional view of the historical antecedents of the epiphany of Christianity.

The notion that Christianity did not make its epiphany full-grown and fully-armed, like Pallas Athene, is of course in itself not a matter of controversy. In the orthodox tradition of the Church it has always been recognized that the incarnation of God in Christ is the culminating act of a long religious drama. The text of the New Testament itself bears the stamp of the doctrine that the coming of Christ is the fulfilment of Scripture; and it has been one of the most fruitful commonplaces of orthodox exegesis to trace the process of revelation backwards from Jesus to the Prophets, from the Prophets to Moses, from Moses to Abraham. The concept of progressive revelation is thus in itself quite familiar; but, in the orthodox Christian tradition hitherto, this concept has only been applied to the Judaic tributary that has flowed into the river of Christianity out of the Syriac World. Latterly, however, it has been discovered by our modern Western scholarship that the mundane area of catchment of these living waters has been of a wider range than is covered by the single domain of Jewry, notwithstanding the immensity of this Jewish empire in the spiritual dimension. It has come to be realized that the Hellenic World, too, has played some part in catching and transmitting the waters by which the river has been fed, and that the number of the tributaries of Christianity has to be reckoned as not one but two, whose respective names are Judaism and Hellenism.[1] This discovery is not at all sensational; for it merely confirms empirically what was to be expected *a priori* in view of the historical background out of which Christianity emerged. Christianity was born into a world which was the product of a collision between the Syriac and the Hellenic cultures.

To minds that look out upon the Universe through Christian eyes this traditionally Christian concept of a progressive revelation surely need not turn into a stumbling-block in the process of being extended from a Jewish to a Hellenic field. But other minds may challenge the concept in principle and in all its applications, traditional or critical. Why *should* revelation come gradually? Why should not God have declared himself to Man once for all in some

[1] This view has been presented, by anticipation, in V. C (i) (*d*) 5, vol. v, p. 434, above.

instantaneous blaze of His divine light? The decisive answer to this impatient question is that 'with men this is impossible' though 'all things are possible with God'.[1] Human life in This World is imprisoned in the Time-dimension; and this means that, under mundane conditions, the apprehension of spiritual truth, like all other human activities, must be a process that has its own specific pace. On this showing, the gradualness of revelation is not an arbitrary decree of an omnipotent God but is a necessary consequence of the mundane limitations of Man; and the evidence which goes to show that revelation does come to Man in this gradual way will accordingly remind us that God is master of this, as of every, situation. It is not in a waterspout but in a gentle shower that the golden rain pierces the brazen carapace of Danae's dungeon. And God's method of progressive revelation may be accurately described, in Newman's famous phrase, as 'an economy of truth', if the word 'economy' is taken in its proper meaning of a masterly dispensation, without any connotation of dishonest short measure.

But what is truth? For it is one thing to dispense pure truth in doses that have been adjusted to the capacity of the recipient, and another thing to dole out a truth that has been slyly diluted with falsehood. 'Have you not', some reader may ask, 'been virtually accusing God of practising a fraud when, without denying that the Gospels may be God's revelation, you argue that the Gospels contain elements that are not historical, in the sense that certain recorded acts were not in fact performed, and certain reported words were not in fact uttered, by the person who is credited with them, or in the circumstances assigned to them, by the Evangelists?' This question is perhaps best answered by counter-questioning the questioner. Is God's economy, we may ask, to be dictated to God by Man? Is God to be prohibited by a human veto from revealing Himself through *Dichtung* if He will, as well as through *Wahrheit*? Are not all human modes of expression at God's disposal? Is no divine truth revealed in the story of a fictitious Lazarus and an anonymous Dives? And, if, as a matter of fact, the Parables have been recognized by the Church as being revelation without being history, are we debarred from accepting other elements in the Gospels on the same footing because, unlike the Parables, they do not proclaim themselves to be fiction, but are cast, like epic poetry or 'folk-tales', in the form of statements of fact?

But is it credible that God should have revealed himself in 'folk-lore'? To this last question the answer is that it is in 'folk-lore' if anywhere—for it is certainly not on ballot-papers—that *Vox*

[1] Matt. xix. 26.

Populi becomes *Vox Dei*. And this answer has good authority; for it has been given in one of the sayings that are attributed to Jesus in an early collection which 'the Higher Critics' call 'Q':

'In that hour Jesus rejoiced in spirit and said: "I thank thee, O Father, Lord of Heaven and Earth, that thou hast hid these things from the wise and prudent and hast revealed them unto babes. Even so, Father; for so it seemed good in thy sight." '[1]

[1] Luke x. 21 = Matt. xi. 25–6.

---

[1] In the cross-references in this index, references in small capitals (e.g. ANATOLIA at the end of the heading Achaeans) are to other main headings, while references in ordinary type are to sub-divisions of the same main heading.

with, v. 239, 241, 245; official title of Emperor, vi. 3; Phoenicians, relations with, v. 123; vi. 203; political unity under, v. 86–7; prolongation of, v. 53; rally-and-relapse of, vi. 302; range of, iv. 471; v. 238; religious policy of, v. 677, 704–5; vi. 29–33, 38, 43 n., 45, 129–30; rise of, iv. 102, 480; subject peoples, treatment of, vi. 202–3 (see also above under Jews); successor states of, iv. 316 n., 408 n.; v. 547, 576; vi. 342; temple-states in, iv. 518. See also under BABYLONIA; CYRUS II; DARIUS I; GREECE; JEWS: revolts; JUDAISM; SCYTHIANS.

Açoka Maurya, Emperor: abortive attempt to establish Buddhism as official philosophy, v. 680–3, 705; character of, vi. 253; inscriptions of, v. 131, 498, 499, 500; vi. 76; philosophical convictions of, v. 131, 132, 145 n., 682, 695; vi. 251, 252; reign of, v. 131; vi. 193, 252; vegetarianism of, v. 682, 701; war, renunciation of, v. 682; vi. 199.

Action, field of, iv. 233; v. 376, 589; vi. 175.

Actium, Battle of (31 B.C.), iv. 70 n., 92, 508; v. 63, 117, 594; vi. 37 n., 55 n., 87, 187, 192, 217, 284, 287.

Adadnirari III, King of Assyria, vi. 442.

Adoptionism, v. 653 and n., 654; vi. 271–5. See also under CHRISTIANITY.

Adrianople, Battle of (A.D. 378), iv. 324 n., 440–2, 443, 444, 450, 468; v. 228–9; vi. 192, 209, 231, 284, 311 n.

Aedesius, vi. 250.

Aegina, iv. 207–8.

Aegospotami, Battle of (404 B.C.), iv. 63, 483; vi. 183, 291, 493.

Aelian of Praeneste, vi. 72.

Aenêsidêmus, v. 548 n., 558.

Aeolians, the, iv. 20.

Aeschylus: Agamemnon, cited, iv. 256; vi. 21 n., 519; Philostratus's relation to, vi. 357–8 n.; spiritual evolution of, iv. 255–6 n.; Supplices, cited, vi. 271 n.; Zeus, presentation of, vi. 179 n.

Aetius, v. 279, 471, 472–3, 553.

Aetolia, v. 210.

Aetolian Confederacy, the, iv. 147 n., 309, 310, 311; v. 38 n.; vi. 288.

Afghanistan: art of, v. 198; Great Britain, relations with, v. 305–8, 323; vi. 201 n., 302 n.; India—juridical frontier with, v. 307 and n.; — relations with, v. 304, 306; vi. 301; language of, v. 516 n., Westernization of, vi. 103 and n., 105, 234.

Afghans, the, v. 304, 311.

Africa: North West—Arab invasion of, iv. 322, 327, 331, 341, 488; v. 221, 241, 247; vi. 223; — barbarians, difficulty of subjugating, v. 205; — French conquests in, v. 45, 323, 324 and n., 573 n.; — Justinian's campaigns in, iv. 326, 327, 332 n., 390; — Rif War, v. 461; vi. 227, 235 n.; — Roman conquests in, v. 64, 65 (see also under VANDALS); partition of, ·v. 207; South—caste system in, iv. 229, 230; — national elements, relations between, iv. 293, 294–5; — Union of, iv. 174, 186, 295; Tropical—cultural influence of on Western World, v. 482; — industrialism, effect of, v. 166; — languages of, v. 522–3; — opening up of, v. 45–6, 295 n., 321, 522–3.

Afrikaans, v. 493–4.

Agathocles, Despot of Syracuse, iv. 590; vi. 183, 253.

Agesilaus II, King of Sparta, v. 463 n.; vi. 395.

Agesistrata, vi. 392, 400, 402 n., 403, 404.

Agiatis, vi. 405.

Agis IV, King of Sparta: archaism of, v. 388; vi. 376, 432; arrest of, vi. 390, 531; betrayal of, vi. 386, 390, 420, 421; Cleomenes, relation to, vi. 405; conscientiousness of, v. 435; cult of, vi. 512; dead body, tending of, vi. 404, 524; death of, vi. 219, 391, 399–400, 403–4, 524, 527; gentleness of, v. 78, 388, 398; vi. 219, 378, 392; idealism of, vi. 240, 288; illegality of his proceedings, vi. 220; Leonidas, plot against, vi. 524 n.; mother, relations with, vi. 379–80, 392, 400; reforms of, vi. 381, 385, 432, 507, 524 n.; reign of, vi. 512; rescue of, attempted, vi. 402 n.; Stoic influence on, vi. 249 n.; takes sanctuary, vi. 385; trial of, vi. 391, 393, 394, 395, 524.

Agrigentum, v. 212; vi. 235.

Agrippa, M. Vipsanius, v. 47.

Ahab, King of Israel, iv. 467–8.

Ahmad of Qâdyân, Ghulâm, v. 175 n.

Ahmad Shâh Durrânî, v. 306 n.

Ahmadîyah sect, the, v. 174–5, 176, 188; vi. 329.

Ahiqar Romance, the, vi. 440 n.

Ainu, the, iv. 94; v. 45, 95; vi. 208, 330.

341, 342. *See also under* ASSYRIA; SUMER AND AKKAD.

Babylonic Civilization: *abandon* and self-control, examples of, v. 402–3; archaism, examples of, vi. 94, 95; articulation into national states, v. 122; barbarians, pressure of, iv. 102, 103, 116, 475, 486; v. 122; breakdown of, iv. 101; challenges, response to, iv. 116, 477–9; culture of, iv. 51, 439 *n.*, 473–4, 483; v. 347 *n.*; — astrology, iv. 23–4, 37; v. 56–7, 176, 362, 403, 426, 540, 554; vi. 19, 21, 33, 328; — folk-tales, vi. 442, 443, 447, 455, 459; — mythology, vi. 130; — philosophy, v. 57; — script, iv. 51, 54; disintegration of, *see above under* abandon, archaism; *and below under* minority, proletariat, promiscuity, rally-and-relapse, saviours, Time of Troubles, unity; Egyptiac Civilization—contact with, v. 143 *n.*; — intrusion upon, v. 118; environment, physical, iv. 43–5; expansion of, v. 117–18; extinction of, iv. 1, 44, 101, 102; v. 57, 347, 370; fossilized remnant of, iv. 101 *n.*; v. 125 *n.*; Hellenic Civilization—contact with, iv. 81; vi. 442–3; — intrusion of, iv. 100; v. 64, 608 *n.*; Indic Civilization, contact with, v. 274; languages of, v. 499; marches of, iv. 475, 486, 487; militarism of, iv. 143; vi. 199; minority, dominant, v. 40–1, 94, 122, 369, 426; nomads, pressure of, iv. 471, 477, 478; v. 121 *n.*, 261; proletariat, external, v. 261, 600; vi. 330 (*see also above under* barbarians, nomads); proletariat, internal, v. 94, 117 *seqq.*, 369, 370; promiscuity, examples of, v. 499, 529–30; vi. 45; rally-and-relapse of, vi. 308; religion of, iv. 101 *n.*; v. 121, 125 *n.*, 148, 369, 402, 403, 529–30, 554, 652 and *n.*; vi. 15, 19, 32, 33, 37, 45–6, 47 *n.*, 94, 95, 329; rulers, deification of, v. 652 and *n.*; saviours with the sword, vi. 189, 190, 199; Sumeric Civilization, relation to, iv. 43; v. 5, 148; Syriac Civilization—absorption by, iv. 43, 44, 81, 100, 101; v. 122–3, 370; — contact with, iv. 100, 101 *n.*, 102, 103 *n.*, 471, 475, 486; v. 122, 369, 370; vi. 45, 442; — intrusion upon, v. 118, 119; — relation to, iv. 43; Time of Troubles, iv. 44; v. 120, 122, 261, 274 *n.*, 304 *n.*, 370; vi. 308, 327; unity, sense of, vi. 19, 47 *n.*; universal state, *see* BABYLONIA: New Empire.

Bacon, Francis: *Of the Proficience and Advancement of Learning*, cited, iv. 123–4 *n.*

Bactria, Kingdom of: administrative devices in, v. 443; Buddhism in, v. 132–3, 139; conquest of India by rulers of, iv. 20–1, 99; v. 53, 64 *n.*, 131–2, 133 *n.*, 275, 361, 628 *n.*; vi. 450 *n.*; Kushan Empire, relation to, v. 133 *n.*, 139, 275 *n.*; nomad invasion of, v. 133 *n.*, 143 *n.*, 144, 239, 275, 278, 602 *n.*; Oxus-Jaxartes Basin, relations with, v. 133 *n.*, 249, 275, 278; range of, v. 133 and *n.*; Seleucid Monarchy, relation to, v. 133 *n.*, 601–2 and *n.*, 628 *n.*; successor states of, v. 133, 139, 144.

Bagehot, Walter: *Physics and Politics*, cited, iv. 134 *n.*

Bahaism (and Bahā'īyah sect), v. 174–5, 176, 187 *n.*, 188, 665; vi. 329.

Bahā'u'llāh, v. 176.

Bālāditya, v. 279.

Balance of Power, the, iv. 148, 149, 283, 299 *n.*, 582 *n.*; v. 619, 625.

Balbinus, D. Caelius, Emperor, vi. 54.

Balder, worship of, v. 150.

Balkan Peninsula, the: languages of, iv. 328; Slav invasions of, v. 327–8, 332, 343, 344 *n.*, 359 *n.*, 398, 399 *n.*, 605 *n.*, 607 *n.* *See also under* BULGARIANS.

Balkan War, First, iv. 77 *n.*

Bandinelli, Roland, *see* ALEXANDER III, Pope.

Barbarians: alien cultural tinge, effects of, v. 3–4 *n.*, 348, 351–4, 357–8, 449 *n.*; vi. 229; as founders of universal states, v. 54, 448–50; as hostages in hands of a civilized Power, v. 459–60, 461, 472–3; as mercenaries, v. 459–60, 461 and *n.*, 462–6, 467–8, 470, 472, 476; assimilation of, by civilizations, iv. 372; v. 459–66; badges adopted by, v. 229 and *n.*, 248; cultural individuality, development of, v. 468; demoralization of, after conquest of a disintegrating universal state, v. 201 *n.*, 710 *n.*; dress of, v. 470 and *n.*; elimination of, question of, v. 334; infusion of fresh blood by, iv. 16–17, 18 and *n.*; militarism of, iv. 486; military despotism of, v. 213 *n.*; military technique of, v. 209; vi. 229–30; poetry produced by—epic, 233–5, 252 *seqq.*, 265, 288–9, 296 *seqq.*, 310, 325, 327–8, 338, 596–606, 607–14; vi. 325–6, 330–1, 440–1; — lyric, v. 234, 235; political institutions of, v. 213 *n.*;

Christ (*cont.*).

as Son of Man, vi. 163 *n.*, 353, 395 *n.*, 414.

Ascension of, vi. 475.

asceticism, attitude towards, vi. 382.

at Bethany, vi. 385.

baptism of, iv. 625; vi. 156, 273 and *n.*, 362, 451, 488.

betrayal of, iv. 534; vi. 386, 387, 390, 420, 421.

birth of, iv. 625; vi. 163 *n.*, 174-5, 268-9, 269-70 *n.*, 273 *n.*, 274 *n.*, 344, 450-1, 469 *n.*

burial of, vi. 474, 526.

Challenge-and-Response illustrated in life of, v. 72-3.

children, blessing of, iv. 249.

cleansing of the Temple, iv. 537; vi. 378, 384-5, 425-6, 525.

clothing of, vi. 400, 420-1.

crucifixion of, vi. 400-4, 426, 484-5, 492, 525; as foolishness to philosophers, v. 74; vi. 150-4, 243, 265, 347: as stumbling-block to futurists, v. 74; vi. 150, 155-6; women present at, vi. 403-4 and *n.*, 421, 474.

death of, vi. 401, 403, 473; prediction of, v. 74, 392-3; vi. 165, 383-4.

denunciation of Scribes and Pharisees, iv. 238, 246; vi. 380, 489.

descent from the Cross, vi. 404, 526.

desertion of, by his followers, v. 74, 393; vi. 389, 392, 395.

disputation with doctors of law, vi. 487.

divinity of, iv. 625-6; vi. 261, 273 *seqq.*, 352-3, 359; declaration of, vi. 273 *n.*, 352, 362, 394, 488; recognition of—by disciples, v. 392, vi. 165, 384, 490; — by John the Baptist, vi. 488; — by witnesses of crucifixion, vi. 401, 525.

entry into Jerusalem, vi. 384, 420, 481, 525, 530.

flight into Egypt, vi. 470.

Gentiles, attitude towards, iv. 246, 247; vi. 7-8.

incarnation of, question of moment of, iv. 625 *n.*

infancy of, vi. 451, 456, 470.

John the Baptist, relation to, vi. 185, 378, 380, 488.

kingship of, vi. 155, 163 and *n.*, 396 *seqq.*, 430, 471; analogies to in Judaism and Zoroastrianism, vi. 163 *n.*

Last Supper, vi. 386-7, 388, 426, 427, 492-3, 525, 531.

lineage of, vi. 273-4 *n.*, 378-9, 469.

Magi, journey of, vi. 524 *n.*

Messiahship of, vi. 163 *n.*, 383-4, 394.

miracles of, v. 25; vi. 380, 382, 452-3.

mocking of, vi. 352 and *n.*, 398-9, 400, 402, 421-2, 481 *seqq.*, 525, 531-2.

Mother, relations with, vi. 379-80, 401.

non-violence of, iv. 467; v. 72-3, 74, 78, 382, 390, 393, 589; vi. 178-9, 260-1, 377, 378, 392, 430, 527-8, 531.

on Mount of Olives, vi. 388.

on way to crucifixion, vi. 399-400.

parables of, iv. 247, 466; v. 166, 563; vi. 358, 380, 455, 538.

Paschal Lamb, identification with, vi. 426-7.

piercing of his side, vi. 403, 426, 525.

popularity of, vi. 381-2, 385, 471.

questioning of, v. 396; vi. 385.

rejection of, by Jews, iv. 246, 263; v. 544, 658; vi. 155, 156.

resurrection of, vi. 478.

reversal of roles illustrated from life of, iv. 246-9.

sayings of, iv. 132, 133, 237, 238, 246, 247, 248-9, 363-4, 370, 378, 510, 534, 537, 545, 583; v. 72, 73, 75, 179, 180, 392, 396, 487, 561; vi. 11, 16 *n.*, 99, 155, 156-7, 166, 260-1, 353, 354, 355, 358, 380, 393, 399, 401, 501, 502-3, 533, 534, 539.

story of:

correspondences with stories of Hellenic heroes, vi. 268-9 and *n.*, 376 *seqq.*; points of, vi. 378-405; possible explanations of— chance, vi. 418-29; — folk-memory, vi. 447 *seqq.*; — identical causes producing identical results, vi. 429-31; — imitation of one hero by another, vi. 431-3; — influence of story of one hero upon that of another, vi. 486 *seqq.*; — ritual, vi. 476 *seqq.*, 525; — tableaux, influence of, vi. 508 *seqq.*; tables, vi. 407-17, 476; verbal correspondences, vi. 414-17, 418, 500 *seqq.*, 533; visual correspondences, vi. 381-2, 384, 387 *seqq.*, 398, 399, 404, 411-12, 524 *seqq.*

correspondences with stories of: the Buddha, vi. 448-9 and *n.*, Hêraklês, vi. 269 *n.*, 465-76; Socrates, vi. 486-95, 533-4.

folk-lore elements in, vi. 448 *seqq.*

temptation of, vi. 451, 452, 470.

Transfiguration of, v. 392; vi. 165.

trials of: before High Priests, vi. 352, 353, 393 *seqq.*, 421, 490, 492; be-

exiles from, v. 168, 188; Irish
Free State, foundation of, vi. 68 n.;
literature of, iv. 291; vi. 66 and n.,
330; position of, iv. 293 n.; self-
idolization of, iv. 291 seqq.; Western,
barbarians surviving in, v. 207, 320.
Irenaeus of Lyon, Saint: *Contra
Haereses*, cited, v. 407–8 n.
Irene, Empress, iv. 274, 595.
Irene (Maria Lecapena), wife of Bul-
garian Tsar Peter, iv. 387, 388.
Irish language, the, vi. 63, 65–7, 68 n.,
69, 70, 95 and n.
Irrigation systems, decay of, iv.
42 seqq.
Isaac I Comnenus, Emperor, iv. 355
n., 601 n., 619 n., 620.
Isaurians, the, iv. 76, 325 and n.; v.
206 n., 297 n., 354 n.
Ishtar, worship of, v. 82, 148–9, 437.
Isidorus of Miletus, iv. 21, 54.
Isis, worship of, v. 81, 138, 149–50,
360–1, 531, 538, 553; vi. 46, 48.
Islam: as reaction against Hellenism,
vi. 113; as Syriac universal church,
v. 128, 137, 359, 370–1, 661, 672,
673, 675–6, 677; *fanā'*, conception
of, vi. 143 n.; genesis of, v. 230,
235, 359, 676; gentleness and violence, alternation between, v. 128–9,
130–1, 175 n., 662, 665; God, conception of, vi. 38, 40–1, 42, 44;
headgear, significance of, vi. 102–3
n., 104; Hinduism, relation to, v.
667, 668; vi. 47 n.; iconoclasm
of, vi. 116–17; indigenous inspiration of, v. 368, 370–1, 676; vi. 329;
iktisāb, doctrine of, v. 424, 430,
615; Jewish and Christian elements
in, v. 220 n., 230, 235, 359; vi.
143 n.; Judaism, relation to, v. 658;
vi. 38, 40, 42; Khārijīs, v. 73 n.,
129; law in relation to, vi. 18;
Meccan stone, v. 688 n.; militancy
of, v. 175 and n., 674; political
character of, v. 359 n., 658–9, 672,
673 seqq.; propagation of, iv. 67,
69 n., 75, 231–2, 496, 497; v. 674,
677, 678; Qadarīyah movement, v.
424 n.; *qismet*, concept of, v. 430–
1; religious toleration of, iv. 226,
630; v. 674 and n., 675–6, 678, 706;
vi. 204–5 and n.; schism between
Sunnis and Shī'īs, v. 17 n., 73 n.,
130; Sufism, iv. 29–30, 69 n.; vi.
143 n.; syncretism between other
religions and, iv. 68–9; v. 111, 537,
667, 668; transformation of, by non-
Arab converts, v. 677; variations
upon, v. 174–5; Zoroastrianism, relation to, iv. 226; v. 674 n.; vi. 44 n.

See also under 'ABBASID CALIPHATE;
BERBERS; CATHOLIC CHURCH;
EGYPT; MONGOLS: religion
MUHAMMAD, Prophet; NOMADS
SALJŪQS; SHI'ISM; UMAYYAD CALI-
PHATE.
Islamic Civilization: Arabic Civilization, relation to, iv. 82 and n.;
articulation into national states; iv.
81–2; breakdown of, iv. 107; disintegration of, iv. 107; futurism,
examples of, vi. 102–3, 106; nationalism, operation of, iv. 81–2, 107;
political unity of, iv. 82 n., 113;
survival of, iv. 1; Time of Troubles,
iv. 105, 107; universal state, absence
of, iv. 106 (*see also* Pan-Islamic
Movement); Western Civilization,
absorption by, iv. 79, 81–2, 105,
106–7.
Ismā'īl Shāh Safawī, iv. 107; v. 310;
and Shī'ī insurrection in Anatolia,
v. 365; campaign against Uzbegs,
iv. 499; career and policy of, v.
661–2, 664, 665, 666 n., 680, 706;
militarism of, v. 175 n., 661 seqq.; vi.
199, 260.
Ismā'īlīs (Assassins), the, v. 129, 130,
131, 175 n.
Isocrates of Athens, v. 55.
Israelites, the: Assyrians, relations
with, iv. 367; vi. 38; deportation of,
iv. 367; v. 118, 120, 123, 387,
536; vi. 120, 481; Egypt, relations
with, v. 611; vi. 39, 43, 451 n.;
Palestine, invasion of, vi. 39, 43;
Philistines, relations with, vi. 43;
primitive religion of, v. 119 and n.;
Prophets, spiritual experiences of,
v. 433–4; return of, from exile,
v. 370 n.; vi. 17, 121 n. *See also
under* HEBREWS; JEWS.
Itali, the, v. 211 and n., 213.
Italian language, the, v. 502.
Italy:
archaism in, vi. 52.
as battlefield of Europe, iv. 18–9, 22.
as education of Western Society, iv.
52, 198–200, 215, 274–5, 283–4,
341, 344, 406, 407; v. 627; vi.
340–1.
atrocities committed by, iv. 129.
Church and State, relations between,
iv. 219.
City-states: *abandon* and self-control,
examples of, v. 403; as dominant
institution of Western World, iv.
352, 405–6; as empire builders, iv.
276, 285; v. 622–3; as Hellenic
ghost, iv. 352 n., 406; consolidation
of, into principalities, iv. 544;